The Politics of International Economic Relations

FOURTH EDITION

Joan Edelman Spero

First published in the UK by
the Academic Division of
Unwin Hyman Ltd, 1977

Second edition 1980
Third edition 1985
Fourth edition 1990

Reprinted 1992, 1993 and 1994
by Routledge
11 New Fetter Lane, London EC4P 4EE

© 1990 St Martin's Press Inc.

Printed and bound in Great Britain by
Mackays of Chatham PLC, Chatham, Kent

British Library Cataloguing in Publication Data
A catalogue reference for this book is available from the British Library.

ISBN 0–415–08430–X

Preface

The first edition of *The Politics of International Economic Relations*, published in 1977, was written to fill a void in the study of international relations—the gap between international politics and international economics. Since 1977 that gap has narrowed significantly. International political economy has emerged as a new and increasingly prominent field of political science. Theoretical and empirical analyses of the politics of international economic relations appear regularly in professional journals and books. Although the most important bridge building has come from the political scientists, economists are also including political variables in their analyses and applying economic theory to the study of political behavior. At the same time, a new generation of students in a variety of fields is being made aware of the interrelationship of economics and politics and is learning to use and integrate the tools of both fields.

Much has happened since 1977 to reinforce this academic evolution. Above all, the turbulence in the world economy has highlighted the political dimension of international economic relations. The persistent problems of the dollar, the dislocations in the international trading system, the international oil crisis, the problem of developing country debt—these and a host of other world issues have obliged scholars to reexamine the assumptions that have separated their disciplines for a century.

The focus of the analysis and organization of *The Politics of International Economic Relations* has not changed. The problems of the systems of interdependence in the West, of dependence of the South on the North, and of independence between East and West continue to provide, in my view, a valid approach to the politics of international economic relations.

In this fourth edition I have added new material that reflects both the academic changes and the events in the years since the third edition was published. For example, the monetary chapter explores efforts at exchange rate management since the Plaza and Louvre agreements; the trade chapters examine issues being negotiated in the Uruguay Round of multilateral trade negotiations; the chapters on multinational corporations discuss the more critical attitude toward foreign investment in the United States and the more receptive policies in developing countries; and the chapter on oil explores the decline of OPEC. Similarly, a new chapter on financial flows to developing countries analyzes private bank lending and the less-developed country (LDC) debt crisis, and the East-West chapter includes an analysis of Mikhail Gorbachev's *perestroika* as well as a new section on China.

Each edition of this book has reflected a different dimension of my professional experience. At the time the first edition appeared in 1977, I was assistant professor of political science at Columbia University. When the second edition was published in 1980, I was ambassador of the United States to the United Nations Economic and Social Council. The third edition was published in 1985 when I was senior vice president of international corporate affairs at American Express Company. At present, I am senior vice president and treasurer of American Express. Over the years, my academic and government perspectives have merged with the practical aspects of trade, monetary, and investment issues I have learned as a corporate officer and now as a financial executive. Since this is now a "three-dimensional" book—drawing on academic, governmental, and private sector experience—I believe it presents a more rounded and fuller accounting of the world political economy environment.

Of course, a good deal more than my own experience has gone into this edition. I owe an immense debt of gratitude to Jeffry Frieden, for his thorough review of the manuscript, and to Kristin Brady, Stephen Gaull, Christiana Horton, Deirdre Maloney, and Kathleen McNamara, who contributed research support. I also owe special thanks to Andrew Bartels, Toby Gati, Lisa Lamas, Charles Levy, Edward Morse, Richard O'Brien, and John Sewell for their insights and counsel, and to Anita Andersen, Blanca Avila, Victoria Handwerk, and Karen Sheffron, who held the whole project together. I would also like to thank the following reviewers for their time and efforts: Don Babai, Harvard University; Larry Elowitz, Georgia College; Alex Hybel, University of Southern California; David Lake, University of California at Los Angeles; and Robert M. Stern, University of Michigan.

In addition, I would like to thank St. Martin's Press and its fine editorial staff, which has long supported this book and encouraged me to update it regularly. St. Martin's prodding, combined with the understanding that the demands of corporate life often conflict with meeting production deadlines, provided the necessary balance that enabled me to complete this and other editions.

Above all, I am grateful to my husband, Michael, and my sons, Jason and Benjamin, for their support, encouragement, and forbearance.

Contents

Conclusion: Toward a New International Economic Order?   *350*

Introduction: The Link between Economics and Politics

The interaction of politics and economics is an old theme in the study of international relations. From seventeenth-century mercantilists to twentieth-century Marxists, students of relations among states have dealt with the problems of international political economy. Yet in the twentieth century, the study of international political economy has been neglected. Until recently, politics and economics were divorced from each other and isolated in the analysis and theory, if not in the reality, of international relations.

One reason for this divorce is the theoretical heritage of modern Western academe. The heritage that has shaped much of the modern study of politics and economics—and that is responsible for the artificial separation of economics and politics—is liberalism. Liberal theorists rejected the age-old concept of a unified political and economic order and replaced it with two separate orders.

First, argued the liberals, an economic system is based on the production, distribution, and consumption of goods and services; these economic processes operate under natural laws. Furthermore, they maintained, there is a harmony in these laws and in the economic system, and such natural harmony operates best and to the benefit of all when political authority interferes least with its automatic operation. The liberals considered economic activity to be the preserve of private enterprise, not of government.

Second, they contended that the political system consists of power, influence, and public decision making. Politics, they asserted, unlike economics, does not obey natural laws or harmony. Politics is unavoidable and government is necessary for essential services—defense, law, and order. But,

1

for them, government and politics should not interfere with the natural economic order. Indeed, in an international system, the liberals' only hope for peace and harmony is for politics to be isolated from economics and for the natural and harmonious processes of free trade to operate among nations, bringing not only prosperity but also peace to all.[1]

Such theoretical separation led to, and was reinforced by, the specializations of modern academe. Since the nineteenth century, economics and political science have developed as separate disciplines, focusing on separate processes; and each to a great extent has ignored the common ground where the two overlap and interrelate. Consequently, international political economy has been fragmented into international politics and international economics. Economists, for the most part, ignored the role of political factors in international economic process and policy,[2] whereas students of international politics tended to ignore economic issues in relations among states.[3]

Two political and economic developments following World War II reinforced this formal division of analysis. In the early postwar years, the major world powers reached an agreement on postwar international economic relations. In the West, the Bretton Woods system of international economic management established the rules for commercial and financial relations among the major industrial states. In the East, Soviet hegemony in Eastern Europe provided the foundation for a separate and stable international economic system. Finally, during the first postwar decade, the greater part of the Third World remained politically and economically subordinate. As a result of the agreed-upon structures and rules of international economic interaction, conflict over economic issues was minimized, and the significance of the economic aspect of international relations seemed to recede. The emergence of the Cold War also caused international economic relations to recede. The problems of international relations that preoccupied decision makers and observers alike were security issues: the Soviet Union's domination of Eastern Europe and the development of Soviet nuclear capability, the division of Germany, the forging of the North Atlantic Treaty Organization (NATO) and American nuclear strategy, the Korean conflict, Vietnam, and the problems of limited war. Thus, analysis of international relations focused on security and security-related issues.

Conditions after 1970 undermined the separation of economics from the study of international politics. Military tensions eased as the United States and the Soviet Union demonstrated a willingness and an ability to reach agreements on security issues, thus alleviating some of the tension of the Cold War. The war in Vietnam ended, and the European countries completed the task of freeing their colonies. ·

At the same time, the broad agreement on economic rules established after World War II collapsed. In the West, the Bretton Woods system of management broke down. The renewed economic vigor of Western Europe and Japan, the strain on the United States' balance of payments, the oil crisis, inflation, and the growth of freewheeling international capital markets have led to the disintegration of the international monetary system developed after World War II. The growth of the European Economic Community as an economic power, the dynamism of Japanese trade, and domestic economic problems of slower growth and unemployment threaten established commercial relations. New international patterns of production posed a multifaceted challenge to the traditional economic and political order. In the East, the Soviet Union and the Communist states of Eastern Europe found their closed system too restrictive for economic development and have turned to the West for trade and technology. China has also signaled its willingness to increase its economic ties with the developed countries. China and the Soviet Union have launched ambitious policies of domestic economic reform. In the South, the now independent Third World countries have made demands for changes in financial flows. How they will be integrated into the world economy has become a major issue. Some less-developed countries—the so-called Four Tigers of Asia, for example—have more robust economies which threaten sensitive sectors in the industrialized states. A few Southern countries have burst onto the international economic scene with their newfound oil wealth. The majority of Third World countries face numerous obstacles to development, and are wrestling with ways to improve the benefits they receive from the international economic system. With the disintegration of postwar economic consensus, economic issues have reemerged alongside security issues as a focus of international relations.

Thus, in order for theory and analysis to maintain touch with reality, it has become necessary to bridge the gap between economics and politics, to explore the interface between economics and politics in the international system. This study will examine one aspect of that interface: the way in which international politics shapes international economics.

The Political Dynamics of International Politics

Until recently, students of international politics who analyzed the interaction between economics and politics almost always examined the way in which economic reality affects politics.[4] There is, for example, a body of thought that maintains that economic resources determine strategic and diplomatic power. Analysts have pointed out the ways in which a country's gross national product, the quantity and quality of its resources, and its international trade and financial position determine its military strength. The literature demonstrates that the impact of economics on politics is quite important. The early industrialization of Great Britain in the nineteenth century, for example, was a significant resource base for British political power and an important factor in Great Britain's domination of that century's international economic and political structure. Similarly, the United States' economic power was important in creating U.S. military and political dominance in the twentieth century.

Just as economic factors influence political outcomes, so political factors influence economic outcomes. Students of international politics, however, have often overlooked the political determinants of international economic relations. Although not denying the effect of economics on politics, this book will be concerned with that other side of the coin that has been frequently ignored: the political dynamics of international economics.

There are three ways in which political factors affect economic outcomes. *First, the political system shapes the economic system*, because the structure and operation of the international economic system is, to a great extent, determined by the structure and operation of the international political system. *Second, political concerns often shape economic policy*, because economic policies are frequently dictated by overriding political interests. *Third, international economic relations themselves are political relations*, because international economic interaction, like international political interaction, is a process by which state and nonstate actors manage, or fail to manage, their conflicts and by which they cooperate, or fail to cooperate, to achieve common goals. Let us now look in more detail at these three political dimensions of international economics.

The Political System and the Economic System

The structure and operation of the international economic system are to a great extent determined by the structure and operation of the international political system. Throughout modern history, production, distribution, and consumption have been affected by diplomatic and strategic factors.

During the mercantilistic period between the fifteenth and eighteenth centuries, economic interaction had two principal political characteristics. First was the rise of powerful nation states from the ruins of medieval universalism and local particularism: the emergence of new centralized political units—England, France, Spain, Sweden, Prussia, and Russia—whose policy was the consolidation of power, both internally, vis-à-vis local power structures, and externally, vis-à-vis other states. Second, in the mercantile political system, was the competition among these many nearly equal states. Because power was distributed fairly equally, relatively minor changes could be important to a state's overall power position. There were certain limits to competition. There was a common political culture, including a consensus on royal legitimacy. In addition, state administration was weak, armies were small and mercenary, and, therefore, military and diplomatic objectives were limited.

The impact of the political structure on the economic structure of mercantilism was profound. The economic realm became the main arena for political conflict. The pursuit of state power was carried out through the pursuit of national economic power and wealth, and the process of competition, limited by political reality, was translated into economic competition. All international economic transactions were regulated for the purpose of state power.

Because mercantilists believed that wealth and power were closely associated with the possession of so-called precious metals, governments organized their international trading structures for the purpose of maintaining a favorable balance of trade to accumulate these metals. There were controls on exchange markets and the international movement of precious metals, along with regulation of individual and general commercial transactions through tariffs, quotas, and prohibitions of some transactions. States gave subsidies to export and import substitution industries and sometimes engaged in production or trade.

Mercantilist states also acquired colonies for the purpose of favorable trade balances and for the political goal of self-sufficiency. The mercantile interests of the metropole were served by strict state regulation of the colonial economy. It was the reaction to such mercantilist policies—the regulation of production and exports and imports and the control of shipping—that led the American colonies to rebel against England.

Thus in the mercantile period, it was the nature of the emerging state and the state system that in large part determined economic interaction—and when that political structure changed, when Great Britain rose to political dominance, the economic system also changed.[5]

In the nineteenth century, the political system was characterized by the balance of power on the continent and by Great Britain's power overseas. On the continent, Russia and France were constrained by the territorial realignments of the Congress of Vienna, and the four major continental powers were controlled through their own rivalries. This enabled Great Britain to play a balancing and mediating role. With its geographic position off the European continent and its predominance on the seas, Great Britain was able to control Europe's access to the rest of the world by denying overseas colonies to continental states. This naval power combined with the decline of the continental powers meant that the greater part of the non-European world was independent or under British rule.

Because of this political system of a balance of power on the continent and British power overseas, Great Britain achieved a head start in economic development and was able to establish an international economic system that centered on Britain. The basis of this system was free trade.

The political roots of free trade may be traced back to the Napoleonic period, when the French emperor imposed the continental system: an economic embargo on Great Britain. The Napoleonic embargo encouraged a transformation of the British economy from trade with the Continent to trade overseas. After the defeat of France and the end of the embargo, Britain continued on the established path. With the repeal of the Corn Laws, the navigation laws, and the gradual removal of tariffs, however, Britain devised an exchange system of domestic manufactures for overseas raw materials. Treaties with and among other European states expanded the system to the Continent, and trading dominance was reinforced by British investment overseas. In the nineteenth century, vast amounts of capital flowed out of Great Britain to the United States, Canada, Latin America, and the nontropical areas of the empire, and the city of London emerged as the world's financial center.

Thus in the nineteenth century, military and political dominance enabled Britain to adopt and internationalize a liberal economic system. But once again, when the political system began to change at the end of the nineteenth century—when British power waned—the liberal economic system also began to decline, and a new imperialist system emerged.[6]

The roots of nineteenth-century imperialism are complex and elusive, but two political factors were crucial to its growth. The first was the decline of British dominance that stemmed from the rise of rival political, military, and economic powers: in particular, the United States and Germany. And second, the disruptive influence of these new powers was reinforced by the emergence of modern nationalism. The increasingly powerful rival states, and Britain as well, were motivated by the unruly forces of national identity, national pride, and the quest for national self-fulfillment and power. More nearly equal power relations and the new nationalism led to a highly competitive international system, one increasingly less constrained by Great Britain's balancing and overseas domination, which had stabilized the earlier nineteenth-century system.

These political changes permitted the operation of other forces: the political pressures of a newly powerful capitalist class, along with the military; the escapades of various adventurers (explorers and fortune hunters); technological and communications developments, which facilitated control of overseas territories; and the action and reaction dynamic of imperial competition. International political conflict increased, but often it was acted out not in Europe—at least not until 1914—but, rather, in Asia and Africa. In only a few decades, much of Asia and virtually all of Africa were divided up by Western Europe and the United States.

This new imperialism was the basis for a new international economic system. European political domination led to economic domination and exploitation. As in the days of mercantilism, colonies were integrated into an international economic system designed to serve the economic interest of the metropole. The political victors controlled investment and trade, regulated currency and production, and manipulated labor, thus establishing structures of economic dependency in their colonies that endured far longer than their actual political authority.[7]

The imperialist system and the residual domination of the United Kingdom in the West finally collapsed under the strain of World Wars I and II. In the post–World War II period, a new political and economic system emerged based on the hostile confrontation of the two superpowers. Politically, the new system was bipolar. In the West, there was a hierarchy, with the United States as the dominant political and military power over a weakened Europe and Japan; in the Third World, most of the nations remained politically subordinate to the old imperial powers; and in the East, the Soviet Union was the overwhelmingly dominant political and military power. And finally, East and West confronted each other in the Cold War.

This international political system determined the postwar international economic system. For political reasons, the East and West were isolated into two separate economic systems. In the East, the Soviet Union imposed a Communist international economic system based on the concept of a socialist commonwealth and, for political reasons, sought to make the other members of the socialist commonwealth economically dependent on the Soviet Union and economically isolated from the West. In the West, U.S. military and political dominance was matched by U.S. economic dominance. The United States' liberal vision shaped the economic order in the West. The principles of the international economic system were again as in the period of British hegemony: free-trade and free-capital movements.[8] With such a system, U.S. trade, U.S. investment, and the U.S. dollar predominated. Thus, politics shaped economics in the postwar era. And in the 1970s and 1980s, as before, it was to a great extent the changing political scene that caused the breakdown of the postwar economic system. The decline of U.S. power and increasing pluralism in the West, a superpower détente, and new political pressures from the less-developed countries transformed the international economic system.

Political Concerns and Economic Policy

In addition to influencing economic systems, political factors also influence economic policies. Throughout history, as we have seen, national policy has shaped international economics. In the mercantile period, governments regulated economic activity and acquired colonies. In the nineteenth century, the British repealed the Corn Laws and the navigation acts and adopted free trade. At the end of that century, public policy turned to the annexation of territory in Asia and Africa. In the years since World War II, foreign policy has focused on a multilateral, free-trading system.

These national policies were, in turn, determined by internal political processes. Economic policy is the outcome of a political bargaining process in which different groups representing different interests conflict over different preferred policy outcomes. Group conflict occurs, for example, between groups favoring low tariff barriers and those advocating protection, between advocates of foreign economic assistance and its opponents, and between those favoring energy independence and those advocating reliance on foreign sources of energy. The outcome of political conflict is determined by power. The different strengths of the competing groups affect the outcomes of foreign economic policy. Thus mercantilism may be viewed as the outcome of a political conflict between particularist local powers and the rising power of the central government; free trade was the product of a conflict between the landed class, which advocated protection, and the rising bourgeois class, which supported free trade; imperialism reflected the political power of the ascendant military and capitalist classes; and U.S. liberalism was determined by the support it enjoyed among powerful business and labor groups.

Very often, overriding strategic and diplomatic interests determine the political bargaining process. Economic policy is frequently either shaped by political concerns or becomes an explicit tool of national strategic and diplomatic policy. Trade policy is often consciously linked with political goals. Embargo has been an economic tool of political warfare throughout history. France applied an embargo to weaken Great Britain during the Napoleonic wars; the League of Nations called for an embargo of Italy after its invasion of Ethiopia in an effort to end that aggression in 1935; the United States since 1949 has frequently embargoed trade with Communist countries in an effort to weaken military capability; the 1973 Arab oil embargo of the United States and the Netherlands was an effort to alter their pro-Israeli foreign policy; and in 1980, the United States tried to use economic pressure to force Iran to release its American hostages.[9]

Trade policy has also been used for defensive military purposes. Alexander Hamilton argued that the fledgling United States should establish a domestic manufacturing system through trade protection to avoid dependence on foreign sources of supply that could be cut off in time of political conflict or war.[10] The 1988 U.S. trade law restricted purchase by foreigners of industries important for U.S. national security.

Foreign aid is another familiar economic tool used for strategic and diplomatic ends. The Marshall Plan, under which the United States gave $17 billion in outright grants to Western European countries to rebuild their economies after World War II, was designed to make Western Europe impervious to aggression by the Soviet Union. Foreign economic assistance to less-developed countries has been used to win friends for the West or the East during the Cold War. Foreign aid has also been used by former colonial powers to retain political influence in those newly independent former colonies.

International Economics as International Politics

Finally, international economic relations, in and of themselves, constitute political relations. International politics may be defined as the "patterns of political interaction between and among states."[11] And as with all politics, international politics involves goal-seeking behavior and a process of deciding who gets what, when, and how.[12]

Interaction in the international system ranges from conflict to cooperation. At one extreme is pure conflict, as when the interests of actors (such as states) or nonstate actors (such as multinational corporations) are diametrically opposed: if one actor realizes its goal, the other cannot achieve its objective. For example, in a conflict over territory, one state will gain the territory and the other will lose it. At the other extreme is cooperation. In such a situation, actors have a common interest, and all benefit from the pursuit of this shared interest. Allies, for example, have a common interest in ensuring their common defense, or colonies have a common interest in achieving independence, or trading partners have a common interest in maintaining beneficial trading relations.

Most international interaction contains elements of both conflict and cooperation. Even in situations of extreme conflict, there is often an element of cooperation. For example, despite the confrontation between the United States and the Soviet Union over placing missiles in Cuba in 1962, both superpowers' interest in preventing the escalation of these conflicts into nuclear war and holocaust led to cooperation as their resolution. Conversely, in situations involving high levels of cooperation, there is often an element of conflict; and even when actors share interests, there is usually conflict over specific interests and specific solutions. For example, all states may want to establish and maintain a stable international monetary system; but some of these states may prefer a particular type of monetary system, such as a fixed exchange rate or a floating exchange rate regime, which satisfies their more specific national interests. Thus within a framework of common goals, states disagree over the best means to achieve their common end.

In domestic politics, goal-seeking behavior is regulated by government, which has the authority to make decisions for a society and the power to enforce those decisions. The characteristic that distinguishes international politics from internal politics is the absence of government. In the international system, no legitimate body has the authority to manage conflict or achieve common goals by making and enforcing decisions for the system; instead, decision-making authority is dispersed among many governmental, intergovernmental, and nongovernmental groups.

Because there is no international government, the central problems of international politics are the adjustment or management of conflict and the achievement of cooperation. The means by which state and nonstate actors manage, or fail to manage, their conflicts and the ways in which they cooperate, or fail to cooperate, to achieve common goals are the central subject of international politics. Over the centuries, actors have deliberately or inadvertently devised rules, institutions, and procedures to manage international conflict and cooperation. These forms of managing international order have varied over time, space, and issues. They range from balances of power to alliances to international organizations, from hegemony to colonialism to international law. When there are effective rules, institutions, and procedures, conflict takes place within agreed-upon limits, and cooperation is facilitated. But when there are no effective rules, institutions, and procedures, conflict may be unregulated and cooperation may be impossible to achieve. In such a situation, therefore, international conflict may escalate into war.

The subject of international economic relations may also be viewed as the management of conflict and cooperation in the absence of government. As with all international political interaction, economic interaction ranges from pure conflict to pure cooperation. Some economic relations lead to high levels of conflict. Wealth is an important goal of groups in international politics, and the pursuit of wealth in the presence of scarce resources leads to conflict—over access to markets, the control of raw materials, and the control of the means of production. Such conflict often is linked to conflicts over power and sovereignty. The confrontation of producers and consumers over the price of oil, for example, is a challenge by the producers to the power of both the developed countries and the oil companies. The concern in Canada, Europe, and the Third World about multinational corporations is, in part, a reaction to the infringement of their sovereignty. Much international economic interaction, however, has a high level of cooperation. Many states share the goals of a stable monetary system, expanding trade relations, and rising production, although they differ over the means of achieving these ends. Some favor fixed exchange rates, whereas others prefer a float. Some advocate tariff reductions on textiles, whereas others forcefully oppose them. Some favor growth through free trade, whereas others feel that free trade inhibits growth. Some consider multinational corporations to be a vital road to economic growth, whereas others believe that they perpetuate underdevelopment.

As with all international politics, states have deliberately or inadvertently established rules, institutions, and procedures to manage international conflict and cooperation.[13] International economic management thus varies with the time, place, and issue. Mercantilism, free trade, and imperialism have been different historical forms of trade management. At different times, the gold standard and the dollar system have regulated international monetary relations. Sometimes, as during the nineteenth-century gold standard or the twentieth-century dollar system, the management is effective. But at other times, as during the Great Depression of the 1930s, the monetary crisis of 1971 to 1973, or the trade wars of the 1980s, the management breaks down. In some relations, such as those among the developed market economies, there are complex and effective management rules, institutions, and procedures. In other relations, such as those between developed and less-developed countries, there either are no rules, institutions, and procedures, or they are the subject of great disagreement. Finally, in some areas, such as international trade, complex rules have been formally established, international organizations created, and informal procedures devised. In other areas, such as international production, international management relies on more rudimentary forms of control. This book is a study of the way that actors have managed or have failed to manage international economic relations since World War II.

Three Systems

To understand the nature of international economic conflict and cooperation and their management, this study will examine management in three subsystems of the larger international economic system: the Western system of interdependence, the North-South system of dependence, and the East-West system of independence. This delineation of the international economy into three subsystems, especially that of separating the Western from the North-South systems, is artificial because interactions and problems overlap all systems in the real world. Nevertheless, political processes and political problems are different in the three subsystems.

The Western system includes the developed market economies of North America, Western Europe, and Japan.[14] These states are wealthy, highly developed, and capitalistic. They have their major international economic interactions with one another and are linked in a dense system of mutual economic interaction. Since World War II there has been a vast increase in economic interaction among the developed market economies. Increased interaction in the financial and monetary field has been caused by the common international use of the American dollar, reductions in barriers to financial flows, and the internationalization of financial markets. There has also been a great increase in international trade owing to economic growth, trade liberalization, a decrease in transportation costs, and the broader horizons of business people. Production has also become international, with the increased flow of direct investment and the reorganization of production and marketing on a global scale.[15]

These and other forms of increased interaction have led to a significant degree of interdependence—that is, actors or events in one part of the system have the ability to influence actors or events in another part of the system.[16] Thus, individual countries' economic policies and events are increasingly sensitive to the economic policies and events of other members of the system. The monetary, trade, and investment policies in one country in the Western system now have a direct impact on the monetary, trade, and investment policies in other countries in the system, and governments are discovering that the national economy is more and more open to external influence. Some Western countries are more sensitive or more vulnerable than other countries are. The United States, in particular, has been able to control the impact of interdependence better than some other nations have, partly because the international aspect of the U.S. economy is smaller than that of other members of the system and partly because of U.S. economic power.[17]

Although contributing to economic prosperity, interdependence has also created a political problem. Interdependence seems to have grown faster than the means of its management. From the perspective of the individual state, interdependence interferes with national policy and a nation's ability to control its economy. Greater interaction increases the number of disturbances with which national decision makers must cope; for now disturbances arise not only from within the economy but also from without. Interdependence also creates forces that interfere with the traditional measures of national economic policy. Thus interdependence weakens national management.

A series of economic problems have intensified the dilemmas that interdependence poses to the developed countries: inflation, sluggish and, at times, stagnant economic growth, and high rates of unemployment have plagued the advanced capitalist countries in the 1970s and 1980s. There is confusion among economists and policymakers over how best to respond to these problems. The consensus on Keynesian economic policies that guided the West's tremendous economic expansion after World War II has eroded and, despite a growing orientation to freer market policies such as those of the United States under President Reagan and the United Kingdom of Prime Minister Thatcher, no new consensus has emerged. Thus, Western leaders must confront the problems that interdependence poses to their economies at a time when there is a significant debate about appropriate domestic economic policy. Under such conditions, leaders may find it difficult to respond forcefully and effectively to the challenge of interdependence. The complexity of domestic economic issues coupled with the problems posed by interdependence may also increase international economic friction. Leaders searching for remedies for domestic problems may turn to national solutions and seek to reduce the international economic contacts that complicate their tasks. At the same time, international management is inadequate. The present structures and leadership are incapable of responding to the malaise of advanced capitalism or controlling interdependence. As a result, there is growing tension between national and international management. In Part Two we shall examine the problem of interdependence and the possibility of managing it.

The second subsystem of international economic interactions is the

North-South system of relations among the developed market economies and the Third World—the less-developed economies of Africa, Asia, and Latin America. Unlike the Western system, which is composed of relatively similar and equal actors, the North-South system is one of disparity and inequality between North and South in gross national product per capita. In 1986, the developed market economies had an average gross national product of $12,960 per capita, whereas the less-developed countries had an average gross national product of $610 per capita.[18] Although in relative terms the lot of some developing countries seems to be improving, the absolute differences in income remain. And in many cases, the gap between North and South is widening.

The main problem of this unequal system is dependence. Whereas interdependence means a high level of mutual economic interaction and mutual sensitivity, dependence denotes highly unequal economic interaction and highly unequal sensitivity. Dependence exists when a Southern country has a high level of economic interaction with a Northern country, when that interaction is of great importance to the national economy and when, therefore, the Southern country is influenced by actors or events in the Northern state. The Northern country, on the other hand, does not have a high level or a qualitatively important economic interaction with the Southern state and is not influenced by actors or events in the Southern country. Interdependence is a relatively symmetrical relationship; dependence is an asymmetrical relationship.

Dependence usually takes one or more forms. First, it can be trade dependence. Most Southern countries earn a large percentage of their gross national products from trade with the North. Most of the Third World countries have a small internal market and thus depend on the larger Northern markets for the sale of their product. Thus a dependent country is highly sensitive to factors in the North—both market and political—that shape Northern demand and thus influence their trade. Furthermore, a large percentage of Southern countries' exports is often concentrated in a single or small number of primary products, which reinforces sensitivity to foreign demand by making the country highly vulnerable to fluctuations in demand for the principal product. Also, a large percentage of Southern countries' trade is often directed to a particular Northern market, which again accentuates the sellers' sensitivity and vulnerability to the demand conditions of that single market. Finally, many of the Southern countries that do have strong export sectors frequently manufacture products, such as steel and textiles, that threaten floundering but politically powerful industries in the North. Trade dependence, then, is characterized by the Southern economy's dependence on trade with the North and the high levels of sensitivity to those factors that influence that trade.

A second form of dependence is in the area of investment. A large percentage of the domestic stock of investment in Third World countries is often owned by Northern investors. Northern foreign investment tends to control the sectors most crucial to technological development, modern industrial development, and exports.

A third form of dependence is financial. Financial dependence exists when a less-developed country with a balance-of-payments difficulty becomes dependent on external balance-of-payments assistance through the International Monetary Fund, which then reserves the right to help determine that country's domestic and foreign economic policy. Another indication of the South's financial dependence on the North is Third World indebtedness to private banks. In the 1970s, many developing countries borrowed extensively from Northern private commercial banks. By 1982, Third World long-term debt owed to private financial institutions in developed countries amounted to $359 billion, and by 1988 that figure had risen to $570 billion.[19] Foreign aid also creates dependence and may reinforce Northern trade and investment dominance.

Usually, these economic dependencies—trade, investment, finance— are reinforced by other types of relationships with the North: cultural ties, alliances and treaties, more informal political ties, and military links ranging from military aid to military intervention.

In political terms, the dependent Southern country is subject to political decisions made by institutions in which it has little say. The most obvious example of exclusion from management of the underdeveloped countries has been in the major economic institutions of the North—the International Monetary Fund, the International Bank for Reconstruction and Development, and the General Agreement on Tariffs and Trade—institutions that were created by the developed countries and reflect their dominant power. In the broader sense, the economic decisions of the developed Northern countries affect the economic development of the dependent countries. The agricultural, trade, and monetary policies of the North all directly affect the South. Thus, the less-developed countries feel that the system is illegitimate because they do not have access to decision making and because they are excluded from its management.

This political structure also means that the management decisions made by the North reflect the interests, desires, and goals of the North, not those of the South. And this adds another dimension to dependency—the feeling among the underdeveloped countries that not only do they not share in the management of the system but also that they do not share in the resources and the benefits of the system, and that the system exists to perpetuate the South's dependent status. The impact of dependence is seen as the perpetuation of dependency and underdevelopment.

Thus, the political interest of less-developed countries is (1) to share in the management of the system and (2) thereby to benefit to a greater extent from the system. Their goal is to change the system of dependence. Over the years, the Southern countries have pursued different strategies in an effort to alter their dependence. By the 1970s, with the coincidence of the erosion of the Bretton Woods system and the discovery by the South of the oil weapon, the less-developed countries called for a new international economic order involving sweeping changes in the rules governing international economic relations. In the 1970s, most Southern countries turned from proposals for radical restructuring to a more pragmatic effort to increase benefits from the prevailing regime. In Part Three we shall examine the problem of dependence and the attempts of Third World countries to manage that dependence.

The final international economic subsystem we shall consider is that between the East and the West. The relationship between the developed market economies of the West and the planned economies of the Communist states of Eastern Europe, the Soviet Union, and China has been one of independence, whose partners have few interactions and little impact on one another. The Cold War forced each side to isolate its system from the other. Led by the United States, the West established a set of legal and administrative barriers to trade with the East, whereas the East followed a policy of economic and political isolation within a socialist commonwealth. Reinforcing the political choice of independence was the divergence of the two economic systems. The socialist states and the developed market states created their own, separate economic institutions. The socialist states, for example, did not participate in the International Monetary Fund (IMF), the General Agreement on Tariffs and Trade (GATT), and the International Bank for Reconstruction and Development. East-West trade was small, and there were no capital or investment flows.

Had the system remained independent, there would have been little interest in examining the East-West system of management. But in recent years, the political and economic bases for independence and isolation have changed. The détente of the 1970s and new economic problems in the East led to efforts to increase East-West economic interaction. In the 1980s, under the leadership of Mikhail Gorbachev the Soviet Union is seeking to restructure its economy *(perestroika)* and open up its society and policy *(glasnost)*. China has also sought to restructure its economy and open up its international economic relations. These policies have a potential impact on relations with the West ranging from greater trade and financial flows to possible membership in Western economic institutions such as the IMF and the GATT. The problem to be examined in Part Four is this attempt to move away from independence toward greater international economic interaction.

NOTES

1. For readings on the classical liberal school, see Adam Smith, *An Inquiry into the Nature and Causes of the Wealth of Nations*, ed. Edwin Cannan (New York: Modern Library, 1937); James Mill, *Elements of Political Economy*, 3rd rev. ed. (London: Henry G. Bohn, 1844); John Stuart Mill, *Principles of Political Economy*, 7th ed. of 1871, ed. J. W. Ashley (London: Longmans, Green & Co., 1909). For twentieth-century liberals, see Norman Angell, *The Great Illusion 1933* (New York: Putnam's, 1933); Cordell Hull, *Memoirs*, 2 vols. (New

York: Macmillan, 1963). For a critique of the political implications of liberal theory, see Edward Hallett Carr, *The Twenty Years' Crisis, 1919–1939: An Introduction to the Study of International Relations*, 2nd ed. (New York: St. Martin's Press, 1962); Kenneth N. Waltz, *Man, the State, and War: A Theoretical Analysis* (New York: Columbia University Press, 1954, 1959).

2. There are, of course, important exceptions. See, for example, Richard Cooper, *The Economics of Interdependence* (New York: McGraw-Hill, 1968); Charles P. Kindleberger, *Power and Money: The Economics of International Politics and the Politics of International Economics* (New York: Basic Books, 1970); François Perroux, *L'Economie du XXe Siècle* (Paris: Presses Universitaires de France, 1961); Paul A. Baran and Paul M. Sweezy, *Monopoly Capital: An Essay on the American Economic and Social Order* (New York: Modern Reader, 1966). The last citation represents one school that is an exception to the general isolation of economics and politics, the Marxists.

3. Again, there are exceptions: see, for example, David P. Calleo and Benjamin M. Rowland, *America and the World Political Economy* (Bloomington: Indiana University Press, 1973); Klaus Knorr, *Power and Wealth: The Political Economy of International Power* (New York: Basic Books, 1973). Political scientists have recently become interested in the political implications of international economic interdependence. See, for example, Robert O. Keohane and Joseph S. Nye, Jr., *Power and Interdependence: World Politics in Transition* (Boston: Little, Brown, 1977); Edward L. Morse, *Modernization and the Transformation of International Relations* (New York: Free Press, 1976). Other studies in international political economy have been made by "practitioners" and scholars with a joint economics and political science background: see, for example, Harold Malmgren, *International Economic Peacekeeping in Phase II* (New York: Quadrangle Books, 1972); Susan Strange, *Sterling and British Policy, A Political Study of an International Currency in Decline* (New York: Oxford University Press, 1971). More and more, economic issues are being addressed by scholars of international politics. See, for example, issues of the journal *International Organization;* Robert O. Keohane, *After Hegemony: Cooperation and Discord in the World Political Economy* (Princeton: Princeton University Press, 1984); Robert Gilpin, *The Political Economy of International Relations* (Princeton: Princeton University Press, 1987).

4. See, for example, Klaus Knorr, *The Power of Nations: The Political Economy of International Relations* (New York: Basic Books, 1975); Paul Kennedy, *The Rise and Fall of the Great Powers: Economic Change and Military Conflict from 1500 to 2000* (New York: Random House, 1987).

5. For a classic study of mercantilism, see Eli F. Hecksher, *Mercantilism*, 2 vols., trans. Mendel Shapiro (London: Allen & Unwin, 1936), especially vol. 1, pp. 19–30. See also Jacob Viner, "Power Versus Plenty As Objectives of Foreign Policy in the Seventeenth and Eighteenth Centuries," *World Politics*, I (October 1948), 1–29.

6. See Robert Gilpin, "The Politics of Transnational Economic Relations," in Robert O. Keohane and Joseph S. Nye, Jr., eds., *Transnational Relations and World Politics* (Cambridge, Mass.: Harvard University Press, 1972), pp. 55–56; Alexander K. Cairncross, *Home and Foreign Investment, 1870–1913: Studies in Capital Accumulation* (Cambridge: Cambridge University Press, 1953); Albert H. Imlah, *Economic Elements in the Pax Britannica: Studies in British Foreign Trade in the Nineteenth Century* (Cambridge, Mass.: Harvard University Press, 1958).

7. The literature on nineteenth-century imperialism is vast. For political interpretations, see Carlton J. H. Hayes, *A Generation of Materialism, 1871–1900* (New York: Harper & Row, 1941); William Langer, *The Diplomacy of Imperialism* (New York: Knopf, 1935); Parker T. Moon, *Imperialism and World Politics* (New York: Macmillan, 1926); Joseph A. Schumpeter, *Imperialism and Social Classes* (Oxford: Basil Blackwell, 1951). For economic interpretations, see Michael Barratt Brown, *The Economics of Imperialism* (Harmondsworth, England: Penguin, 1974); John A. Hobson, *Imperialism: A Study* (Ann Arbor: University of Michigan Press, 1965); V. I. Lenin, *Imperialism: The Highest Stage of Capitalism* (New York: International Publishers, 1969). For overall analyses of different theories, see Benjamin J. Cohen, *The Question of Imperialism* (New York: Basic Books, 1973); George Lichtheim, *Imperialism* (New York: Praeger, 1971); E. M. Winslow, *The Pattern of Imperialism* (New York: Columbia University Press, 1948).

8. Stephen Krasner has examined patterns in international economic regimes and has

devised a theoretical explanation for why a structure of hegemony—such as existed in the nineteenth century and after World War II—is most conducive to the development of a liberal international trading system. See Stephen Krasner, "State Power and the Structure of International Trade," *World Politics*, 28:3 (April 1976), 317–347. For another perspective on post-1945 American international economic policy—that liberalism was a mask for the United States' imperial domination—see Harry Magdoff, *The Age of Imperialism: The Economics of U.S. Foreign Policy* (New York: Monthly Review Press, 1969).

9. See, for example, Yuan-Li Wu, *Economic Warfare* (Englewood Cliffs, N.J.: Prentice-Hall, 1952); Albert O. Hirschman, *National Power and the Structure of Foreign Trade* (Berkeley and Los Angeles: University of California Press, 1945).

10. Alexander Hamilton, "Report on the Subject of Manufactures," in Arthur Harrison Cole, ed., *Industrial and Commercial Correspondence of Alexander Hamilton Anticipating His Report on Manufactures* (New York: A. M. Kelley, 1968), pp. 247–320. For a general discussion of nineteenth-century ideas about how economic policy can serve military power, see Edward Meade Earle, *Makers of Modern Strategy* (Princeton, N.J.: Princeton University Press, 1943), esp. "Adam Smith, Alexander Hamilton, Friedrich List: The Economic Foundations of Military Power," pp. 117–154.

11. Donald J. Puchala, *International Politics Today* (New York: Dodd, Mead, 1971), p. 1.

12. Harold D. Lasswell, *Politics: Who Gets What, When, How* (Cleveland, Ohio: World Publishing, 1958).

13. Scholars studying international political economy are paying more attention to how international economic regimes—the constellations of rules, institutions, and procedures that bring order to international economic activity—are developed and maintained. See, for example, Robert O. Keohane and Joseph S. Nye, Jr., *Power and Interdependence: World Politics in Transition* (Boston: Little, Brown, 1977); Oran R. Young, "International Regimes: Problems of Concept Formation," *World Politics*, 32:3 (April 1980), 331–356; Stephen Krasner, ed., *International Organization*, 36 (1982): Special issue on regimes.

14. One might also add Australia, New Zealand, and South Africa.

15. Richard N. Copper, *The Economics of Interdependence* (New York: McGraw-Hill, 1968).

16. Oran Young, "Interdependencies in World Politics," *International Journal*, 24 (Autumn 1969), 726.

17. Cooper, *The Economics of Interdependence;* Keohane and Nye, Jr., *Power and Interdependence;* Robert O. Keohane and Joseph S. Nye, Jr., "Power and Interdependence Revisited, International Organization," 41:4 (Autumn 1987), pp. 725–753; Edward L. Morse, *Modernization and the Transformation of International Relations* (New York: Free Press, 1976); Kenneth N. Waltz, "The Myth of National Interdependence," in Charles P. Kindleberger, ed., *The International Corporation* (Cambridge, Mass.: MIT Press, 1970) pp. 205–223.

18. World Bank, *World Development Report 1988* (Washington, D.C.: World Bank, 1988), p. 223.

19. World Bank, *World Debt Tables: External Debt of Developing Countries*, 1988–1989 Volume I (Washington, D.C.: World Bank, 1988), p. X.

Part One

An Overview

1

The Management of International Economic Relations since World War II

During and after World War II, governments developed and enforced a set of rules, institutions, and procedures to regulate important aspects of international economic interaction. For nearly two decades, this order, known as the Bretton Woods system, was effective in controlling conflict and in achieving the common goals of the states that had created it. There were three political bases for the Bretton Woods system: the concentration of power in a small number of states, the existence of a cluster of important interests shared by those states, and the presence of a dominant power willing and able to assume a leadership role.[1]

The concentration of both political and economic power in the developed countries of North America and Western Europe enabled them to dominate the Bretton Woods system. They faced no challenge from the Communist states of Eastern Europe and Asia, including the Soviet Union, which were isolated from the rest of the international economy in a separate international economic system. Although the less-developed countries were fully integrated into the world economy, they had no voice in management because of their political and economic weakness. Finally, Japan, weakened by the war and lacking the level of development and the political power of North America and Western Europe, remained subordinate and outside the management group for much of the Bretton Woods era. The concentration of power facilitated the economic system's management by confining the number of actors whose agreement was necessary to establish rules, institutions, and procedures and to carry out management within the agreed-upon system.

Management was also made easier by a high level of agreement among the powerful on the goals and means of the international economic system. The foundation of that agreement was a shared belief in capitalism and liberalism. The developed countries relied primarily on market mechanisms and private ownership.

They also agreed that the liberal economic system required governmental intervention. In the postwar era, government has assumed responsibility for the economic well-being of its citizens, and employment, stability, and growth have become important subjects of public policy. The welfare state grew out of the Great Depression, which created a popular demand for governmental intervention in the economy, and out of the theoretical contributions of the Keynesian school of economics, which prescribed governmental intervention to maintain adequate levels of employment.

For the international economy, the developed countries favored a liberal system, one that relied primarily on a free market with the minimum of barriers to the flow of private trade and capital. The experience of the 1930s, when proliferation of exchange controls and trade barriers led to economic disaster, remained fresh in the minds of public officials. Although they disagreed on the specific implementation of this liberal system, all agreed that an open system would maximize economic welfare.

Some also believed that a liberal international economic system would enhance the possibilities of peace, that a liberal international economic system would lead not only to economic prosperity and economic harmony but also to international peace.[2] One of those who saw such a security link was Cordell Hull, the U.S. secretary of state from 1933 to 1944. Hull argued that

> unhampered trade dovetailed with peace; high tariffs, trade barriers, and unfair economic competition, with war . . . if we could get a freer flow of trade—freer in the sense of fewer discriminations and obstructions—so that one country would not be deadly jealous of another and the living standards of all countries might rise, thereby eliminating the economic dissatisfaction that breeds war, we might have a reasonable chance of lasting peace.[3]

A belief in governmental intervention and cooperation at the international level also evolved from the experience of the 1930s. The failure to control beggar-thy-neighbor policies, such as high tariffs and competitive devaluations, contributed to economic breakdown, domestic political instability, and international war. The lesson learned was that, as Harry D. White, a major architect of the Bretton Woods system, put it:

> the absence of a high degree of economic collaboration among the leading nations will . . . inevitably result in economic warfare that will be but the prelude and instigator of military warfare on an even vaster scale.[4]

To ensure economic stability and political peace, states agreed to cooperate to regulate the international economic system.

The common interest in economic cooperation was enhanced by the outbreak of the Cold War at the end of the 1940s. The economic weakness of the West, it was felt, would make it vulnerable to internal Communist threats and external pressure from the Soviet Union. Economic cooperation became necessary not only to rebuild Western economies and to ensure their continuing vitality but also to provide for their political and military security. In addition, the perceived Communist military threat led the developed countries to subordinate their economic conflict to their common security interests.

The developed market economies also agreed on the nature of international economic management, which was to be designed to create and maintain a liberal system. It would require the establishment of an effective international monetary system and the reduction of barriers to trade and capital flows. With these barriers removed and a stable monetary system in place, states would have a favorable environment for ensuring national stability and growth. The state, not the international system, bore the main responsibility for national stability and growth. Thus, the members of the system shared a very limited conception of international economic management: regulation of the liberal system by removing barriers to trade and capital flows and creating a stable monetary system.

Finally, international management relied on the dominant power to lead the system. As the world's foremost economic and political power, the United States was clearly in a position to assume that responsibility of leadership. The U.S. economy, undamaged by war and with its large market, great productive capability, financial facilities, and strong currency, was the dominant world economy. The ability to support a large military force plus the possession of an atomic weapon made the United States the world's strongest military power and the leader of the Western alliance. The European states, with their economies in disarray owing to the war, their production and markets divided by national boundaries, and their armies dismantled or weakened by the war, were not in a position to assume the leadership role. Japan, defeated and destroyed, was not then even considered part of the management system.

The United States was both able and willing to assume the leadership role. U.S. policymakers had learned an important lesson from the interwar period. The failure of U.S. leadership and the country's withdrawal into isolationism after World War I were viewed as major factors in the collapse of the economic system and of the peace. U.S. policymakers believed that after World War II the United States could no longer isolate itself. As the strongest power in the postwar world, the United States would have to assume primary responsibility for establishing political and economic order. With the outbreak of the Cold War, yet another dimension was added to the need for American leadership. Without such leadership, it was believed, the economic weakness in Europe and Japan would lead to Communist political victories.

Furthermore, the Europeans and Japanese—economically exhausted by the war—actively sought this leadership. They needed American assistance to rebuild their domestic production and to finance their international trade. The political implications of U.S. leadership, therefore, were viewed as positive, because it was felt that U.S. economic assistance would alleviate domestic economic and political problems and encourage international stability. What the Europeans feared was not U.S. domination but U.S. isolation: the history of the late entry into the two world wars by the United States was fresh in their minds.

Throughout the Bretton Woods period, the United States mobilized the other developed countries for management and, in some cases, managed the system alone. The United States acted as the world's central banker, provided the major initiatives in international trade negotiations, and dominated international production.

This coincidence of three favorable political conditions—the concentration of power, the cluster of shared interests, and the leadership of the United States—provided the political capability equal to the tasks of managing the international economy. It enabled the Europeans and Japan to recover from the devastation of the war and established a stable monetary system and a more open trade and financial system that led to a period of unparalleled economic growth.

By the 1970s, however, the Bretton Woods system was in shambles, and the management of the international economy was gravely threatened. Changes in power, leadership, and the consensus on a liberal, limited system undermined political management.

Although the developed countries remained the dominant political and economic powers, states outside the group challenged their right to manage the system. The less-developed countries sought to increase their access to the management and, thus, to the rewards of the international economic system. The Soviet Union and the countries of Eastern Europe have sought greater participation in the international economy.

More importantly, power shifted internally. In the 1960s, Europe experienced a period of great economic growth and dynamism in international trade. Six and then ten European countries united to form the European Economic Community, an economic bloc rivaling the U.S. economy and a potential political force. Japan's economic development was even more spectacular. In the 1960s, Japan became a major world economic power and joined the developed countries' condominium. At the same time a weakened dollar and a weakening balance of trade undermined U.S. international economic power.

Europe and Japan became more and more dissatisfied with the prerogatives that leadership gave the United States. The clearest example of this dissatisfaction was the growing European and Japanese criticism of the dollar system and U.S. payments deficits. The United States, for its part, was increasingly dissatisfied with the costs of leadership. Whereas the Europeans and Japanese criticized U.S. deficits, the United States criticized their refusal to allow it to devalue the dollar. As domestic economic problems emerged in the late 1960s, U.S. leaders began to feel that the costs of economic leadership outweighed its benefits.

The relaxation of security tensions reinforced the changing attitudes toward American leadership. Détente and the lessening of the perceived security threat weakened the security argument for Western economic cooperation and U.S. leadership. Europe and Japan were no longer willing to accept U.S. dominance for security reasons, and the United States was no longer willing to bear the economic costs of leadership for reasons of security.

Though U.S. dominance was increasingly unsatisfactory for the United States as well as for Europe and Japan, no new leader emerged to fulfill that role. Europe, although economically united in a common market, lacked the political unity necessary to lead the system. West Germany and Japan, the two strongest economic powers after the United States, were unable to manage the system by themselves and, in any case, were kept from leadership by the memories of World War II.

Finally, by the 1970s, the agreement on a liberal and limited system, which was the basis of Bretton Woods, had weakened. The most vociferous dissenters from the liberal vision of international management were the less-developed countries. In their view, the open monetary, trade, and financial system perpetuated their underdevelopment and subordination to the developed countries. They sought to make that development a primary goal and responsibility of the system.

For many in the developed countries as well, liberalism was no longer an adequate goal of management. The challenge to liberalism in the developed countries grew out of its very success. The reduction of barriers to trade and capital enabled an expansion in international economic interaction among the developed market economies: larger international capital flows, the growth of international trade, and the development of international systems of production. As a result, national economies became more interdependent and more sensitive to economic policy and events outside the national economy. The problem was heightened, because this sensitivity grew at a time when states were more than ever expected to ensure domestic economic well-being. Because of the influence of external events, states found it increasingly difficult to manage their national economies, and those economies became more and more troubled as governments became unable to cope with rising inflation and unemployment.

Interdependence led to two reactions and two different challenges to liberalism. One reaction was to erect new barriers to limit economic interaction and, with it, interdependence. An open international system, in the view of many, no longer maximized economic welfare and most certainly undermined national sovereignty and autonomy. Some argued that liberalism was no longer an adequate guide for policy in an increasingly tariff free world economy, where nontariff barriers are deeply inbedded in national economic policy and economic behavior is the main impediment to trade. Pressures grew for protection and managed trade, and efforts to build regional groupings, such as the EC or a North American system, grew.

Another reaction was to go beyond liberalism, beyond the idea of a limited management to new forms of international economic cooperation that would manage interdependence. An open system, according to this viewpoint, maximized welfare but required, in turn, new forms of international management that would assume responsibilities and prerogatives formerly undertaken by the state. These views led to efforts to coordinate national macroeconomic policies.

The shift in power and especially in U.S. leadership as well as the weakening of the liberal consensus eroded political management. Without an effective system of control, the international economy entered a period of instability: the fixed exchange rate system collapsed; states began to put up new barriers to trade; a handful of oil producers forced the powerful developed countries to submit to their demands; and the Third World called for a new international economic order. With less effective management, economic conflicts escalated to the highest political levels and became contests of political power.

While the Bretton Woods system collapsed, new forms of management gradually evolved. These new forms of management were built on the foundation of the Bretton Woods system: the dominance of the developed market economies, the persistent liberal consensus, and continuing U.S. leadership with more multilateral forms of management. These new forms of management were also built on the Bretton Woods institutions, which were gradually reformed and complemented to adapt to the new conditions of the end of the twentieth century. In the monetary system, the IMF became less important in exchange rate management and more important as a manager of the debt crisis of developing countries. Increasingly, a Group of Seven industrial countries undertook the management of the exchange rate regime and pursued greater coordination of national economic policies. In the trade arena, two new GATT negotiating rounds sought to develop new rules to contain and manage new forms of protectionism, to extend the multilateral trading regime to new sectors of trade, such as services and intellectual property, and to reflect more the concerns of developing countries. These multilateral efforts at reform were complemented by the growing importance of regional trade management systems, most notably the European Community, which grew to twelve members committed to complete the creation of a common internal market. Another regional system that emerged in the 1980s was the North American market, codified in the U.S.-Canada Free Trade Agreement.

In the 1980s, many developing countries took a more pragmatic approach to multilateral management, seeking to work within the prevailing regime rather than to establish a new international economic order. In particular, those developing countries that moved rapidly toward industrialization—the so-called New Industrializing Countries, or NICs—sought to play a greater role within the system. They pursued export-oriented policies and became active participants in the GATT. For a time it seemed that these rapidly growing countries would also become more integrated into the world financial system, especially through their new access to private capital markets. However, the heavy borrowing of many NICs, particularly those in Latin America, instead led to the LDC debt crisis, which posed a threat not only to their development and political stability but also to the international financial regime itself. In the 1980s (as in the oil crisis of the 1970s), management of the debt crisis posed a challenge for both developed and developing countries.

Finally, changes in domestic and international policy in the two key Communist countries, the Soviet Union and China, opened up the possibility of greater East-West economic interaction. Gorbachev's *perestroika*, or restructuring, sought to move the Soviet economy more in the market direction and to open up trade, finance, and investment relations with the West. China's reform had similar implications. While it remained highly unlikely that the Eastern states would become part of the market system, these reforms did raise important questions about the political desirability and economic feasibility of removing some of the barriers to East-West economic interaction.

The main political problem facing the international economy, and a crucial problem of all international relations, is how new forms of political management develop and whether those forms will be able to deal with the three key problems of our time: the control of interdependence in the face of the economic malaise in the North, the achievement of equity and the end of Third World dependence, and the improvement of East-West economic relations.

NOTES

1. On the idea of the need for a leader, see Charles P. Kindleberger, *The World in Depression, 1929–1939* (Berkeley and Los Angeles: University of California Press, 1973). For a theoretical analysis of the role of leadership in international cooperation, see Norman Frohlich, Joe Oppenheimer, and Oran Young, *Political Leadership and Collective Goods* (Princeton: Princeton University Press, 1971).

2. Kenneth Waltz, *Man, the State and War* (New York: Columbia University Press, 1969). For a discussion of how liberal ideas motivated U.S. foreign economic policy after World War II, see David P. Calleo and Benjamin M. Rowland, *America and the World Political Economy* (Bloomington: Indiana University Press, 1973).

3. Richard N. Gardner, *Sterling-Dollar Diplomacy in Current Perspective: The Origins and Prospects of Our International Economic Order*, expanded ed. (New York: Columbia University Press, 1980), p. 9.

4. Gardner, *Sterling-Dollar Diplomacy in Current Perspective*, p. 8.

Part Two

The Western System

2

International
Monetary Management

In July 1944, representatives of forty-four nations met on an estate in Bretton Woods, New Hampshire, to create a new international monetary order. Foremost in their minds was the collapse of the international monetary system in the 1930s. In those years, economic nationalism—competitive exchange rate devaluations, formation of competing monetary blocs, and the absence of international cooperation—contributed greatly to economic breakdown, domestic political instability, and war. The goal at Bretton Woods was to establish an international economic system that would prevent another economic and political collapse and another military conflict. It was the international consensus that previous monetary systems that relied primarily on market forces had proved inadequate.[1] At Bretton Woods, officials were prepared to establish a publicly managed international monetary order.

United States policymakers involved in creating the new economic order had concluded that the failure of U.S. leadership was a major cause of the economic and political disaster. During World War II, U.S. leaders thus decided that the United States would have to assume the primary responsibility for establishing a postwar economic order. That order would be designed to prevent economic nationalism by fostering free trade and a high level of international interaction. A liberal economic system, ensured by international cooperation, would provide the foundation for a lasting peace. Thus, in two years of bilateral negotiation, the United States and the United Kingdom, the world's leading economic and political powers, drew up a plan for a new system of international monetary management.[2]

The Anglo-American plan, approved at Bretton Woods, became the first publicly managed international monetary order. For a quarter of a century, international monetary relations were stable and provided a basis for growing international trade, economic growth, and political harmony among the developed market economies. Then, in the 1970s, the Bretton Woods system collapsed under the strain of growing interdependence and weakening U.S. monetary power. Monetary management in the 1970s and 1980s focused efforts to maintain order and stability in international monetary affairs in an environment of economic interdependence and a more plurilateral distribution of power.

In this chapter we shall examine monetary management in the period since World War II: the functioning and breakdown of Bretton Woods and international monetary relations in the post–Bretton Woods era. We will examine how nations have sought to provide the two central functions of an international monetary system: liquidity and adjustment.

Just as any national economy needs an accepted money, so the international economy requires an accepted vehicle for investment, trade, and payments. Unlike national economies, however, the international economy lacks a central government that can issue currency and manage its use. Historically, this problem has been solved through the use of gold and national currencies. In the nineteenth and first half of the twentieth centuries, gold played a key role in international monetary transactions. Gold was used to back currencies; the international value of currency was determined by its fixed relationship to gold; and gold was used to settle international accounts.

The British pound was a supplement to gold. Based on the dominant British economy, it became the reserve, transaction, and intervention currency. After World War II, as we shall see, the U.S. dollar became the key international currency. Dollars were held as reserves by central banks; the dollar became the unit for international trade, investment, and finance; and dollars were used to intervene in exchange markets to maintain fixed exchange rates. Although the use of the dollar eventually became a central problem for managing the system, efforts to replace it, including the creation of an international money, failed.

An international monetary system must also have means for adjusting imbalances in international payments. In national economies, payments imbalances among regions are adjusted more or less automatically through movement of capital and through common fiscal and monetary policy. In international economic relations, disequilibriums in payments can be settled by financing, by changing domestic economic policy to shift trade and investment patterns, by rationing the supply of foreign exchange through exchange controls, or by allowing the exchange rate to change. Effective adjustment can be promoted by international cooperation but it requires above all *alteration of domestic policies to achieve international solutions*, a politically difficult task. In the Bretton Woods era, adjustment was based on a fixed exchange rate system supplemented by financing, exchange controls, exchange rate changes, and adaptation of national policies. After Bretton Woods, the system was based on frequent exchange rate changes supplemented by financing and changes in national economic policies. The tension between international adjustment needs and domestic political re-quirements is a central dilemma of international monetary relations.

The Original Bretton Woods Agreement

In actuality, Bretton Woods never functioned as the United States and the others who signed the agreement had planned. The new order was intended to be a system of limited management by international organizations. Two public international organizations, the International Monetary Fund (IMF) and the International Bank for Reconstruction and Development (IBRD, known as the World Bank), were, for the first time in history, to perform certain monetary functions for the international system.

The rules of Bretton Woods, set forth in the articles of agreement, provided for a system of fixed exchange rates. Public officials, fresh from what they perceived as a disastrous experience with floating rates in the 1930s, concluded that a fixed exchange rate was the most stable and conducive basis for trade. Thus, all countries agreed to establish the parity, or value, of their currencies in terms of gold and to maintain exchange rates within 1 percent, plus or minus, of parity. The rules further encouraged an open system, by committing members to the convertibility of their respective currencies into other currencies and to free trade.[3]

The IMF was to be the keeper of the rules and the main instrument of public international management. Under the system of weighted voting, the United States exerted a preponderant influence in that body. IMF approval was necessary for any change in exchange rates, and it advised countries on policies affecting the monetary system. Most importantly, it could advance credits to countries with payments deficits. The IMF was provided with a fund, composed of member countries' contributions in gold and in their own currencies. The original quotas were to total $8.8 billion. In the event of a deficit in the current account, countries could borrow from this fund for up to eighteen months and, in some cases, for up to five years.

Despite these innovations in public control, the original Bretton Woods agreement mainly emphasized national and market solutions to monetary problems. It was expected that national monetary reserves, supplemented when necessary by IMF credits, would finance any temporary balance-of-payments disequilibriums. No provision was made for the creation of new reserves; new gold production was considered sufficient. In the event of structural disequilibrium, it was expected that there would be national solutions—a change in the value of the currency or an improvement by other means of a country's competitive position. Few means were given to the IMF, however, to encourage such national solutions.

The Bretton Woods planners expected that after a brief transition period—of no more than five years—the international economy would recover and the system would enter into operation. To facilitate the postwar recovery, the planners created another institution, the International Bank for Reconstruction and Development, or World Bank, to make loans to make possible a speedy postwar recovery and also to promote economic development.[4]

From 1945 to 1947 the United States actively pressed for implementation of the Bretton Woods institutions. The United States provided resources to the IMF and the World Bank and urged other countries to do likewise. To permit postwar recovery and facilitate the implementation of the Bretton Woods agreement, the United States gave financial assistance: $3 billion in relief funds and, more importantly, a $3.75 billion loan to Great Britain, which was expected to enable that country to complete its reconstruction and return the pound to convertibility.

By 1947, however, the United States concluded that the Bretton Woods system was not working and, in fact, that the Western system was on the verge of collapse. World War II, it became clear, had destroyed the European economic system, which had been based largely on international trade. The sources of Europe's foreign earnings had been wiped out. Its productive capacity had been destroyed or disrupted; its overseas earnings had turned into debts; its shipping was decimated; and its payments deficit was large and growing. Western Europe was faced with vast import needs, not only for reconstruction but also for mere survival.[5]

The Bretton Woods institutions were unable to cope with this problem. The IMF's modest credit facilities were insufficient to deal with Europe's huge needs and, in any case, the IMF could make loans only for current-account deficits and not for capital and reconstruction purposes. Only the United States' contribution of $570 million was actually available for World Bank lending. In addition, because the World Bank relied on U.S. financial markets to float its bonds, it was obliged to follow a conservative lending policy, making loans only when repayment was assured. By 1947 the IMF and the World Bank themselves admitted they could not deal with the system's economic problems.[6]

The economic crisis of 1947 was directly linked with political problems. Germany lay in ruins economically and politically. The governments of Italy and France, faced with pressures from powerful labor unions, were highly unstable. Britain, partly due to its economic difficulties, was withdrawing from India and Palestine and abandoning its political and security commitments to Greece and Turkey. More importantly, the Soviet Union seemed willing and able to take advantage of the West's economic plight and political instability to further its aim of territorial expansion in Europe. The Soviet Union had forcibly established Communist governments in the countries it occupied at the end of the war: Hungary, Rumania, Poland, and

Bulgaria, and it had pressured Iran and Turkey for territorial concessions. Communist guerrillas were making significant headway in Greece, and large Communist parties in the governments of Italy and France tried to take advantage of labor unrest. The Soviet Union also refused to cooperate with the Allies on a postwar settlement for Germany.

After 1947, because of these circumstances, the Bretton Woods system of international monetary management evolved from limited management by international organization to management by the United States.

Unilateral U.S. Management

From 1947 to 1960, the United States was both able and willing to manage the international monetary system. The strength of the U.S. economy, the lessons of the interwar period, and security incentives made U.S. leadership acceptable economically and politically at home. The Europeans and Japanese also accepted U.S. management. Economically exhausted by the war, they needed U.S. assistance to rebuild their domestic production, finance their international trade, and provide a setting for political stability. Thus, after 1947, the United States began to manage the international monetary system, by providing liquidity and adjustment.

By 1947 it was clear that gold and the pound could no longer serve as the world's money. Gold production was insufficient to meet the demands of growing international trade and investment. Because of the weakness of the British economy, the pound was no longer able to serve as the primary world currency. The only currency strong enough to be used to meet the rising demands for international liquidity was the dollar. The strength of the U.S. economy, the fixed relationship of the dollar to gold ($35 an ounce), and the commitment of the U.S. government to convert dollars into gold at that price made the dollar as good as gold. In fact, the dollar was better than gold, as it earned interest and could be used for trade and finance.

There was, however, a major stumbling block to the dollar's emergence as the world's key currency: a huge dollar shortage. The United States was running huge trade surpluses, and its reserves were immense and growing. For the system to work, it would be necessary to reverse this flow: the United States had to run a payments deficit. That is just what happened.

From 1947 until 1958, the United States encouraged an outflow of dollars, which provided liquidity for the international economy. Dollars flowed out through U.S. aid programs: the Truman plan for aid to Greece and Turkey, aid to underdeveloped countries, and, most important, the Marshall Plan, which from 1948 to 1952 gave sixteen Western European countries $17 billion in outright grants. U.S. military expenditures in NATO countries and for the war in Korea provided another source of dollar liquidity. Thus, the dollar became the world's currency, and the United States became the world's central banker, issuing dollars for the international monetary system.

In addition to providing liquidity, the United States managed imbalances in the system. It facilitated short-term adjustment through foreign aid and military expenditures, which helped offset the huge U.S. trade surplus and the European and Japanese deficits. In addition, the United States abandoned the Bretton Woods goal of convertibility and tolerated European and Japanese trade protection and discrimination against the dollar. For example, the United States absorbed large volumes of Japanese exports while accepting Japanese restrictions against U.S. exports. It supported the European Payments Union, an intra-European clearing system that discriminated against the dollar, and it promoted European exports to the United States. Finally, the United States used the leverage of Marshall Plan aid to encourage devaluation of many European currencies to support national programs of monetary stabilization.

To encourage long-term adjustment, the United States nurtured European and Japanese trade competitiveness. Policies for economic controls on the defeated Axis countries were scrapped. Aid to Europe and Japan was designed to rebuild productive and export capacity. In the long run it was expected that such European and Japanese recovery would benefit the United States by widening markets for U.S. exports.

The system worked well. Europe and Japan recovered and then expanded. The U.S. economy prospered partly because of the dollar outflow, which led to the purchase of U.S. goods and services. Yet by 1960, the U.S.-managed system was in trouble.

Multilateral Management under U.S. Leadership

The economic foundation of the U.S. management of the international monetary system was confidence in the U.S. dollar. This confidence was based on the strength of the U.S. economy, the enormous U.S. gold reserves, and the commitment to convert dollars into gold. But ironically, the system also relied on a process that eventually undermined the very confidence on which the structure was built: the constant outflow of dollars from the United States. The U.S. deficit and the foreign holding of dollars provided sufficient liquidity for international transactions. If, however, the deficit continued, and if outstanding dollar holdings abroad became too large in relation to gold reserves, confidence in the dollar—and thus in the entire system—would be jeopardized.[7]

By 1958 the United States no longer sought a payments deficit. The European and Japanese recoveries were nearly complete. Balances of payments were improving, and official reserves were growing steadily. By the end of 1959, European and Japanese reserves equaled those of the United States. U.S. gold holdings, however, had fallen from $24.4 billion at the end of 1948 to $19.5 billion at the end of 1959. More importantly, dollars held abroad had risen from $7.3 billion in 1948 to $19.4 billion at the end of 1959. The excess of U.S. gold holdings over foreign dollar holdings had fallen from $18.1 billion to $0.5 billion. In 1960, for the first time, foreign dollar holdings exceeded U.S. gold reserves.[8] The U.S. deficit was out of control. Private long-term capital outflow, caused to a great extent by direct investment abroad and foreign military and aid expenditures, led to a rising payments deficit (see Table 2-1).

The first run on the dollar, which occurred in November 1960 when speculators converted dollars into gold, signaled the end of the unilateral system of U.S. management. The dollar system did not collapse. The United States was still able to play a strong leadership role, and the dollar and the U.S. economy remained healthy. But the United States could no longer manage the system alone. Henceforth, it would be obliged to join in collective management, to seek the cooperation of other members of the system, and to make concessions.

At the end of the 1950s, the IMF, largely inactive in the period of U.S. unilateral management, began to play a more important role, largely by lending funds to Europeans and others to finance temporary payments disequilibriums. Increases in the Fund's quotas at this time facilitated the more active role. The principal functions of monetary management, however, were performed by a multilateral group of the major states. One important new form of multilateral management was central bank cooperation. Since 1930, European central bankers had met together regularly at the Bank of International Settlements (BIS) in Basel, Switzerland, but the United States had never become a member and had never participated in their frequent meetings.[9] After the dollar crisis of 1960, however, high officials of the United States' central bank, the Federal Reserve, joined the monthly meetings although the United States did not join the BIS.

U.S. participation enabled the Basel group to control important aspects of the international monetary system. The bankers provided ad hoc crisis management by supporting currencies that came under pressure. The group also regulated the price of gold. In 1961 the bankers agreed to control gold speculation by centralizing gold dealings through a "gold pool," buying gold when it fell below $35 an ounce and selling it when it rose above that limit. The bankers also cooperated in exchange markets and began to play an important role in the burgeoning Eurocurrency market (see below) by investing, intervening, and accumulating information. Finally, the

Table 2-1 U.S. International Transactions, 1946–88 [millions of dollars; quarterly data seasonally adjusted, except as noted. Credits (+), debits (−)]

Year or quar-ter	Merchandise[1][2]			Investment income[3]			Net mili-tary trans-actions	Net travel and trans-portation receipts	Other services net[3]	Balance on goods and services[4]	Remit-tances, pensions, and other unilateral transfers[1]	Balance on current account[4]
	EXPORTS	IMPORTS	NET	RECEIPTS	PAYMENTS	NET						
1946	11,764	−5,067	6,697	772	−212	560	−493	733	310	7,807	−2,922	4,885
1947	16,097	−5,973	10,124	1,102	−245	857	−455	946	145	11,617	−2,625	8,992
1948	13,265	−7,557	5,708	1,921	−437	1,484	−799	374	175	6,942	−4,525	2,417
1949	12,213	−6,874	5,339	1,831	−476	1,355	−621	230	208	6,511	−5,638	873
1950	10,203	−9,081	1,122	2,068	−559	1,509	−576	−120	242	2,117	−4,017	−1,840
1951	14,243	−11,176	3,067	2,633	−583	2,050	−1,270	298	254	4,399	−3,515	884
1952	13,449	−10,838	2,611	2,751	−555	2,196	−2,054	83	309	3,145	−2,531	614
1953	12,412	−10,975	1,437	2,736	−624	2,112	−2,423	−238	307	1,195	−2,481	−1,286
1954	12,929	−10,353	2,576	2,929	−582	2,347	−2,460	−269	305	2,499	−2,280	219
1955	14,424	−11,527	2,897	3,406	−676	2,730	−2,701	−297	299	2,928	−2,498	430
1956	17,556	−12,803	4,753	3,837	−735	3,102	−2,788	−361	447	5,153	−2,423	2,730
1957	19,562	−13,291	6,271	4,180	−796	3,384	−2,841	−189	482	7,107	−2,345	4,762
1958	16,414	−12,952	3,462	3,790	−825	2,965	−3,135	−633	486	3,145	−2,361	784
1959	16,458	−15,310	1,148	4,132	−1,061	3,071	−2,805	−821	573	1,166	−2,448	−1,282
1960	19,650	−14,758	4,892	4,616	−1,237	3,379	−2,752	−964	638	5,191	−2,367	2,824
1961	20,108	−14,537	5,571	4,999	−1,245	3,754	−2,596	−978	732	6,484	−2,662	3,822
1962	20,781	−16,260	4,521	5,618	−1,324	4,294	−2,449	−1,152	911	6,127	−2,740	3,387
1963	22,272	−17,048	5,224	6,157	−1,561	4,596	−2,304	−1,309	1,037	7,244	−2,831	4,414
1964	25,501	−18,700	6,801	6,824	−1,784	5,040	−2,133	−1,146	1,161	9,724	−2,901	6,823
1965	26,461	−21,510	4,951	7,437	−2,088	5,349	−2,122	−1,280	1,480	8,378	−2,948	5,431
1966	29,310	−25,493	3,817	7,528	−2,481	5,047	−2,935	−1,331	1,496	6,095	−3,064	3,031
1967	30,666	−26,866	3,800	8,020	−2,747	5,273	−3,226	−1,750	1,742	5,838	−3,255	2,583
1968	33,626	−32,991	635	9,368	−3,378	5,990	−3,143	−1,548	1,759	3,693	−3,082	611
1969	36,414	−35,807	607	10,912	−4,869	6,043	−3,328	−1,763	1,964	3,524	−3,125	399
1970	42,469	−39,866	2,603	11,747	−5,516	6,231	−3,354	−2,038	2,329	5,773	−3,443	2,331
1971	43,319	−45,579	−2,260	12,707	−5,436	7,271	−2,893	−2,345	2,649	2,423	−3,856	−1,433
1972	49,381	−55,797	−6,416	14,764	−6,572	8,192	−3,420	−3,063	2,965	−1,742	−4,052	−5,795
1973	71,410	−70,499	911	21,808	−9,655	12,153	−2,070	−3,158	3,406	11,244	−4,103	7,140
1974	98,306	−103,811	−5,505	27,587	−12,084	15,503	−1,653	−3,184	4,231	9,392	[5]−7,431	1,962
1975	107,088	−98,185	8,903	25,351	−12,564	12,787	−746	−2,812	4,853	22,984	−4,868	18,116
1976	114,745	−124,228	−9,483	29,286	−13,311	15,975	559	−2,558	5,027	9,521	−5,314	4,207
1977	120,816	−151,907	−31,091	32,179	−14,217	17,962	1,528	−3,565	5,679	−9,488	−5,023	−14,511
1978	142,054	−176,001	−33,947	42,245	−21,680	20,565	621	−3,573	6,459	−9,875	−5,552	−15,427
1979	184,473	−212,009	−27,536	64,132	−32,960	31,172	−1,778	−2,935	6,214	5,138	−6,128	−991
1980	224,269	−249,749	−25,480	72,506	−42,120	30,386	−2,237	−997	7,793	9,466	−7,593	1,873
1981	237,085	−265,063	−27,978	86,411	−52,329	34,082	−1,183	144	9,278	14,344	−7,460	6,884
1982	211,198	−247,642	−36,444	83,549	−54,883	28,666	−274	−992	9,320	278	−8,956	−8,679
1983	201,820	−268,900	−67,080	77,251	−52,376	24,875	−243	−4,227	9,908	−36,766	−9,480	−46,246
1984	219,900	−332,422	−112,522	85,908	−67,419	18,489	−2,099	−8,604	9,760	−94,975	−12,102	−107,077
1985	215,935	−338,083	−122,148	88,837	−62,901	25,936	−3,431	−10,049	9,600	−100,093	−15,010	−115,103
1986	223,969	−368,516	−144,547	90,110	−66,968	23,142	−4,372	−9,344	11,600	−123,520	−15,308	−138,828
1987	249,570	−409,850	−160,280	103,756	−83,381	20,375	−2,368	−10,281	12,035	−140,519	−13,445	−153,964
1986:												
I	54,113	−89,546	−35,433	24,352	−17,357	6,995	−1,403	−2,456	2,817	−29,485	−2,972	−32,457
II	56,946	−90,807	−33,861	22,248	−17,533	4,715	−1,283	−2,070	2,870	−29,629	−4,085	−33,714
III	56,268	−92,989	−36,721	21,845	−15,729	6,116	−1,076	−2,407	2,800	−31,288	−4,249	−35,537
IV	56,642	−95,174	−38,532	21,667	−16,350	5,317	−605	−2,410	3,112	−33,118	−4,003	−37,121
1987:												
I	56,791	−96,662	−39,871	24,791	−19,715	5,076	−78	−2,597	2,813	−34,657	−2,967	−37,624
II	59,864	−99,416	−39,552	22,429	−20,737	1,692	−179	−2,516	2,828	−37,727	−3,125	−40,852
III	64,902	−104,567	−39,665	23,289	−22,222	1,067	−851	−2,521	2,983	−38,987	−2,980	−41,967
IV	68,013	−109,205	−41,192	33,248	−20,709	12,539	−1,261	−2,648	3,412	−29,150	−4,373	−33,523
1988:												
I	75,300	−110,484	−35,184	26,554	−25,395	1,159	−1,033	−2,121	3,362	−33,817	−3,121	−36,938
II	79,606	−109,757	−30,151	23,426	−25,366	−1,940	−914	−1,676	3,693	−30,988	−2,751	−33,739
III[p]	82,306	−110,839	−28,533	26,830	−27,167	−337	−934	−1,463	3,491	−27,776	−3,118	−30,894

[1]Excludes military.
[2]Adjusted from Census data for differences in valuation, coverage, and timing.
[3]Fees and royalties from U.S. direct investments abroad or from foreign direct investments in the United States are excluded from investment income and included in other services, net.
[4]In concept, balance on goods and services is equal to net exports and imports in the national income and product accounts (and the sum of balance on current account and allocations of special drawing rights is equal to net foreign investment in the accounts), although the series differ because of different handling of certain items (gold, capital gains and losses, etc.), revisions, etc.
See next page for continuation of table.

Year or quarter	U.S. assets abroad, net [increase/capital outflow (–)]				Foreign assets in the U.S., net [increase/capital inflow (+)]			Allocations of special drawing rights (SDRs)	Statistical discrepancy	
	TOTAL	U.S. OFFICIAL RESERVE ASSETS[b]	OTHER U.S. GOVERNMENT ASSETS	U.S. PRIVATE ASSETS	TOTAL	FOREIGN OFFICIAL ASSETS	OTHER FOREIGN ASSETS		TOTAL (SUM OF THE ITEMS WITH SIGN REVERSED)	OF WHICH: SEASONAL ADJUSTMENT DISCREPANCY
1946		– 623								
1947		– 3,315								
1948		– 1,736								
1949		– 266								
1950		1,758								
1951		– 33								
1952		– 415								
1953		1,256								
1954		480								
1955		182								
1956		– 869								
1957		– 1,165								
1958		2,292								
1959		1,035								
1960	– 4,099	2,145	– 1,100	– 5,144	2,294	1,473	821		– 1,019	
1961	– 5,538	607	– 910	– 5,235	2,705	765	1,939		– 989	
1962	– 4,174	1,535	– 1,085	– 4,623	1,911	1,270	641		– 1,124	
1963	– 7,270	378	– 1,662	– 5,986	3,217	1,986	1,231		– 360	
1964	– 9,560	171	– 1,680	– 8,050	3,643	1,660	1,983		– 907	
1965	– 5,716	1,225	– 1,605	– 5,336	742	134	607		– 457	
1966	– 7,321	570	– 1,543	– 6,347	3,661	– 672	4,333		629	
1967	– 9,757	53	– 2,423	– 7,386	7,379	3,451	3,928		– 205	
1968	– 10,977	– 870	– 2,274	– 7,833	9,928	– 774	10,703		438	
1969	– 11,585	– 1,179	– 2,200	– 8,206	12,702	– 1,301	14,002		– 1,516	
1970	– 9,337	2,481	1,589	– 10,229	6,359	6,908	– 550	867	– 219	
1971	– 12,475	2,349	– 1,884	– 12,940	22,970	26,879	– 3,909	717	– 9,779	
1972	– 14,497	– 4	– 1,568	– 12,925	21,461	10,475	10,986	710	– 1,879	
1973	– 22,874	158	– 2,644	– 20,388	18,388	6,026	12,362		– 2,654	
1974	– 34,745	– 1,467	⁵366	– 33,643	34,241	10,546	23,696		– 1,458	
1975	– 39,703	– 849	– 3,474	– 35,380	15,670	7,027	8,643		5,917	
1976	– 51,269	– 2,558	– 4,214	– 44,498	36,518	17,693	18,826		10,544	
1977	– 34,785	– 375	– 3,693	– 30,717	51,319	36,816	14,503		– 2,023	
1978	– 61,130	732	– 4,660	– 57,202	64,036	33,678	30,358		12,521	
1979	– 64,331	– 1,133	– 3,746	– 59,453	38,752	– 13,665	52,416	1,139	25,431	
1980	– 86,118	– 8,155	– 5,162	– 72,802	58,112	15,497	42,615	1,152	24,982	
1981	– 110,951	– 5,175	– 5,097	– 100,679	83,032	4,960	78,072	1,093	19,942	
1982	– 121,153	– 4,965	– 6,131	– 110,058	93,746	3,593	90,154		36,085	
1983	– 49,777	– 1,196	– 5,006	– 43,576	84,869	5,845	79,023		11,154	
1984	– 22,304	– 3,131	– 5,489	– 13,685	102,621	3,140	99,481		26,760	
1985	– 32,636	– 3,858	– 2,829	– 25,950	129,900	– 1,196	131,096		17,839	
1986	– 97,991	312	– 2,000	– 96,303	221,253	35,507	185,746		15,566	
1987	– 75,987	9,149	1,162	– 86,297	211,490	44,968	166,522		18,461	
1986: I	– 15,626	– 115	– 206	– 15,305	39,050	2,719	36,331		9,033	3,006
II	– 24,515	16	– 211	– 24,320	50,128	15,838	34,291		8,100	– 2,786
III	– 26,213	280	– 1,592	– 24,901	69,884	15,779	54,104		– 8,133	– 3,876
IV	– 31,635	132	10	– 31,777	62,192	1,171	61,020		6,565	3,655
1987: I	11,072	1,956	67	9,049	33,100	13,977	19,122		– 6,547	4,141
II	– 22,878	3,419	– 170	– 26,127	50,660	10,332	40,327		13,071	– 2,615
III	– 25,292	32	252	– 25,567	71,658	611	71,047		– 4,399	– 4,658
IV	– 38,891	3,741	1,012	– 43,645	56,072	20,047	36,025		16,342	3,138
1988: I	6,591	1,503	814	5,903	26,066	24,670	1,395		4,282	3,747
II	– 18,972	39	– 801	– 18,210	65,495	5,946	59,549		– 12,784	– 3,585
IIIᵖ	– 39,630	– 7,380	1,931	– 34,181	48,027	– 2,902	50,928		22,498	– 5,205

⁵Includes extraordinary U.S. Government transactions with India.
⁶Consists of gold, special drawing rights, foreign currencies, and the U.S. reserve position in the International Monetary Fund (IMF).
NOTE: Quarterly data for U.S. official reserve assets and foreign assets in the United States are not seasonally adjusted.
SOURCE: *Economic Report of the President* (Washington, D.C.: U.S. Government Printing Office, January 1989), pp. 424–425.

bankers regularly exchanged information about national policies affecting the international monetary system.

A second management system developed at this time was the Group of Ten, composed of finance ministers. The Group of Ten was formed in December 1961 when representatives of ten industrial countries—Belgium, France, Germany, Italy, the Netherlands, Sweden, Canada, Japan, the United Kingdom, and the United States—met to create the General Arrangements to Borrow, a $6 billion fund for exchange rate management that was under the control of its ten members.[10] It soon became a forum for discussion and exchange of information, a vehicle for negotiating monetary reform, as well as a mechanism for crisis management. In 1968, for example, the Group stopped a dollar crisis and eased pressure on the U.S. gold supply by creating a two-tier gold system: a private market in which the price of gold could fluctuate freely and a public market in which the group agreed to sell one another gold at $35 an ounce. The Group of Ten was complemented by Working Party Three of the Organization for Economic Cooperation and Development (OECD), where finance ministers discussed economic policies, exchanged information, and studied the operation and reform of the monetary adjustment process.

A series of bilateral arrangements between the United States and other members of the Group of Ten supported this multilateral management system. These arrangements included currency swap arrangements and standby credit lines to be used by central bankers for crisis management; special U.S. bonds (known as Roosa bonds after their architect) that countries agreed to hold in lieu of converting dollars into gold; and German agreements to purchase U.S. military equipment and to continue to hold large amounts of U.S. dollars to offset the cost of U.S. troops stationed in Germany.

Finally, the United States sought to shore up the system by improving the U.S. balance of payments and reestablishing confidence in the weakening dollar. Unilateral U.S. efforts included an interest equalization tax on foreign securities designed to make borrowing in the United States less desirable and thus to reduce capital outflows, capital restraints on U.S. foreign investment, the tying of foreign aid, a decrease in duty-free tourist allotments, and programs to encourage U.S. exports. United States fiscal and monetary policy, however, remained unconstrained by balance-of-payments disequilibriums, and the United States maintained an expansionary economic policy despite its growing balance-of-payments difficulties.[11]

Multilateral management mechanisms not only prevented and contained currency crises, but also achieved a major reform of the system. In the early 1960s, inadequate liquidity was seen as a crucial problem. Once the United States, as was expected, solved its balance-of-payments problems, there would be a liquidity shortage and a need to provide alternative forms of international money. The problem of the future, it was believed, would not be too many dollars but too few.[12] In 1968, after five years of negotiations by the Group of Ten, an agreement was reached to create Special Drawing Rights (SDRs), artificial international reserve units created by the IMF, which could be used to settle accounts among central banks. Significantly, the new form of international liquidity would be managed not by the United States alone but by the Group of Ten jointly, for the Europeans were given a veto power on the creation of new SDRs.[13] The $6 billion of the new "paper gold" created was small compared with total world reserves at that time, close to $100 billion in 1970.[14] Nevertheless, for the first time in history, the international monetary system had an internationally created and managed asset.

The SDR agreement was the height of multilateral cooperation. Yet just at this point the system began to crack. Continuing currency crises in 1967 and 1968 heralded the eventual demise of the Bretton Woods monetary regime.

Breakdown of Bretton Woods

Several structural changes that emerged in the 1960s and early 1970s led to the breakdown of the Bretton Woods system. One change was the development of a high level of monetary interdependence. The return to convertibility of the Western European currencies at the end of 1958[15] and of the Japanese yen in 1964 made possible the huge expansion of international financial transactions. Multinational banks became the vehicles for large international financial flows. Beginning in the 1960s, the number of multinational banks increased rapidly. In 1965, only 13 U.S. banks had branches abroad, but by the end of 1974 there were 125 U.S. banks with foreign branches. The assets of the U.S. banks' foreign branches rose from about $9 billion in 1965 to over $125 billion in 1974. Concomitantly, there was an expansion of foreign banks in the United States. The number of foreign branches and agencies in New York City, for example, rose from 49 in 1965 to 92 in 1974. The total assets of these branches and agencies in the same period rose from $5 billion to $29 billion, and by the end of 1974 foreign banks operating in the United States had total assets of $56 billion.[16]

Monetary interdependence was also a result of the internationalization of production. Multinational corporations that controlled large liquid assets became sophisticated in moving their capital from country to country to take advantage of interest rate spreads or expected exchange rate adjustments. In the 1960s and 1970s, as crises multiplied and risks increased, the movements of such capital became an important part of financial management.[17]

A final source of monetary interdependence in this period was the Eurocurrency market. Eurocurrencies are national currencies—dollars, marks, francs, pounds, yen—held and traded outside their home country, primarily in Europe. For example, branches of U.S. banks or foreign banks in London accept dollar deposits and lend those deposits in the form of dollars. The Eurocurrency markets originated in the late 1950s, primarily with Eurodollars, and grew to huge proportions in the 1960s and 1970s, reaching almost $1 trillion by 1978 (see Table 2-2).[18] The market flourished largely because it is controlled neither by state regulation nor by constraints of domestic money markets. It thus has been able to establish highly competitive interest rates that have attracted huge sums. Because it consists largely of short-term money, funds in the Eurocurrency market are highly mobile and highly volatile.

These new forms of monetary interdependence made possible huge international capital flows that put great strain on the international mone-

Table 2-2   The Growth of the Eurodollar and Eurocurrency Markets ($ billions 1964–86)

Year	Size	Eurodollars as Percent of Total
1964	20	83
1965	24	84
1966	29	83
1967	36	84
1968	50	82
1969	85	84
1970	110	82
1971	145	76
1972	200	78
1973	305	73
1974	375	77
1975	460	78
1976	565	79
1977	695	76
1978	895	74
1979	1220	72
1980	1515	74
1981	1954	79
1982	2168	80
1983	2278	81
1984	2386	82
1985	2846	75
1986	3683	72
1987	4509	66

SOURCE: Morgan Guaranty Trust Company, *World Financial Markets*, various issues.

tary system. In a fixed exchange rate regime, as we have seen, governments facing balance-of-payments disequilibriums have several policy alternatives. If the disequilibrium is small or short-term, governments can finance the imbalance or impose exchange controls. If the disequilibrium is structural they can either change the value of their currencies—devalue or revalue—or alter domestic fiscal or monetary policy to restore balance. However, political leaders were often reluctant to take politically risky measures to address structural imbalances. The failure to resolve these disequilibriums led to large speculative international capital movements. Efforts to intervene in exchange markets to prevent change were overwhelmed by rapid and massive international financial flows, which made it impossible to maintain the fixed value of currencies within a plus or minus one percent. Crises developed and governments were forced eventually to alter both exchange rates and national economic policies.

Monetary interdependence also increasingly interfered with national economic management, especially with national monetary policy. Interest rates, for example, became a less-effective means of managing the national economic system. Low interest rates, used to stimulate an economy, can lead to an outflow of capital to countries with higher interest rates. In April and May 1971, a lowering of interest rates in the United States led to an outflow of capital. Conversely, high interest rates used to manage inflation may be defeated by capital inflows attracted precisely by those higher interest rates. Such was the case in Germany in 1969 and 1971. The need to defend fixed exchange rates in an interdependent system also interfered with domestic monetary management. In 1969 and 1971, Germany's attempts to deflate its economy and to control inflation were seriously challenged by the need to absorb large amounts of dollars to maintain the value of the deutsche mark.

For a long time the United States was the one country that was not interdependent in this sense. United States national economic policy was not influenced by the international position of the dollar or by monetary interdependence. Large capital flows had less effect on the huge U.S. economy than on the smaller European and Japanese economies. Furthermore, as long as other countries would absorb dollar outflows, the United States did not have to take domestic measures to balance international accounts. Thus, in the 1960s the United States was able to rely on special balance-of-payment measures and avoid restrictive monetary or fiscal policy. Nevertheless, the U.S. economy was constrained by the international monetary system. By the late 1960s, the dollar was overvalued partly because of inflation induced by expenditures on the Vietnam War and partly because other countries had altered their exchange rates to account for inflation, even though the value of the dollar had not been altered. This overvalued dollar contributed to large investment outflows and led to declining exports and increasing imports (see Table 2-1), which had an adverse impact on domestic economic performance.

The solution for any country, aside from the United States, in this position would have been to devalue the currency or deflate the economy to reestablish a competitive trade position. Neither was politically attractive. The United States was willing to have others revalue but did not want the domestic political problem of devaluing the dollar. Other countries holding vast sums of dollars and enjoying trade surpluses refused to allow a realignment of currencies. The Europeans and the Japanese demanded instead a deflationary U.S. policy, arguing that the dollar outflow and the expansion of the U.S. economy were causing inflation abroad. This call for restraint was in direct conflict with U.S. domestic economic objectives as well as with President Nixon's political desires for reelection in 1972—and his desire to stimulate the U.S. economy in 1970 to provide a better setting for that election.

In addition to interdependence, increased pluralism also eroded monetary management. By the mid-1960s, the United States was no longer the dominant economic power it had been for almost two decades. Europe and Japan—with higher levels of growth, and per-capita income approaching that of the United States—were narrowing the gap between themselves and the United States. A more pluralist distribution of economic power led to a renewed sense of political power and to increasing dissatisfaction with U.S. dominance of the international monetary system and, in particular, with the privileged role of the dollar as the international currency. The Europeans and Japanese resented the prerogatives that the monetary system provided for the United States. They were concerned that U.S. domestic policies were undertaken with little or no regard for their international economic consequences and critical of the fact that the United States could carry out unlimited foreign expenditures for political purposes—military activities and foreign aid—without the threat of payments constraints. Such prerogatives of U.S. dominance were acceptable to a war-weary Europe and Japan confronting a hostile Soviet Union. They were less acceptable to a recovered and revitalized Europe and Japan faced with a less hostile neighbor.

The continuing decline of the dollar accentuated the problem of pluralism. Despite large and persistent deficits, it had seemed possible until 1965 that the dollar drain might be reduced or eliminated and that confidence in the system could be preserved. But the Vietnam conflict and the refusal of the Johnson administration to pay for both it and its domestic social programs through taxation resulted in an increased dollar outflow to pay for the military expenses as well as in rampant inflation, which led to further deterioration in the U.S. balance-of-trade position (see Table 2-1). By the end of the 1960s, large U.S. payments deficits seemed chronic. Pluralism also made monetary management more difficult. One example of the problem was the long and difficult negotiation over the SDR reform, which lasted five years and almost failed several times. By the time an agreement was reached, the problem of liquidity shortage, which it had been intended to solve, had been transformed into liquidity excess.

In short, monetary interdependence grew faster than international management. New problems created by interdependence, including huge international capital flows, strained the fixed exchange rate system and interfered with national economic management. In the face of these problems, there was decreased cooperation, an absence of leadership, and, finally, a breakdown in management.

From 1968 to 1971, international monetary management was paralyzed. Despite the expansion of the bilateral swaps and the creation of new multilateral swaps, the central banks were unable to control the large currency flows and to contain currency crises. The Group of Ten was unable to move on further monetary reform and fell to bickering over currency realignment and national economic policies.

Most important, the United States abdicated monetary leadership and pursued a policy of "benign neglect." It let others defend the existing exchange rate system; permitted a huge foreign dollar buildup; and remained passive during currency crises. The United States also followed its domestic policies regardless of international consequences and disregarded the inflationary consequences of the huge dollar outflow in other parts of the system. And the United States no longer sought to mobilize the system for reform.

By late summer 1971, benign neglect was no longer a sustainable policy. In the summer and spring of 1971, there was a run on the dollar, and for the first time in the twentieth century, the United States showed a trade deficit (see Table 2-1). The U.S. gold stock declined to $10 billion versus outstanding foreign dollar holdings estimated at about $80 billion, inflation was rampant, and unemployment widespread. Political problems due to the economic situation led to pressure from all political quarters to do something.

On August 15, 1971, President Nixon—without consulting the other members of the international monetary system—announced a new economic policy: henceforth, the dollar would no longer be convertible into gold, and the United States would impose a 10-percent surcharge on dutiable imports.[19] August 15, 1971, marked the end of the Bretton Woods period.

The shock of August 15 was followed by efforts by the Group of Ten under U.S. leadership to patch up the system of international monetary management. The first attempt was an agreement reached at the Smithsonian Institution in Washington, D.C., in December 1971. The United States, feeling able to alter the rules and to improve its position, took a forceful leadership role in the negotiations. The United States used the import surcharge and dollar inconvertibility as weapons to force European and Japanese compromises, while at the same time agreeing to devalue the dollar. The Smithsonian agreement provided for a 10-percent devaluation of the dollar in relation to gold, a realignment of other exchange rates, and greater flexibility in rates that would float within a plus or minus 2.25 percent of parity, over twice the range of the Bretton Woods agreement.

The Smithsonian agreement was intended to be temporary and would give the participants time to negotiate long-term reform. In 1972 the Committee on Reform of the International Monetary System and Related Issues was established with the IMF to reform the international monetary system. Composed of the Group of Ten plus ten representatives of the developing countries, the so-called Committee of Twenty was charged with devising ways to manage world monetary reserves, establishing a commonly accepted currency, and creating new adjustment mechanisms. ·

When he announced the agreement at the Smithsonian, President Nixon called it "the greatest monetary agreement in the history of the world." In fact, the Smithsonian agreement provided little more than temporary crisis control. It prevented deterioration in the system—a further hardening of trade restrictions, capital controls, and multiple exchange rates—but did not solve the fundamental problems of managing interdependence. The increased flexibility in and realignment of exchange rates were insignificant in the face of differing national policies and huge international capital flows. And the dollar, still the center of the system, remained inconvertible into gold.

"The greatest monetary agreement in the history of the world" lasted a little over a year. Soon massive currency flows led to new pressures on the Smithsonian rates, and national currency controls to hold back the pressure on the new rates proliferated. In June 1972 Great Britain and Ireland floated their currencies, and a new currency crisis began in January and February 1973. Even a second 10-percent devaluation of the U.S. dollar at that time could no longer save the fixed exchange rate system. By March 1973, all of the major world currencies were floating. Management was left to the market and in a minor way to central bankers who intervened in exchange markets on a somewhat cooperative basis to prevent extreme fluctuations.

The effort of the Committee of Twenty to achieve reform also was unsuccessful. The committee's reform plans centered on a system of stable but adjustable exchange rates and the provision of new forms of international liquidity. But while the committee debated, massive changes occurred in the international monetary system. Fixed exchange rates were replaced by the float. Inflation erupted, fueled by U.S. inflation combined with an enormous dollar outflow and worldwide commodity shortages. Different national rates of inflation made stability impossible and increased national desires for floating exchange rates to enable a degree of isolation from external inflation.[20]

Finally, while the committee debated, a handful of oil exporters engineered a dramatic rise in the price of petroleum (see Chapter 9). Within a year, the price of oil quadrupled. As a result, huge sums—an estimated $70 billion in 1974 alone—were transferred from the oil-consuming countries, primarily from the developed market economies, to the oil-producing states.[21] This price change created a major new problem of financial recycling. Under the ideal free-trade model, the surplus earnings of the oil-producing states would have been channeled back to the oil-consuming countries in the form of revenue from the import of goods and services from the oil consumers. But the transfer of resources to the oil-producing states had been too large for them to absorb. Despite huge development needs and arms expenditures, these states as a whole could not take in enough imports to make up for the loss to the consuming countries. In 1974, the current-account surplus of the oil-producing states was over $70 billion, and by 1980, a second round of precipitous oil price increases had pushed it above $114 billion.[22]

Many of the oil-consuming countries did not reduce their oil consumption sufficiently to eliminate their deficits or increase exports sufficiently to cover the gap. Thus, they had to borrow to pay for their deficits, and the only sources for such borrowing were the countries with surpluses from oil earnings. This was the recycling problem that, less than a decade later, was transformed into the less-developed countries' external debt crisis (see Chapter 6).

After 1974, surpluses were recycled primarily through private banks, which accepted the deposits of the oil-exporting countries and lent these funds to the oil-importing countries. Smaller amounts were recycled through government securities and direct loans and investment by the oil-producing states and through international institutions (such as the IMF and the World Bank), which borrowed from the oil producers and made loans to the oil consumers. Thus, the private system, especially the banking system, was the primary monetary manager. Throughout the 1970s, private banks remained the principal recyclers and, in the process, accumulated large Eurocurrency deposits and equally large international loan portfolios. Despite its effectiveness, reliance on the private market posed certain problems. The role of the private banks in recycling required increasing their ratio of assets (loans) to capital, thus bringing into question the financial stability of the banking system. Furthermore, many developing countries that borrowed heavily from commercial banks were eventually unable to service their loans. By the early 1980s, as we shall see, the resulting debt crisis raised serious questions about the strength of the international financial markets.

The float, inflation, and the monetary consequences of the oil crisis overwhelmed the Committee of Twenty. In January 1974, the committee concluded that because of the turmoil in the international economy, it would be impossible to draw up and implement a comprehensive plan for monetary reform.[23]

For a year and a half, the world focused on the overwhelming problem of coping with the immediate consequences of the oil shock: inflation, recession, and recycling. Then, in November 1975, heads of government of the major monetary powers—the United States, the United Kingdom, France, West Germany, Japan, and Italy—met at the French chateau of Rambouillet to decide on the framework for a new monetary system. This meeting was the first of what would become regular annual economic summits of the seven major industrial powers.[24] At the IMF meeting in January 1976, the final details were hammered out on the Second Amendment to the Articles of Agreement of the International Monetary Fund.

On paper, the Second Amendment seemed to signal a return to multilateral public management of the international monetary system. It called for an end to the role of gold and the establishment of the SDR as the principal reserve asset of the international monetary system. It legitimized the de facto system of floating exchange rates but permitted return to fixed exchange rates if an 85-percent majority approved such a move. And it called for greater IMF surveillance of the exchange rate system and management of national economic policies to promote a stable and orderly system.[25]

In reality, the monetary powers had not reformed the system of public management; they had merely codified the prevailing nonsystem. The Second Amendment did not resolve the problem of the dollar; its guidelines for managing exchange rates were undefined; its calls for appropriate national policies and national cooperation with the fund carried little obligation; its mechanisms for institutionalizing cooperation were fragile; and it was implemented in an unstable international economic environment. The Second Amendment signaled the beginning of a period characterized as much by national and regional as by multilateral management.

Management Dilemmas
in the Post–Bretton Woods Era

The interdependent, pluralist international monetary system that has prevailed since 1976 has confronted several major management problems. One is the long-standing dilemma of the dollar. Despite continuing challenges to the dollar's credibility and persistent dissatisfaction abroad with U.S. economic policies, the U.S. dollar survives as the world's major currency. Throughout the 1970s and 1980s, foreign exchange constituted approximately 90 percent of official reserves excluding gold, and the dollar accounted for an average of 70 percent of official holdings of foreign exchange in those years.[26]

The dollar has retained its central role through this period despite widespread dissatisfaction with the dollar both when it is seen as excessively weak as in the late 1970s or as excessively strong as in the first half of the 1980s. As in the Bretton Woods system, the size of the U.S. economy and its highly developed financial markets as well as U.S. political stability make it desirable and feasible to use the dollar. The U.S. government continues to support the dollar's role while other countries with strong economies and stable polities have been reluctant to allow their currencies to play a central international role. For years, West Germany and Japan, fearing loss of control over their domestic economies, restricted their capital markets to make it difficult for foreigners to hold deutsche marks and yen. Efforts to enlarge the role of the SDR, including changing its valuation and raising interest rates, have been unsuccessful. SDRs account for less than 5 percent of official reserves.[27]

There has been, nonetheless, a shift away from the dollar as the exclusive reserve and transaction currency. In 1978 the dollar accounted for 76 percent of official holdings of foreign exchange, while deutsche marks accounted for 11 percent and yen for 3 percent. By 1986 the dollar share had fallen to 67 percent while the deutsche mark had risen to 15 percent and the yen to 7 percent.[28] Eurodollars accounted for 76 percent of the Eurocurrency market in 1978 and for 71 percent in 1987.[29] Holding and using currencies other than the dollar became more attractive in the 1980s as the U.S. balance of payments weakened dramatically, while other countries, particularly Japan and Germany, accumulated payments surpluses. The expectation that the dollar would have to decline to reflect the worsening payments situation made it prudent to diversify currency holdings.

Furthermore, in the 1980s a number of countries liberalized financial regulations making it easier for their currencies to be used and held abroad. Japan, for example, took a number of steps to internationalize the yen. It eliminated exchange controls, removed restrictions on Euroyen activities of Japanese institutions, and increased access of foreign financial institutions to Japanese capital markets. Importantly, these steps were taken under pressure from the United States to open up financial markets to foreign institutions and to allow the yen to become an international currency and were negotiated bilaterally with the United States as part of the so-called yen-dollar talks.[30]

Floating exchange rates (as opposed to the fixed rates of Bretton Woods) are another central characteristic and major problem of the prevailing system.[31] Although many of the IMF's lesser members maintain some form of fixed exchange rates, most major currencies float against one another. Proponents had argued that a float would provide for relative stability and rationality in exchange rates through the stabilizing effect of speculation. Prompt exchange rate changes, they contended, would result in more effective current-account adjustment. Trade deficits and inflation would lead to exchange rate depreciation, increased competitiveness of exports, and decreased competitiveness of imports and would thereby restore the trade balance. A float would also make possible greater autonomy for national policy in an era of interdependence, by freeing economic policy from external balance of payments constraints of maintaining a fixed exchange rate.

Floating exchange rates have operated effectively in several ways: they have not disrupted international trade and investment, as many critics feared, and they were probably the only system that could have endured the serious economic shocks of the 1970s and 1980s, including the oil and debt crises and inflation differentials. They also encouraged the long-term movement of exchange rate changes generally in a direction to correct payments imbalances. However, there have been several serious problems with the floating rate system. Exchange rates have been highly unstable, frustrating a smooth and rapid adjustment process. Most major currencies have been subjected to wide and often inexplicable fluctuations, especially in short-term rates.

One reason for exchange rate movements lies in the emergence of globally integrated international financial markets. We have already noted the significance of the Eurocurrency markets that developed in the 1960s and 1970s and contributed to growing financial interdependence and the end of the fixed exchange rates of Bretton Woods. In the 1980s the internationalization of financial markets increased exponentially, driven by several powerful forces.[32] Most developed countries—the United Kingdom, France, Germany, Canada, Australia, and Japan—abolished relaxed exchange controls, opened domestic markets to foreign financial institutions, and removed domestic regulatory barriers. As a result of deregulation, national financial markets became integrated into the global market enabling larger amounts of capital to flow more freely across national boundaries.

A revolution in telecommunications, information processing, and computer technologies made possible a vastly increased volume, speed, and global reach of financial transactions. Finally the growing sophistication of financial players reinforced deregulation and the technology revolution. In the 1960s and 1970s, as we have noted, the multinational corporation, with its pool of funds and its worldwide borrowing needs, contributed to growing international financial flows. In the 1980s, the concentration of capital in institutions, such as pension funds, money market funds, and insurance companies, reinforced the trend to sophisticated, global management of large pools of capital. Professional managers of such funds, operating in an environment of volatile prices, exchange rates, and interest rates, were increasingly willing to move money across international boundaries to diversify risk and take advantage of market differentials.

As a result of these multiple forces, global financial markets exploded in size and became a major influence on the floating exchange rate system. World financial flows now exceed goods flows by a factor of 50 to 1. By 1987, financial flows from the Eurocurrency markets had grown to $271 billion, 31 percent in bank lending and 69 percent in bonds.[33] The emergence of a highly integrated world capital market facilitated enormous international funds flows that respond as much to political risk and interest rate differentials as to trade balances. Thus, for example, high real American interest rates and the search for a political safe haven in the early 1980s attracted a large flow of capital to the United States (see Table 2–1). These flows maintained the strength of the dollar despite the deteriorating U.S. current account position and the strengthening trade balances of other industrial countries, particularly Germany and Japan. The result was persistent instability in foreign exchange markets (see Figure 2–1).

Figure 2–1   United States: Exchange Rates [1] and External Balances

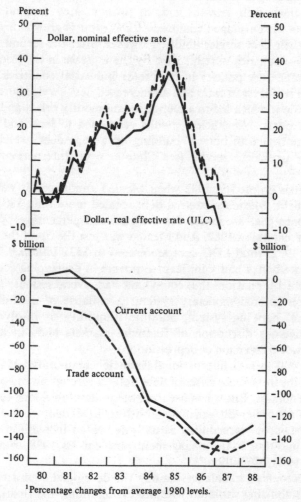

[1] Percentage changes from average 1980 levels.

SOURCE: Organization for Economic Cooperation and Development; *OECD Outlook 41*, (Paris: OECD, June 1987), p. 57.

Massive financial imbalances that have not been adjusted through market mechanisms are another problem of the prevailing monetary system. We have seen how the oil crises of the 1970s created a financial imbalance that swamped efforts to recreate a fixed exchange rate regime. So, in the 1980s the debt crisis and the massive U.S. budget and trade deficits created a serious adjustment problem.

As we have seen, a rapid increase in bank lending to developing countries was a major solution to the problem of recycling OPEC financial surpluses. In the period before 1979, the private system of recycling worked well. Lending helped promote the developing countries' productive capacities, maintained their growth, and, in turn, created demand for OECD exports from the developed countries. LDC exports grew along with debt, enhancing their debt service ability. However, after the second oil crisis of 1979, debtor countries were hit hard by the increase in the price of oil; by restrictive monetary policies in the major industrial countries that led to record-high real interest rates and an increased debt service burden; and by world recession, which led to a plunge in commodity prices and in demand for LDC exports. Nonetheless, banks continued to lend and developing countries continued to borrow, building up a huge debt, which they were increasingly unable to service (see Chapter 6 on International Financial Flows).

The crisis erupted in 1982 when Mexico announced it was unable to service its debt. Mexico's external debt totaled more than $80 billion and included loans that accounted for a significant percentage of the largest U.S. banks' capital in 1982. And Mexico was just the tip of the iceberg. At the end of 1982, total LDC debt amounted to $831 billion.[34] The world's major private banks had significant exposure in developing countries. Default by the debtor nations thus could have had several serious consequences for the international monetary system: a collapse of confidence in the international banking system, possible illiquidity or insolvency of the banks, dangerous disruption of financial markets and—in a worst-case scenario—world recession or depression.

As we will see, the international financial community has succeeded in containing the immediate crises of debt default through an ongoing series of debt reschedulings. But it has been unable to develop a long-term solution that would restore credit worthiness both to LDC debtors and their creditors. Indeed, debt rescheduling actually led to an increase in outstanding LDC debt and thus in the management problem. By 1988, total LDC debt had grown to $1,320 billion.[35]

Unprecedented imbalances among the developed countries created an equally destabilizing situation. Despite expectations, the floating exchange rate system has not assured effective current account adjustment and has not prevented the development of large, unsustainable external deficits and surpluses. In the 1980s, the United States accumulated two massive and unprecedented deficits. The budget deficit was created by inappropriate domestic policies: the lowering of taxes that was not matched by a decline in government spending. The causes of the trade deficit are many and complex: an overvalued dollar; strong U.S. economic growth in comparison with other developed countries; lower demand in traditional markets for U.S. agricultural exports; the increased competitiveness of foreign companies even as the competitiveness of U.S. industry declined; the rise in protectionist barriers; and the Third World debt crisis, which lowered demand for U.S. exports (see Chapter 3).

The twin deficits called for adjustments in U.S. economic policies, which were not forthcoming. Improvements in the budget deficit were blocked by a political conflict between a president opposed to raising taxes and a Congress opposed to spending cuts. An improvement in the trade deficit was hampered by the budget crisis as well as by the resistance of the administration to adopt domestic policies that would lead to devaluation of the dollar. Instead of adjusting, the United States used its unique position in the international monetary system to finance its deficits. As in the past, the central role of the dollar in the international financial system enabled the United States to more or less automatically finance its deficits through foreign capital inflows. In the 1980s, the amount of such financing dwarfed that of previous years. In 1981 the United States had positive net international investment of $141 billion. In 1985, the United States became a net debtor with a negative net investment position of $112 billion. By 1986 the figure was negative $269 billion, and it reached negative $368 billion in 1987.[36] Despite the changed U.S. international position, the dollar remained strong for the first half of the 1980s, buoyed by high real U.S. interest rates and the search for a political safe haven.

United States dependence on such capital inflows created a serious threat to the dollar, which remained the basis of the international monetary system. At some point, the trade deficit would undermine confidence in the U.S. currency and lead to a decline in the dollar. Furthermore, because much of the capital inflow sustaining U.S. imbalances was short-term, a loss in confidence could lead to a precipitous, free fall of the dollar and a serious shock to the system. The question was whether U.S. domestic policy adjustments combined with international economic cooperation could assure that the decline of the dollar would lead to a soft, not a hard, landing.

The mirror image of the U.S. trade deficit were the trade surpluses of Japan and West Germany. By 1987, Japan had a trade surplus of $96.5 billion and Germany a surplus of $70 billion. Of growing importance also were growing surpluses of the newly industrialized countries in Asia, such as Taiwan, which had a 1986 surplus of $16.9 billion and Korea with a 1986 surplus of $4.2 billion.[37]

Finally, the prevailing system has not, as was hoped, resolved the dilemma of interdependence. With the practical exception of the United

States, countries have not been able to pursue national economic policies without regard to international constraints. Especially in the new world of global financial interdependence, national autonomy has proved illusory. Yet achieving the level of international cooperation necessary in such an interdependent world has proved equally difficult.

National, Regional, or Multilateral Management?

The period since 1976 has been one of muddling through, characterized as much by national and regional as by multilateral management. The monetary powers have cooperated to stabilize the system during periods of crisis and have periodically sought to coordinate economic policies in order to achieve long-term stability. Policy coordination has, however, been limited in scope and in success. Despite the growth of interdependence, national governments have been either unwilling or unable to adjust national economic policies to international economic needs.

The most successful effort at international monetary cooperation is the European Monetary System (EMS).[38] Members of the European Community, with their high level of intra-EC trade and their Common Agricultural Policy, which is based on common prices and relies on stable exchange rates, have an especially strong interest in stabilizing exchange rates among themselves. In December 1978, member states agreed to create a "zone of monetary stability in Europe": a system with fixed, although adjustable, exchange rates among the members and a floating rate with the outside world; the creation of a European Currency Unit (ECU), a basket of currencies serving as a basis for fixing exchange rates, a means of settlement and a potential future reserve asset; and a network of credit arrangements and plans for a future European Monetary Fund for financing payments imbalances and supporting the fixed rates. All of the then members of the EMS except the United Kingdom agreed to participate in the exchange rate mechanism (ERM) by maintaining fixed exchange rates with 2.5 percent fluctuation margins. Fixed rates were to be maintained by convergent national economic policies and, when necessary, by intervention in currency markets financed by mutual lines of credit. The U.K.'s opposition to the ERM was both economic (the special role of the pound sterling as an international currency and as the currency of an oil exporter) and political (the need to subject its domestic economic policy to international constraints, especially to the policies of West Germany, which had the strongest economy and currency in the EMS).

The European Monetary System has succeeded in creating a zone of monetary stability. Since 1978, members have maintained greater exchange rate stability with each other than in previous periods and greater stability than the rest of the world (see Figure 2–2). Central banks have cooperated

Figure 2–2   Value of the European Currency Unit

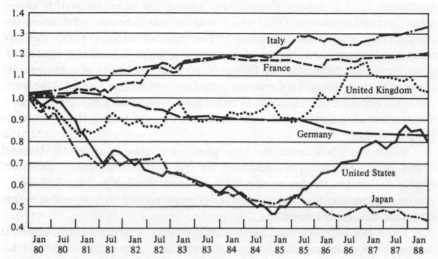

SOURCE: The Boston Company Economic Advisors, Inc.

closely to manage the system and governments have been able to achieve some coordination of macroeconomic policies, which has led to a convergence of prices, costs, and money supplies. The deutsche mark as the strongest currency has become the informal reference currency for the EMS and German monetary policy, which has been deflationary, has become the standard for the EMS members.

EMS success has not been complete. The European Monetary Fund, which was to have been a quasi-central bank and the institutional framework for the EMS, has not been established. In 1989, central bankers agreed to the long-term objective of creating a European central bank but recognized that members would first have to harmonize economic and monetary policies over a period of years.[39] There have been numerous realignments of rates, and fixed rates have been made possible by exchange controls on weaker currencies. The Italian lira has had wider 6 percent fluctuation margins. Furthermore, despite growing internal support for EMS membership, the United Kingdom as well as the new members of the EC—Greece and Portugal—remain outside the EMS. Nevertheless, by fixing rates and forcing coordination of national economic policies, the EMS has produced lower inflation and less misalignment of rates than would have occurred had unguided market forces prevailed. Finally, although the ECU has not, as intended, become a major reserve unit or a means of settlement between EC monetary authorities, it has established a permanent role in international financial markets as a major currency of denomination for banking and securities market transactions.

In the 1990s, the European Monetary System will confront important challenges. The European Community has agreed to create a fully liberalized internal market by 1992, which will include removing all controls on capital flows among member states.[40] The need for national policy coordination, including coordination of monetary policies in such a system, will pose important challenges to Europe's zone of stability. In addition, in order to achieve the goals of creating a unified trading and financial market, the EMS will have to include those states now outside the EMS, particularly the United Kingdom, which continues to resist subjecting its policies to EMS discipline.

While the EMS countries have pursued a zone of stability, United States policy has been characterized by two conflicting trends: periodic efforts to improve the functioning of the system through multilateral cooperation and resistance to the inevitable consequences of interdependence for U.S. domestic economic policy.

From 1977 to 1981 the Carter administration emphasized multilateral management of international economic relations. A principal objective in the early Carter years was to achieve world recovery from the recession of the mid-1970s through multilateral cooperation. The U.S. strategy for global economic growth was based on the "locomotive theory," which called for coordinated national economic policies and for countries with payments surpluses—that is, Germany and Japan—to follow expansionary policies that would serve as engines of growth for the rest of the world. The multilateral strategy seemed to achieve some success in 1978 when Germany, France, and Japan agreed at the economic summit to pursue more expansionary policies, and the United States agreed, as a trade-off, on a program to curb inflation and energy consumption. The agreement seemed to be a major milestone, demonstrating that the world's economic powers were capable of coordinating national economic policies and that the United States could still be the driving force behind multilateral management.[41] However, the 1978 dollar crisis, which immediately followed the agreement, demonstrated that governments, especially the U.S. government, were still reluctant to alter domestic policies for international reasons. Then the oil crisis of 1979 and the fear of inflation led to the abandonment of the goal of economic stimulation.

The dollar crisis of 1978 followed a familiar pattern. More rapid growth and greater inflation in the United States than the rest of the world led to trade and current account deficits, plummeting confidence in the ability of the United States to pursue stringent economic policies and a continuing decline in the dollar. Initially, the United States resisted defending the dollar. Then, the government sought to resolve the problem through external policies and limited domestic policies: intervening in foreign exchange markets, doubling the swap network with West Germany, selling SDRs and gold, voluntary wage and price guidelines, and fiscal constraints.

Finally the United States was forced to take major domestic and international measures. On November 1, 1978, President Carter announced a new restrictive economic and dollar defense program: a restrictive monetary policy, the mustering of $30 billion in foreign currencies for possible intervention in foreign exchange markets, a policy of active intervention in those markets, and an expansion of the sale of U.S. gold.[42] The package was a major departure in U.S. policy. For the first time since World War II, the United States altered domestic economic policy for international monetary reasons.

Initially, it seemed that the thrust of U.S. policy was permanently altered and that the United States accepted its interdependence. In 1979, when the dollar again came under pressure, the Federal Reserve announced a major new policy designed to bring U.S. inflation under control. Before October 1979, the Federal Reserve had concentrated on raising or lowering interest rates through open market operations and raising or lowering the discount rate, the rate at which the Federal Reserve makes loans to member banks, as the principal policies for controlling the supply of money and credit. In 1979, the Federal Reserve turned, instead, to monetarism, that is, managing the size of the nation's money supply. By focusing on the size and growth of certain monetary aggregates and by responding immediately to changes in the size of those aggregates, the Federal Reserve hoped to bring inflation under control and to return stability to the international monetary system.[43]

In 1981, however, with the election of Ronald Reagan, the policy of combining international cooperation with domestic policy changes was altered to U.S. unilateralism in international monetary relations. Domestically, the Reagan administration combined the tight monetary policy and the monetarist approach, begun in 1979, with an expansionary fiscal policy known as supply-side economics.[44] The United States pursued a tight monetary policy, based on strict adherence to monetary targets, in order to fight inflation. Yet at the same time, it raised expenditures, especially for defense, and—according to supply-side theory—reduced taxes in an effort to stimulate savings, investment, and growth.

The United States reverted to economic unilateralism in its international monetary policy. Departing from previous U.S. policy, the Reagan administration officially rejected intervention in foreign exchange markets and ceased efforts to coordinate national economic policies. Although the impact of U.S. policies on the world economy was profound and often disruptive, the United States carried out its abrupt shift and continued to conduct its policies, not only without serious consultation, but also without taking into account their impact on other countries. The United States also conducted domestic economic policy without taking into account the international repercussions on the U.S. economy.

There were many beneficial effects of the new U.S. policies: inflation subsided, and as confidence grew, the dollar turned from a weak to a strong currency. But there were also heavy costs. With an expansionary fiscal policy, the United States relied heavily on tight monetary policy applied through rigid monetary targeting to bring inflation under control. This policy sharply increased the volatility of U.S. and, thus, world financial markets, while the rejection of intervention exacerbated exchange rate volatility. More important, the tight monetary policy drove interest rates at home and abroad to unprecedented high levels. High U.S. interest rates led to a dollar that was overvalued in trade terms and to dislocations in exchange markets (see Figure 2-1). The policy also contributed to the most severe economic decline since the Great Depression.

Other developed countries were faced with difficult policy choices: raising their interest rates above the level warranted by their economic situation and thus avoiding an outflow of capital to the United States but dampening growth; keeping rates low and allowing capital to flow to the United States; or imposing capital controls. The decision of most was to avoid capital controls and raise interest rates. But in the end, they found themselves with the worst of both worlds: recession as well as capital outflows.[45] The consequences for the developing countries were far worse: declining exports and greater debt service costs, the recipe for the debt crisis. The repercussions on the United States were also serious. A high dollar plus world recession led to a decline in U.S. exports and massive merchandise trade deficits (see Figure 2-3). The drop in U.S. exports in turn retarded American growth. The monetary system whose purpose was to foster trade and investment was now disrupting it.

Despite its unilateralism in exchange rate policy, the United States, as we shall see, was willing to cooperate in the management of the debt crisis (see Chapter 6). The debt crisis altered somewhat the United States' attitude toward worldwide financial stability. At the time of the Mexican crisis, the Federal Reserve eased its stringent monetary policy in order to lower worldwide interest rates; the United States became more willing to intervene in limited situations to smooth volatile foreign exchange markets; and, in a reversal of previous policy, the United States supported increases in IMF quotas in order to enable the fund to play a role in debt management.

Despite growing pressure from the other members of the system to restore some degree of multilateral monetary management, the United States continued to pursue a unilateral policy, arguing that the best thing the United States could do for the system would be to get its own house in order. United States monetary and fiscal policy remained out of balance and highly disruptive and the United States did not believe it had to alter its policies to achieve stability in exchange markets. It was not until 1985, when economic dislocations became unsustainable politically and economically, that the United States returned to a more multilateral policy.

Figure 2–3   Exchange Rates of Major Currencies against the Dollar (percentage deviations with respect to dollar parities of October 1987 monthly averages of daily figures*)

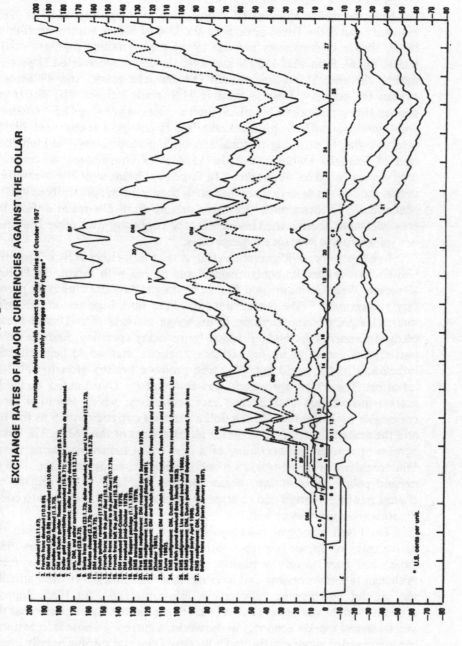

EXCHANGE RATES OF MAJOR CURRENCIES AGAINST THE DOLLAR

Percentage deviations with respect to dollar parities of October 1987
monthly averages of daily figures*

1. £ devalued (18.11.67).
2. French franc devalued (10.8.69).
3. DM floated (30.9.69) and revalued (26.10.69).
4. £ floated (23.6.72).
5. Swiss franc floated (23.1.33); dollar devalued, yen, and Lira floated (13.2.73); major currencies de facto floated.
6. Dollar gold convertibility suspended (16.8.71); major currencies de facto floated.
7. DM and Dutch guilder floated; Swiss franc revalued (9.5.71).
8. Smithsonian realignment; dollar formally devalued (18.12.71).
9. DM.
10. DM revalued (29.6.73); DM revalued (18.10.73).
11. Swiss franc floated (23.1.33); dollar devalued, yen, and Lira floated (13.2.73).
12. DM, Dutch guilder revalued (17.9.73).
13. French franc left the joint float (19.1.74).
14. French franc revalued (10.7.76).
15. French franc left the joint float (15.3.76).
16. DM revalued (mid-October 1976).
17. Other Snake realignment (April–March 1979).
18. EMS introduced (mid-March 1979).
19. First EMS realignment: DM revalued (lira September 1979).
20. EMS realignment: DM and Dutch guilder revalued, French franc and Lira devalued (24.3.81).
21. October 1981.
22. EMS realignment: DM and Dutch guilder revalued, French franc and Lira devalued (22.2.82).
23. EMS realignment: DM, Dutch guilder and Belgian franc revalued (late March 1983).
24. EMS realignment: Lira devalued (mid-July 1985).
25. EMS realignment: DM, Dutch guilder and Belgian franc revalued, French franc devalued (early April 1986).
26. EMS realignment: DM, Dutch guilder and Belgium franc revalued (early January 1987).

* U.S. cents per unit.

59

By 1985, a serious misalignment in world exchange rates had developed. The dollar appreciated sharply due to the combination of tight monetary and loose fiscal policies in the United States and to conflicting rather than complementary policies in the major trading partners of the United States. From mid-1980 to mid-1985 the dollar appreciated 21 percent against the yen, 53 percent against the deutsche mark, and 49 percent against the pound.[46] Despite massive U.S. trade deficits, the dollar remained strong because of high U.S. interest rates, a growing U.S. economy, and confidence in U.S. political stability. Exchange markets were highly volatile owing to differing national economic performances, the globalization of financial markets, and the absence of coordinated government intervention in exchange markets. In large part because of the overvalued dollar, the U.S. trade deficit reached crisis proportions, politically as well as economically. Protectionist pressures arising from the trade deficit increased, finally forcing the United States to cooperate with other countries in a joint effort to manage exchange rates.

In a September 1985 secret meeting at the Plaza Hotel in New York, the United States ended its benign neglect and agreed with Japan, the United Kingdom, West Germany, and France to cooperate more closely in monetary management.[47] The participants agreed to work together on economic matters, especially intervention in exchange markets. The United States pledged to narrow its budget deficit by reducing spending, and the other participants agreed to pursue economic policies that would help ease the imbalances in the world economy and promote healthy growth with low inflation. The Plaza agreement was followed by coordinated exchange market intervention and interest rate reductions, which led to a more reasonable exchange rate for the dollar vis-à-vis currencies such as the yen and the deutsche mark (which meant all currencies of the EMS). The Plaza agreement marked the beginning of a new era in monetary management. Finance ministers of the world's monetary powers, recognizing the need to expand policy coordination, began meeting regularly to coordinate exchange rate intervention and to attempt—not always successfully—to coordinate economic policy as well.

The Plaza agreement was significant in another way: it marked the active entry of Japan into the world management system. Before 1985, Japan had been largely a passive member of the management system. Although Japan's economy and international trade had grown dramatically, the yen did not become fully convertible until 1980. By 1985, Japan's economic weight was second only to that of the United States. Japan has the second largest market economy in the world, a currency whose international use is increasing significantly, and a massive financial surplus heavily invested abroad, especially in the United States. In 1985, as the United States shifted from a net creditor to a net debtor, Japan became the world's largest net creditor, attaining a $241 billion net external credit position in 1987, up from only $7 billion in 1976. Any efforts to stabilize the system and to coordinate economic policies would be meaningless without Japan.

Japan's new strength created new vulnerabilities, including the threat of closure of the trading system because of rising protectionism, especially in Japan's critical U.S. market; the uncertainty of financial investments due to a collapsing dollar; and increasing political pressure on Japan to open its markets, liberalize its financial system, and alter its domestic policies to help manage the world economy. Gradually, although reluctantly, Japan began to respond to its changed economic and political environment. From the time of the Plaza agreement, Japan played an active role in international monetary negotiations and in the efforts to agree on and implement appropriate domestic economic policies. Increasingly, international economic management hinged on the cooperation of the big three economic powers: the United States, West Germany, and Japan.

The new cooperative approach begun with the Plaza agreement was formalized at the May 1986 economic summit in Tokyo. There, the newly formed Group of Seven (created by the addition of Canada and Italy) not only reaffirmed the importance of cooperative intervention in exchange markets, but also affirmed that close coordination of domestic economic policies was needed to stabilize the system. The Group of Seven agreed to monitor the basic economic policies and performance of each country— inflation, interest rates, growth, unemployment, deficits, trade balance— and to recommend remedial action whenever the policy of one country was thought to be damaging others. The stated goal was to coordinate domestic economic policies to attain steady growth with a minimum of inflation.

But stated goals and policy action are quite different. International coordination of domestic fiscal and monetary policy remained elusive. While finance ministers and central bankers often agreed on appropriate policies, political constraints—the need for legislative approval and the reluctance to relinquish sovereignty over macroeconomic policy—limited actual coordination. Some steps were taken. In 1986, the United States passed legislation to slow the growth of the U.S. federal budget deficit. Germany and Japan took limited steps—lowering discount rates—to stimulate their economies to offset the decline in U.S. growth. But agreement could not be reached on the appropriate levels of U.S. budget cutting or of growth stimulation in Japan and Germany.

There were also disagreements on the appropriate exchange rate for the dollar. Japan and Germany feared a large decline of the U.S. currency would damage their trade as well as the value of their investments in the United States and argued that a significant dollar decline would upset financial markets. The United States, on the other hand, wanted to use the dollar decline to improve the trade imbalance and deflect congressional pressure for protectionist trade legislation and argued that a larger decline of the dollar would not upset capital inflows into the United States, needed to finance the trade and budget deficits. As disagreement persisted, cooperation in exchange market intervention broke down and exchange markets became unstable.

In February 1987, the world's monetary powers met at the Louvre in Paris to attempt once again to stabilize the international monetary system. Officials announced to the world that exchange rates had come into the proper relationship, and that they would oppose further substantial shifts and would cooperate to stabilize exchange rates at prevailing levels. The participants agreed on informal, flexible, and unannounced target ranges for intervention in exchange markets. At the Louvre, officials again sought to coordinate domestic policies. Germany and Japan agreed to take modest but significant steps to stimulate domestic demand, and the United States reaffirmed its commitment to reduce its budget deficit.[48]

The Louvre agreement was both a major step in the effort to establish international economic management and another example of the problem of coordinating economic policy. With one important exception, the Group of Seven did not live up to its stated commitments to coordinate policy. The German government, faced with a public that had a historical fear of inflation, was reluctant to pursue serious stimulative policies; and the U.S. Congress and administration were unable to agree on a significant deficit reduction package. Japan, however, did move toward stimulating domestic demand by pursuing a more expansionary fiscal policy and by reorienting from reliance on export-led growth to development of domestic demand.[49]

As Group of Seven cooperation disintegrated, private investors, fearing a dollar devaluation, reduced inflows of funds to the United States, forcing central banks to buy dollars to stabilize exchange rates and prevent a crash of the U.S. currency. As a result, the bond market began a severe decline; international equity markets collapsed in October 1987; and the dollar began what seemed like a free fall, declining 15.6 percent vis-à-vis the yen and 13.4 percent vis-à-vis the deutsche mark from September to the end of December.

The October crisis galvanized the key actors to make domestic economic policy changes. The United States eased monetary policy and Congress passed a limited deficit reduction bill, the Gramm-Rudman-Hollings bill; West Germany and other European countries lowered interest rates; and Japan's cabinet approved a stimulative budget. Finally, in December 1987, the Group of Seven announced that appropriate steps had been taken to stabilize exchange rates and that there should be no further significant shifts in the value of the dollar. They implemented massive coordinated action by central banks to stabilize the dollar and to signal their intent to the world. Throughout 1988, the Group of Seven met regularly and acted effectively to stabilize exchange markets. Cooperation in monetary policy increased and progress was made on the coordination of fiscal policy. Japan, in particular, successfully pursued a stimulative domestic economic policy. The United States made some limited progress in reducing its budget and trade deficit. As a result, exchange rates, including the dollar, stabilized. However, the long-term success of international monetary cooperation of the Group of Seven continued to depend on the ability of the key monetary actor, the United States, to pursue policies that would reduce its twin deficits.

Monetary Management in the 1990s

It remains to be seen whether states will muster the political will and skill to manage the system. Gone are those simpler days when the United States, along with the United Kingdom, could draw up a constitution for a world monetary order. In a world in which monetary power is more widely dispersed, management will depend not on the preferences of a dominant power but on the negotiation of several key powers, primarily the United States, West Germany, and Japan. While monetary power is now more widely dispersed, it is not equally dispersed. The United States remains the most powerful monetary actor. Without an active U.S. role within the multilateral system, effective management is impossible.

Management will also be complicated by the conflict between interdependence and national sovereignty. Managing interdependence requires the coordination of national economic policies and the imposition of international discipline over policies that have always been the prerogative of national governments. The experience of the European Monetary System and the groping efforts of the Group of Seven to coordinate policy indicate both the need for and the difficulty of achieving such coordination. Numerous ideas for achieving coordination and stability have been proposed, ranging from managed floats to formulas for fixing exchange rates to a return to a modified gold standard or a standard based on a basket of commodities.[50] Ultimately, they all depend on the ability of countries to achieve adequate coordination of macroeconomic policies. Indeed, some believe that such coordination is impossible and that discipline and management are best left to the market place.

In a multilateral system, improvement in management will be slow. It will depend on trial and error and the development of common law as opposed to formal constitutions, as in the days of Bretton Woods or even the Second Amendment. Such a process is not necessarily bad, as constitutions often do not work as planned. The Bretton Woods agreement, for example, never operated as the United States intended. But in the Bretton Woods period, there was a dominant power to step in and establish new rules for regulating conflict. Today, although the United States is necessary, it is not sufficiently dominant to fulfill its earlier role. The danger in this present multilateral system is that with incomplete management, crises may go unregulated, cumulate, and wreak havoc.

It is possible—although by no means certain—that states will develop means not only of crisis management but also of crisis prevention. The consensus among the powerful on the need for cooperation and joint management persists in word if not always in deed. The leaders of the developed states have time and again stressed the necessity of interdependence and of cooperating to maintain economic prosperity and political stability. Mechanisms for consultation and policy coordination still operate, but what will be done with them remains to be seen.

NOTES

1. For earlier systems of management, see Robert Triffin, *The Evolution of the International Monetary System: Historical Reappraisal and Future Perspectives* (Princeton, N.J.: International Finance Section, Department of Economics, Princeton University, 1964); Stephen V. O. Clarke, *Central Bank Cooperation, 1924–1931* (New York: Federal Reserve Bank of New York, 1967).

2. See Richard N. Gardner, *Sterling-Dollar Diplomacy in Current Perspective: The Origins and Prospects of our International Economic Order* (New York: Columbia University Press, 1980), Chs. 1 and 2.

3. Ibid., Chs. 3–5, 7; J. Keith Horsefield, ed., *The International Monetary Fund, 1945–1965: Twenty Years of International Monetary Cooperation*, vol. 1 (Washington, D.C.: IMF, 1969), pp. 10–118.

4. Edward S. Mason and Robert E. Asher, *The World Bank Since Bretton Woods* (Washington, D.C.: Brookings Institution, 1973), pp. 11–36.

5. See United Nations Economic Commission for Europe, *A Survey of the Economic Situation and Prospects of Europe* (Geneva: United Nations, 1948); United Nations Economic Commission for Europe, *Economic Survey of Europe in 1948* (Geneva: United Nations, 1949).

6. Mason and Asher, *The World Bank Since Bretton Woods*, pp. 105–107, 124–135.

7. See Robert Triffin, *Gold and the Dollar Crisis: The Future of Convertibility* (New Haven, Conn.: Yale University Press, 1960).

8. International Financial Statistics, Supplement 1972, pp. 2–3.

9. The Bank for International Settlements was a consortium of European central banks originally established in 1930 to implement a plan for rescheduling German reparations and to provide a forum for central bank discussion.

10. Switzerland joined in 1964 to make the Group of Ten in fact a group of eleven.

11. G. L. Bach, *Making Monetary and Fiscal Policy* (Washington, D.C.: Brookings Institution, 1971), pp. 111–150.

12. See Walter S. Salant et al., *The United States Balance of Payments in 1968* (Washington, D.C.: Brookings Institution, 1963).

13. Stephen D. Cohen, *International Monetary Reform, 1964–1969* (New York: Praeger, 1970); Fritz Machlup, *Remaking the International Monetary System: The Rio Agreement and Beyond* (Baltimore: Johns Hopkins University Press, 1968).

14. International Monetary Fund, *Annual Report 1972* (Washington, D.C.: IMF, 1972), p. 28.

15. This was convertibility for nonresidents. Full convertibility came in 1961.

16. Richard A. Debs, "International Banking," an address to the tenth annual convention of the Banking Law Institute, New York City, May 8, 1975, p. 3.

17. Sidney M. Robbins and Robert B. Stobaugh, *Money in the Multinational Enterprise: A Study in Financial Policy* (New York: Basic Books, 1973); Lawrence B. Krause, "The International Economic System and the Multinational Corporation," *The Annals*, 403 (September 1972), 93–103.

18. There are many theories regarding the origins of the Eurodollar market. See, for example, Paul Einzig, *The Euro-Dollar System: Practice and Theory of International Interest*

Rates, 4th ed. (New York: St. Martin's Press, 1970); Geoffrey Bell, *The Eurodollar Market and the International Financial System* (New York: John Wiley, 1973).

19. On the crisis, see Susan Strange, "The Dollar Crisis 1971," *International Affairs*, 48 (April 1972), 191–215.

20. Committee on Reform of the International Monetary System and Related Issues (Committee of Twenty), *International Monetary Reform: Documents of the Committee of Twenty* (Washington, D.C.: IMF, 1974), p. 8.

21. International Monetary Fund, *Annual Report 1975* (Washington, D.C.: IMF, 1975), p. 12.

22. International Monetary Fund, *Annual Report 1983* (Washington, D.C.: IMF, 1983), p. 21.

23. Committee on Reform, International Monetary Reform, pp. 216, 219.

24. See George de Menil and Anthony M. Solomon, *Economic Summitry* (New York: Council on Foreign Relations, 1983).

25. International Monetary Fund, *Proposed Second Amendment to the Articles of Agreement of the International Monetary Fund: A Report by the Executive Directors to the Board of Governors* (Washington, D.C.: IMF, March 1976).

26. International Monetary Fund, *Annual Report 1987* (Washington, D.C.: IMF, 1987), pp. 58, 60.

27. Ibid., p. 58.

28. Ibid.

29. See Morgan Guaranty Trust Company, *World Financial Markets*, March 1979, December 1986 issues.

30. See Edward J. Lincoln, *Japan: Facing Economic Maturity* (Washington, D.C.: The Brookings Institution, 1988), p. 210.

31. See, for example, Group of Thirty, *The Problem of Exchange Rates: A Policy Statement* (New York: Group of Thirty, 1982); Henry C. Wallich, Otmar Emminger, Robert V. Roosa, and Peter B. Kenen, *World Money and National Policies* (New York: Group of Thirty, 1983); John Williamson, *The Exchange Rate System* (Cambridge, Mass: MIT Press, 1983).

32. On internationalization see: *Recent Innovations in International Banking*, (Basel, Switzerland: April 1986); Maxwell Watson, Donald Mathieson, Russell Kincaid, and Eliot Kalter, *International Capital Markets: Developments and Prospects* (Washington, D.C.: International Monetary Fund, February 1986); Maxwell Watson, Russell Kincaid, Caroline Atkinson, Eliot Kalter, and David Folkerts-Landau, *International Capital Markets: Developments and Prospects.* (Washington, D.C.: International Monetary Fund, December 1986).

33. See *World Financial Markets*, Sept./Oct. 1987.

34. See World Bank, *World Debt Tables* (Washington, D.C.: World Bank, 1988).

35. Ibid.

36. "International Investment Position of the United States," *Survey of Current Business*, June 1988, p. 78.

37. International Monetary Fund, *International Financial Statistics*, May 1988 (Vol. XLI, No. 5) (Washington, DC: IMF, 1988) for Japan, West Germany and Korea. For Taiwan, see Central Bank of China (R.O.C.), *Financial Statistics*, November, 1987 (Taipei: Central Bank of China, 1987).

38. See Horst Ungerer et al., *The European Monetary System, 1979–1982*, Occasional Paper no. 19 (Washington, DC: International Monetary Fund, 1983); Horst Ungerer et al., *The European Monetary System: Recent Developments*, Occasional Paper no. 48 (Washington, DC: International Monetary Fund, 1986); Directorate General for Economic and Financial Affairs, EC, "The Creation of a European Financial Area, "*European Economy*, no. 36 (Brussels: Commission of the European Community, May 1988); Daniel Gros and Niels Thygesen, "The EMS: Achievements, Current Issues and Directions for the Future," CEPS Paper no. 35 (Brussels: Centre for European Policy Studies, 1988).

39. European Community, Committee for the Study of Economic and Monetary Union, *Report on Economic and Monetary Union in the European Community* (The Delors Report), April 12, 1989.

40. Lord Cockfield, *White Paper on Completing the Internal Market* (Brussels: Commission of the European Community, 1985).

41. On 1978 agreement, see de Menil and Solomon, *Economic Summitry*, pp. 23–29, 47–48.

42. The restrictive monetary policy consisted of a record increase in the discount rate from 8.5 to 9.5 percent and the imposition of a reserve requirement on certificates of deposit. The "war chest" included enlarged swaps with the central banks of West Germany, Japan, and Switzerland; the issuance of U.S. Treasury securities denominated in foreign currencies; a drawdown in IMF reserves; and the sale of SDRs.

43. On monetarism, see Milton Friedman and Anna Jacobson Schwartz, *A Monetary History of the United States 1867–1960* (Princeton, N.J.: Princeton University Press, 1963), the twelfth volume of a series, Studies in Business Research, of the National Bureau of Economic Research.

44. See: Bruce R. Bartlett, ed., *The Supply Side Solution* (Chatham, N.J.: Chatham House, 1983); Victor A. Canto et al., *Foundations of Supply-Side Economics: Theory and Evidence* (New York: Academic Press, 1983); Lawrence Robert Klein, *The Economics of Supply and Demand* (Baltimore: Johns Hopkins University Press, 1983).

45. See: Kenneth King, *U.S. Monetary Policy and European Responses in the 1980's*, Chatham House Paper 16 (London: Routledge, 1982); Sylvia Ann Hewlett, Henry Kaufman, and Peter B. Kenen, eds., *The Global Repercussions of U.S. Monetary and Fiscal Policy* (Cambridge, Mass.: Ballinger, 1984).

46. U.S. Department of Commerce, *U.S. Trade Performance in 1985 and Outlook* (Washington, D.C.: U.S. Government Printing Office, 1986), pp. 105–106.

47. On the period from the Plaza agreement to the Louvre agreement see Yoichi Funabashi, *Managing the Dollar: From the Plaza to the Louvre* (Washington, D.C.: Institute for International Economics, 1988).

48. Ibid, pp. 177–210.

49. See: *Report of the Advisory Group on Economic Structural Adjustment for International Harmony* (chaired by Haruo Maekaza), submitted to Prime Minister Nakasone on April 7, 1986.

50. See: John Williamson, *The Exchange Rate System* (Washington D.C.: Institute for International Economics, 1985); John Williamson and Marcus Miller, *Targets and Indicators: A Blueprint for International Coordination of Economic Policy*. (Washington D.C.: Institute for International Economics, 1987); International Monetary Fund; *Exchange Arrangements and Exchange Restrictions: Annual Report, 1987* (Washington D.C.: International Monetary Fund, 1987).

3

International Trade
and Domestic Politics

Trade policy is the stuff of domestic politics. Tariffs, quotas, and nontariff barriers are familiar issues for a broad range of economic groups, from farmers to manufacturers to labor unions to retailers. Because trade policy often determines prosperity or adversity for these groups, it is also the subject of frequent and often highly charged domestic political conflict.

In the United States, the Constitution accentuates the political conflict over trade policy by giving Congress the power to levy tariffs and regulate foreign commerce while at the same time giving the president authority in foreign policy. Conflict within Congress and between Congress and the executive branch is a central characteristic of U.S. trade policy. Because members of Congress are responsible to their constituents and, therefore, responsive to their economic concerns, there is often pressure within Congress for a trade policy that protects those special interests. Furthermore, the demands of relatively few interest groups directed at Congress may snowball into national trade policy, as occurred with the Smoot–Hawley Tariff Act of 1930, the most protectionist law of the century.[1]

While Congress tends to link trade policy with particular domestic interests, the United States executive branch often links trade policy with larger foreign policy and foreign economic goals. Thus, for example, since the 1930s, U.S. presidents have advocated open trade as the preferred economic policy, for broad economic and strategic reasons. Presidents, however, must have congressional approval for any agreement to reduce trade barriers. Yet the very process of approval raises the threat of interest group opposition. Presidents have tried to overcome this legislative constraint by asking Congress to delegate authority to the President to conclude trade agreements without subsequent congressional approval. Since 1934, Congress has regularly delegated such power for specifically limited periods of time and with specific constraints.

Domestic politicization in the United States and throughout the world has been an important constraint on international management. In this chapter we shall examine the evolution of trade management in the face of domestic political constraints.[2]

The Havana Charter

The same factors that led to the creation of a managed international monetary system after World War II also led to the first attempt to subject trade to systematic international control. Protectionism and the disintegration of world trade in the 1930s created a common interest in an open trading order and a realization that states would have to cooperate to achieve and maintain that order. The retreat into protectionism in the interwar period led not only to economic disaster but also to international war. In the postwar era, mechanisms for guarding against such economic nationalism and reducing and regulating restrictions on trade would have to be created. In the United States, policy was shaped by Secretary of State Cordell Hull, who was the major advocate of the liberal theory that open trade would lead to economic prosperity and international peace.[3]

The interwar experience also led to the willingness of the United States to lead the system. As the State Department explained:

> The only nation capable of taking the initiative in promoting a worldwide movement toward the relaxation of trade barriers is the United States. Because of its relatively great economic strength, its favorable balance of payments position, and the importance of its market to the well-being of the rest of the world, the influence of the United States on world commercial policies far surpasses that of any other nation.[4]

Despite the perception of a common interest in management and an open system and despite the willingness by the United States to lead the system, domestic political conflict made it difficult to translate the generally perceived common goals into an international order for trade. The conflict between domestic politics and international management began with the Havana Charter, the first attempt to build an order for international trade. The charter was an essential part of the plan to create a new, internationally managed economic system in the postwar era and, like the rest of that plan, was a product of strong U.S. leadership.

United States efforts to create an open system dated from the Reciprocal Trade Agreements Act of 1934, a product of Cordell Hull's liberal vision. Under that act, the United States concluded numerous agreements reducing the high tariffs of the early 1930s. During World War II, the

United States obtained from its allies commitments to a postwar international commercial order based on the freeing of international trade. In 1945, the United States presented a plan for a multilateral commercial convention to regulate and reduce restrictions on international trade. The convention offered rules for many aspects of international trade—tariffs, preferences, quantitative restrictions, subsidies, state trading, international commodity agreements—and provided for an International Trade Organization (ITO), the equivalent of the IMF (International Monetary Fund) in the area of trade, to oversee the system. In 1946 the United States called for an international conference to discuss this U.S. proposal and to implement a new trading order.[5]

Agreement on a new international order for trade, however, was more difficult to achieve than was agreement on a monetary order. The process of negotiation was very different from that of Bretton Woods, in which the United States and the United Kingdom dominated the decision making and there was little disagreement on the features of the desired system. The United States clearly played a leadership role in the negotiation process, but because each participant faced important domestic political constraints, the United States was not able to impose its plan on others. Britain, for example, insisted on provisions for its Imperial Preference System; other Europeans insisted on safeguards for balance-of-payments problems; and the less-developed countries demanded provisions for economic development. The result was a long-delayed international negotiation. Discussion began in 1943, but the final negotiations did not take place until 1947. In the end, the Havana Charter was a complex compromise that embodied in some way the wishes of everyone, but in the end it satisfied no one.[6]

Nevertheless, the charter might have become operational had it not been for domestic politics in the United States. Although the United States under the Roosevelt and Truman administrations had been a strong advocate of a new trading order and had led the international system through the complex negotiating process, Congress prevented the United States from adhering to the Havana Charter. The traditionally high tariff policy of the Republican party; the opposition of both the protectionists, who felt that the charter went too far, and the liberals, who felt that it did not go far enough toward free trade; and the opposition of business groups that opposed compromises on open trade and at the same time feared increased governmental involvement in trade management coalesced in a majority against the United States' own charter. After delaying for three years, the Truman administration finally decided in 1950 that it would not submit the Havana Charter to Congress, where it faced inevitable defeat. Once the United States withdrew, the charter was dead.[7] Despite a prevailing norm of international cooperation and strong and persistent U.S. leadership, an agreement on international control of trade proved elusive.

Multilateral Management under U.S. Leadership

The demise of the Havana Charter meant that trade management would be more limited than was originally envisaged. The consensus for an international trading order survived, embodied in GATT (General Agreement on Tariffs and Trade), which had been drawn up in 1947 to provide a procedural base and establish guiding principles for the tariff negotiations then being held in Geneva. Intended to be a temporary treaty to serve until the Havana Charter was implemented, GATT, by default, became the world's trading organization.

GATT reflected the prevailing agreement on open trade: the economic consensus that open trade would allow countries to specialize according to their comparative advantage and thereby achieve higher levels of growth and well-being, and the political consensus that a liberal trading regime would promote not only prosperity but also peace. The major rule for implementing free trade was the GATT principle of nondiscrimination. All of the contracting parties, that is, member states, agreed to adhere to the most-favored-nation principle, which stipulated that "any advantage, favour, privilege or immunity granted by any contracting party to any product originating in or destined for any other country shall be accorded immediately and unconditionally to the like product originating in or destined for the territories of all other contracting parties."[8] The only exceptions to this general rule of equal treatment were for existing preferential systems and future customs unions and free-trade associations. A second element of nondiscrimination in the GATT was the provision for national treatment designed to prevent discrimination against foreign products after they enter a country. Under GATT rules, a country must give imports the same treatment as it gives products made domestically in such areas as taxation, regulation, transportation, and distribution.[9]

GATT also established an international commercial code with rules on such issues as dumping and subsidies. The most important rule prohibited the use of quantitative restrictions, such as quotas, except for balance-of-payments or national security reasons. GATT also provided a mechanism for resolving disputes under this commercial code.

There were, however, important departures from these rules. Provisions in the original GATT treaty and amendments made in the 1950s established a separate regime for agricultural trade. GATT rules on agriculture reflected the powerful political influence of agricultural groups in the contracting parties of GATT and the resultant policies of government intervention to protect domestic prices and producer incomes and to assure food security. GATT rules reflected, in particular, the domestic policies of the United States, which pressed for an agricultural regime that would enable the United States to preserve the policy of production controls, price supports, export subsidies, and import protection implemented in the

1930s. Thus, for example, export subsidies on primary agricultural products were permitted as long as those subsidies did not interfere with established market shares, a concept alien to GATT rules for goods trade. GATT rules on quantitative restrictions facilitated their use in agriculture and, in 1955, the United States even obtained a waiver under GATT rules from the application of these rules that gave the United States special permission to impose quotas on agricultural products.[10]

There were also important gaps in the coverage of GATT as compared with the Havana Charter. Provisions for economic development, commodity agreements, restrictive business practices, and trade in services, for example, were not included. In addition, other topics not of great concern at the time, such as relations with state trading countries, were left undeveloped in the code. These departures from GATT norms and gaps in GATT coverage eventually became a major problem for the management of international trade. Finally, GATT's institutional mechanisms had important weaknesses. The dispute settlement mechanism was lengthy, allowed parties to delay or block decisions, and was not binding.

In addition to establishing trade principles, GATT provided a set of rules and procedures for what was to be the principal method of trade management in the postwar period: multilateral trade negotiations. The agreement contained a commitment to enter into such negotiations and provided guidelines for them. The most important rule was reciprocity, the concept that tariff reductions should be mutually advantageous. Although not part of the original GATT, the principal supplier procedure by which negotiations were to take place among actual or potential principal suppliers also became a negotiating rule of GATT.

From a temporary treaty, GATT became not only an established commercial code but also an international organization with a secretariat and a director general to oversee the implementation of its rules, manage dispute settlement, and provide a forum and support for multilateral trade negotiations.

Whereas GATT provided the framework for achieving trade liberalization, the United States put that framework into action. With the coming of the Cold War, Cordell Hull's vision of trade liberalization took on new significance as a key to a prosperous West and Western security in the face of Soviet aggression. United States economic strength and the lure of foreign markets were a further reason for U.S. interest in leading trade liberalization.

United States leadership was made possible by a new domestic approach to trade policy.[11] In order to avoid the pressure of special interest groups for protection, Congress delegated to the President, for a specific period of time, the authority to reduce tariffs by specific amounts without subsequent congressional approval. This negotiating authority, begun in 1934, was periodically renewed throughout the postwar period. Later, when nontariff barriers were negotiated, Congress agreed to consider proposals for their removal without allowing amendments and within a short time frame. In addition, Congress created a quasi-judicial system of trade remedies that channeled grievances of specific industries to fact-finding agencies outside the Congress. Finally, the decision-making process in Congress was concentrated in two powerful committees that dominated trade policy and that supported a liberal trading order.[12]

In the two decades following World War II, the United States led the system by helping Europe and Japan rebuild production and by pushing for trade liberalization. In the early years, the Marshall Plan, or the European Recovery Program as it was officially known, was the tool of U.S. leadership in Europe. As we have seen, the United States played a key role in financing international trade and encouraging long-term European trade competitiveness through the Marshall Plan. The United States also used the plan as a lever to encourage regional trade liberalization in Europe. During the war and the immediate postwar period, significant barriers to trade had been erected throughout Europe, which underscored the trade restrictions in effect since the 1930s. The United States pushed actively for the liberalization of trade and payments among Western European countries and, in some cases, made available the funds for such liberalization, even though this conflicted with the larger U.S. goal of nondiscrimination on an international basis and even though regional liberalization sometimes involved direct discrimination against the United States.[13]

The United States also took an important leadership role with Japan. During the Occupation, the supreme commander for the Allied forces and his administration directly controlled Japanese trade and the Japanese monetary system. Until the 1960s, the United States helped the recovery and development in Japan by keeping the U.S. market open for Japanese goods while at the same time accepting Japanese protectionist policies, many of which had been instituted under the Occupation. The United States also supported Japanese membership in GATT and urged the Europeans, unsuccessfully, to open their markets to Japanese exports.[14]

Finally, the United States took a leading role in multilateral trade negotiations. The idea of creating a more open system through negotiations to remove tariffs and other trade barriers had originated with the U.S. Reciprocal Trade Agreements Act of 1934, which had led to a series of bilateral negotiations. Tariff reductions in these negotiations were based on reciprocity (that is, mutual advantage), a system that headed off potential domestic political opposition to tariff reduction within the United States. The reductions negotiated bilaterally were broadened under the most-favored-nation agreements that the United States had established with numerous countries under various commercial treaties.

In the postwar period, this procedure of bilateral negotiations was expanded to a series of multilateral trade negotiations conducted by the members of GATT. The United States, with the world's largest economy and a huge share of international trade, was the essential motivating force in these negotiations. Because the United States was, in many cases, one of the world's principal suppliers, its participation was required under GATT's negotiating rules. Because the U.S. market was so important, there was little possibility of achieving reciprocity in tariff negotiations without the United States. Most importantly, without U.S. initiatives, the negotiations would probably never have taken place. Initiatives by the United States were responsible for the eight major trade negotiations from the Geneva Round in 1947 to the Uruguay Round, which began in 1986. The U.S. negotiators were necessary participants—mobilizing others, seeking compromises—in the actual negotiations.

Furthermore, throughout the 1940s and 1950s, the United States accepted limited benefits from the trade negotiations. Although tariffs were reduced on a reciprocal and mutually beneficial basis, U.S. trading partners gained more than the United States did. Because of European and Japanese exchange controls that persisted through the 1950s, the trade concessions had a limited effect on U.S. exports. Because the United States did not impose controls, Europe and Japan gained immediate benefit from the tariff reductions. The United States accepted such asymmetrical benefits because of a commitment to European and Japanese recovery, because it expected to benefit from the reductions when the exchange controls were removed, and because it sought to maintain the momentum of establishing a more open trading system.

The system worked very well for the developed countries. Most quotas and exchange rate barriers were eliminated. Although restrictions remained in agricultural products, there was substantial liberalization of trade in manufactured products.[15] The rapid growth of trade was an important source of economic prosperity. The high point of trade management of this period was the Kennedy Round, which culminated in 1967. Although states were unable to reach any significant agreement on agricultural trade, tariffs on nonagricultural products in the developed countries were reduced by about one-third.[16] After the Kennedy Round reductions, tariffs on dutiable, nonagricultural products were reduced to an average of 9.9 percent in the United States, 8.6 percent in the six EC (European Community) states, 10.8 percent in the United Kingdom, and 10.7 percent in Japan.[17]

Structural Change and Protectionism

After 1967, however, important changes in the international trading system began to emerge and to undermine the GATT system of management and the liberal international trading order created by GATT. Over the next two decades, structural changes led to domestic political challenges to international management of trade and to new forms of protection. Governments sought, with only limited success, to stem the tide of protectionism and to modernize the international trading regime. Thus, the conflict between national and international approaches to management—the same conflict we have seen in the international monetary system—came to plague international trade management.

As in the case of monetary relations, a central force for change was increased interdependence. Interdependence increased the level of political sensitivity to trade as trade came to affect more sectors and more jobs. After World War II, economic growth, trade liberalization, decreasing transportation costs, and broadening business horizons led to a surge in trade among the developed market economies.[18] Merchandise trade among the developed countries more than quadrupled between 1963 and 1973; increased over two-and-one-half times from 1973 to 1983; and grew almost one-and-one-half times again between 1983 and 1986.[19] From 1960 to 1986, the percentage of GDP derived from trade (exports plus imports) doubled to 14.4 percent in the United States, gained 40 percent to an average 63 percent in the original six EC countries, while remaining fairly constant at 17.3 percent in Japan.[20] The role of trade was even greater in certain sectors. For example, in 1979, 5.5 percent of U.S. consumer goods and 12 percent of U.S. business equipment purchases came from abroad. By 1987, the figures for consumer goods had grown to about 12 percent, whereas foreign business equipment outlays exceeded 40 percent.[21] Interdependence in certain sectors was reinforced by the emergence of the global company which sources parts from around the world. One example is the Boeing Company, which produces commercial jetliners. In 1980, imported parts accounted for 2 to 3 percent of airplanes produced by Boeing. By 1988, imported parts represented 28 percent of Boeing airplanes.[22]

Another dimension of trade interdependence was growing convergence of the developed countries' economies. The rapid accumulation of physical and human capital, the transfer of technology, and the growing similarities of wages narrowed the differences in factor endowments, which are the basis for comparative advantage and trade. In 1970, for example, labor costs in the United States and West Germany were over twice the labor costs in Japan. By 1986, the costs were roughly equal.[23] Similarly, in 1970, U.S. manufacturing productivity was 58 percent greater than West Germany and 105 percent greater than Japan in 1970. By 1986, these figures had fallen to 20 percent and 2 percent, respectively.[24] Convergence altered the nature of comparative advantage, leading to more complex specialization and fostering the global company and intraindustry trade. Also, because of economic convergence, small changes in factor costs led to large shifts in comparative advantage and thus in trade, production, and employment—and to political reaction to those shifts.

A second change that increased protectionist pressures was the shift in competitiveness worldwide. Changes in factor endowments altered the competitive positions of several industries in the developed countries, including autos, steel, textiles, shipping, and consumer electronics. In some sectors, the shift favored the developing countries. Lags in capital investment in the developed countries plus rising labor productivity, lower labor costs, and aggressive export policies in some of the LDCs led to a shift in comparative advantage toward the newly industrialized countries (NICs), such as Taiwan, Korea, and Brazil.[25] In other cases, because of differing levels of investment and research, of management effectiveness and labor productivity, as well as exchange rate changes, the shift occurred among the developed countries. The reasons for this shift in competitiveness among developed countries has become a subject of significant debate. In the United States, for example, debate has focused heavily on declining U.S. competitiveness vis-à-vis Japan, which has been evidenced by greater Japanese investment per employee, greater productivity growth, and greater average growth of total gross fixed capital formation.[26]

The main economic manifestations of the shift in competitiveness were serious competition from imports and surplus capacity—that is, a demand inadequate to maintain price, profit, and employment at politically acceptable levels—in industries that had been the mainstays of many economies.[27] The major political manifestation was pressure from these sectors for protection. The combination of interdependence and changes in competitiveness made national economies more sensitive to external events and provoked domestic producers to mobilize for protection from foreign competition.

A third change contributing to protectionism were disruptions in the economic system in the 1970s and 1980s. Trade management from the end of World War II until the end of the Kennedy Round took place in an environment of unprecedented growth and stability. From 1960 to 1970, growth in the OECD countries averaged almost 5 percent per year, unemployment stood at 2.7 percent, and the volume of world trade grew at an average annual rate of 8.5 percent.[28] Throughout this period, the U.S. trade balance was strongly positive, providing the basis for a national consensus for liberalizing trade (see Table 2-1). In such an expanding world economy, economic groups were able to perceive the advantages of cooperation and trade liberalization.

In the 1970s and 1980s, these favorable conditions altered dramatically and contributed to the new protectionism. The 1970s was the era of stagflation, slow growth combined with rampant inflation. In the wake of the oil crisis, the developed countries' real GNP growth dropped to 2.7 percent between 1974 and 1979, while their inflation exploded to double digits, reaching a high of 13.4 percent in 1974.[29] Unemployment in the OECD countries increased to an average of 4.9 percent for the period 1974 to 1979.[30] Stagflation increased pressures on governments to adopt beggar-thy-neighbor policies such as trade restrictions.

The floating exchange rate system also contributed to growing protectionism. In the 1970s, monetary problems led to trade measures designed to protect payments balances such as exchange controls and special duties. The breakdown in the system of fixed exchange rates also complicated the process of trade negotiations. In a fixed rate system, negotiators had been able to estimate the impact of agreements on their trade and payments. Under floating rates, such calculations were much more difficult. As a result of these economic changes, world trade grew by only 5 percent between 1970 and 1980.[31]

In the early 1980s, deep recession put a brake on trade. Deflationary policies led to a steady decline in inflation from 12.9 percent in 1980 to 2.5 percent in 1986.[32] At the same time, growth ground to a halt. The years 1980 to 1982 witnessed the lowest average growth rate—0.73 percent per year—of any three-year period since the end of World War II.[33] Unemployment rose to levels once thought politically unacceptable. By the end of 1983, recession had pushed total unemployment in the OECD countries to a record 8.5 percent.[34] Significantly, unemployment was concentrated in those industries with the highest levels of foreign competition. For example, in December 1982, when total U.S. unemployment reached its peak of 10.6 percent, unemployment in the auto industry stood at 23.2 percent, and in the primary metals (steel) industry, it was 29.2 percent.[35] Because of the recession, world trade stagnated. The volume of world trade growth slowed to 1.2 percent in 1980, 0.8 percent in 1981, and actually fell by 2.2 percent in 1982.[36]

By the second half of the 1980s, the economic environment improved. Growth among the developed countries rose to 3.2 percent in 1985 and 2.8 percent in 1986, while inflation fell to 4.5 percent in 1985 and to 2.5 percent in 1986.[37] World trade also expanded, growing 3.5 percent in 1986 and 4.0 percent in 1987.[38] Because of labor market rigidities, however, unemployment remained high and persisted as a force for protection. In 1986, unemployment in the developed countries still stood at 8.3 percent, with U.S. unemployment at 7.0 percent, Japanese at 2.8 percent, and the EC at 11.2 percent.[39] In the 1980s, the exchange rate system emerged as a central problem for trade management. As we have seen, the misalignment of exchange rates was a major factor in the emergence of massive trade and payments imbalances. In particular, the overvaluation of the dollar and corresponding undervaluation of the yen and deutsche mark were a major cause of the U.S. trade deficit and the resultant rise in protectionism in the United States.

Pluralism

In the 1970s and 1980s, the rise of Japan and the European Economic Community and the relative decline of the United States complicated the system of trade management. Trade problems and a decline in power combined with growing protectionist pressures left the United States less willing and less able to lead the system. At the same time, the EC and Japan were not prepared to assume a leadership role. Absent strong leadership, management where power is more evenly shared proved a major challenge to the system.

Since 1958 the European Community has emerged as the world's largest trading bloc. The EC has established a customs union with free internal trade in goods, a common external tariff, and a common agricultural policy. Trade of EC countries has grown rapidly from 24.5 percent of total world trade in 1960 to 38.8 percent in 1986.[40] Trade among EC member states has grown even faster. From 1960 to 1986, intra-EC trade as a share of total world trade increased more than two-and-one-half times from 8.4 percent in 1960 to 22.0 percent in 1986.[41] As a result, intra-EC trade as a share of total EC member-state trade burgeoned from 34.4 percent in 1960 to 56.8 percent in 1986.[42] In building this trading system, the Community has weakened the principal of nondiscrimination basic to the GATT and has thus posed challenges to liberalization of the larger international system. In addition, its preoccupation with building a common market and its continuing political fragmentation weakened the EC's ability to play a central management role in the multilateral system.

The EC's first goal was to build a customs union with internal free trade and a common external tariff among the six, then ten, and finally twelve European states that the EC comprises. Such customs unions are permitted as an exception to the GATT rules of nondiscrimination.[43] The European effort to establish such a union was supported by the United States, which, since the days of the Marshall Plan, actively encouraged a European union as a way of strengthening the West. When it looked as if the EC might increase trade discrimination, the United States, by initiating the Kennedy Round, sought to ensure that European integration would remain open and nondiscriminatory. The success of that round suggested that Europe would remain committed to multilateralism and liberalism. However, by the 1970s and 1980s, Europe showed signs of moving in the opposite direction.

The Community's Common Agricultural Policy (CAP) blocked imports into the community and artificially stimulated competition in other markets (see p. 88). The EC also entered into preferential trading arrangements, which were explicitly outlawed under the GATT rule of nondiscrimination. Beginning in 1958 with an agreement with the then French colonies in Africa, the EC has negotiated preferential agreements with most of the Mediterranean Basin, much of Africa, and even with some developed countries of Western Europe. The Community has viewed such agreements as aid to underdeveloped countries and as adjustments for the discriminatory effects of CAP. Although the preferences have not had so great a trade diversionary impact as CAP has—at least not for the developed market economies—the United States has viewed them as an important departure from the postwar agreement on nondiscrimination.

The enlargement of the community to include the United Kingdom, Denmark, Ireland, then Greece, and finally Spain and Portugal created further problems. This expansion not only increased the size of the agricultural protectionist regime and the existing preferential system but also became a force for the extension of EC preferences. Some of the European Free Trade Area (EFTA) countries, which for political reasons did not join the EC, as well as many Commonwealth countries, became linked with the EC through preferential trade agreements.

In the 1980s, EC attention focussed on the new policy of completing the creation of a common internal market by 1992.[44] In 1985, the community announced a plan to remove over 300 nontariff barriers to intra-EC trade ranging from harmonizing standards to eliminating delays at borders to allowing cross border sales of services such as banking and insurance to tax harmonization. The thrust of the internal market program was decidedly liberal, based as it was on efforts to remove nontariff barriers to free trade. However, as the Community worked toward its 1992 deadline, questions began to emerge about its impact on the multilateral trading system. Talk of "Europe for the Europeans" raised concerns about increasing barriers to the outside world through, for example, extension of national protectionist policies to the Community as a whole or through harmonization of standards and regulations that would discriminate against non-European goods and services. Other questions concerned treatment of foreign firms that had invested in Europe and whether they would be considered "European" for purposes of cross-border sales of services and for government procurement. Concern was raised about the EC commitment to multilateral liberalization of trade. The considerable energies required to complete the internal market could divert attention from and willingness of the EC to participate in multilateral trade liberalization. Finally, despite significant progress in economic cooperation, the EC remained a community of sovereign states, which limited its ability to play a leadership role in multilateral trade management like that of the United States.

The rise of Japan as a force in the world economy and world trade has also complicated trade management. As late as 1960, Japan was a minor economic power, with a 3-percent share of world GNP. By the 1980s, Japan had become the second largest developed economy after the United States.

Japan accounted for 10 percent of world GNP,[45] and for 8.3 percent of world trade, making it a trading power on a par with West Germany.[46]

Behind this rapid change in position was the Japanese economic miracle: an annual real growth in GNP of 10 percent from 1950 to 1970. Starting from a position of relative technological backwardness, Japan achieved this remarkable growth rate through its ability to absorb and adapt foreign technology, the availability of labor due to the movement of people out of agriculture and a growing population, and heavy investment in manufacturing.[47] Government policies played a central role in the Japanese miracle. Targeted industries, such as steel, oil refining, petrochemicals, automobiles, aircraft, industrial machinery, electronics, and computers, were promoted through tax incentives as well as financing provided by government lending institutions and private savings encouraged by government policies.

Export expansion and import protection played a central role in government policy. Because of Japan's dependence on imports of raw materials and capital goods essential for growth, government plans and private industry strategies placed heavy emphasis on limiting "nonessential" imports and fostering exports.[48] Government provided industry with significant protection from import competition through tariffs and quantitative restrictions as well as administrative regulations, such as import licensing and import deposits. While the other developed countries were liberalizing trade through multilateral negotiations, Japan retained barriers on virtually all imports. At the same time, tax incentives, export financing assistance, and an undervalued yen encouraged Japanese exports. Finally, government carefully controlled foreign investment. Thus, in the 1950s and 1960s, Japan created an industrial base heavily biased against imports and oriented towards exports.[49]

After 1973, growth slowed due to the end of the process of technological catch-up, lower investment rates, and other factors, such as slower population growth and rising energy costs. Industrial development shifted from heavy industry, such as steel, to more sophisticated industries, such as automobiles and electronic products.[50] Nevertheless, Japan's average growth rate of 4.3 percent from 1974 to 1985 exceeded that of other industrial economies. In the 1970s, Japanese government policy also changed. Although the government still took a lead role in certain strategic sectors, such as computers, the role of government in industrial development began to decline as Japanese industry reached greater maturity.[51]

Beginning in 1970, Japan gradually liberalized trade policy. Quotas on many goods were eliminated; significant across-the-board tariff cuts were instituted; and the yen began to appreciate. Following the Tokyo Round, Japanese tariff barriers were roughly comparable to those of the United States.[52] Japan's strategy of export promotion, however, not only remained but also was reinforced by the oil crises of 1970 and 1974, which accentuated Japan's sense of dependence on and vulnerability to imports of raw materials. Overall, by the end of the 1970s, it seemed that Japan was on its way to full integration in the liberal trading system.

Instead, by the 1980s, Japan had become a source of trade friction due to the seemingly chronic Japanese merchandise trade surplus. In 1970, Japan had a trade surplus of $4.3 billion. Following several years of negative balances caused by the oil crisis, Japan's merchandise trade surplus reached $18.3 billion in 1978. In the 1980s, however, Japan's trade surplus surged, reaching $44.3 billion in 1984, $56 billion in 1985, $92.8 billion in 1986, and $96.4 billion in 1987.[53] Most visible was Japan's growing imbalance in trade with the United States, its principal trading partner. While the bilateral Japan-EC surplus grew from $9.9 billion in 1980 to $24 billion in 1987, its surplus with the United States grew from $7.3 billion in 1980 to $53 billion in 1987.[54]

The principal cause of the massive surplus was an imbalance in macro-economic policies, particularly between the United States and Japan, which was reflected in capital flows and exchange rate relations. Japan maintained a high savings rate fostered by government policies, which dated from the era when Japan needed high levels of investment for economic develop-ment. However, because of slower growth and investment and a policy of government fiscal austerity, there was insufficient demand for these savings within Japan. As the Japanese government eliminated exchange controls and other limits on Japanese foreign investment, surplus yen began to flow abroad in response to demand, primarily from the United States. United States savings rates were low, while demand for funds in the growing U.S. economy was too high to be satisfied from U.S. sources alone. For much of the 1980s, U.S. business was investing heavily and the U.S. government was generating huge budget deficits that had to be financed. Japan provided much of that financing. The flow of yen to the United States was a major factor in the decline in the value of the yen and a rise in the value of the dollar. This exchange rate imbalance with an overvalued dollar and an undervalued yen made Japanese goods more competitive worldwide es-pecially vis-à-vis U.S. products.

Differing domestic demand was also an important dimension of the macroeconomic imbalance. As the United States stimulated its economy in the early 1980s, imports of consumer goods increased more than 150 per-cent from $34.4 billion in 1980, to $87.0 billion in 1987.[55] The Japanese were well positioned to take advantage of this surge in consumer demand. For decades, Japanese manufacturers had concentrated on export-led growth and on developing the U.S. market. Since the 1970s, they had focussed on developing products targeted at the U.S. consumer. Japanese automobiles and consumer electronic products, for example, were well designed for the U.S. market, of high quality, and, due to productivity improvements and a declining yen, increasingly price competitive. At the same time, because of slower growth and fiscal austerity, Japanese demand, especially demand for competitive U.S. machine tools and heavy equipment, was restrained.

These macroeconomic differences were accentuated by continuing barriers to imports into Japan. With the exception of agriculture, most Japanese tariff and quota barriers had been removed. However, nontariff barriers deriving from the earlier era of cooperation between government and business—what has been called "Japan Inc."—remained a problem. Government procurement policies favored Japanese telecommunications and computer manufacturers. Regulation was used effectively to block imports. For example, patent approvals were delayed until Japanese producers became competitive. Inspections and approvals by foreign testing agencies were rejected by some ministries, and the process of regulatory approval was often long and not transparent. Industrial targeting, as in the case of computers, was still used to discriminate against foreign goods. In addition, private patterns of behavior, such as so-called *keiretsu* behavior or preference of Japanese for dealing with other Japanese suppliers as well as the complex Japanese distribution system, formed barriers to foreign access to Japanese markets. For U.S. industry that was less export oriented, overcoming these public and private barriers proved especially difficult.

As a result of this combination of factors, the bilateral U.S.-Japan trade imbalance soared in the 1980s. Even after the Plaza agreement of 1985 when the value of the dollar began to decline, Japanese surpluses continued to grow. In part this was due to the so-called J-curve effect, whereby the impact of a depreciation is initially an increase in a deficit as the cost of goods already contracted for import rises. Persistent depreciations of the dollar from 1985 to 1987 accentuated the J-curve effect and masked the turnaround in the physical volume and yen value of U.S.-Japan trade. Furthermore, the trade impact of dollar depreciation was reduced, because Japanese exporters, dependent on the U.S. market, increased prices less than the magnitude of the dollar depreciation in order to retain their market share.

The political consequence of the Japanese trade surplus was increasing trade friction between Japan and its trading partners. Pressures grew for protection against Japanese imports and for action to open Japanese markets. In the West, the Japanese surpluses were often attributed not to macroeconomic imbalances but to unfair trade practices by Japan. Protectionist pressures were accentuated by the traditional Japanese export strategy of capturing market share. This strategy led to swift penetration of certain foreign markets, which led to equally swift foreign political reaction in such powerful sectors as semiconductors and automobiles. Finally, the slow process of decision making in Japan, where consensus must be formed before action is taken, exacerbated growing Western criticism of Japan as a free rider in the system.[56]

Growing Western exasperation seemed unfounded in Japan. From a Japanese perspective, the country had moved far and fast under Western prodding to liberalize trade. Under heavy pressure, Japan had opened up a variety of protected markets, such as telecommunications, cigarettes, beef, citrus, and airport construction. It had liberalized its financial markets, opening the securities and trust banking business to foreigners.[57] Furthermore, Western governments subjected Japan to numerous highly protectionist VRAs. In the mid-1980s, under pressure from the West and from a revalued yen, Japan had stimulated domestic demand and moved toward reducing its dependence on export-led growth. After the Plaza agreement, net exports measured in terms of physical volume and net receipts in yen declined. Imports from the developing countries increased dramatically. As seen from Japan, foreign profligacy, especially U.S. macroeconomic policy and declining Western productivity and competitiveness, were the root of the problem.[58]

Finally, one of the most important developments in the 1970s and 1980s was the erosion of U.S. dominance of the international trading system and the related decline in U.S. support for a multilateral trade regime. While the United States remained the world's largest economy and largest trading power, it was no longer overwhelmingly preponderant as in the first two postwar decades. In 1950 the United States accounted for 26.1 percent of trade among developed market economies; by 1980 that figure had fallen to 18.3 percent.[59] Furthermore, after 1970 the United States began to experience what seemed to be chronic merchandise trade deficits. The huge and traditional (since 1893) U.S. merchandise-trade surplus turned in 1971 into a persistent and growing merchandise trade deficit.[60] The United States traditional surplus with Japan turned into deficit in 1965, and its traditional surplus with Western Europe diminished and in 1983 became a deficit.[61] In the 1980s, U.S. trade deficits soared due to several factors: an overvalued dollar; strong U.S. economic growth in comparison with other developed countries; the declining rate of increase in U.S. productivity relative to other industrialized countries; lower demand for U.S. agricultural exports; the increased competitiveness of foreign companies in many traditional sectors even as the competitiveness of U.S. industry declined; the rise in the number of protectionist barriers; and the Third World debt crisis, which resulted in sharply reduced imports by debtor countries that had been important U.S. markets. In 1987 the U.S. merchandise trade deficit reached its nadir of $167 billion.

The erosion of United States' trading dominance was accentuated by interdependence. Between 1970 and 1980, trade as a percentage of U.S. GNP rose from 8.7 percent to 17.5 percent.[62] Interdependence was a new condition for the United States. In contrast with Europe and Japan, whose economies had long been dependent on trade, international trade had been important but not vital to the United States because of its vast continental market. As the United States faced more competition at home and abroad, the political consensus for a multilateral, open trading regime led by the United States began to erode.

The decline of U.S. trade preponderance and the swelling trade deficit raised questions about U.S. international competitiveness. The ability of countries to compete in foreign trade depends on productivity, which, in turn, depends on investment in both physical and human capital as well as on research and development. Much of the deterioration of the U.S. trading position in the 1980s was attributable to the overvalued dollar. Indeed, following the devaluation of the dollar in 1985, U.S. exports rebounded and regained some world market share.

Nonetheless, several indicators also suggest a relative decline in U.S. competitiveness. While the United States retains the highest level of productivity, it has been losing ground. Total factor productivity—output per combined unit of labor and capital—in the U.S. business sector has grown more slowly than that of other industrialized countries since the 1960s.[63] Since 1972, investment in relation to GDP increased only 3.1 percent in the United States—less than half the Group of Seven average of 7.1 percent— while in Germany it rose 33 percent, and in Japan, 24.6 percent.[64] While overall research and development expenditures in the United States have kept pace with those of other developed countries, much of that expenditure has been for military purposes. Nondefense research and development spending relative to GDP in the United States has increased only 3 percent since 1970, while that of Germany increased 31 percent and that of Japan 55 percent. In terms of human capital, the United States is also losing ground. In 1965, for example, 80 percent of the patents awarded in the United States went to U.S. citizens, whereas by 1986, this figure was only 55 percent.[65] Not all evidence suggests a U.S. decline, however. In terms of relative unit labor costs, Japan and Germany have increased from 1980 levels, while the United States has actually declined.[66] Furthermore, U.S. industry has adapted to changing competition by increasing automation, downsizing, mergers, and streamlining operations. Overall, evidence suggests the United States has lost some of its relative position, largely as a result of gains in Japan.

Finally, in the 1970s and 1980s, U.S. support for multilateralism was further undermined by changes in the domestic political system that had developed to deflect protectionist pressures from special interest groups.[67] A series of congressional reforms weakened the power of the committees that had virtually exclusively controlled U.S. trade policy, while the growing importance of nontariff barriers imbedded in a variety of national policies meant that these committees that had traditionally controlled trade could no longer claim exclusive jurisdiction over trade issues. In addition, the quasi-judicial system established to manage trade grievances began to break down both under the weight of complaints and because President Reagan often rejected the findings as leading to protectionism. The pressures then spilled back to Congress, which came to feel that the administration was rigid and uncooperative on trade policy. The result was increasing efforts by Congress to reform U.S. trade law to reduce presidential discretion and to oblige retaliation against countries found in violation of international trade agreements.

As a result of these changes, domestic pressures for protection increased and became increasingly effective. As trade problems developed, more industries organized into special interest groups to put pressure on Congress and the executive for relief from foreign competition. Beginning in the late 1960s following the Kennedy Round, vulnerable industries, such as textiles, steel, electronics, and shoes, began to put strong pressure on Congress to alleviate import competition.[68] In 1970, organized labor officially shifted its policy from support for free trade to active lobbying for protection. Proposals for sectoral protectionist legislation increased in Congress and put pressure on the President to negotiate bilateral agreements outside the GATT to avert legislated quotas and tariffs. At the same time, U.S. industries facing barriers to market access abroad increasingly turned to the U.S. government for help in breaking down foreign barriers. As markets became increasingly global, many high-technology, export-oriented industries, such as microelectronics and supercomputer industries, chafed under restrictions on access to foreign markets. Their goal was to use access to U.S. markets as bargaining leverage to open up foreign markets.[69]

As the trade problem deepened and spread from sensitive industries to the entire economy in the 1980s, many U.S. industry, labor, and political leaders came to believe the United States was no longer benefiting from the system and was being subjected to unfair treatment by its trading partners and by the trading regime. Japan, in particular, was singled out as a country that benefited from the liberal trading order and access to U.S. markets while maintaining barriers to its own market.[70] Proposals for broad-based protectionist legislation increased in Congress. In 1988, Congress enacted omnibus trade legislation, which tightened U.S. trade law to give the president less discretion in case of unfair trade practices by foreign competitors and to require the executive branch to identify and achieve changes in the policy of countries that have unfair trade practices.[71]

In response to persistent congressional pressures, the Reagan administration sought nonlegislative ways to resolve trade conflicts: negotiated voluntary export restraint agreements as in automobiles (see p. 86); negotiations to open overseas markets, such as the Market Opening Sector Specific (MOSS) talks between the U.S. and Japan; and aggressive use of the U.S. trade provisions, which authorizes the U.S. government to retaliate against countries deemed not to be allowing U.S. exports fair market access. Finally, the United States negotiated a broad-based bilateral trading agreement with Israel in 1986 and a more important agreement with Canada in

1987. The U.S.-Canada Free Trade Agreement reduced a number of trade and investment barriers between the two countries, established rules on trade in services, and put in place a new dispute settlement mechanism between the two countries. Although the free-trade agreement was described as a reinforcement of the multilateral regime and a model for future GATT agreements on investment and services, it was potentially a departure from the postwar U.S. policy of multilateralism in international trade.[72]

Despite the important shift in the domestic political consensus, the United States remained committed to the multilateral system. As it negotiated VRAs and bilateral free-trade agreements, the United States also continued efforts to reform the GATT system and to further trade liberalization through multilateral negotiations. United States initiatives launched both the Tokyo and the Uruguay Rounds of multilateral trade negotiations. And a key provision of the 1988 trade legislation authorized the President to enter into multilateral trade negotiations, which Congress agreed to approve under fast-track procedures.

The New Protectionism

The result of these structural changes in the global trading economy was a surge in protectionist policies in developed countries. The new protectionism took several forms.

One form was nontariff barriers (NTBs) to trade. In part, the NTB problem grew out of the very success of the GATT. GATT had been designed to liberalize trade by removing quotas and tariffs. With the success of such liberalization in manufactured products, the major remaining barriers to trade were nontariff barriers such as government procurement policies, customs procedures, health and sanitary regulations, national standards, and a broad range of other laws and regulations that discriminate against imports or offer assistance to exports. Regional policy, agricultural policy, and consumer and environmental protection are other examples of nontariff measures that have trade-distorting consequences.

Furthermore, the success of the GATT in trade liberalization actually increased the use of nontariff barriers. Because governments can no longer use tariffs and quotas as tools of national economic policy, they have tried to shape comparative advantage through a variety of national industrial policies. States have used subsidies and tax preferences to help ailing industries, such as steel and shipbuilding. They have provided a variety of incentives for the development of new, technologically sophisticated industries, such as airframes and computers. And they have used a combination of tax and financial incentives as well as requirements for local content, export performance, and technology transfer for foreign investors.

Countries now had to reduce nontariff trade barriers to maintain what had already been achieved, let alone continue the process of liberalization. However, the control of nontariff barriers is far more difficult than the regulation and removal of tariffs and quotas. Such policies are usually an integral part of national economic and social policies. Because they are often carried out for reasons other than trade protection, NTBs have traditionally been considered national prerogatives not subject to international negotiation. Nontariff barriers also pose practical negotiating problems. Because NTBs take many different forms and because many different governmental bodies have authority over them, it is not possible to conduct broad international negotiations, such as those over tariffs. The reduction of nontariff barriers requires international agreements to coordinate and harmonize a broad range of policies, for which GATT offers few guidelines.[73]

Another form of the new protectionism were voluntary restraint agreements (VRA), also known as voluntary export restraints (VER). VRAs were developed as a response to pressure for protection from import-sensitive industries. GATT provides three principal forms of recourse for industries hurt by imports. If foreign competitors are dumping, that is, selling goods abroad at prices below those in the home market, countries are allowed to impose a duty to offset the dumping. Although the anti-dumping law is well developed both domestically and internationally, action can take a long time, and proving dumping cases can be difficult. GATT also permits countries to impose duties to offset foreign subsidies of exported products. However, this is a remedy used only by the United States. Finally, GATT permits certain emergency measures known as safeguard actions. GATT permits governments to impose restrictions on fairly traded imports if an unforeseen surge in imports resulting from a trade concession causes or threatens serious injury to a domestic industry. Such safeguard actions must be applied to all countries; protection must be limited in time and be gradually removed; and importing countries must adopt meaningful adjustment policies. For several reasons, however, this GATT provision has rarely been invoked. It must be applied to all countries, whereas governments have preferred to target certain suppliers for import controls. GATT also requires the importing country to grant compensatory concessions to all affected exporting countries. Furthermore, GATT does not clearly define "serious injury" and offers inadequate guidance—for example, on consultative procedures, duration, and adjustment—for implementing and regulating safeguards actions. Thus, governments have turned increasingly to VRAs, which are outside the GATT framework.[74]

Under such agreements, which are usually bilateral and sometimes secret, low-cost exporters "voluntarily" restrict sales to countries where their goods are threatening industry and employment. There is a long history of such agreements. In the 1950s and 1960s, for example, the United States negotiated a number of voluntary export controls with Japan and many LDCs, under which exporters restricted their sales in the U.S. market.

Two agreements—the Longterm Textile Arrangement of 1962 and the subsequent Multi-Fiber Arrangement of 1974—were negotiated multilaterally and within the GATT context (see Chapter 7). These earlier agreements were unusual steps, exceptions to normal GATT procedures. In the recent period, however, VRAs have become an accepted mode of trade regulation.[75] In the 1970s and 1980s, VRAs proliferated in various sectors—textiles, steel, automobiles, electronics, and footwear—and covered trade among the industrial nations themselves.

In the United States, the typical pattern has been a surge of imports, followed by massive filings of unfair trade actions, followed by pressure on Congress for protectionist legislation, followed, in turn, by a negotiated voluntary export restraint agreement as a way to reduce imports without resolving the legal cases and without legislating protection.

Steel was the first major industry subjected to VRAs among developed market economies. In 1968, faced with surging imports and under pressure from proposed legislation to limit steel imports, the Johnson administration negotiated VRAs with the European Community and Japan, which set specific tonnage limits on each for their steel exports to the United States.[76] In 1978, in response to new surges of imports and large number of anti-dumping cases, the Carter administration instituted the trigger price mechanism (TPM), which established a "fair value" reference price for steel based on Japanese production costs. All European and Japanese imports entering the United States below that price were presumed to be dumped and were subject to a fast-track anti-dumping investigation. By 1982, due to a rise in the dollar and renewed import competition, the TPM was on the rocks. Numerous trade actions against foreign producers and proposed legislation to cut imports forced the Reagan administration to negotiate VERs with not only the EC, Japan, and Australia, but also Argentina, Brazil, Mexico, Korea, and South Africa.[77]

In the 1980s, VRAs among developed countries grew. The most important industry to be added to the list was automobiles, which account for 15 percent of world manufactured goods exports.[78] A surge in Japanese exports led to legal and political pressure to keep Japanese automobiles out of Western Europe and the United States. The first VRA on automobiles was in 1976 between the United Kingdom and Japan. The following year, France negotiated an agreement with Japan. In 1981, in response to proposed legislation to limit Japanese imports, the Reagan administration and Japan agreed to a VER. Agreements with West Germany, Canada, the Netherlands, Belgium, and Luxembourg followed.[79] By the latter half of the 1980s, VRAs had spread to high-technology sectors.

The GATT regime became increasingly irrelevant in the face of the new protectionism. GATT had been designed to manage import restrictions, especially quantitative restrictions and tariffs, not nontariff barriers and voluntary export controls. Furthermore, countries often preferred politically negotiated bilateral solutions to GATT's multilateral rules and procedures. Finally, with increasing government intervention in the economy, shifting comparative advantage and surplus capacity in many sectors, and frequent departures from GATT rules, many policymakers and analysts began to argue for a regime based on managed trade, not on the GATT principle of open trade. A managed-trade regime would recognize the reality, indeed the desirability, of government intervention in national economies to decide comparative advantage and intergovernmental agreements to shape international trade flows.[80] Proposals for such a regime ranged from an outright advocacy of tariff barriers as a tool of national policy[81] to proposals for global negotiations to allocate world production[82] to a set of regimes based on varying levels of government intervention, anywhere from managed trade in surplus sectors to free trade in the advanced sectors.[83]

New Issues

In addition to the new protectionism, trade management in the 1980s had to confront trade problems in sectors that had not yet been brought under GATT rules and process. One such challenge for GATT was both old and new protectionism in agriculture. As we have seen, agriculture was subject to a separate GATT regime and did not benefit from the liberalization process of the postwar era.

National agricultural policies of most developed countries remained interventionist and protectionist. Since the 1930s, the U.S. government has intervened in domestic agricultural markets to maintain agricultural prices and the income of U.S. farmers. It has supported domestic prices by purchasing surplus commodities, production controls, and deficiency payments, and further managed the domestic market through export subsidies and import quotas. Japan's government, led by a political party that has depended heavily on electoral support from farmers and also motivated by a deep concern for food security resulting from wartime shortages, has widespread import restrictions to maintain domestic agricultural prices above world price levels and to provide farmers with incomes comparable to nonfarmers.

The European Community maintains farm incomes through its Common Agricultural Policy (CAP). The CAP establishes common, artificially high internal prices, which it maintains through the purchase of surpluses and a flexible external tariff on agricultural imports, which ensures that imported products are more expensive than domestic products and that imported products can only assume the slack that the EC producers cannot fill. Because the CAP has no production controls, high prices for agricultural products have generated large food surpluses, which are exported with the help of export subsidies.

Although protection was extensive, the exemption of agriculture from the rules of international trade did not become a serious problem until the

1980s. Conflict was limited because agricultural trade grew steadily, driven by economic growth, rising incomes, and improved diets. However, in the 1970s, burgeoning populations, inappropriate agricultural policies in developing countries and the Eastern bloc, unfavorable weather conditions, and overall global inflation led to a dramatic rise in the demand for food imports and in the price of agricultural products. Rising prices and expected long-term food shortages led both importing and exporting countries to increase production.[84] Favorable market conditions combined with government encouragement resulted in soaring food production.[85]

As production increased, world demand for agricultural products declined. Per capita food consumption grew at a slower rate; supply far outdistanced demand; world commodity markets collapsed; and agricultural producers in many developed countries faced the worst economic crisis since the 1930s. Governments that protected their domestic markets and maintained high domestic prices by a combination of domestic price supports, purchase of excess supplies, and import protection found themselves with growing mountains of surplus commodities. To reduce these surpluses, governments increased export subsidies and dumped agricultural products on the already strained international market. Export subsidies further depressed prices and had a serious negative effect on exporting countries, such as Canada, Australia, and a number of developing countries that had relatively less intervention at home and that now faced greater competition abroad.[86] The budgetary costs of the agricultural trade war were also high. The costs of the CAP, estimated at $60 billion in 1986, created a budget crisis in the EC. United States expenditures for price and income support rose sixfold from 1982 to 1986 when they surpassed $26 billion.[87] Conflicts over agricultural policy increased. Even Japan, a large net importer of agricultural products, was criticized as never before for its protectionist policies.

GATT was unable to restrain the agricultural trade war, because domestic agricultural programs and export subsidies received special treatment under its rules. The combination of trade war and budgetary costs led countries for the first time in the postwar period to consider seriously multilateral negotiations that would change the GATT regime for agriculture and lead to reform of domestic agricultural policies.

In addition to agriculture, other sectors not adequately covered by the GATT raised important management issues in the 1980s. As the structure of international production and trade evolved, the developed countries tried to adapt GATT to cover industries of increasing importance in international trade.

One challenge was posed by the growing importance of services in the national economies and international trade of the developed countries. Services, or invisibles, differ from goods in that they cannot be stored and, therefore, require some form of direct relationship between the buyer and seller. The international trade of services thus requires some form of commercial presence in foreign markets. Consumer services are provided directly to retail customers by such businesses as restaurants, hotels, and travel agencies and tend to be produced, sold, and consumed within the same market. Producer services—banking, securities trading, insurance, law, advertising, accounting, data processing—are used in the intermediate production of manufactured goods and other services and are more frequently traded internationally.

By the late 1970s, services in the United States accounted for two-thirds of the GNP and for more than 50 percent of the GNPs in twelve other developed countries. Within the service sector, producer services experienced particularly rapid growth. As the economies of the developed countries matured, services came to play an ever greater role in the production and distribution of goods.[88] During the 1970s and 1980s, services also became a major factor in international trade among developed countries.[89] The liberalization of goods and capital markets created business opportunities for firms trading in services, while the revolution in telecommunications and computer technologies made possible the rapid transmission of data at long distance and enabled services to be offered across national boundaries. By 1986, for example, U.S. exports of services amounted to $148.4 billion, equivalent to 39.8 percent of U.S. exports.[90] Because of problems both in defining services and collecting data, worldwide exports of services are difficult to quantify with any degree of certainty. Many estimates put this figure around $600 billion.[91] Services account for between 20 percent[92] and 30 percent[93] of world trade.

Services trade has grown despite widespread nontariff barriers. Many service industries, such as telecommunications, banking and insurance, and law and accounting, are highly regulated and often involve state-owned industry. Frequently, such regulation discriminates against foreign services providers by denying access to national markets or by imposing constraints on activities of foreign firms operating in domestic markets. Such barriers include discriminatory treatment of foreign firms in licensing and taxation; policies through which a section of the market is reserved for domestic industry; investment performance requirements; discriminatory government procurement; and government monopolies.[94] Barriers to trade in services have not been subject to the process of liberalization, because services are not covered by the GATT regime. Although there have been efforts to establish liberalizing rules for such services as insurance in the OECD, by and large services have been outside the international trade regime.

As services grew in importance in the developed countries, service industries, particularly those in the United States and the United Kingdom, began to organize to press governments for adaptation of the trading regime to cover services. In the United States, for example, the service industry successfully pressed for a change in U.S. trade law to make trade rules and remedies applicable to services as well as goods.[95] As a result, services barriers began to receive greater attention in bilateral U.S. trade relations. The service sector in the developed countries also sought to make the inclusion of services in the GATT a goal of the Uruguay Round of multilateral trade negotiations.

Intellectual property is another new trade issue.[96] The comparative advantage of many of the most competitive industries of the developed market economies has become increasingly dependent on their advanced technology, which is expensive and time consuming to develop. Such technology can sometimes be easily and quickly copied and used to produce products at a much lower cost than that incurred by the developer, thus undermining the competitive ability of the firm that developed the technology. The cost of computer software, for example, derives largely from developmental costs. Yet such software can often be easily copied and sold at a price far below the cost to the developer. Similarly, the cost of developing pharmaceutical products is high, while drugs can be easily copied, produced, and sold below the cost to the developer.

For this reason and to encourage the development of technology, most developed countries protect the developer of technology through patent, trademark, and copyright laws. However, intellectual property protection differs among the developed countries and frequently is nonexistent in developing countries. As high-technology firms have increased in importance in trade and as their concern about intellectual property has increased, they have argued that such pirating undermines their ability to compete internationally and, thus, disrupts trade. Because efforts to standardize and expand protection for intellectual property through the World Intellectual Property Organization (WIPO) have not led to common rules and dispute settlement procedures, they and their governments argued that GATT should be broadened to cover intellectual property.

Finally, some developed countries also pressed for GATT rules to eliminate trade-restrictive and trade-distorting effects of government investment policies and practices.[97] Trade-related investment measures (TRIMs) include local content requirements, which require domestic sourcing; licensing requirements, which stipulate that an investor license production locally and often limit the amount of royalties; product mandating requirements, which oblige an investor to supply certain markets with specific products; trade-balancing requirements, which mandate arbitrary export or import levels; and export-performance requirements, which oblige an investor to export a percentage of its production.

The Tokyo and Uruguay Rounds

The Tokyo and Uruguay Rounds—the seventh and eighth rounds of multilateral trade negotiations—attempted to respond to the changed international trading system, to reform the postwar system of trade management by developing rules in new areas, and by addressing nontariff barriers to trade. The Tokyo Round, begun in 1973 and completed in 1979, started the process of trade reform.

The Tokyo Round of Multilateral Trade Negotiations (MTN) was the result of a U.S. initiative launched after the dollar crisis of 1971. Begun in 1973 in the midst of the oil crisis, deep recession, and rising protectionism, it took place in an economic and political environment less propitious than that of earlier trade negotiations. Nevertheless, its goals were more ambitious than those of earlier rounds. Previous negotiations sought to lower quotas and tariff barriers, primarily on nonagricultural products, and to implement GATT goals and rules. The Tokyo Round continued the pursuit of tariff reduction and also tried to regulate uncharted areas of international trade such as nontariff barriers; safeguards (i.e., the use of unilateral measures such as voluntary export restraint agreements); tropical products, which were of interest to developing countries; agriculture; and several sectors in which there were still unresolved problems.

In April 1979—six-and-a-half years after the first meeting in Tokyo—the multilateral trade negotiations were concluded.[98] Some of the goals of the participants had been achieved: tariffs on manufactured products were reduced; codes on certain nontariff barriers (NTBs) were drawn up; and changes were made in the application of GATT rules to the LDCs (see Chapter 7). Other efforts collapsed, including the liberalization of trade in agriculture and, most critically, the effort to regulate safeguards.

The most important outcome of the Tokyo Round was the progress made on regulating nontariff barriers to trade. The Tokyo Round agreement included several new codes that significantly modified the GATT system by extending trade management to nontariff barriers to trade. For example, the Code on Subsidies and Countervailing Duties was a step toward dealing with national industrial policies. The code recognized subsidies on manufactured products (but not raw materials) as nontariff barriers to trade. It allowed countries unilaterally to impose countervailing duties when a subsidy led to a material injury in the importing country and, with authorization from the other signatories, to impose such duties if subsidies led to injury to exports in third markets. A dumping code established comparable rules for anti-dumping measures. The Code on Government Procurement recognized government purchasing policies as NTBs and set rules for giving equal treatment to both national and foreign firms bidding for contracts from official entities. Although the number of government agencies covered by the code was small, it established an important precedent. Other codes covering product standards and customs valuation and licensing established rules for regulating these NTBs. The NTB codes not only established rules but also provided for surveillance and dispute settlement mechanisms. Each code set up a committee of signatories, some of which had powers only to consult (i.e., to oversee) and some of which were given dispute settlement authority.[99]

Despite the new departure signified by the NTB codes, there remained important limits to their effectiveness. Because the NTB codes apply only to the signatories, they diverged for the first time from the GATT principle of most-favored-nation status (MFN) or nondiscrimination. Whereas the developed countries signed and ratified the MTN codes, most of the developing countries were not convinced of their value and chose not to sign, thus leaving themselves open to discrimination that is legal under GATT's rules. The codes are also incomplete. The Code on Subsidies and Countervailing Duties, for example, does not specify which forms of government intervention beyond direct export subsidies are to be considered trade barriers.[100] Even more serious was the failure to reach agreement on a safeguards code to bring rapidly proliferating VRAs under multilateral management. The pivotal, unresolvable issue in the safeguards negotiations was selectivity, the desire of some GATT contracting parties, most importantly the EC, to target safeguards measures instead of applying them on a MFN basis.[101]

The efforts to extend trade management to include agriculture also met with little success. The negotiations were unable to reconcile two opposing views of the purpose and nature of international control in agriculture. The United States, because of its competitive advantage in agriculture, advocated liberalization of agricultural trade including the modification of the European Community's CAP. The EC, on the other hand, urged the use of commodity agreements to stabilize world prices and long-term supply and refused to negotiate on the fundamentals of CAP. Japan was also unwilling to liberalize trade in agriculture. The result was thus minimal: an agreement to consult about certain agricultural problems, including those connected with meat and dairy products. The sectoral negotiations yielded only one important result: an agreement on civil aircraft that liberalizes trade in this industry. Finally, only limited progress was made on improving GATT's dispute settlement mechanism. Thus, although the MTN was an important step, it was only a limited one, [102] and it was to prove inadequate to stem the burgeoning protectionist pressures of the 1980s.

Following the Tokyo Round, pressures on the GATT system increased. Departures from GATT rules, such as voluntary export restraints, grew; the agriculture trade war erupted; and trade conflicts became more frequent and more heated. Nevertheless, the postwar political consensus supporting open trade remained alive, if not well. The leaders of the developed countries used summit and OECD meetings to reiterate their commitment to open trade principles and to resolving specific conflicts, even as they negotiated managed-trade agreements. New forms of international dialogue were tried. Bilateral meetings, most notably between the United States and Japan, were used to try to resolve specific trade conflicts, and multilateral meetings, such as regular quadrilateral meetings of the United States, Japan, the European Community, and Canada, were begun to try to resolve systemic issues.

The precarious nature of the multilateral trading regime was revealed in 1982, when GATT held its first ministerial meeting since the 1973 meeting that launched the Tokyo Round. The agenda of the meeting was ambitious: a review of the Tokyo codes on NTBs; action on GATT dispute-settlement procedures; continuation of the negotiations on a safeguards code; efforts to bring agriculture under the GATT regime; and consideration of new codes on trade in high technology and services. The meeting ended in failure. The ministers made virtually no progress on any issues under discussion and could pledge only to "make determined efforts" to ensure that their countries' trade policies were consistent with GATT's rules.[103] Perhaps the most positive result of the ministerial meeting was the widening recognition that the international trading system faced collapse.

The following year, the Reagan administration, aided by the economic recovery in the United States, supported by Japan and the GATT secretariat, began a campaign to launch a new round of multilateral trade negotiations. Initially the EC, confronted with severe unemployment and recession, argued that the time was not right. However, in 1985, the world's trade officials agreed to launch a new round of multilateral trade negotiations and established a committee to develop an agenda. In September 1986, a special session of the GATT contracting parties meeting in Punta del Este, Uruguay, officially launched the negotiations, which came to be known as the Uruguay Round and set a target date of 1990 for their completion. The Uruguay Round negotiations began in 1987.

The ministerial declaration issued at Punta del Este instituted a standstill on new trade-restrictive or distorting measures and called for the elimination by the end of the Uruguay Round of measures inconsistent with the provisions of the GATT. The trade ministers also established fifteen negotiating groups that fell into four broad categories.

Some groups focused on issues that had been taken up in earlier negotiating rounds, including those (such as tariffs) that had long been on the GATT agenda as well as others (such as subsidies and safeguards) that had not been resolved satisfactorily in the Tokyo Round. Most important, and perhaps most difficult, among these issues was safeguards. As we have seen, GATT rules on safeguard actions have been ineffective and relatively easy to circumvent through new protectionist measures, such as voluntary restraint agreements (VRAs). The success or failure of the Uruguay Round on the safeguards issue will, in large part, determine whether the GATT will retain influence over the international trading system as protectionist measures continue to multiply outside of GATT disciplines. Although the 1986 ministerial declaration called for "a comprehensive agreement on safeguards," the political difficulty of reaching such an agreement remained significant. As in the Tokyo Round, the central conflict centered on selectivity. The EC insisted on the need for selectivity. The United States advocated safeguard actions taken either on a most-favored-nation or "consensual selectivity" basis. The developing countries—for whom the safeguards negotiations were a top priority in the Uruguay Round—strongly advocated the most-favored-nation position.

A second set of negotiations focused on concerns of developing countries, such as tropical products, natural resource-based products, textiles, and clothing. Due to the increasingly active role of the developing countries in the GATT, successful completion of these negotiations was essential to their continued involvement in the GATT system (see Chapter 7).

A third set of negotiating groups had mandates to reform existing GATT rules or mechanisms. Dissatisfaction with existing GATT dispute settlement mechanisms had been mounting for years. Countries were able to delay or block resolution of a dispute; there was no effective mechanism for enforcing decisions or overseeing their implementation; and protection of third countries affected by the dispute was inadequate. The ministerial declaration at Punta del Este instructed the negotiating group on dispute settlement to "improve and strengthen the rules and procedures of the dispute settlement process." Negotiations moved rapidly in this negotiating group due to broad agreement on the need to expedite dispute settlement procedures and to the absence of any significant North-South division. By the end of 1988, negotiators had agreed on several measures to streamline procedures and speed up decisions in the dispute settlement process. These reforms were implemented on a provisional basis in 1989.

The negotiations on the functioning of the GATT system (FOGS) were intended to strengthen the role of GATT as an institution. The negotiating group focused on ways to enhance GATT surveillance of trade policies and practices; to improve the overall effectiveness and decision making of the GATT by involving ministers; and to strengthen GATT's relationship with the IMF and World Bank. Because there was a significant degree of consensus on what needed to be done, negotiations on FOGS proceeded smoothly. By the end of 1988 agreement was reached on the establishment of a new trade policy review mechanism to examine and publicize national trade policies on a regular basis. Negotiators agreed to begin implementing this mechanism in 1989 rather than wait until the conclusion of the Uruguay Round.

Finally, some groups sought to broaden the scope of the GATT to cover nontraditional areas. One of the most significant and controversial decisions made at Punta del Este was the agreement to include the so-called new issues—services, intellectual property rights, and investment—in the round. The opposition to their inclusion was led by a small group of developing countries, which feared that GATT rules developed for the new issues could be used by the industrialized countries to overwhelm their fledgling industries and to undermine domestic policies that the developing countries considered critical to their national economic development. They argued that the Uruguay Round should concentrate instead on unfinished business from the Tokyo Round and on reform in areas where the GATT had clearly failed to impose adequate international discipline, such as safe-guards, textiles, and agriculture. They also insisted that GATT was not the appropriate forum for the new issues that, they argued, came under the purview of other organizations, such as WIPO for intellectual property or the United Nations for investment.

The industrialized nations stressed the need to modernize the GATT by broading its scope to deal with new areas of trade. As in previous GATT rounds, the United States took the initiative in pushing aggressively for the inclusion of services, intellectual property rights, and investment in the Uruguay Round. The EC and Japan supported the U.S. position, but they were not entirely convinced of the wisdom of increasing the burden of the GATT at a time when so many longstanding problems had yet to be resolved. They also shared some of the concerns of the developing countries about the extent to which GATT rules in the new areas might impinge on their sovereignty in domestic regulation and government policy. In the case of investment in particular, they questioned the appropriateness of using GATT as the forum for management. Finally, while there was a consensus among the developed countries about the principles that would cover some of the new issues (especially services and intellectual property), it proved difficult to come to agreement on specific details of the application of those principles.

The issue that is most likely to determine the ultimate success or failure of the Uruguay Round, however, is not a new issue but an old one: agriculture. As we have seen, agriculture has been treated as an exception in the GATT. Agriculture remains a highly controversial issue, largely because it is so deeply imbedded in the domestic politics of most nations. Although the United States, the EC, and the key agricultural producers have agreed on the need for reform, there is no agreement on how to go about it. The United States ambitiously proposed phasing out all direct farm subsidies and farm trade protection within a decade. The Cairns group—a coalition of fourteen smaller producing nations (including Australia, Argentina, Hungary, and Canada among others)—advocated a similar approach. The EC accepted the need to reduce subsidies, but viewed the U.S. proposal as highly unre-alistic, advocating instead an approach that would allow it to maintain its Common Agricultural Policy. Japan was also unenthusiastic about the U.S. proposal, but generally tried to keep a low profile.

Conclusion

The Uruguay Round will thus be a major test for the multilateral trade regime. The challenge is great. New rules and techniques must be developed to constrain the new protectionism. GATT must be expanded to cover new sectors. In the process, GATT must be expanded from a fragile dispute settlement regime and periodic international negotiation to an effective international organization capable of resolving conflicts, containing protectionist pressures, and promoting liberalization in both old and new sectors. If the Round can make headway in achieving these goals, it will make possible the continued vitality of a multilateral, liberal system.

If it fails, the stage is set for increased reliance on managed trade and a breakdown into regional blocs. As we have discussed, the European Community is forming its own separate trading system that could turn inward. The United States and Canada have signed a free-trade agreement that is intended to complement the GATT but which, without a vital multilateral system, could become the basis for a separate North American market. If such regional systems begin to emerge, there will be severe pressure on Japan to secure market access. Some have proposed a free-trade agreement between the United States and Japan. Others conjecture that, instead, Japan may turn to Southeast Asia as its central trading system. Such managed trade and regionalism bear dangerous resemblances to the blocs of the 1930s.

The continued vitality of a multilateral liberal system will also depend on the development of plurilateral management. Economic power is now more evenly dispersed. The United States as the largest (although no longer the dominant member) will have to continue to provide leadership for the system. This will be possible only if the United States can redress its trade imbalance and revitalize its competitiveness. At the same time, Europe and Japan must define new, more active roles in trade management. Europe will have to find the appropriate balance between looking inward towards the creation of an internal market and its need to look outward to the multilateral trading system. Because of its size and its role in world trade, reestablishing a reasonable balance between Japan and its trading partners, as well as integrating Japan into the management of the international trading system, will be a central challenge for the remainder of the century. Finally, as development outside the developed market economies proceeds, all will need to address the new role, first, for the newly industrialized countries and, then, for other developing countries.[104]

NOTES

1. E. E. Schattschneider, *Politics, Pressures and the Tariff* (Englewood Cliffs, N.J.: Prentice-Hall, 1935). See also: Robert A. Pastor, *Congress and the Politics of U.S. Foreign Economic Policy, 1929–1976* (Berkeley and Los Angeles: University of California Press, 1976) and Stefanie Ann Lenway, *The Politics of U.S. International Trade: Protection, Expansion and Escape* (Marshfield, Mass.: Pitman Publishing, 1985).

2. The analysis in this chapter concentrates on trade relations among developed market economies. For issues involving the underdeveloped countries, see Chapter 6 of this text; for East-West trade issues, see Chapter 10.

98   The Western System

3. See, for example, Richard N. Gardner, *Sterling-Dollar Diplomacy in Current Perspective: The Origins and Prospects of Our International Economic Order* (New York: Columbia University Press, 1980), p. 9.

4. Ibid., p. 102.

5. Ibid.; Clair Wilcox, *A Charter for World Trade* (New York: Macmillan, 1949). The trade charter was not exclusively an American idea; British planners were also closely involved in the process. See E. F. Penrose, *Economic Planning for the Peace* (Princeton, N.J.: Princeton University Press, 1953).

6. See Gardner, *Sterling-Dollar Diplomacy*, Chaps. 8 and 17; Wilcox, *A Charter for World Trade*; Committee for Economic Development, Research and Policy Committee, *The United States and The European Community: Policies for a Changing World Economy* (New York: CED, November 1971).

7. Gardner, *Sterling-Dollar Diplomacy*, Chap. 17; William Diebold, Jr., *The End of the I.T.O.* (Princeton, N.J.: International Finance Section, Department of Economics and Social Institutions, Princeton University, 1952).

8. Kenneth W. Dam, *The GATT: Law and International Economic Organization* (Chicago: University of Chicago Press, 1970), p. 392.

9. Ibid., pp. 396–397.

10. Dale E. Hathaway, *Agriculture and the GATT: Rewriting the Rules* (Washington, D.C.: Institute for International Economics, September 1987), pp. 103–113.

11. For an analysis of the process of making trade policy in the period, see Raymond A. Bauer, Ithiel de Sola Pool, and Lewis Anthony Dexter, *American Business & Public Policy: The Politics of Foreign Trade* (Chicago: Aldine, Atherton, 1972).

12. I. M. Destler, *American Trade Politics: System Under Stress* (Washington, D.C.: Institute for International Economics and New York: Twentieth Century Fund, 1986), pp. 9–36.

13. William Diebold, Jr., *Trade and Payments in Western Europe: A Study in Economic Cooperation 1947–1951* (New York: Harper & Row, 1952); Robert Triffin, *Europe and the Money Muddle: From Bilateralism to Near Convertibility, 1947–1956* (New Haven, Conn.: Yale University Press, 1957).

14. Robert S. Ozaki, *The Control of Imports and Foreign Capital in Japan* (New York: Praeger, 1972), pp. 5–9; Warren S. Hunsberger, *Japan and the United States in World Trade* (New York: Harper & Row, 1964).

15. See, for example, Gardner Patterson, *Discrimination in International Trade: The Policy Issues, 1945–1965* (Princeton, N.J.: Princeton University Press, 1966); Karin Koch, *International Trade Policy and the GATT, 1947–1967*, Stockholm Economic Studies XI (Stockholm: Almquist & Wiksell, 1969).

16. John W. Evans, *The Kennedy Round in American Trade Policy: The Twilight of the GATT?* (Cambridge, Mass: Harvard University Press, 1971), p. 282. For other studies of the Kennedy Round, see Ernest H. Preeg, *Traders and Diplomats: An Analysis of the Kennedy Round Negotiations Under the General Agreement on Tariffs and Trade* (Washington, D.C.: Brookings Institution, 1970); Thomas B. Curtis and John R. Vastine, *The Kennedy Round and the Future of American Trade* (New York: Praeger, 1971).

17. Robert E. Baldwin, *Non-Tariff Distortions of International Trade* (Washington, D.C.: Brookings Institution, 1970), p. 1.

18. Richard N. Cooper, *The Economics of Interdependence: Economic Policy in the Atlantic Community* (New York: McGraw-Hill, 1968), pp. 59–80.

19. General Agreement on Tariffs and Trade, *International Trade 1986–87* (Geneva: GATT, 1987) p. 158.

20. International Monetary Fund, *International Financial Statistics* (Washington, D.C.: IMF, January 1968 and April 1988), various pages; International Monetary Fund, *Direction of Trade Statistics Yearbook 1987* (Washington, D.C.: IMF, 1987), various pages; Organization for Economic Cooperation and Development, *Main Economic Indicators* (Paris: OECD, April 1988), p. 174.

21. Allen Sinai, "The 'Global' Factor and the U.S. Economy," *Economic Studies Series*, No. 27, Shearson Lehman Brothers, October 6, 1987, p.1.

22. *New York Times*, May 5, 1988, p. 1.

23. Council on Competitiveness, *Competitiveness Index: Trends, Background Data and Methodology* (Washington, D.C.: Council on Competitiveness, 1988), Appendix II.

24. Ibid.

25. See Richard Blackhurst, Nicolas Marian, and Jan Tumlir, Adjustment, *Trade and Growth in Developed and Developing Countries*, GATT Studies in International Trade, No. 6 (Geneva: General Agreement on Tariffs and Trade, 1978); William Diebold, Jr., "Adapting Economics to Structural Change: The International Aspect," *International Affairs* (London) 54:4 (October 1978), 573–588.

26. Paul R. Krugman and George N. Hatsopoulos, "The Problem of U.S. Competitiveness in Manufacturing," *New England Economic Review* (January/February 1987), 22; Organization for Economic Development and Cooperation, *OECD Economic Outlook 42* (Paris: OECD, December 1987), pp. 41, 178.

27. See Susan Strange, "The Management of Surplus Capacity: or How Does Theory Stand Up to Protectionism 1970s Style?" *International Organization*, 33:3 (Summer 1979), 573–588.

28. *Economic Report of the President* (Washington D.C.: GPO, 1988), pp. 373, 374; General Agreement on Tariffs and Trade, *International Trade, 1986–87* (Geneva: GATT, 1987), p. 10. Unemployment figures are for the G-7 countries.

29. Organisation for Economic Cooperation and Development, *OECD Economic Outlook 42* (Paris: OECD, December 1987), pp. 174, 184.

30. Ibid., p. 190.

31. General Agreement on Tariffs and Trade, *International Trade, 1986–87*, p. 10.

32. *OECD Economic Outlook 42*, p. 184.

33. Ibid., p. 174.

34. Ibid., p. 190.

35. U.S. Department of Labor, Bureau of Labor Statistics.

36. International Monetary Fund, *Annual Report 1987* (Washington, D.C.: IMF, 1987), p. 16.

37. *OECD Economic Outlook 42*, pp. 174, 184.

38. General Agreement on Tariffs and Trade, Press Release, GATT/1432, 29 February 1988, p. 4.

39. *OECD Economic Outlook 42*, pp. 5, 28.

40. International Monetary Fund, *Direction of Trade Annual, 1960–64*; IMF, *Direction of Trade Annual, 1970–74*; IMF, *Direction of Trade Statistics Yearbook 1987*; IMF, *International Financial Statistics Yearbook 1985*.

41. Ibid.

42. Ibid.

43. See Jacob Viner, *The Customs Union Issue*, Studies in the Administration of International Law and Organization, vol. 10 (New York: Carnegie Endowment for International Peace, 1950).

44. See Paolo Cecchini, ed. *The European Challenge, 1992: The Benefits of a Single Market* (Hants, England: Wildwood House, 1988); Lord Cockfield, *White Paper on Completing the Internal Market* (Brussels: Commission of the European Community, 1985); Jacques Pelkmans and Alan Winters, *Europe's Domestic Market*, Chatham House paper No. 43, Royal Institute of International Affairs (London: Routledge, 1988); Michael Calingaert, *The 1992 Challenge from Europe: Development of the European Community's Internal Market* (Washington, D.C.: National Planning Association, 1988).

45. Keizai Koho Center, *Japan 1987: An International Comparison* (Tokyo: Japan Institute for Social and Economic Affairs, 30 April, 1987), p. 9.

46. *International Financial Statistics Yearbook 1987* (Washington, D.C.: IMF, 1987); International Monetary Fund, *Direction of Trade Statistics Yearbook 1987* (Washington, D.C.: IMF, 1987).

47. See Edward Denison and William Chung, "Economic Growth and Its Sources," in Hugh Patrick and Henry Rosovsky, eds., *Asia's New Giant* (Washington, D.C.: Brookings Institution, 1976), pp. 63–151.

48. Philip H. Trezise and Yukio Suzuki, "Politics, Government, and Economic Growth in Japan," in Patrick and Rosovsky, op. cit., pp. 753–811; Chalmers Johnson, *MITI and the Japanese Miracle* (Stanford, Calif.: Stanford University Press, 1982).

49. Lawrence B. Krause and Sueo Sekiguchi, "Japan and the World Economy," in Patrick and Rosovsky, op. cit., pp. 397–410.

50. Edward J. Lincoln, *Japan Facing Economic Maturity* (Washington, D.C.: Brookings Institution, 1988), pp. 14–68.

51. Ezra Vogel, *Comeback Case by Case: Building the Resurgence of American Business* (New York: Simon and Schuster, 1985).

52. C. Fred Bergsten and William R. Cline, *The United States-Japan Economic Problem* (Washington, D.C. Institute for International Economics, 1987), pp. 53–119.

53. *International Financial Statistics Yearbook 1988*, p. 445.

54. International Monetary Fund, *Direction of Trade Statistics Yearbook 1987* (Washington, D.C.: IMF, 1987), pp. 243, 245, and *Direction of Trade Statistics Yearbook 1988* (Washington, D.C.: IMF, 1988), p. 243.

55. Bureau of Economic Analysis, *Survey of Current Business* (Washington, D.C.: Department of Commerce, July 1984), p. 60; *Survey of Current Business*, May 1988, p. 11.

56. See Clyde V. Prestowitz, Jr., *Trading Places: How America Allowed Japan to Take the Lead* (New York: Basic Books, 1988).

57. C. Fred Bergsten and William R. Cline, *The United States-Japan Economic Problem* (Washington, D.C.: Institute for International Economics, 1987), pp. 53–119.

58. See Makoto Kuroda, "Japan's Trade Surplus is Declining Fast," *Amex Bank Review*, Vol. 15, No. 3, March 24, 1988, pp. 2–3.

59. *International Financial Statistics Yearbook 1985* (Washington, D.C.: IMF, 1985).

60. *Economic Report of the President* (Washington, D.C.: GPO, 1988), pp. 364–365.

61. Ibid., p. 367.

62. *International Financial Statistics Yearbook 1985, International Financial Statistics*, April 1988 (Washington, D.C.: IMF 1985 and 1988).

63. *OECD Economic Outlook 42*, p. 41.

64. Council on Competitiveness, *Competitiveness Index*, Special Supplement, May 1988, p. 7.

65. Council on Competitiveness, *America's Competitive Crisis: Confronting a New Reality* (Washington, D.C.: Council on Competitiveness, 1987), p. 17.

66. *OECD Economic Outlook 42*, p. 70.

67. See I.M. Destler, *American Trade Politics: System Under Stress* (Washington, D.C.: Institute for International Economics, 1986).

68. See U.S. Congress, House Committee on Ways and Means, Foreign Trade and Tariff Proposals, Hearings, 90th Cong., 2d Sess. (1968).

69. On the politics of supporters of free trade see: I. M. Destler and John S. Odell, *Anti-Protection: Changing Forces in the United States Trade Politics* (Washington, D.C.: Institute for International Economics, September 1987) and Helen V. Milner, *Resisting Protectionism: Global Industries and the Politics of International Trade* (Princeton, N.J.: Princeton University Press, 1988).

70. Helen V. Milner and David B. Yoffie, "Between Free Trade and Protectionism: Strategic Trade Policy and a Theory of Corporate Trade Demands," *International Organization*, 43, 2 (Spring 1989), pages 239–272.

71. See Clyde V. Prestowitz, *Trading Places*, op. cit.

72. P.L. 100–418, Omnibus Trade and Competitiveness Act of 1988.

73. See William Diebold, Jr., ed., *Bilateralism, Multilateralism and Canada in U.S. Trade Policy* (Cambridge, Mass.: Ballinger, 1988); Jeffrey J. Schott and Murray G. Smith, eds., *The Canada-United States Free Trade Agreement: The Global Impact* (Washington, D.C.: Institute for International Economics, 1988); Paul Wonnacott, *The United States and Canada: The Quest for Free Trade* (Washington, D.C.: Institute for International Economics, 1987).

74. Robert E. Baldwin, *Non-Tariff Distortions of International Trade* (Washington, D.C.: Brookings Institution, 1970); William Diebold, Jr., *The United States and the Industrial World: American Foreign Policy in the 1970s* (New York: Praeger, 1972), pp. 123–140; J. M. Finger, H. K. Hall and D. R. Nelson, "The Political Economy of Administered Protection," *The American Economic Review*, vol. 72, 1982, pp. 452–466; Stanley D. Metzger, *Lowering Non-Tariff Barriers: U.S. Law, Practice and Negotiating Objectives* (Washington, D.C.: Brookings Institution, 1974).

75. See 97th Cong., 2d sess., *The Mercantilist Challenge to the Liberal International*

Trade Order, a study prepared for the use of the Joint Economic Committee, Congress of the United States, December 29, 1982 (Washington, D.C.: U.S. Government Printing Office, 1982), pp. 8–31.

76. See Brian Hindley and Eri Nicolaides, *Taking the New Protectionism Seriously, Trade Policy Research Centre*, Thames Essay No. 34 (London: Trade Policy Research Centre, 1983).

77. Ingo Walter, "Structural Adjustment and Trade Policy in the International Steel Industry," in Cline, *Trade Policy in the 1980s*, pp. 497–500; Gary C. Hufbauer & Diane T. Berliner, Kimberly A. Elliot, *Trade Protection in the United States: 31 Case Studies* (Washington, D.C.: Institute for International Economics, 1986), pp. 156, 176; Ingo Walter, "Structural Adjustment and Trade Policy in the International Steel Industry," in Cline, *Trade Policy in the 1980s*, p. 489.

78. Hufbauer, pp. 170–173.

79. General Agreements on Tariffs and Trade, *International Trade 1986–87*, p. 29.

80. See Robert B. Cohen, "The Prospects for Trade and Protectionism in the Auto Industry," in Cline, *Trade Policy in the 1980s* (Washington, DC: Institute for International Economics, 1983), p. 527–563.; Gary C. Hufbauer et al. *Trade Protection in the United States: 31 Case Studies* (Washington D.C.: Institute for International Economics, 1986), pp. 249–262.

81. See Paul R. Krugman, ed., *Strategic Trade Policy and the New International Economics* (Cambridge, Mass.: MIT Press, 1988).

82. This is the view of the Cambridge Economic Policy Group. See their journal, the *Cambridge Economic Policy Review*.

83. Albert Bressand, "Mastering the World Economy," *Foreign Affairs*, 16:4 (Spring 1983), 747–772.

84. Robert B. Reich, "Beyond Free Trade," *Foreign Affairs*, 16:4 (Spring 1983), 773–804. See also Stephen S. Cohen and John Zysman, *Manufacturing Matters: The Myth of the Post-Industrial Economy* (New York: Basic Books for the Council on Foreign Relations, 1987).

85. See Raymond Hopkins and Donald F. Puchala, eds., "The Global Political Economy of Food," *International Organization*, 32 (Summer 1978), entire issue.

86. Dale E. Hathaway, *Agriculture and the GATT: Rewriting the Rules* (Washington: Institute for International Economics, September 1987), p. 43.

87. See Robert L. Paarlberg, *Fixing Farm Trade: Policy Options for the United States* (Cambridge: Ballinger Publishing for the Council on Foreign Relations, 1988), pp. 13–40.

88. *Economic Report of the President* (Washington, D.C.: Government Printing Office), 1988, p. 144.

89. See Ronald Kent Shelp, *Beyond Industrialization* (New York: Praeger, 1981); Thomas M. Stanback, Jr., Peter J. Bearse, Thierry J. Noyelle, and Robert A. Karasek, *Services: The New Economy* (Totowa, New Jersey: Allanheld, Osmun, 1981).

90. David C. Mowery, *International Collaborative Ventures in U.S. Manufacturing* (Cambridge, Mass.: Ballinger, 1988); Geza Feketekuty, *International Trade in Services: An Overview and Blueprint for Negotiations* (Cambridge, Mass.: Ballinger, 1988); Steven S. Wildman and Stephen E. Siwek, *International Trade in Films and Television Programs* (Cambridge, Mass.: Ballinger, 1988); Lawrence J. White, *International Trade in Ocean Shipping Services* (Cambridge, Mass.: Ballinger, 1988); Ingo Walter, *Global Competition in Financial Services: Market Structure, Protection, and Trade Liberalization* (Cambridge, Mass.: Ballinger, 1988); Thierry J. Noyelle and Anna B. Dutka, *International Trade in Business Services: Accounting, Advertising, Law, and Management Consulting* (Cambridge, Mass.: Ballinger, 1988); Jonathan David Aronson and Peter F. Cowhey, *When Countries Talk: International Trade in Telecommunications Services* (Cambridge, Mass.: Ballinger, 1988); Daniel M. Kasper, *Deregulation and Globalization: Liberalizing International Trade in Air Services* (Cambridge, Mass.: Ballinger, 1988).

91. *International Financial Statistics Yearbook 1987*, p.701.

92. Coalition of Service Industries; British Invisibles Export Council, *Annual Report and Accounts 1986–87* (London: British Invisible Exports Council, 1987), p.34.

93. U.S. Department of Commerce, *U.S. Trade: Performance in 1985 and Outlook* (Washington, D.C.: GPO, 1986), p.2.

94. Coalition of Service Industries. Derived from IMF figures by Boston Economic Advisors, Inc.

95. See Spero, "Removing Trade Barriers"; William Diebold, Jr., and Helena Stalson,

"Negotiating Issues in International Services Transactions," in Cline, *Trade Policy in the 1980s*, pp. 581-609.

96. U.S. Congress, *Trade and Tariff Act of 1984*, Public Law 98-573, October 30, 1984.

97. See Robert P. Benko, *Protecting Intellectual Property Rights: Issues and Controversies* (Washington, D.C.: American Enterprise Institute for Public Policy Research, 1987); R. Michael Gadbaw and Timothy J. Richards, eds., *Intellectual Property Rights: Global Consensus, Global Conflict?* (Boulder, Colorado: Westview Press, 1988); Helena Stalson, *Intellectual Property Rights and U.S. Competitiveness in Trade* (Washington, D.C.: National Planning Association, 1987).

98. Business Roundtable, "Negotiations on International Investment in the Uruguay Round: A Preliminary Statement," March 1988; U.S. Trade Representative, Submission of the United States to the Negotiating Group on Trade-Related Investment Measures, June 1987.

99. See U.S. Senate, Committee on Finance, *Trade Agreements Act of 1979, Report on H.R. 4537 to Approve and Implement the Trade Agreements Negotiated Under the Trade Act of 1974, and for Other Purposes*, 96th Cong., 1st sess. (Washington, D.C.: U.S. Government Printing Office, 1979); Stephen D. Krasner, "The Tokyo Round: Particularistic Interests and Prospects for Stability in the Global Trading System," *International Studies Quarterly*, 23:4 (December 1979), 491-531; Thomas R. Graham, "Revolution in Trade Politics," *Foreign Policy*, 36 (Fall 1979), 49-63.

100. See U.S. Senate, Committee on Finance, MTN Studies No. 4, *MTN and the Legal Institutions of International Trade*, report prepared at the request of the Subcommittee on International Trade, 96th Cong., 1st sess. (Washington, D.C.: U.S. Government Printing Office, 1979).

101. See Gary C. Hufbauer, "Subsidy Issues After the Tokyo Round," in Cline, *Trade Policy in the 1980s*, pp. 327-361.

102. See Alan W. Wolff, "The Need for New GATT Rules to Govern Safeguard Actions," in Cline, *Trade Policy in the 1980s*, pp. 363-391.

103. See John H. Jackson, "GATT Machinery and the Tokyo Round Agreements," in Cline, *Trade Policy in the 1980s*, pp. 159-187.

104. GATT Press Release, No. 1328, November 29, 1982. See also Jeffrey J. Schott, "The GATT Ministerial: A Postmortem," *Challenge* (May-June 1983), 40-45.

4

The Multinational Corporation and the Issue of Management

Foreign direct investment is not a new phenomenon.[1] From the time that people began to trade with one another, they set up foreign commercial operations. Foreign commercial investment reached a high point in the development of the large mercantile trading companies, such as the British East India Company and the Hudson's Bay Company. Beginning in the eighteenth century, but more importantly in the nineteenth century, there was direct foreign investment in agriculture, mining, and manufacturing as distinct from the earlier forms of commercial investment. By the early 1890s, several U.S. manufacturers—Singer (the first large multinational corporation), American Bell, and Standard Oil, to mention but a few—had large manufacturing investments abroad. By World War I, according to one study, U.S. direct foreign investment amounted to an estimated $2.65 billion, 7 percent of the United States' GNP (gross national product) of that time.[2]

In another sense, international investment is quite a new phenomenon. The nature and extent of international business have changed dramatically since World War II, creating a new and powerful form of international investment, the multinational corporation. Whereas multinational corporations were the focus of much attention in the 1960s and 1970s because of the controversy they provoked as people first became aware of their existence, they remain equally important today because their existence has become a fact of life. They are now permanent—and influential—players in the international arena.

The Multinational Corporation

Multinational corporations range from companies that extract raw materials to those that manufacture consumer goods such as soft drinks or high-technology products like computers to those that offer services such as insurance or banking. These multinational corporations differ not only in what they do but also in how they do it, their level of technology, their organizational structure, and the structure of the market for their products. Nevertheless, certain characteristics common to many multinational corporations can be used to describe this phenomenon and to identify the problems it creates.

A multinational corporation is a firm with foreign subsidiaries that extend the firm's production and marketing beyond the boundaries of any one country.[3] Multinational corporations are not simply large corporations that market their products abroad; they are firms that have sent abroad a package of capital, technology, managerial talent, and marketing skills to carry out production in foreign countries. In many cases, the multinational's production is truly worldwide, with different stages of production carried out in different countries. Marketing also is often international. Goods produced in one or more countries are sold throughout the world. Finally, multinational corporations tend to have foreign subsidiaries in many countries. One analyst defined a multinational corporation as one with investments in six or more foreign countries and found that such firms accounted for 80 percent of all foreign subsidiaries of major U.S. corporations.[4]

Multinational corporations are among the world's largest firms. In 1985, each of the top two hundred multinationals had sales in excess of $4 billion. The top five multinationals had sales well over $50 billion each, and the largest—General Motors—had sales in 1985 of over $96 billion. The sales of each of the top ten multinational corporations in 1985 were over $29 billion, more than the GDP (gross domestic product) of eighty countries (not counting the Soviet Union and Eastern Europe). Indeed, General Motors' 1985 sales were larger than the GDP of one hundred and four countries (not counting the Soviet Union and Eastern Europe) and well ahead of Austria, Belgium, Denmark, Norway, and Switzerland.[5] These corporate giants also tend to be oligopolistic. Some are able to dominate markets because of their sheer size, others (even some small- and medium-size firms) because of their access to financial resources, control of technology, or possession of a special, differentiated product.[6]

The organization of multinational organizations takes various forms. Generally, foreign subsidiaries are directly owned by the parent through either sole ownership or joint venture with public or private groups. The internalization theory of multinational activity explains why sole ownership has been the preferred scheme from the enterprise's point of view.[7] Companies that operate successfully abroad must have some peculiar advantage, which is often some sort of specialized knowledge, such as managerial or marketing techniques or new production processes. Since knowledge is a public good (i.e., it is impossible to exclude anyone, even competing firms, from profiting from it once it becomes generally known), companies cannot afford to use open market practices such as exporting or licensing if they wish to profit from developing that knowledge. As a result, the company "internalizes" the market by setting up a wholly owned foreign subsidiary that can ensure maximum control over the use of that knowledge.

Joint ventures and licensing are other structuring options available to multinationals. In certain countries they are the only avenues available, due to restrictive investment policies of host countries. Another option that has become more common recently in certain industries is the strategic alliance. Strategic alliances are partnerships between separate, sometimes competing, companies from different countries. The companies are drawn together because each needs the complementary technology, skills, or facilities of the other; nonetheless, the scope of the relationship is strictly defined, leaving the companies free to compete outside the relationship. The purposes of the alliances range from research and development to designing industry standards to sharing distribution or marketing networks in a way that both benefits the companies and reduces their risks. The catalyst for these arrangements has been the rapidity of technological change and the skyrocketing costs of development, especially in high-technology sectors.[8]

Decision making for multinationals tends to be centralized, though management structures vary from company to company, and policy control emanates from the parent company when the international aspects of a firm's business become important. The classic evolution of international investment has been from semi-independent foreign operations to the integration of international operations within a separate international division to the integration of international operations within the whole company. As a result, although multinational corporations have decentralized many decisions to the local level, key decisions involving foreign activities, such as the location of production facilities, distribution of markets, location of research and development facilities, long-range planning, and especially capital investment, tend to be made by the parent company.[9]

Yet another organizational characteristic is the integration of production and marketing on an international scale. Production may take place in different stages in several different countries, and the final product may be marketed in still other countries. The European Ford Escort, for example, includes parts from fifteen different countries, which are assembled in the United Kingdom and Germany and then sold throughout Europe. Integrated production and the need for central decision making and central planning are made possible by central control and central management.

Multinationals often are mobile and flexible. Some are tied to specific countries by the need for raw materials or by a large capital commitment. Others, however, are able to shift their operations across national boundaries for the purposes of company profits, markets, security, or survival. As part of their effort to transcend national borders, many multinationals try to create global staffs that are drawn from many countries to serve in yet others. Mobility and flexibility are related to the company's central decision-making structure and resources.

The centralized, integrated organizational structure reinforces the multinational corporations' tendency to make decisions with concern for the firm and the international environment and not with concern for the particular states in which it is operating. Their size, centralized organization, and integrated production and marketing are powerful resources that the firms can use to follow their international goals or policies.

The special characteristics of multinational corporations can cause conflict with states, and their international scope has been known to create political problems. Most importantly, multinational corporations may seek goals or follow policies that are valid from the firm's international perspective but that are not necessarily desirable from the national perspective. The policies and goals of multinational corporations may conflict with the policies and goals of the states in which they operate. There is also a related jurisdictional problem. Legally, multinational corporations have many different national identities and are therefore subject to many different jurisdictions. Because no one entity or country is responsible for overall jurisdiction and because jurisdiction is often unclear, it is sometimes difficult for states to exert legal control over resident multinational corporations.

Force for Change: The Spread of the Multinationals

The spread of multinational corporations, and especially of U.S. multinationals, has been characteristic of the contemporary world economy. From 1971 to 1986, the stock of U.S.-owned direct investment abroad measured by book value rose from $86.2 billion to $259.9 billion.[10] Direct investment by other developed countries, though smaller than U.S. investment, also rose sharply. From 1971 to 1984, the stock of direct investment by West Germany rose from $7.3 billion to $51.1 billion, that of the United Kingdom from $16.2 billion to $101.2 billion, and that of Japan from only $4.4 billion to $71.4 billion (see Table 4-1).

Much of the growth of multinational corporations has taken place within the developed market economies. Over 95 percent of the recorded flows of direct foreign investment originates in the OECD countries, and approximately three-quarters of this investment flows to other OECD countries (see Tables 4-2 and 4-3). By the 1960s, foreign investment had come to play an important role in the economies of the developed states.

Table 4-1 Outward Stock of Foreign Direct Investment (billions of dollars)

	1960[1]	1971	1978	1984[2]
Australia	0.2	0.65	1.61	4.12
Canada	2.5	6.47	14.47	33.04
FRG (W. Germany)	0.8	7.3*	30.25	51.16
Japan	0.5	4.44	26.81	71.43
Netherlands	7.0	13.8*	28.00	44.80
U.K.	10.8	16.23	36.68	101.18
U.S.	32.8	86.20	164.11	236.56

Inward Stock of Foreign Direct Investment (billions of dollars)

	1960[1]	1971	1978	1984[2]
Australia	NA	6.65	10.10	17.83
Canada	12.9	27.73	42.30	61.44
FRG (W. Germany)	NA	NA	33.33	29.79
Japan	0.1	0.85	2.16	5.47
Netherlands	NA	NA	14.59	18.16
U.K.	5.0	9.29	21.30	51.42
U.S.	7.6	13.92	42.47	164.58

[1]Estimates from John M. Stopford and John H. Dunning, *Multinationals: Company Performance and Global Trends* (London: MacMillan Publishers, 1983), p. 5 ("based on data provided by national governments, private sources and the IMF").

[2]1984 figures are slightly distorted because of the overvaluation of the U.S. dollar. West Germany's inward stock of foreign investment as measured in deutschemarks, for example, increased by 25 percent between 1978 and 1984, though the U.S. dollar figures cited here imply a decline.

Source: United Nations Center on Transnational Corporations. United Nations, *Transnational Corporations in World Development: Trends and Prospects* (New York: United Nations, 1988), pp. 518–526.

Canada, which traditionally has had widespread and high levels of foreign investment, was the most extreme case. At the end of 1973, companies whose equity was controlled abroad accounted for 58 percent of the capital in Canadian manufacturing, 75 percent in petroleum and natural gas, 58 percent in other mining and smelting, and 34 percent of all other industries outside agriculture and finance. By 1981, even though those figures had declined, they were still quite high: 50 percent in manufacturing, 44 percent in petroleum and natural gas, 46 percent in other mining and smelting, and 26 percent of all industries outside agriculture and finance.[11] In 1984, 20 percent of Canada's GNP was accounted for by branches of subsidiaries of foreign multinationals.[12]

Penetration is noteworthy, although less extensive, in Europe. In the early eighties, foreign multinationals in the United Kingdom accounted for 19 percent of industrial output and 15 percent of industrial employment. At the same time, foreign-owned enterprises in West Germany accounted for 26 percent of industrial production, and in France, for 25 percent. Capital stock of foreign affiliates accounted for approximately 13 percent of GNP

Table 4-2 Outflows of Foreign Direct Investment by Country and Region, 1970–1985 (millions of dollars)

Country/Region	1970	1975	1980	1981	1982	1983	1984	1985
DEVELOPED MARKET ECONOMIES								
Australia	111.0	161.5	468.6	711.0	792.7	622.2	1779.4	1824.6
Austria	11.0	25.5	101.5	209.9	147.9	183.9	77.9	37.6
Belgium and Luxembourg	156.0	234.3	204.3	116.7	−62.9	358.1	295.2	272.1
Canada	300.0	896.0	3697.6	5970.1	318.0	5318.3	3388.7	4913.2
Denmark	29.0	78.9	195.2	140.3	79.5	160.3	95.3	—
Finland	52.0	25.5	130.2	141.5	229.6	258.7	412.1	328.0
France	373.0	1335.6	3100.2	4583.4	2843.9	1699.7	2134.1	2201.3
Germany, Federal Republic of	873.0	2015.5	4177.9	4103.5	2771.1	3185.6	4356.3	4934.6
Italy	110.0	346.0	744.5	1383.2	1028.9	2128.4	1975.2	1833.7
Japan	355.0	1760.5	2394.8	4917.1	4526.4	3602.5	5945.1	6427.1
Netherlands	519.0	2293.5	5983.1	4750.8	3323.1	3757.5	5093.3	3175.0
New Zealand	1.0	20.6	115.8	99.0	444.9	77.0	64.6	60.9
Norway	32.0	171.2	253.8	179.2	305.8	356.0	548.4	1034.6
Portugal	—	8.5	14.3	18.9	9.9	18.2	10.3	22.3
South Africa	17.0	121.4	756.2	645.0	−9.9	160.3	184.5	47.7
Spain	43.0	168.8	311.1	271.2	508.9	243.7	249.1	251.8
Sweden	213.0	435.9	624.7	834.8	951.7	1054.0	1044.5	1278.3
Switzerland	—				—	491.7	1139.8	3627.8
United Kingdom	1310.0	2968.6	11379.3	12292.7	7188.2	8281.5	8075.0	11206.3
United States	7589.0	14217.7	21898.6	12497.6	6204.1	3574.3	5686.5	15236.1
Subtotal	12094.0	27285.6	56551.8	53866.0	31601.8	35532.0	42555.0	58712.9

Country/Region	1970	1975	1980	1981	1982	1983	1984	1985
DEVELOPING COUNTRIES								
Latin America and Caribbean	NA	116.2	413.6	164.4	409.3	299.7	88.6	119.0
Africa	NA	45.8	99.8	68.3	48.9	49.7	55.7	26.4
Western Asia	NA	97.4	402.6	−65.9	289.6	367.3	127.6	211.2
Other Asia and Oceania	NA	45.7	166.7	134.6	441.8	312.1	324.9	819.7
Subtotal	NA	305.0	1082.7	301.4	1189.6	1028.9	596.8	1176.3
Total of listed countries	12094.0	27590.5	57634.5	54167.4	32791.4	36560.9	43151.8	59889.2

SOURCE: United Nations Centre on Transnational Corporations, *Transnational Corporations in World Development: Trends and Prospects* (New York: United Nations, 1988), pp. 503–510.

Table 4-3 Inflows of Foreign Direct Investment by Country and Region, 1970–1985 (millions of dollars)

Country/Region	1970	1975	1980	1981	1982	1983	1984	1985
DEVELOPED MARKET ECONOMIES								
Australia	898.0	450.4	1833.9	2242.8	2189.3	2861.7	400.8	1594.1
Austria	95.0	78.9	238.2	332.5	272.7	289.7	145.6	224.4
Belgium and Luxembourg	318.0	956.7	1550.1	1384.3	1486.0	1299.9	400.8	1037.7
Bermuda	NA	748.3	940.0	–582.8	1777.0	388.9	295.0	1215.8
Canada	866.0	709.1	521.9	–2771.0	–1925.4	1596.0	2090.0	–1093.5
Denmark	104.0	267.1	105.4	100.2	134.7	64.1	9.2	—
Finland	18.0	68.0	27.3	17.7	–9.9	16.0	53.3	63.0
France	622.0	1562.6	3290.3	2457.4	1596.4	1733.9	2408.8	2526.2
Germany, Federal Republic of	595.0	667.8	286.3	306.6	783.8	1806.6	738.0	710.7
Greece	50.0	24.3	672.9	520.0	437.2	439.4	485.9	446.7
Iceland	5.0	42.4	22.5	53.2	36.1	–23.4	13.6	24.1
Ireland	32.0	157.8	286.3	204.0	241.8	168.9	119.9	161.4
Italy	606.0	633.8	584.4	1129.6	642.5	1185.5	1281.3	1003.2
Japan	94.0	230.7	286.3	188.7	441.6	406.2	–10.3	629.5
Netherlands	537.0	1245.7	2266.0	1173.5	1128.3	1392.9	1693.3	1185.9
New Zealand	23.0	132.3	200.4	311.3	268.3	191.4	160.9	155.3
Norway	64.0	214.9	59.9	682.7	431.7	332.5	–201.9	–13.2
Portugal	—	114.1	157.5	174.5	145.7	141.1	195.8	252.8
South Africa	335.0	184.6	–10.4	73.1	344.5	68.4	433.6	–450.8
Spain	222.0	681.1	1492.9	1711.0	1787.4	1628.1	1773.3	1949.5
Sweden	108.0	80.1	251.2	180.4	180.0	54.5	155.8	265.0
Switzerland	—	—	—	—	—	642.5	777.0	1249.9
United Kingdom	850.0	3337.7	10129.8	5899.3	5351.1	5170.7	–283.9	5520.4
United States	1464.0	2634.7	16906.9	25410.9	13877.4	11972.8	25348.5	19169.6
Subtotal	7906.0	15223.2	42099.9	41799.8	31018.0	33828.3	38484.0	37836.8

Country/Region	1970	1975	1980	1981	1982	1983	1984	1985
DEVELOPING COUNTRIES								
Southern Europe	22.0	156.0	153.5	225.6	147.9	157.1	191.8	175.7
Africa	369.0	475.8	243.2	1770.8	1657.2	1608.9	1497.8	1726.5
Latin America and Caribbean	815.0	3316.0	6219.4	7735.1	6447.7	3478.2	3421.9	4530.0
Western Asia	142.0	690.5	292.3	15.3	373.4	301.2	615.1	547.9
Other Asia and Oceania	486.0	1647.3	3197.1	5267.8	4827.5	4720.0	4773.3	4494.9
Subtotal	1834.0	6285.6	10105.5	15014.6	13453.6	10265.4	10499.9	11475.0
Total of listed countries	9740.0	21508.9	52205.4	56814.3	44471.6	440983.7	48983.9	49311.7

SOURCE: United Nations Centre on Transnational Corporations, *Transnational Corporations in World Development: Trends and Prospects* (New York: United Nations, 1988), pp. 503–510.

111

in the United Kingdom, 5 percent in Germany, and 3 percent in France during the same period.[13]

Several factors have contributed to the enormous growth of the multinational corporation. Technology and organizational sophistication created the possibility of expansion. The development of communications, transportation, and techniques of management and organization have made possible centralization, integration, and mobility. The computer, telecommunications, and the development of corporate organization, which initially came to a great extent from the United States and were used by U.S. firms, have been important factors in the dominance of U.S. corporations.

Governments also encouraged multinational expansion. The elimination of restraints on capital flows and trade made expansion of direct investment possible. Canadians and Europeans created incentives to attract foreign investment.[14] Although the United States federal government has not officially courted foreign investment, in recent years individual states have taken the lead, even competing with one another for foreign manufacturing plants.[15]

There were also incentives for individual firms to move abroad. Various theories explain the motivation for the spread of multinational corporations.[16] The product cycle theory argues that firms expand abroad in response to a threat to export markets. Firms develop new products and processes that they introduce abroad through exports. When their export position is threatened, they establish foreign subsidiaries with lower costs or better market access in an attempt to retain their advantage. When the firm finally loses its advantage, it may move on to new products or attempt to create new advantages by altering the product.[17]

Internalization theory, as described above, contends that firms expand abroad in order to "internalize" inefficient markets. This phenomenon is common domestically, when companies integrate vertically or horizontally in order to take advantage of economies of scale or assured production sources. According to this theory, the same motivation has prompted companies to expand internationally.

The monopoly or oligopoly theory of foreign investment contends somewhat similarly that firms move abroad to exploit the monopoly power they possess through such factors as unique products, marketing expertise, control of technology and managerial skills, or access to capital.[18] In the battle for profits and market share, firms engaged in oligopolistic competition may move abroad as part of their overall competitive strategy. They may move aggressively to exploit a new foreign market in the hope that this action will give them a permanent advantage over their competition. Conversely, a company whose competitors have just entered a foreign market might be forced to go international defensively, in order to block their opponent's move or at least prevent the competitor from gaining a survival-threatening advantage.

Yet another theory posits that firms expand abroad to take advantage of locational advantages, such as less-expensive labor and technology, large markets, or lower taxes and tariffs.[19] Each of these theories provides useful insights into why companies choose to enter foreign markets.[20] The impressive increase in international activity recently can be explained by these theories in conjunction with the particular circumstances of today's changing international economy.

For example, the rapid growth of multinational corporations in Europe after 1955 is explained by a combination of favorable factors: the economic recovery of Europe, which provided an attractive market; the return to convertibility of European currencies, which enabled the unrestricted repatriation of earnings and capital; greater political stability both internally and internationally; and the formation of the European Community, with its promise of a large market and its discrimination against third-party imports.[21]

More recently, investment in the United States by European and Japanese corporations has accelerated. Whereas in the early 1960s, the stock of foreign direct investment in the United States was negligible, by 1980 the United States had about $83 billion in foreign direct investment, and by 1986 this had grown to almost $209 billion. In 1970, the stock of direct foreign investment into the United States was only about 20 percent of U.S. direct investment abroad. By 1986 that figure reached over 80 percent.[22]

There were several reasons for the increased interest of foreign corporations in investment opportunities in the United States. One was the increased size and aggressiveness of non-U.S. firms while the European and Japanese economies grew rapidly. Another was that the decline of the dollar in the 1970s and the late 1980s brought down the cost of acquiring U.S. firms, making them more attractive to foreign corporations. This circumstance coincided with corporate restructuring in the United States, which left many companies up for sale, and with the search by U.S. surplus trading partners for safe places to invest their money. A further incentive to invest in the United States was an increasingly protectionist U.S. trade policy, especially in such vulnerable sectors as electrical equipment and automobiles. Thus, production in the United States itself guaranteed continued access to the huge U.S. market. And finally, foreign investors have been attracted to the huge U.S. market and by the relative political stability, especially compared with that of many developing countries and even many European nations.

One interesting new dimension of foreign investment in the United States was the influx of foreign banks and securities firms, which were attracted to the United States by their multinational clients who had already settled there, by profits to be made in U.S. financial markets, and by the low cost of acquiring U.S. banks. The growth of Japanese banks has been particularly important in recent years, keeping pace with the spread of

Japanese business and foreign investment. Japan is now the world's leading surplus nation and capital exporter, and the United States is one of its favorite sites for investment. Approximately 45 percent of Japanese off-shore equity investment went to the United States in 1987, amounting to $14.7 billion. These investments are not merely in manufacturing: non-manufacturing investments, especially trade, sales, banking, finance, insur-ance, and real estate, made up 70 percent of Japanese foreign investment in North America by March 1988.[23]

Japanese financial institutions have challenged U.S. supremacy in the banking and securities areas. In 1985, Japanese banks overtook U.S. banks as the world's biggest lenders.[24] Although only one of the top ten banks in the world measured by assets was Japanese in 1978, twelve of the top fourteen were Japanese by the end of 1986,[25] and four of the top ten securities firms ranked by capital were Japanese.[26]

It was the combination of the unique characteristics of multinational corporations and their phenomenal growth among the developed market economies that caused international management problems. Multinational policy and interests threatened to conflict with national policy and interests in three areas: economic efficiency, growth, and welfare; national economic control; and the national political process.

Efficiency, Growth, and Welfare

Modern governments have given high priority to the public policy goals of economic efficiency, growth, and improvement in the standard of living. In evaluating the impact of multinational corporations on developed market economies and determining the management problems raised by multina-tionals, one must judge the effect of those firms on economic performance.

Proponents of multinational corporations argue that the new corporate form is a mechanism for increasing economic efficiency and stimulating growth. By transferring capital, technology, and know-how and by mobiliz-ing idle domestic resources, multinational corporations (argue their advo-cates) increase world efficiency, foster growth, and thereby improve wel-fare.[27]

Critics of multinational corporations, on the other hand, believe that these international firms may reduce efficiency and stifle growth. Without competition, multinational corporations may be able to limit their produc-tion, maintain artificially high prices, earn monopoly rents, and thus reduce efficiency. They may actually hinder national growth by absorbing local capital instead of providing new capital, by applying inappropriate technol-ogy, and by employing expatriate, not indigenous, managers. And, as critics point out, global efficiency and growth do not necessarily maximize effi-ciency and growth for individual national economies.[28]

Over the years, much research has been devoted to empirical and theoretical analyses of multinationals.[29] Most studies of the economic impact of multinational corporations on their host developed market economies conclude that their overall effect is positive. One such case is Canada. Because of its significant penetration, foreign investment has been an important public issue in Canada and the subject of several official and semiofficial studies and much private scholarly examination. All these studies have concluded that foreign investment has favorably affected the Canadian economy.[30]

One of the earlier reports, although critical of foreign investment, concluded that direct foreign investment, especially U.S. investment, was a key factor in Canadian economic development generally and an important factor specifically in capital formation, export promotion, and the balance of payments. Furthermore, the report concluded, it was important that this investment was direct and not portfolio investment, for direct investment brought not only financial resources but also a package of product, technology, management, and market access. The report noted that there were problems with direct foreign investment, that it may have stunted the domestic Canadian capital market and damaged the initiatives of local entrepreneurs, but it concluded that "the host country typically benefits and often substantially from foreign direct investment."[31]

Similar conclusions have been reached in Europe. The 1981 Caborn report adopted by the Parliament of the European Community, which called for greater regulation of multinational corporations, found that multinational enterprises raise the level of world economic activity and have "favourable impacts on productivity, growth rates and overall level of employment, on the dissemination of new products and processes and also of managerial know-how."[32] Other benefits cited in studies of individual European economies include improvements in balance of payments, research and development, the level of technology, and increased dynamism.[33]

Despite indications of overall benefits from multinational corporations, such investment is not without costs for the host state. Costs are incurred because behavior that is rational for the corporation may be less beneficial to the host country. Several concerns have been revealed in public and private studies.[34] The fear of technological dependence is one. Although access to advanced technology is one of the primary economic benefits of multinational corporations for the host developed countries, that access may stifle domestic research and development. The concentration of research and development in the home state, primarily the United States, may discourage research and development activities in the host state and result in the subordination of the host to technology controlled from abroad. There is a related concern that host states may pay excessive costs for imported technology, because the control of technology by a multinational enables the parent to charge a monopoly rent for its use.[35] A similar concern arises concerning management skills. The transfer of managerial talent to host countries can be a source of efficiency and growth, but the use of foreign managers may also deny nationals opportunities to use and develop their skills.

Yet another concern grows out of the multinational corporations' oligopolistic character. The entrance of foreign competitors may stimulate domestic competition and thus encourage efficiency, but it may also reduce competition and threaten existing domestic industries. Even such market dominance by multinational corporations may be beneficial if it brings with it new technologies and other economic efficiencies. But if it does not introduce such improvements, it may decrease efficiency. Special concern is voiced by states when multinational corporations acquire existing national firms. Acquisition may give the firm access to capital, technology, and other resources and thereby improve its performance, but it may simply indicate a transfer of ownership, adding no new efficiencies.

Some concern has been expressed regarding the import orientation of multinational corporations. An official Canadian study, known as the Gray report, found that subsidiaries in Canada preferred to seek supplies and services within the company, as opposed to within the country. This preference for importing from the parent may provide the highest-quality goods and services, but it may retard the development of Canadian manufacturing and service sectors and thus limit the spillover effect that foreign investment has on the rest of the Canadian economy.[36] Other concerns have been voiced concerning export policy. Although the evidence suggests that multinational corporations have an equal or better export record than their domestic counterparts do, the practice of restricting exports and limiting markets of individual subsidiaries is not unknown in multinational corporations. Finally, there is concern concerning the multinational corporations' balance-of-payments impact. It is difficult to judge the entire payments ramifications of multinational corporations, but there is a feeling that the consequences may be negative in the long run.

In evaluating the problems created by the conflict between multinational corporations and their host states over economic efficiency, growth, and welfare, one must go beyond economic analyses. Equally important is the way in which the host country's citizens view the impact of multinationals on the national economy.

A survey of public opinion in Western Europe was conducted in 1974 and 1976 and involved nearly thirteen thousand people in the nine countries that were then members of the EC. The poll revealed that although many Europeans were critical of multinationals, they generally believed that multinationals have a positive economic impact. Foreign investment was seen as a modernizing force that keeps prices down, aids economic development, and improves business methods. Still, many Europeans were concerned about the disruptive effects that multinationals might have on the international monetary system and, especially, about the multinationals' ability to shift production without regard to the consequences for the home country.[37] Among national elites, opinions varied: business people and senior civil servants were the most favorable; politicians, academics, and clergy were more circumspect; and trade unionists, students, and youth leaders were generally critical.[38]

Another study showed that elites in Canada and Europe considered national income effects, balance-of-payment effects, and employment effects to be of most concern in terms of the economic effects of multinationals. The overall impact on national income was generally considered positive for the host nation, although opinion on the balance-of-payment effects was more divided, tending toward the negative. Opinion was also divided on employment effects of multinationals. Although most agreed that foreign companies paid higher wages, they also felt that other benefits for workers were worse.[39]

In sum, the multinationals' economic impact on the host economy seems generally positive, and the public generally perceives that positive impact. Yet there are real economic concerns in specific areas. The important issue for the developed host countries is not whether foreign investment is economically worthwhile but whether it is possible to increase the benefits and decrease the costs of direct foreign investment.

For much of the 1960s and 1970s, examination of the effect of multinational corporations focused on the host states, with the implicit assumption that the home state was the recipient of economic benefits. In recent years, however, the assumption that multinational corporations are good for the home economy has come under fire. Some analysts and influential interest groups in the United States, particularly labor union representatives, feel U.S. direct foreign investment has had a negative effect on the U.S. economy by favoring foreign investment over foreign trade and production in the United States, exporting jobs instead of goods, allowing tax revenues to escape, and impairing domestic economic development by sending capital abroad instead of using it at home. Although these arguments have increasing political significance, several studies of the impact of foreign investment on the U.S. economy reveal that investment has not taken place at the expense of domestic investment, trade, or employment.[40]

National Economic Control

A second area of potential multinational-state conflict in developed countries is the interference of multinational corporations in the national control of the economy. As developed states have sought to manage their economies to improve economic efficiency, growth, and welfare, concern about external constraints on that control by multinational corporations has emerged.

The concern with national control is clearly revealed in studies of elite and public attitudes toward foreign investment. In a survey of European public opinion, most of the negative views on multinationals centered on fears that they might erode the national control of the economy.[41] Many respondents saw major differences between U.S. and European multinationals: corporations based in the United States were viewed as typically powerful, dynamic, and well organized but also uncontrollable and morally suspect; whereas multinationals based in Europe were seen as socially committed, humane, and loyal as business partners.[42] Various studies of Canadian attitudes reveal that the most adverse feeling toward multinational corporations involved the loss of control. Canadians generally believe that there is a trade-off between the economic benefit of multinational corporations and their adverse effect on control over national affairs.[43]

The sense of lost control reflects, in part, an intangible feeling that as a result of foreign investment, decisions crucial to the national economy are made outside the nation. The perception is not that these decisions are adverse, just that they are made elsewhere. The tendency of multinational corporations to centralize decisions in the parent suggests that the fears that decision making shifts from host to investing country are often justified. Interestingly, the intangible fear of loss of decision making is not related to the level of foreign investment. Canadians, who have a vast amount of foreign investment, are no more concerned than are the English, who have much less. The French, with a low level of investment, on the other hand, evidence a high level of concern. The fear of lost control seems to be related more to different national expectations regarding the need for independence than to the actual threat to that independence.[44]

The fear of lost control of sensitive industries is particularly acute. Countries, including the United States, have always been concerned about foreign ownership of such sectors as communications, transportation, and finance. Increasingly, public officials feel that industries with a large influence on the economy, such as the automotive or petroleum industries, or those in the vanguard of scientific and technological development, such as computers or electronics, should remain under national control.[45] Such concern emerged in the United States in 1987 when the Japanese company, Fujitsu Ltd., tried to acquire an 80 percent share in Fairchild Semiconductor Corporation, a large supplier of computer chips for the U.S. military. Various U.S. government officials argued strongly that the sale ought to be blocked on national security grounds. Ironically, Fujitsu was proposing to buy the 80 percent share that already belonged to another foreign firm, the French company Schlumberger, Ltd. Apparently the concern of government officials was not simply that it was foreigners who wanted to buy Fairchild, but that it was the Japanese in particular, with whom U.S. semiconductor competition has been particularly fierce. In this case, the issue never came to decision because Fujitsu withdrew its offer as a result of the controversy.

Since that time, however, as foreign investment in the United States has increased, public opinion has been increasingly wary of foreign investors, especially in the sensitive high-technology industries.

Whereas multinational corporations have often played an important role in achieving national goals, there is a concern that they are less responsive to national economic planning than are domestically owned firms operating primarily in the national market.[46] The concern is, first, that activity rational for an international firm may not be in tune with that planned for the national economy and, second, that the multinational has the capacity to circumvent mechanisms for implementing national plans. Because multinational corporations have access to outside financing, they are not as dependent as domestic industry is on national governmental finance and thus may not respond to governmental incentives to invest in certain industries or certain regions. Because they have fewer links with the national economy and polity, it is feared, multinational corporations are less likely to cooperate voluntarily with national planning goals.

The Gray report, for example, expressed a concern that multinational corporations might interfere with the Canadian government's goal of increasing investment in manufacturing and discouraging overdevelopment of resource extraction. The report pointed out that foreign fabricating and manufacturing firms that integrate vertically backwards to obtain secure supplies of natural resources are less likely to respond to Canadian needs and economic capabilities because their raison d'être is shaped heavily by their committed investment elsewhere.[47]

A greater concern is that multinational corporations may evade national taxation. Through its central control of pricing, the multinational corporation can take profits in countries where taxes are low and avoid showing profits and paying taxes in those countries where taxes are high. Because transactions of subsidiaries of the same multinational are not arm's length transactions, that is, not determined by free-market prices, the central decision-making unit can artificially fix the prices of those transactions. These so-called transfer prices can be manipulated to minimize taxes. A multinational can, for example, inflate the price of imports or decrease the value of exports among affiliated companies in order to minimize the earnings of a subsidiary in a high-tax country. This issue emerged in the United States when certain states proposed using a "unitary tax" formula for computing state taxes of multinational corporations. The purpose of the unitary tax is to prevent multinationals from manipulating transfer prices to their own benefit. Rather than taxing the company on its state revenues, the state would tax it according to a complex formula based on its world-wide earnings. This provoked a strong reaction, particularly from Japanese and British corporations, who threatened to stop investing in states that used unitary tax formulas. Eventually unitary taxes were repealed.

Another dimension of interference in national control is in what one author called the "national order."[48] Multinational corporations, it is charged, are less bound by national social codes and economic relationships. Thus, the links between business and government that exist in Europe and in Japan and that are a tool for national economic management may be more tenuous and less effective between national governments and multinational corporation management.

Another aspect of the national order is labor-business relations. It has been argued that foreign multinationals have followed labor policies inimical to national labor policies. It has been charged that they are more willing than national firms, for example, to discharge employees and are less willing to consult employees in making decisions that will affect them. Europe is particularly sensitive to this because of its commitment to labor rights and employment protection, but these concerns have also surfaced in the United States. In 1988, the British construction company Beazer tried to buy Koppers, a Pittsburgh-based construction materials and chemicals company. In order to stir up public opposition to the takeover, Koppers' management successfully played up fears that Beazer, as an insensitive foreign company, would close the plant or fire workers.

Interference by Home Governments of Multinationals

Another dimension of the problem of control is not the threat from the multinational itself but from the multinational's home government to the host country, primarily the threat from the United States to the host countries of U.S. multinational corporations. Such interference occurs when U.S. laws are applied beyond U.S. borders through subsidiaries of the multinational corporation (MNC).[49]

One area of U.S. interference has been through extraterritorial application of U.S. export controls. The Trading with the Enemy Act of 1917, the Export Control Act of 1949, and its successors, the Export Administration Acts of 1969 and 1979, have been used by the U.S. government to control dealings of foreign affiliates of U.S. corporations. The Trading with the Enemy Act empowers the President to regulate all commercial and financial transactions by U.S. citizens with foreign countries or nationals in time of war or national emergency. The act has been invoked to prohibit all trade with Cuba, North Korea, North Vietnam, and, until recently, China. The Export Control and Export Administration acts give the executive branch the authority to "prohibit or curtail" all commercial exports, including technical know-how, to Communist or other specified countries from U.S. companies or their foreign subsidiaries on the basis of national security, foreign policy, or short supply. Because U.S. courts hold the parent firm criminally liable for the acts of its foreign affiliates, there is a great incentive for multinational corporations to cooperate with these U.S. regulations.

There have been cases in which the United States has blocked U.S. subsidiaries' transactions abroad that were legal under the laws of the host country. In 1982, in a highly politicized episode, the United States ordered U.S. multinational corporations operating abroad to comply with a U.S. embargo on the export of high-technology products to the Soviet Union for use in the construction of a natural gas pipeline from the Soviet Union to Western Europe. The sanctions, originally promulgated in December 1981, following the imposition of martial law in Poland, were extended in June 1982 to subsidiaries of U.S. companies abroad and foreign companies working under U.S. license. The embargo applied to technology that had been purchased when there were no controls on exports from the United States. The incident provoked a serious conflict between the United States and its European allies, who saw the U.S. action as a unilateral and retroactive application of extraterritorial jurisdiction. Some European governments issued formal orders requiring the resident companies to honor the contracts, and when the companies complied, the United States imposed penalties on them, including the revocation of all export licenses.

The U.S. government, however, has not always prevailed. Resistance by the French government and courts led the United States to withdraw its restriction on the sale of trucks made in France by a U.S. firm to the People's Republic of China. And after five months, the U.S. decision to extend the pipeline embargo to foreign subsidiaries of U.S. corporations and licenses was reversed following an agreement by the North Atlantic Treaty Organization (NATO) allies to study East-West trade. Numerous other cases suggest that the U.S. government is often willing to accede when foreign governments insist.[50]

Another area of U.S. (as well as EC and West German) interference has been through antitrust legislation. The Sherman and Clayton acts seek to prevent restraint of competition both within the United States and in U.S. import and export trade. The U.S. courts have asserted a wide-ranging extraterritorial jurisdiction of these laws, including application to the subsidiaries of U.S. multinational corporations. The fact that a U.S. corporation is a parent of a foreign subsidiary has been held sufficient for jurisdiction by U.S. courts. On this basis, the U.S. government has attempted to force, not always with success, disclosure of information by foreign subsidiaries. It has forced U.S. parents to divest themselves of foreign affiliates or to alter the behavior of their affiliates, even though that ownership or behavior was legal under the host country's laws. United States courts, for example, forced a U.S. beer company to divest itself of a subsidiary in Canada and obliged American parents to order their subsidiaries to cease to operate in a radio cartel in Canada, even though this cartel had been approved by the Canadian government.

In another case, U.S. courts claimed jurisdiction in a private antitrust claim against foreign companies joining in a uranium cartel outside the United States and with the expressed consent of their governments. But instead of the defendant firms, the relevant governments, including Canada and the United Kingdom, appeared in court and argued that the United States could not exercise jurisdiction because it had provoked the cartel by embargoing the use of foreign-origin uranium in U.S. nuclear reactors; because the cartel was, as a result, created as a matter of government policy; and because laws outside the United States do not regard cartel formation as unlawful. The court not only rejected these arguments but also criticized the governments for appearing in place of the firms. Largely in reaction to the uranium case, the United Kingdom enacted legislation to block such action by foreign governments.[51]

Finally, there has been intervention through the United States' balance-of-payments policies. In the 1960s, the U.S. government tried to improve its balance of payments by asking U.S. corporations to limit their new foreign investment in developed countries, to increase the amount of foreign investment financed by borrowing abroad, and to increase the return of earnings and short-term assets from their foreign affiliates. This had a serious impact on investment abroad, particularly in Europe, where the policy threatened to dampen economic growth, hurt the balance of payments, and dry up local capital markets when U.S. corporations borrowed on local capital markets instead of borrowing in the United States. The capital restraints were ended in the 1970s following the emergence of the float and the improvement in the U.S. balance-of-payments position. Given the internationalization of capital markets in the 1980s, it is unlikely that similar controls could be imposed today.

The U.S. government has also used multinational corporations to pressure South Africa to end its apartheid policy. The Comprehensive Anti-Apartheid Act of 1986 prevents U.S. companies and their foreign branches from providing new loans to the South African government or engaging in new investment in South Africa. Canada, the European Community, the Commonwealth nations, and the Nordic nations have passed similar laws prohibiting new investment, and the Nordic countries and Australia and Canada do not allow new bank loans. Periodically, Congress has considered stricter legislation, such as requiring mandatory disinvestment by U.S. multinationals or imposing a full-trade boycott on South Africa.

In addition to federal actions directed at ending apartheid, many U.S. state and local governments have taken a strong stance against apartheid by enacting partial or total disinvestment policies, prohibiting investment of state-run funds in companies that do business in South Africa, or refusing to make purchases from or give contracts to firms that do business in South

Africa. Although the state and local governments are not in a position to mandate that U.S. companies withdraw from South Africa, their laws force multinationals to choose between their U.S. business and their South African business.

Federal, state, and local laws have been successful in inducing U.S. corporations to leave South Africa. From 1984 to 1988, for example, 141 U.S. companies withdrew their equity investments from South Africa (although some of these maintained other economic links). Whether this withdrawal will have its intended effect on South Africa's apartheid policies is unclear, but it is significant that so many governments consider manipulation of multinationals to be a legitimate means of influencing national control within South Africa.

In conclusion, the potential for the multinational corporations' interference with national control is very real. However, if one considers the volume of transactions carried out by multinational corporations, the number of actual threats to national control is relatively small. Like the problem of the MNC's impact on economic efficiency, growth, and welfare, the problem is one of minimizing costs and maximizing benefits.

Multinationals and the National Political Process

One final but important area in which multinational corporations may interfere is in the politics of the home and host states. As with any corporation in the home or host country, the multinational is a powerful political actor that can, and at times does, seek to influence law and public policy and that does have an impact on the political environment. The nature and significance of the multinational corporation's effect on national politics in developed countries are areas that have not been sufficiently examined and about which little is known.

There are several ways in which multinational corporations might attempt to influence politics in host countries. In the most extreme case, they might overthrow an unfriendly government or keep a friendly regime in power. They might intervene in elections through legal or illegal campaign contributions or take action to support or oppose particular public policies. Finally, multinational corporations might influence the national political culture, that is, shape public political values and attitudes. In all of these actions, the firm may act on its own, at the instigation or with the support of the home government.[52]

In the case of Canada, the Gray report, which considered these possibilities, concluded that multinational corporations have little direct impact on Canadian public policy. The influence of foreign investment, according to that study, was in shaping alternatives available to Canadian decision makers. For example, because of the structure of Canadian industry and the fact that some firms are foreign controlled, public policy is limited in its efforts to rationalize industry.[53] The U.S. Senate Subcommittee on Multinational Corporations found that multinational corporations have engaged in legal and illegal payments in developed countries, but the subcommittee did not suggest just how such payments influenced public policy.[54]

Multinational corporations may also affect public policy in the home state. One study of U.S. foreign policy found that the direct influence of any particular corporation is likely to be balanced by countervailing powers, even though corporate groups may shape policy. The most important influence, the study concluded, was the ability of business generally to influence the political consensus from which U.S. foreign policy is drawn. The predominance of the liberal approach to international economic relations is an example of this intangible yet significant influence.[55]

A somewhat different view emerged from the hearings of the Senate Subcommittee on Multinational Corporations. These hearings suggested that multinational corporations at times become an important part of the dynamic of U.S. foreign policymaking by initiating demands, providing information, and at times cooperating in the execution of policy. Another impression is that multinational corporations at times follow policies independent of, and perhaps in contradiction to, official governmental policy.[56]

Another effect of multinational corporations on national politics is through their influence on social structure. One study suggested that multinational corporations are altering both national and international class structures, creating new social, economic, and political divisions. According to the study, there is a new class structure emerging that consists of a transnational managerial class favoring a liberal international economic order; a large class of established labor with secure employment and status in their local communities, which has been the primary object and beneficiary of social legislation and economic management; and a group of social marginals that has not been integrated into the new industrial society and that suffers the system's social costs. The study found that this new class structure, shaped by the multinational enterprise, will create new social conflicts not suited to control by presently established institutions.[57]

In conclusion, concern has risen in recent years, and with that concern, conflict has been generated over the multinational corporation. The regulation of multinational corporations, however, has not become such a highly politicized and controversial issue in the Western system as it has in the Third World. Although some believe that multinational corporations should be managed to maximize benefits, there is a general perception of the importance of international investment. As the former prime minister of Canada, Pierre Trudeau, explained,

I don't worry over something which is somewhat inevitable, and I think the problem of economic domination is somewhat inevitable, not only of the

United States over Canada but perhaps over countries of Europe as well. . . . These are facts of life, and they don't worry me. I would want to make sure that this economic presence does not result as I say in a real weakening of our national identity. I use that general expression too. The way in which I do that is to try and balance the benefits against the disadvantages. It is obvious if we keep our capital and keep out technology, we won't be able to develop our resources and we would have to cut our standard of consumption in order to generate the savings to invest ourselves and so on. . . . Each country wants to keep its identity or its sovereignty, to speak in legal terms. It has to instantly make assessments, and when we make assessments it is to try and select those areas which are important for our independence, for our identity.[58]

Management of Multinational Corporations

Compared with the control of money and trade, the international management of multinational enterprise has been extremely limited. One reason for the absence of an international order for investment is that multinational corporations have only recently become an issue in international economic relations among the developed market economies. The need for monetary and trade orders became clear as a result of the crisis of the 1930s, which was a crucial force behind the establishment of the postwar management mechanisms. In investment, however, no such international crisis and no consensus have arisen in the West. It was not until the 1960s that these firms became important international economic phenomena.

Even when multinational corporations came to be seen as an international problem in the West, the extent of that problem was perceived as rather limited (for Southern perceptions, see Chapter 8). The fear of economic costs and loss of national control has been balanced by the perception of economic benefits to be gained from foreign investment.

One factor shaping these generally positive perceptions of multinational corporations is the dominant liberal philosophy. International investment, like international finance and trade, is viewed as economically rational and beneficial. The role of large corporations in politics is not seen as dangerous in countries where domestic corporations play such roles. This general receptivity to international capital affects reactions to multinational corporations. It is interesting that the principal dissent comes from the labor leaders in the United Kingdom, France, and Canada. Furthermore, France and Japan, the two countries whose national policies evidence the greatest opposition to multinational corporations, are countries for which liberalism is not part of the national philosophical tradition.

Another reason for the limited perceived threat has been the power relationship between the multinational corporations and the governments of the developed countries. In the developed countries, the multinational corporation is not perceived as a major threat to governmental power. Whereas firms can influence economic performance and interfere with a nation's economic management, they cannot undermine the authority of these powerful, sophisticated governments. Although multinational corporations control sensitive sectors, they do not, except in Canada, loom so large in the national economy that governments feel they must acquiesce to their strength. Furthermore, Western governments possess not only the expertise—lawyers, accountants, economists, business experts—to regulate multinational corporations but also the confidence that they can devise means for control.

Yet another reason for the limited perception of threat in the West is that virtually all developed states have their own multinational corporations. The position of the developed market economies' governments as both home and host moderates their desires to restrict multinational corporations, for any restriction would limit national corporations. Reinforcing this limited concern over foreign investment in the late 1970s and early 1980s was the troubled economic scene in the West, one of the more prominent features of which has been a decline in new capital formation. There has thus been a reluctance to question the source of any new capital investment.

A final dimension of the limited threat and lack of international control of multinational corporations is the absence of United States interest in such management. Concern about foreign investment in the United States, especially by the Japanese, has been rising. Nevertheless, U.S. perception of a need for management, crucial to the development of international monetary and trade orders, has not existed in the field of international investment. The lack of perceived problems for U.S. political and economic systems, the dominant liberal ideology, and the political significance of the large multinational corporations in U.S. politics has made U.S. leadership more interested in promoting than controlling foreign investment.

As multinationals have become more important and better understood, the trend toward liberalizing regulations on multinationals has been echoed throughout the Northern states, as we will see in the following discussions of national, regional, and international management.

National Management

Most efforts to control multinational corporations in the present international system occur within the host country. Although policy in developed market economies has been receptive to foreign investment, there have been some attempts to regulate foreign corporations to maximize economic benefits and to minimize the loss of control.

The most important form of regulation is the control of initial capital investment. States have sought to restrict key sectors for national investment and to regulate the degree of foreign ownership or control in sectors open to foreign investment. Although all countries have some form of key sector control—transportation, communications, and defense industries are commonly restricted industries—few of the developed market economies have comprehensive regulations or even a clear national policy regarding foreign investment.[59]

For many years, Japan followed a comprehensive, restrictive policy.[60] In investment as well as trade, Japan's public philosophy and governmental policy differ from those of other Western countries. Postwar policy was originally based on the Foreign Exchange Control Law of 1949 and the Foreign Investment Law of 1950, which provided governmental authority to screen all new foreign investment, with a view to limiting that investment, and to prevent the repatriation of earnings and capital of foreign investors. Government policy was highly restrictive. New foreign investment was limited to a few industries, and within those industries, foreign ownership was limited to no more than 49 percent. When purchasing existing industry, foreigners were limited at most to a 20 percent ownership of unrestricted industries and a 15 percent interest in the many restricted industries.

While restricting direct foreign investment, Japan tried to obtain the benefits of multinational corporations by purchasing advanced technology through licensing agreements instead of acquiring technology through foreign control. As a result of these comprehensive, restrictive policies, foreign investment in Japan has been quite low (see Table 4–1).

Starting in 1967, as Japan's balance of payments strengthened and foreign pressure for liberalization increased, Japanese policy changed. The number of restricted industries was reduced, and 100 percent foreign ownership was permitted in many industries. In 1980, the Japanese government passed the Foreign Exchange and Foreign Trade Control Law. This legislation liberalized foreign exchange controls, removed formal entry restrictions on foreign direct investment (with the exception of primary industries related to agriculture, forestry, fisheries, mining, petroleum, leather, and leather manufactures) and permitted 100 percent foreign control through new investment or acquisition.

In the mid-1980s Japan relaxed controls in the financial services sector, allowing foreign institutions to obtain securities and trust bank licenses and encouraging the Tokyo Stock Exchange to open membership to foreigners. There remains a review process through the Committee on Foreign Exchange and Other Transactions in the Ministry of Finance, which evaluates foreign investment according to criteria such as effects on national security, impacts on domestic enterprise in the same or related business, smooth performance of the national economy, reciprocity with the home country of the investor, and the need for approval for capital export transactions. One of the most effective barriers to foreign investment is the existence of industry associations that can effectively restrict foreign investment. Another barrier is the fact that many Japanese financial and industrial firms hold each other's stock, a policy promoted by the Japanese government since World War II. This makes foreign acquisitions of Japanese firms virtually impossible. Finally, though the Japanese government has allowed some liberalization, it has always retained the power to restrict foreign investment at any time at its own discretion.

On the other hand, the Japan External Trade Organization (JETRO), once an export-promoting organization, has been turned into an investment-attracting organization; and the Japan Development bank is now providing favorable rates on loans to foreign investors. As a result of liberalization, foreign investment in Japan has risen, although Japan still has very low levels of foreign investment inflow in comparison with those of other OECD countries (see Table 4–3).[61]

Canada also drew up a policy for regulating the inflow of foreign investment in the seventies. The Canadian Foreign Investment Review Act of 1972 established the Foreign Investment Review Agency (FIRA) to screen virtually all new direct foreign investment in Canada. Its coverage was comprehensive (including new businesses), most acquisitions, the expansion of existing foreign-owned firms into nonrelated businesses, and change of foreign ownership. As a matter of national policy, FIRA refused takeovers in the fields of broadcasting, rail and air transportation, newspapers, nuclear energy, and banking. Evaluation of the benefit to Canada of foreign investment was determined by criteria such as contribution to employment, new investment, exports, processing of raw materials, purchase of supplies in Canada, access to sophisticated technology, improved productivity, and competition, as well as the degree of Canadian equity participation.

FIRA also insisted that foreign investors fulfill performance requirements in return for permission to invest in Canada. These commitments included import substitution requirements, export targets, research and development expenditures to be made in Canada, local equity participation guarantees, and exclusive production-in-Canada arrangements. Many investors were deterred by such requirements from making application to FIRA. Others complied. But FIRA's restrictions brought a negative reaction from the United States, which in 1982 filed a complaint with the GATT charging that FIRA's performance requirements were illegal. In 1983, a GATT panel found that Canadian requirements forcing companies investing in Canada to buy a certain proportion of their goods and services in Canada were illegal under GATT but that its export performance requirements were compatible with GATT.[62]

In 1984, the Foreign Investment Review Act was replaced by the Investment Canada Act, which is designed to promote, rather than discourage, foreign investment. Foreign investment is still screened, but only those investments exceeding C$5 million and C$50 million for direct and indirect investments respectively are subject to the screening procedure, greatly decreasing the number of foreign investments subject to review. The stated purpose of the review is to ensure that the investment be "of net benefit to Canada."[63] Under the U.S.-Canada Free Trade Agreement, U.S. firms will have even greater opportunities for Canadian investment, because indirect acquisitions will eventually be exempted from any review, and the threshold for review of direct acquisitions will be raised.[64]

Other states also screen new investment. Britain and France rely on an ad hoc consideration of applications for new direct foreign investment. Investments that might create foreign dominance of an important economic sector, damage national research and development, interfere with official plans for industrial rationalization, or create excessive concentration are reviewed by the appropriate ministries or agencies. There are no formal statutory guidelines for evaluating foreign investment, but in practice, judgments tend to favor investments that benefit employment, balance of payments, research and development, and exports; create new enterprises instead of acquiring existing firms; encourage national management at both the national and the parent level; and fit in with governmental plans for industrial reorganization.

In general, investment policy in the mid-1960s was restrictive, but since then many countries have been highly receptive to foreign investment.[65] The United Kingdom, for example, has been traditionally favorable to foreign investment, and, under the Conservative government since 1979, it has abandoned any government planning role, preferring to leave investment decisions to the operation of a free market. In 1985 the government of the United Kingdom permitted a merger between Westland, a British helicopter manufacturer, and the U.S. company United Technologies, despite strong pressure to favor the development of a Euro-consortium to strengthen European air industry cooperation. In 1988, the Swiss chocolate company, Nestlé, was allowed to buy Rowntree despite strong nationalistic protests. Nonetheless, even in a fundamentally liberal environment, such as Great Britain's, the desire for a national presence, or even a national champion in certain industries, has occasionally prevailed. When British Caledonian Airways was up for sale in 1987, both the Scandinavian carrier SAS and British Air made a bid for control. The government subtly discouraged SAS by declining to guarantee retention of route licenses; the British Air bid succeeded, allowing it to expand significantly its size and route capacity, providing England with a strong national airline carrier to compete in the post-1992 internal market.

U.S. controls on foreign investment have traditionally been limited to the International Investment and Trade in Services Act (IITSA) of 1976, which established a mechanism to monitor foreign investment, and the International Emergency Economic Powers Act of 1977, which empowers the President to block foreign acquisitions of U.S. companies or compel divestiture of an already acquired domestic company if he determines there is an extraordinary threat to the national security, foreign policy, or economy. Various other sectoral controls limit foreign investments in areas such as aviation, atomic energy, and communications. As foreign investment in the United States increased dramatically in the eighties, more attention was given to regulation. The Bryant Amendment to the Omnibus Trade Bill of 1988, which was defeated, would have required foreign investors to file certain proprietary information with the Department of Commerce for public disclosure. A provision of the 1988 trade bill extends the scope of the IITSA to prohibit foreign investment in a broader range of industries relating to the national security of the United States, and permits a presidential "veto" at the time of the takeover. Other proposed legislation includes a Foreign Ownership of U.S. Banks Limitation Act aimed at limiting ownership by countries with whom trade is restricted under the Export Administration Act, and a Hostile Foreign Takeover Moratorium Act, which would place a six-month moratorium on hostile takeovers of U.S. corporations funded by debt instruments.

Motivating these recent efforts was increasing economic nationalism. There is a growing concern in the United States over excessive dependence on foreign capital to finance growth, and a loud minority would like to see even stricter limits on foreign investment.[66] Proponents of this minority view argue that the United States is sacrificing its long-term competitiveness by becoming dependent on Japanese and other foreign technology. In the automobile sector, for example, there are many American-Japanese joint ventures in which the production of sophisticated parts takes place in Japan and the final product is assembled in the United States. Some fear that the United States is losing its production capability in this process, its companies reduced to "screwdriver factories" where the high-technology parts are made abroad and the workers are only capable of producing low-technology parts and assembling all the pieces. In Japan, it is argued, workers are learning sophisticated production techniques that will allow them to become the unchallenged champions in automobile production in a short time.[67] Anti-foreign sentiment lies below the surface of the U.S. consciousness, but some U.S. companies are discovering that it can be easily stirred and are using this knowledge as a tool for trying to prevent foreign takeovers of their companies.

Nonetheless, the prevailing view in the United States stills defends the benefits of foreign investment for the United States and would like to see a more liberal economic environment for foreign investment here and abroad. Judging by the actions of most U.S. states, one would assume that foreign investment is highly desirable. State governors are competing intensely at times to attract new foreign manufacturing plants. In return for the jobs and the economic stimulus of the new plants, they are willing to offer tax incentives, regulatory breaks, and other inducements. This has been taken to such a degree that a backlash has developed, in which U.S. companies argue that they are being discriminated against by their own local governments, which favor foreign companies and allow them to produce in the United States much less expensively than U.S. companies. It remains to be seen which of these two opposing points of view will prevail; but there is no doubt that the United States is facing an important new wave of protectionism and economic nationalism that is not likely to disappear in the near future.

Aside from imposing entry requirements, countries may also attempt to manage the behavior of multinational corporations once established in their state. The ability to control the multinational corporations' behavior is crucial to management, because it involves activities that affect national economic performance and national control, such as taxation, labor policy, capital movements, and competition policy. Indeed, governments in the developed countries closely regulate the operations of those firms—both national and multinational—operating within their borders. However, with some exceptions, the developed countries' governments have not sought to impose special or differential regulation on the operation of multinational corporations. Controls on intracorporate capital flows and intracompany charges, for example, would be difficult to apply, could provoke retaliation, and could act as a deterrent to foreign investment, which is viewed positively in the developed market economies. Furthermore, governments in the developed countries have the administrative and legal capacity to control the MNCs through legislation, regulation, and administrative practice, which applies to domestic as well as foreign corporations. Finally, the principle of national treatment—meaning that foreign-owned enterprises are to be treated no less favorably than are domestically owned enterprises—acts as a deterrent to discrimination against MNCs. Although national treatment is not universally accepted and is inconsistently applied, it is embodied in certain bilateral treaties such as the friendship, commerce, and navigation treaties with the United States and in the multilateral codes of the OECD (see p. 138) and thus serves as a constraint on government policy. Exceptions to national treatment do exist in the areas of government subsidies, government purchasing, work permits and immigration policy, and participation in industry groups that set sectoral policy.

Governments have also applied informal pressure on firms to fulfill certain "performance requirements" in areas such as plant or export expansion and to adhere to national labor practices. They have carefully monitored foreign investors' adherence to national tax legislation and foreign exchange laws. As governments, especially in Europe, have expanded their intervention in the national economy through law and regulation, foreign investors have been increasingly obliged to adopt practices—for example, labor relations policies—consistent with those of the host country. Finally, where there has been a conflict of law or policy between the host and the home state, as in the case of the U.S. extraterritorial application of export controls, the governments of the host countries have insisted on asserting their jurisdiction over the resident MNCs. As we have already discussed, several European countries required resident companies to ignore U.S. restraints on pipeline exports to the Soviet Union.[68]

Finally, there have been increasing attempts in the major home country, the United States, to regulate home country MNCs. Concerns with balance-of-payments deficits led to capital control measures; organized labor has expressed concern over export of jobs and the tax "loopholes" enjoyed by multinational corporations; and the investigation of the Senate Subcommittee on MNCs in the mid-1970s revealed a broad range of potential foreign policy problems posed by multinationals. In 1977, Congress enacted legislation to prohibit the use of bribery and illicit payments for political purposes by U.S. corporations operating abroad. And in the late 1970s and early 1980s, several states in the United States, in an effort to raise new revenues and to offset the ability of multinational corporations to select the state or country of lowest taxation, enacted unitary tax legislation that taxed both foreign and domestic corporations on their worldwide income instead of on income earned in that particular state. The result was an outcry from Japan and Europe, alleging violation of tax treaties that eliminated double taxation.

Because the developed market economies have been unwilling to restrict too severely the multinational corporations, many have tried to minimize their costs in other ways. Many states and regions, such as the EC, have tried to strengthen their domestic industry. Such policies, as part of broader industrial policies, include governmental encouragement and support of industrial concentration and rationalization of national industry, research and development, maintenance of key industries or companies, and development of national capital markets and national managerial skills. Methods include governmental financial assistance, tax preferences, government participation in industry, encouragement of mergers, financing of research and training programs, and "buy national" procurement policies. Within the European Community, many of these policies are being made illegal, which has discouraged the growth of "national champions." Nonetheless, in certain industries, such as defense, strong domestic suppliers have been encouraged (i.e., GEC-Marconi in the United Kingdom and Matra in France) and in other instances steps have been taken to strengthen individual countries' competitive positions in preparation for the creation of the internal market in 1992 (see Chapter 3). The Spanish government, for example, has encouraged mergers of Spanish banks in order to prevent local market dominance by non-Spanish banks after 1992. But the main emphasis within the European Community is on promoting certain competitive pan-European "sunrise" industries to fight U.S. and Japanese dominance (see section on regional management).

At times, Canada has also encouraged national industry to compete with multinational corporations or to reduce the need for foreign investment. During the 1970s and early 1980s, while the Liberal Party was in power, various steps were taken in this direction. The Canada Development Corporation (CDC), 49 percent financed by the Canadian government, was set up in 1971 to invest seed money in new Canadian businesses, to provide capital for existing businesses threatened with foreign takeover, and to mobilize private Canadian investment behind Canadian corporations. The CDC invested in both new and existing Canadian industry and was involved in an attempt to capture control of existing foreign investment. A National Economic Policy was also established to retain domestic control of Canadian energy sources. In 1975, a government firm called Petro-Canada was established to gain more secure Canadian access to sources of petroleum. In 1983, the Canadian government created a new mechanism for promoting national industrial objectives, including promoting the Canadian ownership of industry. The Canada Development Investment Corporation (CDIC), wholly owned by the government, was made the holding company for the CDC, Petro-Canada, and other nationally owned corporations. The CDIC was expected to be more responsive to government policy than the CDC, which was only partly controlled by the government.

After 1984, when the Conservative (Tory) Party took power, this trend was partially reversed. The CDC, CDIC, and National Energy Policy were dismantled, although Petro-Canada still exists. It was also during this period that the FIRA was replaced with the Investment Canada Act and that the U.S.-Canada Free Trade Agreement was negotiated. Concern about foreign investment is still high, particularly with respect to Canada's fear of cultural domination by the United States. Canada maintains restrictive foreign investment policies in culturally sensitive industries such as books and films, which were entirely excluded from the U.S.-Canada Free Trade Agreement. Nonetheless, Canadian government policy as a whole has shifted away from officially promoting Canadian economic nationalism.

In addition to national policy, interest in some broader form of management has emerged from time to time.

Regional Management

Regional common markets and free trade areas have provided new opportunities for regional management of multinational corporations. Within the context of such agreements there is room for substantial control or liberalization of investment policies.

One potentially important forum for the multilateral management of multinational corporations is the EC. A European solution figures prominently in the European critics' analysis of foreign multinational investment in Europe.[69] Two approaches to regional policy have been suggested. One approach, prevalent in the seventies, was to develop European Community regulations to limit the autonomy of MNCs in areas of frequent national conflict such as labor relations. The other approach has been the Community's encouragement of large European corporations, capable of competing globally with U.S. and Japanese corporations in high-technology sectors. The control function has not been developed as far as expected, in part because of the liberal, pro-business climate of Europe in the 1980s. Instead, the emphasis has been on the second approach in an effort to close the high-technology gap before the internal market is completed in 1992. However, it is possible that the control issues will reemerge as a priority if the political left grows stronger in Europe.

European regional management faces major obstacles.[70] In addition to political opposition on some of these issues, a more basic problem concerns the authority of the EC to pass binding regulation on its member countries. Members of the community have consistently refused to delegate to the EC any national authority for regulation of industrial policy. A French proposal in 1965 for community regulation of foreign investment was rejected by the other members, who opposed a restrictive policy. In 1973, a commission of the EC proposed a number of community regulations regarding MNCs, including the protection of employees in event of a takeover and cooperation in monitoring MNC activities. It led nowhere. The Caborn report, adopted by the European Parliament in 1981, called for maximizing the positive effects of multinational corporations and minimizing their negative effects by "the establishment of an appropriate framework of countervailing power at the international level through legislation, guidelines, codes, multilateral agreements, and through greater cooperation and exchange between states."[71] Specifically, it recommended binding EC regulations in the areas of information disclosure, transfer pricing, and merger controls.

Although no specific directives aimed at non-EC investment have been passed, the European Community has moved ahead on several directives that would shape foreign as well as EC corporations' practices and address some of the concerns mentioned in the Carborn report. The most important areas are accounting and information disclosure and antitrust policy, especially merger control. A number of directives—the EC form of legislation—in the area of company law are designed to increase the transparency of the activities of large conglomerates. The Seventh Company Law Directive, adopted in 1983, calls for the consolidation of financial reporting to enable a fair review of the business as a whole. The First and Fourth directives had already specified the type of information to be published in public companies' accounts. The draft of the Ninth Directive would oblige groups of companies to define and publish the relationships between parents and subsidiaries and increase the rights of subsidiaries against the parent. The draft of the Thirteenth Directive would lay down rules for the conduct of takeover bids, particularly with regard to information disclosure.

Another area of concern has been the promotion of greater participation and consultation rights for employees. The proposed Fifth Company Law Directive, to harmonize the structure of EC public companies, includes a provision for employee participation at the board level. Another proposed directive, known as the Vredeling proposal, calls for greater consultation between management and labor regarding company policy and plans.[72] Though interest in these actions stagnated because of liberalization and deregulation in the early 1980s, they may receive renewed interest in the future.

The Community's industrial policy, although not yet comprehensive in coverage, has been considerably strengthened in recent years. This policy, which permeates the 1992 program, is designed to build EC industrial champions to counter U.S. and Japanese industrial and technological dominance. The Single European Act, which came into force in 1987, added a chapter to the EC Treaty (the Treaty of Rome) entitled "research and technological development," which states that "the Community's aim shall be to strengthen the scientific and technological basis of European industry and encourage it to become more competitive at [sic] international level."[73] This is to be realized through EC financial support for basic R&D, the opening up of national public sector procurement contracts, technical standardization, and the removal of fiscal and legal barriers to joint ventures and other forms of cooperation. This has resulted in numerous jointly funded research consortia in the areas of telecommunications, industrial technology, and information technologies and has also encouraged a steady increase in the number of cross-border mergers occurring in Europe.

The Community has made it clear that, while it wishes to maintain a liberal policy, it does not intend to allow foreign companies to reap the greatest benefit from the 1992 barrier-free internal market. This is bound to mean that a degree of Community preference will prevail and that foreign-based multinationals will not have the same access to EC programs as local companies, unless some reciprocity is recognized in the multinationals' home countries.

There is no Community policy specifically to regulate inward foreign investment, although individual EC states have their own regulations. However, Community action could be taken to disallow state financial inducements that act as subsidies for foreign investors or to refuse to allow goods produced with less than an acceptable local content to circulate freely in the Community. This would curtail the operations of so-called "screwdriver plants," which simply assemble foreign-made components within the EC and thereby avoid external tariffs. In 1988, for example, France received permission from the EC to block the import of 300,000 television sets that were produced by Japanese companies but assembled in the EC. France claimed that these televisions did not qualify as European because of the high foreign content.

In addition to regional management through the EC, which is the best known and most complex regional internal market existing today, recent steps have been taken to create other regional areas for trade and investment liberalization. New Zealand and Australia have had a free-trade area for many years, and have just strengthened it through the Closer Economic Relationship agreement to include substantial liberalization of investment and harmonization of regulatory barriers. The U.S.-Canada Free Trade Agreement has similar provisions, which will increase cross-border competition in manufacturing by eliminating most tariffs and will enable service industries, such as banks and insurance companies, to compete directly for business in both countries. Previously, for example, U.S. financial institutions were not allowed to own more than 25 percent of federally regulated Canadian-controlled financial institutions, and Canadian companies were not allowed to offer Canadian government securities in the United States. Both of these policies have been changed under the U.S.-Canada Free Trade Agreement.

International Management

International regulations and agreements have tended to encourage the expansion of multinational corporations. Western international law enacted before World War II offered protection for foreign investment. The traditional law of prompt, adequate, and effective compensation in the case of nationalization and various patent and copyright conventions was designed for this purpose, and the postwar agreements reinforced this general trend. The IMF's provisions regarding currency convertibility allow the repatriation of capital and earnings and thus facilitate the international flow of capital. The GATT's tariff reductions smooth international production and transfers within the multinationals. And the OECD's Code on Liberalization of Capital Movements establishes the norms of nondiscrimination between foreign and domestic investors within a country, freedom of establishment, and freedom of transfer of funds.

Although there has been some marginal international regulation through various international agencies and international conventions, whose authority covers certain aspects of multinational operations,[74] there were until the 1970s few attempts to manage multinational corporations at an international level, and most of those attempts failed.

One such effort died with the Havana Charter.[75] The management of international investment had not been a part of the U.S. scheme for a new postwar economic order. Ironically, in response to strong pressure from U.S. business groups, the U.S. delegation at Geneva in 1947 proposed a draft article on foreign investment. The article, intended to codify the prevailing Western liberal attitude toward foreign investment and the rights of capital-exporting countries, provided for protection against nationalization and discrimination. Once the matter was placed on the negotiating agenda, however, its character quickly changed. The underdeveloped countries, led by the Latin American states, were able to redefine the proposed article to protect not capital exporters but capital importers. Provisions of the Havana Charter allowed capital-importing countries to establish national requirements for the ownership of existing and future foreign investment and to determine the conditions for further investments. The inclusion of the investment provisions was a major reason for the opposition of U.S. business to the Havana Charter and for its eventual failure. GATT, its successor, contains no provisions for investment, although negotiations on trade-related investment measures were included in the Uruguay Round.

Throughout the 1950s and early 1960s, a do-nothing attitude prevailed. Attempts to write international foreign investment laws, such as the United Nations' Economic and Social Council efforts in the 1950s and those of GATT in 1960 on restrictive business practices, surfaced but led nowhere.[76]

In the late 1960s, as concern increased, more comprehensive proposals for a system of international control were drawn up. The most far-reaching proposals called for a body of international law under which multinational corporations would be chartered and regulated and for an international organization to administer these regulations.[77] Other proposals advocate the development of a GATT for investment[78]. This intergovernmental general agreement would consist of a few fundamental concepts of substance and procedure on which there might be a general international consensus and would establish an agency to investigate and make recommendations about the creation or infringement of rules (much as the GATT organization has done). Such an agency would not have compulsory authority, but it would have the power to publicize its findings and thus appeal to public opinion.

Although such a comprehensive, self-sufficient supra-national body or even GATT Code for Investment seem unlikely, other options are available. These include amending existing GATT articles to include investment, drawing up a separate agreement committing only its signatories to apply GATT principles to investment, or prosecuting investment issues that are trade related through the GATT dispute framework in order to set GATT precedents covering investment. Currently, the United States is participating in Uruguay Round GATT negotiations that include certain trade-related investment measures (TRIMS) (see Chapter 3). Although this does not mean that GATT is ready to deal with investment issues head on, the GATT is considering those investment issues that affect trade. These issues\include local content requirements, local equity requirements, technology transfer or export requirements, remittance restrictions, and incentives. If successful, the TRIMS negotiations could be the first step in broadening the GATT to cover investment issues.

The OECD has been another forum for devising a regime for international investment. In 1976, largely in response to pressure from both less-developed and developed countries, the developed market states agreed on a voluntary code of conduct for multinational corporations. One factor leading to the OECD agreement was the new interest of the U.S. government and U.S. business in such an international code. Public revelations of corporate bribery and illegal political activity created domestic pressures for regulating U.S. corporations. United States business sought to deter, through an international agreement, congressional legislation and to internationalize any constraints placed on U.S. firms.

The stated goal of the OECD code is to maximize international investment. It suggests guidelines for corporate behavior, such as greater disclosure of information, cooperation with the laws and policies of host governments, less anticompetitive behavior and fewer improper political activities, respect for the right of employees to unionize, and cooperation with governments in drawing up voluntary guidelines for corporate behavior. As part of the multinational agreement, the OECD countries further agreed on guidelines for government policy regarding multinational corporations, including nondiscrimination against foreign corporations, equitable treatment under international law, respect for contracts, and government cooperation to avoid beggar-thy-neighbor investment policies. Finally, the developed countries agreed to establish consultative procedures to monitor and review the agreed-upon guidelines. Although the OECD code is voluntary and its guidelines are often deliberately vague, it is a step toward the development and implementation of international norms.[79]

Another limited international solution was offered by the United Nations. Largely as a result of the pressures from the Third World Countries, in 1974 and 1975 two new organizations were established within the United Nations system: the Center on Transnational Corporations, which gathers and generates information on multinational corporations and also the intergovernmental Commission on Transnational Corporations, which acts as a forum for considering issues related to multinational corporations, for conducting inquiries, and for supervising the center. The commission's activities have focused on the development of an international code of conduct for multinational corporations. Because the commission is such a large, public governmental forum and because the positions of the member countries differ (thirty-three are developing countries, five are socialist, and ten are developed market economies), the bargaining process has been tedious and often confrontational; agreement has been difficult. After well over a decade, the negotiations on a code of conduct remained deadlocked on a number of issues. Most difficult were the definition of a transnational corporation—with the developed market countries wanting to include state-owned transnationals of the Eastern bloc and the socialist states unwilling to accept this definition—as well as the demand of the developed market economies for assurances on the treatment of MNCs by host governments in return for concessions governing the MNCs' behavior. In the 1980s, as interest shifted from controlling to encouraging foreign investment, the code negotiations languished.

The center has been active since its formation in 1975. It has attempted to remedy the dearth of information on multinationals by studying their operations and effects, offering technical advice to member countries, and making policy recommendations to the commission. In the process, the center has commissioned and compiled information on multinationals and has made available services to countries whose lack of information could place them at a negotiating disadvantage with foreign corporations.[80]

Other steps have been taken in the United Nations toward regulating various MNC activities. The United Nations Conference on Trade and Development (UNCTAD) formulated a code in 1980 on restrictive business practices that establishes principles and rules for controlling anticompetitive behavior, such as abuse of market power or restraint of competition. Other agreements have been reached concerning consumer protection, and transborder data flows. Negotiations are taking place in various parts of the United Nations system on technology transfer and international patent agreements.[81]

One final form of international management of multinational corporations involves not a unified and centralized order but, rather, a complex system of bilateral or multilateral negotiations among states, possibly leading to a series of agreements on specific matters or to methods for mediating conflicts. Conflicting national laws, in such areas as taxation, antitrust regulations, patents, export controls, and balance-of-payments controls, may be harmonized through such negotiation. In the area of taxation, for example, the OECD has written a draft convention containing proposals regarding many issues of taxation. Although never implemented, the treaty has guided subsequent bilateral negotiations and treaties among the developed market economies.[82]

Another bilateral approach might be the establishment of arbitration, adjudication, or simply consultation procedures that would accompany regulations or take the place of regulations when rules cannot be agreed upon. Although the World Bank has set up such an organization, called the International Center for the Settlement of Investment Disputes, very few nations have recognized it, and few disputes have been submitted to it. It is possible, however, to create institutions or processes to which countries or companies and countries desiring a solution can turn. Such commissions exist in the socialist states to manage state-corporate disputes, and the U.S.-Canada Free Trade Agreement includes a provision for a strong bilateral dispute settlement panel to resolve trade disputes and continue reviewing each country's trade remedy laws.

In conclusion, the international management of multinational corporations has focussed on promoting foreign direct investment. Not until the

1970s were there any significant attempts to establish rules of conduct, and even then the political impetus came largely from the developing countries. Despite some international tension and national uneasiness regarding multinational corporations, there is no dominant perception of a common interest in control in the developed market economies or in the one country that might mobilize the system for common action—the United States. Until there is a change in the international consensus, the international control of multinational corporations will remain limited. Thus, the future of management in the coming years is not with international order but with national regulation.

NOTES

1. Direct investment involves control, whereas portfolio investment involves capital movement but not control. This chapter focuses on direct investment in the developed market economies. See Chapter 8 for a discussion of investment problems in North-South relations.

2. Mira Wilkins, *The Emergence of Multinational Enterprise: American Business Abroad from the Colonial Era to 1914* (Cambridge, Mass.: Harvard University Press, 1970), p. 201.

3. Although the majority of multinational corporations do in fact own subsidiaries abroad, there are some corporations that are strongly linked to foreign companies by subcontracting agreements or nonequity alliances. In a sense these companies are multinationals, too, although they fall outside the traditional definition.

4. Raymond Vernon, *Sovereignty at Bay: The Multinational Spread of U.S. Enterprises* (New York: Basic Books, 1971), p. 11.

5. United Nations, *Transnational Corporations in World Development: Trends and Prospects* (New York: United Nations, 1988), pp. 335–340; World Bank, *World Development Report 1987* (New York: Oxford University Press, 1987), pp. 206–207.

6. See Stephen Hymer and Robert Rowthorn, "Multinational Corporations and International Oligopoly: The Non-American Challenge," in Charles P. Kindleberger, ed., *The International Corporation* (Cambridge, Mass.: MIT Press, 1971), pp. 57–91.

7. The internalization theory is based on work done by Ronald H. Coase on the theory of the firm. See Coase's "The Nature of the Firm," *Economica* (1937), 386–405. For further developments of this theory, see Oliver Williamson, *The Economic Institutions of Capitalism: Firms, Markets and Relational Contracting* (New York: Free Press, 1985).

8. On joint ventures, see R.E. Caves, *Multinational Enterprise and Economic Analysis* (Cambridge, England: Cambridge University Press, 1982) and David C. Mowery, ed., *International Collaborative Ventures in U.S. Manufacturing* (Cambridge, Mass.: Ballinger Publishing Company, 1988).

9. Louis T. Wells, Jr., "The Multinational Enterprise: What Kind of International Organization?" in Robert O. Keohane and Joseph S. Nye, Jr., eds. *Transnational Relations and World Politics* (Cambridge, Mass.: Harvard University Press, 1972), pp. 97–114; John M. Stopford and Louis T. Wells, Jr., *Managing the Multinational Enterprise: Organization of the Firm and Ownership of the Subsidiaries* (New York: Basic Books, 1972); Stefan H. Robock et al., *International Business and Multinational Enterprises* (Homewood, Ill.: Richard D. Irwin, Inc., 1977), pp. 399–450.

10. *Survey of Current Business*, August 1987 (Washington, D.C.: U.S. Government Printing Office, 1987). Note that these figures are cited at book value, which means that they represent the historical value of the investments, that is, what they cost at the time of acquisition with no adjustment for inflation or changing market values since then. This means that the U.S. investments, which were generally made earlier, are undervalued. Although the increase in other countries' foreign direct investment is significant, the contrast would not be as sharp if all investments were measured at current market value.

11. A. E. Safarian, *Governments and Multinationals: Policies in the Developed Countries* (Washington, D.C.: British-North American Committee, 1983), p. 14.

12. John Dunning and John Cantwell, *IRM Directory of Statistics of International Investment and Production* (New York: New York University Press, 1987), Table A-8.

13. Ibid.

14. For national incentives, see Stephen E. Guisinger, *Investment Incentives and Performance Requirements* (New York: Praeger Publishers, 1985); Earl H. Fry, *The Politics of International Investment* (New York: McGraw-Hill, 1983), pp. 127-160; OECD, *Investment Incentives and Disincentives and the International Investment Process* (Paris: OECD, 1983).

15. Susan and Martin Tolchin, *Buying into America: How Foreign Money Is Changing the Face of Our Nation* (New York: Times Books, 1988); James Moses, *State Investment Incentives in the USA* (London: The Economist Publications, Ltd., 1985).

16. For a comparative survey of the theories that follow, see Peter J. Buckley and Mark Casson, *The Economic Theory of the Multinational Enterprise* (New York: St. Martin's Press, 1985) and Alan M. Rugman, ed., *New Theories of the Multinational Enterprise* (New York: St. Martin's Press, 1982).

17. Vernon, *Sovereignty at Bay*, pp. 65-77; Raymond E. Vernon, "The Product Cycle Hypothesis in a New International Environment," *Oxford Bulletin of Economics and Statistics*, vol. 41(1979), 255-67.

18. See Stephen H. Hymer, *The International Operations of National Firms: A Study of Direct Foreign Investment* (Cambridge, Mass: MIT Press, 1976); Charles P. Kindleberger, *American Business Abroad: Six Lectures on Direct Investment* (New Haven, Conn.: Yale University Press, 1969), pp. 1-36.

19. See John Fayerweather, "International Transmission of Resources," in *International Business Management: A Conceptual Framework* (New York: McGraw- Hill, 1969), pp. 15-50.

20. The "eclectic theory" of multinational activity is an attempt to integrate elements of the above theories into one unified theory. See John Dunning, "Explaining Changing Patterns of International Production: In Defence of the Eclectic Theory," *Oxford Bulletin of Economics and Statistics* 41 (November 1979): 269-96.

21. Richard N. Cooper, *The Economics of Interdependence: Economic Policy in the Atlantic Community* (New York: McGraw-Hill, 1968), pp. 89-91.

22. *Survey of Current Business*, August 1987, Tables 9 and 10.

23. Japan Economic Institute, "Japan's Fiscal 1987 Foreign Direct Investment," *JEI Report* no. 23B (June 17, 1988), 9-13.

24. Randall Jones, "Japan's Role in World Financial Markets," *JEI Report* no. 42A (November 14, 1986).

25. "The Top 500 Banks in the World," *American Banker*, July 26, 1988, p. 34; United Nations, *Transnational Corporations in World Development: Trends and Prospects* (New York: United Nations, 1988), p. 114.

26. United Nations, *Transnational Corporations in World Development: Trends and Prospects* (New York: United Nations, 1988), p. 119.

27. See Harry G. Johnson, "The Efficiency and Welfare Implications of the International Corporation," in Kindleberger, ed., *The International Corporation*, pp. 35-56; Kindleberger, *American Business Abroad*.

28. See Stephen Hymer, "The Efficiency (Contradictions) of Multinational Corporations," *American Economic Review*, 60 (May 1970), 441-448.

29. See John H. Dunning, "Multinational Enterprises and Nation States," in A. Kapoor and Phillip D. Grub, eds., *The Multinational Enterprise in Transition* (Princeton, N.J.: Darwin Press, 1972), pp. 402-410; Raymond Vernon, "A Program of Research on Foreign Direct Investment," in C. Fred Bergsten, ed., *The Future of the International Economic Order: An Agenda for Research* (Lexington, Mass.: Lexington Books, 1973), pp. 93-113; Karen Hladik, *International Joint Ventures: An Economic Analysis of U.S.-Foreign Business Partnerships* (Lexington, Mass.: Lexington Books, 1985).

30. See Royal Commission on Canada's Economic Prospects, *Final Report* (Ottawa: Queen's Printer, 1958); Task Force on the Structure of Canadian Industry, *Foreign Ownership and the Structure of Canadian Industry* (Ottawa: Privy Council Office, 1968); *Foreign Direct Investment in Canada* (The Gray Report) (Ottawa: Information Canada, 1972). For private studies, see Charles A. Barrett, *The Future of Foreign Investment in Canada* (Ottawa: The Conference Board of Canada, 1984); A.E. Safarian, *Foreign Direct Investment: A Survey of*

Canadian Research (Montreal: Institute for Research in Public Policy, 1985). For a somewhat more skeptical view, see Steven Globerman, *U.S. Ownership of Firms in Canada* (Montreal and Washington, D.C.: Canadian-American Committee, 1979). For a critical analysis, see Kari Levitt, *Silent Surrender: The Multinational Corporation in Canada* (New York: St. Martin's Press, 1970).

31. Task Force, *Foreign Ownership and the Structure of Canadian Industry*, p. 37.

32. (Caborn Report) European Communities, European Parliament, Working Documents 1981-1982, *Report on Enterprises and Governments in Economic Activity*, Doc. 1–169/81, May 15, 1981, p. 5.

33. Giles Y. Bertin, "Foreign Investment in France," in Isaiah A. Litvak and Christopher J. Maule, eds., *Foreign Investment: The Experience of Host Countries* (New York: Praeger, 1970), pp. 105–122; Dunning, "Multinational Enterprises and Nation States," pp. 406–408; John H. Dunning, "The Role of American Investment in the British Economy," *Political and Economic Planning*, Broadsheet No. 508 (February 1969); Stephen Young, *Foreign Multinationals and the British Economy* (New York: Croom Helm, 1988).

34. See Task Force, *Foreign Ownership and the Structure of Canadian Industry*, and *Foreign Direct Investment in Canada*; United Nations, *Transnational Corporations in World Development*; Jack N. Behrman, *National Interests and the Multinational Enterprise: Tensions Among the North Atlantic Countries* (Englewood Cliffs, N.J.: Prentice-Hall, 1970), pp. 32–84; Jean-Jacques Servan-Schreiber, *The American Challenge* (New York: Atheneum, 1968); Susan and Martin Tolchin, *Buying into America*.

35. On this point, see Johnson, "The Efficiency and Welfare Implications of the International Corporation."

36. Task Force, *Foreign Direct Investment in Canada*, pp. 183–211.

37. Georges Peninou et al., *Who's Afraid of the Multinationals? A Survey of European Opinion on Multinational Corporations* (Hampshire, England: Saxon House, 1978), pp. 59–62.

38. Ibid, pp. 93–97.

39. John Fayerweather, "Elite Attitudes Toward Multinational Firms" in J. Fayerweather, ed., *Host National Attitudes Toward Multinational Corporations*, 1982.

40. See Cooper, *The Economics of Interdependence*, pp. 98–103; Robert G. Gilpin, Jr., *U.S. Power and the Multinational Corporation: The Political Economy of Foreign Direct Investment* (New York: Basic Books, 1975). For an evaluation of the impact of U.S. multinationals' overseas activities on the United States, see C. Fred Bergsten, Thomas Horst, and Theodore Moran, *American Multinationals and American Interests* (Washington, D.C.: Brookings Institution, 1978); Robert Stobaugh et al., *Nine Investments Abroad and Their Impact at Home* (Boston: Division of Research, Harvard Graduate School of Business Administration, 1976); Richard T. Frank and Richard T. Freeman, *Distributional Consequences of Direct Foreign Investment* (New York: Academic Press, 1978); AFL-CIO, 16th Constitutional Convention, *Resolution on International Trade and Investment*, October 1985.

41. Peninou et al., *Who's Afraid of the Multinationals?* pp. 59–62. See also Joseph La Palombara and Stephen Blank, *Multinational Corporations in Comparative Perspective* (New York: The Conference Board, 1977), pp. 6–8.

42. Peninou et al., *Who's Afraid of the Multinationals?* pp. 69–70.

43. J. Alex Murray and Lawrence Le Duc, "Changing Attitudes Toward Foreign Investment in Canada," in John Fayerweather, *Host National Attitudes Toward Multinational Corporations* (New York, N.Y.: Praeger Publishers, 1982), pp. 216–235.

44. John Fayerweather, "Elite Attitudes Toward Multinational Firms: A Study of Britain, Canada, and France," *International Studies Quarterly*, 16 (December 1972), 472–490.

45. See, for example, French attitudes toward sensitive industries, in Allan W. Johnstone, *United States Direct Investment in France: An Investigation of the French Charges* (Cambridge, Mass.: MIT Press, 1965), pp. 32–34.

46. See Behrman, *National Interests and the Multinational Enterprise*, pp. 69–84.

47. Task Force, *Foreign Direct Investment in Canada*, p. 428.

48. Behrman, *National Interests and Multinational Enterprise*, pp. 73–76.

49. See Behrman, *National Interests and the Multinational Enterprise*, pp. 88–127.

50. Ibid., pp. 104–113.

51. Mark R. Joelson, "International Antitrust: Problems and Defenses," *Law and Policy in International Business*, 2 (Summer 1970), 1121–1134.

52. See similar possibilities outlined in Task Force, *Foreign Direct Investment in Canada*, pp. 301–306.

53. Ibid., pp. 305–307.

54. See U.S. Senate, 93rd Cong., 1st and 2nd sess., and 94th Cong., 1st and 2nd sess., *Multinational Corporations and United States Foreign Policy*, hearings before the Subcommittee on Multinational Corporations of the Committee on Foreign Relations (Washington, D.C.: U.S. Government Printing Office, 1975).

55. Dennis M. Ray, "Corporations and American Foreign Relations," *The Annals*, 403 (September 1972), 80–92.

56. See U.S. Senate, *Multinational Corporations and United States Foreign Policy* for a discussion of International Telephone & Telegraph; Jerome Levinson, "The Transnational Corporations and the Home Country," in *Conference on the Regulation of Transnational Corporations*, February 26, 1976 (New York: Columbia Journal of Transnational Law Association, 1976), pp. 17–22.

57. Robert W. Cox, "Labor and the Multinationals," *Foreign Affairs*, 54 (January 1976), 344–365.

58. In Fayerweather, *Foreign Investment in Canada*, p. 32.

59. For a good summary of national approaches to the management of foreign direct investment, see Linda M. Spencer, *American Assets: An Examination of Foreign Investment in the United States* (Arlington, Va.; Congressional Economic Leadership Institute, 1988), pp. 19–27. See also: Earl H. Fry, op. cit. and OECD, *Investment Incentives and Disincentives*.

60. See M. Y. Yoshino, "Japan As Host to the International Corporation," in Kindleberger, *The International Corporation*, pp. 345–369; Lawrence B. Krause, "Evolution of Foreign Direct Investment: The United States and Japan," in Jerome B. Cohen, ed., *Pacific Partnership: United States-Japan Trade: Prospects and Recommendations for the Seventies* (Lexington, Mass.: Lexington Books for Japan Society, 1972), pp. 149–176; Noritake Kobayashi, "Foreign Investment in Japan," in Litvak and Maule, eds., *Foreign Investment: The Experience of Host Countries*, pp. 123–160.

61. See Japan Economic Institute, "Recent Trends in U.S. Direct Investment in Japan," Report No. 23A (June 15, 1984), and "Foreign Direct Investment in Japan" Annual Updates for 1985 (August 16, 1985), 1986 (October 10, 1986) and 1987 (April 17, 1987), *JEI Report* (Japan Economic Institute, Washington, D.C.). See also Dennis Encarnation, "American-Japanese Cross-Investment: A Second Front of Economic Rivalry" in Thomas McCraw, ed., *America versus Japan* (Boston: Harvard Business School Press, 1986).

62. See Safarian, *Governments and Multinationals*, pp. 14–20. For a critical review of FIRA, see Christopher C. Beckman, *The Foreign Investment Review Agency: Images and Realities* (Ottawa: The Canadian Conference Board, 1984).

63. On Investment Canada, see *Investment Canada, Annual Report 1986–87* (Minister of Supply and Services Canada, 1987) and Thorne, Ernst & Whinney, *Canada's Investment Canada Act: An Executive Summary* (Toronto: Thorne, Ernst & Whinney, 1986).

64. See A.E. Safarian, "The Canada-U.S. Free Trade Agreement and Foreign Direct Investment," *Trade Monitor* No. 3, May 1988, C.D. Howe Institute, p. 16ff.; Earl Fry and Lee H. Radebaugh, *The Canada/U.S. Free Trade Agreement: The Impact on Service Industries* (Provo, Ut.: Brigham Young University, 1988); and *The Canada-U.S. Free Trade Agreement* (Ottawa: Department of External Affairs, 1987).

65. Charles Torem and William Laurence Craig, "Developments in the Control of Foreign Investment in France," *Michigan Law Review*, 70 (December 1971), 285–336; Safarian, *Governments and Multinationals*, pp. 20–24.

66. See Tolchin, *Buying into America* and Robert B. Reich, "Corporation and Nation," *The Atlantic*, May 1988.

67. Robert Reich and E. Mankin, "Joint Ventures with Japan Give Away Our Future," *Harvard Business Review*, No. 2 (March-April 1986), pp. 78–86.

68. See Cynthia Day Wallace, *Legal Control of the Multinational Enterprise* (The Hague: Martinus Nijhoff, 1982); John Robinson, *Multinationals and Political Control* (New York: St. Martin's Press, 1983).

69. See Schreiber, *The American Challenge*.

70. See J. J. Boddewyn, "Western European Policies Toward U.S. Investors," *The Bulletin*, March 1974, pp. 45–63; Raymond Vernon, "Enterprise and Government in Western Europe," in Vernon, ed., *Big Business and the State: Changing Relations in Western Europe*

144   The Western System

(Cambridge: Harvard University Press, 1974), pp. 3–24; Behrman, *National Interests and the Multinational Enterprise*, pp. 161–172.

71. Caborn Report, p. 7.

72. For an analysis that argues that the EC has imposed significant controls on MNCs, see Robinson, *Multinationals and Political Control*. For a survey of European Community initiatives and their status, see *Business Guide to EC Initiatives*, American Chamber of Commerce in Belgium, 1988.

73. Article 130f (1), "Treaty Establishing the European Economic Community (as amended by the Single European Act, July 1, 1987)," *Treaties Establishing the European Communities* (Luxembourg: Office for Official Publications of the European Communities, 1987), p. 239.

74. For example, the International Civil Aviation Organization, the International Labor Organization, and the World Health Organization.

75. See Clair Wilcox, *A Charter for World Trade* (New York: Macmillan, 1949), pp. 145–148.

76. United Nations Economic and Social Council, *Report of the Ad Hoc Committee on Restrictive Business Practices* (New York: United Nations, 1953); General Agreement on Tariffs and Trade, *Decisions of the Seventeenth Session* (Geneva: GATT, December 5, 1960), p. 17.

77. See George W. Ball, "Cosmocorp: The Importance of Being Stateless," *Columbia Journal of World Business*, 2 (November–December 1967), 25–30.

78. Paul M. Goldberg and Charles Kindleberger, "Toward a GATT for Investment: A Proposal for Supervision of the International Corporation," *Law and Policy in International Business*, 2 (Summer 1970), 195–323.

79. Organization for Economic Cooperation and Development, *International Investment and Multinational Enterprises* (Paris: OECD, 1976). Experience with the OECD guidelines to date indicates that they may indeed have some impact on the operations of multinationals within member states. See, for example, R. Blanpain, *The Badger Case and the OECD Guidelines for Multinational Enterprises* (Deventer, the Netherlands: Kluwer, 1977). For OECD reviews, see Organization for Economic Cooperation and Development, *National Treatment for Foreign Controlled Enterprises in OECD Member Countries* (Paris: OECD, 1978); Organization for Economic Cooperation and Development, *International Direct Investment: Policies, Procedures and Practices in OECD Member Countries* (Paris: OECD, 1979); OECD, *Controls and Impediments Affecting Inward Direct Investments in OECD Countries* (Paris: OECD, 1987).

80. For a compendium of the center's publications, see United Nations, Center on Transnational Corporations, *Bibliography on Transnational Corporations* (New York: United Nations, 1988). The center's periodical, *CTC Reporter*, carries summaries and announcements of the center's work.

81. Black, Blank, and Hanson, *Multinationals in Contention*, pp. 221–225; Werner Feld, *Multinational Corporations and U.N. Politics: The Quest for Codes of Conduct* (Elmsford, N.Y.: Pergamon Press, 1980); Debra Lynn Miller, "Panacea or Problem? The Proposed International Code of Conduct for Technology Transfer," *Journal of International Affairs* (Spring–Summer 1979), 43–62.

82. See Seymour J. Rubin, "The International Firm and the National Jurisdiction" and "Developments in the Law and Institutions of International Economic Relations," in Kindleberger, *The International Corporation*, pp. 179–204, 475–488.

Part Three

The North-South System

5

The North-South System
and the Possibility
of Change

Management problems of the North-South system are quite different from those of the Western system. For the interdependent system of developed market economies, the dilemma is whether it is possible to achieve the necessary political capability to manage mutually beneficial international economic relations. In the North-South system of dependence, the management dilemma is whether it is possible to achieve the necessary political capability to create a system that is mutually beneficial for all.

In the Western system, control is facilitated by a perceived common interest in the system. In the North-South system, there is less perception of a common interest. The developed market economies feel that the system of dependence, although perhaps not perfect, is legitimate, because it gives them benefits that they believe extend to the system as a whole. The Southern states feel that the system is illegitimate because they have not enjoyed enough of its economic rewards. From their viewpoint, the system has not adequately promoted their economic development.

The management processes of the North-South system are also quite different from those of the Western system. In the West, there is a relatively highly developed system consisting of international organizations, elite networks, processes of negotiation, agreed-upon norms, and rules of the game. Although power is unequally distributed in the West, all members have access to both formal and informal management systems. In North-South relations, in contrast, there is no well-developed system with access for all. The South has been regularly excluded from the formal and informal processes of system management. North-South relations are controlled by the North as a subsidiary of the Western system. Understandably, the North perceives this structure as legitimate, whereas the South generally perceives it as illegitimate.

Since the end of World War II, developing countries have persistently sought to change their dependent role in international economic relations. As we shall discuss, their efforts to achieve growth and access to decision making have varied over time and from country to country. Southern strategies have been of several types: isolation from the international economic system, efforts to change the economic order, and integration into the prevailing system. These strategies have been shaped to a significant degree by the central question of whether it is possible to achieve growth and development within the prevailing international economic system. The dominant liberal philosophy argues that such development is not only possible but also most likely under a liberal economic regime. Two contending theories—Marxist theory and structural theory—challenge the liberal analysis and argue that the system itself is at the root of the development problem.

The Liberals

Liberalism, as we have seen, is the dominant theory of the prevailing international economic system. Liberal theories of economic development argue that the existing international market structure provides the best framework for Southern economic development.[1] The major problems of development, in this view, lie in the domestic economy of the developing country in the form of market imperfections; unproductive or inadequate land, labor, and capital; and social and political rigidities. The best way to improve these weaknesses is through market-oriented domestic policies. Given appropriate internal policies, the international system—trade, foreign investment, and foreign aid—can play a crucial role in development.

Trade, according to liberal analyses, acts as an engine of growth, and specialization according to comparative advantage and international trade increases income. Specialization and trade in products particularly suited to the national factor endowment promote more efficient resource allocation and greater technology and managerial skills; encourage capital inflow through the financial system and through international investment; and stimulate competition. Foreign investment is seen to bring in other managerial and technological skills that can increase productivity. Private financial flows from developed countries can be used to fund investment in infrastructure and productive facilities. And foreign aid from developed market economies, although not a market relationship, is believed to help fill resource gaps in less-developed countries by, for example, providing capital, technology, and education.

From the liberal viewpoint, the correct international Southern strategy for economic development is to foster those domestic changes necessary to promote foreign trade, foreign investment, and foreign financial flows.

The Marxists

Marxist or dependency theories take the opposite view of the international market system.[2] Southern countries, it is argued, are poor and exploited because of their history as subordinate elements in the world capitalist system, and this condition will persist for as long as they remain part of that system. The international market is under the monopolistic control of the developed economies and thus operates to the detriment of the underdeveloped countries tied to it. International market operations enable the developed countries to extract the economic wealth of the underdeveloped countries for their own use.

Trade between North and South is an unequal exchange, as control of the international market by the developed capitalist countries leads to declining prices for the raw materials produced by the South and rising prices for the industrial products produced by the North. Thus, the terms of trade of the international market are biased against the South. In addition, international trade encourages the South to concentrate on backward forms of production that prevent development.

Foreign investment further hinders and distorts Southern development, often by controlling the most dynamic local industries and expropriating the economic surplus of these sectors through the repatriation of profits, royalty fees, and licenses. According to many Marxists, there is a net outflow of capital from the South to the North. In addition, foreign investment contributes to unemployment by establishing capital-intensive production, aggravating uneven income distribution, displacing local capital and local entrepreneurs, adding to the emphasis on production for export, and promoting undesirable consumption patterns.

Another dimension of capitalist creation and perpetuation of underdevelopment is the international financial system. Trade and investment remove capital from the South and necessitate Southern borrowing from Northern financial institutions, both public and private. But debt service and repayment further drain Third World wealth. Finally, foreign aid reinforces the Third World's distorted development, by promoting foreign investment and trade at the expense of true development and by extracting wealth through debt service. Reinforcing these external market structures of dependence, according to Marxist theory, are clientele social classes within the underdeveloped countries. Local elites with a vested interest in the structure of dominance and a monopoly of domestic power cooperate with international capitalist elites to perpetuate the international capitalist system.

Because international market operations and the clientele elite perpetuate dependence, any development under the international capitalist system is uneven, distorted, and, at best, partial. For the Marxists, the only appropriate strategy for development is revolution: total destruction of the international capitalist system and its replacement with an international socialist system.

The Structuralists

Structural theory, which has had a significant influence on the international economic policy of the South, falls between liberalism and Marxism.[3] Structuralist analysis, like Marxist analysis, contends that the international market structure perpetuates backwardness and dependency in the South and encourages dominance by the North. According to this view, the market tends to favor the already well endowed and to thwart the less developed. Unregulated international trade and capital movements will accentuate, not diminish, international inequalities.

The structural bias of the international market, according to this school, rests in large part on the inequalities of the international trading system. Trade does not serve as an engine of growth but actually widens the North-South gap. The system creates declining terms of trade for the South. Inelasticity of demand for the primary product exports of the less-developed countries and the existence of a competitive international market for those products lead to lower prices for Third World exports. At the same time, the monopoly structure of Northern markets and the rising demand for manufactured goods lead to higher prices for the industrial products of the North. Thus, under normal market conditions, international trade actually transfers income from the South to the North.

Structuralists also argue that international trade creates an undesirable dual economy. Specialization and concentration on backward export industries by the Southern economies do not fuel the rest of the economy as projected by the liberals. Instead, trade creates an advanced export sector that has little or no dynamic effect on the rest of the economy and that drains resources from the rest of the economy. Thus, trade creates a developed and isolated export sector alongside an underdeveloped economy in general.

Foreign investment, the second part of the structural bias, often avoids the South, where profits and security are lower than in the developed market economies. When investment does flow to the South, it tends to concentrate in export sectors, thereby aggravating the dual economy and the negative effects of trade. Finally, foreign investment leads to a flow of profits and interest to the developed, capital-exporting North.

Economic Change

Although the structuralist analysis of the international market is quite similar to the Marxist analysis, the two theories diverge on a critical point.

Structuralist theory argues that the international system can be reformed, that the natural processes can be altered. Although the various theorists differ on preferred reforms—foreign aid, protection, access to Northern markets—they all believe that industrialization can be achieved within a reformed international market and that such industrialization will narrow the development gap.

Marxist theory, on the other hand, contends that the capitalist system is immutable and that the only change possible is revolution: destruction of the international capitalist system and its replacement with an international socialist system. Marxists explain the impossibility of reform in two ways.

One explanation is that developed capitalist economies are unable to absorb the economic surplus or profits generated by the capitalist system of production.[4] Capitalist states cannot absorb their rising surplus internally through consumption, because the worker's income does not grow as fast as capitalist profits do. To prevent unemployment and the inevitable crisis of capitalism resulting from overproduction and underconsumption, the developed market economies invest excess capital in and export excess production to the underdeveloped countries. Another way to absorb the rising surplus and prevent the crisis of capitalism, according to some, is to invest in the military at home, which in turn leads to pressure for expansion abroad. By absorbing economic surplus, foreign expansion prevents or at least delays the collapse of the capitalist system. Thus, dominance, dependence, and imperialism are essential and inevitable dimensions of capitalism.

A second explanation of the necessity of capitalist imperialism derives from the North's need for Southern raw materials.[5] According to this argument, capitalist economies depend on Southern imports, and the desire to control access to those supplies leads to Northern dominance.

Empirical examination reveals important weaknesses in the Marxists' analysis. Although some economic ties with the South are important to the developed countries, they are not crucial to the North's economic well-being. Indeed, as we shall discuss, the problem for the less-developed countries is that they are not important enough for the North.

First, the underconsumption arguments are weak, because the developed market economies are able to absorb their economic surplus. While the developed economies have had difficulties maintaining aggregate demand at acceptable levels, they have managed the problem internally through modern economic policies: income redistribution, fiscal and monetary policy, and public and social expenditures. Although the developed countries have had serious economic problems—sluggish growth, surplus industrial capacity, inflation—these cannot be adequately explained by underconsumption theories.

Second, foreign investment, especially in less-developed markets, is not of vital importance to the developed market economies, as illustrated by the case of the United States, the principal foreign investor. Foreign investment is a relatively small percentage of total U.S. investment. In 1987, U.S. foreign direct investment amounted to $309 billion, whereas its total investment was in the trillions of dollars. Furthermore, the South is not the main area of U.S. foreign investment and is, in fact, declining in importance. In 1987, the developing countries accounted for 23 percent of all U.S. direct foreign investment, whereas the developed market economies accounted for 76 percent. In 1960, U.S. direct foreign investment in the South accounted for 35 percent, versus an investment of 61 percent in the developed market economies.[6]

Moreover, income from the developing countries is not of vital economic importance to the United States. In 1987, Southern earnings accounted for 30 percent of total U.S. earnings on foreign direct investment, about 2.2 percent of total business earnings, and an infinitesimal part of its total GNP.[7] Although Southern investment is a small part of total foreign investment, returns for many years were greater in the less-developed countries. In 1982, the rate of return on U.S. investments in the Third World was 15.8 percent, as compared with a 8.2 percent return in the North.[8] This situation was reversed in 1986. The rate of return on investments in developed countries was 17.5 percent, while it was 11.8 percent in the developing countries. In 1987, the rate of return on investments in developed countries was 20.3 percent and 13.7 percent for investments in developing countries.[9] In sum, U.S. investment in and earnings from the developing countries are significant but hardly crucial to the overall U.S. economy.

Trade with the South as a whole is also not of overwhelming economic importance to the North. In 1987, exports from developed to developing countries accounted for 21 percent of exports of the developed market economies, of which 17 percent was exports to oil-exporting LDCs. In the same year, imports of the developed countries from the LDCs were 22 percent of total imports of which 24 percent was from oil exporters.[10] The minor overall importance to the United States of trade with the South is demonstrated by the fact that in 1987, U.S. exports to developing countries represented only 1.8 percent of the U.S. GNP.[11]

In sum, the case for dependence as a necessary outlet for capitalist surplus is not sustainable. The underdeveloped countries provide significant earnings for the developed market economies and are important investment and export outlets, but they are not necessary for the North.

Northern dependence on Southern raw materials is also limited. Raw materials in general are not as significant as Marxist theory suggests, and, where they are significant as with oil, raw material dependence may work to the detriment of the developed countries, not to their advantage. The United States, and to a greater extent the Europeans and Japanese, depend on the import of certain raw materials, but in only a few cases are the major suppliers of these materials Southern countries.[12] Furthermore, foreign dependence is declining as growth in overall consumption of raw materials declines due to changing growth patterns, conservation, technological improvements, and substitution.

In conclusion, the arguments that dominance and exploitation of the South are necessary for the capitalist economies as a whole do not stand the empirical test. The South is important but not vital.

There is, however, the Marxist argument that dependence, although not important to the capitalist economies as a whole, is necessary for the capitalist class that dominates the economy and polity.[13] According to these theories, capitalist groups, especially those managing the multinational corporations, seek to dominate the underdeveloped countries in their quest for profit. Because these groups control the governments of the developed states, they are able to use governmental tools for their class ends.

To evaluate this theory, it is necessary to determine whether the capitalist class as a whole has a common interest in the underdeveloped countries, even though most capitalists do not profit, as has been shown, from foreign trade and investment. One theorist argues that the entire capitalist class has an interest in dominance and foreign expansion, including those capitalists having no relation to or profit from such expansion.[14] This is true, he explains, because there is a common interest in expansion that maintains the system as a whole. Yet the preceding analysis of the macroeconomic importance of the Third World suggests that the less-developed countries are not economically necessary to the North and that certain Northern groups, such as the petroleum industry, enjoy most of the benefits of economic ties with the South. Thus, the capitalist class as a whole does not have an interest in the South and in dominance, because only a small percentage of that class profits from dominance and because the system itself is not dependent on dominance.

A stronger argument is that some powerful capitalists, such as the managers of multinational corporations, have a crucial interest in the South and in Northern dominance. Clearly, certain firms and certain groups profit from the existing structure of the international market. The question is the role of these firms and these groups in Northern governmental policy. Certainly, those groups interested in Northern economic dominance can affect the foreign policies of developed countries.[15] But they do not inevitably dominate foreign policy in the developed market economies. In the Middle East, for example, despite the importance of oil earnings and petroleum, U.S. foreign policy has not always reflected the interests of the U.S. oil companies.

On balance, then, dominance is important to the developed market economies and is especially important to certain groups within those economies. But dominance is neither necessary nor inevitable. Under the right political circumstances, change is possible. The problem is that the South has only limited ability to demand change from the North. Economically underdeveloped and politically fragmented, the South has limited leverage on the North. As we shall discuss, because the South is not vital for the North, the developed countries need not respond to Southern demands for change.

Development Strategies

Since the end of World War II, developing countries have pursued several different strategies in an effort to alter their dependence. In finance, trade, investment, and commodities, they have sought greater rewards from the greater participation in the international economic system. Over the years, those strategies have alternated between seeking to change the system and seeking to accommodate to it.

During the formative period of Bretton Woods, those developing states that were independent—primarily the Latin American countries— attempted to incorporate their goal of economic development and their view of appropriate international strategies for development into the North's plans for the new world economic order. The political and economic weakness of the developing world at this time doomed their efforts. At Bretton Woods, they sought, and failed, to ensure that development—meaning development for both industrial and developing countries—would have the same priority as reconstruction did in the activities of the new International Bank for Reconstruction and Development. At Havana, they argued for modification of the free trade regime: for the right to protect their infant industries through trade restrictions such as import quotas and for permission to stabilize and ensure minimum commodity prices through commodity agreements. Some LDC interests, such as the right to form commodity agreements and to establish regional preference systems to promote de-·velopment, were, in fact, included in the Havana Charter. But these provisions were lost when the charter was not ratified and the GATT took its place.

In the 1950s and 1960s, developing countries abandoned these first efforts to shape the international system and turned inward. Faced with an international regime that they believed did not take their interests into account and that excluded them from management, developing countries turned to policies of national autarky. The stress on isolation from international markets was reinforced by the preoccupation of developing countries with decolonization and by the belief that the end of colonial political exploitation would foster economic development.

In this period, the main development policy was import substitution. Developing countries protected local industry through tariffs, quantitative controls, and multiple exchange rates and favored production for local consumption over production for export. Government became actively involved in promoting economic development, largely by channeling resources to the manufacturing sector. Autarky did not mean total isolation from the international system. Trade with the North continued to flow. Developing countries also encouraged foreign direct investment, especially in manufacturing, as a way of fostering domestic productive capacity. As a result, there was a major movement of multinational corporations into developing countries. LDCs also tried with some success to persuade developed countries to provide foreign aid for development. As decolonization swept the Third World and competition with the Soviet Union shifted to the South, aid became a useful political tool in the Cold War as well as a way for colonial powers to retain links with their former colonies. In this period, aid became a regular feature of North-South relations.

Toward the end of this period, elements of a new strategy began to emerge. The strategy of isolation from the international system gradually came to be seen as a failure. Import substitution created uncompetitive industries and weakened traditional exports. The influx of foreign investment came to be seen as a threat to sovereignty and development. Foreign aid proved inadequate to assure economic growth. Instead of relying on domestic change, developing countries began to argue that only changes in the international system could promote development. As independent developing countries became more numerous, they began to meet with each other and to develop plans for changing the prevailing international economic regime. The hope was that such common action would increase the bargaining leverage of the South and enable the less-developed countries to negotiate that change with the North.

In the 1960s, developing countries gradually began to work together to press for changes in the system. They created the Group of Seventy-Seven to act as a permanent political bloc to represent developing country interests in U.N. forums. In Third World conferences and United Nations forums where the South commanded a majority, the less-developed countries pushed through declarations, recommendations, and resolutions calling for economic reforms.

The developing countries achieved some largely procedural changes. They persuaded the GATT to include economic development as one of its goals. The United Nations established the United Nations Conference on Trade and Development, which the South intended to be its international economic forum. UNCTAD provided the developing countries with a new economic doctrine that followed the ideas of the structuralists. According to the view developed by UNCTAD's first secretary general, Raul Prebisch, the natural operation of the market works against developing countries because of a long-term decline in developing countries' terms of trade and because of Northern protectionism. What is needed is a redistribution of world resources to help the South: restructuring of trade, control of multinational corporations, and greater aid flows.

The strategy of seeking to change the international system reached its apex in the 1970s with the South's call for a New International Economic Order (NIEO). The NIEO grew out of the threat and the promise of the economic crises of the 1970s. The combination of food shortages, the rapid increase in the price of oil, and a recession in the developed countries undermined growth prospects in much of the South and made developing countries desperate for change. At the same time, the success of the oil-producing and -exporting countries in forcing changes in the political economy of oil held out the prospect of new leverage on the developed countries. Developing countries sought to use their own commodity power and to link their interests with OPEC, their fellow members of the Group of Seventy-Seven, to demand changes in the global economic system. The NIEO included a greater Northern commitment to the transfer of aid and new forms of aid flows; greater control of multinational corporations and greater MNC transfer of technology to developing countries; and trade reforms including reduction of developed country tariff barriers and international commodity agreements.

Success of the NIEO depended on Southern unity, the credibility of the commodity threat, and the North's perception of vulnerability. It foundered on all three. Southern unity was weakened by the differential impact of the food, energy, and recession crises; by the growing gap between the NICs and the least-developed countries; and by traditional regional and political conflicts. The credibility of the commodity threat was undermined by the inability to develop other OPECs, by OPEC's unwillingness to link the oil threat to Group of Seventy-Seven demands in any meaningful way, and by declining demand for Southern raw materials. And, in the end, the North did not perceive any significant vulnerability to Southern threats. The North was willing to enter into a dialogue about changing the international economic system—as in the 1975 to 1977 Conference on International Economic Cooperation (CIEC)—but it was unwilling to make any substantive changes.

By the 1980s, developing countries had effectively abandoned the hope of reforming the international system and were once again thrown back on their own resources. The recession of the 1980s made developed countries even less responsive to demands for systemic change and less willing to dispense foreign aid. The failure of the NIEO led developing nations to pursue different routes to development.

The Group of Seventy-Seven survived in the U.N., but Southern unity became increasingly irrelevant to the development strategy of most Southern states. The developing countries were increasingly fragmented. A number of countries in Asia achieved rapid growth largely by integrating into the system, welcoming foreign investment and exporting manufactured products to developed countries. Other advanced developing countries, such as Brazil and Mexico, relied on a relatively closed internal market. The interests of these countries increasingly departed from those poorer countries, especially in Africa, which existed at the poverty line and relied on foreign assistance for survival. Even the NICs were divided. Those in Asia became concerned about growing protectionism in the United States; others, especially Latin American countries that had borrowed heavily from commercial banks, faced the debt crisis; others such as Mexico and Venezuela faced the collapse of oil prices and the growing conflicts within OPEC.

The issue for developing countries, as the end of the twentieth century approached, remained little different than it had been in 1945: whether it is possible to achieve growth and development within the prevailing system and, if so, how.

NOTES

1. For examples of liberal theory, see Gottfried Haberler, *International Trade and Economic Development* (Cairo: National Bank of Egypt, 1959); Ragnar Nurkse, *Equilibrium and Growth in the World Economy* (Cambridge, Mass.: Harvard University Press, 1961); Harry G. Johnson, *Economic Policies Toward Less Developed Countries* (New York: Praeger, 1967); Gerald M. Meier, *International Trade and Development* (New York: Harper & Row, 1963); Gerald Meier, ed., *Pioneers in Development* (New York: Oxford University Press, 1984); Jagdish Bhagwati, *Essays in Development Economics: Wealth and Poverty* (vol. 1), and *Dependence and Interdependence* (vol. 2) (Cambridge: MIT Press, 1985).

2. For examples of Marxist theory, see Samir Amin, *Accumulation on a World Scale* (New York: Monthly Review Press, 1974); Samir Amin, *Unequal Development: An Essay on the Social Formations of Peripheral Capitalism* (New York: Monthly Review Press, 1976); Paul A. Baran, *The Political Economy of Growth* (New York: Monthly Review Press, 1968); Arghiri Emmanuel, *Unequal Exchange: A Study of the Imperialism of Trade* (New York: Monthly Review Press, 1972); Andre Gunder Frank, *Capitalism and Underdevelopment in Latin America*, rev. ed. (New York: Monthly Review Press, 1969); Harry Magdoff, *Imperialism: From the Colonial Age to the Present* (New York: Monthly Review Press, 1978); Dan Nabudere, The Political Economy of Imperialism (London: Zed Press, 1977); Theotonio Dos Santos, "The Structure of Dependence," in K. T. Fann and Donald C. Hodges, eds., *Readings in U.S. Imperialism* (Boston: Porter Sargent, 1971). See also the special issue of the *Review of Radical Political Economics*, "Facing the 1980s: New Directions in the Theory of Imperialism," 11 (Winter 1979).

3. For examples of structuralist theory, see Gunnar Myrdal, *Rich Lands and Poor: The Road to World Prosperity* (New York: Harper & Row, 1957); Raul Prebisch, *The Economic Development of Latin America and Its Principal Problems* (New York: United Nations, 1950); Johan Galtung, "A Structural Theory of Imperialism," *Journal of Peace Research*, 8 (1971), 81–117.

4. Paul A. Baran and Paul M. Sweezy, *Monopoly Capital: An Essay on the American Economic and Social Order* (New York: Monthly Review Press, 1966). These authors define economic surplus as "the difference between what a society produces and the costs of producing it" (p. 9). For a critical analysis of the concept, see Benjamin J. Cohen, *The Question of Imperialism: The Political Economy of Dominance and Dependence* (New York: Basic Books, 1973), pp. 104–121.

5. See, for example, Pierre Jalee, *Imperialism in the Seventies*, trans. R. and M. Sokolov (New York: Third World Press, 1972).

6. *Statistical Abstract of the U.S. 1974* (Washington, D.C.: U.S. Government Printing Office, 1974), p. 781; U.S. Bureau of the Census, U.S. Department of Commerce, *Survey of Current Business*, 68:8 (August 1988), p. 49.

7. *Survey of Current Business*, 68:8 (August 1988), p. 45; 68:7 (July 1988), p. 86.

8. Ibid.

9. *Survey of Current Business*, 68:8 (August 1988), p. 45.

10. International Monetary Fund, *Direction of Trade Statistics, Yearbook 1988* (Washington, D.C., IMF, 1988), pp. 8, 12.

11. Ibid., p. 406

12. Commodity Research Bureau, *1986 CRB Commodity Yearbook* (Jersey City, New Jersey, 1986).

13. See Arthur MacEwan, "Capitalist Expansion, Ideology and Intervention," *Review of Radical Political Economics*, 4 (Spring 1972), 36–58; Thomas Weisskopf, "Theories of American Imperialism: A Critical Evaluation," *Review of Radical Political Economics*, 6 (Fall 1974), 41–60.

14. MacEwan, "Capitalist Expansion, Ideology and Intervention."

15. See Senate, *Multinational Corporations and United States Foreign Policy*, hearings before the Subcommittee on Multinational Corporations of the Committee on Foreign Relations, 93rd Cong., 2nd sess. (Washington, D.C.: U.S. Government Printing Office, 1975).

6

International
Financial Flows

International Financial Flows

The effort of the South to obtain financial capital for development is a central theme in North-South relations. Developing countries, short of their own funds, traditionally turned to capital surplus countries for private funds in the form of bank loans and the purchase of bonds to finance infrastructure and productive facilities. In the nineteenth century, for example, British capital helped build United States railroads and industry; and in the first half of the twentieth century, foreign capital flowed to Latin America to finance industrialization. In the first twenty-five years of the Bretton Woods era, public funds for development replaced private lending in North-South financial relations. Foreign aid, virtually nonexistent before World War II, came to account for a large portion of financial transfers to developing countries in the postwar period. Then, in the 1970s and early 1980s, private financial flows re-emerged as commercial banks in the developed countries financed public works and private industry in many developing countries. In this chapter, we examine the evolution of financial flows, both public and private, in North-South relations.

Foreign Aid and the Postwar Order

Although foreign aid was one of the most innovative developments in North-South relations in the Bretton Woods era, it was not part of the original postwar vision of the developed countries. To be sure, the International Bank for Reconstruction and Development (IBRD), now known as the World Bank, was established along with the IMF as one of the two international institutions of the Bretton Woods system. Recognizing the massive needs for financing and the disruption of capital markets after the

159

war, the founders of Bretton Woods set up this unique public multilateral institution to finance the rebuilding of war-torn countries and the development of members of the Bank. With capital provided by member states, the World Bank was to borrow in private capital markets and make loans at market rates to cover foreign exchange needs of borrowing countries.

After the war, the less-developed countries sought to ensure that development would have the same priority as reconstruction and that they would have access to World Bank financing. However, the developed countries that dominated the World Bank unanimously agreed that European postwar reconstruction would be the first priority for the Bank. Furthermore, the United States and other developed countries rejected the developing country argument that public capital was needed for economic development. In the view of the North, a combination of domestic capital and new funds from trade expansion was the appropriate route to growth. External capital, where necessary, would have to be private and would be obtained by promoting foreign direct investment and by trade liberalization, which would improve export opportunities for investors. In those rare cases where public external financing might be appropriate, financing should be limited in amount and offered on market or hard, not concessional or soft, terms.[1] Thus, in its first five years, one-half of World Bank lending went to European reconstruction and development; the other half was extended to developing countries on hard terms.[2]

Northern policy on bilateral aid closely resembled that in international forums. In the early postwar period, the United States was the only country able to transfer significant resources to the less-developed countries. The rhetoric at this time suggested that bilateral aid for development would be a major aspect of U.S. foreign policy. In the famous "Point Four" of his inaugural address in 1949, President Harry S Truman called for "a bold new program . . . for the improvement and growth of underdeveloped areas."[3] The reality, however, was different. Emphasis was to be on self-help; where external capital was needed, it should be primarily private; and where private capital was unavailable, external financing should come primarily from the World Bank. United States economic aid was very limited. The Export-Import Bank gave market-term loans for financing U.S. trade, and the technical assistance program offered a small number of grants. Between 1950 and 1955, bilateral overseas development aid (that is, public transfers of funds) from all of the developed market countries averaged $1.8 billion a year, and multilateral flows amounted to $100 million a year.[4]

The Link between Aid and Foreign Policy

In the mid-1950s, Northern policies shifted. One reason was the emergence of the less-developed countries as increasingly active, albeit weak, actors in international relations. In the two decades following World War II, much of Africa and Asia achieved political independence. By 1965, 85 out of 118 members of the United Nations were developing countries. As the less-developed countries became more numerous, they also became more outspoken and somewhat more united and specific in their demands for international economic reform, including more financial aid. Gradually, the newly independent countries began to coordinate policies within the U.N. system and to meet together in international conferences of developing countries where they formulated common demands on the North.

The emergence of the new Third World became significant when the Soviet Union decided to make the developing world an arena of competition in the Cold War. Following the Communist takeover of China in 1949 and the Korean conflict of 1950, the United States began a program of military assistance to developing countries bordering the Soviet Union and the People's Republic of China and to certain Middle Eastern countries.[5] After Stalin's death in 1953, the Soviet Union for the first time contributed to United Nations technical assistance programs, entered into trade agreements with Southern countries, and provided financial assistance to Egypt, India, Syria, Indonesia, and Afghanistan. Then, in 1956, Soviet Premier Nikita Khrushchev announced that competition with the West would be expanded to the less-developed countries.[6]

The Soviet Union's threat to the West's position of dominance in the developing world led the United States for the first time to conclude that economic assistance to the South could be a powerful tool in the Cold War.[7] One influential study expressed well the U.S. view:

A comprehensive and sustained program of American economic assistance aimed at helping the free underdeveloped countries to create the conditions for self-sustaining growth can, in the short run, materially reduce the danger of conflict triggered by aggressive minor powers, and can, say in two to three decades, result in an overwhelming preponderance of societies with a successful record of solving their problems without resort to coercion or violence. The establishment of such a preponderance of stable, effective and democratic societies gives the best promise of a favorable settlement of the Cold War and of a peaceful, progressive world environment.[8]

According to economic analysis at the time, the growth of the less-developed countries was constrained primarily by insufficient capital investment, which was in turn limited by insufficient savings and/or foreign exchange. External financial assistance, it was argued, would fill this resource gap. Capital flows plus technical assistance to improve the use of both domestic and external capital would create the conditions for self-sustaining economic growth. Economic growth, in turn, would provide a constructive outlet for nationalism, foster social progress, develop political leadership, and encourage confidence in the democratic process.[9] Aid would serve U.S. foreign policy by "help[ing] the societies of the world develop in ways that will not menace our security—either as a result of their own internal dynamics or because they are weak enough to be used as tools by others.''[10] This focus on foreign aid as part of U.S. political and security policy has been a central theme in U.S. aid policy throughout the post-war era.

France and the United Kingdom, motivated both by security concerns and by the desire to maintain political and economic relationships with their former colonies, adopted similar policies.[11] As a result, bilateral foreign aid programs expanded dramatically. The United States established the Development Loan Fund (DLF) in 1958 and rapidly increased its size. Major new aid programs for Latin America were drawn up after Vice-President Richard M. Nixon was stoned and mobbed on a trip to Latin America in 1958 and after the Cuban Revolution of 1960. Between 1961 and 1969, $4.8 billion was sent from the United States to Latin America. Overall, annual U.S. aid increased from $2.0 billion in 1956 to $3.7 billion in 1963.[12] British aid doubled from $205 million in 1956 to $414 million in 1963, and French aid rose from $648 million in 1956 to $863 million in 1963.[13] Between 1960 and 1962, new development aid authorities were created in Canada, Japan, the United Kingdom, Denmark, Sweden, and Norway.

Multilateral aid also increased. As Europe recovered from the war, World Bank lending shifted to developing countries, and the Bank's capital was increased to allow greater lending. In 1956, World Bank members created the subsidiary International Finance Corporation (IFC) to promote private investment in developing countries. In 1960, the International Development Agency (IDA) was established as a separate institution closely integrated with the World Bank with a mandate to make soft or highly concessional loans. In 1958, the United States, reversing its long-standing opposition, agreed to the establishment of the Inter-American Development Bank and provided $350 million of the bank's initial capital of $1 billion.[14] African and Asian development banks followed in 1964 and 1966, respectively.

Thus, in the 1950s and 1960s aid emerged as a new form of international economic interaction. Never before in history had states voluntarily transferred funds on concessional terms to other countries; never before had multilateral institutions played such a role in economic relations. While aid thus ushered in a new form of international relations, it did not, as we shall examine, change the balance of economic power between North and South.

Stagnation of Aid

Although aid became a regular North-South economic interaction, Northern political support for public financial assistance to developing countries was uneven and the flow of aid proved to be highly erratic.

Between 1960 and 1970, total aid flows from all the industrialized countries remained roughly constant in real terms. Most European countries regularly increased their aid as their economies strengthened. Germany and Japan became major donors in the late 1950s and 1960s, in part because of reparation payments after the war and partially as a reflection of their high domestic growth rates. The Nordic countries and the Netherlands, motivated by a sense of moral responsibility, provided dramatic increases in aid flows throughout the 1960s and 1970s.

At the same time, however, official development assistance from the United States, the United Kingdom, and France declined. United States aid, for example, declined from $3.5 billion in 1967 to $3.0 billion in 1973, but in real resource value (constant 1967 dollars), it fell to $2.0 billion.[15] In 1973, U.S. overseas development aid fell to a postwar record low of $2.97 billion.[16]

One reason for the shift in U.S. aid policy was disillusionment after a period of high expectations about the link between aid and foreign policy. The heavy emphasis of the U.S. aid program on the foreign policy benefits of foreign assistance led to disappointment when the political and security goals of economic assistance were not realized. The long and frustrating war in Vietnam played an important role in this dissatisfaction. Aid did not fulfill predictions of leading to economic development, democratic government, and political stability. Growth was uneven, instability seemed to increase with development, and aid did not necessarily win friends and influence people.[17] Meanwhile, the cost of aid grew, and willingness to assume such costs decreased in the face of growing U.S. external payments and budget deficits and the cost of the war in Vietnam.[18]

The South's political and military significance also diminished. As the strategic relationship between the United States and the Soviet Union stabilized and the superpower conflict moderated, "winning" or "losing" Third World allegiances became less important to each side. Both also discovered that it was difficult to win friendship through economic assistance. The South thus began to look less suitable as a testing ground for rival forms of political and economic organization. Proportionally greater amounts of shrinking United States aid were devoted to a few militarily strategic countries: India, South Vietnam, and Indonesia in the early 1970s, and later on Egypt, Israel, and Central America. At the same time, a shrinking share of development aid went to needy but less strategically important countries.

The link between foreign aid and foreign policy also became less important for France and the United Kingdom.[19] Although sub-Saharan Africa remained important for French prestige and economic benefit, its significance for French security disappeared, and its role in French foreign policy generally declined. Similarly, as Britain cut its military commitments east of the Suez Canal and moved toward a more Atlantic-oriented foreign policy, its political and security motivations for aid to the Commonwealth faded.

Overall aid flows stagnated as European and Japanese increases in aid flows were offset by decreases in aid from the United States, the United Kingdom, and France. Furthermore, after 1960 the South was increasingly burdened with debt service on earlier public financial flows. From 1965 to 1969, the rise in debt service payments on the official and officially guaranteed loans to eighty less-developed countries exceeded the rise in gross flows of new capital aid. As a result, the net transfer of resources fell slightly during this period.[20]

The stagnation, and in some cases decline, in aid flows also disillusioned Southern governments. A few developing countries, such as Burma, rejected aid and turned to other self-help policies.[21] Most developing countries tried to increase the amount and improve the conditions of aid by acting together to negotiate with the developed countries. In the early 1960s, they expanded their earlier coordination by forming the Group of Seventy-Seven, a united Southern bloc, to improve their bargaining position and to confront the North with common demands for changes in the international economic system (see also Chapter 7). Acting primarily in the United Nations, they sought to increase aid flows by pressing the Northern countries to transfer first 1.0 percent and then 0.7 percent of their respective GNPs to developing countries. They also proposed improvements in the terms of aid: more soft loans and grants, longer duration of loans, easing the debt burden, and ending the policy of tying aid to purchases in the donor country.[22] Finally, the Group of Seventy-Seven sought to limit Northern control by increasing the multilateral component of aid and by making aid transfers more automatic. One such proposal was to allocate newly created SDRs (Special Drawing Rights) to underdeveloped countries, IDA, or regional development banks.[23]

The strategy of Southern unity was largely unsuccessful. Although the North (with the exception of the United States) eventually agreed to transfer 0.7 percent of its GNP to developing countries, in most cases this goal was not met. The developed countries also rejected other reform proposals including the SDR-aid link.

Financial Flows in the 1970s: Politicization and Privatization

The 1970s witnessed two important developments in the North-South financial relationship: the politicization and the privatization of financial flows. On the one hand, the issue of aid flows became highly politicized as Southern countries confronted developed countries with demands for a new international economic order. At the same time, the share of aid in total flows from North to South declined due to a massive surge in private commercial bank lending to certain developing countries.

The setting for the political confrontation over aid was the commodity crises of the 1970s. The rapid increases in the price of food and oil in the early 1970s were major shocks for many developing countries, in some cases stimulating rapid growth for commodity exporters and in other cases drawing away scarce resources for vital food and energy imports. These shocks created new needs and greater demands for economic aid in the developing countries while at the same time undermining the political support for aid in the developed countries. The crises posed a major threat to Southern economies but weakened the South's ability to address the threat, because they affected the South in different ways and thereby accentuated the divisions among the developing countries.

The food crisis had its roots in postwar development strategies aimed at industrialization. Development funds were channelled to industry and agricultural prices kept low to feed the growing urban population. The resulting neglect of agriculture in many developing countries reached catastrophic proportions in the 1970s and continued to touch large areas of the Third World in the 1980s. Southern food production in the postwar era has not kept up with a rapidly expanding population.[24] In Asia, application of agricultural technology developed during the green revolution and effective government policy improved the production of wheat and rice. But South America and especially Africa, where coarse grains and starch roots remain the basic staple diet, were helped less by the green revolution. As a result, the South became dependent on the North for food imports to meet the gap between production and consumption. Imports strained the South's balance of payments, and food shortages and nutritional deficiencies became a characteristic of Southern underdevelopment.

Until the 1970s, major increases in Northern production and international food aid helped fill the supply and foreign exchange gap. But in the early seventies, a decline in Northern food production led to a sharp rise in world food prices, severe food shortages, and balance-of-payments crises for many Southern states. From 1970 to 1980, the cost of developing country imports of agricultural products rose 20 percent annually.[25] As food stocks fell and prices rose, the volume of Northern food aid was greatly reduced.

After 1975, there appeared to be improvements in the food crisis. For humane reasons and out of self-interest, the developed countries sought to improve the world's food system. After 1973, both bilateral and multilateral food aid increased, and from 1973 to 1981, overall food aid quintupled in current prices and doubled in constant prices.[26] In 1974 the International Fund for Agricultural Development (IFAD), with initial funding of $1 billion, was created to provide aid for agricultural development in the poorest countries. Overall food production in the developing countries rose and the cost of cereal imports as a percentage of export earnings dropped.[27]

The reality, however, was less promising. In much of the South, improvements in agricultural production and food aid were offset by population increases. Although Asia achieved a 21-percent increase in per capita production between 1975 and 1985, South American per capita output increased only 6.9 percent in the same period.[28] In Africa, the food crisis actually worsened in the late 1970s and 1980s because of the combination of a rapidly growing population, economic policies that discouraged food production by keeping food prices low, and poor soil management. From the early 1970s to the early 1980s, per-capita food production in Africa declined about 1.1 percent per year. As a result, Africa's food import bill rose 17 percent in 1982 to $1 billion, an amount equivalent to the total U.S. aid program in Africa.[29] A sub-Saharan crisis in 1984–1985 provoked a huge outpouring of emergency aid, but the underlying problems of inadequate agricultural production and of anti-agriculture government policies in countries did not change. Finally, the willingness of developed countries to support nonemergency food aid programs decreased.

The second crisis for the South in the 1970s was that of oil and energy. Price increases that took the cost of a barrel of oil from $1.80 in 1971 to over $35 in 1981 threatened development in countries without oil resources and caused new divisions within the South between oil exporters and importers, and between oil importers able to obtain commercial loans and those dependent on aid. The rising price of oil and oil-related products, such as petrochemical fertilizers, caused the current account deficit of LDC oil importers to increase from $11.3 billion in 1973 to $46.3 billion in 1975, and to $89.0 billion in 1980.[30] A secondary effect of the oil crisis was severe recession in the North. The resultant decrease of prices and quantities of imports from the South further aggravated the balance-of-payments crisis. Finally, even the oil exporters were not exempt from negative effects of the oil crisis. Certain countries, such as Mexico and Nigeria, mismanaged their new revenues, overborrowed while they were prosperous, and were badly hurt when oil prices eventually declined.

Middle-income oil importers financed current account deficits and maintained their growth by borrowing from private commercial banks. This borrowing from private financial markets was a major development in North-South financial flows. It marked the beginning of what seemed to be a new era for development finance but which turned out to be the onset of the developing country debt crisis.

The new borrowing of developing countries was made possible by changing policies of commercial banks. Until the late 1960s, less-developed countries, with their slow growth and bad credit records, appeared as undesirable markets for Northern banks. Thus, bank lending to the developing countries was limited primarily to short-term trade finance. In the late 1960s and early 1970s, however, many banks from the OECD countries became attracted to the profits in international markets. With rapid growth and rising exports, many developing countries appeared capable of servicing increased debt. As a result, banks were willing to expand from short-term trade finance to longer-term project lending. Interest in lending to developing countries was reinforced by the inflow of petrodollar deposits following 1973 that left banks with vast amounts of funds available for lending and only limited markets for such lending in the slowly growing developed countries. Finally, bank lending was actively encouraged by the governments of developed countries, which saw it as a mechanism for recycling (see Chapter 2).

With an ample supply of petrodollars on deposit, massive demand from the LDCs, and official encouragement from the OECD governments, bank flows to LDCs surged. Large loans were made at floating interest rates calculated as a percentage over the interbank lending rate and were syndicated or divided up among many banks. From 1973 to 1975, oil-importing developing countries' annual borrowing from private financial institutions went from $6.5 billion to $14.2 billion. By 1978, the annual flows reached $19.5 billion, and in 1981, they peaked at $35.7 billion.[31] By 1977, the total private debt of the developing countries reached $167 billion; by 1979, it had increased to $248 billion.[32]

In the 1970s, the rapid growth of bank lending did not pose a problem for developing country borrowers. Lending helped expand productive capacity and maintained growth, even after the first oil shock. From 1973 to 1980, middle-income oil importers achieved an average annual GDP growth of 5.7 percent, whereas the industrial countries' GDP grew at only 2.8 percent per year.[33] Furthermore, because developing countries' exports increased, their ability to service debt remained strong. Finally, debt service was eased by inflation, which meant that real interest rates were low or negative.

Not all countries, however, had access to private financial markets. Low-income developing countries, unable to borrow from banks, remained dependent on concessional flows. Fortunately, although overall aid flows did not rise by much after the first oil shock, flows to the low-income countries—especially from multilateral agencies and OPEC—did increase and helped offset the effects of the oil price rise (see Tables 6-1 and 6-2).

The external shocks of the 1970s proved very damaging to the prospects for development in the low-income countries and even for the maintenance of existing levels of real per-capita income. Higher oil costs combined with recession drained foreign exchange and forced a curtailment of imports necessary for development and survival. The decrease in energy consumption meant a drop in overall production and consumption, which were already precariously low. For the low-income countries, any hope for growth hinged on increasing the real value of their official development assistance (ODA).

Table 6-1 Total Net Resource Receipts of Developing Countries from All Sources, 1956–1987 ($ billion at current prices)

	1956	1964	1970	1975	1976	1977	1978	1979	1980	1981	1982	1983	1984	1985	1986	1987
I. Official Development Assistance	3.2	5.9	8.23	20.95	20.35	20.98	28.10	31.93	37.33	36.63	34.24	33.3	34.4	36.9	44.4	48.1
1. Bilateral	3.0	5.5	7.16	7.11	16.49	16.15	22.09	25.69	29.54	28.70	26.79	25.7	26.7	28.5	34.9	38.1
a) DAC countries	3.0	5.5	5.66	9.79	9.50	10.08	13.12	16.33	18.11	18.28	18.53	18.5	19.8	21.9	26.4	30.1
b) OPEC countries	—	—	0.39	5.68	5.17	4.28	6.90	6.96	8.73	7.61	5.51	3.9	3.7	3.0	3.9	3.0
c) CMEA and other donors	—	—	1.11	1.64	1.81	1.79	2.07	2.40	2.70	2.81	2.75	3.3	3.2	3.6	4.6	5.0
2. Multilateral agencies	0.2	0.4	1.07	3.84	3.87	4.83	6.01	6.24	7.79	7.93	7.45	7.6	7.7	8.4	9.5	10.0
II. Grants by private voluntary agencies	—	0.4	0.86	1.34	1.35	1.49	1.65	1.95	2.31	2.02	2.31	2.3	2.6	2.9	3.3	3.5
III. Nonconcessional flows	—	—	10.95	34.31	34.89	44.56	57.91	57.72	56.41	62.27	56.63	36.6	44.7	41.2	34.3	37.5
1. Official or officially supported	—	—	3.96	10.53	12.66	15.74	19.21	18.72	22.49	22.14	22.63	16.5	20.9	19.1	15.3	12.0
a) Export credits	—	0.4	2.68	5.62	8.13	10.28	9.92	10.58	13.58	13.34	(11.45)	7.4	7.1	4.6	(0.3)	(0.7)
b) Multilateral	—	—	0.71	2.53	2.54	2.69	3.09	4.16	4.85	5.68	(6.68)	7.2	8.2	7.9	7.7	6.8
c) Other official and private flows	—	—	0.57	2.38	1.99	2.81	4.2	3.98	4.06	3.12	(4.5)	1.9	5.6	6.6	7.9	5.9
2. Private	2.5	2.3	6.99	23.78	22.23	28.82	38.70	39.00	33.92	47.13	34.0	20.1	23.8	22.1	19.0	25.5
a) Direct investment	2.5	1.7	3.69	11.36	8.31	9.82	11.59	13.42	10.54	16.13	(11.00)	9.9	11.4	6.7	12.2	20.0
b) Bank sector	—	0.5	3.00	12.00	12.70	15.80	23.2	24.9	22.00	29.00	21.00	9.1	11.4	10.6	5.2	5.0
c) Bonds lending	—	—	0.30	0.42	1.22	3.20	3.91	0.68	1.38	2.00	2.00	1.1	1.0	4.8	1.6	0.5
Total receipts (I + II + III)	5.7	8.6	20.04	56.60	56.59	67.03	87.66	91.60	96.05	107.92	93.18	72.2	81.7	81.0	82.0	89.1

Source: Organization for Economic Cooperation and Development, *Development Co-operation*, various years (Paris: OECD, various years).

Table 6-2   Total Resource Flows to Developing Countries by Major Types of Flow, 1950–1987 (percentage shares of long-term total flows)

	1950–55	1960–61	1970	1975	1980	1983	1984	1985	1986	1987
I. Official Development Finance (ODF)	52.5	60.9	48.1	46.0	49.1	48.7	56.5	60.7	65.2	66.5
1. Official Development Assistance (ODA)	52.5	55.9	41.8	37.3	38.4	35.9	41.9	45.7	52.3	53.9
A. Bilateral	52.5	53.6	36.5	30.5	30.6	27.8	32.0	35.2	41.1	42.8
a) OECD countries	52.5	45.8	27.9	17.2	19.0	19.8	23.7	27.6	31.3	NA
b) OPEC countries	—	—	1.9	10.0	2.6	4.6	4.4	2.9	4.4	NA
c) CMEA countries	NA	5.2	4.9	2.6	2.6	3.1	3.5	4.4	4.9	NA
d) Other countries	NA	2.6	1.8	0.7	0.3	0.3	0.5	0.3	0.4	NA
B. Multilateral	NA	2.3	5.3	6.8	7.8	8.0	9.9	10.5	11.3	11.1
2. Other ODF	NA	5.0	6.3	8.6	10.7	13.0	14.6	15.0	12.9	12.6
Of which: Bilateral	NA	2.7	2.8	4.2	5.9	5.3	5.8	5.0	3.6	4.9
Multilateral	NA	2.3	3.5	4.4	4.8	7.7	8.8	9.9	9.3	7.6
II. Total export credits (official and private)	NA	14.0	13.2	10.1	13.6	8.0	8.8	1.5	2.4	−0.8
III. Private flows (excluding export credits)	47.5[1]	25.1	38.7	44.2	37.2	43.1	34.6	37.7	32.4	34.3
1. Direct investment	NA	18.8	18.2	20.0	10.5	8.3	11.2	9.8	14.1	22.5
2. Bank sector	NA	6.3	14.8	21.1	23.0	31.8	20.0	17.2	6.0	5.6
3. Bond lending	NA	—	1.5	0.7	1.4	0.5	0.6	5.7	4.2	0.6
4. Other private	NA	—	4.2	2.4	2.3	2.5	2.9	5.0	8.2	5.6
Of which: Nongovernmental organizations	NA	—	4.2	2.4	2.3	2.5	2.9	3.9	3.9	3.9
Total resource flows (I + II + III)	100.0	100.0	100.0	100.0	100.0	100.0	100.0	100.0	100.0	100.0

[1]All nonconcessional flows, including export credits and official nonconcessional aid.

Source: OECD, Twenty-five Years of Development Co-operation: A Review (Paris: OECD, 1985), p. 165 and OECD, Development Co-operation reports of 1986, p. 48; 1987, p. 46; and 1988, p. 47.

In the face of these crises, the South sought to increase public financial flows to the developing countries and to make those flows more automatic. The major strategy of the 1970s was Southern unity and confrontation. In the 1960s, the developing countries had tried with little success to increase their bargaining strength and obtain greater concessions from the North by acting as a block in negotiating with the developed countries. With the onset of the oil crisis of the 1970s, the South felt that it had obtained new leverage in negotiating with the North and tried to use that leverage to obtain a variety of structural changes, including more aid on better terms.

Ironically, the action of the oil-producing states—which posed a severe threat to the South—also served as a force for Southern unity and cooperation. One effect was psychological. The ability of a unified OPEC (Organization of Petroleum Exporting Countries) to attain significant rewards from the North demonstrated the potential effectiveness of Southern unity in bargaining with the North. It also created, at least temporarily, a sense of Southern solidarity.

The oil crisis, too, held out the hope of a new bargaining chip for the South. The oil-producing countries could hurt the North by withholding petroleum or raising prices, or they could offer the North inducements such as energy agreements or an energy dialogue. If the oil-producing states remained part of the Southern bloc, then the oil stick or the oil carrot could be linked to demands for systemic reform, and the balance of power could be altered. Some oil-producing states, especially Venezuela and Algeria, encouraged the linkage of Southern development demands with raw materials threats or inducements. However, others, in particular the Gulf states, played little or no role in the Southern group and had no interest in using their oil weapon for broader purposes.

In the heady days following OPEC's initial success, the South boldly tried to force systemic reform on the North. In the spring of 1974, the Group of Seventy-Seven issued a call for a new international economic order that included changing the system of financial flows (see Chapter 7). The Declaration and Action Programme on a New International Economic Order (NIEO) called for a link between SDR allocation and development finance, the implementation of the 0.7-percent-of-GNP goal for industrial country foreign aid established by the United Nations, and greater participation by the less-developed countries in IBRD, IDA, and IMF decision making.[34] Throughout the 1970s, the developing countries consistently urged the realization of the new international economic order in their multilateral negotiations with the developed countries.

The North, itself a victim of the energy and recession crises, firmly resisted the South's efforts to create the New International Economic Order. Southern stridency and Northern resistance increased the contentiousness of relations in this period. The South was able to force the North to discuss the concept of reform at the United Nations and other multilateral forums, but it was not able to make the North actually negotiate for systemic change, nor was the South able to play its oil card to force the North to respond. The OPEC countries, in the end, were not willing to link the price and availability of oil to the NIEO.

Because of Southern pressure and the Northern desire to alleviate the crises of the 1970s, however, there was some improvement in financial flows, especially multilateral flows, to the South. As has been noted, food aid increased. The IMF was also gradually adapted to respond to the developing countries' problems. Several temporary mechanisms were created to deal with balance-of-payments crises following the two oil shocks: an oil facility was created in 1974 to finance the payments deficits caused by the increase in petroleum prices; a trust fund was financed by the sale of IMF gold; the Supplementary Finance Facility was created in 1979 to help alleviate serious payments imbalances; and an enlarged access policy allowed countries with protracted and structural balance-of-payments problems to borrow larger percentages of their quotas. There were also permanent changes in the IMF that benefited the developing countries: the Extended Fund Facility was created in 1974 to make money available for longer periods and in larger amounts than the usual IMF drawings, and the Compensatory Finance Facility, which helps countries suffering from severe drops in primary commodity prices, was enlarged and extended to cover cereal imports.[35]

As the United States and other developed countries gave increasing emphasis to multilateral aid, the World Bank also expanded in the 1970s. In addition to its traditional support for infrastructure projects, the bank began to make loans for basic human needs projects, including the development of subsistence farming, minimally adequate housing, and rudimentary health care.[36] In the late 1970s, the bank increased its lending for energy development. In response to the second oil crisis, it launched structural adjustment lending, a form of medium-term balance-of-payments support to enable countries to adapt the structure of production to prevailing world conditions, especially to changes in the cost of energy and food.[37] Finally, the bank sought to promote commercial lending to developing countries through cofinancing: mixed projects combining private and World Bank funding.[38]

Another success of the 1970s was the ability of the oil-importing developing countries to obtain aid from the new rich, the oil producers. Throughout the 1970s, the attempt to obtain aid from the oil exporters was an important and successful strategy of the South. Significant OPEC financial flows explain in part Southern acquiescence to the increase in oil prices that devastated their economies. The old poor appealed to the new rich on the basis of Third World solidarity, and their history of common action and shared problems made the oil producers receptive to some of the South's demands. In the 1970s, because major oil producers were unable to absorb their new wealth, they found it relatively easy to assist in development finance. During that time, the North also looked to the oil producers for development finance. New IMF facilities and IFAD, for example, were based in part on financing by OPEC members.

Although the South was unable to achieve its vision of a new international economic order based in part on increased aid flows and significant changes in decision making, there were important changes in financial flows during the 1970s: greater concessional flows to the low-income developing countries; more multilateral aid; and a new source of aid from OPEC.

The Impact of Financial Flows

By the early 1980s, after a quarter century of concessional flows, it was possible to assess the impact of foreign aid.[39] From an economic standpoint, the reviews were mixed but positive.

Overall growth of developing countries was significant. As a group, they achieved an average annual growth rate of GDP of 6.1 percent between 1965 and 1980 and 3.8 percent between 1980 and 1986, compared with 3.6 percent and 2.5 percent for the industrial market economies during the same periods.[40] However, in per-capita terms, this growth was less dramatic. From 1965 to 1986, per-capita GNP rose at an annual rate of 2.9 percent in the less-developed countries versus 2.3 percent in the industrialized countries.[41] Growth also aggravated the unequal distribution of income in much of the South, where national income remained or became even more concentrated in the hands of a few. In general, measures of income distribution within noncommunist developing countries worsened between 1960 and 1980.[42]

Growth rates were also very uneven, leading to greater differentiation among developing countries. One group, the newly industrializing countries (NICs), experienced phenomenal growth and became important players on the world economic stage. A number of factors, including foreign aid, led to self-sustaining growth in the four "Asian tigers"—South Korea, Taiwan, Hong Kong, and Singapore—and in Mexico and Brazil. By the 1970s, these countries "graduated" from concessional flows and were able to tap private capital markets. Another set of upper-middle-income countries that bridged the development gap was the oil-exporting countries. Other LDCs, most notably China and India, which account for two-thirds of the population of the developing countries, had important successes in the fields of food self-sufficiency and growth. These and other middle-income countries maintained fairly strong growth rates.[43]

Other developing countries, however, including many African nations and others such as Burma, Bangladesh, and Haiti, experienced no growth during this period or even found themselves worse off. These least-developed countries (LDCs) were the hardest hit by the commodity crises especially in food and energy. Furthermore, they had no access to commercial credit, which made them almost completely dependent on aid.

In absolute terms, there is still a tremendous gap between rich and poor. In 1986, GNP per capita in the industrial market economies was $12,960; but in the developing countries it was only $610.[44] Nonetheless, by the early 1980s, standards of living had improved universally. Importantly, life expectancy increased and infant mortality decreased significantly. Moreover, the proportion of people living in absolute poverty in noncommunist developing countries decreased by a third between 1960 and 1980.[45] Unfortunately, as we shall see, the crises of the 1980s halted, or even reversed, that process.

Aid was only one of many factors that produced these results. Concessional flows seem to have made a positive contribution to GNP growth, but their role is difficult to quantify. Although aggregate data show little or no correlation between aid and growth for developing countries as a whole, individual country studies show clearer correlations. It appears that aid can add significantly to growth in individual countries, particularly when accompanied by other sensible development policies. One study estimates that reasonable amounts of aid used reasonably efficiently can add 0.6 percent to 1.5 percent to the annual growth rate of a developing country.[46]. On the other hand, aid is ineffective when applied through misguided donor or recipient programs or when other structural domestic barriers counteract its effect.

Aid definitely contributed to growth in certain countries such as Pakistan, South Korea, and Taiwan, which received massive aid inflows. Even in these cases, however, aid was important because of other factors such as effective private initiatives.[47] On the other hand, in some countries, such as Mexico and Thailand, growth took place without significant aid.[48] Finally, there are cases of countries such as Bangladesh that received foreign aid, but whose growth rates were still far below average.

Quality of life, including health, would certainly be worse in most developing countries had it not been for substantial medical and poverty-alleviation aid. In many cases, aid has been responsible for real increases in health and welfare. Unfortunately, in some cases aid has merely prevented bad situations from becoming worse.

In general, aid strategies have improved as practitioners have learned more about development. Many disappointing episodes in the early days resulted in later, more sophisticated, realistic, and carefully planned strategies. For example, the early efforts at rapid industrialization were replaced by greater recognition of the role of agriculture in development. Early emphasis on aggregate growth was tempered by concern for poverty alleviation, meeting basic human needs, and equity. At the same time, individual project lending was supplemented with comprehensive structural lending, and greater emphasis on free-market solutions. Most recently, planners have recognized the importance of analyzing the environmental impact of new projects.[49]

Finally, aid has had a political, as well as an economic, impact. The aid policies of most Northern states have reinforced their economic links with recipient countries and occasionally have given them extra leverage in their relations with the South. The United States, for example, has used aid to discourage the expropriation of existing investment. The Foreign Assistance Act provides that U.S. aid must be withheld in the event of nationalization or expropriation without prompt, adequate, and effective compensation. Many donor countries have also encouraged new foreign investment by providing information, sharing the costs of investment surveys, and guaranteeing such investment against risk. Aid also supports trade links by encouraging the use of donor goods, especially through tied aid, and discouraging the development in some cases of competing industry.[50]

Aid is frequently used to influence economic policies in recipient countries. The United States, for example, places economic conditions on aid that shape monetary and fiscal policy, investment policy, and international economic policy, such as exchange rate and nationalization policy. Through the supervision of aid projects, the aid bureaucracies in all countries have become involved in decision making in recipient countries. Such economic influence occurs in multilateral aid programs as well. The World Bank, for example, has used its aid to promote market-oriented reforms in developing countries.[51]

Aid can also be used to support the preferred internal and external policies of the recipient governments. The United States, for example, has given emergency support in economic crises to the Philippines in 1987 and to Mexico in 1982 and 1988. Also, the withdrawal or threatened withdrawal of aid has been used to express disapproval of or opposition to internal and external policies. The United States withheld aid from Haiti in 1987 and from Panama in 1988. And, reflecting the political/security focus of the U.S. foreign aid program, assistance has been used to promote foreign policies, such as granting basic rights and supporting countries in conflict with the Soviet Union (for example, Pakistan).[52]

Aid has not always enhanced the North's bargaining power. The degree of Northern dominance through aid varied not only in some "objective" measurement of Northern influence but also in the eye of the beholder. Donors often felt that aid was given for altruistic reasons and without political strings; alternatively, donors often felt that aid was given for political reasons but that its effect was nil or even counterproductive. The recipients, on the other hand, often felt that aid constituted not influence but intervention in national policy.[53]

The Aid and Debt Crises of the 1980s

While the promise of public and private financial flows was great at the end of the 1970s, that promise had turned sour by the mid-1980s. The combination of recession and new conservative governments in the North increased the focus on nonconcessional flows and private market solutions and decreased the flow of aid. World economic crises turned private bank flows into the debt crisis. As a result, total financial flows to developing countries (concessional and commercial) fell greatly.

Two external shocks hit the developing countries between 1979 and 1981. First, the second oil crisis of 1979 caused a surge in the price of oil to a high of $35 in 1981 (see Chapter 9). Second, anti-inflationary policies in the developed countries and a steep recession (see Chapter 2) caused a precipitous drop in commodity prices and an adverse shift in the LDCs' terms of trade (see Chapter 7). Although a handful of developing countries were able to increase their exports of manufactured products to the North, demand for most of the South's products stagnated. The industrial recession also intensified protectionist pressures that further limited the export of manufactured goods. At the same time, the rise in the value of the dollar reduced commodity prices and increased the cost of many LDC imports denominated in dollars. Anti-inflationary policies combined with fiscal deficits in the developed countries led to unprecedented high interest rates and a resultant rise in the debt burden. Finally, these international shocks were aggravated by inappropriate domestic economic policies in many of the LDCs, especially increased government spending that exacerbated fiscal deficits.

The effects of these shocks were an increase in the trade deficit of developing countries from $22.2 billion in 1979 to $91.6 billion in 1981; increases in interest payments frm $24.3 billion in 1979 to $41.8 billion in 1981; and a current account deficit that rose from $31.3 billion in 1979 to $118.6 in 1981. By 1981, interest payments almost offset new private lending. By 1982, when the debt crisis struck, interest payments exceeded new lending by $3.5 billion.[54]

With recession, domestic political opposition to foreign aid expenditures grew in the North. At a time of domestic unemployment and—at least in the United States—a cutback in domestic welfare programs, increased or even constant expenditures on foreign aid were politically impossible. Opposition to foreign aid was reinforced by an ideological challenge to economic aid as a route to development and a tool of foreign policy. Conservative governments elected to power in the 1980s in the United States and the United Kingdom argued that foreign aid had only a limited role to play in the development process. According to the view of the Reagan and Thatcher governments, economic recovery and development in both the developed and the developing countries had to be based on a return to free-market principles. The developing countries above all had to provide incentives and commercial opportunities for private enterprise, both domestic and foreign. Economic aid would be limited in amount, would not compete with private efforts, and would have as its main purpose the support of private enterprise and free markets. According to this view, much foreign aid—especially aid from multilateral institutions—did not meet these criteria.

In the 1980s, foreign economic aid also lost much of its political rationale, at least for the United States. With a strong East-West defense orientation, the Reagan administration was more interested in increasing its defense budget, in offering military assistance instead of foreign aid for development, and in granting bilateral rather than multilateral aid.

From 1980 to 1983, these economic and political changes led to another decline in multilateral aid, although levels still remained higher than in the late 1970s. The United States reduced its contributions to the International Development Association (IDA), cut back on its commitment to IFAD, resisted capital increases in the World Bank, and dragged its heels on increasing IMF quotas. The United States also pushed for changes in the use of multilateral aid. It vetoed projects such as energy funding which, it contended, were commercially viable. It argued that countries like India and China should not benefit from concessional funds because they could go to private markets for capital. Finally, the United States sought to attach conditions to aid flows so that they would promote private enterprise and investment capital. The United Kingdom under Prime Minister Thatcher also decreased its official development assistance by almost 38 percent during this period, both bilaterally and multilaterally.

As a result of the recession's pressures, aid from the OECD countries actually fell from $27.3 billion in 1980 to $25.6 billion in 1981, before rebounding in 1982 to $27.9 billion. From 1980 to 1981, U.S. aid fell from $7.1 billion to $5.8 billion, then rose in 1982 to $8.3 billion. In constant prices, however, OECD and U.S. aid continued to decline.[55]

While overall aid stagnated, bilateral aid became increasingly defense oriented instead of development oriented. In 1973, 22 percent of U.S. bilateral aid was for political/strategic purposes, and 78 percent was for development. By 1985, 67 percent of the total was for political/strategic purposes, and 33 percent was for development assistance.[56] The changing political economy of oil (see Chapter 9) also undermined OPEC's interest in aid transfers. Beginning in 1980, OPEC aid decreased in absolute amounts, as a percentage of GNP, and as a percentage of total official development assistance. From 1980 to 1985, total OPEC aid fell by more than 50 percent, from $8.7 billion to $3.0 billion (see Table 6–1).

By the mid- to late-1980s, however, some concessional aid was restored. New surplus countries, such as Japan, began extending more aid to the developing countries. As Japan's trade and financial surplus soared, it came under pressure from the United States to recycle those surpluses in part to developing countries. The United States saw this as a way to alleviate pressures on the United States for aid flows. At the same time, Japanese leaders sought to define a greater world role for Japan. They perceived that leadership in the Third World was a role that Japan could assume without threatening the United States and without taking on military responsibilities forbidden under Japan's constitution and unacceptable to the Japanese public. Thus, Japanese aid increased significantly, from $3.1 billion in 1981 to $5.6 billion in 1986, terms were eased, and the scope of recipients broadened. In 1987, Japan announced that it planned to recycle $20 billion (in addition to $10 billion it had previously pledged) to these countries through bilateral loan programs and multilateral institutions. By 1988, over 70 percent of these funds had been committed.[57]

Despite budgetary problems, the United States became more receptive to the need for some concessional flows in particularly hard-hit areas such as sub-Saharan Africa and also as a means of promoting "growth with adjustment" as a way out of the debt crisis under the Baker Plan. Following the announcement of the Baker Plan in 1985, the United States approved a $75 billion increase in the World Bank's authorized capital; agreed to fund a new World Bank agency, the Multilateral Investment Guarantee Agency (MIGA), to insure foreign direct investment in developing countries; and provided new funds for the concessional lending arm of the World Bank, the International Development Agency (IDA). However, the lopsided distribution of United States aid to strategic countries was not changed.

The Onset of the Debt Crisis

Private flows changed dramatically in the 1980s. The rise in the price of oil (see Chapter 9), combined with restrictive monetary policies in the major industrial countries, led to record-high real interest rates and world recession. As a result, the LDC debtor nations faced declining terms of trade—plunging commodity prices and a threefold increase in the price of oil—and falling export volumes.

By 1982, external LDC debt was 264 percent above 1975 levels. The highly indebted countries, consisting of (in order of exposure), Brazil, Mexico, Argentina, Venezuela, Nigeria, Philippines, Yugoslavia, Morocco, Chile, Peru, Colombia, Ivory Coast, Ecuador, Bolivia, Costa Rica, Jamaica, and Uruguay, by 1982 had outstanding debt 305 percent higher than in 1975 (see Table 6-3 and Figure 6-1). Borrowing from private commercial sources accounted for an ever greater portion of total debt (see Figure 6-1), rising from 60 percent of the highly indebted countries' debt in 1975 to 76 percent by 1982 (see Table 6-3).

Because of rising interest rates, developing countries also faced sharp

Figure 6-1   Debt Outstanding for All Debtor Countries

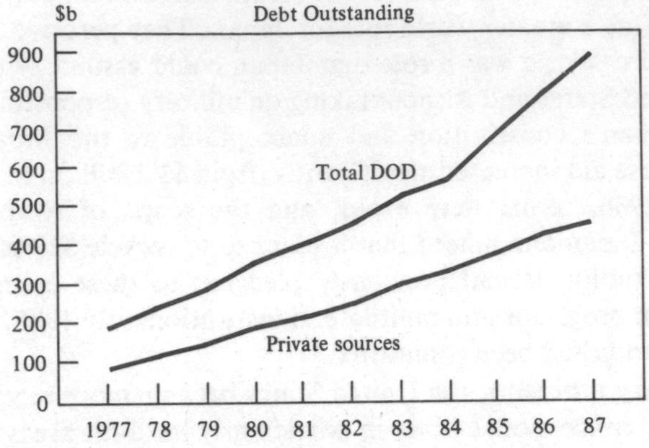

SOURCE: World Bank, *World Debt Tables, 1988* (Washington, D. C.: World Bank, 1988), p. 5.

increases in the cost of servicing their greatly increased debt. By 1982, the debt service ratio, measured by the dollar value of interest and principal amortization payments as a percentage of the dollar value of exports, rose to 21 percent for all debtors and to 38.8 percent for the highly indebted countries (see Table 6-4).

Before 1979 borrowing had been for relatively long terms of three to five years. But as lenders became cautious in 1979 to 1981, they turned increasingly to short-term credits, which made the borrowers much more vulnerable to a change in the lenders' willingness to continue the flows. Significantly, in many, although not all, cases, this new lending was used for consumption, not for increases in productive capacity. In some countries, including Argentina, Venezuela, and Mexico, some lending was dissipated in capital flight.

A few critics warned of danger. But the ease of adjustment in the 1970s to increased lending to developing countries, inaccurate predictions about world recovery and declining interest rates, plus the system's ability to manage earlier debt reschedulings with no lasting consequences for the international system, led to complacency on the part of bankers and government officials in both the developed and less-developed countries. The system was set for crisis.

The first signs of the increasingly fragile structure of international debt came in 1981 and early 1982. Argentina's decision to suspend payments on its $37 billion in external debt following its defeat by Great Britain in the 1982 Falklands war lowered confidence in the capital markets, which responded by shortening maturities and demanding repayment of some short-term obligations. A number of countries found themselves in a severe liquidity squeeze.

Table 6-3 Highly Indebted Countries (U.S. $ millions)

	1970	1975	1980	1981	1982	1983	1984	1985	1986	1987
SUMMARY DEBT DATA										
Debt Stocks (EDT)	—	—	288,925	350,588	391,234	421,923	438,080	453,398	481,538	527,296
Long-Term Debt	31,448	76,640	205,396	246,209	278,973	334,403	358,168	377,606	420,798	457,808
Public and Publicly Guaranteed	17,923	49,510	148,215	171,164	200,721	250,080	278,707	307,580	360,391	402,171
Private Nonguaranteed	13,525	27,130	57,181	75,045	78,252	84,323	79,460	70,025	60,407	55,636
Use of IMF Credit	201	1,251	2,988	4,111	6,221	12,287	14,692	18,305	20,129	21,830
Short-Term Debt	—	—	80,541	100,267	106,040	75,233	65,221	58,027	40,611	47,658
PUBLIC AND PUBLICLY GUARANTEED LONG-TERM DEBT BY SOURCE										
Debt Outstanding Including Undisbursed	23,778	66,702	188,466	221,245	253,446	302,033	326,357	351,199	403,514	451,442
Official Creditors	13,550	29,932	61,651	71,033	79,150	88,657	93,101	107,907	132,199	162,481
Multilateral	5,629	13,849	32,174	38,049	44,010	48,984	49,614	58,508	71,576	85,377
IBRD	4,249	9,444	21,274	25,385	28,743	33,268	31,451	37,867	47,032	57,631
IDA	147	285	412	409	406	402	398	386	449	545
Bilateral	7,921	16,083	29,477	32,984	35,140	39,673	43,487	49,399	60,623	77,103
Private Creditors	10,228	36,771	126,815	150,212	174,296	213,376	233,256	243,292	271,315	288,961
Suppliers	3,955	7,163	11,294	13,001	12,770	12,616	11,281	12,832	13,720	13,980
Financial Markets	5,779	28,483	115,042	136,847	161,234	200,544	221,816	230,332	257,488	274,895

SOURCE: World Bank, *World Debt Tables, 1988* (Washington, D.C.: World Bank), p. 30.

Table 6-4   Debt Indicators in Developing Countries, 1975–1987 (percent)

Country Group and Debt Indicator	1975	1980	1981	1982	1983	1984	1985	1986	1987[1]
All Developing Countries									
Debt service ratio	13.7	16.2	17.9	21.0	19.7	19.5	21.8	22.6	21.0
Debt-GNP ratio	15.7	20.7	22.4	26.3	31.4	33.0	35.9	38.5	37.6
Highly Indebted Countries									
Debt service ratio	24.0	27.1	30.7	38.8	34.7	33.4	33.9	37.7	32.7
Debt-GNP ratio	18.1	23.3	25.6	32.4	45.4	47.5	49.5	54.1	55.9
Low-income Africa									
Debt service ratio	10.2	13.6	14.6	14.2	14.2	15.1	17.9	19.9	34.7
Debt-GNP ratio	25.2	39.8	44.2	48.0	55.1	62.0	68.9	72.1	76.2

Notes: Data are based on a sample of ninety developing countries. The debt service ratio is defined as the dollar value of external debt payments (interest and amortization) on medium- and long-term loans expressed as a percentage of the dollar value of exports of goods and services. The debt-GNP ratio is defined as the dollar value of outstanding medium- and long-term debt expressed as a percentage of dollar GNP.
[1]Estimated. Ratios do not assume further buildup of arrears. This accounts for the sharp increase in the debt service ratio for low-income Africa in 1987.
SOURCE: World Bank, *World Development Report 1988* (New York: Oxford University Press, 1988), p. 31.

The trigger for the debt crisis was Mexico's announcement in August 1982 of its inability to service its foreign debt. Mexico's ambitious growth policies had resulted in an overheated and increasingly inflationary economy and surging budget deficits. The weakening world oil market (see Chapter 9) reduced the value of Mexico's oil exports, which comprised three-fourths of its total export earnings; higher interest rates and growing debt drove up the annual cost of debt service; the greatly overvalued peso led to a surge in Mexico's imports; and the situation was aggravated by capital flight.[58] An upcoming presidential election made the government particularly unwilling to take far-reaching measures to avert a crisis. One month after the July 1982 election, a financial panic erupted.

The Mexican debt crisis posed a major challenge to the world's financial system. Until 1982, external debt problems like Mexico's had been rare and had generally involved relatively small amounts of commercial bank borrowings. By contrast, Mexico's external debt totaled more than $85 billion and included loans that accounted for a significant percentage of the capital of the largest U.S. banks in 1982. Moreover, Mexico was just the tip of the iceberg. At the end of 1982, loans to Argentina, Brazil, Mexico, Venezuela, and Chile alone amounted to over $260 billion. Brazil by itself had borrowed $91 billion.[59] The world's major private banks, especially U.S. banks, had significant exposure in these countries (see Table 6–5).

In the developed countries, the LDC debt crisis was treated primarily as

SOURCE: IBCA Banking Analysis; cited in *Financial Times*, January 5, 1989, p. 15.

Table 6-5   World's Top 100 Banks

	1982 ($bn)	1987 ($bn)
Net profits	16	30*
Equity capital	146	300
South American and Mexican exposures	182	237
Bank provisions	0	65
Net exposures/equity (%)	125	57

*estimated

a threat to the international financial system. Defaults by debtor nations could have led to a collapse of confidence in the international banking system, possible illiquidity or insolvency of the banks, dangerous disruption of the financial markets, and, in a worst-case scenario, world recession or depression.[60] As a Federal Reserve Bank study later put it: "International bankers and policy makers faced a threat of financial disorder on a global scale not seen since the Depression."[61] Central bankers, finance ministers, and heads of government, determined to prevent any such danger to the international financial system, cooperated to manage the crisis. The United States played an important leadership role in mobilizing international management. In the process, the central banks and the IMF also assumed significant roles.

Within two days of the 1982 crisis, the United States forwarded to Mexico $2 billion in prepayments for oil and in credits for the purchase of U.S. agricultural products. It also helped arrange a $1 billion bridging loan from a group of central banks acting through the BIS. The principal foreign creditor banks agreed to postpone debt service fees for three months. Under pressure from the United States, Mexico and the IMF began negotiations for a longer-term arrangement. Thus, the immediate crisis was averted.

In November 1982, Mexico and the IMF reached an accord. In exchange for $3.84 billion in IMF credits between 1983 and 1985, Mexican authorities agreed to carry out a strict austerity program that included reducing the budget deficit, limiting public sector external borrowing, and reducing or eliminating subsidies and public works projects. Significantly, the IMF refused to conclude its agreement until the commercial banks agreed to lend an additional $5 billion to Mexico. This was the first time that the IMF insisted on large complementary financing from banks as an essential element of an IMF lending agreement. At the same time, the Mexican government, acting on behalf of all Mexican borrowers and its private creditors, agreed to begin negotiations to postpone debt repayments and lengthen repayment timetables.[62]

As bank lending to developing countries abruptly halted after August 1982, the debt crisis spread rapidly through Latin America and the rest of the developing world. By December 1982, Brazil, with $91 billion in foreign debt, was in trouble. By the end of 1983, Brazil, almost all the other Latin American countries, and a number of African countries had rescheduled their debts.[63] By the end of 1983, more than twenty-five countries around the world, with a combined outstanding bank debt of more than $200 billion, had gone into arrears.

Debt Crisis Management

Mexico became the model for managing these debt crises. Each country was handled separately as its debts came due or as it fell into arrears, according to what came to be called the case-by-case approach. Although the process thus varied from country to country, a pattern of crisis management emerged. The debt problem was handled as a temporary liquidity problem that could be managed through domestic austerity programs, rescheduling debt payments, and some new lending. The key elements of debt management became negotiation of a loan from and an economic stabilization agreement with the IMF, debt rescheduling with commercial banks, and new public and private lending.

Reaching agreement with the IMF on a loan and a domestic austerity program—a condition of IMF borrowing—became a central part of debt rescheduling. Although its loans were small compared with total indebtedness, the IMF provided a vehicle for imposing and surveying national economic policies deemed necessary for debt repayment. The IMF could hold up its lending and all rescheduling if a debtor did not agree to certain policies. It could also hold up disbursements of monies if a country did not meet agreed-upon economic commitments.

In this first period of the debt crisis from 1982 to 1984, IMF economic programs focussed on austerity policies. Budget deficits were to be reduced through spending restraint, reduced subsidies, and higher taxes. External imbalances were to be improved by slowing domestic demand, raising the volume of exports, and cutting the prices of tradeable products. Inflation was to be controlled by tight monetary policy, competitive exchange rates, positive real interest rates, limits on wage increases, and fiscal austerity. These changes were expected to enable debtor countries to overcome what was seen as a temporary liquidity problem, so they could service their debts and return to normal access to commercial credit markets.

A second central element of debt rescheduling was an agreement between creditor banks and the debtor government. The banks were represented by an advisory committee, a group of lead banks with significant financial exposure in the country, which had to reach agreements not only with the debtor but also with other smaller creditor banks. The debtor government represented all domestic debtors. Negotiations focused on new terms and conditions of outstanding medium- and long-term loans. Short-term trade credits by and large were serviced and not rescheduled, while other short-term loans were rescheduled in many cases. Repayment schedules were extended, grace periods given on principal repayment, and rates adjusted. But debtors were always expected to service debts fully, and no debt relief such as reduction of interest or principal was provided.

Creditor banks were also expected to provide new financing for debtor countries. The commitment of new lending by creditor banks to a debt-plagued country became an essential element of any debt-rescheduling package. Central banks and the IMF became deeply involved in pressing creditors to continue lending to debtor countries. Indeed, in what has been called coerced lending, the central banks and the IMF virtually required private banks to commit additional funds to debtor countries, according to a quota allocation system based on each bank's exposure in the country.[64]

Finally, creditor governments, whose various credit-granting institutions, such as export credit agencies, had outstanding loans to debtor countries, themselves had to reschedule. This was done through the Paris Club of government creditors, which negotiated as a group with debtor countries. The Paris Club handled virtually all debt rescheduling for poorer debtors such as those in Africa that were never able to borrow significantly from commercial banks and whose debt was owed mostly to government entities.[65]

From 1982 to 1984, the strategy of debt management through austerity, rescheduling, and new lending seemed to work. Cooperation among key parties in developing a system of crisis management averted the feared world financial crisis. Through the IMF, concerted lending by commercial banks, and ongoing trade finance, monies continued to flow to debtor countries, enabling them to make interest payments to banks. Debtors, following IMF-imposed policies, reduced their budget deficits by cutting back on public and private investment. For the heavily indebted countries, the rate of growth in investment was minimal in 1981 at only 0.4 percent and fell by 13.1 percent in 1982, 21 percent in 1983, and by 2.1 percent in 1984. In the same period, real growth in imports, including capital equipment for development projects or parts for manufactured products for export, grew at a rate of 2.3 percent in 1981, then fell by 14.1 in 1982, by 20.4 in 1983, and by 1.1 percent in 1984 (see Table 6–6). Largely by restraining imports, the major debtors generated large trade surpluses that brought them close to current account balance. For example, by suppressing domestic demand and encouraging nonoil exports, Mexico went from a $7 billion deficit on current account in 1982 to a $5 billion surplus in 1983. Brazil's trade surplus increased from $800 million in 1982 to $6.5 billion in 1983 and in 1984 even higher exports led to a small current account surplus.[66]

Following the initial crises, some improvements were made in the debt

Table 6-6 Highly Indebted Countries and the World Economy, 1980–1988

	1980	1981	1982	1983	1984	1985	1986	1987	1988[1]
					PERCENTAGE REAL CHANGE				
Economic Growth Indicators									
Industrial Country Output	1.3	2.0	−0.4	2.8	4.5	3.1	2.7	3.3	3.9
World Trade[2]	1.3	2.4	−1.0	3.0	9.9	4.0	2.6	4.3	7.5
HIC GDP[3]	5.6	0.6	−0.4	−2.9	1.9	3.7	3.4	1.7	2.0
HIC Investment[3]	9.4	0.4	−13.1	−21.0	−2.1	4.5	1.9	0.8	−2.9
HIC per Capita Consumption[3]	3.4	0.3	−2.2	−4.1	−1.7	0.2	2.6	−1.4	−0.6
HIC Exports[3]	1.1	−6.6	0.0	5.0	9.3	2.2	0.7	0.4	6.4
HiC Imports[3]	8.2	2.3	−14.1	−20.4	−1.1	−1.6	4.0	−1.7	2.0
					U.S. $ BILLIONS				
Total External Debt	289.0	351.0	391.0	422.0	438.0	454.0	482.0	527.0	529.0
Net Flows to HICs	28.6	43.7	34.6	19.1	13.3	6.0	4.5	6.2	7.6
Net Resource Transfers to HICs	8.8	18.3	3.7	−9.9	−19.9	−26.5	−25.8	−21.8	−31.1

[1]Preliminary estimates.
[2]Volume.
[3]Constant 1980 U.S. dollars.
SOURCE: World Bank, *World Debt Tables* (Washington, D.C.: World Bank, 1988), p. xvii.

management system. Initially, debt reschedulings covered only one year, so frequent reschedulings became regular events. In 1984, Mexico and its creditors reached the first multiyear rescheduling agreement (MYRA), which lasted four years, provided for a fourteen-year final maturity, lower interest rates, monitored by the banks of Mexico's economic performance over the long term, and the banks' right to refuse to proceed with a second phase of rescheduling if Mexico did not meet its economic targets. The Mexican agreement became a model for other MYRAs.

The creditor governments also ensured that the IMF had adequate resources to continue its crisis management role. Not surprisingly, the debt crisis placed serious financial strains on the Fund and decreased its resources. In 1983, members agreed to increase IMF quotas by almost fifty percent. At the same time, the Group of Ten agreed to increase the General Arrangements to Borrow (GAB) and to allow IMF members other than the Group of Ten access to GAB credits if their problems seriously threatened the international monetary system.[67] Finally, the breathing room created by debt management gave creditor banks time to reduce their exposure to developing country debtors by increasing their capital and restraining further lending to LDCs.

Despite these successes, the first phase of debt management neither resolved the debt problem nor brought it under adequate long-term control. Indeed, the strategy actually undermined the long-term ability of the indebted countries to service their debts. Austerity policies, which dramatically reduced domestic demand and imports, also brought growth to a halt. Cutbacks in investment and imports removed catalysts for growth. Devaluations designed to improve balance-of-payments adjustment made it more costly in local currency to service external debt and aggravated the fiscal problems of the government, which had to purchase foreign exchange for debt service.

A few debtor countries—particularly Korea and Turkey—made quick structural adjustments and resumed growth. Most, however, fell into recession. Most seriously affected were the highly indebted countries. Real GDP growth for the highly indebted group fell by 0.4 percent in 1982 and by 2.9 percent in 1983 before rising by 1.9 percent in 1984—half the rates of the 1960s and 1970s, and barely faster than population growth (see Table 6–6).

Because GDP and exports grew slowly or not at all, the debt service capacity of the major countries did not improve. Furthermore, because of concerted lending and increased loans from the IMF and World Bank, external debt outstanding increased further from $391 billion in 1982 to $454 billion in 1985 (see Table 6–3). From 1982 to 1985 the ratio of debt to GNP for the highly indebted countries rose from 32.4 to 49.5. Although the debt service ratio (total debt service to exports of goods and services) for these countries improved due to falling interest rates, it became clear that the debt crisis was more than a temporary liquidity problem (see Table 6–4).

In September 1985, the United States took the lead in calling for a new debt strategy. In a speech to the annual meeting of the World Bank and IMF, Treasury Secretary James Baker recognized that normal access of LDC debtors to commercial lending could only be restored through growth.[68] He proposed a three-part plan to restore growth in fifteen of the most heavily indebted countries and to complement the ongoing country-by-country debt restructuring efforts.

First, debtor governments would implement market-oriented structural changes to remove economic inefficiencies that were seen as impediments to growth. Reforms included trade liberalization such as reducing tariffs and quotas; financial liberalization such as improved access for foreign direct investment; deregulation, including reducing subsidies, interest rate controls and exchange rate regulations; and privatization of state-owned industry. Second, the Baker Plan called on commercial banks to provide $20 billion in new loans over three years. Finally, the multilateral development banks, particularly the World Bank, were to increase disbursements by $3 billion per year. Increased World Bank structural adjustment lending was to facilitate domestic reform. The combination of economic reforms and new financial flows was expected to lead to a growth in output and exports and, eventually, to a return to solvency and access to credit markets.

The Baker plan, however, did not lead to a resurgence of growth. While countries such as Mexico, Chile, and Uruguay pursued structural adjustment policies, others such as Brazil, Argentina, and Peru did not implement significant reforms. Efforts to carry out structural reforms were limited by political constraints. Fragile democratic regimes in countries like Brazil and Argentina found it difficult to implement reforms that would remove protection from important political constituencies. In addition, there were real differences of view about the desirability of market-oriented as opposed to government-led approaches to growth.

Economic reality also left little room for maneuver. Inadequate tax systems left countries dependent on tariffs for revenue and made widespread tariff reduction difficult. Financial liberalization was set back by increased government demands on the banking system for debt financing and by persistent financial crises. Despite fiscal austerity, public sector deficits remained large because foreign debt service constituted such a large share of government expenditures—about 30 percent in many countries.[69] Public deficits contributed to high inflation and high interest rates, which, in turn, worsened the debt service burden. Anti-inflation programs were overwhelmed by fiscal imbalances.[70] Large public financing needs squeezed out private savings while high interest rates and the uncertainty created by high and unstable inflation rates damaged investors' confidence.

External conditions were also unfavorable. Growth in the developed countries slowed; there was a persistent weakness in nonoil commodity prices; and turmoil in OPEC led to a sharp drop in oil prices after 1985. As a result, the overall terms of trade moved sharply against the major debtors from 1985 to 1987, falling at an average annual rate of 6.7 percent.[71] Lower inflation and lower interest rates in the industrial countries were not enough to offset the decline in the terms of trade.

Finally, the financial inflows prescribed by the Baker Plan were not forthcoming. Commercial banks continued to lend large amounts of new money to the major debtor countries as part of rescheduling agreements. By 1988, they had largely met the $20 billion target of new loans set by the Baker Plan. However, due to debt servicing by LDCs to banks, net commercial bank flows to debtor countries were actually negative. In 1986, LDC debtors had a net outflow to commercial banks (see Figure 6-2). Public financial flows were a mixed picture. World Bank commitments to the highly indebted countries met the Baker Plan target, increasing from $9.2 billion in 1981-1982 to $12.9 billion in 1986-1987. Net transfers, however, told a far different story. In 1986, net transfers were far short of the $3 billion per year goal and in 1987 they were actually a negative $0.6 billion.[72]

Figure 6-2   Net Resource Transfers to Developing Countries, 1973 to 1987

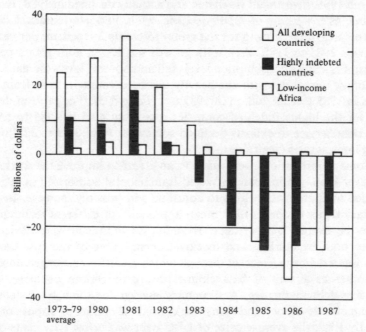

Note: Net resource transfers are defined as disbursements of medium- and long-term external loans minus interest and amortization payments on medium- and long-term external debt.
Source: World Bank, *World Development Report 1988* (New York: Oxford University Press, 1988), p. 30.

Critics argued that World Bank flows should have been even greater and that the Bank should have played a more active role in promoting financial flows. Bank officials, on the other hand, pointed out that lending was constrained by the economic crisis in the debtor countries, which left them short of matching funds to invest in new projects and unwilling or unable to implement structural adjustment programs. They also pointed out the growing limits on Bank lending imposed by a shortage of capital.

IMF flows to the heavily indebted countries actually declined. In 1983, the Fund transferred $6.5 billion to these countries, providing an important offset to the contraction of private flows. In 1986 and 1987, IMF flows to the heavily indebted countries were negative. In 1987 repayments to the Fund exceeded new disbursements by 1.4 billion.[73] In response to criticism, the Fund pointed out that the reverse flow occurred, in part, because of repayments for the heavy outflows during the early years of the debt crisis and, in part, because debtors had not implemented economic reforms required for IMF lending.[74]

While some improvements were made after 1985, the Baker Plan did not fulfill its goal of achieving sustained growth in major debtor countries. Table 6–6 presents various indicators for this period. After recovering briefly in 1985, investment stagnated and actually declined in 1988. Exports of goods as a percent of GDP declined while imports remained largely constant. Real GDP growth for the group rose only 2.4 percent per year for the period 1985 to 1988. Per-capita growth was lower, averaging 1 percent per year. Per-capita consumption levels fell and poverty levels increased.

Total external debt for the heavily indebted countries rose from $454 billion in 1985 to $528 billion in 1987 (see Table 6–3). The ratio of debt to GNP for the highly indebted countries rose from 49.5 in 1985 to 55.9 in 1987. Debt service to exports declined somewhat from 33.9 to 32.7 due to falling interest rates (see Table 6–4).

Some modifications were made in an effort to improve the working of the Baker Plan. An increase in World Bank capital authorized in 1988 was intended to enable bank flows to continue and possibly increase. In 1987, Secretary Baker endorsed the "menu approach" of different techniques to reduce the overall level of debt. Included on the menu were devices developed both by markets and by governments. One of the first developments was a debt swap market through which creditors exchanged debt with each other as a way of balancing exposure to certain countries or of balancing debt maturities. A secondary market for the sale of debt at a discount also developed and many banks used the market to dispose of LDC debt. By 1988, the average price of LDC debt was below fifty cents on the dollar (see Figure 6–3).

Debt-equity swaps were also on the menu. These involved the exchange of bank debt for equity investments in debtor countries and required debtor

Figure 6–3   Secondary Market Prices for Developing Country Loans, March 1986–February 1988[1] (in percentage of face value)

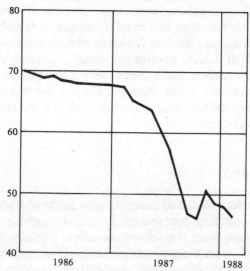

[1]Weighted average prices for 15 heavily indebted countries, where weights are staff estimates of unguaranteed outstanding commercial bank debt at end-1986, adjusted for maturing short-term debt.

SOURCE: International Monetary Fund, *World Economic Outlook* (Washington, D.C.: International Monetary Fund, April 1988), p. 19.

government participation. A creditor bank might swap debt on its own behalf or sell debt to an investor at a discount. The bank or the investor exchanged the debt for local currency at the debtor central bank at a rate below full face value but above the amount the investor paid the bank. The currency was then used to make a local equity investment. The commercial bank thus reduced its debt exposure by selling it or turning it into a real asset; the debtor country lowered its debt and promoted new investment; and the investor obtained favorable financing for investment.

Some countries, especially Chile and Mexico, used debt-equity swaps to reduce overall debt. Most LDCs, however, controlled such swaps in order to minimize various problems. Swaps could be inflationary if a country simply created local currency to finance them. So, monetary policy was used to offset swaps and the amount of swaps allowed has been limited. There is also a question whether investment would have taken place anyway at less cost for the debtor government. Thus, countries have restricted the type of investment eligible for swaps. And debt-equity swaps also raise political issues about control of the national economy traditionally associated with foreign investment. For this reason, some countries do not allow swaps and others have periodically closed the swap window, as Mexico did in 1988.

Other items on the menu were exit bonds made available to creditors as part of a rescheduling. Exit bonds gave creditors a lower rate of interest but exempted them from providing new money as part of concerted lending packages. One variation of an exit bond developed by the Mexican government offered to swap existing debt for fixed interest bonds whose principal was collateralized by a U.S. government bond purchased by the Mexican government. Overall, these menu items were helpful in reducing the debt service burden, but only at the margins. Despite the Baker plan and the menu modification, debtor economies stagnated and the system continued to lurch from crisis to crisis.

Debt Fatigue

By 1987, the debt crisis had entered a new phase characterized by debt fatigue and disintegrating cooperation among the participants. The first sign of change came from the debtor countries. Initially, debtor governments had, by and large, been willing participants in the debt management system developed after 1982. Their cooperation stemmed partly from a sense of responsibility for solving their problems and partly from lack of leverage with the creditor banks and governments. The major source of LDC leverage would have been to threaten or actually to default on their debt. But unless they acted simultaneously, default would have damaged their economies more than those of the creditors. Furthermore, the case-by-case approach acted as an effective deterrent to cooperation among debtor countries. When one country faced financial problems and was in the midst of rescheduling, other countries had just concluded agreements with creditors and were in no mood to reopen the debate. Sequential rescheduling negotiations in which each debtor government sought to take advantage of its own special situation discouraged cooperation or even sharing information among debtors. As slow or no growth persisted and the debt burden grew, social and political tensions within debtor countries rose, and dissatisfaction with the system emerged. With access to credit markets an elusive goal, economically painful and politically difficult policies designed to satisfy creditors became less acceptable. As early as 1984, the newly elected Argentine government resisted a proposed IMF austerity program as unduly severe economically and a threat to the fragile democratic political consensus and threatened to refuse to pay the interest on its debt. At the same time, Argentina joined with other Latin American debtor countries in the so-called Cartagena Group to make specific proposals for easing the debt service burden, including limiting debt payments to a "reasonable" percentage of export earnings and relaxing IMF austerity programs by giving priority to economic growth.[75] In 1985 the newly elected government in Peru announced it would limit its debt service to 10 percent of exports. These actions, however, had little impact on the debt management system. Argentina was discouraged by Brazil and Mexico and eventually signed an agreement with the IMF; Peru was treated as a pariah by both creditors and debtors; and the Cartagena group did not become a debtor cartel.

By 1987, however, conditions had changed. Bolivia, Costa Rica, the Dominican Republic, Ecuador, and Honduras had unilaterally suspended all or part of their debt service. Most important, Brazil, in the first challenge to the system by a major debtor, suspended payments on its $110.5 billion of medium- and long-term debt. The Brazilian moratorium was designed to obtain better terms including some form of debt relief in its debt-rescheduling negotiations. A Brazilian default would have forced creditor banks to suffer substantial losses and could have started a chain reaction among debtor governments.

Rather than improving its leverage, however, the moratorium weakened Brazil's ability to extract concessions from creditor banks and governments. Banks throughout the developed world responded to Brazil's action by increasing their reserves for possible losses on LDC loans. Having gradually increased their equity capital after 1982, banks were better able to withstand the losses to earnings that resulted from this action. The banks thus called Brazil's bluff and demonstrated that banks were more willing to suffer earnings losses than to give in to Brazil and to the precedent of debt relief. Banks also reduced trade credit lines and delayed disbursement of loans. Governments, especially the United States, put pressure on Brazil to return to the fold. Brazil also received little support from other debtors. A summit meeting of Latin America's major debtors called for lower interest rates and reduction in debt-service payments but led to no common action. One year after declaring its moratorium, Brazil reentered negotiations with creditor banks and eventually concluded a new rescheduling agreement.

Although Brazil's moratorium was unsuccessful, it demonstrated growing debtor dissatisfaction with the debt management system. This dissatisfaction was increasingly used by opposition parties in debtor countries that based their electoral platforms on debt relief. For example, in 1988, debt was a major issue in elections in Mexico, where the opposition party that advocated debt relief offered a serious challenge to the previously dominant governing party, and in Venezuela, where the winning candidate advocated debt relief.

There was restiveness among creditor banks as well. While debtors had been divided and unable to form a debtor cartel, creditors had been united from the beginning through the advisory committees, which were a form of creditor cartel. Now, creditor unity had begun to weaken. Small and regional banks and even some larger banks, which did not see long-term future business in the debtor countries, sought to limit or reduce their lending to LDC debtors. Most set aside significant reserves for losses on LDC loans. Some sold all or part of their portfolios at a discount in the debt market. These banks resented being called upon to make new loans to debtor countries at a time when the actual value of loans in the secondary market was below face value and when prospects for a return to solvency seemed dim. It became increasingly difficult for the lead creditor banks and governments to persuade these banks to provide new money as part of the restructuring packages. Pressure on big banks increased, not only from reluctant creditors and from the secondary market where loan values were significantly discounted, but also from the stock markets where values of the major banks with exposure in developing countries were depressed because of the LDC debt overhang. Following the increases in reserves in 1987, more banks became interested in reducing lending to LDC debtors and many major lenders sold debt in the secondary market.

Finally, banks from different countries took different positions in the restructuring negotiations. For example, differences in regulatory and tax treatment between countries led banks to have different positions on setting up reserves against potential losses on LDC loans, and this led to opposing views on concessions to debtor countries. Debt-restructuring packages became harder to negotiate because of the divisions among banks and raised concern that overall new flows would decline. In 1988, the World Bank predicted that commercial bank lending would fall far short of the private sector financing needed by the debtor countries[76]; an organization representing banks from around the world announced that private flows would not meet the demand[77]; some bankers began to call for a new strategy involving debt relief and greater involvement by creditor country governments[78]; and members of Congress offered plans to reduce debt service.[79]

Despite growing pressures, the United States continued to insist on the viability of the Baker Plan and to oppose any form of debt relief. The Reagan administration argued that the strategy allowed banks to reduce exposure to LDC debt, helped stabilize the financial system, and made it possible, given favorable conditions, for the debtors to grow and to reduce debt through the menu approach. In the administration's view, it was inappropriate and politically infeasible for creditor country governments to ask taxpayers to "bail out" the banks or the LDC debtors.

In the face of initial U.S. opposition, other industrial countries also began wavering in their support of the U.S. government. Britain, France, and Germany supported debt relief for the poorest debtors in Africa whose debt was largely to governments. In 1987, with U.S. acquiescence, they approved the creation of an Expanded Structural Adjustment Fund in the IMF to provide greater funds for the least-developed countries to adjust to market changes. Despite U.S. resistance, the heads of state at the 1988 Toronto Summit agreed on a plan to alleviate the debt service burden for the poorer sub-Saharan African countries. The plan gave these debtors various options for lowering interest rates, stretching out repayments, and actual forgiveness of debt to developed country governments. This was the first recognition of a need for debt relief.

Also at the Toronto Summit, and later at the 1988 World Bank/IMF meeting, the Japanese government called on the Group of Seven to develop new forms of debt relief for middle-income debtors. The Japanese offered a proposal for the exchange of debt for securities and for a central role for the IMF. The Japanese proposal for a new approach to debt management was part of its efforts to develop a new role as a world power in developing countries and complemented its new aid initiatives.[80]

By the end of 1988, almost everyone, except the U.S. government, recognized that the Baker Plan needed revision. The World Bank said that the time had come for the international debt strategy to enter a new phase. As the Bank put it: "The declining interest of commercial banks in sovereign risk lending to highly indebted countries coupled with the continued uncertainties arising from the debt overhang may be a signal that it is time to rework the 1985 consensus."[81] The challenge described by the Bank was to develop new ways for debtor countries both to restructure their economies and to obtain adequate funds to renew investment and thus development over the long term. At risk was not only economic development for the developing countries but also economic benefits for the developed countries that exported large amounts to debtor countries. Also at stake, as the Mexican election and the elections in other Latin American countries revealed, was the political stability of democratic regimes in many debtor countries.

One of the first initiatives of the new administration of President George Bush was to face up to these realities. In December 1988, even before his inauguration, President-elect Bush announced "a whole new look" on U.S. policy toward the world's debtor countries.[82] As the Bush administration worked to develop a new approach, pressure for change increased. The new Mexican President called for debt reduction in his inaugural address in January and, then, in March rioting and hundreds of deaths followed the imposition of austerity measures by the newly elected Venezuelan government, which demonstrated dramatically the political threat.

In March 1989, Treasury Secretary Nicholas Brady announced a new LDC debt strategy.[83] Although it was vague on many details, the strategy called for a shift in emphasis from new lending to debt reduction by banks and stated that World Bank and IMF resources should be available to debtor countries with sound economic reform policies for use in encouraging debt reduction. Bit by bit, details on the "Brady initiative" began to emerge. First, it became clear that debt reduction would be added to a menu of options that still included new money from banks. In terms of debt reduction, the United States proposed mostly voluntary exchanges of old debt for new bonds: either bonds paying market rates but exchanged for bank loans at a discount, or bonds paying sharply reduced interest but exchanged at par value. It was envisaged that principal and at least one year of interest on the new bonds would be secured by a country's existing reserves or funds from

IMF or World Bank loans. The Treasury proposal also envisioned lending by international financial institutions to countries to buy back debts at secondary market prices.

Support for the Brady initiative came promptly from Japan, which pledged $4.5 billion in loans to be provided in parallel with IMF and World Bank loans. Many of the debtor countries also welcomed the Brady initiative, seizing on the hope for substantial reductions in their bank debts. However, other industrial countries, particularly the United Kingdom and Germany, remained wary and expressed concern that the Brady initiative was transferring risks from the private sector to the public. Other analysts, while welcoming the new direction in policy, worried that the Brady initiative did not go far enough fast enough to turn around the economic and political situation in the debtor countries.

Implementation of the Brady initiative was left to negotiations between banks and specific debtor countries. Negotiations over Mexican debt provided the first test case. After months of stalled talks between Mexico and bank representatives, a new debt reduction agreement was reached in late July 1989, under pressure from Secretary Brady and with the assistance of U.S. officials. The agreement, which followed the main points for debt resolution set out by Secretary Brady earlier in the year, covered $54 billion of the $69 billion owed by Mexico to private banks. The Mexican plan specified three options for the banks: (1) swapping old loans in return for thirty-year bonds which pay interest at the same rate as the old loans but which are valued at 35 percent less than the old loans; (2) swapping old loans for thirty-year bonds with the same value, but with a lower, fixed interest rate; or (3) agreeing to lend new money (or recycle interest received from Mexico) for four years, at levels equal in amount to 25 percent of the bank's exposure. In return, the agreement called for a guarantee of the interest payments on the bonds for eighteen months, to be financed by funds from the IMF, the World Bank, Mexico, and Japan.[84]

The Mexican agreement was seen by many as a new departure, for it represented the first time that private banks accepted debt forgiveness and voluntarily reduced debt levels. It was estimated that the agreement would bring $2.5 billion of new money into the Mexican economy over four years, and would reduce Mexico's interest payments, estimated at $9.6 billion in 1989, by $1.5 billion a year.[85] The involvement of the two international organizations—the IMF and the World Bank—and the Japanese participation in the process were also seen as positive precedents for further debt negotiations. However, it was uncertain to what degree the agreement would help resolve Mexico's long-term economic problems. Critics of the agreement called for a more ambitious program, asserting that radical levels of debt reduction (some argued for total debt forgiveness) were necessary to resolve the crisis. Without adequate relief, argued the critics, Mexican growth would continue to stagnate, capital flight would persist, and Mexico would be unable to attract needed foreign direct investment.

It was not clear whether the Mexican formula could be applied to other debt-burdened nations whose economies were not as strong as Mexico's. The amount of debt reduction needed for countries such as the Philippines might be too large to negotiate successfully. Securing the large amounts of money needed for collateral financing of other debt reduction agreements would be problematic. Finally, the Mexican agreement represented a delicate balance between voluntary, private negotiations and government intervention. A comprehensive resolution to the debt crisis that used the Mexican example as its model would be difficult without strong leadership by public officials in bringing lenders and borrowers to agreement.

The Impact of the Debt Crisis on Third World Strategy

The cumulative effect of the crises of the 1970s and 1980s was a growing differentiation among Third World countries—oil and nonoil, NIC and least developed, debtor and nondebtor, and so on. As the strains within the group grew, the Southern bargaining chips proved ineffective, and as the stalemate with the North persisted, the South's solidarity and sense of direction began to crack.

The developing countries de-emphasized the NIEO and focused, instead, on the need for immediate action to alleviate the South's problems. In a variety of forums—meetings of the nonaligned movement, UNCTAD—they called for expanded lending and more structural adjustment lending by the World Bank; an increase in IMF quotas; allocations of new SDRs to developing countries; easing of IMF conditionality; new IMF lending facilities; and increases in official development assistance.[86] The North, they argued, should respond in its own self-interest. In an interdependent world, economic vitality in the North was intimately linked with Southern growth, which needed to be reactivated through financial flows to and trade with the Third World. Specifically, argued the South, the debt crisis posed a serious problem for Northern banks, Northern economies, and the entire international financial system. It was thus imperative for the developed countries— and in their own self-interest—to devise new mechanisms to ensure financial flows to developing countries.

The developed countries rejected the South's program. Budget problems placed severe limits on their ability and willingness to make even modest concessions to the developing countries. Furthermore, the North, and especially the United States, argued that the developing countries would benefit from growth in the North and from domestic reforms in the South, and that special measures such as those proposed by the South were inappropriate and, indeed, counterproductive.

Finally, the North's rejection reflected a new strategy for negotiating with the developing countries. From the very beginning, the North had never wanted to negotiate with the South as a bloc. The program of the group was more radical than that of individual developing countries. In the Northern view, their policies had become increasingly divorced from political reality, and their tone had become increasingly strident. The North, pointing out the diversity among the developing countries, had always preferred to deal with the South bilaterally or regionally.

Indeed, throughout the era of Southern unity, the Northern states continued to feel that the real business of dealing with the South took place in bilateral relations or in forums such as the IMF, the World Bank, and the GATT, in which the South did not act as a bloc. The unity of the South during the 1960s and 1970s had forced the North to negotiate with it as a bloc in United Nations forums. The crises of the 1970s and 1980s fragmented the South and made it politically possible to pursue a predominantly bilateral or regional approach.

The debt crisis reinforced this strategy of returning to the bilateral or regional negotiations. The differential impact of the crisis, combined with the concern about the potential for a debtors' cartel, led the North to follow successfully a policy of negotiating with the debtor countries on a case-by-case basis.

The debt crisis also shifted the focus of North-South interaction. In the 1960s and 1970s, the politics of financial flows centered on concessional flows and flows to the most needy. With the onset of the debt crisis, the issue shifted to nonconcessional flows to assist the debtor states. The political attention of the developed countries thus turned to debt rescheduling, balance-of-payments lending to the debtor countries, and ways to enable the debtor countries to resume some level of economic growth so that they could repay their debts and avert political instability. Attention focused on the more advanced developing countries whose potential debt defaults posed a serious threat to the developed market economies. Thus, the debt crisis further fragmented the South and weakened the least-developed countries that were not eligible for major private commercial lending.

The Future of Aid and Financial Flows

As a result of the crises of the 1970s and 1980s, the future of international financial flows to developing countries is uncertain. The South's continuing political and economic weakness, and fragmentation, as well as competing demands on the North's resources because of internal economic problems and shifting Northern diplomatic strategies, have undermined the political basis for aid flows. The debt crisis has turned commercial flows into a drain for most LDC debtors.

There may be some counterbalancing forces. One such force would be a crisis of conscience growing out of the recognition of the desperate plight of the South, especially the least-developed countries. The problems of sub-Saharan Africa in the 1980s, for example, led to special aid measures for that region. A crisis of conscience would certainly have an impact on temporary relief measures such as food aid and some balance-of-payments assistance for the poorest of the Southern states. But moral responsibility, as the history of aid demonstrates, is a weak reed on which to base demands for resource transfers. It might lead to temporary relief in crisis situations, but such reactions are usually ephemeral and clearly not the basis for any major shift in aid.

A more sustained source of optimism may be found in the balancing effect of the variety of donors that now participate in resource transfers to the South. As we have seen, the shifting sources of resources transfers have evened out over the long run. As the United States and the United Kingdom were pulling back on Third World aid in the 1960s, the Nordic countries and others increased their aid. As the majority of the North felt the impact of the recession caused by the oil crisis, OPEC donors made up the difference. As the United States faced current budgetary and fiscal crises in the late 1980s, Japan became willing and able to take up some of the financial burden of resources transfers to the Third World. By 1988, Japan had become the largest aid donor. Although this does not guarantee the stability of future flows, it suggests that the diversification of Northern donors may reduce some of the risk for developing countries.

It is also possible that the North will find a new concern for international economic management. The food, energy, and debt crises have affected the North as well as the South. Although the economic disorder in the North has been less severe, it has created an interest in improving the functioning of market forces. Even in the United States under President Reagan, the desire to improve the market's functioning eventually led to a greater willingness to intervene in the market and to support multilateral management. In the future, such global issues as the environment may call for greater North-South cooperation. Such international cooperation might benefit the South and, in some cases, might require the inclusion of certain Southern states in management. Depending on how these leading Southern states define their relation to the other less-developed countries, the South may benefit not so much from its specific demands as from the recognition that the problems that the South faces are also faced, albeit somewhat differently, by the North.

Perhaps the greatest potential source of change in Northern attitudes is the growing importance of the Southern economies to the industrialized countries. Markets in the Third World are expanding, especially in the newly industrialized countries, and are becoming increasingly important for Northern exports. The percentage of Northern merchandise exports going to the developing countries rose from 23 percent in 1973 to 28 percent in

1980.[87] As a result of the debt crisis, exports from industrial countries to developing countries fell from 30 percent of all exports in 1981 to 20 percent in 1987.[88] The share of U.S. exports going to Latin America and the Caribbean fell by 27 percent during the same time period.[89] In order to restore this demand, the Northern states may consider it in their interest to promote continued Southern economic development. Although the immediate threat of financial collapse subsided as banks increased their equity capital and set up reserves for LDC loan losses, the continuing LDC debt exposure remained a threat to the strength of many commercial banks[90] (see Table 6-5). The developing countries will be able to service their debts to Northern banks only if they can maintain their economic growth. Thus, new financial flows or reduction of outflows for debt service may increasingly be seen by the Northern countries as a way to protect their economic interests.

In conclusion, there are few signs of change. The growing bilateralism in aid and the fragmentation of the South mean that certain Southern countries—for example, the debtors or those that are important markets for the North—will be in a better position to obtain financing from the developed countries. Ironically, it is the countries that are least eligible for funds by this criteria that may be the most needy. Thus, financial flows may reinforce the growing differentiation of the South. Some Third World states—Brazil, Taiwan, and South Korea—will cross the development gap, but most will fall behind. The result of the recent economic disorder, therefore, will most likely not be the end of Third World dependence but the creation of a new and more miserable Fourth World.

NOTES

1. On early financing priorities for the World Bank, see Henry J. Bitterman, "Negotiation of the Articles of Agreement of the International Bank for Reconstruction and Development," *The International Lawyer*, 5 (January 1971), 59–88; Edward S. Mason and Robert E. Asher, *The World Bank Since Bretton Woods* (Washington, D.C.: Brookings Institution, 1973), pp. 1–35.

2. *The World Bank Since Bretton Woods*, pp. 178–179.

3. "The Inaugural Address of the President," U.S. Department of State, *The Bulletin*, 20 (January 30, 1949), 125.

4. Goran Ohlin, *Foreign Aid Policies Reconsidered* (Paris: Organization for Economic Cooperation and Development, 1966), p. 66.

5. See "Military Assistance and the Security of the United States, 1947–1956," a study prepared by the Institute of War and Peace Studies of Columbia University, in U.S. Senate, *Foreign Aid Program*, a compilation of studies and surveys under the direction of the Special Committee to Study the Foreign Aid Program, 85th Cong., 1st sess. (Washington, D.C.: U.S. Government Printing Office, 1957), pp. 903–969.

6. See Marshall I. Goldman, *Soviet Foreign Aid* (New York: Praeger, 1967), pp. 60–167; Robert S. Walters, *American and Soviet Aid: A Comparative Analysis* (Pittsburgh, Pa.: University of Pittsburgh Press, 1970), pp. 26–48.

7. Several official and unofficial reports at this time showed that there was a link between U.S. security and Southern economic development. See *Report to the President on*

Foreign Economic Policies (Washington, D.C.: U.S. Government Printing Office, 1950); International Development Advisory Board, *Partners in Progress, A Report to the President* (March 1951); U.S. Mutual Security Agency, Advisory Committee on Underdeveloped Areas, *Economic Strength for the Free World: Principles of a U.S. Foreign Development Program*, a report to the director for mutual security (Washington, D.C.: U.S. Government Printing Office, 1953).

8. U.S. Senate, *Foreign Aid Program*, 1957, p. 20.

9. See Max F. Millikan and W. W. Rostow, *A Proposal: Key to an Effective Foreign Policy* (New York: Harper & Brothers, 1957), pp. 34–38.

10. Ibid., p. 39. For an analysis of the role of aid in political development, see Robert A. Packenham, *Liberal America and the Third World: Political Development Ideas in Foreign Aid and Social Science* (Princeton, N.J.: Princeton University Press, 1973).

11. See Ohlin, *Foreign Aid Policies Reconsidered*, pp. 27–36. See also Teresa Hayter, *French Aid* (London: Overseas Development Institute, 1966); Overseas Development Institute, *British Aid—A Factual Survey* (London: Overseas Development Institute, 1963–1964).

12. Organization for Economic Cooperation and Development, *Flow of Financial Resources to Less-Developed Countries*, 1956–1963 (Paris: OECD, 1964), p. 19.

13. Ibid.

14. Baldwin, *Economic Development and American Foreign Policy*, p. 204.

15. Organization for Economic Cooperation and Development, *Development Cooperation 1974 Review* (Paris: OECD, 1974).

16. Ibid, p. 133.

17. Samuel P. Huntington, *Political Order in Changing Societies* (New Haven, Conn.: Yale University Press, 1968), pp. 1–92.

18. See Samuel P. Huntington, "Foreign Aid for What and for Whom," *Foreign Policy*, 1 (Winter 1970–1971), 161–189; Samuel P. Huntington, "Does Foreign Aid Have a Future?" *Foreign Policy*, 2 (Spring 1971), 114–134.

19. On French and British aid during this period see Teresa Hayter, *French Aid*, and Bruce Dinwiddy, ed., *European Development Policies: The United Kingdom, Sweden, France, EEC and Multilateral Organizations* (London: Praeger Publishers for the Overseas Development Institute, 1973).

20. United Nations Conference on Trade and Development, *Debt Problems of Developing Countries* (New York: United Nations, 1972), p. 1.

21. See "The Policy of Self-Reliance: Excerpts from Part III of the Arusha Declaration of February 5, 1967," *Africa Report*, 12 (March 1967), 11–13; Henry Bienen, "An Ideology for Africa," *Foreign Affairs*, 47 (April 1969), 545–559. On Burma, see Mya Maung, *Burma and Pakistan: A Comparative Study of Development* (New York: Praeger Publishers, 1971) and David I. Steinberg, *Burma: A Socialist Nation in Southeast Asia* (Boulder, Colo.: Westview Press, 1982).

22. United Nations Conference on Trade and Development, *Towards a New Trade Policy for Development* (New York: United Nations, 1964), pp. 79–89; United Nations Conference on Trade and Development, *Towards a Global Strategy of Development* (New York: United Nations, 1968), pp. 32–44.

23. See Y. S. Park, *The Link Between Special Drawing Rights and Development Finance* (Princeton: Princeton University, Department of Economics, International Finance Section, September 1973).

24. On the food crisis see: Raymond Hopkins and Donald Puchala, eds. "The Global Political Economy of Food," *International Organization* 32 (Summer 1978); World Bank, *World Development Report 1986*, Chapter 4.

25. Food and Agricultural Organization, *Commodity Review and Outlook 1981–1982* (Rome: Food and Agricultural Organization, 1982), p. 4.

26. Organization for Economic Cooperation and Development, *Development Cooperation: 1983 Review* (Paris: OECD, 1983), p. 136.

27. Ibid., p. 135.

28. Robert L. Paarlberg, "U.S. Agriculture and the Developing World" in *Growth, Exports & Jobs in a Changing World Economy: Agenda 1988* (New Brunswick, N.J.: Transaction Books, 1988).

29. Henry Bienen, "The United States and Sub-Saharan Africa," in John P. Lewis and

Valeriana Kallab, eds., *U.S. Foreign Policy and the Third World: Agenda* 1983 (New York: Praeger for the Overseas Development Council, 1983), p. 77. See also Carol Lancaster, "Africa's Economic Crisis," *Foreign Policy*, No. 52 (Fall 1983), 149–166.

30. International Monetary Fund, *Annual Report*, 1983 (Washington, D.C.: IMF, 1983), p. 33.

31. Ibid., p. 33.

32. See also World Bank, *World Debt Tables: External Debt of Developing Countries* (Washington, D.C.: World Bank, 1983), p. xiii.

33. World Bank, *World Development Report 1988* (New York: Oxford University Press, 1988), p. 37.

34. "Declaration and Action Programme on the Establishment of a New International Economic Order," in Guy F. Erb and Valeriana Kallab, eds., *Beyond Dependency: The Developing World Speaks Out* (New York: Praeger, 1975), pp. 193–194.

35. See John Williamson, *The Lending Policies of the International Monetary Fund* (Washington, D.C.: Institute for International Economics, 1982).

36. See: Robert L. Ayres, *Banking on the Poor* (Washington, D.C.: Overseas Development Council, 1983). For a highly critical study of the World Bank, see Teresa Hayter, *Aid as Imperialism* (Harmondsworth, England: Penguin Books, 1971).

37. See G.K. Helleiner, "Policy-Based Program Lending: A Look at the Bank's New Role," in Richard E. Feinberg and Valeriana Kallab, eds., *Between Two Worlds: The World Bank's Next Decade* (New Bruswick, N.J.: Transaction Books, 1986).

38. Richard E. Feinberg, "Bridging the Crisis: The World Bank and U.S. Interests in the 1980s," in Lewis and Kallab, eds., *U.S. Foreign Policy and the Third World: Agenda 1983*, pp. 141–149.

39. For excellent overviews of aid see: Robert Cassen and Associates, *Does Aid Work? Report to an Intergovernmental Task Force* (Oxford: Claredon Press, 1986). This study was commissioned by the Development Committee of the World Bank and the IMF. See also: John P. Lewis and Valeriana Kallab, eds., *Development Strategies Reconsidered* (New Brunswick, N.J.: Transaction Books, 1986). For a critical view of the role of aid see: Peter Bauer, *Equality, The Third World, and Economic Illusion* (Cambridge, Mass.: Harvard University Press, 1981). On development theory see W. Arthur Lewis, "The State of Development Theory," *American Economic Review*, Vol. 74, No. 1 (March 1984); and Albert O. Hirschman, "The Rise and Decline of Development Economics," in *Essays in Trespassing: Economics to Politics and Beyond* (Cambridge: Cambridge University Press, 1981).

40. World Bank, *World Development Report 1988*, p. 225.

41. Ibid., p. 223.

42. Irman Adelman, "A Poverty-Focussed Approach to Development Policy," in John P. Lewis and Valeriana Kallab, eds, *Development Strategies Reconsidered*, p. 53.

43. World Bank, *World Development Report 1988*, pp. 224–225.

44. Ibid., p. 223.

45. Irman Adelman, "A Poverty-Focussed Approach to Development Policy," pp. 52–53. Absolute poverty level defined in World Bank terms as below an annual per capita income of less than US $50 in constant 1960 dollars.

46. Robert Cassen, *Does Aid Work*, pp. 24–25.

47. Irving Brecher and S. A. Abbas, *Foreign Aid and Industrial Development in Pakistan* (Cambridge, Mass.: Harvard University Press, 1972); Gustav F. Papenek, *Pakistan and Development: Social Goals and Private Incentive* (Cambridge, Mass.: Harvard University Press, 1967); Irma Adelman, ed., *Practical Approaches to Development Planning: Korea's Second Five-Year Plan* (Baltimore: Johns Hopkins University Press, 1969); Neil H. Jacoby, *U.S. Aid to Taiwan* (New York: Praeger, 1966).

48. Roger D. Hansen, *Mexican Economic Development: The Roots of Rapid Growth* (Washington, D.C.: National Planning Association, 1971).

49. John P. Lewis, "Overview: Development Promotion: A Time for Regrouping," in John P. Lewis and Valeriana Kallab, eds., *Development Strategies Reconsidered*, pp. 3–46.

50. See Joan M. Nelson, *Aid, Influence and Foreign Policy* (New York: Macmillan, 1968), pp. 69–90. On aid tying, see "Aid Tying and Mixed Credits," Chapter 10 in OECD, *Twenty-five Years of Development Cooperation* (Paris: OECD, 1985), pp. 241–250.

51. See G. K. Helleiner, "Policy-Based Program Lending," and Joan M. Nelson, "The Diplomacy of Policy-Based Lending," in Feinberg and Kallab, *Between Two Worlds*.

52. Howard Wriggins, "Political Outcomes of Foreign Assistance: Influence, Involvement, or Intervention?" *Journal of International Affairs*, 22 (1968), 217–230.

53. International Monetary Fund, *World Economic Outlook* (Washington, D.C.: IMF, April 1984), p. 205.

54. World Bank, *World Development Report 1983*, p. 182; Organization for Economic Cooperation and Development, *Development Cooperation: 1983 Review*, p. 52.

55. John W. Sewell and Christine E. Contee, "U.S. Foreign Aid in the 1980s: Reordering Priorities" in John W. Sewell, Richard E. Feinberg, and Valeriana Kallab, eds., *U.S. Foreign Policy and the Third World: Agenda 1985–6*, p. 99.

56. Organization for Economic Cooperation and Development, *Development Cooperation: 1987 Review* (Paris: OECD, 1987), p. 327.

57. On increased Japanese lending see: Toshihiko Kinoshita, *"Japan's Current "Recycling Measures": Its Background, Performance and Prospects,"* Export-Import Bank of Japan, 1988 (mimeo).

58. William R. Cline, "Mexico's Crisis, the World's Peril," *Foreign Policy*, no. 49 (Winter 1982–1983), pp. 107–120.

59. World Bank, *World Debt Tables 1985–1986* (Washington, D.C.: World Bank, 1985), pp. 254, 274, 278, 326, 358.

60. On systemic problems see Jack M. Guttentag and Richard Herring, *The Lender of Last Resort Function in an International Context*, Essays in International Finance (Princeton: International Finance Section, Princeton University, 1983).

61. Edward J. Frydl and Dorothy M. Sobol, "A Perspective on the Debt Crisis, 1982–1987," Federal Reserve Bank of New York, *Seventy-Third Annual Report* (New York: Federal Reserve Bank of New York, 1988), p. 5.

62. "Mexico under the IMF," *The Economist*, August 20, 1983, pp. 19–20. Also see Karin Lissakers, "Dateline Wall Street: Faustian Finance," *Foreign Policy*, no. 51 (Summer 1983), 160–175; M.S. Mendelsohn, *Commercial Banks and the Restructuring of Cross-Border Debt* (New York: Group of Thirty, 1983).

63. E. Brau and R.C. Williams, with P.M. Keller and M. Nowak, *Recent Multilateral Debt Restructuring with Official and Bank Creditors* (Washington, D.C.: International Monetary Fund, December 1983).

64. See Jack Guttentag and Richard Herring, *The Current Crisis in International Banking* (Philadelphia: University of Pennsylvania, Wharton Program in International Banking and Finance, October 1983).

65. See Peter M. Kelleo with Nessanke E. Weerasinghe, *Multilateral Official Debt Rescheduling Recent Experience* (Washington, D.C.: International Monetary Fund, May 1988).

66. Frydl and Sobol, "A Perspective on the Debt Crisis, 1982–1987," p. 19.

67. International Monetary Fund, *Annual Report, 1983* (Washington, D.C.: IMF, 1983), pp. 87–88.

68. "Statement of the Honorable James A. Baker III before the Joint Annual Meeting of the International Monetary Fund and the World Bank, Seoul, Korea," *Treasury News*, October 8, 1985, Washington, D.C.

69. Jeffrey Sachs and Harry Huizinga, "U.S. Commercial Banks and the Developing-Country Debt Crisis," *Brookings Papers on Economic Activity*, 2 (Washington, D.C.: Brookings, 1987), p. 560.

70. See World Bank, *World Development Report 1988* (Washington, D.C.: World Bank, 1988), pp. 55–71.

71. Ibid., p. 192.

72. Ibid., p. 30.

73. Ibid.

74. See International Monetary Fund, *World Economic Outlook*, April 1988.

75. *Wall Street Journal*, June 25, 1984, p. 31.

76. World Bank, *World Development Report 1988*, p. 3.

77. *Investors Daily*, September 14, 1988, p. 14.

78. See for example, "Third World Debt: A Reexamination of Long-Term Management:

Report of the Third World Debt Panel of the Economic Policy Council of UNA-USA,"
September 7, 1988 (New York: UNA-USA, 1988).

79. One proposal called for banks to forgive three percent of interest and principal over
a three-year period. See Senator Bill Bradley, "The Debt Crisis as a U.S. Job Crisis," speech at
the National Press Club, Washington, D.C., July 24, 1986. Other proposals would create a
debt restructuring facility to buy LDC loans at a discount and to lower debt service. See: U.S.
Congress, *Omnibus Trade and Competitiveness Act of 1988*, PL 100–418 (Washington, D.C.:
U.S. Government Printing Office, August 23, 1988), Sec. 3111–3113; James D. Robinson III,
"A Comprehensive Agenda for LDC Debt and World Trade Growth," *The Amex Bank Review
Special Papers,* Number 13, March 1988.

80. "Statement by the Hon. Satoshi Sumita, Governor, the Bank of Japan and Alternate
Governor of the Fund and the Bank for Japan at the Joint Annual Discussion," Press Release
12, September 27, 1988, IMF/The World Bank Group.

81. World Bank, *World Debt Tables 1988*, p. xi.

82. "Bush Backs U.S. Shift on World Debt," *New York Times*, December 20,
1989, B10.

83. "Statement of the Honorable Nicholas F. Brady to the Brookings Institution and the
Bretton Woods Committee Conference on Third World Debt," *Treasury News*, March 10,
1989, Washington, D.C.

84. "Relief from Washington as Brady Plan Passes Its Test," *Financial Times*, July 25,
1989, 3. See also "Brady's Mexican Hat-Trick," *The Economist*, July 29, 1989, 61–62.

85. *The Economist*, July 29, 1989, 61; and "Mexico Pins Hopes on Debt Agreement,"
Wall Street Journal, July 25, 1989, A-15.

86. See Overseas Development Institute, *UNCTAD VI: Background and Issues*, Briefing
Paper No. 4, 1983.

87. World Bank, *World Bank Development Report 1984* (Washington, D.C.: World
Bank, 1984), p. 15.

88. International Monetary Fund, *Direction of Trade Yearbook 1988* (Washington,
D.C.: IMF 1988), p. 8.

89. Ibid., pp. 406–407.

90. William Seidman, Chairman, Federal Deposit Insurance Corporation. "Import of
LDC Debt Situation on Financial Condition of the FDIC." Testimony before the Committee
on Banking, Finance and Urban Affairs, U.S. House of Representatives, January 5, 1989.

7

Trade Strategy

Most Southern economies are highly dependent on trade with the North. Export earnings constitute a large share of their GNP, and imported goods are crucial to their development. Yet many developing countries believe that the international market has not promoted their development and that they have been excluded from the trade management system established by the North. Since World War II, the less-developed countries have pursued several strategies to achieve their goals of development and independence: isolation from the international trading system, seeking to force changes in the system, and integrating into the prevailing regime.

Isolation from the Postwar Trading Order

In constructing the postwar trading order, the wartime and postwar planners from the North assumed that a system based on free trade would benefit both developed and developing countries. In their view, free trade would lead to the most efficient and profitable use of national factors of production, increase national income and foreign exchange earnings, attract foreign private capital, and thus stimulate Southern development.[1]

The Southern states felt, however, that free trade threatened their strategy of import substitution, which was based on promoting domestic industrial development behind protective walls. The economic rationale for this development policy was the infant-industry argument that protection from foreign competition for an initial stage would allow domestic industrial producers to attain optimum size and economies of scale within the domestic market. Once the infant stage was completed, protection could be removed and free trade resumed.[2] Protection had historically been a route to development in the North and, it was hoped, would help Southern industrialization and development as well. Such protection also appealed to the less-developed countries as a way of saving precious foreign exchange by decreasing imports.[3]

Thus, in the negotiations leading up to the Havana Charter, the Southern countries argued that their developing country status required special treatment under the free-trade rules proposed by the North. They sought exemptions from the new rules including the ability to use import quotas and tariffs to protect infant industry, to establish new preferential trading systems, and to enter into commodity agreements to stabilize and ensure minimum commodity prices. They also wanted to obtain tariff concessions from developed countries without having to offer concessions in return.[4]

Because the North wanted approval by the less-developed countries for the new trade charter, the South was able to achieve some limited modifications in the Havana Charter, especially a new chapter that recognized the special needs of developing countries. In order to promote economic development, developing countries could increase bound (i.e., legally negotiated) tariffs, impose quantitative restrictions or quotas on imports, establish regional preference systems, and enter into commodity agreements. However, these exceptions to free trade could be taken only with the prior approval of the ITO (International Trade Organization) and/or the parties to trade agreements involved and had to follow restrictive guidelines.[5]

The inclusion of the less-developed concerns into the system ended with the death of the Havana Charter. The General Agreement on Tariffs and Trade (GATT), which replaced the charter as the constitution of the new trading order, was designed as an interim measure and included none of the provisions for development that the South had fought to include in the Havana Charter. All that was left was a GATT article that authorized a country under certain restricted conditions to use tariffs and quantitative restrictions to assist economic development or deal with payments imbalances.[6]

GATT's negotiating process also effectively excluded the developing countries from the international management of trade. GATT's reciprocity rule stated that all trade concessions had to be mutual. But the South, with its small markets, had little to exchange for concessions in its favor. GATT followed the technique of negotiating trade concessions among the importing countries and principal suppliers of any particular item. Because there were no principal suppliers, many products of interest to the less-developed countries, such as raw materials, were left out of the GATT negotiations. Even when the developing countries were the principal suppliers, they were unable to put products or issues of interest to them on the agenda, because the South represented only a minority of the GATT membership and power. The less-developed countries were also hampered by the lack of staff and resources to sustain difficult and sophisticated trade negotiations with the powerful developed countries.

Thus, GATT was a rich man's club. By the end of the 1950s, its thirty-seven members included twenty-one developed countries and only sixteen developing countries. While virtually all the developed nations were members, many developing countries, including Argentina and Mexico, did not join GATT. Those Southern countries that did join did not participate actively in the multilateral trade negotiations. GATT tariff negotiations reduced barriers to manufactured goods of interest to developed countries while barriers to exports of concern to developing countries were generally left intact. Because Southern products were not covered in tariff negotiations, developing countries were not legally bound to lower tariffs on manufactured goods and actually raised tariffs on these products. In addition, most developing country members used GATT's balance-of-payments exemptions to protect their markets.[7]

The primary strategy of developing countries in this period was to insulate themselves from the international market and to pursue industrialization through import substitution. Many developing countries, particularly those in Latin America, either continued the protection introduced before or during the war or established new protectionist barriers in an attempt to develop an internal market for domestic production. Very high rates of protection for domestic industry were ensured through tariffs that were sometimes several hundred percent or more, exchange controls, multiple exchange rates for different products, import licensing, and outright bans on the importation of goods produced domestically.[8] Protection provided powerful incentives for the development of local production to replace imports by providing an assured market and by channeling domestic savings into industry through increased industrial profits.[9]

From Import Substitution to Trade Expansion

The strategy of isolation from the international trading system led neither to development nor to independence and may have actually aggravated the negative impact of international trade on the South. Import substitution fostered some industrialization, but at a high price. Too often, the new industries were inefficient and their output costly and uncompetitive. Faced with small domestic markets, most developing countries could not achieve adequate scales of production to build efficient industry. Furthermore, policies that encouraged the importation of capital-intensive equipment and favored profits over wages discouraged the growth of demand for labor and thus did not contribute to employment.

Import substitution also did not help the balance of payments. Production of high-cost domestic manufactures came at the expense of export-oriented industrial production and of traditional agricultural exports. Furthermore, protection did not decrease imports but, rather, changed the composition of those imports. Instead of importing finished products, Southern countries now imported raw materials, parts, and capital goods.[10] And the systems of licensing and exchange controls created new rigidities in

Southern economies that discouraged competition and promoted ineffi-
ciency.[11]

Industrialization through import substitution also damaged agriculture. New investment in agriculture was limited; real earnings declined as
industrial profits rose; and income inequalities between agriculture and
industry were exacerbated. As a result, people began to leave the coun-
tryside for the town, but the new industry in the cities could not absorb the
burgeoning urban population. Thus, unemployment and income inequalities worsened.[12]

By the end of the 1950s, the governments of many Southern states
concluded that their international trade and economic development policies
could not be based on import substitution alone and would have to focus on
export expansion. It came to be felt that focusing on export growth while
continuing to protect domestic markets could maximize efficiency of production and increase earnings and foreign exchange available for development, much as the liberals had always argued. According to the less-
developed countries, however, such benefits could not occur without a
restructuring of the international trading system, for that system prevented
export growth.

First, contended the less-developed countries, there was a long-term
deterioration in the South's terms of trade.[13] The prices of raw materials
exported by the developing countries were declining in relation to the prices
of manufactured products imported from the developed countries. Because
of trade unions and monopoly markets in the developed market economies,
it was argued, increased productivity in manufacturing in the North was
absorbed by higher wages and profits and did not lead to a fall in the price
of manufactures. On the other hand, because of unemployment and the
absence of labor organization in the less-developed countries plus the existence of a competitive international market for Southern raw materials,
increased productivity in primary products led not to increased wages or
profits but to a decline in prices. The terms of trade also turned against the
South because of an inelastic demand in the North for primary products.
An increase in the production of raw materials led to a decline in price
rather than to an increase in consumption. Finally, the prices of Southern
products tended to fall because of the development of synthetics and
substitutes—for example, nylon replacing cotton—in the North.

The structural decline in terms of trade for primary producers was
aggravated by Northern protectionist policies. According to the South, the
development of competitive, mechanized Northern agriculture through protectionist systems, the development of domestic mineral extraction under
protectionist national security policies, and Northern taxes on tropical
foodstuffs accentuated the declining position of commodity exports. Another problem of the international market, according to the South, was the
inherent instability of commodity prices. In their view, fluctuations in prices

and, thus, in export earnings hindered investment and disrupted development planning.

Finally, the South felt that its real potential to export manufactured
products was constrained by Northern dominance of the international market. The head start of the North, which gave the developed countries
established positions in international markets, as well as Northern protection prevented the expansion of Southern manufactured exports. The South
was particularly critical of Northern protectionist measures (for example,
the practice of imposing a higher tariff on intermediate or finished products
than on raw materials). Such "cascading" tariffs meant that the effective
rate of protection of the finished product was much higher than the nominal
rate was. Differential tariffs favored the import of raw materials from the
less-developed countries, discouraged the import of processed or semiprocessed products, and thus discouraged the development of Southern
industry. Unusually high tariffs or import quotas were imposed on many
Southern manufactures, such as textiles, footwear, and leather goods, that
competed effectively with Northern industries. Where there were no tariff
or quantitative restrictions, the North often forced "voluntary" export
restraint agreements on Southern states.[14] Such nontariff barriers as health
standards, labeling requirements, and customs procedures posed difficult
hurdles for the Southern states with their lack of marketing expertise and
experience.[15]

These constraints on developing country exports were reflected in the
South's diminished role in international trade. The Southern share of world
exports dropped from 31.6 percent in 1950 to 21.4 percent in 1960. In the
same period, the trade of the developed market economies grew from 60.4
percent of total world exports to 66.8 percent, and the socialist states went
from 8.0 percent of total world exports to 11.8 percent. Between 1950 and
1960, exports from the developed countries grew 8.7 percent, whereas those
of the less-developed countries grew only 3.5 percent.[16]

As the South turned from isolation to trade expansion, exclusion from
GATT's trade-management system became unacceptable, and Southern political pressure for a change in the GATT system increased. At Third World
conferences and at the United Nations and within GATT itself, developing
states pushed for greater consideration of their trade problems. Southern
pressure was reinforced by the independence of many colonial states and by
the expansion of the Cold War to the developing world. As part of its new
initiatives in the South, the Soviet Union proposed an international conference on trade and the creation of a world trade organization outside
GATT. The North persuaded the South to reject the Soviet proposal in favor
of reform within GATT.

For the developed countries, reforming the GATT meant little more
than studying the problems of developing countries. In 1957, the contracting
parties of GATT appointed a panel of experts to examine the problems of

Southern trade. The panel's report, published in 1958, focused on the problems of trade in primary products: Northern trade barriers, the deterioration in the price of exports from the less-developed countries, and Southern import-substitution policies. The panel also noted that tariff barriers to Southern manufactured exports remained higher than tariffs on developed country exports despite GATT liberalization.[17] The report led to the 1958 GATT Programme for the Expansion of International Trade, and to the establishment of a GATT committee to consider problems of Southern exports of primary products and manufactured goods and to make recommendations for the expansion of Southern export earnings.

Developing countries used this new committee and the ongoing trade rounds to push for better access to Northern markets through unilateral concessions from developing countries, including a standstill on tariff and nontariff barriers for exports of Southern states, elimination of quantitative restrictions inconsistent with GATT rules, duty-free entry for tropical products, elimination of customs duties on primary products important to the trade of less-developed countries, reduction and elimination of customs tariffs on semiprocessed and processed Southern exports, and reduction by the North of internal taxes and revenue duties on products produced primarily or wholly in Southern states. The Northern countries, however, were prepared to agree only to a set of goals, not a policy commitment.[18] The less-developed countries, frustrated with the realities of trade and with the structure of management, turned to a new strategy: changing the GATT not from within but through an assault from without.

Unity and Confrontation

Beginning in 1961, the South developed a united front to press the North for changes in trade management and in the operation of the international trading system. In Third World conferences and in the United Nations General Assembly, where the South commanded a majority, the less-developed countries pushed through their demands for trade and other economic reforms. A key plank in the Southern platform was a call for an international conference on trade and development. Confronted with the South's persistence and growing unity plus its increasing numerical control of the General Assembly, the North agreed to convene a United Nations Conference on Trade and Development (UNCTAD), which was held in 1964.[19]

The Southern countries then focused on achieving trade reform through UNCTAD. They formed the Group of Seventy-Seven, named for the co-sponsors of the Joint Declaration of the Developing Countries made to the General Assembly in 1963.[20] The declaration spelled out for the first time its common goals for trade reform:

The existing principles and patterns of world trade still mainly favour the advanced parts of the world. Instead of helping the developing countries to promote the development and diversification of their economies, the present tendencies in world trade frustrate their efforts to attain more rapid growth. These trends must be reversed.[21]

In order to make international trade "a more powerful instrument and vehicle of economic development,"[22] the Seventy-Seven offered a series of goals for UNCTAD ranging from the improvement of institutional arrangements to the progressive reduction and early elimination of all barriers and restrictions impeding Southern exports (without reciprocal concessions on their part), to increased exports of primary products to the developed countries, and the stabilization and establishment of fair prices.[23] The Group of Seventy-Seven, which retained its original name but which eventually came to include 127 states, became a permanent political group representing Southern interests within the UN system.

UNCTAD also became a permanent United Nations organization.[24] Its doctrine, which has served as a basis for united Group of Seventy-Seven action, was developed by UNCTAD's first secretary-general, Raul Prebisch.[25] In UNCTAD's structuralist analysis of North-South relations, the world is divided into a center, or the developed countries, and a periphery, or the less-developed countries. The market works against the less-developed countries because of the long-term structural decline in Southern terms of trade and because of Northern protectionist policies that discriminate against Southern exports. As a result, the South has "a persistent tendency toward external imbalance," what Prebisch called the "trade gap." Unless measures are taken to counteract the structural bias against the South and to fill the trade gap, argues UNCTAD, the underdeveloped countries will not be able to meet reasonable growth targets.

UNCTAD has also worked with the Southern states to develop specific proposals for reforming the system and has fostered Southern bloc unity. Southern unity within UNCTAD gradually spread to other forums such as the IMF, the World Bank, as well as the United Nations.

Despite the creation of UNCTAD, the united Southern front did not greatly alter the management of trade or the operation of the international market. Maintaining Southern unity proved difficult. Many cleavages—political and ideological, differing levels of development, and different relations with Northern states—divided the South. Although there had been no problem reaching agreement on common general goals, these differences made it difficult to reach agreement on specific, short-term policies. The cleavages also tended to prevent the group from establishing priorities and contribute to the accumulation and escalation of demands, which politicized conflict and confrontation with the North and prevented serious bargaining.[26] The South was also weakened by a united front of Northern opposition to the creation of a powerful UNCTAD, unwillingness to treat UNCTAD as a legitimate negotiating forum, and insistance on dealing with trade issues in GATT. The South's marginal economic importance, its declining importance as an area of superpower competition, and its own internal divisions enabled the North to defeat, weaken, or ignore the South's proposed resolutions. Thus, the South was unable to achieve its goals of a change in institutional structure, increased exports of Southern manufactures, and improvement in Southern commodity trade.

Despite opposition from the North, the South was able in 1964 to obtain the establishment of UNCTAD as a permanent organization within the framework of the United Nations. UNCTAD also led to changes in GATT.[27] Faced with an attempt to replace GATT as the principal forum for trade management, the North agreed to add to the GATT agreement a new section on trade and development, Part IV, which came into operation in 1965. It called on states to refrain from increasing trade barriers against products of special concern to the less-developed countries, give priority to the reduction and elimination of such barriers, and implement a standstill on internal taxes on tropical products. More important, Part IV provides for exceptions to the free-trade rules for the less-developed countries: it eliminates the rule of reciprocity in trade negotiations and accepts commodity agreements to stabilize and ensure more equitable prices. Finally, the new section called for joint action to promote trade and development, which was the basis for establishing a Trade and Development Committee in GATT to work on the elimination and reduction of trade barriers.

The institutional changes in UNCTAD and GATT had little impact. UNCTAD cannot compel its members to take action: it can only make proposals and create public pressure on the members to comply. Part IV of GATT is similarly nonbinding. The continued weakness of the developing countries in the GATT was evidenced during the Kennedy Round negotiations of 1964 to 1967 (the first trade negotiation that followed the implementation of Part IV). Although developing countries participated for the first time in an active way and although their participation was encouraged by the developed countries, the results of the Round for the South were slim. Restrictions against Southern manufactures, such as textile products and clothing, remained higher than the norm; agricultural protectionism, including that on tropical products, remained intact; and quantitative restrictions and nontariff barriers continued to limit Southern exports generally.[28]

The South's limited ability to change Northern policy was revealed again in the case of Southern demands for a scheme to expand the industrial exports of developing countries.[29] Growth of manufactured exports, it was argued, could not be achieved alone by eliminating obstacles such as tariffs and quotas. It would also be necessary to give industrial exports from less-developed countries preferential access to Northern markets (that is, lower tariffs for the products of less-developed countries than for those of the developed countries). Preferences would help Southern industries overcome the problem of high initial costs of infant industries and, by opening larger markets, would enable them to achieve economies of scale, lower their costs, and eventually compete in world markets without preferences.[30]

Following years of conflict over the concept of a general system of preferences (GSP), agreement was reached in 1968 on the principle of establishing a preferential scheme, and in 1971, GATT authorized the preference scheme through a waiver of its most-favored-nation requirement. However, there were important limits on GSP schemes implemented by the Northern states.[31] Because the North was unable to agree on a common general system, individual states adopted similar but different schemes. These individual preference schemes are temporary—for example, the U.S. scheme, passed in 1975, lasted for ten years and had to be renewed by Congress. The main schemes are subject to ceiling limitations on the quantity or value of any particular import receiving preferences. In addition, many products have been excluded from preferential treatment including many import-sensitive goods for which the South enjoys a comparative advantage.[32] Geographical coverage is also uneven. For example, Taiwan was included in the U.S. scheme but not in that of the EC. The developed countries have also reserved the right to refuse to grant preferences to any state they choose, although only the United States has actually taken such action in the case of OPEC.[33]

Furthermore, evidence suggests that only a few countries, including South Korea and Hong Kong, have benefitted from GSP and that these countries could have competed in international markets without any preferences.[34] The least-developed countries export few goods that enable them to make effective use of the preference schemes. And ironically, GATT's success in general trade liberalization tends to eliminate the difference between preferential treatment and general treatment and to erode the advantages of preferences.[35]

The story of commodity schemes, the third Southern demand, was shorter and even less successful.[36] Commodities represent a huge share of Southern exports and foreign exchange earnings. In 1978, for example, over 80 percent of the South's export earnings came from primary commodities.[37] In 1986, 48 percent of the South's export earnings came from primary commodities.[38] The problems of commodity trade are numerous: price fluctuations that affect foreign exchange earnings; Northern protectionism and discriminatory tax policies; and competition from synthetics and substitutes.[39] Southern proposals to UNCTAD have been equally numerous: commodity agreements to stabilize prices and to establish remunerative and equitable prices; compensatory finance schemes to ease earnings fluctuations; the liberalization of Northern protection against Southern commodities; and aid for products facing competition from substitutes and synthetics. Until the oil crisis and its aftermath, the North successfully resisted all such proposals.[40]

In sum, Southern unity and confrontation without further leverage proved to be weak bargaining tools. The UNCTAD "victories" led to only minor revisions in Southern dependence. The result was more frustration and hostility from the developing world.

Commodity Power
and the New International Economic Order

Suddenly, in the early 1970s, OPEC's ability to seize control of the international oil system suggested that Southern producers could pose a serious threat to the North by withholding or threatening to withhold supplies of raw materials (see Chapter 9). At the time, it seemed that the North was becoming dependent on a variety of raw material imports from the South. While overall consumption was rising, high-grade Northern supplies of many materials were being depleted, and extraction in the North was becoming increasingly expensive. Because supplies in the less-developed countries were plentiful and production costs were low, demand for raw material imports from the less-developed countries was increasing.[41]

An economic boom in the developed countries at the end of the 1960s and the beginning of the 1970s led to a surge in Northern demand for raw materials from the developing countries. Inflation and the uncertainties of floating exchange rates led to a shift of speculative funds into commodities, further increasing demand and creating price increases and supply shortages. Furthermore, as the oil crisis demonstrated, the North's ability to ensure access to supplies through political and military action was weakened by the end of colonialism and the waning influence of the West in Third World governments. Not surprisingly, many developing countries concluded that the North was now vulnerable to commodity threats.

The credibility of the threat was enhanced by a growing Southern ability to control access to their raw materials. New, skilled cadres in many Southern states had acquired expertise in the raw materials industry and in world commodity market conditions and operations (see Chapter 8). Greater national control over raw material production facilitated the control of supplies. Moreover, as frustration with the North grew, the South's political leaders become more willing to use these new skills to manipulate raw material supplies.

The South's discovery of commodity power led to a new period in North-South relations. Southern states united to use aggressively the commodity weapon and other economic and political resources at their disposal to persuade the North to restructure the international economic system (for commodity cartels, see Chapter 9). At Third World Conferences in 1974, 1975, and 1976, the Group of Seventy-Seven drew up a coordinated program for a "new international economic order" (NIEO). The Declaration and Action Programme on the Establishment of a New International Economic Order adopted in 1974 by a special session of the General Assembly reflected the South's new sense of power. The declaration proclaimed that

> the present international economic order is in direct conflict with current developments in international political and economic relations. . . . The developing world has become a powerful factor that makes its influence felt in all fields of international activity. These irreversible changes in the relationship of forces in the world necessitate the active, full and equal participation of the developing countries in the formulation and application of all decisions that concern the international community.[42]

While the Southern program for the new international economic order touched all areas of international economic interaction, the South placed special emphasis on trade reform. It called for a reduction in Northern tariff barriers on a nonreciprocal basis, improvement in the preference schemes implemented by the developed countries, more effective adjustment assistance in the developed countries to ease the cost of more imports in the less-developed countries and to defuse political opposition, and international commodity agreements. A central element of the Southern program was a proposed Integrated Programme for Commodities that was to consist of an international agency and a common fund of $6 billion to support the prices of ten commodities.[43]

The ability of the less-developed countries to change the old economic order depended in part on Southern unity. The South stood a much better chance of forcing the North to make concessions if it could link its various potential commodity threats and, in particular, the oil threat, the inducement of an international agreement on oil prices, or if OPEC's considerable financial power could be linked to other Third World demands. However, unifying this heterogeneous group of states continued to be a difficult task. The impact of rising oil prices on the oil-importing developing countries and the growing economic divergence between the newly industralized countries (NICs) and the other less-developed countries were particularly divisive.

Nevertheless, the South demonstrated a surprising degree of cohesion. Over a decade of common action gave the group an understanding of how to conduct international negotiations. In this period, some oil producers, Algeria and Venezuela in particular, played a leadership role in mobilizing a common Southern front and linking the oil issue to other Third World demands. The credibility of the South's threat to the North was enhanced by the projections of most resource economists at this time that demand for developing country raw materials would rise due to the rapid growth in consumption of durable goods and the depletion of known mineral resources.[44] A minority view at the time argued that oil was the exception, that commodity power was a short-term phenomenon based on temporary shortages, and that even if there were scarce resources producers would not be able to coordinate their actions as OPEC had to threaten the North[45] (see Chapter 9).

Because of the perceived seriousness of the commodity threat, coupled with Northern concerns about growing financial linkages with the developing countries, the tremendous financial power of the capital-surplus oil exporters, and a growing interest in Southern markets, the developed countries were willing to enter into negotiations with the South on the issue of a new international economic order. Thus, they agreed to several special sessions of the United Nations General Assembly to discuss the NIEO and they supported a special producer-consumer negotiation.

European countries that were more vulnerable to supply interruption were the most receptive to the NIEO demands. The EC, for example, agreed to the first Lome Convention between the Community and forty-six associated African, Caribbean, and Pacific (ACP) states. The agreement increased aid to the ACP states and gave them a greater voice in aid management; provided for preferential access for ACP products to EC markets without reciprocal advantages for EC products; and created a compensatory finance scheme, Stabex, to stabilize the export earnings of the associated states from twelve key commodities.[46]

The United States—more self-sufficient and, thus, less vulnerable to external supply control—felt that the developed market economies should not make impetuous bargains with the South based on what it saw as a temporarily unfavorable situation. In the view of U.S. policymakers, the only threat came from the oil-producing states. When the Southern oil consumers recognized that OPEC was damaging their economies, the United States believed they would turn on the oil producers. Eventually the cyclical factors that led to temporary Northern vulnerability would disappear and commodity prices would fall.

As the 1970s wore on, the North did come to feel less vulnerable. The oil countries, in particular the Gulf states, were not willing to use their leverage on behalf of other developing countries. Furthermore, as raw material prices began to decline, it became clear that the rise in commodity prices in the 1970s was a cyclical and not a structural phenomenon. Finally, developing countries were unable to unite to create cartels similar to OPEC.

The various negotiations on the establishment of a new international economic order (held in the 1970s) revealed the limits of Southern power. One example was the Conference on International Economic Cooperation (CIEC), which met from 1975 to 1977. It linked Northern interest in an energy dialogue with OPEC (see Chapter 9) to Group of Seventy-Seven desires for negotiations on other raw materials, finance, and development as well as energy. The results of CIEC were meager: an agreement in principle to establish a common fund for commodity-price stabilization, a promise by the North to redouble its efforts to reach the 0.7-percent-of-GNP aid target, and a pledge by the North to give $1 billion to the least-developed countries. The common fund was eventually adopted by UNCTAD in 1980 but never implemented because of an inadequate number of ratifications. The 0.7-percent target was not reached. And the $1 billion for the least-developed countries had, by and large, already been committed. The conference was unable to reach agreement on the key issues of oil price and supply and international monetary reform.[47]

The Group of Seventy-Seven also used UNCTAD to put forth programs for NIEO demands. The main UNCTAD effort focused on the proposal for an Integrated Programme on Commodities. It called for the negotiation of international commodity agreements (ICAs) for raw materials exports important to developing countries and the establishment of a common fund to stabilize the prices of developing country commodities.

ICAs are accords among producers and consumers designed to stabilize or increase the price of particular products. They may be of three types or combinations thereof: buffer-stock schemes such as that of the International Tin Agreement, whereby price is managed by purchases or sales from a central fund at times of excessive fluctuation; export quotas such as those used by the International Coffee Agreement, whereby price is managed by assigning production quotas to participating countries in order to control supply; and multilateral contracts, whereby the importing countries contract to buy certain quantities at a specified low price when the world market falls below that price and the exporting countries agree to sell certain quantities at a fixed price when the world market price exceeds the maximum.

UNCTAD's efforts to implement international commodity agreements foundered on the traditional problems of ICAs. Producers who would like to use ICAs to raise prices and consumers who want only to stabilize prices often have difficulty agreeing on objectives. When they have been able to reach agreement, ICAs have been plagued by such problems as temptations to cheat when prices rise, variations of price and supply among different qualities of the same commodity, encouragement of using substitutes, the difficulty of imposing drastic production or export reductions, the high cost of financing buffer stocks, and the political and financial difficulty of managing an ICA when there is a long-term downward trend in commodity prices. Moreover, most Northern governments oppose ICAs as inefficient, encouraging waste and the misallocation of resources, helpful to only a few developing countries, and actually damaging to others faced with higher prices due to ICAs.[48] Despite UNCTAD efforts, few ICAs—tin, sugar, coffee, cocoa, natural rubber, and tropical timber—have been negotiated. Most of these date back to the 1960s and are not a result of UNCTAD's efforts. Only the rubber and tropical timber agreements were formally concluded under UNCTAD and the latter provides only for cooperation and consultation on product and market development, conservation and reforestation, and not price stabilization.[49]

UNCTAD's common fund never saw the light of day.[50] Following Northern resistance to the South's proposed $6 billion fund, UNCTAD eventually agreed in 1980 on a less ambitious $400 million plan. However, the agreement never received the ratifications needed to set it into operation.

Although the Southern vision of the new international economic order was never implemented, there were some additional limited achievements in the 1970s. One was the establishment of compensatory financing facilities that attempted to stabilize or increase the export earnings of developing countries by compensating them when the fall in the price of a commodity lead to a decline in export earnings. A Compensatory Financing Facility created by the IMF in 1963 was greatly expanded in 1975, 1979, and again in 1988. It allowed IMF members to borrow from the fund in excess of their regular quota limits when commodity prices and thus export earnings fell below normal levels.[51] Another compensatory financing facility was the EEC Stabex scheme set up under the Lome Convention of 1975. It established a fund to pay the associated ACP states compensation when the market price for certain commodities fell below a certain level. Wealthier associated states received an interest-free loan, whereas the poorest states received a grant.

The developing countries also achieved some success in the GATT's Tokyo Round of multilateral trade negotiations that took place from 1975 to 1979.[52] Their main goal was to obtain what came to be known as "special and differential treatment" that would exempt developing countries from GATT's rules on reciprocity and most-favored-nation obligations. During the Tokyo Round, the developing countries succeeded in obtaining a series of agreements that built the principle of special and differential treatment of developing countries into the GATT rules. These agreements gave permanent legal authorization for GSP preferences and preferences in trade between developing countries. They also authorized "more favorable" treatment for developing countries on nontariff barriers and special favorable treatment for the least-developed developing countries.[53]

As a balance to special and differential treatment, the developed countries insisted on the inclusion of a "graduation clause" in the GATT articles. It set forth the principle that as Southern countries reached higher levels of development, preferential treatment would be withdrawn and countries would be expected to assume the full rights and obligations of the GATT.[54] The developing countries, especially the NICs, unsuccessfully opposed this principle, which they saw as a device that the North could use to withdraw preferential treatment unilaterally whenever the developing countries began to threaten the Northern economies. One problem with the graduation provision was that it included no criteria or standards for graduation.

In addition to this amendment of the GATT, developing countries were able to obtain special and differential provisions in the various codes negotiated during the Tokyo Round. For example, Southern countries were permitted under the government procurement code to rely on domestic purchases when they were necessary to protect infant industries and balance-of-payments positions. Similarly, standards code did not bind Southern countries when its provisions conflicted with development, financial, and trade needs. And the subsidies code excused developing countries from most obligations.[55]

The developing countries achieved little else in the Tokyo Round. The failure to reach agreement on a safeguards code (on safeguards, see Chapter 3) left in place many of the new Northern protectionist policies such as VERs. As the target of many of these policies, the developing countries had particularly sought strict rules governing the application of safeguard measures; explicit criteria of actual, not potential, injury to producers in importing states; and controls on selectivity, that is, the ability of individual exporters to be singled out and subjected to safeguard actions. The developing countries were dissatisfied with the results of the Tokyo Round, and many chose not to ratify the code agreements.

By the close of the 1970s, the South's strategy based on unity, commodity power, and the NIEO had reached a dead end. While the Group of Seventy-Seven continued to call for its vision of a new international economic order in the United Nations and UNCTAD, developments in the international market were changing the South's bargaining power and creating a very different economic order.

The New Order for the 1980s

Trade between the developed and developing countries underwent several changes that altered the politics of North-South trade in the 1980s. Despite the predictions of experts that the world faced a future of ever-diminishing raw materials, the soaring commodity prices of the mid-1970s turned out to be a cyclical phenomenon. If anything, the long-term trend seemed to be a decline and not an increase in the growth of world demand for raw materials. In the 1970s and 1980s, rates of growth of GNP in the developed countries fell from the rapid rates of the 1960s, thus slowing demand for commodities. Demand also declined as output in the Northern states shifted from manufacturing, which requires raw materials, to services, which use far fewer raw materials (see Chapter 3). The dramatic rise in prices in the 1970s encouraged conservation, greater recycling, and the substitution of traditional materials by synthetics or by technology and energy-intensive materials. This decline in demand growth combined with a new capacity created by investment during the commodity shortages of the 1970s led to excess capacity, oversupply, and weakening of prices.[56]

Prices of non-oil commodities of developing countries fell by 24 percent between 1980 and 1986. They then recovered somewhat, rising 14 percent between 1986 and 1988[57] (see Figure 7–1). As a result, from 1980 to 1986, the terms of trade fell by 9 percent for low-income developing countries, by 8, 6, and 4 percent, respectively, for lower-middle, middle, and upper-middle income developing economies. During the same time period the industrial countries' terms of trade improved by 9 percent.[58]

The decline in prices seriously affected the poorest of the developing countries who still relied heavily on commodity exports. For example, Zambia's exports, over 90 percent of which are copper, declined by over one-half between 1980 and 1985. In the same period, Liberia's export earnings, largely from iron ore and rubber, and Bolivia's earnings, largely from tin, declined by nearly 40 percent.[59] Although cyclical factors may boost demand for certain raw materials and while certain developing country exporters may benefit from shifts in demand for commodities, commodity power will not be an effective bargaining tool for the South.

While many of the poorest developing countries were caught in the collapse of commodity prices, others were developing strong manufacturing capabilities and increasing their exports of manufactured products. In the 1970s, export-oriented industrialization policies of a number of developing countries began to bear fruit. Lower labor costs in labor-intensive industries, such as textiles and shoes, and production innovations often acquired from the North, as in the case of steel, enabled certain developing countries to compete successfully in Northern markets

From 1965 to 1986, the share of manufactured goods in exports from

Figure 7–1   Real Non-Oil Commodity Prices

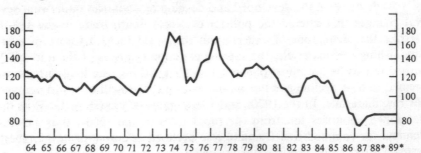

aOECD import price index deflated by OECD manufactures export prices.
bWeighted average of food, tropical beverages, vegetable oilseeds and oils, agricultural raw
   materials, minerals, ores, and metals prices.
cTotal index as in (b) deflated by OECD manufactures export prices.
*OECD projections from 1988 I onwards.
SOURCES: UNCTAD, OECD.

the developing countries more than doubled, reaching 51 percent of the total value of their exports in 1986.[60] Southern manufactures also came to represent a large share of Northern imports. Between 1963 and 1987 Southern manufactures increased from 4 to 13 percent of their share of industrial country manufactured imports.[61] By 1987, 30 percent of U.S. imports of manufactured products came from developing countries, up from 15 percent in 1972. In 1987, Japan obtained 30 percent of its manufactured imports from the South, up from 18 percent in 1972.[62] Southern manufactured exports also increased as a percentage of total consumption in the North. Despite growing protectionism, for example, the LDCs' exports of clothing rose from 4.0 percent of the consumption by developing countries in 1970 to 16.3 percent in 1980; footwear increased from 2.6 percent to 16.3 percent; leather products from 6.2 percent to 17.3 percent; and radios and televisions from 1.1 percent to 6.7 percent.[63]

The principal beneficiaries of this change in the structure of trade have been the newly industrializing countries (NICs), especially the so-called four tigers of Asia—South Korea, Taiwan, Singapore, and Hong Kong.[64] In the 1950s and early 1960s, the East Asian NICs, with the exception of Hong Kong, had followed successful import substitution policies. Domestic production of consumer nondurables replaced imports, resulting in a period of rapid growth. However, in the 1960s and 1970s, import substitution reached its limits. Expansion into machinery and consumer durables would have required extending protection and investment into more capital-intensive sectors; the costs of deepening import substitution would have been high given the small domestic markets in these countries; and domestic industries would not have been able to take advantage of economies of scale without expanding into foreign markets.

The four tigers also realized they needed the foreign exchange earnings to import essential goods. Poorly endowed with natural resources, they needed foreign exchange to pay for raw materials imports. For South Korea and Taiwan, which were receiving extensive foreign assistance, export earnings would eventually have to replace foreign aid as a source of financing. However, import substitution discriminated against export sectors. Protection raised the cost of imported inputs essential for many export industries and thus decreased the export competitiveness. In addition, import substitution was often accompanied by overvalued currencies that increased the price of exports.

The switch to export-led growth policies did not mean eliminating all protection. All the tigers except Hong Kong retained many import tariffs and quantitative restrictions. Outward-oriented policies did mean eliminating the bias against exports: maintaining realistic exchange rates that did not discriminate against exports, reducing import barriers for inputs to the export sector, as well as removing any other export disincentives such as export taxes. In South Korea, Taiwan, and Singapore, outward-oriented policies also involved government promotion of exports through favorable credit terms for exporters, tax incentives, undervalued exchange rates that decrease export prices, encouragement of foreign investment in export industries, and direct subsidies for targeted sectors. Government intervention has been criticized for targeting certain sectors, such as the heavy and chemical industries in South Korea, which have been relatively less successful than industries that were "chosen" by the markets. However, general export incentives clearly aided the competitiveness of the NICs. Exports also increased through "offshore assembly" or "sourcing" arrangements, whereby multinational companies were encouraged to invest for export (see Chapter 8).

These strategies have led to a dramatic increase in exports. The four tigers' share of world trade tripled to 6 percent between 1960 and 1986.[65] The four tigers alone account for over 60 percent of the manufactured exports from developing countries. With the addition of several other middle-income countries such as Brazil, Mexico, and Argentina, the share by the NICs of manufactured exports from developing countries has reached almost 75 percent.[66] The four tigers' share in OECD imports of manufactured goods increased from 1.3 percent in 1964 to 7.5 percent in 1985.[67] More importantly, outward-oriented strategies have resulted in higher growth rates than inward-oriented policies (see Figure 7–2).[68]

The success of the four tigers, however, created strong pressures for

Figure 7-2   Growth Rates of Forty-one Developing Countries Grouped by Trade Orientation

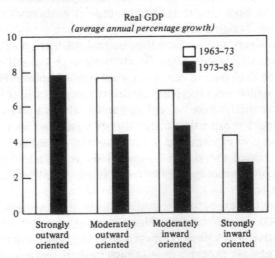

Real GDP
(average annual percentage growth)

□ 1963–73
■ 1973–85

Note: Averages are weighted by each country's share in the group total for each indicator of the trade groups.

Source: World Bank, *World Development Report 1987* (New York: Oxford University Press, 1987), p. 84.

protection. In the 1980s, the United States, which in 1986 absorbed 38 percent of the four tigers' exports of manufactured goods and 34 percent of all their exports, removed GSP privileges from these countries, limited imports of textiles, footwear, and steel and other items, and put pressure on the Asian NICs to allow their currencies to appreciate vis-à-vis the dollar.[69] The United States also put pressure on South Korea and Taiwan to remove domestic protection and open their markets to U.S. goods and services.

The trade problems of the Asian NICs were characteristic of North-South trade relations generally. Southern manufactured imports posed a significant threat to important industrial sectors with high concentrations of employment in the North and thus provoked powerful political pressures for protection. As a result, North-South trade in manufactures was increasingly subjected to trade barriers, especially voluntary export restraints.

The classic example was textiles.[70] The South has a comparative advantage in significant portions of the textile industry, which are labor-intensive and require simple technology. Those same segments of the textile industry, however, represent an important share of the GDP and employment of the developed countries. Furthermore, the textile industry tends to be geographically concentrated and well organized politically, making it a powerful force in domestic trade politics in all the developed countries.

In 1962, as the LDCs became competitive in Northern textile markets, the members of GATT negotiated the Long-Term Arrangement Regarding International Trade in Cotton Textiles (LTA) that allowed for such departures from GATT as quotas on textile imports and regulation of market share. Restrictive bilateral agreements were then negotiated within the framework of the LTA. In 1974, when LDCs had become competitive in artificial fibers and wool, GATT contracting parties concluded the Arrangement Regarding International Trade in Textiles, known as the Multi-Fiber Arrangement (MFA). It creates a multilateral framework for restricting trade in textiles, under which specific bilateral controls are negotiated. Over the years, MFA agreements have been regularly extended and made more restrictive, by broadening the coverage and lowering the growth in market share of the LDCs. By 1986, 61 percent of Southern exports of textile yarn and fabrics and 78 percent of Southern exports of clothing were subjected to import restrictions.[71] Originally intended as temporary safeguard measures, the textile agreements have become virtually permanent, and they have significantly limited textile exports of the LDCs.[72]

The case of textiles was repeated, in less comprehensive but equally pernicious ways, in many other sectors. Voluntary export restraints (VERs) increasingly restricted Southern access to Northern markets. Forty-seven percent of all export restraint arrangements in place in 1987 applied to exports from developing countries.[73]

As a result of the new importance of manufactures and new forms of protectionism, the trade policy of the LDCs focused more and more on access to the markets of the developed countries in general and on controlling VERs in particular. GATT's inability to conclude a safeguards agreement remained a critical problem for the South. The importance of manufactured exports also raised the graduation issue. As the NICs became more competitive in a variety of manufactured products, the Northern governments claimed that they no longer deserved special privileges such as GSP or special and differential treatment in GATT. In several forums, the North began to demand that the NICs graduate and assume the same commitments and responsibilities in the international trading system as the developed countries had.

In the 1970s, the South became not only an important exporter of manufactured products to the North, but it also became a more important market for the developed countries. From 1973 to 1981, the developing countries' share of the merchandise exports from the developed countries rose from 17 to 26 percent. Owing to the onset of the debt crisis, the share of the developing countries in total merchandise exports from the developed countries fell to only 19 percent in 1987.[74] In 1980, 37 percent of U.S. exports went to developing countries, up from 29 percent in 1973. By 1986 that share had dropped to 32 percent.[75]

The LDC debt crisis demonstrated the significance of Southern trade for the North. In an effort to generate foreign exchange to service their debt, developing countries reduced imports through austerity policies, rationing of foreign exchange, and import restrictions. Imports by the highly indebted countries grew at an average of 5.5 percent from 1973 to 1980 and fell by 6.3 percent per year on average between 1980 and 1987.[76] From 1980 to 1987, total U.S. exports increased 8 percent, but exports to Latin America dropped 19 percent; worldwide U.S. exports of manufactured goods fell 23 percent, but manufactured exports to Latin America fell 32 percent.[77] At the same time, in order to increase foreign exchange earnings, debtor countries tried to export more to the North, thus aggravating protectionist pressures. United States imports from the heavily indebted countries increased by 18 percent between 1980 and 1987.[78]

The New Pragmatism and the Old Stalemate

The new realities of the 1980s altered the trade strategy of the developing countries. The South's demand for a new international economic order was undermined by the collapse of commodity power, including the OPEC threat; by deep cracks in the Group of Seventy-Seven's solidarity, as several advanced developing countries were integrated into the existing international economic order; and by the weakened economic position of the South, especially the debt crisis. Meanwhile, the North was becoming both more protectionist at home and more insistent on market-oriented policies abroad. As we have seen, one of the main elements of Northern policies for developing country debtors was the implementation of domestic market-oriented reforms and international liberalization (see Chapter 6). The South's main bargaining chip in such a situation was to persuade the North that maintenance of world economic stability and prosperity depended on improving the lot of the developing countries.

The new forces of the 1980s also called into question the effectiveness of the South's preferred forums for management, especially UNCTAD and the United Nations. The South continued to use these forums to call for a new international economic order, but in the 1980s the Group of Seventy-Seven focused, instead, on more pragmatic measures to deal with the South's economic crisis. According to the South, the world economic crisis called for special measures to promote global recovery, especially measures to assist the South, which was most seriously affected by the crisis. In trade, this would mean greater access for the South to the markets of the North: dismantling protectionism, halting subsidy and dumping investigations, suspending countervailing and antidumping duties, implementing structural adjustment policies, expanding the GSP, and offering favorable treatment to the developing countries for trade in services. In commodities, the Group of Seventy-Seven called for less radical reforms than it had in the 1970s: interim commodity agreements to help stabilize commodity prices until ICAs can be negotiated; expansion of the IMF's buffer stock financing facility and compensatory financing facility; a new compensatory financing facility to cover the export-earnings shortfalls of countries dependent on commodity exports; and assistance in processing, marketing, transporting, and distributing Southern commodities.[79]

Although the South moved away from its strident NIEO proposals, it did not move far enough for the North. In the view of the developed market countries, the principal measures to be taken by the international community were those that would preserve the liberal international trading and financial system. What the South called emergency measures, for instance, interim commodity agreements, looked like fundamental deviations from the liberal order to the North. Thus, in the 1980s, the North-South dialogue in the United Nations system increasingly became a dialogue of the deaf. UNCTAD meetings produced only meager results.[80] And Group of Seventy-Seven efforts in the United Nations General Assembly to launch a set of global negotiations led nowhere.[81]

As the strategy of confrontation and the NIEO collapsed, developing countries shifted their focus to the GATT. One reason for the shift was the pressure of the developed countries, especially the United States, for a new round of multilateral negotiations. As the 1980s progressed, frustration with the existing trade regime grew in both the industrialized countries and the developing countries (see Chapter 3). Developed countries wanted a new multilateral trade round to bring agriculture and the so-called "new" areas of trade (services, intellectual property rights, and investment) under GATT discipline. There was also a growing sense of alarm at the proliferation of protectionist measures both outside of and in violation of GATT rules. The United States, in particular, became convinced that without significant reform of GATT rules and procedures, the GATT system would become increasingly divorced from economic reality and would ultimately collapse.

The dramatic export success of the newly industrialized countries was another motivation behind the drive for a new multilateral trade round. As concern mounted over the NICs' deepening penetration of U.S. and European markets, the industrialized countries accused the NICs of "free riding" on the international system by continuing to take advantage of the special treatment accorded developing countries by the GATT and by GSP programs despite overwhelming evidence that they had now become internationally competitive exporters. The industrialized countries insisted that the time had come for the NICs to "graduate" from developing country status (and the attendant benefits) and to be fully integrated into the GATT system, thereby becoming subject to obligations consonant with their new economic stature. As part of this push for "graduation," in January 1989 the United States removed the four tigers of Asia (Hong Kong, Korea, Singapore, and Taiwan) from the list of nations eligible for GSP privileges.

The industrialized countries also complained that the NICs engaged in unfair trade practices, ranging from export subsidies and dumping to restrictions on foreign imports and direct investment. The developed countries, especially the United States, also criticized the NICs for maintaining undervalued currencies which served to promote exports. Consequently, the number of bilateral trade disputes and unilateral trade actions initiated against these countries by the United States and by EC member states rose dramatically. The United States instituted trade negotiations with Korea and Taiwan over access to their markets for cigarettes, beef, beer, wine, and insurance. The EC entered into negotiations with Korea over the lack of patent protection.

While most concern focused on the NICs, developed countries also increased pressure on the non-NIC developing countries to liberalize their domestic trade and economic regimes, arguing that protectionist policies and demands for "special and differential" treatment made little economic sense. This change in approach was most evident in the growing emphasis of the World Bank and the IMF on the need for developing countries to undertake "structural" market-oriented economic reforms. A parallel approach was evident in the U.S. determination to use a new trade round to circumscribe the definition and application of "special and differential" treatment, to reform the GATT provision permitting developing countries to institute trade restrictions for "balance of payments" reasons, and to persuade developing countries to bind—and perhaps reduce—a substantial portion of their tariff schedules.

At the same time, the developing countries had become increasingly dissatisfied with what they regarded as the meager gains of previous trade rounds. Although, as we have discussed, some developing countries had participated in GATT negotiations, most had chosen to take a passive rather than active role, largely out of the conviction that the GATT—as a "rich man's club"—had little to offer poor countries with no substantial political or economic leverage. Since tariff reductions agreed in the GATT were applied on a most-favored-nation (MFN) basis, developing countries felt they could reap the benefits of GATT negotiations without necessarily participating. Furthermore, since most developing countries played a very small role in international trade, they had little incentive to engage in pragmatic bargaining and preferred to take an ideological stance marked by North-South confrontation, as discussed earlier in this chapter.

By the late 1980s, however, developing countries had become more dependent than ever on trade, and their stake in the maintenance of a liberal international trading regime had risen proportionately. In 1970 the ratio of exports to gross domestic product in developing countries was 11 percent. By 1987, that ratio had grown to 22 percent.[82] A handful of countries—the NICs—had become highly successful exporters in a relatively short time, and other developing countries were eager to follow in their footsteps. Given the failure of the inward-looking economic policies of the past, the example of successful export-led growth of the NICs, and the continuing commodity and debt crises, the developing countries were forced to reevaluate their development strategies. Slowly but surely, a number of developing countries began reforming their domestic economic policies, liberalizing their trade regimes, and shifting toward a more export-oriented growth strategy.[83]

The importance of actively participating in the GATT was underlined by rising protectionism against developing country exports. Between 1981 and 1986 the EC, Japan, and the United States collectively increased the application of "hard-core" nontariff barriers from 19 to 21 percent of their imports from developing countries, compared to an increase from 13 to 16 percent for imports from other industrialized countries (see Table 7-1). When one looks at individual export sectors, the figures are even more telling. As indicated in Table 7-2, nontariff barriers were applied by the industrial market economies to 55 percent of iron and steel imports and 31 percent of manufactures imports (nonchemicals) from developing countries, including 80 percent of clothing imports, and 27 percent of footwear imports.

Market access thus became a priority trade issue for the developing countries in the 1980s. Despite market access problems in Japan and Europe, the primary focus of this fear was the United States, which for many developing countries was by far their largest export market. As the United States continued to toughen its trade laws and as nontariff barriers con-

Table 7-1   Industrial Country Imports Subject to "Hard-Core" NTBs,
1981 and 1986 (percent)

| | Source of Imports | | | |
| | INDUSTRIAL COUNTRIES | | DEVELOPING COUNTRIES | |
Importer	1981	1986	1981	1986
EC	10	13	22	23
Japan	29	29	22	22
United States	9	15	14	17
All industrial countries	13	16	19	21

Note: "Hard-core" NTBs represent a subgroup of all possible NTBs. They are the ones most likely to have significant restrictive effects. Hard-core NTBs include import prohibitions, quantitative restrictions, voluntary export restraints, variable levies, MFA restrictions, and nonautomatic licensing. Examples of other NTBs that are excluded include technical barriers (including health and safety restrictions and standards), minimum pricing regulations, and the use of price investigations (for example, for countervailing and antidumping purposes) and price surveillance. Percentage of imports subject to NTBs measures the sum of the value of a country's import group affected by NTBs, divided by the total value of its imports of that group. Data on imports affected in 1986 are based on 1981 trade weights. Variations between 1981 and 1986 can therefore occur only if NTBs affect a different set of products or trading partners.
SOURCE: UNCTAD, 1987.

tinued to multiply, many developing countries came to view the GATT as their only chance of imposing discipline on U.S. trade policy and ensuring continued access to U.S. markets. This view was reinforced by the negotiation of a free-trade arrangement between the United States and Canada, which some countries saw as an indication that the United States was turning away from multilateralism. The European Community's renewed efforts after 1985 to achieve full economic integration similarly provoked fear that the GATT system was on the verge of disintegrating into protectionist regional and bilateral trading blocs. Developing countries also hoped that the Uruguay Round would force Japan to offer greater access to its markets.

Finally, by the mid-1980s there was greater recognition of the diversity of interests among developing countries and the problems that posed for the traditional bloc approach to relations with the North. At one extreme were the NICs, some of which seemed on the verge of joining the exclusive club of industrialized nations. At the other extreme were the least developed of the developing countries, clinging to the frayed margins of the international trading system. In the middle lay a wide range of countries at different levels of economic development, each differing in its degree of export dependence, in comparative advantage, and in its political and social objectives. In the face of such diversity, many developing countries came to believe that their interests would best be served by a pragmatic rather than ideological or bloc approach to negotiations in the GATT.

Table 7-2   Import Coverage Ratios of a Subgroup of NTBs Applied by
Selected Industrial Market Economies, 1981 and 1986

| | Source of Imports | | | | | | | |
| | WORLD | | INDUSTRIAL COUNTRIES | | DEVELOPING COUNTRIES | | CPES | |
Product coverage	1981	1986	1981	1986	1981	1986	1981	1986
Ore and metals (27, 28, 67 and 68)	12.7	24.7	13.1	29.4	8.6	12.8	26.2	30.0
Iron and steel (67)	29.0	64.2	26.8	65.2	24.8	54.6	58.1	68.2
Nonferrous metals (68)	3.8	6.4	1.9	6.0	6.1	6.4	7.9	8.0
Chemicals (5)	13.2	12.7	13.8	12.9	11.4	12.6	10.5	13.5
Manufactures, not chemicals (6 and 8, less 67 and 68)	18.6	20.5	15.4	17.8	31.3	31.0	41.3	43.0
Leather (61)	8.2	13.9	5.5	17.9	9.9	9.9	3.9	8.5
Textile yarn and fabrics (65)	37.3	39.6	18.6	21.2	57.6	61.4	74.3	75.6
Clothing (84)	67.3	67.4	40.2	38.9	77.1	77.9	74.8	74.9
Footwear (85)	71.3	32.5	65.1	24.1	71.0	27.0	81.5	62.4

Note: The figures in the table are to be regarded as preliminary and subject to revision. Numbers in parentheses refer to SITC codes. The import coverage ratios (the sum of the value of a country's import groups affected by NTBs divided by the total value of its imports of these groups) have been computed using 1981 import trade weights. Computations have been made at the tariff-line level and results aggregated to relevant product group levels. The data cover a broad range of NTBs, including para-tariff measures (for example, variable levies, seasonal tariffs, and countervailing and antidumping duties), quantitative restrictions (including prohibitions, quotas, nonautomatic licensing, state monopolies, voluntary export restraints, and restraints under MFA and similar textile arrangements), import surveillance (including automatic licensing), and price control measures. Standards to comply with health and technical regulations as well as excise taxes are not included because the data base information coverage is not even for all countries. The industrial market economies covered are Austria, Canada, EC (excluding Portugal and Spain), Finland, Japan, New Zealand, Norway, Switzerland, and the United States.
SOURCE: UNCTAD 1987.

Initially the developing countries resisted the call by the developed countries for a new trade round and argued that instead of discussing new issues, GATT talks should focus on old, unresolved issues. For example, Brazil proposed addressing the elimination of nontariff barriers and the Multi-Fiber Agreement, liberalization in trade of tropical products, restraint in the use of antidumping and subsidy actions, and an improved dispute settlement mechanism.[84] Using the threat of nonparticipation in the round to bargain for greater attention to Southern concerns, the LDCs achieved some concessions such as a special negotiating group and a commitment to an early agreement on tropical products. With these concessions in hand, they concurred in the 1986 agreement to launch the Uruguay Round and entered the negotiations determined to be active participants in the GATT process. In order to participate in the round, Mexico became a contracting party to the GATT in 1986, and a number of other developing countries, including China, Bolivia, Guatemala, Honduras, and El Salvador, initiated proceedings to accede to the General Agreement.

The most active and cooperative developing country participants in the negotiations were those that believed they had a great deal at stake: most of the NICs and developing countries from the next tier, such as the ASEAN nations. A handful of countries chose to pursue a hard line, making traditional Group of Seventy-Seven demands, for example, for unqualified "special and differential" treatment. The hard-line countries were led by Brazil and India, which had large domestic markets and continued to rely on import substitution and included others that felt they would lose from liberalization.

Although most developing countries were reluctant to mar the appearance of Southern unity, many chose to pursue a more pragmatic strategy. Believing that only those who played the game had any chance of winning concessions, they worked with developing and industrialized countries alike in an effort to reach agreements on issues of importance to them. As a result, despite clear differences in priorities between the industrialized and developing countries, the Uruguay Round negotiations did not split along North-South lines. Instead, coalitions developed along issue lines which, in contrast to early rounds, often included both industrialized and developing countries. One pivotal coalition was the so-called "Cairns group" of thirteen agricultural exporting nations—nine of them developing countries—that was organized in 1986 to pressure the United States and the EC to find a solution to the problem of excess production and subsidization of agricultural products. Many other North-South informal groupings developed in the course of the negotiations on issues as varied as nontariff barriers, dispute settlement procedures, trade in services, tariffs, and tropical products.

Since the most important goal of the developing countries was increased access to industrialized country markets, they tended to focus their efforts in the Uruguay Round negotiations on such issues as enforcing the standstill and rollback of protectionist measures agreed to at the beginning of the trade round; bringing agriculture and textiles under GATT discipline; strengthening safeguards and discipline over "gray area" measures; eliminating nontariff barriers to trade; tightening GATT rules (e.g., the antidumping code) to limit the ability of developed countries to invoke their trade laws against alleged offending nations; and reforming the dispute settlement mechanism and other GATT procedures in order to improve surveillance and enforcement. The developing countries continued to insist on special treatment in recognition of their development needs, although a number of them indicated a willingness to be flexible on the precise form taken by such special treatment.

Concerning the so-called "new" issues under negotiation (services, intellectual property, and investment), the majority of developing countries were either lukewarm or hostile. They saw services, intellectual property, and investment negotiations as efforts aimed at changing developing country policies in areas not appropriately covered by GATT. Only a handful of countries (the Asian NICs) expressed a qualified willingness to consider entering into agreements on these topics—and that was primarily because they suspected that they would be better off entering into multilateral agreements than being subjected to bilateral pressure from the developed countries, especially the United States. All the developing countries insisted that any concessions on the "new" issues would be linked to progress made on the more traditional issues of importance to them.

The 1990s

Thus, as the decade of the 1980s drew to a close, the developing countries found themselves once again reevaluating their trade and developing strategies. Having concluded that the traditional strategies of import-substitution and North-South confrontation yielded few concrete benefits, many developing countries turned to more pragmatic policies. They started to reform their economic and trade policies to become more outward-looking, and they increasingly sought to negotiate deals with the North while maintaining a public facade of Southern unity. The cracks in that facade widened, however, as the disparity between Third and Fourth Worlds grew and as the diversity of Southern interests became more apparent. With the increasing disparity between the NICs and the rest of the South, the advanced developing countries may move away from the Southern bloc and seek separate deals with the North. Some observers have suggested that the NICs may be co-opted into the North, even becoming members of the Organization for Economic Cooperation and Development, the primary international economic organization of the industrialized countries.[85] Others have advocated the formation of a new Pacific economic forum that would include the United States, Japan, and the rapidly growing Asian countries.[86]

In addition, various countries and regions of the South will maintain special trading relationships with countries and groups in the North. The special EC-ACP relationship has been maintained as the Lome Agreement has been periodically renegotiated.[87] In the 1980s, the United States passed trade legislation and negotiated a series of bilateral treaties giving the countries of the Caribbean Basin preferential access to U.S. markets. In 1987, the United States and Mexico negotiated a special bilateral trade agreement that some, including President Reagan, suggested should be expanded to a full free-trade agreement along the lines of the U.S.-Canada agreement. And Japan has strengthened economic ties with other countries in the Pacific Basin region. Indeed, it seemed that in the 1990s, Japan and the NICs of Asia might form a powerful new economic bloc linked by trade, investment, and aid relationships.

Efforts to develop Southern regional ties have been largely unsuccessful. Both the Latin American Free Trade Area (LAFTA) and the Association of South East Asian Nations (ASEAN), for example, have produced limited results.

The South's search for bargaining leverage will continue to be tested as it attempts to persuade the North that it is in the self-interest of the industrialized countries to make changes that will help the developing countries export, earn more, service their debts, and provide markets for Northern products. Strong protectionist pressures in both traditional manufacturing sectors and agriculture will make it difficult, although not impossible, for the North to respond to the South. As the preferred Southern forums (e.g., UNCTAD) become less and less effective, the South must find new ways to enhance its effectiveness in the traditional institutions preferred by the North, such as the GATT. Finally, the South must determine not only what it wants to achieve but also what it can achieve. The last decade has seen the beginning of a new pragmatism in the South. But the new pragmatism has, as yet, led nowhere for the majority of developing countries. If industrialized country protectionism and the South's weakness in trade negotiations continue, many developing countries now hoping to emulate the NICs will be forced to reassess their strategy of export-led growth and to reassess, once again, their role in the international trading system. The 1990s will continue to test the relationship between trade and development, and the outcome will profoundly affect both the future of Southern policies and the international trading system.

NOTES

1. Clair Wilcox, *A Charter for World Trade* (New York: Macmillan, 1949), p. 141.
2. Economic Commission for Latin America, *The Economic Development of Latin America and Its Principal Problems* (Lake Success, N.Y.: United Nations, 1950); Economic Commission for Latin America, *Theoretical and Practical Problems of Economic Growth* (New York: United Nations, 1951).
3. Ian Little, Tibor Scitovsky, and Maurice Scott, *Industry and Trade in Some Developing Countries: A Comparative Study*, published for the Development Centre of the Organization for Economic Cooperation and Development, Paris (London: Oxford University Press, 1970), pp. xvii–xxii, 1–29. For an example of the economic argument underlying import substitution policies, see Gunnar Myrdal, *An International Economy* (New York: Harper & Row, 1969), pp. 275–284.
4. Wilcox, *A Charter for World Trade*; Williams Adams Brown, Jr., *The United States and the Restoration of World Trade* (Washington, D.C.: Brookings Institution, 1950), pp. 97–104, 152–158.
5. Wilcox, pp. 140–167; Brown, pp. 178–180, 203–211, 217–222.
6. Only four less-developed countries—Ceylon (Sri Lanka), Cuba, Haiti, and India—sought and obtained permission to impose quantitative restrictions under Article 18. The limitations imposed by the contracting parties, however, destroyed much of the benefit of their use. Article 18 was revised in 1955 to provide a greater possibility for withdrawal or modifica-

tion of concessions previously made and to enable the use of quantitative restrictions for balance-of-payments reasons. But once again, the many safeguards included rendered it of little use to the South. Sidney Wells, "The Developing Countries, GATT and UNCTAD," *International Affairs*, 45 (January 1969), 65–67; Karin Koch, *International Trade Policy and the GATT, 1947–1967* (Stockholm: Almquist & Wiksell, 1969), pp. 227–232.

7. Steffan B. Linder, "The Significance of GATT for Underdeveloped Countries," in *Proceedings of the United Nations Conference on Trade and Development*, 5 (1964), 502–532; Robert Hudec, *Developing Countries in the GATT Legal System* (London: Trade Policy Research Center, 1987), p. 24.

8. Although it was not permitted under GATT, the South was able to follow protectionist policies under IMF rules, which allowed quantitative restriction for balance-of-payments reasons, or under GATT waivers, or because they were not members of GATT.

9. Little et al., *Industry and Trade in Some Developing Countries*, pp. 1–29. For the Latin American experience with protection, see Economic Commission for Latin America, *The Process of Industrial Development in Latin America* (New York: United Nations, 1966), pp. 21–35.

10. For the limits of import substitution, see Little et al., *Industry and Trade*, pp. 1–29; United Nations Conference on Trade and Development, *Toward a New Trade Policy for Development*, Report by the Secretary-General (New York: United Nations, 1964), pp. 21–22.

11. Anne O. Krueger and Constantine Michalopoulos, "Developing-Country Trade Policies and the International Economic System," in Ernest H. Preeg, ed., *Hard Bargaining Ahead: U.S. Trade Policy and Developing Countries* (New Brunswick: Transaction Books, 1985), pp. 40–45.

12. World Bank, *World Development Report, 1986* (New York: Oxford University Press, 1986), Chapter 4.

13. The argument here is that of Raul Prebisch: see United Nations Conference on Trade and Development, *Toward a New Trade Policy for Development*. For a summary of Prebisch's argument and the arguments of the critics of the theory of declining terms of trade, see A. S. Friedeberg, *The United Nations Conference on Trade and Development of 1964: The Theory of the Peripheral Economy at the Centre of International Political Discussions* (Rotterdam: Rotterdam University Press, 1969), pp. 33–67.

14. One of the most flagrant examples of restrictive export agreements was the Long-Term Arrangement Regarding International Trade in Cotton Textiles, which was negotiated in the GATT. The North, in particular the United States, forced the less-developed exporters (as well as Japan) to agree to "voluntarily" limit their cotton textile exports with the threat that the alternative—national import quotas imposed by national legislatures—would be worse. Later, the cotton agreement was expanded to a Multi-Fiber Arrangement.

15. For the Southern view of trade barriers, see United Nations Conference on Trade and Development, *Toward a New Trade Policy for Development*; United Nations Conference on Trade and Development, *Towards a Global Strategy of Development* (New York: United Nations, 1968). For other analyses, see Harry G. Johnson, *Economic Policies Toward Less Developed Countries* (New York: Praeger, 1967), pp. 78–110; Alexander J. Yeats, *Trade Barriers Facing Developing Countries* (London: Macmillan, 1979).

16. Economic Commission for Latin America, *Economic Survey 1969* (New York: United Nations, 1969), pp. 61, 62.

17. *Trends in International Trade: A Report by a Panel of Experts* (Geneva: The Contracting Parties to the General Agreement on Tariffs and Trade, October 1958). The experts were Roberto de Oliviero Campos, Gottfried Haberler, James Meade, and Jan Tinbergen.

18. Koch, *International Trade Policy and the GATT, 1947–1967*, pp. 235–244.; Hudec, *Developing Countries in the GATT Legal System*, pp. 39–46.

19. For a history of events leading up to UNCTAD I, see Cordovez, "The Making of UNCTAD"; Friedeberg, *The United Nations Conference on Trade and Development of 1964*; Charles L. Robertson, "The Creation of UNCTAD," in Robert W. Cox, ed., *International Organization: World Politics* (London: Macmillan, 1969), pp. 258–274.

20. For an analysis of the Group of Seventy-Seven, see Bronislav Gosovic, *UNCTAD, Conflict and Compromise: The Third World's Quest for an Equitable World Economic Order Through the United Nations* (Leiden, Netherlands: A. W. Sijthoff, 1972), pp. 271–292. For a

discussion of Southern unity, both in the Group of Seventy-Seven and UNCTAD, see Robert L. Rothstein, *Global Bargaining: UNCTAD and the Quest for a New International Economic Order* (Princeton: Princeton University Press, 1979), pp. 118–122.

21. United Nations General Assembly, 18th Session, Official Records: Eighteenth Session, Supplement No. 7 (A 5507), p. 24.

22. Ibid.

23. Ibid., p. 25.

24. In Branislav Gosovic, *UNCTAD, Conflict and Compromise*, p. 271. On UNCTAD see Joseph S. Nye, "UNCTAD: Poor Nations' Pressure Group," in Robert W. Cox and Harold K. Jacobson, *The Anatomy of Influence: Decision Making in International Organization* (New Haven, Conn.: Yale University Press, 1973), pp. 348–349.

25. For a statement of the UNCTAD doctrine, see United Nations Conference on Trade and Development, *Towards a New Trade Policy for Development and Toward a Global Strategy of Development*.

26. See Gosovic, *UNCTAD, Conflict and Compromise*, pp. 279–286, on Southern cleavages and pp. 293–301, for the Northern bloc within UNCTAD. There is also a group composed of the socialist states of Eastern Europe, Group D. For an analysis of bargaining within the Northern bloc over commodity issues, see Rothstein, *Global Bargaining*, pp. 123–125.

27. On the addition of Part IV generally, see Kenneth W. Dam, *The GATT: Law and International Economic Organization* (Chicago: University of Chicago Press, 1970), pp. 236–244; Hudec, *Developing Countries in the GATT Legal System*, pp. 56–60.

28. United Nations Conference on Trade and Development, *The Kennedy Round, Estimated Effects on Tariff Barriers: Report by the Secretary General of UNCTAD*, Parts I and II (New York: United Nations, 1968); International Bank for Reconstruction and Development and International Development Agency, *Annual Report 1968* (New York: IBRD and IDA, 1968), pp. 33–34.

29. For a history of the issue of preferences, see Gosovic, *UNCTAD, Conflict and Compromise*, pp. 65–93; and Tracy Murray, *Trade Preferences for Developing Countries* (New York: John Wiley, 1977), ch. 1. For a study of U.S. policy, see Ronald I. Meltzer, "The Politics of Policy Reversal: The American Response to the Issue of Granting Trade Preferences to the Developing Countries, 1964–1967" (Ph.D. diss., Columbia University, 1975).

30. United Nations Conference on Trade and Development, *Toward a New Trade Policy for Development*, pp. 65–75.

31. For the details of the various preference schemes, see United Nations Conference on Trade and Development, *Operations and Effects of the Generalized System of Preferences: Fourth Review* (New York: United Nations, 1979).

32. United Nations Conference on Trade and Development, *Proceedings of the United Nations Conference on Trade and Development, Third Session* (13 April to 21 May 1972), vol. 2, Merchandise Trade (New York: United Nations, 1973), pp. 104–140; Tracy Murray, "How Helpful Is the Generalised System of Preferences to Developing Countries?" *Economic Journal*, 83 (June 1973), 449–455; U.S. Code, *Congressional and Administrative News*, 93rd Cong., 2nd sess., 1974, vol. 2 (St. Paul: West Publishing, 1975), pp. 2398–2399; U.S. House of Representatives, Committee on Ways and Means, 98th Cong., 2nd Sess., *Summary of Provisions of H.R. 3398, Trade and Tariff Act of 1984* (Washington, D.C.: U.S. Government Printing Office, 1984).

33. United States Congress, House of Representatives, Committee on Ways and Means, *Report to the Congress on the First Five Years' Operation of the U.S. Generalized System of Preferences (GSP)*, 96th Cong., 2nd sess. (Washington, D.C.: U.S. Government Printing Office, 1980).

34. Rolf J. Langhammer and Andre Sapir, *Economic Impact of Generalized Tariff Preferences* (London: Trade Policy Research Centre, 1987).

35. For an analysis of the effects of tariff reductions on GSP, see Thomas B. Birnberg, "Trade Reform Options: Economic Effects on Developing and Developed Countries," in William R. Cline, ed., *Policy Alternatives for a New International Economic Order: An Economic Analysis* (New York: Praeger, 1979), pp. 234–239.

36. For histories of the commodity issue, see Gosovic, *UNCTAD, Conflict and Compromise*, pp. 93–114; and Carmine Nappi, *Commodity Market Controls: A Historical Analysis*

(Lexington, Mass.: D.C. Heath, 1979). For recent developments, see F. Gerard Adams and Jere R. Behrman, *Commodity Exports and Economic Development* (Lexington, Mass.: Lexington Books, 1982).

37. Independent Commission on Development Issues, *North-South: A Program of Survival* (Cambridge, Mass.: MIT Press, 1980), p. 141.

38. *World Development Report, 1988* (New York: Oxford University Press, 1988), p. 245.

39. For background on the problems the commodity market poses for developing countries, see David L. McNicol, *Commodity Agreements and Price Stabilization* (Lexington, Mass.: D.C. Heath, 1978), pp. 15–24; Alton D. Law, *International Commodity Agreements* (Lexington, Mass.: D.C. Heath, 1975), ch. 1.

40. Gosovic, *UNCTAD, Conflict and Compromise*, pp. 99–101.

41. World Bank, *Commodity Trade and Price Index, 1986* (New York: Oxford University Press, 1986), Tables 5 and 16.

42. "Declaration and Action Programme on the Establishment of a New International Economic Order," in Guy F. Erb and Valeriana Kallab, *Beyond Dependency: The Developing World Speaks Out* (Washington, D.C.: Overseas Development Council, 1975), p. 186. For another summary of NIEO proposals, see Branislav Gosovic and John G. Ruggie, "On the Creation of a New International Economic Order," *International Organization*, 30 (Spring 1976), 309–345.

43. The mechanisms for increasing and stabilizing prices were to include buffer stocks, a common fund for financing such stocks, multilateral purchase and supply agreements for particular commodities, and compensatory finance. For details on the Integrated Programme for Commodities, see United Nations Conference on Trade and Development, "An Integrated Programme for Commodities and Indexation of Prices," in Karl P. Sauvant and Hajo Hasenpflug, eds., *The New International Economic Order: Confrontation or Cooperation Between North and South?* (Boulder, Colo.: Westview, 1977), pp. 85–102. For an analysis of the negotiations surrounding the program, see Rothstein, *Global Bargaining*, Part I.

44. See, for example, C. Fred Bergsten, "The Threat from the Third World," *Foreign Policy*, 11 (Summer 1973), 102–124, and "The New Era in World Commodity Markets," *Challenge*, 17 (September-October 1974), 34–42; Donella H. Meadows et al., *The Limits to Growth: A Report for the Club of Rome's Project on the Predicament of Mankind* (New York: Universe Books, 1972).

45. See, for example, Stephen D. Krasner, "Oil Is the Exception," *Foreign Policy*, 14 (Spring 1974), 68–84; Raymond Mikesell, "More Third World Cartels Ahead?" *Challenge*, 17 (November-December 1974), 24–27.

46. This first Lome Convention was renewed and revised in 1979 and 1984. Negotiation on Lome IV will be begun in 1990. See Isebill V. Gruhn, "The Lome Convention: Inching Towards Interdependence," *International Organization*, 30 (Spring 1976), 240–262; John Ravenhill, "What Is to be Done for the Third World Commodity Exporters? An Evaluation of the STABEX Scheme," *International Organization*, 38 (Summer 1984), 537–574; For background on Lome II, see Carol C. Twitchett, "Lome II Signed," *Atlantic Community Quarterly*, 18 (Spring 1980), 85–89; Jonathan Fryer, "The New Lome Convention: Marriage on the Rocks but No Separation," *International Development Review*, 1 (1980), 53–54.

47. For details of this analysis, see Jahangir Amuzegar, "Requiem for the North-South Conference," *Foreign Affairs*, 56 (October 1977), 136–159.

48. Johnson, *Economic Policies Toward Less Developed Countries*, pp. 137–149.

49. In 1985, one of the most effective and long-lasting ICAs, the International Tin Agreement, collapsed when the tin buffer stock ran out of funds. For background on the various ICAs, see Nappi, *Commodity Market Controls*, pp. 61–83. On the International Rubber Agreement, see Ursula Wassermann, "UNCTAD: International Rubber Agreement, 1979," *Journal of World Trade Law*, 14 (May-June 1980), 246–248; and UN Report, January 20, 1984, pp. 5–6.

50. For background on the common fund, see Nappi, *Commodity Market Controls*, ch. 6; Paul D. Reynolds, *International Commodity Agreements and the Common Fund* (Lexington, Mass.: D.C. Heath, 1978).

51. The facility originally allowed countries to access 25 percent of the quota. It was later increased to 83 percent of the quota for shortfalls in export earnings or for an increase in the

price of cereal imports with a combined access limit of 105 percent. In 1988, a contingency mechanism was added to provide additional funding in response to adverse external developments. Borrowers must repay the fund in five years when, it is expected, the cyclical decline of prices will have been reversed. See International Monetary Fund, *Annual Report 1988*, pp. 49–50.

52. For background on the Southern countries and the Tokyo Round, see Bela Belassa, "The Developing Countries and the Tokyo Round," *Journal of World Trade Law*, 14 (March-April 1980), 93–118; Thomas R. Graham, "Revolution in Trade Politics," *Foreign Policy*, 36 (Fall 1979), 49–63; Stephen D. Krasner, "The Tokyo Round: Particularistic Interests and Prospects for Stability in the Global Trading System," *International Studies Quarterly*, 23 (December 1979), 491–531; Hudec, *Developing Countries in the GATT Legal System*, pp. 71–102.

53. For background, see General Agreement on Tariffs and Trade, *The Tokyo Round: Report by the Director-General of GATT* (Geneva: GATT, 1979); Hudec, p. 85.

54. For background on the graduation issue, see Isaiah Frank, "The Graduation Issue for the Less Developed Countries," *Journal of World Trade Law*, 13 (July-August 1979), 289–302.

55. GATT, *The Tokyo Round: Report by the Director-General of GATT*, pp. 166–177.

56. Raymond F. Mikesell, "The Changing Demand for Industrial Raw Materials," in John W. Sewell, Stuart K. Tucker, and contributors, *Growth, Exports, and Jobs in a Changing World Economy: Agenda 1988* (New Brunswick: Transaction Books, 1988), pp. 139–166).

57. International Monetary Fund, *World Economic Outlook, 1988* (Washington, D.C.: International Monetary Fund, 1988) p. 141.

58. *World Development Report, 1988*, pp. 242–243.

59. Mikesell, "The Changing Demand for Industrial Raw Materials," p. 140 and 155.

60. *World Development Report 1988*, p. 245.

61. General Agreement on Trade and Tariffs, *International Trade 1987–88* (Geneva: GATT, 1988), Table AC3.

62. GATT, *International Trade*, various issues.

63. World Bank, *World Development Report, 1983* (New York: Oxford University Press, 1983), p. 14.

64. For background on the NICs see: Organization for Economic Co-operation and Development, *The Newly Industrializing Countries: Challenge and Opportunity for OECD Countries* (Paris: OECD, 1988); Lawrence B. Krause, *Introduction to Foreign Trade and Investment: Economic Growth in the Newly Industrializing Asian Countries* (Madison, Wisc.: University of Wisconsin Press, 1985), p. 22; Neil McMullen and Louis Turner, with Colin L. Bradford, *The Newly Industrializing Countries: Trade and Adjustment* (London: Allen and Unwin, 1982); and David Yoffie, *Power and Protectionism: Strategies of the Newly Industrializing Countries* (New York: Columbia University Press, 1983).

65. IMF, *World Economic Outlook 1988*, p. 80.

66. Albert Fishelow, "Making Liberal Trade Policies Work in the 1980s," in Roger Hansen, ed., *U.S. Foreign Policy and the Third World, Agenda 1982* (New York: Praeger, 1982), pp. 56–57.

67. OECD, *The Newly Industrializing Countries: Challenge and Opportunity for OECD Industries*, p. 19.

68. Other factors have been crucial to the East Asian NICs' success. The four tigers all have a highly educated and skilled workforce that is highly disciplined and motivated. The four also have high savings rates, which has provided the credit for investment and enabled them to avoid heavy external borrowing. To the extent that they relied on foreign borrowing, it was usually channeled into export sectors that provided the foreign exchange necessary to service the debt. In addition, until recently these countries had a relatively stable political environment. Authoritarian regimes in South Korea, Singapore, and Taiwan allowed the political elites greater freedom to determine economic policies resulting in greater continuity of economic policies. These countries had either undergone land reform or never had a landed class, and so they did not have political pressure from an entrenched privileged class. In addition, the political legitimacy of these governments rested heavily on their economic success. Economic growth has led to a decrease in absolute poverty, a more equitable income distribution and an improvement in living conditions that has eased political pressures. These governments also

felt insecure surrounded by Communist countries and believed that economic strength would increase their independence and security. In addition, under these authorization governments, trade unions and minimum wages were discouraged, which kept wages from increasing significantly.

69. GATT, *International Trade 1987-1988*, Tables A14-A17.

70. Martin Wolf, "Managed Trade in Practice: Implications of the Textile Arrangements," in William R. Cline, ed., *Trade Policy in the 1980s* (Washington, D.C.: Institute for International Economics, 1983), pp. 455-482.

71. World Bank, *World Development Report 1987* (New York: Oxford University Press, 1987), p. 142.

72. Wolf., pp. 468-469.

73. United Nations, *World Economic Survey 1988* (New York: United Nations, 1988), p. 34.

74. GATT, *International Trade 1987-88*, Table AA10.

75. *Economic Report of the President, 1988* (Washington, D.C.: U.S. Government Printing Office, 1988), p. 367.

76. *World Development Report 1988*, p. 197.

77. U.S. Department of Commerce, *Highlights of U.S. Export and Import Trade* (Washington, D.C.: U.S. Government Printing Office, various issues).

78. GATT, *International Trade 1987-1988*, Table AA-7.

79. United Nations Conference on Trade and Development, *The Buenos Aires Platform; Final Document of the Fifth Ministerial Meeting of the Group of 77* (March 28-April 9, 1983) (New York: United Nations, 1983).

80. United Nations Conference on Trade and Development, *Report of the United Nations Conference on Trade and Development on its Sixth Session* (June 6-July 2, 1983) (New York: United Nations, 1983).

81. See Jagdish N. Bhagwati and John Gerard Ruggie, eds., *Power, Passions, and Purpose: Prospects for North-South Negotiations* (Cambridge, Mass.: MIT Press, 1984).

82. International Monetary Fund, *International Financial Statistics, Supplement on Trade Statistics, No. 15* (Washington, D.C.: International Monetary Fund, 1988), pp. 50-51.

83. The shift was incremental rather than dramatic, however, since the domestic political influence of the export sector—although growing throughout the decade—remained minimal in most countries. As one analyst put it, the political balance between trade-liberalizing and trade protectionist forces is the critical "knife's edge" on which national trade policy turns.

84. Carlos Luiz Marone and Carlos Alberto Primo Braga, "Brazil and the Uruguay Round," Paper presented for the Conference on the Multilateral Trade Negotiations and Developing Countries (Washington, D.C., September 15-18, 1988.)

85. Richard Holbrooke, Roderick MacFarquhar, Kazuo Nukazawa, and Evelyn Colbert, "The Evolution of the East Asian Rim of the Pacific," *Draft Report to The Trilateral Commission* (March 1988), pp. 75.

86. For a critical discussion of such proposals, see Roger D. Hansen, "North-South Policy—What Is the Problem?" *Foreign Affairs*, 58 (Summer 1980), 1104-1128.

87. ACP nations are concerned however, that their benefits have been diluted by privileges the EC has given to other developing countries on certain items, such as on tropical products, during the Uruguay Round negotiations. They also fear they will lose other benefits as the EC moves toward a unified market and standardizes the individual preferential arrangements each country has with the former colonies.

8

Managing the Multinational Corporation

The issue of managing multinational corporations is of greater concern in the less-developed countries than in the developed countries.[1] Multinational corporations have greater power in the South than in the North, and some evidence suggests that the costs of the power of multinationals have been greater in the less-developed world than in the developed world. Thus, developing countries have sought to develop public policies to shift the perceived imbalance of power between host government and foreign corporations and to regulate multinational corporations in order to capture more of the benefits of direct foreign investment.

Power: The Local Economy

The importance of foreign investment in the South varies from country to country. In some states, it is relatively insignificant, whereas in others it plays a key role. Multinational corporations have tended to concentrate in a few less-developed countries. Eighteen countries alone account for 86 percent of all private foreign investment in the South.[2] In these countries, in particular, foreign investment possesses considerable power.

The power of multinational corporations grows out of their structural position within the relatively small and underdeveloped economies of many Southern states.[3] Because agricultural and service sectors still account for much of the gross national product of the developing states, the multinational corporations play a relatively small part in their total GNP. But foreign investment often accounts for a large share of critical sectors.

Historically, Northern firms controlled the South's extractive sector, long the key to development. Multinationals, for example, controlled oil in the Middle East, copper in Chile and Zambia, and bauxite in Jamaica and Guyana. In many cases, even when the ownership and control of production have been transferred from multinational corporations to state-owned companies, the developing countries remain dependent on the multinationals for processing, shipping, marketing, and distributing their raw materials. For example, in 1980, despite widespread nationalization of the petroleum industry in the developing countries, 43 percent of all crude oil produced outside North America and the socialist countries was either produced or purchased by the seven major international oil companies, and 24 percent was produced or purchased by smaller international oil companies or trading companies.[4] In 1982, 46 percent of the world's bauxite capacity, 50 percent of its alumina capacity, and 45 percent of its aluminum capacity were owned by six large multinational corporations.[5]

A second and newer sector of Northern control is manufacturing. Since World War II, the developing countries have sought to expand their industrial sector as a primary means of development and have offered incentives for investment in manufacturing. The multinational corporations have often taken the lead in these new growth sectors. Foreign investment is growing most rapidly in manufacturing and is thus moving to dominate certain sectors of the new Southern industry. For example, foreign affiliates control 32 percent of production, 32 percent of exports, and 23 percent of the employment of Brazil's manufacturing sector. In Singapore foreign affiliates control 63 percent of production, 90 percent of exports, and 55 percent of employment in manufacturing.[6]

Foreign firms also represent a significant percentage of the largest and most powerful firms in Southern economies. Foreign investment in the Third World generally is found in industries dominated by a small number of large firms. For example, U.S. foreign investment is found in such highly concentrated industries as petroleum, chemicals, transportation, insurance, food products, electronics, and machinery.[7] The large firms that dominate such industries have more power to control supply and price than do firms in more competitive industries. Thus, the oligopolistic structure of foreign investment means that significant economic power is concentrated in the hands of a few large foreign firms.[8]

Power: Local Government

Such a situation of economic dominance, however, need not mean the removal of decision making from national control. In principle, Southern governments could assert the control necessary to retain decision making at home. Host state laws could be passed to regulate multinational corporations, and host governments could impose restrictions on multinational corporations when investment agreements are negotiated. To impose such controls, Southern governments could use the one important bargaining advantage they possess: control over access to their territories.[9] Control over access to resources that the multinational wants—local raw materials, labor, and markets—could be used by developing countries to impose controls on foreign investors.

In practice, however, the bargaining advantage of control over access is offset by the bargaining tools of the multinational corporation. The foreign investor often controls resources such as capital, technology, and access to foreign markets that the less-developed countries need for development. The South's desire for the benefits of direct foreign investment—for example, the ability to exploit a valuable raw material deposit or the possibility of expanding industrialization through new factories—poses a dilemma to policymakers in those countries. On the one hand, officials want to regulate the multinationals so as to maximize national benefits and minimize national costs. But on the other hand, they do not want to make regulation so restrictive that it will deter potential investors.

Related to the desire to regulate and the fear of overregulating is the problem of uncertainty.[10] Before a foreign investment is actually made, potential investors are uncertain about the operation's eventual success and final cost. For example, a corporation proposing to explore for and develop oil in a less-developed country cannot be certain of the ultimate success of the project until it has prospected and built up an extracting capability, that is, until it has determined whether oil will be discovered and at what price. Similarly, a corporation proposing to manufacture sewing machines for a local foreign market may not be able to determine the potential of that market and the final costs of production. Another risk faced by the corporation is the political instability in Third World host states and the uncertainty of the effect of political change and possible turmoil on investment. For foreign investors, such uncertainties serve to reduce the attractiveness of the local factors of production and the local market and thus weaken the hand of the host country.

Another factor weakening the bargaining power of the less-developed countries is the absence of competition for investment opportunities. The availability of alternative sources of raw materials and cheap labor elsewhere can diminish the bargaining ability of any one Southern state. At times, the oligopolistic nature of multinational corporations—the fact that few companies dominate the industry and that those companies may collaborate with one another to decrease competition—can also weaken the hand of the developing countries.[11]

Furthermore, even if a country resolves the dilemma in favor of regulation, there remain constraints on the country's ability to carry out regulatory policies. The ability of Southern governments to control multinational corporations is shaped by the availability of the skilled persons necessary to draft and enforce laws and to negotiate agreements to regulate foreign investment. Without skilled lawyers, financial experts, and specialists in the particular businesses that the state seeks to regulate, Third World governments are no match for the multinational corporation.

Another governmental problem has been the ability of multinationals to intervene in the host state's domestic political process to advance their corporate interests. Multinational corporations are able to use their resources in legal or even illegal political activities in host countries. Tactics such as public relations activities, campaign contributions, bribery, and economic boycotts are available to the corporation. In their ability to intervene in domestic politics, multinational corporations are, in one sense, no different from national corporations; the problem they pose is not in the area of foreign investment but in their ability as private institutions to influence the government.

There are, however, several characteristics of multinational corporations that distinguish them from national corporations and that make their participation in host politics a problem for the Southern states. Because multinational corporations are foreign-owned, they are not considered legitimate participants in the national political process. Their interests may not necessarily be those of the host state; their policies may, in varying degrees, reflect their own corporate interests or the interests of their home state. For these reasons, numerous states have barred foreign firms from political activities. Political participation by multinational firms carries the connotation and, at times, the reality of a challenge to national sovereignty. In addition, multinational corporations bring many resources to their political activities. Their financial resources and international structure can be powerful political tools.

Multinational corporations also can derive great power from their relationship with the government of their parent corporations. Investment in Southern states tends to be highly concentrated according to the home country. United States investment, for example, is predominant in Latin America, whereas French investment is dominant in the former French colonies in sub-Saharan Africa.[12] In the home country, these giant corporations often play a powerful political role. The ability of a multinational to pressure its home government to take certain actions and follow specific foreign policies to influence host governments adds to the imbalance between southern governments and multinational corporations.[13]

In sum, because of their powerful position within the Third World's economies and vis-à-vis the Third World's governments, multinational corporations can affect economic efficiency and welfare and influence politics in Southern host countries. The crucial question then, is, how have these corporations used their power?

Efficiency, Growth, and Welfare

Proponents argue that foreign investment has a positive effect on Southern economic development.[14] Such investment fills resource gaps in less-developed countries and improves the quality of factors of production. One of the most important contributions is capital. Multinational corporations bring otherwise unavailable financial resources to the South through the firm's own capital and its access to international capital markets. Figures indicate that an important share of the flow of capital to less-developed countries comes from foreign investment. In the 1960s and 1970s, direct foreign investment accounted for approximately 15 percent of total flows, averaging $7 billion a year. These flows declined relatively in the early 1980s. Nonetheless, in 1987, direct foreign investment flows to developing countries reached approximately $20 billion, which represented 22 percent of the total flows to developing countries[15] (see Table 6–1).

Multinational corporations also contribute crucial foreign exchange earnings to the developing world through their trade effect. First, the marketing skills and knowledge of foreign markets of the multinational corporations and their competitive products, it is argued, generate exports and thus increase the foreign exchange earnings of the host countries. Foreign affiliates of multinational corporations have contributed to the growing role of developing countries in world trade (see Chapter 7). For example, foreign affiliates of U.S. firms in developing countries more than doubled their share of world trade between 1966 and 1983. In Latin America, U.S. affiliates outperformed domestic industries as exporters.[16] Furthermore, the manufacture for the local market of products that otherwise would have been imported also saves precious foreign exchange.

A second crucial resource gap filled by the multinational, according to proponents of foreign investment, is technology. The desire to obtain modern technology is perhaps the most important attraction of foreign investment for developing countries. Multinational corporations allow Southern states to profit from the sophisticated research and development carried out by the multinational and make available technology that would otherwise be out of the reach of less-developed countries. Foreign firms train local staff, stimulate local technological activities, and transfer technology throughout the local economy.[17] Thus, technology improves the efficiency of production and encourages development.

Third, say proponents, foreign investment improves the quality of labor in the South. It provides needed managerial skills that improve production, and it creates jobs and trains workers. Multinationals are depending less on expatriate labor and providing more opportunities for local professionals to manage and operate their facilities. The rapidly growing service sector, in particular, promotes the development of high-level skills in its local workforce.

Supporters contend, finally, that multinational corporations have a positive impact on welfare. The creation of jobs, the provision of new and better products, and programs to improve health, housing, and education for employees and local communities, it is thought, improve the standard of living in the Third World.

This positive view of the role of multinational corporations in growth, efficiency, and welfare has been challenged by critics of the multinationals. In the 1970s, a new body of critical analysis of multinational corporations emerged. It argued that, at best, those policies adopted because they are best for the multinational are not necessarily best for the subsidiary or the host state and that, at worst, the multinational exploits less-developed countries and perpetuates dependence.[18]

Multinational corporations, explain these critics, do not bring in as much foreign capital as their proponents suggest. The financing of foreign investment is done largely with host-country, not foreign, capital.[19] For example, between 1958 and 1968, U.S. manufacturing subsidiaries in Latin America obtained 80 percent of all their financing locally, through either borrowing or subsidiary earnings.[20] Furthermore, according to the critics, multinational corporations, because of their strength, often have preferred access to local capital sources and are able to compete successfully with and thus stifle local entrepreneurs. Critics contend that such local financing is often used to acquire existing nationally owned firms. One study of the Mexican economy revealed that 43 percent of U.S. multinational corporations entered Mexico by acquiring existing firms and that 81 percent of these firms were formerly owned by Mexicans.[21] And in Brazil, 33 percent of U.S. multinational corporations began operations in Brazil by acquiring local firms. In the late 1960s and early 1970s, acquisitions accounted for 50 percent of the new multinational affiliates in Brazil, 63 percent of which were formerly owned by Brazilians.[22]

Some critics believe that foreign investment in less-developed countries actually leads to an outflow of capital. Capital flows from South to North through profits, debt service, royalties and fees, and manipulation of import and export prices. Such reverse flows are, in themselves, not unusual or improper. Indeed, the reason for investment is to make money for the firm. What certain critics argue, however, is that such return flows are unjustifiably high. They point to the fact that, in the seventies, profits in developing countries were substantially higher than profits in developed market economies. The average return on book value of U.S. direct foreign investment in the developed market economies between 1975 and 1978 was 12.1 percent, whereas the average return in developing countries was 25.8 percent.[23]

Furthermore, contend the critics, profits represent only a small part of the effective return to the parent. A large part of the real return comes from the licensing fees and royalties paid by the subsidiary to the parent for the use of technology controlled by the parent. In 1972, the payment by foreign affiliates for the use of technology accounted for 30 percent of total dividend income and 60 percent of all income from manufacturing received by U.S. parent corporations.[24] Critics do not argue that subsidiaries should not pay the parent for research and development costs incurred by the parent that eventually benefit the subsidiary. Rather, the critics contend that the subsidiaries in less-developed countries pay an unjustifiably high price for technology and bear an unjustifiably high share of the research and development costs. The monopoly control of technology by the multinational corporation enables the parent to exact a monopoly rent from its subsidiaries.[25] And the parent chooses to use that power and to charge inordinately high fees and royalties to disguise high profits and avoid local taxes on those profits, according to the critics.

Yet another mechanism of capital outflow—of disguising profits and evading taxes—identified by critics is trade. Much of the trade by multinational subsidiaries in developing countries is intracompany trade. Often, subsidiaries located in less-developed countries are obliged by agreements with the parent to purchase supplies from and to make sales to the parent.[26] The parent thus is able to manipulate the price of such intracompany imports and exports—the transfer price—to benefit the firm. Critics of multinational corporations argue that firms have used this transfer price mechanism to underprice exports and overprice imports and thereby to remove capital from the South.[27] In one study of an extreme case, it was argued that the overpricing of pharmaceutical imports into Colombia amounted to $3 billion.[28]

The negative effects of such decapitalization would be limited if, in the process of removing capital, the multinational corporations made a significant contribution to local development. Critics contend that the contribution of multinational corporations is limited or negative. Technology, they feel, is not the great boon for the South that the proponents of multinational corporations suggest. The high cost of technology has already been mentioned. Another criticism is that the importation of technology stunts the development of local technological capabilities.[29] Yet another problem is the appropriateness of technology. Although some foreign investment has entered the South to take advantage of abundant Southern labor and thus has contributed to employment, some multinational corporations bring advanced, capital-intensive technology developed in and for developed countries that does not contribute to solving the problem of unemployment in less-developed states.[30]

Critics also argue that multinational corporations do not benefit Southern labor. They make only a small contribution to employment, and they discourage local entrepreneurs by competing successfully with them in local capital markets by acquiring existing firms, by using expatriate managers instead of training local citizens, and by hiring away local skilled workers.[31] Finally, the trade benefits from the multinational corporations, according to the critics, are limited by restrictive business practices. Written agreements between parent and subsidiary may include clauses confining exports and requiring subsidiaries to produce only for the local market. Management policy, similarly, may hold down subsidiary production and marketing.[32]

In sum, say the critics, multinational corporations create a distorted and undesirable form of growth. They often create highly developed enclaves that do not contribute to the expansion of the larger economy. These enclaves use capital-intensive technology that employs few local citizens; acquire supplies from abroad, not locally; use transfer prices and technology agreements to avoid taxes; and send earnings back home. In welfare terms, the benefits of the enclave accrue to the home country and to a small part of the host population allied with the corporation.

Not only does the enclave not contribute to local development, say the critics, but it often hinders it.[33] In other words, the enclave economy develops at the expense of the local economy and thus of local welfare. It absorbs local capital, removes capital from the country, destroys local entrepreneurs, and creates inappropriate consumer demands that turn production away from economically and socially desirable patterns.

Despite more and more empirical studies examining the economic impact of multinational corporations on the developing countries, it is impossible to reach any general or definitive conclusion about the overall effect of multinationals on development. The influence of foreign investment varies from country to country, from sector to sector, from firm to firm, and from project to project. Some case studies demonstrate the beneficial impact of direct foreign investment; others, the detrimental effects. The principal effect of the criticism of multinationals that began in the 1970s has been to alter the political reality of foreign investment in the developing countries. No longer do governments assume that foreign investment will automatically promote development. Instead, as we shall see, developing country governments have tried to regulate that investment to maximize the rewards and minimize the costs to the host economy.[34]

National Political Process

The evidence suggests that multinational corporations have at times intervened in political processes in their host states. While most foreign investors do not become actively involved in host country politics, some multinational corporations have taken both legal and illegal actions within host states to favor friendly governments and oppose unfriendly governments, to obtain favorable treatment for the corporation, and to block efforts to restrict corporate activity. They have engaged in such legal activities as contributing to political parties, lobbying with local elites, and carrying out public relations campaigns.[35] They have also engaged in illegal activities (illegal contributions to political parties),[36] bribes to local officials,[37] and refusals to comply with host laws and regulations.[38] They have also used such extralegal methods as international boycotts to pressure an unfriendly government.[39]

Multinational corporations have also used their power in the politics of the home state to obtain foreign policies favorable to corporate interests. They have helped shape the liberal world vision that the U.S. government has sought to implement since World War II and that has favored foreign direct investment. They have worked for specific legislation, such as the Hickenlooper amendment, which enables the U.S. government to cut off aid to any country nationalizing U.S. investments without compensation; the Gonzalez amendment, which requires the United States to vote against any multilateral bank loan to a nationalizing country; the Overseas Private Investment Corporation, which insures foreign investment in many Southern countries; and the trade legislation which withdraws General System of Preference (GSP) tariff benefits from any country that expropriates U.S. companies without compensation.[40] This legislation protects foreign investment and often links the interests of the corporation with the foreign policy interests of the United States. At times, corporations have gone beyond legislation to seek governmental support for their opposition to unfavorable regimes in host countries.[41]

Not only have corporations sought to shape home government policy, but they have also served as tools of that policy. For example, in 1988 the United States used multinationals to put pressure on the Panamanian government of General Noriega by forbidding subsidiaries and branches of U.S. companies to issue any direct or indirect payments to the Noriega government. In the 1980s, it encouraged foreign investment to move to Jamaica following the change from a restrictive to a more open regime under Edward Seaga. However, multinational corporations do not necessarily advance the foreign policy of their home government. For example, foreign oil companies operating in Angola actively opposed U.S. sanctions on the Angolan government, because the sanctions conflicted with their own interests.

One of the most notorious examples of multinational interference in host country politics that served as a catalyst for host country policies to restrict multinational corporations was the intervention of the International Telephone & Telegraph Company in Chile in the early 1970s.[42] From 1970 to 1972, ITT actively sought, first, to prevent the election of Salvador Allende as the president of Chile and, once Allende was elected, to engineer his overthrow. In the process, ITT not only resorted on its own to a variety of illegal or extralegal activities but also tried to involve the U.S. government in both open and clandestine activities against Allende and was solicited by the U.S. government to serve as an agent of its policy.

The main reason for ITT's political intervention was concern that Chiltelco, ITT's profitable telephone company, would be nationalized without compensation if the Marxist candidate, Allende, won the 1970 Chilean election for president. As a result, ITT gave funds to conservative Chilean newspapers opposing Allende. It also tried unsuccessfully to get help from the U.S. Central Intelligence Agency in channeling funds to the conservative candidate opposing Allende. When Allende was elected, ITT conferred with the CIA on ways to destabilize his government. At one point, the company drafted an eighteen-point program of economic and political disruption to be carried out by the U.S. government and other multinational corporations. Included in the program were restricting public and private credit, boycotting Chilean copper, delaying fuel delivery and shipments of small arms and ammunition, and instituting an anti-Allende propaganda campaign and CIA activity. In March 1972, newspaper reports of ITT's attempts to overthrow Allende led to a Senate inquiry that revealed the extent of the company's intervention.[43] On the next day, the Allende government broke off negotiations with ITT regarding compensation for Chiltelco.

The intervention of ITT into Chilean politics is not an example of the typical behavior of multinational corporations in Southern states; most multinational corporations do not pursue such ruthless politics of intervention. But there are enough examples of intervention to suggest that multinational corporations are in a position to exercise political influence and may use that position to favor what the companies perceive corporate interest to be. In that sense, multinational corporations have posed real or perceived threats to the autonomy of Southern political processes.

Management of Foreign Investment by Less-Developed Countries

In the 1950s and 1960s, most developing country governments encouraged foreign investment and placed few restrictions on the operation of foreign investors in their states. By and large, less-developed countries accepted the prevailing international liberal regime based on national treatment; prompt, adequate, and effective compensation in the event of expropriation; and the right of foreign investors to appeal to their home country governments for assistance. Latin America was the exception. Since the turn of the century, Latin American countries have adhered to the Calvo Doctrine, which asserts the right of host nations to nationalize foreign investments and make their own determination of what constitutes fair compensation; thus they reject the right of foreign investors to appeal to their home governments for help. Even in periods when foreign direct investment has been actively encouraged in Latin America, the Calvo Doctrine has been maintained.[44] In the 1970s, many Southern governments adopted the Latin American position, altering their open-door policies.

A shift in public attitudes toward foreign investment was an important factor behind this change. As nationalist sentiment developed in the late 1950s and 1960s, the multinational corporation came to be seen as a threat to economic and political independence.[45] Furthermore, the development process increased demands for improved economic welfare, housing, transportation, and jobs.[46] To satisfy these new pressures and to preserve their own political power, Southern elites turned against the multinational corporation.[47] Opposition to multinational corporations thus became a politically useful and powerful platform for Southern elites.

In the 1970s, exposés of political intervention by multinational corporations in Southern politics outraged Southern publics and led to a new spurt of antimultinational opinion. The ITT scandal played an important catalytic role in public mobilization against multinational corporations. The initial revelations led to a U.S. Senate inquiry into multinationals in general, which revealed other instances of their intervention in politics.[48] Publicity regarding ITT and Chile also led to a unified Southern outcry against multinational corporations and to a United Nations investigation of them.[49]

The new critical economic analysis that pointed out the detrimental effects of foreign investment also contributed to changing public attitudes toward multinational corporations. As one critic of multinational corporations observed:

> Serious and competent economists can make a strong case against a permissive attitude toward private foreign investment and thus bring respectability even to attitudes originally based upon an unthinking, emotional reaction.[50]

A second factor behind the new policies toward multinational corporations was a shift in power from the multinational to the host government. One reason for the change in the power relationship was what one analyst called the "learning curve."[51] Over the years, host governments developed significant expertise in monitoring and regulating foreign investment. They trained cadres in the legal, financial, and business skills necessary to regulate foreign subsidiaries. This movement up the learning curve made it possible for host governments to develop the laws and bureaucratic structures for managing multinational corporations.[52]

Decreasing uncertainty also contributed to the shift in power. Analysts have pointed out that a distinction must be made between the bargaining position of a host country vis-à-vis a potential investor and its bargaining position vis-à-vis an investor who has already made a significant and successful investment in its country.[53] When a country is seeking investment, it is in a weak bargaining position. Foreign investors are uncertain about the success of the proposed operation and its final cost. To overcome these uncertainties and to attract investment, host countries must follow permissive policies regarding investment. But once a foreign investment is made and is successful, the bargaining relationship changes, and the power of the host country increases. The host country now has jurisdiction over a valuable multinational asset. As uncertainty decreases, the host government comes to regret and resent earlier permissive policies and agreements. The operation's success leads the host government to seek revision of agreements with foreign investors, whereas the company's financial commitment and interest weaken its bargaining position and ability to resist new terms for operation.

A third factor contributing to the power shift was the increasing competition for investment opportunities in the South. The greater numbers of foreign investors and countries with major multinational corporations meant that Southern states had more alternatives in choosing foreign investors. These alternatives are important at the level of individual investments, allowing greater competition and thus better terms for the host countries. They are also important in that they allow the Southern states to diversify investment away from one traditionally dominant Northern home state. Thus, for example, Japanese multinationals have emerged as an alternative to U.S. firms in Latin America, and U.S. companies have in turn emerged as an alternative to French firms in Africa.[54]

This shift in power from foreign investor to host government has clearly been the case in raw materials, such as copper and oil, where host-government policy has evolved from permissive policies to attract investment, to more strict application of local laws in such areas as taxation and labor policy once the foreign investment has been successful, and to eventual ownership of equity or direct involvement in business decision making on such matters as price or supply.[55] It is less clear whether the shift in power applies to manufacturing. Some analysts argue that it is more difficult for developing countries to control global manufacturing firms with worldwide production and worldwide marketing, because local subsidiaries remain dependent on the parent for supplies, capital, technology, and markets.[56]

In the 1970s, these various forces of change led to new Southern attempts to regulate multinational corporations. As discussed, one such abortive effort was launched in the United Nations (see Chapter 4). Part of the Southern plan for the New International Economic Order was an attempt to bring multinational corporations under international control. In 1974, the United Nations made two major statements on the NIEO: the Declaration of the Establishment of the New International Economic Order and the Charter of Economic Rights and Duties of States. Both of these documents asserted the full sovereignty of each nation over its natural resources and all economic activities including the right of nationalization. The Declaration of the Establishment of the NIEO made no reference to any compensation, and the Charter simply said that any compensation should be "appropriate." Although the United Nations did establish a Center on Transnational Corporations, the attempt to draw up an international code of conduct proved impossible. The real effort to control multinational corporations came at the national level and, in the case of the Andean Common Market (ANCOM), at the regional level (ANCOM's original members were Bolivia, Chile, Colombia, Ecuador, Peru, and Venezuela).[57]

The most publicized Southern attempts to manage multinational corporations have been nationalizations of local subsidiaries. Peru's government, for example, nationalized the International Petroleum Corporation, various banks, and the fishmeal and fish oil industry.[58] Chile and Zambia have taken over their copper industries,[59] and many oil-producing states have nationalized their oil industries.[60] Nationalization, although highly visible, is not the main method of Southern management or the prevailing trend of Southern attempts at control. In fact, after reaching a peak in 1975, nationalization declined dramatically.[61]

More important than well-publicized nationalizations were new laws, regulations, and bureaucratic structures designed to strengthen governmental control and to increase the host country's share of the economic rewards from foreign investment.[62] Attempts to manage the multinational corporation through such laws and policies varied from country to country and within countries from industry to industry. Nevertheless, certain trends emerged. Governments often put strict limits on the entry of new investment. Many countries enacted investment laws limiting the sectors in which foreign investment is permitted. Banking, communications, transportation, and public utilities are commonly reserved for national ownership. Restrictions were also placed on the amount of equity that foreigners may hold in local companies. For example, Mexico's foreign investment law of 1973 banned foreign investment entirely in sectors like those mentioned above and confined foreign equity and management control to 49 percent or less in many other sectors, including mineral exploitation, automobile manufacturing, and petrochemical by-products. One-hundred percent ownership was only allowed in a limited number of sectors: nonelectric equipment and machinery, electronics, machine tools, electronic machines and appliances, biotechnology, transportation equipment, chemicals, and hotels.[63] Several states also controlled the takeover of nationally owned firms by multinational corporations. Mexico, for example, required prior authorization before allowing a foreign investor to acquire 25 percent of the capital stock or 49 percent of the fixed assets of a nationally owned firm and gave Mexican investors a chance to make the purchase in place of the foreigner. In 1989 Mexico's restrictions on foreign investment were relaxed.

Some countries sought with varying degrees of success to reduce the level of existing foreign investment. In the ANCOM Uniform Code on Foreign Investment, reserved sectors were to be closed not only to new but also to existing foreign investment. Foreign firms operating in reserved sectors were to offer at least 80 percent of their shares for sale to national investors.[64] ANCOM's effort foundered due to the conflicts among its member states and the difficulty of implementing such strict divestiture procedures. India was more successful in its divestitive efforts. Between 1977 and 1980, India reduced foreign ownership in almost four hundred companies by requiring the issue of shares to the Indian public.[65]

Through these sectoral and equity restrictions and reinforced by new domestic abilities to enforce these restrictions, governments sought to encourage new forms of foreign participation—joint ventures, licensing agreements, management contracts, and turnkey arrangements—to replace total or majority ownership. The goal was to "unbundle" the foreign investment package: to separate technology, managerial skills, and market access from equity and control.[66] As a result, joint ventures, production sharing, and technical assistance agreements became more common, and many multinational corporations accepted less than majority ownership of affiliates in developing countries.[67] By the early seventies, 38 percent of the affiliates of U.S.-based corporations in developing countries were co-owned or minority-owned. Multinationals based in other countries have shown even more flexibility: by the late sixties, the proportion of minority-owned affiliates of corporations based in Europe was 49 percent, and that of other (primarily Japanese) corporations was 82 percent.[68]

Developing countries also sought to regulate behavior by the multinationals after entry. Restrictions on profit and capital repatriation were widely implemented throughout the developing world. The Andean Group, for example, limited remittances of profits and capital to 20 percent of registered investments. A number of countries, such as Mexico, supervise technology and licensing agreements.[69] Some countries require registration and greater disclosure of such information as capital structure, the technology used and restrictions on its use, and reinvestment policies.[70]

An additional control technique relies not on restrictions but on positive incentives. Inducements, such as tax advantages or exemptions from import restrictions, have been used to encourage companies to invest in new fields or to use new technologies, to invest in export industries and in less-developed regions of the country, and to increase sectoral competition. Brazil has relied on such positive tools of public policy to manage multinational corporations. In the 1970s the Brazilian Industrial Development Council distributed incentives to foreign investors to regulate them and direct their investments into desirable sectors of the economy.[71]

Another technique is the support of state-owned industry. In many industries with high barriers to entry, government-owned enterprise is the only viable national alternative to foreign investment. In both Mexico and

Brazil, for example, state-owned corporations have been formed in such basic industries as petroleum, steel, finance, utilities, and transportation.[72] Significantly, the emphasis on state-owned industry as a strategy for balancing foreign investment contributed to greater borrowing from foreign commercial banks in order to invest in national industry.[73]

A final method of control was the producer cartel (see Chapter 9). Various exporters of raw materials—particularly oil, copper, and bauxite—tried to manage multinational corporations by cooperating to increase prices as well as the national share of profits and national ownership. Until now, only OPEC, the oil producers' cartel, has used this technique successfully.

The 1980s: The New Pragmatism

In the 1980s, the Southern strategy of control and confrontation shifted toward more pragmatic policies toward multinational corporations. Although developing countries continued to closely monitor and control the activities of foreign investors, multinational corporations gradually came to be seen less as a threat and more as a potential opportunity for promoting growth and development.

The new pragmatism was the result of several converging forces. The decline in direct foreign investment flows to developing countries played an important role. Restrictive policies enacted in the 1960s and 1970s deterred some direct investment and led foreign investors to turn to nonequity arrangements as a way of gaining access to LDC markets.[74] Particularly troublesome for political investors were controls on remittance of earnings. Depressed economic conditions and low rates of return in most developing countries during the 1980s were an important factor in the decline in investment flows. For example, rates of return on U.S. foreign direct investment in Latin America fell from 18.8 percent in 1980 to 2.4 percent in 1983 before rising to 10.8 percent in 1985. Rates of return on U.S investment in other developing countries fell from 41.3 percent in 1980 to 22.5 percent in 1983 and to 18.6 percent in 1985.[75] The debt crisis further discouraged investment by making capital repatriation from many developing countries difficult or impossible. These unfavorable conditions in developing countries contrasted with rapid growth, rising rates of return, and few restrictions on foreign investment in many developed countries.

As a result, multinational corporations shifted their investment towards the developed countries and away from developing countries. Between 1982 and 1985, the share of foreign direct investment flowing to developing countries fell from 30.2 percent to 23.3 percent (see Table 8-1).[76] The largest drop came in Latin America, where foreign direct investment fell from 14.4 percent of total world investment flows in 1982 to 9.1

Table 8-1   Distribution of Foreign Direct Investment Inflows, by Major
Region, 1975–1985 (percentage)

Country Groups by Region	1975	1980	1981	1982	1983	1984	1985	Annual Averages 1975–1980	Annual Averages 1981–1985
Developed market economies	70.6	80.5	73.6	69.8	76.8	78.5	76.7	76.6	75.2
United States	12.1	32.4	44.7	31.1	27.0	51.7	38.9	24.6	39.2
Western Europe	47.0	41.0	29.7	32.9	37.0	19.8	33.7	43.3	30.4
Japan	0.9	0.6	0.4	0.9	0.9	—	1.2	0.3	0.6
Other	10.2	6.7	1.2	4.5	11.6	6.7	2.8	8.4	4.5
Developing countries	29.3	19.3	26.4	30.2	23.2	21.3	23.3	23.4	24.8
Africa	2.3	0.4	3.2	3.8	3.6	3.1	3.4	2.5	3.3
Latin America and the Caribbean	15.3	11.9	13.6	14.4	7.7	7.0	9.1	12.5	10.5
Western Asia	3.3	0.6	—	0.7	0.7	1.2	1.0	1.9	0.8
Other Asia and Oceania	7.4	6.1	9.3	10.8	10.7	9.6	9.1	6.2	9.9
Southern Europe	0.9	0.2	0.4	0.2	0.2	0.4	0.4	0.3	0.4
World[a]	100	100	100	100	100	100	100	100	100
Billions of dollars	21.5	52.2	56.8	44.5	44.1	49.0	49.3	32.1	48.7

[a]Excluding the centrally planned economies of Europe.
SOURCE: UNCTC, *Transnational Corporations in World Development: Trends and Prospects* (New York: United Nations, 1988), p. 76.

percent in 1985.[77] In contrast, flows of investment to the rapidly growing countries of Asia were unchanged. Foreign investors were attracted to these countries by large domestic markets as in China, Indonesia, and Thailand; skilled, low-cost labor and well-developed infrastructure for export-oriented manufacturing as in Hong Kong, Malaysia, Singapore, and Taiwan; petroleum and other natural resources as in Indonesia and Malaysia; and generally more favorable policies regarding foreign investment in certain countries.[78]

The debt crisis was another factor leading to a shift in LDC attitudes toward foreign direct investment. (On debt, see Chapter 6). Ironically, the ready availability of bank capital in the 1970s had enabled developing countries to adopt the restrictive policies that contributed to the fall in direct investment flows in the 1980s. As we have seen, in the 1970s, commercial bank flows replaced both direct investment and foreign aid as a source of development finance for many middle-income Southern countries. In the 1980s, however, the debt crisis increased the attractiveness of foreign direct investment as source of capital for growth. As a result of the crisis, both foreign and domestic sources of capital for investment were channeled to debt service. While foreign banks continued to lend to debtor countries, usually under pressure from their governments and the IMF, new lending

was devoted to debt service and not investment. Although they were important borrowers from the World Bank, the middle-income debtors were
no longer major recipients of foreign aid that had been redirected to the
least-developed countries. In addition, domestic sources of capital were
consumed by foreign debt service. As discussed, due to the debt crisis,
investment and with it growth in the highly indebted countries collapsed.
Increasingly, foreign direct investment emerged as one of the few possible
sources of needed foreign capital and foreign exchange. Furthermore, unlike debt service, earnings on foreign investment are related to the success of
an investment project and not to the vagaries of international interest rates.

More receptive policies toward foreign investment were also part of the
prescription of developed countries and multilateral institutions for resolving the debt crisis. Improved access for foreign direct investment was one of
the pillars of the Baker Plan for more liberal policies in debtor countries. A
more positive approach to foreign investment was also fostered by the
World Bank. The Bank's structural adjustment lending encouraged the
easing of restrictions on foreign investment, and the Bank established a
Multilateral Investment Guaranty Agency (MIGA) to insure and, thereby,
promote direct investment in developing countries. In Pakistan and other
nations, the World Bank has encouraged governments to allow private
foreign investors to build and operate major infrastructure facilities, such
as power plants and highways. These projects are occasionally even owned
by the foreign investors, but eventually ownership and operation of the
facilities is transferred back to the government or to local private enterprises. Furthermore, debt-equity swaps that were part of the menu for
reducing commercial bank debt involved exchanging financial debt for
foreign equity investment.

At the same time, developed countries generally took a more aggressive
role on the issue of access for foreign investment to the markets of developing countries. The U.S. Trade and Tariff Act of 1984, for example, broadened the definition of barriers to market access to include investment as well
as trade barriers, and the United States used the trade approach to push for
access to markets for U.S. firms. In addition, the developed countries
pushed for new investment provisions as part of the Uruguay Round (see
Chapter 3).

This encouragement to open their policies and be more receptive to
foreign investment fit well with the change in development strategies of
many Southern countries. In the 1980s, many developing countries shifted
from state-led investment to private-sector investment strategies. The clearest manifestations of this new approach were the privatization policies of
several developing countries. In an effort to promote more efficient and
competitive industry and to reduce the financial burden on government
budgets, many developing countries divested a number of state-owned
companies to the private sector.

Privatization policies complemented the new emphasis on export-led growth. As discussed, in this period many developing countries turned to the type of export-led development strategy that had been successful in the Asian NICs (see Chapter 8). In several of the NICs, promotion of foreign investment in the export sector was part of the export-led growth strategy. These countries attracted foreign direct investment in the export sector through export processing zones (EPZs) or by contractually requiring foreign firms to export in return for the right to invest (see below). Also related to the new emphasis on export-led growth was the growing interest of developing countries in obtaining access to modern technologies. Desire for advanced technology increased LDC receptivity to MNCs, the major holders of such technology.

These various forces converged in more liberal policies towards direct foreign investment. The new liberalism did not reverse established restrictive policies. Countries continued to control the entry and operations of foreign investors; most laws, regulations, and institutions put in place to control foreign investment remained; while countries opened up some sectors, such as those that exported or involved high technology, they maintained tightly closed policies in others (for example, the service sector); and the liberalization trend applied more to Asia and Africa than to Latin America where long-held concern about foreign investment inhibited change. Nevertheless, there was a clear trend towards encouraging foreign direct investment by reducing restrictions placed on the entry and operations of multinational corporations and by streamlining procedures and offering incentives to foreign investors.

New investment laws and policies adopted in the 1980s removed a variety of restrictions placed on foreign investors. A number of developing countries, including Korea, Mexico, and the ANCOM members, increased the number of sectors open to foreign investment. The opening tended to be in high-technology or export-oriented industries. In some countries, existing laws were implemented more flexibly. For example, IBM was given an exemption from Mexico's stringent limitation on foreign control of the informatics sector in order to set up a wholly owned subsidiary to produce microprocessors in Mexico. In return, IBM accepted a number of obligations regarding, for example, location of research and development in Mexico and exports from Mexico.[79] Privatization actions also involved foreign investors and not infrequently involved debt-equity swaps. Argentina allowed foreign private participation in petroleum extraction and telecommunications. In the case of telecommunications, foreign participation was financed in part with a debt-equity swap. Brazil sold part of its steel industry to foreign interests. Chile allowed foreign investors to use debt-equity swaps to buy stock in a state holding company. And the Philippines permitted foreign banks to convert their loan exposures into equity in its National Steel Company.[80]

Controls on operations were also eased in many developing countries. For example, Algeria eliminated requirements that the local partner exercise control, and Ancom removed restrictions on profit remittances. Policies requiring gradual divestiture, in Mexico and ANCOM for example, were relaxed. Restrictions on operations were relaxed in certain preferred sectors. Venezuela and others, for example, exempted foreign investment in electronics, informatics, and biotechnology from limitations on reinvestment of profits, remittances, repatriation of capital, and divestiture requirements.[81] A number of developing countries, such as Algeria, India, Indonesia, Korea, Mexico, and the Philippines, also simplified administrative procedures for approving foreign direct investment. Finally, certain socialist countries, such as Ethiopia, Mozambique, North Korea, and China, passed new laws making foreign investment possible, primarily through joint ventures. China's liberalization policy was the most dramatic. Starting from scratch in 1979, China developed a foreign investment regime and implemented a policy that attracted a significant number of foreign corporations.[82]

A number of other developing countries have set up export processing zones (EPZs). EPZs encourage investment for production of goods for export by making imports and exports free from tariffs or other trade restraints as well as through such techniques as providing infrastructure facilities for manufacturing and offering streamlined regulatory and administrative procedures. Their use has grown dramatically in recent years. While only 10 developing countries had EPZs in 1970, at least 53 Southern countries had them by 1986. Although EPZs are designed for both foreign and domestic producers, many foreign firms have invested in EPZs as a way of gaining access to low-cost labor for the production of such labor-intensive goods as electronics and textiles. Export processing zones have clearly helped promote the export of manufactured products.[83]

As national policies became more accommodating, international efforts to control multinationals also shifted from hostility to greater cooperation. A growing number of Southern countries, primarily in Africa and Southeast Asia, signed bilateral investment treaties (BITs) with developed countries. These treaties are designed to promote foreign investment by providing certain protections and a predictable foreign investment regime. They generally establish terms for entry of foreign investment; basic standards of treatment, such as national treatment or most-favored-nation treatment; conditions for nationalization and forms of compensation; rules for transfer of profits and capital repatriation; and dispute settlement mechanisms.[84] The Multilateral Investment Guarantee Agency (MIGA) was set up under the World Bank to guarantee private investment in developing countries against noncommercial risks, such as currency transfer, expropriation, breach of contract, war, and civil disturbance. Guarantees are con-

tingent upon MIGA's judgment about the economic soundness and development validity of the investment as well as the approval of the host
government.[85]

Meanwhile, negotiations for a United Nations Code on Transnational
Corporations, originally conceived at the time of the NIEO, languished and
seemed increasingly irrelevant. As attitudes toward foreign investment
changed, Southern interest in the code declined. Developed countries remained adamantly opposed to the code and pushed instead for negotiations
on investment under GATT (see Chapter 3). However, developing countries
still wanted to maintain national sovereignty and to control entry and
operations of foreign investors and thus strongly resisted negotiating investment issues, even the so-called trade-related investment measures, in the
GATT.

The 1990s: Cooperation or Conflict?

In the 1980s, there was clearly a shift in Southern attitudes toward
multinational corporations. Developing countries became less confrontational and more and more concerned about promoting desired forms of
investment. Nevertheless, for many developing countries, particularly those
in Latin America, deeply held concerns about the economic and political
consequences of foreign investment remained. Policy continued to be based
on the principle of controlling the access and operations of foreign investment in order to achieve national economic objectives and maintain national sovereignty. In most countries, as we have noted, laws and institutions controlling MNCs remained on the books and powerful domestic
political forces opposed any legal changes. Furthermore, few Latin American countries signed BITS or joined MIGA and developing countries almost
universally opposed the Northern attempt to negotiate foreign investment
in the GATT, which they continued to see as a Northern-dominated institution with a liberalizing mandate.

Views were equally mixed in developed countries. The strong interest of
Northern governments in BITs, MIGA, and a GATT for investment suggested that firms in developed countries would be interested in renewing
investment in the South if developing country policies were more accommodating and national economies more attractive. For many investors in the
developed countries, however, the climate for investment in many developing countries continued to appear inhospitable. Despite some policy
changes, access and operations remained highly constrained from their
point of view. While interest in investment in the rapidly growing countries
of Asia remained high, the depressed economic conditions in most developing countries remained a deterrent to investment.

Thus, the events of the 1980s left unclear whether the hostile relationship between the LDCs and the MNCs had changed fundamentally or whether there was only a temporary truce based on the exigencies of debt and economic recession.

NOTES

1. The terms foreign investment and multinational corporation are used interchangeably in this chapter. Because much, although not all, foreign investment in less-developed countries is made by multinational corporations, this usage should not interfere with the analysis made and the conclusions reached.

2. United Nations Center on Transnational Corporations [hereafter UNCTC], *Transnational Corporations in World Development: Trends and Prospects* (New York: United Nations, 1988), p. 18. The countries are Argentina, Brazil, Chile, China, Colombia, Egypt, Hong Kong, Indonesia, Malaysia, Mexico, Nigeria, Oman, Singapore, Taiwan, Thailand, Trinidad and Tobago, Tunisia, and Venezuela.

3. For a similar analysis of two countries, see Richard S. Newfarmer and Willard F. Mueller, *Multinational Corporations in Brazil and Mexico: Structural Sources of Economic and Noneconomic Power*, report to the Subcommittee on Multinational Corporations of the Committee on Foreign Relations, 94th Cong., 1st sess. (Washington, D.C.: 1975).

4. UNCTC, *Transnational Corporations in World Development: Third Survey* (New York: United Nations, 1983), p. 197.

5. Ibid., p. 210.

6. UNCTC, *Transnational Corporations in World Development: Trends and Prospects*, p. 159.

7. Newfarmer and Mueller, *Multinational Corporations in Brazil and Mexico*, pp. 25–27; United Nations Conference on Trade and Development, *Restrictive Business Practices: The Operations of Multinational Enterprises in Developing Countries, Their Role in Trade and Development*, a study by Raymond Vernon (New York: United Nations, 1972), p. 3.

8. Gary Gereffi and Richard S. Newfarmer, "International Oligopoly and Uneven Development: Some Lessons from Industrial Case Studies," in Richard S. Newfarmer, ed., *Profits, Progress and Poverty: Case studies of International Industries in Latin America* (Notre Dame, Ind.: University of Notre Dame Press, 1985), pp. 385–442.

9. For an analysis of control over access, see Samuel Huntington, "Transnational Organizations in World Politics," *World Politics*, 25 (April 1973), 333–368.

10. See Raymond Vernon, "Long-Run Trends in Concession Contracts," *Proceedings of the American Society for International Law*, Sixty-First Annual Meeting (Washington, D.C.: American Society for International Law, 1967), pp. 81–90; Theodore H. Moran, *Multinational Corporations and the Politics of Dependence: Copper in Chile* (Princeton: Princeton University Press, 1974), pp. 157–162.

11. This applies particularly to collusion by the major international oil companies. See Chapter 9.

12. UNCTC, *Transnational Corporations in World Development: Third Survey*, pp. 336–342.

13. See Dennis M. Ray, "Corporations and American Foreign Relations," in David H. Blake, ed., *The Annals of the American Academy of Political and Social Science: The MNC* (Philadelphia, Pa.: 1972), pp. 80–92.

14. See, for example, Harry G. Johnson, "The Efficiency and Welfare Implications of the International Corporation," in Charles P. Kindleberger, ed., *The International Corporation: A Symposium* (Cambridge, Mass.: MIT Press, 1970), pp. 35–56; Lester B. Pearson, *Partners in Development: Report of the Commission on International Development* (New York: Praeger, 1969), pp. 99–123; United Nations Conference on Trade and Development, *The Role of Private Enterprise in Investment and Promotion of Exports in Developing Countries*, report prepared by Dirk U. Stikker (New York: United Nations, 1968); Herbert K. May, *The*

Effects of United States and Other Foreign Investment in Latin America (New York: Council for Latin America, 1970).

15. Organization for Economic Cooperation and Development, *Development Cooperation: Efforts and Policies of the Members of the Development Assistance Committee, 1988* (Paris: OECD, 1988), p. 47.

16. UNCTC, *Transnational Corporations in World Development: Trends and Prospects*, pp. 161–162.

17. Ibid., pp. 180–183.

18. Leading critics include Celso Furtado, for example, *Obstacles to Development in Latin America* (Garden City, N.Y.: Doubleday, 1970); Stephen Hymer, for example, "The Multinational Corporation and the Law of Uneven Development," in Jagdish N. Bhagwati, ed., *Economics and World Order: From the 1970s to the 1990s* (New York: Macmillan, 1972), pp. 113–140; Ronald Muller, for example, *Global Reach: The Power of the Multinational Corporations* (New York: Simon & Schuster, 1974), written with Richard J. Barnet; Constantine V. Vaitsos, for example, *Intercountry Income Distribution and Transnational Enterprises* (Oxford: Clarendon Press, 1974); Fernando Henrique Cardoso, for example, *Dependencia and Development in Latin America* (Berkeley and Los Angeles: University of California Press, 1979), written with Enzo Faletto. An excellent summary of both critical and "neoconventional" perspectives on multinational corporations, as well as a case study of the Nigerian experience, is Thomas Biersteker, *Distortion or Development? Contending Perspectives on the Multinational Corporation* (Cambridge, Mass.: MIT Press, 1978). See also Theodore H. Moran, "Multinational Corporations and Dependency: A Dialogue for Dependistas and Non-Dependentistas," *International Organization*, 32:1 (Winter 1978).

19. Sidney M. Robbins and Robert Stobaugh, *Money in the Multinational Enterprise: A Study of Financial Policy* (New York: Basic Books, 1972), pp. 63–71; R. David Belli, "Sources and Uses of Funds of Foreign Affiliates of U.S. Firms, 1967–68," *Survey of Current Business* (November 1970) 14–19; Grant L. Reuber, *Private Foreign Investment in Development* (Oxford, England: Clarendon Press, 1973), p. 67; Sanjaya Lall and Paul Streeten, *Foreign Investment, Transnationals and Developing Countries* (London: Macmillan, 1977); L. E. Westphal, Y. W. Ree, and G. Pursell, "Foreign Influences on Korean Industrial Development," *Oxford Bulletin of Economics and Statistics*, 41 (November 1979).

20. Ronald J. Muller, "Poverty Is the Product," *Foreign Policy*, 13 (Winter 1973–1974), 85–88.

21. Newfarmer and Mueller, *Multinational Corporations in Brazil and Mexico*, pp. 67–72.

22. Ibid., pp. 121–125.

23. *Survey of Current Business*, 57 (August 1977), 39; *Survey of Current Business*, 59 (August 1979), 22.

24. Newfarmer and Mueller, *Multinational Corporations in Brazil and Mexico*, p. 17.

25. See Johnson, "The Efficiency and Welfare Implications of the International Corporation"; Walter A. Chudson, *The International Transfer of Commercial Technology to Developing Countries* (New York: United Nations Institute for Training and Research, 1971); Lynn Mytelka, "Technological Dependence in the Andean Group," *International Organization*, 32 (Winter 1978), 101–139.

26. Vaitsos, *Intercountry Income Distribution and Transnational Enterprises*, pp. 42–43.

27. Ibid., pp. 44–54.

28. Ibid., p. 47.

29. Constantine V. Vaitsos, "Foreign Investment Policies and Economic Development in Latin America," *Journal of World Trade Law*, 7 (November–December 1973), 639; Albert O. Hirschman, "How to Divest in Latin America and Why," *Essays in International Finance*, November 1969 (Princeton: International Finance Section, Department of Economics, Princeton University, 1969), pp. 5–6.

30. For a Mexican case study, see Fernando Fajnsylber and Trinidad Martínez Tarragó, *Las empresas transnacionales: expansión a nivel mundial y proyección en la industria mexicana* (Mexico City: Fondo de Cultura Económica, 1976).

31. The International Labor Organization has commissioned a number of studies on the employment impact of foreign direct investment in host developing countries. See, for example, Norman Girvan, *The Impact of Multinational Enterprises on Employment and Income in*

Jamaica (Geneva: ILO, 1976); Juan Sourrouille, *The Impact of Transnational Enterprises on Employment and Income: The Case of Argentina* (Geneva: ILO, 1976); Sung-Hwan Jo, *The Impact of Multinational Firms on Employment and Income: The Case Study of South Korea* (Geneva: ILO, 1976), and *Technology Choice and Employment Generation by Multinational Enterprises in Developing Countries* (Geneva: ILO, 1984).

32. United Nations, *Multinational Corporations in World Development: Third Survey*, p. 195; Vaitsos, *Intercountry Income Distribution and Transnational Enterprises*, pp. 54–59; United Nations Conference on Trade and Development, *Restrictive Business Practices* (New York: United Nations, December 1969), pp. 4–6.

33. For statistical evidence to this effect, see Michael B. Dolan and Brian W. Tomlin, "First World–Third World Linkages: External Relations and Economic Development," *International Organization*, 34 (Winter 1980), 41–64.

34. For analyses of recent empirical studies see United Nations, *Transnational Corporations in World Development, Third Survey*, pp. 132–237; Theodore H. Moran, *Multinational Corporations: The Political Economy of Foreign Direct Investment* (Lexington, Mass.: Lexington Books, 1985).

35. For an interesting case study, see Adalberto J. Pinelo, *The Multinational Corporation As a Force in Latin American Politics: A Case Study of the International Petroleum Company in Peru* (New York: Praeger, 1973).

36. Gulf Oil, for example, contributed $4 million illegally in South Korea (*New York Times*, May 17, 1975, p. 1).

37. Bribes have been made, for example, by United Brands in Honduras for favorable tax treatment, and in arms and airplane sales, such as those of the Northrop Corporation in Saudi Arabia and Brazil. See Yerachmiel Kugel and Gladys Gruenberg, *International Payoffs: Dilemma for Business* (Lexington, Mass.: D.C. Heath, 1977).

38. See, for example, Pinelo, *The Multinational Corporation As a Force in Latin American Politics*, pp. 17–25; Neil H. Jacoby, Peter Nehemkis, and Richard Eells, *Bribery and Extortion in World Business* (New York: Macmillan, 1977).

39. The control of international markets, for example, made possible the boycott by the major international oil companies of Iranian oil in 1951–1953 that contributed to the overthrow of Premier Muhammed Mossadegh.

40. On the Overseas Private Investment Corporation, see U.S. Senate, 93rd Cong., 1st sess., *The Overseas Private Investment Corporation, A Report to the Committee on Foreign Relations, United States, Subcommittee on Multinational Corporations, October 17, 1973* (Washington, D.C.: U.S. Government Printing Office, 1973).

41. See, for example, accounts of the role of the United Fruit Company in the United States overthrow of President Arbenz of Guatemala, in Richard J. Barnet, *Intervention and Revolution: The United States in the Third World* (New York: World Publishing, 1968), pp. 229–232; David Wise and Thomas B. Ross, *The Invisible Government* (New York: Random House, 1964), pp. 165–183; U.S. Senate, Committee on Foreign Relations, Subcommittee on Multinational Corporations, 93rd Cong., 1st sess., *The Overseas Private Investment Corporation, A Report with Additional Views* (Washington, D.C.: U.S. Government Printing Office, 1974).

42. The Hickenlooper amendment was passed in October 1964 (Public Law 88–633, 78 Stat. 1009, Sec. 301). The Gonzalez amendment was passed as part of a general appropriations bill for multilateral banks in January 1974. See Anthony Sampson, *The Sovereign State of ITT* (New York: Stein & Day, 1973).

43. U.S. Senate, *Multinational Corporations and United States Foreign Policy*, vol. 1.

44. Paul E. Sigmund, *Multinationals in Latin America: The Politics of Nationalization*, a 20th Century Fund Study (Madison, Wisc.: The University of Wisconsin Press, 1980).

45. For an analysis of economic nationalism, see Harry G. Johnson, "A Theoretical Model of Economic Nationalism in New and Developing States," *Political Science Quarterly*, 80 (June 1965), 169–185. See criticism by Vaitsos, "Foreign Investment Policies and Economic Development in Latin America," p. 632. For evidence of this rising nationalism, see Jorge Dominguez, "National and Multinational Business and the State in Latin America," paper presented at the 1979 annual meeting of the American Political Science Association, Washington, D.C. See also Richard L. Sklar, *Corporate Power in an African State: The Political Impact of Multinational Mining Companies in Zambia* (Berkeley and Los Angeles: University of California Press, 1975).

46. Samuel P. Huntington, *Political Order in Changing Societies* (New Haven, Conn.: Yale University Press, 1968).

47. Theodore H. Moran, *Multinational Corporations and the Politics of Dependence: Copper in Chile*, pp. 164–166.

48. See U.S. Senate, *Multinational Corporations and United States Foreign Policy*.

49. See United Nations, *Multinational Corporations in World Development and Report of the Group of Eminent Persons to Study the Impact of Multinational Corporations on Development and on International Relations* (New York: United Nations, 1974).

50. Edith Penrose, "The State and the Multinational Enterprise in Less-Developed Countries," in John Dunning, ed., *The Multinational Enterprise* (London: Allen & Unwin, 1971), p. 230. For the role of the new economic analysis in Chile, see Moran, *Multinational Corporations*, pp. 57–88.

51. Theodore Moran, *Multinational Corporations*, p. 164.

52 See Moran, op cit., and Alfred Stepan, *The State and Society: Peru in Comparative Perspective* (Princeton: Princeton University Press, 1978), p. 235.

53. Raymond Vernon, "Long-Run Trends in Concession Contracts"; Moran, *Multinational Corporations*, pp. 157–162.

54. UNCTC, *Transnational Corporations in World Development: Third Survey*, pp. 18–19.

55. Vernon, "Long-Term Trends in Concession Contracts."

56. See Gary Gereffi and Richard S. Newfarmer, "International Oligopoly and Uneven Development: Some Lessons from Industrial Case Studies," in Richard E. Newfarmer, ed., *Progress, Profits, and Poverty*, p. 432. See also Newfarmer and Mueller on Mexico, in their *Multinational Corporations in Brazil and Mexico*, p. 59. In addition, once established in the host economy, multinational corporations form alliances with domestic groups and thereby actually improve their bargaining position vis-à-vis the local government.

57. Even ANCOM resolutions must be enacted nationally.

58. On International Petroleum Corporation, see Pinelo, *The Multinational Corporation as a Force in Latin American Politics*.

59. Moran, *Multinational Corporations*; Sklar, *Corporate Power in an African State*.

60. For oil and other minerals, see Raymond F. Mikesell, ed., *Foreign Investment in the Petroleum and Mineral Industries: Case Studies of Investor-Host Country Relations* (Baltimore: Johns Hopkins University Press, 1971). Two interesting studies of nationalizations in developing countries are by Stephen J. Kobrin, "Foreign Enterprise and Forced Divestment in LDCs," *International Organization*, 34 (Winter, 1980), 65–88; and David A. Jodice, "Sources of Change in Third World Regimes for Foreign Direct Investment, 1968–1976," *International Organization*, 34 (Spring 1980), 177–206.

61. UNCTC, *Transnational Corporations in World Development: Trends and Prospects*, p. 315.

62. For a summary of the policies of various developing host countries toward foreign investment, see United Nations, *Transnational Corporations in World Development: Trends and Prospects*, pp. 261–298. A good summary of the problems that developing countries face in controlling foreign enterprises and a case study of Peru is in Alfred Stepan, *The State and Society: Peru in Comparative Perspective*, pp. 230–289.

63. Rosemary R. Williams, "Has Mexico Kept the Promise of 1984? A Look at Foreign Investment Under Mexico's Recent Guidelines," *Texas International Law Journal*, 23 (1988), 417–441. See also Sandra F. Maviglia, "Mexico's Guidelines for Foreign Investment: The Selective Promotion of Necessary Industries," *The American Journal of International Law*, 80 (1986), 281–304. For a review of Venezuelan foreign investment regulations, see Robert J. Radway and Franklin T. Hoet-Linares, "Venezuela Revisited: Foreign Investment, Technology and Related Issues," *Vanderbilt Journal of Transnational Law*, Vol. 15, No. 1 (Winter 1982), pp. 1–45.

64. Chile withdrew from ANCOM in 1976 rather than impose restrictions on foreign investment. See Dale B. Furnish, "The Andean Common Market's Common Regime for Foreign Investments," *Vanderbilt Journal of Transnational Law*, 5 (Spring 1972), 313–339; Robert Black, Stephen Blank, and Elizabeth C. Hanson, *Multinationals in Contention: Responses at Governmental and International Levels* (New York: The Conference Board, 1978), pp. 174–184; Roger Fontaine, "The Andean Pact: A Political Analysis," *The Washington Papers*, 5, no. 45 (Beverly Hills, Calif.: Sage Publications, 1977).

65. United Nations, *Transnational Corporations: Third Survey*, pp. 60–61.

66. Charles Oman, *New Forms of International Investment in Developing Countries* (Paris: OECD, 1983).

67. United Nations, *Transnational Corporations: Third Survey*, pp. 102–122.

68. Ibid., p. 229.

69. Lacey and Garza, "Mexico—Are the Rules Really Changing?" pp. 572–573.

70. See, for example, Business International Corporation, *Investment, Licensing and Trading Conditions Abroad: Peru* (New York: Business International, 1973).

71. See, for example, Business International Corporation, *Investment, Licensing and Trading Conditions Abroad: Brazil* (New York: Business International, 1973).

72. Newfarmer and Mueller, *Multinational Corporations in Brazil and Mexico*, pp. 55, 112, 150; Peter Evans, *Dependent Development: The Alliance of Multinational, State, and Local Capital in Brazil* (Princeton: Princeton University Press, 1979).

73. Jeffrey Frieden, "Third World Indebted Industrialization: International Finance and State Capitalism in Mexico, Brazil, Algeria and South Korea," *International Organization*, 35, No. 3 (Summer 1981), pp. 407–431.

74. UNCTC, *Transnational Corporations in World Development*: Trends and Prospects, pp. 67–71.

75. Ibid., p. 82.

76. Ibid., p. 76.

77. Ibid., p. 76.

78. Ibid., pp. 82–83.

79. Ibid., p. 269

80. Ibid., pp. 264–265.

81. Ibid., p. 269.

82. Ibid., p. 76–78.

83. Ibid., pp. 169–173.

84. Ibid., pp. 332–337.

85. Ibid., p. 348.

9

Oil and Cartel Power

The most successful effort of Southern countries to alter their dependent relationship with the North was the common action of OPEC (Organization of Petroleum Exporting Countries) in seizing control over the world's oil markets. By acting together in a producer cartel, the Southern oil-exporting states were able to increase not only their economic rewards but also their political power. OPEC's success led to efforts to form other Southern commodity cartels. But the OPEC model would prove difficult to reproduce, and even OPEC eventually confronted the inevitable limitations of a producer cartel.

The Dependency System of International Oil

For most of the twentieth century, the international oil system has been controlled by a producer cartel. Until 1973, that cartel consisted of an oligopoly of international oil companies.[1] The "seven sisters"—five American (Standard Oil of New Jersey, now known as Exxon; Standard Oil of California, now known as Chevron; Gulf, now part of Chevron; Mobil; and Texaco), one British (British Petroleum), and one Anglo-Dutch (Royal Dutch-Shell)—first gained control of their domestic oil industries through vertical integration, that is, by controlling all supply, transportation, refining, and marketing operations as well as by controlling the technology for exploration and refining.

In the late nineteenth century, the oil companies then in existence began to move abroad and obtain control of foreign supplies on extremely favorable terms.[2] After World War I, the seven formed joint ventures to explore for foreign oil fields, and eventually in the 1920s they began to divide up sources of supply by explicit agreements. They were thus able to divide markets, fix world prices, and discriminate against outsiders.[3] Northern political dominance of the oil-producing regions—the Middle East, Indonesia, and Latin America—facilitated the activities of the oil companies. Governments provided a favorable political and military environment and actively supported the oil companies owned by their nationals.

261

In bargaining with the oil companies, the less-developed countries were confronted by an oil oligopoly supported by powerful Northern governments as well as by uncertainty about the success of oil exploration and the availability of alternative sources of supply. It is not surprising that the seven sisters obtained concession agreements that gave them control over the production and sale of much of the world's oil in return for the payment of a small fixed royalty to their host governments.[4]

Beginning in the late 1920s and continuing through the years of the great depression of the 1930s, oil prices tumbled despite the efforts of the seven sisters to stabilize markets. At that time, the United States was the largest producer in the world and exported oil to Europe and elsewhere. Efforts at the government level (including not only the U.S. federal government but more significantly the largest producer state, Texas) succeeded where the seven sisters could not in regulating production in order to create a price floor. Thus, the Texas Railroad Commission emerged as the single most significant political force in the international oil industry.

Changes in this system began to emerge in the decade following World War II. In the 1950s, relatively inexpensive imported oil became the primary source of energy for the developed world. Western Europe and Japan, with no oil supplies of their own, became significant importers of oil. In 1950, U.S. oil consumption outdistanced its vast domestic production, and the United States became a net importer of oil. In the host countries, growing nationalism combined with the great success of oil exploration led to dissatisfaction with concession agreements and to more aggressive policies. In these years, the host governments succeeded in revising concession agreements negotiated before the war. They redefined the basis for royalty payments and instituted an income tax on foreign oil operations. They also established what at the time was considered a revolutionary principle: the new royalties and taxes combined would yield a fifty-fifty division of profits between the companies and their respective host governments.[5] As a result, profits accruing to host governments increased significantly. The per-barrel payment to Saudi Arabia, for example, rose from $0.17 in 1946 to $0.80 in 1956–1957.[6]

Nonetheless, the seven sisters, also known as the majors, continued to dominate the system. By controlling almost all the world's oil reserves outside the Communist states (e.g., production at the wellhead, refining and transportation, and marketing), they were able to manage the price of oil.

The seven sisters maintained control, in part, by preventing incursions by competitors. The majors blocked other companies from entering upstream operations outside North America, that is, crude oil exploration and production, by locking in concession agreements with many oil-rich areas and by the long lead times required for finding and developing oil in territory unclaimed by the majors. Outsiders were also deterred from competing with the seven sisters downstream, that is, in refining, transportation, and marketing operations. Not having their own crude oil supplies, independent refiners had to purchase oil from the majors, who were also their competitors. But the majors deliberately took their profits at the less-competitive and lower-taxed upstream level by charging a high price for crude oil as compared with the final product. The small profits for downstream operations discouraged new entrants.

The management of the price of oil was facilitated by the highly inelastic demand for oil. Because there are no readily available substitutes and because it is difficult to decrease consumption, an increase in the price does not greatly decrease the demand for oil in the short run. Thus, if companies can maintain a higher price for oil, they will not lose sales volumes and so will reap high profits.

Thus, in the 1950s and 1960s, the seven sisters controlled supply by keeping out competitors and by a series of cooperative ventures: joint production and refining arrangements, long-term purchase and supply agreements, joint ownership of pipelines, and some joint marketing outside the United States. They also refrained from price competition. Price management by the majors was designed to keep the price of oil economically attractive but also low enough to discourage competing forms of energy including nuclear energy. Developed country governments did not resist this price management. Europeans added a tax on petroleum in order to protect the domestic coal industry, because lower oil prices would have increased oil consumption at the expense of the politically powerful coal companies and coal miners. In the United States, higher oil prices were supported by the domestic oil industry that needed protection from lower international prices to survive and, as we shall discuss, eventually obtained that protection.[7]

Finally, the dominance of the seven sisters was backed by political intervention. One extreme example occurred in the early 1950s when the government of Iran sought a new agreement with the Anglo-Iranian Oil Company, a predecessor of British Petroleum, and nationalized the company's assets in Iran. The British government became actively involved in the negotiations, imposed an economic embargo on Iran, and threatened military intervention. After trying unsuccessfully to mediate between Britain and Iran, the United States worked with opposition parties and the shah to overthrow the Iranian government. A new concession was soon negotiated under which the U.S. companies replaced Anglo-Iranian.[8]

However, as OPEC would later discover, it is difficult to maintain a producer cartel in the long run. Over time, changes in the international oil industry, the oil-producing states, and the oil-consuming developed countries undermined the dominance of the seven sisters.[9] The oligopolistic structure of the international oil industry was weakened by the entrance of new players. Competition increased both upstream, as new players sought concessions to explore for and produce crude oil, and downstream, as more refineries were built and competition grew in markets for refined oil.

Starting in the mid-1950s, companies previously not active internationally obtained and successfully developed concessions in existing and new oil-producing regions such as Algeria, Libya, and Nigeria. In 1952, the seven majors produced 90 percent of crude oil outside North America and the Communist countries, and by 1968 they still produced 75 percent.[10]

As new production by new producers came on line, the seven sisters were no longer able to restrict supply and maintain the price of oil at the old level. By the end of the 1950s, production increases outdistanced the growth in consumption. United States quotas on the import of foreign oil aggravated the problem. Quotas were instituted in 1958 ostensibly for national security reasons: to protect the U.S. market from lower-priced foreign oil in order to ensure domestic production and national self-sufficiency. In fact, quotas also helped domestic U.S. producers that could not have survived without protection.[11] The quotas effectively cut off the U.S. market for the absorption of the new supplies produced abroad. As a result, in 1959 and 1960, the international oil companies lowered the posted price of oil, the official price used to calculate taxes. This act was to be a key catalyst for producer-government action against the oil companies.

Changes in the oil-producing states also weakened the power of the oil company cartel. In addition to changing elite attitudes, improved skills, and less uncertainty, the emergence of new competitors was critically important in increasing the bargaining power of the host governments. In negotiations with the oil companies, producer states obtained larger percentages of earnings and provisions for relinquishing unexploited parts of concessions.[12] As a result, the oil-producing governments, especially large producers such as Libya and Saudia Arabia, increased their earnings and began to accumulate significant foreign exchange reserves. Monetary reserves further strengthened the hand of the oil producers by enabling them to absorb any short-term loss of earnings from an embargo or production reduction designed to increase the price of oil or to obtain other concessions.

At the same time, host governments began to cooperate with each other. Enfuriated by the price cuts of 1959 and 1960 that reduced their tax receipts, five of the major petroleum-exporting countries—Iran, Iraq, Kuwait, Saudi Arabia, and Venezuela—met in 1960 to discuss unilateral action by the oil companies. At that meeting, the five decided to form an Organization of Petroleum Exporting Countries to protect the price of oil and the revenues of their governments.[13] In its first decade, OPEC expanded from five to thirteen members, who accounted for 85 percent of the world's oil exports.[14] Initially, the new organization had little success. OPEC's influence depended on the ability of its members to cooperate to reduce production and thus to force a price increase. Although OPEC tried, it was unable to agree on production reduction schemes. Nevertheless, the individual oil-producing states succeeded in increasing their revenues. The posted price of oil was never again lowered. And the oil-producing states gradually expanded their experience in cooperation. But not until the 1970s, when other conditions became favorable, would OPEC become an effective tool of the producer states.[15]

Finally, the Western consuming countries became vulnerable to the threat of supply interruption or reduction. As oil became the primary source of energy and as U.S. supplies diminished, the developed-market economies became increasingly dependent on foreign oil, especially from the Middle East and North Africa. By 1972, Western Europe derived almost 60 percent of its energy from oil, almost all of which was imported. Oil from abroad supplied 73 percent of Japan's energy needs. And 46 percent of U.S. energy came from oil, almost one-third of which was imported. By 1972, 80 percent of Western European and Japanese oil imports came from the Middle East and North Africa. By 1972, even the United States relied on the Middle East and North Africa for 15 percent of its oil imports.[16] This economic vulnerability was accentuated by declining political influence in the oil-producing regions and by the absence of individual or joint energy policies to counter any manipulation of supply.

The Process of Change: From Negotiation to Unilateral Power

In the 1970s, OPEC took advantage of these changes and asserted its power as a producer cartel. Favorable international economic and political conditions plus internal cooperation enabled the oil-producing states—especially the Arab oil producers—to take control of prices and, then, to assume ownership of oil investments.

The OPEC revolution was triggered by Libya.[17] Libya had definite negotiating advantages: it supplied 25 percent of Western Europe's oil imports[18]; certain independent oil companies relied heavily on Libyan oil and were more vulnerable than the majors in Libya; and Libya had large official foreign exchange reserves. After Colonel Muammar al-Qaddafi seized power in 1969, the new radical government demanded an increase in the posted price of and the tax on Libyan oil. When the talks with the companies stalled in 1970, the government threatened nationalization and a cut in oil production. It targeted the vulnerable Occidental Petroleum, which relied totally on Libya to supply its European markets. Shortly after production cuts were imposed, Occidental, having failed to gain the support of the majors, capitulated, and the other companies were forced to follow. The settlement provided for an increase in the posted price of and the income tax on Libyan oil. The Libyan action revealed the vulnerability of the independent oil companies like Occidental and the unwillingness of the Western governments or the majors to take forceful action in their support.

At a meeting in December 1970, OPEC called for an increase in the posted price of and income taxes on oil. The companies, seeking to avoid a producer policy of divide and conquer, agreed to negotiate with all oil-producing countries for a long-term agreement on price and tax increases. The governments of the oil-consuming states, although increasingly concerned, allowed the companies to manage relations with the oil producers.[19] Following threats to enact changes unilaterally and to cut off oil to the companies in February 1971, the companies signed a five-year agreement that provided for an increase in the posted price of Persian Gulf oil from $1.80 to $2.29 per barrel, an annual increase in the price to offset inflation, and an increase in government royalties and taxes. In return, the companies received a five-year "commitment" on price and government revenues. In April 1971, a similar agreement, but with a higher price, was reached with Libya. After the devaluation of the dollar in 1971 and 1972 and thus of the real price of oil, the producers demanded and received a new agreement that provided for an increase in the posted price of oil and continuing adjustment to account for exchange rate changes. The price of Persian Gulf oil rose to $2.48.

No sooner had the issue of price and revenue been settled than OPEC requested a new conference to discuss nationalization, that is, control over production. A December 1972 agreement among Saudi Arabia, Qatar, Abu Dhabi, and the companies provided a framework: government ownership would start at 25 percent and rise gradually to 51 percent by 1982. Individual states then entered into negotiations with the oil concessionaires.

The final negotiation between the oil producers and the oil companies took place in October 1973. Despite their successes, the oil producers were dissatisfied. Although surging demand for oil drove up the market price, the posted price remained fixed by the five-year agreements. Thus, the oil companies, not the oil producers, benefited. Furthermore, the companies were bidding for new government-owned oil at prices above those of the five-year agreements.

Finally, increasing inflation in the West and continuing devaluation of the dollar lowered the real value of earnings from oil production. Economic conditions were favorable to OPEC. Because of rapidly rising demand and shortages of supply, the developed market economies were vulnerable to supply interruption. Thus, when OPEC summoned the oil companies for negotiations, they came. Negotiations began on October 8. The oil producers demanded substantial increases in the price of oil; the companies stalled; and on October 12 the companies requested a two-week adjournment of talks to consult with their home governments.

The adjournment was not for two weeks but forever. Political as well as economic conditions now enhanced the bargaining position and escalated the demands of the most powerful oil producers: the Arab states. The fourth Arab-Israeli war had begun on October 6, just two days before the oil talks began. A common interest in supporting the Arab cause vis-à-vis Israel and the supporters of Israel in the consuming states was a force for unity of the Arab members of OPEC in their economic confrontation with the companies and the consumers. On October 16, the Organization of Arab Petroleum Exporting Countries (OAPEC) unilaterally increased the price of their crude oil to $5.12.[20] Other oil producers followed. On December 23, OPEC unilaterally raised the price of Persian Gulf oil to $11.65.

After the autumn of 1973, oil prices were controlled by OPEC. Operating in a market where supplies were limited and demand high, the producers negotiated among themselves to determine the posted price of oil and the production reductions needed to limit supply and maintain price. The key to reducing supply was the role of the major reserve countries and large producers. Saudi Arabia and Kuwait were willing to support the cartel by themselves, absorbing a large part of the production reductions necessary to maintain the price. The role of these two countries was facilitated by the tight oil markets, which meant that price could be managed when necessary by only limited production reductions. Power over price was quickly translated into equity control. All the major oil-producing states signed agreements with the oil companies for immediate majority or total national ownership of subsidiaries located in those states. In the long run, as we shall see, the abrupt movement of control over production from the seven sisters to OPEC would prove to be the real revolution of the 1970s oil crisis.

The monopoly control of oil by OPEC, the unity of the producers, and tight market conditions undermined the position of the oil companies. Furthermore, the companies had little incentive to resist. They were able in most cases to pass the price increases along to consumers and thus did not suffer financially from the loss of control over price. Although no longer either the arbiters of supply and price or the owners of oil concessions, the seven sisters and their many smaller relatives still played a vital role in the international oil scene. As holders of technology and markets, they were needed by the newly powerful producer governments. As their holdings were nationalized, they became vital service contractors to the producer states. Still, it was a far cry from the days when the companies divided up the producing regions among themselves and obtained control of the world's oil for almost nothing.

With the decline of the companies, the Northern consumer governments tried but failed to agree on a common policy toward the producers. The United States urged Western Europe and Japan to form a countercartel that would undermine producer solidarity by presenting a united front and by threatening economic or military retaliation. The Europeans and Japanese—more dependent on foreign sources of oil, less interested in support for Israel, and somewhat fearful of U.S. dominance—instead advised cooperation with the producers. A consumer conference in early 1974 failed to reconcile these opposing views. The only agreement was to establish an International Energy Agency (IEA) to develop an emergency oil-sharing scheme and a long-term program for the development of alternative forms of energy. France, the strongest opponent of the U.S. approach, refused to join the IEA and urged instead a producer-consumer dialogue.

After the conference, consumer governments went their own ways. The United States tried to destroy producer unity by continuing to press for consumer unity and the development of the IEA. The Europeans sought special bilateral political and economic arrangements with the oil producers and resisted consumer bloc strategies. In late 1974, a compromise was reached between the United States and France. The United States obtained France's grudging acceptance of the IEA, although France still refused to join, and France obtained the grudging support of the United States for a producer-consumer dialogue. The Conference on International Economic Cooperation (CIEC), begun in 1975 (see Chapter 7), constituted a recognition, if not a total acceptance, by the United States and the other consumers that they could not alter the power of the producer states over the price of oil and that what they could seek at best was some conciliation and coordination of common interests. Even that coordination proved elusive. In 1977, the CIEC and the effort to achieve a forum for a producer-consumer dialogue failed.

OPEC Management

For five years the management of the international oil system was carried out by OPEC under the leadership of Saudi Arabia. Saudi dominance of OPEC's production and Saudi financial strength enabled that country to manage the oil cartel virtually singlehandedly. Saudi Arabia accounted for close to one-third of OPEC's production and exports, controlled the largest productive capacity and the world's largest reserves of petroleum, and possessed vast financial reserves (see Figure 9-1).

In periods of excess supply, as during the recession of 1975, Saudi Arabia maintained the OPEC price by absorbing a large share of the necessary production reductions. The burden of such reductions was minimal because of the country's huge financial reserves and because even its ambitious economic development and military needs could be more than satisfied at a lower level of oil exports. In periods of tight supply, Saudi Arabia increased its production to prevent excessive price rises. With a small population, limited possibilities of industrial development, and the world's largest oil reserves, Saudi Arabia's future is dependent on oil. Furthermore, with its financial reserves invested largely in the developed countries, it has a stake in the stability of the international economic system.

Figure 9-1   Proved Reserves of Oil at End of 1987.

Oil Reserves Growth, 1967–1987

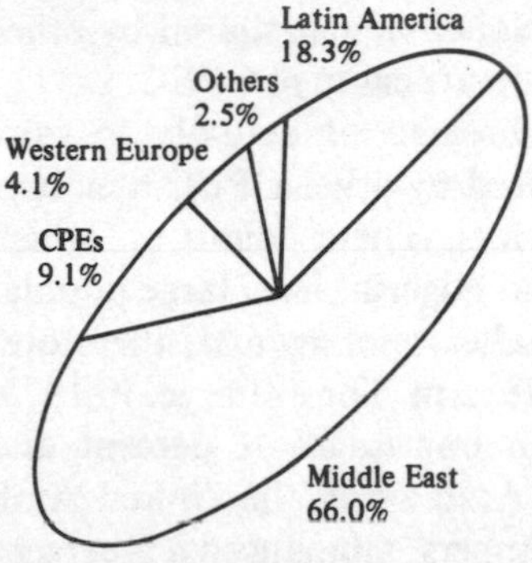

Latin America 18.3%
Others 2.5%
Western Europe 4.1%
CPEs 9.1%
Middle East 66.0%

Total reserves
1967: 418 billion barrels
1987: 896 billion barrels

Proved reserves of oil are generally taken to be those quantities that geological and engineering information indicate with reasonable certainty can be recovered in the future from known reservoirs under existing economic and operating conditions.

Reserves/Production (R/P) ratio. If the reserves remaining at the end of any year are divided by the production in that year, the result is the length of time that those remaining reserves would last if production were to continue at the then current level.

SOURCE OF DATA. The estimates contained in this table are those published by the Oil and Gas Journal in its "Worldwide Oil" issue of 28th December 1987, plus an estimate of natural gas liquids for North America. Reserves of shale oil and tar sands are not included. United Kingdom reserves data are taken from the United Kingdom Department of Energy's Brown Book, published in April 1988; *British Petroleum Statistical Review of World Energy*, June 1988 (The British Petroleum Company p.l.c. 1988).

	Thousand Million Tonnes	Thousand Million Barrels	Share of Total (percentage)	R/P Ratio
North America				
USA	4.2	33.4	3.7	9.0
Canada	1.011	7.7	0.9	11.3
Total North America	5.2	41.1	4.6	9.4
Latin America				
Argentina	0.3	2.3	0.3	14.7
Brazil	0.3	2.3	0.3	11.0
Ecuador	0.2	1.6	0.2	26.4
Mexico	6.8	48.6	5.4	47.9
Venezuela	8.1	56.3	6.3	91.2
Others	0.4	3.2	0.4	11.2
Total Latin America	16.1	114.3	12.9	49.3
Western Europe				
Norway	1.9	14.8	1.6	37.3
United Kingdom	0.7	5.2	0.6	5.5
Others	0.3	2.4	0.3	12.9
Total Western Europe	2.9	22.4	2.5	14.6
Middle East				
Abu Dhabi	12.1	92.2	10.3	*
Dubai	0.5	4.0	0.4	26.5
Iran	12.7	92.9	10.4	*
Iraq	13.4	100.0	11.2	*
Kuwait	12.7	91.9	10.3	*
Neutral Zone	0.7	5.2	0.6	36.8
Oman	0.6	4.0	0.4	19.3
Qatar	0.4	3.2	0.3	25.6
Saudi Arabia	22.7	167.0	18.6	*
Syria	0.3	1.8	0.2	20.7
Others	0.4	2.6	0.3	61.3
Total Middle East	76.5	564.8	63.0	*
Africa				
Algeria	1.1	8.5	0.9	24.6
Angola	0.2	1.1	0.1	8.9
Egypt	0.6	4.3	0.5	12.9
Libya	2.8	21.0	2.3	57.8
Nigeria	2.2	16.0	1.8	34.1
Tunisia	0.2	1.8	0.2	47.0
Others	0.3	2.5	0.3	13.5
Total Africa	7.4	55.2	6.1	29.4
Asia & Australasia				
Japan	†	0.1	†	12.8
Brunei	0.2	1.4	0.2	27.8
Indonesia	1.1	8.4	0.9	17.6
Malaysia	0.4	2.9	0.3	15.3
Other South East Asia	†	0.3	†	19.7
India	0.6	4.3	0.5	18.7
Other South Asia	†	0.2	†	6.5
Australia	0.2	1.7	0.2	7.7
New Zealand	†	0.2	†	21.9
Total Asia & Australasia	2.5	19.5	2.1	15.9
Total NCW	110.6	817.3	91.2	51.6
Centrally Planned Economies (CPEs)				
China	2.4	18.4	2.0	18.2
USSR	8.0	59.0	6.6	12.9
Others	0.2	1.8	0.2	11.0
Total CPEs	10.6	79.2	8.8	13.7
Total World	121.2	896.5	100.0	41.5
Of which OPEC	91.1	670.7	74.8	98.6

*Over 100 years †Less than 0.05

Thus, although the Saudis want a price of oil that is high in terms of Saudi Arabia's cost of production (less that $1 per barrel), they do not want a price high enough to jeopardize the future of an oil-based energy system and the viability of the world economy. The Saudi view is shared by other Gulf states who, with the Saudis, form the moderate camp in OPEC.

The Saudis were willing and able to threaten or actually to raise production to prevent the price increases desired by other OPEC members favoring a more hawkish strategy on oil prices. These countries, which traditionally include Iran, Iraq, Venezuela, and Nigeria, have large populations, ambitious development plans, and smaller reserves and, therefore, seek to maximize their oil revenues in the short term. For example, in 1975, OPEC, over Saudi opposition, approved an immediate 10-percent and subsequent 15-percent price increase. Saudi Arabia and the United Arab Emirates (UAE) split with the other OPEC members, announced a 5-percent increase, and greater production. By June, they had forced the rest of OPEC to limit the price increase to an acceptable 10 percent. In 1978, when oil markets eased, the Saudis maintained the price by absorbing the majority of reductions of production, exports, and earnings. And in 1979 and 1980, when supplies became tight once again, the Saudis increased production to try to prevent a price explosion (see Table 9–1).

In addition to Saudi policy, a propitious environment contributed to the stability of the international oil system. In the mid-1970s, recession in the OECD countries, combined with conservation efforts arising from the increase in price, led to a stabilization of demand for oil. Indeed, demand was about the same in 1977 as it was in 1973.[21] At the same time, the supply of oil was steady and even growing. OPEC production as determined by the Saudis was steady: there were no serious efforts to constrict the supply in order to push up the price. And new sources of oil—from the North Sea, Alaska, Mexico—were coming on line (see Table 9–1).

Political conditions in both the producing and the consuming states also enhanced stability. OPEC states, pursuing ambitious economic development programs, were spending their earnings at a rapid rate. Between 1974 and 1978 their combined current-account surpluses actually declined from $35.0 billion to $5.2 billion.[22] As a result, the oil states had an interest in maintaining production, and therefore earnings, at a high level. In addition, key OPEC states friendly to the West, in particular Saudi Arabia and Iran, were responsive to Western concerns about the dangers of economic disruption from irresponsible management of the price and supply of oil.

The Western countries remained divided and acquiescent and, as time went on, increasingly complacent. Their inability to carry out a major restructuring of energy consumption rapidly was not cause for alarm, because the system seemed to have stabilized at an acceptable level of price and supply. Furthermore, Western foreign policies—the U.S. policy of developing and relying on special relations with Saudi Arabia and Iran, and the European and Japanese policies of general political support for the oil producers—seemed to promise security of supply and stability of price. The Saudi rulers, safe on their throne, friendly to the United States (except on Arab-Israeli issues), and cognizant of their new responsibilities to the world economy, seemed to have OPEC well in hand. The government of the shah of Iran, also apparently stable and reliable, was more hawkish on price than the Saudis but more reliable on supply because it was not directly involved in the Arab-Israeli dispute.

As a result of the effective and moderate Saudi management and a propitious environment, supplies were adequate, and after the beginning of 1974, the price of oil in real terms actually dropped, as the periodic price increases by OPEC were offset by inflation (see Figure 9–2).

The Second Oil Crisis: A System Out of Control

By 1978, however, the political and economic environment had become highly unstable, and the ability and willingness of the Saudis to manage the price of and to ensure the supply of oil had diminished. By the end of the 1970s, the demand for oil imports increased as Western economies moved out of the 1974–1975 recession, as the initial shock effect of the price rise wore off, and as complacency set in with the real decline in the price of oil. While demand increased, the world's supply of oil fell. Iran had sharply curtailed its production. Saudi Arabia was willing to increase its production in the short run, but it kept output below capacity and suggested that it would not increase production ceilings in the future. And Kuwait announced plans to decrease its production.

By the end of 1978, the international oil system was once again vulnerable to disruption. World oil supplies were only barely adequate; any slight decrease in supply or increase in demand would precipitate a world shortage and put serious upward pressure on prices. If a supply reduction or demand increase were small, Saudi Arabia might be able to fill the gap and stabilize the system. But if the shifts were large, even the Saudis might not be able to control the system.

The event that created a world shortage of oil and disorder in world oil markets was the 1978 revolution in Iran. At the beginning of 1978, Iran exported 5.4 million barrels of oil a day, about 17 percent of total OPEC exports. At the end of 1978, as part of a successful effort to depose the shah, oil workers cut off all oil exports from that country. By the spring of 1979, the loss of Iranian oil had been to a great extent offset by increased production in the other oil-producing states. Saudi Arabia, for example, increased its production from about 8.3 million barrels per day in 1978 to about 9.5 million barrels in 1979.[23] However, the effect on oil markets of the

Table 9-1 Crude Oil Production[a] (thousand barrels per day)

	1960	1970	1975	1980	1983	1984	1985	1986	1987
OECD[b]	7,866	11,527	10,756	12,859	13,775	14,300	14,754	14,555	14,257
United States	7,055	9,648	8,375	8,597	8,680	8,735	8,933	8,668	8,297
Canada	526	1,305	1,439	1,424	1,356	1,411	1,457	1,466	1,560
Norway	0	0	189	528	614	700	785	841	943
European Community	223	267	232	1,837	2,617	2,873	2,928	2,952	2,793
United Kingdom	3	2	12	1,619	2,299	2,535	2,533	2,508	2,338
Other countries									
Algeria	183	976	945	1,020	699	638	645	671	635
Indonesia	411	855	1,307	1,576	1,385	1,466	1,235	1,264	1,191
Iran	1,068	3,831	5,350	1,662	2,492	2,187	2,258	1,929	2,451
Iraq	1,004	1,563	2,262	2,514	922	1,203	1,437	1,746	2,076
Kuwait[c]	1,696	2,983	2,085	1,661	1,076	1,117	1,040	1,510	1,230
Libya	0	3,321	1,480	1,830	1,076	1,073	1,069	1,137	972
Mexico	271	420	705	1,936	2,666	2,746	2,733	2,431	2,541
Nigeria	17	1,090	1,783	2,058	1,241	1,393	1,464	1,461	1,286
Saudi Arabia[c]	1,315	3,789	7,075	9,903	5,062	4,649	3,468	5,101	4,262
United Arab Emirates	0	691	1,663	1,702	1,119	1,097	1,146	1,331	1,454
Venezuela	2,846	3,708	2,346	2,165	1,781	1,813	1,621	1,576	1,572
Communist countries									
USSR and Eastern Europe	3,220	7,316	9,933	11,996	12,158	12,019	11,626	12,019	12,197
USSR	2,943	6,976	9,570	11,700	11,864	11,728	11,350	11,754	11,930
Eastern Europe	277	340	363	296	294	291	276	265	267
Bulgaria	4	7	2	3	4	4	4	6	6
Czechoslovakia	3	4	3	2	2	2	2	3	2
East Germany	1	1	1	1	1	1	1	1	1
Hungary	24	39	40	41	40	40	40	40	40

	1960	1970	1975	1980	1983	1984	1985	1986	1987
Poland	4	8	11	7	4	4	4	3	3
Romania	241	281	306	242	243	240	225	212	215
Other									
Albania	15	30	37	NA	NA	NA	NA	NA	NA
China	102	602	1,542	2,113	2,121	2,280	2,496	2,613	2,680
Cuba	1	3	5	5	15	15	17	17	18
Yugoslavia	18	57	74	85	83	83	83	83	78

aUnless otherwise indicated, data are for crude oil and exclude natural gas liquids, shale oil, natural gasoline, and synthetic crude oil.
bIncluding shale oil.
cIncluding about one-half of Neutral Zone production.

SOURCE: Central Intelligence Agency, *Handbook of Economic Statistics, 1988* (Washington, D.C.: CIA), p. 102.

Figure 9–2   Oil Prices, 1972–April 1988

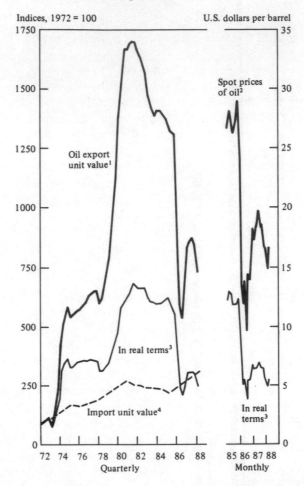

Indices, 1972 = 100   U.S. dollars per barrel

Oil export unit value[1]

Spot prices of oil[2]

In real terms[3]

Import unit value[4]

In real terms[3]

72 74 76 78 80 82 84 86 88
Quarterly

85 86 87 88
Monthly

[1]Unit value of the oil exporting countries (according to the former analytical categories) in terms of U.S. dollars.
[2]Unweighted average of Brent, West Texas Intermediate, and Dubai spot prices in terms of U.S. dollars.
[3]Oil price deflated by import unit value of oil exporting countries.
[4]Import unit value of the oil exporting countries in terms of U.S. dollars.
SOURCE: International Monetary Fund, *Annual Report 1988* (Washington, D.C.: IMF, 1988), p. 18.

loss of Iranian oil could not be completely offset. The crisis led not only to a shortage of supply during the latter part of 1978 and early part of 1979 but also to a greater demand for oil, as consumers tried to augment stocks to protect against anticipated future shortfalls in supply. The result of this perceived shortage and rapid scrambling for stocks was again escalating prices and turbulence in the world oil markets.

The first signal of that turbulence came at the December 1978 OPEC meeting. At that meeting, OPEC agreed to gradually implement price increases amounting to an effective increase of 10 percent for 1979, a rate above the expected Western inflation rates and therefore the first real increase in the price of oil in five years.

This new price, however, did not hold. The Iranian revolution set off panic in the spot market for oil, which spilled over into the long-term contract markets. Most crude oil was then sold by long-term contract between the oil-producing countries and the oil companies at a price determined by OPEC. Oil not under long-term contract was sold in spot markets where the price fluctuates according to market conditions. In 1978 and 1979, those conditions were very tight, creating severe upward pressure on the spot market prices. In early 1979, spot prices rose as much as $8.00 above the OPEC price of $13.34 for Saudi Arabian light crude, their chief traded oil. The differential between the OPEC price under long-term contract and the higher spot price benefited the oil companies, which were able to purchase contract oil at relatively low prices. Many OPEC members, unwilling to allow the companies to benefit from such a situation, put surcharges above the agreed OPEC price on long-term contract oil and even broke long-term contracts in order to sell their oil on the spot markets. Despite its production increases and its refusal to add surcharges, Saudi Arabia was unable by itself to restore order to the world oil markets.

In March 1979, OPEC confirmed that the system was out of control. Instead of gradually implementing the price increase agreed in December 1978, OPEC announced it would immediately implement a 14.5 percent increase. More importantly, OPEC decided that its members would be free to impose surcharges on their oil. The surcharges, which many members immediately instituted, demonstrated that even OPEC and the Saudis were unable to control the price of oil. Furthermore, the OPEC members sought to maintain the tight market, which favored price increases, by agreeing to decrease their production as Iran returned to the oil export market. Despite an agreement by International Energy Agency members to reduce oil consumption by 5 percent for 1979, there was little consumers could do in the short run to stabilize the system. In July 1979, OPEC raised the price again. As the oil minister of Saudi Arabia explained, the world was on the verge of a "free for all" in the international oil system.[24]

By the middle of 1980, the free for all appeared to be coming to an end. High levels of Saudi production and stable world consumption led to an easing of markets. In this climate, Saudi Arabia and other OPEC moderates sought to regain control over prices, reunify price levels, and develop a long-term OPEC strategy for gradual, steady price increases geared to inflation, exchange rate changes, and growth in the developed countries. In September 1980, OPEC discussed the long-term strategy and planned to continue deliberations at a summit meeting of heads of state in November 1980.

But the plan was destroyed by the outbreak of war between Iraq and Iran. On September 22, 1980, Iraq launched an attack on Iran's oil-producing region, and Iran's air force in turn attacked Iraq's oil facilities. The result was a halt in oil exports from these two countries and a reduction in world supplies by an estimated 3.5 million barrels per day—roughly 10 percent of world oil exports. The war dashed all hopes for stability in world oil markets. The OPEC summit was postponed indefinitely, and pressure began to build in the spot market. In December 1980, OPEC members set a new ceiling price of $33 a barrel and spot prices reached $41 a barrel.

The loss of Iraqi and Iranian oil was offset by a high level of world oil stocks, increased production by other Gulf states of an estimated 1 to 1.5 million barrels per day, and the sluggish demand caused by recession and the efforts of members of the International Energy Agency to dissuade companies from entering the spot market in precautionary panic buying, as they had done in 1979. Although such factors prevented panic and chaos, pressure on the spot prices was inevitable, as those countries that had relied on Iraq for oil imports turned to the spot market. As the hostilities continued, spot-market prices gradually rose, thus putting further pressure on long-term prices. Furthermore, damage to the oil production and export facilities in both countries raised questions about oil supplies even after the cessation of hostilities.

As the market conditions disintegrated, the foreign policies of the West, particularly that of the United States, were substantially weakened. The special relationship of the United States with Iran under the shah became one of hostility under the new Islamic government. Even the relationship of the United States with Saudi Arabia seemed threatened. The Camp David agreement between Israel and Egypt had led to a cooling of Saudi-U.S. relations. For the Saudis, the overthrow of the shah, the inability of the United States to keep him in power or even to prevent the holding of U.S. hostages raised doubts about the value and reliability of U.S. support. The events in Iran and an internal insurrection in Mecca in 1980 also raised the specter of internal political instability for both Saudi Arabia and the United States, which Teheran was seeking to foster.

Unstable market conditions and political uncertainty gave rise to widespread pessimistic predictions about the stability of oil prices and the availability of oil in the future. At the height of the second oil shock, experts predicted continuing chronic shortages and periodic interruptions in the supply of oil, at least through the end of the century, by which time alternative energy sources would supposedly be more fully developed. It was also predicted that OPEC market management would keep the price of oil rising approximately 2 percent faster than the rate of inflation.[25] Few observers of the international oil situation in the late 1970s foresaw the profound changes that were to take place as the world moved into the 1980s, changes that not only undermined the ability of the oil oligopoly to manage the price of oil but also threatened the very institutional survival of the OPEC cartel.

OPEC in Decline: The World Oil Glut

OPEC's problems in the 1980s stemmed from its success. The cartel's ability to increase the price of oil eventually transformed the world oil market. The demand for oil fell, non-OPEC production grew, and as a result, a long-term surplus emerged, putting sustained downward pressure on prices. Moreover, the excess supply made it more difficult, if not impossible, for OPEC to manage prices, as it had in the previous decade.

The transformation of the international oil scene was due, in part, to declining demand. Total oil consumption in the industrial countries fell by an estimated 10 percent between 1980 and 1984, after having risen almost continuously for decades (see Table 9-2).[26] Worldwide recession and slow rates of growth in the major consuming countries contributed substantially to this decline. There was also a structural change in consumption patterns. Price increases led to a greater substitution of other fuels for oil, especially in the developed market countries, which rapidly expanded their consumption of coal, natural gas, and, in some countries, nuclear energy. Higher oil prices also stimulated energy conservation and structural adjustment, which were reinforced by government regulations and incentives. Price controls had cushioned the U.S. economy from the effects of the oil-price increases, encouraging imports and discouraging domestic exploration. The removal of controls precipitated a reduction in imports and permanently altered the structure of demand in the United States.[27] In response to the high oil prices, energy efficiency increased. Automobiles became more fuel efficient and homes were better insulated. It is estimated that industry in the non-communist developed countries improved its energy efficiency by a massive 31.1 percent between 1973 and 1982.[28]

Along with the fall in demand, higher oil prices also attracted new suppliers to the international market. OPEC's management task became considerably more difficult, as the OPEC countries lost a substantial portion of their share of world production to non-OPEC producers. OPEC's share of the world oil market fell from 63 percent in 1973 to 48 percent in 1979 to 33 percent in 1983.[29] Non-OPEC production in the oil-exporting developing countries—especially Mexico and, to a lesser extent, China, Egypt, and Malaysia—rose steadily, from 2.8 million barrels per day in 1973 to 7.5 million barrels per day in 1983 (see Table 9-3). In the developed countries, several large reservoirs of new oil came into full operation, most notably in the North Sea, which made Norway and Britain players in the international oil game. In addition, the Soviet Union increased its production and exports in order to boost its foreign exchange earnings.[30]

Table 9-2 Oil Consumption (thousand barrels per day)

	1960	1970	1975	1980	1983	1984	1985	1986	1987
United States	9,795	14,695	16,320	17,055	15,230	15,725	15,725	16,280	16,555
Japan	590	4,000	4,965	5,000	4,330	4,490	4,195	4,255	4,320
Canada	835	1,485	1,660	1,815	1,425	1,445	1,350	1,435	1,510
Western Europe	4,010	12,400	13,230	13,235	11,480	11,400	11,335	11,700	11,890
Belgium, Luxembourg, Netherlands	420	1,290	1,390	1,195	1,030	1,005	1,015	1,140	1,130
France	580	1,950	2,195	2,255	1,800	1,755	1,730	1,745	1,745
Italy	475	1,760	1,915	1,950	1,715	1,640	1,665	1,700	1,750
Spain[a]	120	540	890	1,060	1,000	825	810	805	840
United Kingdom	975	2,030	1,875	1,635	1,480	1,810	1,615	1,570	1,530
West Germany	660	2,570	2,565	2,605	2,205	2,205	2,240	2,375	2,300
Other	780	2,260	2,400	2,535	2,250	2,160	2,260	2,365	2,595

[a]Including the Canary Islands.

SOURCE: Central Intelligence Agency, *Handbook of Economic Statistics, 1988* (Washington, D.C.: CIA), p. 101.

Table 9-3   World Crude Oil Production, 1973–84 (million barrels a day)

	1973	1977	1978	1979	1980	1981	1982	1983	1984
Oil-exporting countries	**31.1**	**31.7**	**30.6**	**31.5**	**27.8**	**23.8**	**19.8**	**18.5**	**19.5**
Saudi Arabia	7.6	9.2	8.3	9.5	9.9	9.8	6.5	4.9	—
Iran, Islamic Rep. of	5.9	5.7	5.4	3.1	1.7	1.4	2.0	2.4	—
Venezuela	3.4	2.2	2.2	2.4	2.2	2.1	1.9	1.8	—
Indonesia	1.3	1.7	1.6	1.6	1.6	1.6	1.3	1.4	—
Nigeria	2.0	2.1	1.9	2.3	2.0	1.4	1.3	1.3	—
United Arab Emirates	1.5	2.0	1.8	1.8	1.7	1.5	1.3	1.1	—
Iraq	2.0	2.5	2.9	3.6	2.8	1.2	1.2	1.1	—
Libyan Arab Jamahiriya	2.2	2.1	2.0	2.1	1.8	1.2	1.2	1.1	—
Algeria	1.1	1.2	1.2	1.2	1.1	1.0	1.0	1.0	—
Kuwait	3.0	2.0	2.1	2.5	1.7	1.1	0.8	1.1	—
Oman	0.3	0.3	0.3	0.3	0.3	0.3	0.3	0.4	—
Qatar	0.6	0.4	0.5	0.5	0.5	0.4	0.3	0.3	—
Natural gas liquids ouput	0.3	0.4	0.4	0.5	0.6	0.7	0.7	0.6	—
Other developing countries									
Net oil exporters	2.8	4.6	5.3	5.8	6.4	6.7	7.3	7.5	7.7
Mexico	0.5	1.1	1.3	1.6	2.1	2.6	3.0	3.0	3.0
China	1.1	1.9	2.1	2.1	2.1	2.0	2.0	2.1	2.1
Egypt	0.2	0.4	0.5	0.5	0.6	0.6	0.7	0.7	0.8
Malaysia	0.1	0.2	0.2	0.3	0.3	0.3	0.3	0.4	0.4
Other	0.9	1.1	1.2	1.3	1.3	1.3	1.3	1.3	1.4
Net oil importers	1.5	1.5	1.5	1.5	1.5	1.7	1.9	2.1	2.3
Argentina	0.4	0.4	0.5	0.5	0.5	0.5	0.5	0.5	0.5
Brazil	0.2	0.2	0.2	0.2	0.2	0.2	0.3	0.3	0.4
India	0.1	0.2	0.2	0.2	0.2	0.3	0.4	0.5	0.6
Romania	0.3	0.3	0.3	0.3	0.2	0.2	0.2	0.2	0.3
Other	0.5	0.4	0.4	0.4	0.4	0.5	0.5	0.6	0.6
Industrial countries	**13.8**	**13.3**	**14.1**	**14.7**	**14.8**	**14.8**	**15.2**	**15.6**	**15.9**
United States	11.0	9.9	10.3	10.2	10.2	10.2	10.3	10.3	10.2
Canada	2.1	1.6	1.6	1.8	1.8	1.6	1.6	1.6	1.6
United Kingdom	—	0.8	1.1	1.6	1.7	1.8	2.1	2.3	2.6
Norway	—	0.3	0.4	0.4	0.5	0.5	0.5	0.6	0.7
Australia	0.4	0.4	0.4	0.4	0.4	0.4	0.4	0.4	0.4
Other	0.3	0.3	0.3	0.3	0.3	0.3	0.3	0.4	0.4
Other countries	**9.1**	**11.4**	**11.9**	**12.2**	**12.5**	**12.5**	**12.6**	**12.7**	**12.7**
U.S.S.R.	8.6	11.0	11.5	11.8	12.1	12.2	12.3	12.4	12.4
Other	0.5	0.4	0.4	0.4	0.4	0.3	0.3	0.3	0.3
Total	**58.3**	**62.5**	**63.4**	**65.7**	**63.0**	**59.5**	**56.8**	**56.4**	**58.1**

SOURCE: International Monetary Fund, *World Economic Outlook* (Washington, D.C.: IMF, 1984), p. 130.

Meanwhile, higher energy prices stimulated increased domestic oil production in the industrialized importing countries. Higher prices and price decontrol in the United States promoted greater investment in the petroleum sector and encouraged new oil companies to enter the market, exploring for new crude sources as well as developing new purchase and distribution lines.[31] As a result of conservation, adjustment, and increased domestic production, the noncommunist developed countries reduced their total demand for imported oil by 40 percent, decreasing their reliance on foreign oil from two-thirds of total consumption in 1979 to less than half in 1983.[32]

Trends in the developing countries were different from the experience of the developed countries. Oil consumption in the developing countries as a whole expanded by approximately 7 percent a year from 1973 to 1979, attributable to relatively high rates of economic growth, generally low domestic oil prices, a lack of oil substitutes, and a limited capacity for conservation. After the second oil shock, however, oil consumption in the developing world rose much more slowly, with most of the increase in consumption attributable to the net oil-exporting countries.[33] A few oil-importing developing countries were able to expand their domestic oil production. Brazil increased its production by 50 percent between 1973 and 1983, and India raised its output fivefold (see Table 9–3).

Downward pressure on oil prices from the sharp drop in demand and the rise in non-OPEC production was exacerbated by an unprecedented drawdown of oil inventories by the international oil companies. Companies had built up their reserve stocks to their highest levels ever during the uncertainties of the 1979–1980 oil shock. Lower oil prices, high interest rates that raised the cost of holding inventories, and, most important, the growing realization that the sluggish world demand for oil was the result of long-term changes in demand patterns and not merely a cyclical phenomenon led to a massive reduction in inventories.[34]

Shifting supply and demand depressed oil prices. On the spot market, prices fell from $40 per barrel in 1980 to $30 per barrel at the end of 1982, further lowering long-term contract prices.[35] As a result, the GNP of the OPEC countries as a whole fell every year during this period. Although Saudi Arabia and some of the high-income OPEC countries were able to maintain positive trade balances, the current-account surpluses of many OPEC members disappeared, constraining their development plans, imports, and, for heavily indebted countries like Nigeria and Venezuela, payment of debt-service obligations.[36] The fall in demand imposed a particularly heavy burden on Saudi Arabia, which, in its informal role as OPEC's market manager, was forced to reduce its production drastically, from a peak of 9.9 million barrels per day in 1980 to less than 5 million barrels per day by 1983, in order to defend OPEC's prices. Saudi oil revenues fell from a peak of $102 billion in 1981 to $37 billion in 1983. The

Gulf countries also reduced their production in support of the Saudi price stabilization effort. As a result, Kuwait's oil revenues fell from a 1980 peak of $19 billion to $9.8 billion in 1983, and the United Arab Emirates oil revenue declined from $18 billion to $11 billion during the same period.[37]

The changing pattern of oil production and consumption increased OPEC's management problems and undermined the cartel's cohesion. As we have seen, the factors that set the stage for OPEC's success in the 1970s had changed by the 1980s. Whereas the demand for oil had been inelastic in the 1970s, conservation and interfuel substitution increased elasticity by the 1980s. Whereas the oil supply seemed inelastic in the 1970s, by the 1980s, new sources had diminished much of the cartel's original advantage as the main source of the world's oil. New non-OPEC suppliers also made the cartel's management more difficult. Finally, as the tight supply eased and prices fell, political differences within the cartel further undermined OPEC's capacity for joint action. Excess supply gave rise to enormous strains within OPEC, and the hardship exacerbated traditional conflicts between those OPEC members seeking to maximize their short-term revenues in order to boost imports and hasten development plans and those like Saudi Arabia and the Gulf states wanting to maintain foreign dependence on OPEC oil for as long as possible by limiting the price increases.

Eventually, OPEC became a victim of the classic cartel problem: cheating. The first episode of cheating occurred between 1981 and 1983. In 1981, several OPEC members—in particular Algeria, Iran, Libya, Venezuela, and Nigeria—undercut the cartel's price-management system by producing over their prescribed ceiling, offering price discounts, and indirectly cutting prices through extended credit terms, barter deals, and the absorption of freight costs by the seller. As long as Saudi Arabia was willing to shore up prices by restraining its own production, these countries were able to violate OPEC's rules without creating a collapse of prices. The Saudis, however, became more and more bitter about having to sacrifice in the face of rampant cheating by their fellow cartel members. Not only were they losing foreign exchange earnings, they were also facing reduced supplies of natural gas that is produced in conjunction with oil and on which the Saudi economy had become dependent.

The expanded volume of oil traded on the spot market after 1978 made it more difficult for OPEC to monitor its members' oil transactions and thus aggravated OPEC's price-management problem. With new non-OPEC sources of supply, greater availability of cheaper oil from OPEC cheaters, slackened demand, and less fear of rising prices, the oil companies saw less need for long-term contracts and more often met their supply needs through the spot market. Whereas in 1973 over 95 percent of all oil was traded on long-term contracts, by 1983 at least 20 percent of the world's oil was traded on the spot market.[38]

The situation was aggravated by continuing disputes over national production allocations within OPEC. Iran, in particular, pressed to maintain or increase its market share at the expense of Saudi Arabia. The Gulf states were reluctant to agree to any production quota unless there was some agreement to end price discounting. Several cartel meetings failed to produce any consensus for dealing with the rampant cheating.

By early 1983, Algeria, Libya, Iran, and Nigeria were selling oil as much as $4 below the $34 OPEC price. Increasingly impatient, Saudi Arabia and its Gulf allies threatened to lower their prices to undercut the cheaters. The threat of a price war was serious. A price collapse would have had severe effects on growth, development plans, military expenditures, and domestic political stability in virtually all of the OPEC-member countries. For indebted oil exporters like Mexico, Venezuela, Nigeria, and Indonesia—and their creditor banks—a sharp drop in prices could have precipitated bankruptcy and a worldwide financial crisis. Other exporters like the United Kingdom, Norway, and the Soviet Union would also suffer from a price fall, as would the oil and banking industries in the United States.

In January 1983, an emergency OPEC meeting collapsed because of the running feud over the distribution of the quotas and price discounting. The international oil markets reacted almost immediately. Spot market prices fell, oil companies began depleting their inventories, and producers came under increasing pressure to reduce their long-term contract prices. The Soviet Union reduced its prices, as did the smaller non-OPEC producers like Egypt. More significantly, the British and Norwegian oil companies proposed to reduce the price of North Sea oil. Meanwhile, Saudi Arabia and the other Gulf producers continued to threaten to cut their prices if some agreement were not concluded.

Finally, in March 1983, OPEC members hammered out an agreement that signaled major changes in the oil-management system. For the first time in the cartel's history, OPEC reduced the price of oil, from $34 per barrel to $29 per barrel. To maintain this price, the members agreed for the first time to a concerted production reduction scheme that limited OPEC output to 17.5 million barrels per day and allocated production among the members. Saudi Arabia formally accepted the role of "swing producer" and committed to adjust its output to support the newly agreed-upon price.[39]

Oil Price Wars

The new production reduction scheme slowed but did not stop the long-term decline in OPEC's power as a price-setting cartel. Sluggish demand and increasing production by countries outside OPEC continued to put downward pressure on oil prices. Domestic economic problems and financial shortages tempted members to break ranks by reducing prices and expanding production to obtain more revenues. As non-OPEC production grew and as non-OPEC producers such as Norway and the United Kingdom lowered prices below that of OPEC, it became more and more difficult for the cartel to reach agreement on production ceilings and quotas among members. In 1984, OPEC lowered the price to $28 per barrel, reduced its production ceiling to 16 million barrels per day, and lowered individual production quotas. Despite OPEC's production allocation scheme, virtually all of the decline in output was absorbed by Saudi Arabia. While other OPEC members either maintained or increased their output, Saudi production declined dramatically. By August 1985, Saudi output had fallen to 2.5 million barrels per day, less than one-fourth of its production in 1980–1981.[40] Saudi foreign exchange earnings suffered a steep decline and the drop in oil production once again impinged on domestic requirements for natural gas.

In the second half of 1985, Saudi Arabia abandoned the role of swing producer. In order to increase its production and restore its market share, Saudi Arabia abandoned selling crude oil on the basis of official OPEC prices and instituted a market-responsive price formula based on the value of products into which its oil was refined, or "netback" sales contracts. Once this happened, OPEC was no longer able to manage the price of oil. In December 1985, OPEC recognized the inevitable. It abandoned the system of fixed official selling prices and concerted production reductions. For the first time since the seven sisters agreed to set prices, the oil cartel agreed to allow prices to be determined by the market.

Largely due to the dramatic increase in Saudi production, OPEC output soared by almost one-third in 1986. The result was volatility and a sharp fall in the price of oil. Spot market prices fell from about $27 to $31 per barrel in November 1985 to $8 to $10 per barrel in July 1986.[41] The collapse of oil prices led to a parallel drop in the value of oil exports to their lowest level since 1973.

Pressure to restore concerted production reductions and higher prices built both within and outside OPEC. In mid-1986, OPEC agreed to interim production reductions and quotas. Then, in December, the cartel reached agreement on new production reductions and quotas and on a new fixed export price of $18 per barrel. Supply control was helped by a slight decline in non-OPEC production due both to voluntary production restraint by non-OPEC exporters and to the shutdown of some high-cost production, especially in the United States. As a result, spot market prices rose to $17 to $19 per barrel in 1987.[42] Once again, the cartel pulled back from a price war and re-established market discipline and prices, albeit at a lower level.

Nonetheless, economic and political conflicts continued to threaten OPEC's ability to implement concerted production reductions. The traditional split remained between the hawks like Iran and Iraq which sought to maximize oil earnings in the short term and the moderates like Saudi Arabia and the Gulf countries which sought to maximize oil earnings over the long-term. This conflict was complicated by an internal civil war over quota allocations. Although a number of OPEC members felt their quota allocations were unfair, the cartel was hopelessly divided and unable to revise the existing agreement. Thus, a number of members resumed cheating by producing over their quotas. The key was the United Arab Emirates, a Gulf state that has a small population and no pressing revenue needs and that thus should have fallen in the camp of the moderates. However, the U.A.E. believed its quota was unfair and in 1988 began pumping twice its allocation. As concerted supply restraint weakened, prices of oil slipped downward.

Another important problem grew out of the Iran-Iraq war. It was a sign of the change in the oil markets that the bombing of oil tankers and shipping facilities in the Persian Gulf did not lead to a run-up in oil prices during the 1980s. The spare capacity of the other OPEC and non-OPEC oil producers, public stocks in consuming countries, as well as the oil-sharing arrangement of the International Energy Agency cushioned any potential threat.

It was the end of the Iran-Iraq war that posed a threat to oil prices. During the war, Iraqi demands for an increase in its quota met implacable resistance from Iran, which insisted on maintaining its second place in OPEC quotas (behind Saudi Arabia) and refused to allow its enemy to improve its relative position. Resolution of the conflict was deferred during the war by leaving Iraq out of the allocation scheme. As long as the war limited the ability of both Iran and Iraq to pump oil, the Iraq-Iran conflict did not threaten OPEC's supply management. However, the cease-fire between the two agreed in mid-1988 posed a serious threat to OPEC's ability to control oil supplies. Iraq was in the process of significantly expanding its production capacity. Both countries faced higher revenue needs for rebuilding and resuming economic development after the lengthy war, and both felt justified in producing more because of postwar needs and because of their reduced production during the war. However, because of the mutual distrust and antagonism arising from the war, OPEC was initially unable to negotiate a new allocation scheme.

At this point, Saudi Arabia intervened. Faced with cheating by the U.A.E., new demands by Iran and Iraq, and the seemingly intractable Iran-Iraq stalemate, Saudi Arabia followed the strategy that it had pursued before. It increased production in an effort to force other OPEC members to resume discipline. OPEC output rose from an estimated 18.5 million barrels per day to an estimated 22.5 million barrels per day. The glut of Saudi oil led to a fall in oil prices to $13 to $14 per barrel by late 1988. In real terms, oil prices were below the 1974 level. The decline in prices hurt the finances of all oil exporters; put severe pressure on indebted oil exporters such as Nigeria, Mexico, and Venezuela; and contributed to political instability in Algeria. By November, action by Saudi Arabia and Kuwait had forced OPEC to agree on a new production agreement to limit production

to 18.5 million barrels per day and raise prices to $18 per barrel. Iran
received its old share allocation and agreed to allow Iraq to return to the
OPEC system with a quota equal to its own. Iraq's increase came at the
expense of other cartel members, especially Saudi Arabia, whose quotas
were decreased. The question was whether the agreement would hold and
for how long, especially when the export capacity of both Iran and Iraq
increased substantially.

The events of the 1980s thus led to a major change in OPEC's power as
a price-setting cartel. Sluggish demand, sustained oversupply, competition
from outsiders, economic temptations to break ranks by reducing prices and
increasing production, and internal political conflicts undermined the role
of the oil-producing cartel. For the foreseeable future, the lack of cohesion
within OPEC will continue to threaten the cartel's effectiveness. In order to
address domestic political and economic problems, expand imports, speed
up development, and service their debts, OPEC members are likely to
pursue competitive export policies. Saudi Arabia can offset some cheating
by other members, but it is no longer willing or able to single-handedly
manage the cartel by playing the role of the swing producer. The Saudi
deterrent of flooding the market with oil will be its principal tool for
establishing cartel discipline.

In the absence of OPEC discipline, some cartel members will protect
themselves from price competition by buying refining and marketing operations in the major oil-consuming countries. During the 1980s, a number of
OPEC members—Venezuela, Libya, Kuwait, Saudi Arabia, and the United
Arab Emirates—acquired downstream operations in the United States and
Western Europe. Moving downstream is intended to protect crude oil exporters when prices fall, because it guarantees an outlet for oil and because
prices for refined products fall less than prices for crude oil. As these OPEC
members develop refining and marketing capacity, their oil operations will
come to resemble the large, integrated oil companies that once dominated
the oil system (see Figure 9–3). They will likely find themselves in even
greater conflict with other OPEC members that remain dependent on crude
oil exports for revenues and seek to maximize oil earnings in the short term.
The downstream strategy, therefore, will further weaken OPEC.

Because OPEC's share of the world oil market is smaller than in the
1970s, price management will also require the cooperation of the non-
OPEC producers. Although Mexico, the main non-OPEC exporter, has
generally cooperated with OPEC, it is not likely that the Mexicans will want
to join OPEC and sacrifice their sovereignty over their oil production and
their relationship with the United States. It is inconceivable that other major
producers like the United Kingdom and Norway will join the cartel, although some informal cooperation with OPEC in maintaining world oil
prices may be possible.

An equally critical issue for the future of OPEC will be the supply and
demand for oil. As supply has increased and OPEC's share has declined, the

Figure 9–3   Composition of the Top 50 Oil Companies

SOURCE: "PIW Ranks World's Top 50 Oil Companies," *Petroleum Intelligence Weekly*, Supplement Issue, December 12, 1988, p.1.

market for oil has become much more like that for other commodities, with a higher degree of cyclical price volatility in response to supply-and-demand fluctuations. As we have seen, soaring prices in the 1970s eventually led in the 1980s to a decline in demand due to conservation and substitution, an increase in supply due to new exploration and production, and a fall in the price of oil. Conversely, the lower price of oil in the 1980s encouraged greater consumption, discouraged investment in exploration and production, and contributed to the depletion of reserves that could constrain supplies in the 1990s. If demand increases or supply falls in the 1990s as a result of these cyclical forces, the price of oil may rise and the oil-producing countries may be able to capitalize on the cyclical upswing. Unless new oil producers emerge and unless the role of oil in the world economy declines dramatically, a new oil system will develop, one based, perhaps, on the dominance of a few oil-exporting countries largely in the Persian Gulf but which will have integrated their operations downstream in the consuming countries.

Other OPECs?

The success of the oil producers in the 1970s led to a revolution in the thinking of Southern raw material producers. Suddenly it seemed that producer cartels could bring the end of dependence. Producer organizations in copper, bauxite, iron ore, bananas, and coffee were either formed or took on new life after October 1973. In a variety of United Nations resolutions, the Third World supported the right of Southern exports to form producer associations and urged the North to "respect that right by refraining from applying economic and political measures that would limit it."[43]

Yet by the late 1970s the prospects for these new producer cartels seemed dim. None had succeeded in maintaining higher commodity prices in the face of depressed market conditions, most were fraught with internal dissension, and a few never even got off the ground. Still, it is worthwhile to examine both their potential and the reasons for their very limited successes. First, it is necessary to review the reasons for the success of the oil producers and thereby to develop a model for effective producer action.

Several market factors set the stage for OPEC's success in the 1970s. The demand for oil imports was high. Oil imports played an important and growing role as a source of energy in the North. Europe and Japan were dependent on foreign sources for oil. Even the once self-sufficient United States had become increasingly dependent on oil imports. In the medium term, the demand for oil and oil imports is also price inelastic. There are no readily available substitutes for petroleum, and there is no way significantly to decrease consumption. Thus, an increase in the price of oil does not immediately lead to a noticeable decrease in demand.

Supply factors also favored OPEC in the medium term. The supply of oil is price inelastic; that is, an increase in its price does not lead to the rapid entrance of new producers into the market. Large amounts of capital and many years are required to develop new sources of oil. In addition, supply inelasticity was not relieved by the stockpiles of oil. In 1973, the developed countries did not have oil reserves to use even in the short run to increase supply and alleviate the effect of supply reductions.

Finally, at the time of the OPEC price increases, there was an extremely tight supply of oil in the international market. Rapidly rising demand in the consuming countries was not matched by rising production. As a result, a few important producers, or even one major producer, could be in a position to influence price by merely threatening to limit supply.

This economic vulnerability of consumers set the stage for OPEC's action. Several political factors, however, determined whether such action would take place, and an understanding of the behavior of interest groups helps explain the ability of the oil producers to take joint action to raise the price of oil.[44]

First, there is a relatively small number of oil-exporting countries. Common political action is more likely when the number of participants is so limited, as the small number maximizes all the members' perception of their shared interest and the benefits to be derived from joint action.

The oil producers were also helped by the experience of more than a decade of cooperation. OPEC encouraged what one analyst described as "solidarity and a sense of community."[45] It also led to experience in common action. Between 1971 and 1973, the oil producers tested their power, saw tangible results from common action, and acquired the confidence to pursue such action. This confidence was reinforced by the large monetary reserves of the major producers. The reserves minimized the economic risks of attempting some joint action such as reducing production or instituting an embargo. The reserves were money in the bank that could be used to finance needed imports if the joint effort to raise the price of petroleum was not immediately successful. According to one analyst, it enabled the oil producers to take a "long-term perspective," to adopt common policies in the first place, and to avoid the later temptation of taking advantage of short-term gains by cheating.[46]

The common political interest of the Arab oil producers in backing their cause in the conflict with Israel reinforced their common economic interest in increasing the price of oil. The outbreak of the 1973 war greatly enhanced Arab cohesiveness and facilitated the OPEC decision of October 16 to raise oil prices unilaterally.

Group theory suggests, however, that the perception of a common interest is often insufficient for common action. A leader or leaders are needed to mobilize the group and to bear the main burden of group action. Leadership was crucial to common oil-producer action. In 1973, the initiative by Arab producers in unilaterally raising prices made it possible for other producers to increase their prices. After 1973 the willingness and ability of Saudi Arabia to bear the major burden of production reductions determined the ability of producers to maintain higher prices.

Producer action was facilitated by the nature of the problem. Manipulating the price was relatively easy because it was a seller's market. Given the tight market, it was not necessary to reduce the supply significantly to maintain a higher price. Ironically, the international oil companies also helped joint-producer action. Producing nations were able to increase their price by taxing the oil companies. The companies acquiesced because they were able to pass on the tax to their customers.[47] Producing nations were also able to reduce the supply simply by ordering the companies to limit production. Increasing governmental control of the companies helped implement these reductions.

Finally, the success of the producers was assured by the absence of countervailing consumer power. The weakness of the corporations and the consumer governments was demonstrated by the Libyan success in 1970 and by subsequent negotiations. The disarray and acquiescence of the oil companies and the oil-consuming governments in 1973 sealed the success of the producing nations. Particularly important was the inability of the developed market economies to take joint action—in contrast with the group action of the producers—to counter the cartel.

In the aftermath of OPEC's success, several factors seemed to suggest that in the short term, and perhaps in the medium term, some producer cartels might succeed. In the near term, economic conditions were propitious for many commodities, particularly for those on which consuming states are highly dependent. The United States, for example, relies on imports of bauxite, tin, bananas, and coffee. Western Europe and Japan, less well endowed with raw materials, depend also on imports of copper, iron ore, and phosphates. Disrupting the supply of many of these commodities, particularly critical minerals, would have a devastating effect on the developed market economies.

In addition, over the short and medium terms, the demand for and supply of these commodities are price inelastic. As discussed earlier, with few exceptions, a price increase for these materials would not be offset by a decrease in consumption, which would lead to an increase in total producer revenues. Similarly, when supply is price inelastic, a rise in price will not immediately lead to the emergence of new supplies, because it takes time and money to grow new crops and exploit new mineral sources. It should be noted that for some critical raw materials, an inelasticity of supply can be cushioned by stockpiles, and developed countries have accumulated such supplies for strategic reasons. Nevertheless, although stockpiles can serve to resist cartel action over the short term, not all commodities can be stockpiled, and stockpiles in many commodities are generally insufficient to outlast supply interruptions that persist for more than a few months.

Tight market conditions favor producers in the short term. As demonstrated by the oil action, a seller's market facilitates cartel action by enabling one or a small number of producers to raise prices, as occurred in 1973–1974. At that time, the simultaneous economic boom in the North and uncertain currency markets that encouraged speculation in commodities led to commodity shortages and sharp price increases. The developed countries were particularly vulnerable to threats of supply manipulation, and the producer countries were in a particularly strong position to make such threats. For example, Morocco (phosphates) and Jamaica (bauxite) took advantage of this situation to raise prices.

In addition to these economic factors, several political conditions also favored producer action, again primarily over the short run. For many commodities—for example, bauxite, copper, phosphates, bananas, cocoa, coffee, natural rubber, and tea—relatively few Southern producers dominate the export market, and some of these producers have formed associations with the goal of price management. Several political developments made producer cooperation more likely in the mid-1970s. One was a new sense of self-confidence. The OPEC experience suggested to other producers that through their control of commodities vital to the North, they might possess the threat they had long sought. Thus, many Third World states felt that they could risk more aggressive policies toward the North.

Another new development stemmed not from confidence but from desperation. The simultaneous energy, food, recession, and inflation crises left most Southern states with severe balance-of-payments problems. Some states may have felt that they had no alternative to instituting risky measures that might offer short-term economic benefits but that would probably prove unsuccessful or even damaging in the long run.

Reinforcing economic desperation was political concern. Political leaders, especially those in the Third World, tend to have short-run perspectives, as the maintenance of their power may depend on achieving short-term gains despite inevitable long-run losses.[48] However, this argument is directly opposite to the OPEC model for a successful producer cartel, wherein monetary reserves enabled the producing nations to take a long-term perspective, to risk short-term losses for long-term gains. In other cases, producers with huge balance-of-payments deficits may be moved to risk long-term losses for short-term gains. And as has been argued, the short-term maximization of revenues may in fact be rational action for the long-term view; that is, if producers feel that their short-term profits will be sufficient to achieve economic diversification and development, they may rationally pursue short-term gains.[49]

The emergence of leaders in some producer groups was yet another new development. Jamaica's unilateral action in raising taxes and royalties on bauxite production and Morocco's unilateral action to raise the price of phosphate altered the conditions for other bauxite and phosphate producers.

Finally, cooperation was sometimes made easier by the nature of the task of managing price and supply. In such commodities as bauxite and bananas, vertically integrated oligopolistic multinational corporations could be taxed according to the OPEC formula. In these and other commodities, production control was facilitated by increasing governmental regulation or ownership of production facilities.

With all of these factors working in favor of cartel success, why then were the raw-material producer associations so unsuccessful after 1974? Some of the reasons for the problems of cartels can be traced to the depressed economic conditions of the late 1970s and 1980s, whereas others are of a more general nature.

Although as we have noted, the demand and supply of many commodities are price inelastic over the short and medium terms, in the long run, the demand and supply are more elastic and thus less conducive to successful cartel action, as is illustrated by the OPEC experience of the 1980s. A rise in price above a certain level will generally lead to a shift in demand to substitutes. Aluminum will be substituted for copper; coffee will be replaced by tea. With time, it is also possible to develop new sources of supply for most commodities. New coffee trees can be planted; new mineral resources, including resources in the seabed, can be exploited. Of course, some of these new supplies may be relatively more expensive, as new production will often have to rely on costly technologies and lower-quality ores. Thus, it should be noted, new production may undermine a cartel, but it may have little effect on price.

Because of the long-term elasticity of demand and supply, the successful survival of a cartel generally depends on two complex factors. First, producers have to manage price so that it does not rise above a level that would encourage the use of substitutes. Such management requires sophisticated market knowledge and predictive ability. Because the threshold price may be lower than the preferred price for many producers, agreement on joint action may be quite difficult to achieve. Second, and equally difficult, the supply response from other producers must be managed. Currently existing cartels have been generally unable to manage successfully either prices or supply: price cutting among fellow cartel members has been common, and few producers have agreed to supply controls.

Despite some incentive for cooperation, there have been major problems in joint action. Although many commodities are supplied by a few producers, these producers often find they have more in conflict than in common. The copper producers, for example, are divided by political as well as economic differences. Moreover, although the foreign exchange crisis may encourage cooperation, it also may facilitate consumer resistance. Producing nations that have no reserves and that rely on the export of one commodity for the bulk of their foreign exchange earnings are not in a position to endure long-concerted corporate or consumer-government resistance. Furthermore, the temptation to take short-term profits from concerted action at the expense of longer-term gains is greater during a balance-of-payments crisis. And although the task of price management may be easy in some cases, as when there is a leader and multinational corporations are present, there are no such advantages for many commodity-producing nations.

One of the greatest barriers to producer cartels has been the task of managing supply. Few countries have a large enough share of production and large enough reserves to assume the kind of leadership role played by Saudi Arabia. No one country or small group of countries is able to bear the burden of supply reduction for the entire commodity group.

Without tight markets, then, supply can be controlled only through buffer stock schemes or export or production reductions—methods that are politically complex and economically costly. Many commodities are perishable and hence cannot be stored in a buffer stock, whereas other commodities require enormous buffer stocks and financing to maintain prices. Export and production reductions are equally difficult to accomplish. Export reduction without production controls poses the same problems of storing and financing as buffer stocks do. And agreements to reduce production are difficult to achieve, as OPEC's experience illustrates, and may be costly in terms of employment.

Perhaps the most devastating blow to the producer associations has been dealt by the stagnant—in some cases falling—demand for their commodities. In 1974 and 1975, as economic activity in the industrialized countries declined, the demand for industrial raw materials fell precipitously. Since then, there has been a steady secular decline in the Northern demand for Southern commodities (see Chapter 7).

Faced with reductions or slow growth in the demand for their commodities, the only hope for the producer associations is to reduce production and supply in order to maintain prices at desired levels. Yet, as we have indicated, most producing nations have found it politically or economically difficult to cut back production, and many cartel members have cut prices in order to increase their international competitiveness. The result has been a general oversupply of many raw materials and a drop in their prices that the cartels have been unable to counteract.

Bauxite, Bananas, and Copper

The problems of producer cartels as well as their potential benefits may be better understood by a brief examination of three attempts by commodity-producing organizations to increase prices: bauxite, bananas, and copper.

In 1974, Jamaica, confronted by rapidly rising import costs for food and petroleum, moved to increase its revenues from bauxite production and to alter its relationship with the six huge multinational companies that owned, processed, and marketed Jamaican bauxite.[50] Despite vigorous protests from the aluminum companies, taxes and royalties on bauxite production were raised, and the new taxes were based not, as before, on the tonnage of bauxite extracted but on the price of aluminum ingots on the North American market. This action increased by over sevenfold the amount collected by the Jamaican government in taxes and royalties on each ton of bauxite.[51] To prevent the companies from shifting production out of Jamaica, the aluminum firms were required to maintain the production levels established by the Jamaican government or to pay taxes on that level whether or not it was actually maintained. Finally, the Jamaican government negotiated long-term agreements with the aluminum companies, providing for increased local refining and government participation in ownership.

The Jamaican actions were followed by other Caribbean bauxite producers, and Jamaica played a leading role in establishing the International Bauxite Association (IBA) in March 1974. Within a few months, the IBA had a membership of eleven (Jamaica, Surinam, Guyana, the Dominican Republic, Haiti, Ghana, Guinea, Sierra Leone, Yugoslavia, Australia, and Indonesia), controlling nearly 85 percent of the noncommunist world's production of bauxite.

The outlook for IBA was optimistic. The consuming states were highly dependent on bauxite imports. None of the six largest consuming nations produced more than 50 percent of its bauxite needs, and most produced very little.[52] The United States, for example, imported 89 percent of its bauxite, and 86 percent of that came from Jamaica.[53] Furthermore, bauxite demand is price inelastic, in large part because the price of bauxite is only a small percentage of the price of aluminum, and most of the price relates to processing costs. Thus an increase in the price of the raw material does not lead to a major increase in the price of the finished product or, in turn, to a significant decrease in consumption. Supply is also price inelastic over the short and medium terms, as huge amounts of capital and many years are needed to develop new sources.

The structure of the market also favored the IBA. Bauxite is sold primarily among subsidiaries of large vertically integrated multinational aluminum corporations, and so the price is subject not to the market but to negotiation. Furthermore, the aluminum multinationals did not have strong incentives to resist pressure for price increases. Because the demand for bauxite, like the demand for petroleum, is inelastic, the multinational companies can pass on price to the end consumer. Thus, if the producing countries can develop bargaining advantages, they can renegotiate the price in their favor. Moreover, geographical and ethnic ties of several key producers—Jamaica, Surinam, and Guyana—facilitated cooperation among them. Perhaps most importantly, Jamaican leadership had demonstrated the benefits of cooperative action.

Despite these positive factors, the IBA's successes were limited. Differing economic and political interests among its members and the resulting lack of cohesiveness proved to be the cartel's central problem. The Caribbean countries, eager to increase prices, maximize government revenues in the short term, and increase national control over the bauxite and aluminum industry, pushed for common pricing and common export taxes. On the other hand, Guinea, in an effort to increase its market share, set its levy well below the Caribbean rate. Australia, as a developed country eager to increase its share of the market for bauxite and related products, did not cooperate in price setting efforts, in imposing a bauxite levy, or in nationalization. Equally troublesome was the rise of new producers outside the IBA. Moreover, a continued slump in the world aluminum market that began with the recession in the mid-1970s and continued into the 1980s, made it difficult for the IBA to act unilaterally to raise prices. Another long-term change was the emergence of substitutes for bauxite such as new plastics that have been used in place of aluminum in the automobile and container industries.[54]

Differing interests of bauxite producers facilitated the development of new sources of supply. From 1974 to 1976, Australia and Guinea, with lower levels of taxation on bauxite exports than most IBA countries, rapidly increased their bauxite production at the expense of the Caribbean producers. Between 1973 and 1976, bauxite production in Jamaica, Surinam, and Guyana dropped more than 25 percent while production in Australia and Guinea rose by 74 percent. This trend away from the Caribbean and its high export levies continued. In 1973, 33 percent of world bauxite production was in Jamaica, Surinam, and Guyana; by 1976 this was down to 22 percent falling to 12 percent by 1988, whereas in the same period, the proportion of the world's bauxite mined in Australia and Guinea went from 29 percent to 45 percent and increased further to 51 percent by 1988. Brazil, which was not a member of the IBA, moved rapidly to increase its production. In 1976, Brazil accounted for only 1 percent of world production. By 1988, Brazil had increased its production ninefold giving it 8 percent of world production.[55]

Yet another problem has been the relative decline of the role of the aluminum multinationals. Although they still dominate bauxite capacity and the international trade in bauxite, the six multinationals, somewhat like the seven sisters before them, have lost their downstream dominance of the market. For example, the control by the majors of noncommunist smelter capacity dropped from 80 percent in 1970 to 40 percent by 1982. By the mid-1980s, aluminum prices were being set by the market, not by the six multinationals. For the IBA, this meant that cartel management by way of taxing the multinationals was no longer possible.

As a result of these problems, the International Bauxite Association has largely given up hope of being the "bauxite OPEC" that some of its more militant members had hoped it would become. Instead, the IBA has concentrated on efforts to forge better relations with the aluminum-producing companies and to dispel the suspicions by the aluminum companies of the IBA that resulted from the association's cartel-like behavior during the 1970s. The focus of these efforts included an unsuccessful attempt by the IBA members to establish an international producer-consumer commodity agreement for bauxite under the auspices of UNCTAD.

In many ways, the situation of the banana producers resembles that of the bauxite exporters.[56] Banana production is highly concentrated, with five countries at the time accounting for 65 percent of the world's banana exports—Ecuador (19 percent), Costa Rica (16 percent), the Philippines (12 percent), Honduras (10 percent), and Panama (8 percent)—and the consuming countries are totally dependent on imports. Furthermore, the demand for bananas is price inelastic in the near term and, under certain conditions, in the long term, largely because, like bauxite, the price of the raw material is only a fraction of the price of the retail product. Temperature-controlled transportation, refining, and distribution account for most of the cost of bananas.[57] Thus, a large increase in the price of bananas does not lead to an equal increase in the retail price of bananas. If the price is not raised to such high levels that consumers turn to substitutes, demand will remain inelastic in the long run. Finally, supply is also inelastic in the short run.

Also as with bauxite, multinationals play a key role in the banana industry. Bananas are sold to subsidiaries of the same multinational corporation that owns and operates the banana plantations. These oligopolistic, vertically integrated multinational corporations are dependent on these sources of supply and are vulnerable because of expensive investments in transportation and refrigeration. Finally, because of their oligopolistic market position, the companies can pass on price increases to consumers without fearing a loss of markets to competitors. The banana-producing countries attempted to take advantage of these favorable conditions. In 1974, several Central American banana-producing countries and Colombia formed a union of banana-exporting countries and agreed to impose an export tax of $1.00 on each box of bananas. The effort failed. Only four countries—Colombia, Costa Rica, Honduras, and Panama—actually imposed a tax; only Panama imposed the agreed-upon $1.00 duty; and soon all reduced the duty sharply.

There were several reasons for the failure of the Unión de Paises Exportadores de Banana (UPEB). The multinational banana companies— United Brands, Standard Fruit, and Del Monte—fought back. They challenged the tax in local courts and refused to pay the government until the courts determined the legality of the duty. They stopped exports, cut production, destroyed crates of bananas, laid off workers, threatened not to reinvest after a hurricane in Honduras, and, in Honduras, resorted to bribery to obtain a tax reduction.[58]

Another problem was the refusal by Ecuador, the largest producer and the country with the greatest ability to expand its production, to join UPEB. Ecuador argued that the tax was not viable without concurrent production reductions and that, in any case, as an oil producer, it did not suffer from the oil price increase, which was UPEB's justification for its tax. Although Ecuador most probably acted out of self-interest, its decision did point out the important long-run problem of excess supply. Although the demand for bananas has grown, the supply has grown even more rapidly. Without some form of supply control, UPEB price rises would collapse. Because bananas are perishable, the form of control would have to be production reductions. Yet these are politically difficult to achieve. Even after catastrophic weather in 1982 destroyed a substantial proportion of the world's banana supply and sent prices soaring, it was clear that once the affected areas had recovered, oversupply conditions would again prevail. Against this backdrop, the UPEB members again attempted in 1983 to introduce more mechanisms to regulate the market through limits on new plantings, output controls, price harmonization, and export taxation. However, disagreements over the distribution of the burdens of these efforts continued. Although the Dominican Republic, Nicaragua, and Venezuela joined UPEB, Ecuador and the Philippines remained outside, and Colombia, although a member, did not collaborate closely with UPEB. As a result, UPEB, like the IBA, sought a producer-consumer agreement through the Food and Agricultural Organization of the United Nations, an effort that ended in failure due in part to UPEB internal dissension.

A third raw material group that has sought to carry out an OPEC strategy is the association of copper producers, CIPEC (Conseil Inter-gouvernemental des Pays Exportateurs de Cuivre). In June 1974 the group, which was formed in 1967, resolved "to control the declining price of copper on world markets."[59] To that end, CIPEC announced in November 1974 that its members would restrict monthly exports of copper by 10 percent and would not increase their inventories of refined copper. In April 1975, the export reduction was increased to 15 percent. All of this was to no avail. Copper prices continued to decline.

At first glance, several market factors would seem to have favored CIPEC. Although the United States then supplied 80 percent of its own copper needs through mining and recycling scrap, Europe imported 85 percent and Japan 86 percent of their respective total consumption.[60] Furthermore, import dependence was increasing. World copper consumption had risen rapidly, and with it imports had also risen. In 1950, for example, imports accounted for 41.1 percent of the industrial world's consumption, whereas in 1973, imports accounted for 51.5 percent of consumption.[61]

Demand is also price inelastic, at least in the short run. Because there are no readily available, adequate substitutes for copper, producers can increase their total earnings by increasing the price. Supply is also inelastic in the short run because of the cost and time involved in bringing new production on line. Moreover, copper stockpiles are usually quite limited.[62]

Several political factors also seemed conducive to CIPEC's success. CIPEC's four original members—Chile, Peru, Zambia, and Zaire—control 55 percent of the noncommunist world's copper exports. If other Third World producers had joined, CIPEC would have accounted for almost two-thirds of the world's exports.[63] In 1975 there was some movement toward expansion: Indonesia became a full member and Australia, Papua New Guinea, Mauritania, and Yugoslavia became associate members. In addition, because the governments of the principal members of CIPEC control all or a majority of production and all of the marketing of copper, they are in a position to carry out policies to control supply. Furthermore, the members had the experience of agreeing and carrying out export reductions in 1974 and 1975.

Despite these favorable conditions, CIPEC had little chance of increasing the price of copper.[64] In the long run, the demand for copper from CIPEC is highly elastic. New sources of raw copper are available, and so unless any increase in the price of copper is relatively modest, new supplies will be developed, including recycled copper. Also, unless any increase is limited, substitutes such as aluminum and plastics will be used.[65]

Finally, the demand for copper is relatively income elastic; that is, an increase in the growth rate of the developed countries will lead to an increase in the demand for copper, whereas a decline in growth will lead to a decline in demand. This elasticity was demonstrated by the rise in price of copper during the economic boom of 1973–1974 and its precipitous drop during the recession of 1974–1975.[66] For producers, this means that except in times of boom in the developed market economies, copper is and will be in surplus supply. Thus, if producers wish to raise or even stabilize prices, they must develop schemes that will absorb huge quantities of copper or prevent its production in the first place. Small reductions such as the 15-percent export cutbacks of 1974–1975 are insufficient.

The problem of developing effective schemes to manage supply is CIPEC's major challenge. One alternative would be to reduce production, but this would be difficult to accomplish, as non-CIPEC producers including the United States would not agree to such reductions and would take advantage of any price rises achieved by CIPEC reductions to increase their sales. One potential producer is the United States, which controls 27 percent of total world reserves and, thus, could disrupt the market. Furthermore, many CIPEC members themselves are not interested in production reductions. Because copper production is labor intensive, any reduction would lead to unemployment and, possibly, to social unrest and political problems for the producer governments. It is probably for this reason that the export reductions of 1974 and 1975 were not matched in most countries by production reductions. In addition, many CIPEC member governments are deeply in debt to foreign creditors and need the foreign exchange they earn on copper exports. Chile and Peru, for example, have strenuously opposed export reductions, and so CIPEC abandoned this tactic in 1977.[67]

Even if CIPEC could have agreed on how to reduce production or how to finance a buffer stock, its members would have had difficulty in agreeing on a common price, as production costs differ from country to country. Thus, what looks like a low price for one producer would provide respectable profits for another. Moreover, there are no common political interests to serve as an incentive for common CIPEC action. Indeed, there has been political conflict among the members. Chile, in particular, has been politically isolated under the Pinochet regime.

One scheme that CIPEC considered was a buffer stock. Under such a program, a central agency would buy copper when the price fell below an agreed-upon floor and would sell it when it rose above that floor. However, because supply is generally way above demand, a buffer stock program would be prohibitively expensive—one estimate suggested a cost of $5 billion, a sum clearly beyond the capabilities of CIPEC.[68] Moreover, outside financing from, for example, the International Monetary Fund or OPEC was not available, because the IMF offers assistance only to producer-consumer groups and OPEC showed little interest in financing CIPEC.

By the early 1980s, the chances of CIPEC's becoming an effective cartel were even more remote. Far from exercising restraint, CIPEC members were maximizing production in spite of a continued slump in the world demand for copper caused by the economic recession, which had affected the copper industry even more than other commodities. Production by CIPEC members reached the point that in 1983, the United States could impose import restrictions on copper to protect its own producers.[69] Chile and Peru, both with debt problems and both able to produce copper efficiently enough to profit from increased copper sales even at depressed world market prices, were the main source of overproduction. Less efficient producers like Zambia suffered more from depressed-market prices and thus argued in CIPEC in favor of production restraints, but to no avail. This experience further illustrates one of the reasons that CIPEC and other commodity-producer associations failed to become effective cartels: divergent economic requirements among their members. Like the IBA and UPEB, CIPEC turned to an unsuccessful effort to manage copper prices through an international agreement between the copper producers and the consumers.

There is a possibility that the producers might try joint action to increase the price of commodity exports, if only out of sheer frustration and even against all rational calculations. However, history suggests that these efforts will fail. In the 1980s, as a result of the continuing inability of commodity exporters to achieve success through cartel action and because of the demonstrated effect of the waning of OPEC's power, developing country commodity exporters have increasingly directed their efforts toward improving their production and marketing capabilities. The producing countries also have sought to achieve other forms of commodity arrangements with consumers through, for example, international commodity agreements. Such arrangements may gather greater support from the consuming countries in the future if there are short-run commodity shortages or disruptive markets that damage developed and developing country producers.[70]

NOTES

1. See: Morris A. Adelman, *The World Petroleum Market* (Baltimore: Johns Hopkins University Press, 1972); J. E. Hartshorn, *Politics and World Oil Economics: An Account of the International Oil Industry in Its Political Environment*, rev. ed. (New York: Praeger, 1962 and 1967); Edith T. Penrose, *The Large International Firm in Developing Countries: The International Petroleum Industry* (Cambridge, Mass.: MIT Press, 1969); Anthony Sampson, *The Seven Sisters: The Great Oil Companies and the World They Made* (New York: Viking, 1975); Federal Trade Commission, *International Petroleum Cartel*, staff report to the Federal Trade Commission submitted to the Subcommittee on Monopoly of the Select Committee on Small Business, U.S. Senate, 82nd Cong., 2nd sess. (Committee Print No. 6) (Washington, D.C.: U.S. Government Printing Office, 1952); John M. Blair, *The Control of Oil* (New York: Pantheon, 1976).

2. See Zuhayr Mikdashi, *A Financial Analysis of Middle Eastern Oil Concessions: 1901–*

1965 (New York: Praeger, 1966); Charles Issawi and Mohammed Yeganeh, *The Economics of Middle Eastern Oil* (New York: Praeger, 1962), pp. 24–40.

3. In 1928, for example, Shell, Standard Oil, and Anglo-Persian (the predecessor of BP) in order to bring order out of soft and volatile markets concluded the "As Is," or "Achnacarry," agreement to divide world markets and stabilize or determine world prices, and in that same year a group of British, Dutch, U.S., and French companies agreed to divide up much of the old Ottoman Empire in the Red Line agreement. Also important was the basing-point pricing system that established a common price at several locations, or basing points, and standard, not actual, freight charges from the basing point to the destination. This system prevented low-cost producers from expanding their market share by reducing prices. See Penrose, *The Large International Firm in Developing Countries*, pp. 180–183.

4. See Mikdashi, *A Financial Analysis of Middle Eastern Oil Concessions*; Issawi and Yeganeh, *The Economics of Middle Eastern Oil*; Gertrude G. Edwards, "Foreign Petroleum Companies and the State in Venezuela," in Raymond F. Mikesell et al., eds., *Foreign Investment in the Petroleum and Mineral Industries* (Baltimore: Johns Hopkins University Press, 1971), pp. 101–128; Franklin Tugwell, *The Politics of Oil In Venezuela* (Stanford, Calif.: Stanford University Press, 1975); Donald A. Wells, "Aramco: The Evolution of an Oil Concession," in Mikesell et al., *Foreign Investment in the Petroleum and Mineral Industries*, pp. 216–236.

5. Wells, "Armaco: The Evolution of an Oil Concession."

6. Adelman, *The World Petroleum Market*, p. 207.

7. See, for example, Robert Engler, *The Politics of Oil: Private Power and Democratic Directions* (Chicago: University of Chicago Press, 1961).

8. Benjamin Shwadran, *The Middle East, Oil and the Great Powers* (New York: Council for Middle Eastern Affairs, 1955), pp. 103–152; J. C. Hurewitz, *Middle East Politics: The Military Dimension* (New York: Praeger, 1969), pp. 281–282.

9. See Penrose, *The Large International Firm in Developing Countries*, pp. 248–263; Adelman, The World Petroleum Market, pp. 196–204.

10. Mira Wilkins, *The Maturing of Multinational Enterprise: American Business Abroad from 1914 to 1970* (Cambridge, Mass: Harvard University Press, 1974), pp. 386–387.

11. See, for example, Engler, *The Politics of Oil*.

12. See footnote 4.

13. For a history of the Organization of Petroleum Exporting Countries, see Zuhayr Mikdashi, *The Community of Oil Exporting Countries: A Study in Governmental Cooperation* (Ithaca, N.Y.: Cornell University Press, 1972).

14. Zuhayr Mikdashi, "The OPEC Process," *Daedalus*, 104 (Fall 1975), 203. The new members were Abu Dhabi, Algeria, Libya, Qatar, the United Arab Emirates, Nigeria, Ecuador, Indonesia, and Gabon.

15. Mikdashi, *The Community of Oil Exporting Countries*, pp. 196–207.

16. Joel Darmstadter and Hans Landsberg, "The Economic Background," *Daedalus*, 104 (Fall 1975), 21.

17. On evolution of events in Libya, see U.S. Senate Committee on Foreign Relations, *Multinational Corporations and United States Foreign Policy: Multinational Petroleum Companies and Foreign Policy*, hearings before the Subcommittee on Multinational Corporations, 93rd Cong., 1st and 2nd sess., Part 5 (Washington, D.C.: U.S. Government Printing Office, 1974).

18. Organization for Economic Cooperation and Development, *Oil Committee, Oil Statistics: Supply and Disposal 1970* (Paris: OECD, 1971), p. 27. There were several reasons for the powerful Libyan position in the European market. The transportation of oil from Libya was much cheaper and safer than the transportation of oil from the Persian Gulf, which, with the closing of the Suez Canal, required a long trip around Africa. Furthermore, in 1970, there had been a decline in the supply of oil from Nigeria because of the civil war, and the pipeline that carried Saudi oil to the Mediterranean had been cut in Syria. Finally, Libyan oil was low in sulfur and therefore desirable for environmental reasons.

19. There was some consultation by the developed market states. The U.S. Department of Justice issued a waiver to oil companies under antitrust law, enabling them to cooperate in bargaining to resist unreasonable demands for higher prices. See U.S. Senate, *Multinational Corporations and United States Foreign Policy*, Part 5, pp. 145–173. President Nixon then sent

Undersecretary of State John N. Irwin to the Middle East to encourage governments to enter into joint negotiations with the companies. Secretary Irwin, however, capitulated to the demand of the shah of Iran for separate negotiations.

20. The Organization of Arab Petroleum Exporting Countries was formed by three Arab states, Kuwait, Libya, and Saudi Arabia, in 1968. It was expanded in 1970 to include Algeria, Abu Dhabi, Bahrain, Dubai, and Qatar.

21. National Foreign Assessment Center, *Handbook of Economic Statistics 1978* (Washington, D.C.: Central Intelligence Agency, 1978), p. 87. For the United States, overall demand was level, although demand for imports increased.

22. International Monetary Fund, *Annual Report 1979* (Washington, D.C.: IMF, 1979), pp. 16, 27.

23. National Foreign Assessment Center, *International Energy Statistical Review* (Washington, D.C: Central Intelligence Agency, November 28, 1979), p. 2.

24. *New York Times*, March 28, 1979, p. 1.

25. Edward L. Morse, "An Overview: Gains, Costs and Dilemmas," in Joan Pearce, ed., *The Third Oil Shock: The Effects of Lower Oil Prices* (London: Royal Institute of International Affairs, 1983), p. 3.

26. International Monetary Fund, *World Economic Outlook: A Survey by the Staff of the International Monetary Fund* (Washington, D.C.: IMF, April 1984), p. 128.

27. Morse, "An Overview," p. 8.

28. Leonard Silk, "The Painful Shift to Costly Oil," *New York Times*, September 28, 1983, Sec. D, p. 1.

29. International Monetary Fund, *World Economic Outlook*, p. 133.

30. Ibid., pp. 130–133.

31. Morse, "An Overview," p. 4.

32. International Monetary Fund, *World Economic Outlook*, p. 128.

33. Ibid., pp. 129–131.

34. Ibid., p. 134.

35. International Monetary Fund, *World Economic Outlook*, p. 135.

36. Morse, "An Overview," pp. 14–15.

37. International Monetary Fund, *International Financial Statistics* (Washington, D.C.: IMF, August 1984).

38. Louis Turner, "OPEC," in Pearce, ed., *The Third Oil Shock*, p. 85.

39. Ibid.

40. International Monetary Fund, *World Economic Outlook* (Washington, D.C.: IMF, April 1986), p. 151.

41. International Monetary Fund, *World Economic Outlook* (Washington, D.C.: IMF, April 1987), p. 98.

42. Ibid., p. 99.

43. Guy F. Erb and Valeriana Kallab, eds., *Beyond Dependency: The Developing World Speaks Out* (New York: Praeger, 1975), p. 206.

44. The following analysis is to a great extent influenced by the theory of collective action developed by Mancur Olson, *The Logic of Collective Action: Public Goods and the Theory of Groups* (Cambridge, Mass.: Harvard University Press, 1965 and 1971).

45. Mikdashi, *The Community of Oil Exporting Countries*, pp. 196–207.

46. S. D. Krasner, "Oil Is the Exception," *Foreign Policy*, 14 (Spring 1974), 78–79.

47. See Raymond F. Mikesell, "More Third World Cartels Ahead?" *Challenge*, 17 (November-December 1974), 24–26, on the OPEC method of taxing multinational corporations.

48. John E. Tilton, "Cartels in Metal Industries," *Earth and Mineral Sciences*, 44 (March 1975), 41–44.

49. Harry G. Johnson, *Economic Policies Toward Less Developed Countries* (New York: Praeger, 1967), pp. 136–162.

50. The six are the Aluminum Company of America, Alcan Aluminum Ltd., Reynolds Metals Company, Kaiser Aluminum and Chemical Corporation, Anaconda Company, and Revere Copper and Brass Company.

51. Carmine Nappi, *Commodity Market Controls* (Lexington, Mass.: D.C. Heath, 1979), p. 123.

52. Anthony Edwards, *The Potential for New Commodity Cartels: Copying OPEC, or Improved International Agreements*? QER Special No. 27 (London: Economist Intelligence Unit, September 1975), p. 41.

53. *Commodity Yearbook 1980*, p. 77. The crucial position of Jamaica in the U.S. market is based on its large production (it is the world's largest producer after Australia and is the largest exporter in the Third World), the low-cost transportation of Jamaican bauxite to U.S. markets, and the low-cost production in Jamaica.

54. Steven Kendall Holloway, *The Aluminum Multinationals and the Bauxite Cartel* (New York: St. Martin's Press, 1988), p. 79-82.

55. U.S. Department of the Interior, *Bureau of Mines, Minerals Yearbook 1986* (Washington, D.C.: U.S. Government Printing Office, 1987), p. 24 and *Minerals Yearbook 1982*, p. 21, *Minerals Yearbook 1977-1978*, p. 108, and *Minerals Yearbook 1975*, p. 243.

56. This discussion involves Latin American producers. The other producers, former British and French colonies, have special agreements with developed countries that guarantee markets and provide price supports and financial aid. See Edwards, *The Potential for New Commodity Cartels*, p. 37.

57. L. Emil Kreider, "Banana Cartel? Trends, Conditions, and Institutional Developments on the Banana Market," *Inter-American Economic Affairs*, 31 (Autumn 1977), 8; Edwards, *The Potential for New Commodity Cartels*, p. 36.

58. Edwards, *The Potential for New Commodity Cartels*, pp. 36-37, for example.

59. K. W. Clarfield et al., *Eight Mineral Cartels* (New York: Metals Week, McGraw-Hill, 1975), p. 57.

60. *Metal Statistics 1968-1978* (Frankfurt: Metallgesellschaft Aktiengesellschaft, 1979), pp. 29-36.

61. Joseph C. Wyman, *Perspective on Copper* (New York: Research Group of Reynolds Securities, Inc., February 1975), p. 6.

62. Edwards, *The Potential for New Commodity Cartels*, p. 52.

63. Raymond F. Mikesell, *The World Copper Industry* (Baltimore: Johns Hopkins University Press, 1979), pp. 20-23.

64. See Chibuzo Nwoke, *Third World Minerals and Global Pricing: A New Theory* (London: Zed Books, 1987).

65. N. Iwase, "Recycling and Substitution," in S. Sideri and S. Johns, eds., *Mining for Development in the Third World* (New York: Pergamon Press, 1980), pp. 266-274.

66. This rise and drop was aggravated by the Japanese accumulation of stocks to hedge against shortages in the boom period and the sales of these stocks during the economic recession.

67. *American Metal Market*, February 9, 1978, p. 10a. See also Theodore Panayotou, "OPEC As a Model for Copper Exporters: Potential Gains and Cartel Behavior," *The Developing Economies* (June 1979), 203-219.

68. Mikesell, *The World Copper Industry*, p. 199.

69. Kenji Takeuchi, John E. Strongman, Shunichi Maeda, and C. Suan Tan, *The World Copper Industry: Its Changing Structure and Future Prospects*, World Bank Staff Commodity Working Papers #15 (Washington, D.C.: World Bank, 1987).

70. Jack A. Finlayson and Mark W. Zacher, *Managing International Markets* (New York: Columbia University Press, 1988).

Part Four

The East-West System

10

East-West
Economic Relations

The planners constructing the new international economic order between 1943 and 1947 both desired and expected that the East would be part of the postwar system. Between the wars, the Soviet Union had been separated from the international economic system by the West's opposition to the Communist regime and by Stalin's autarkic development policy, but it was never completely isolated. From the time of the Russian Revolution until the early 1930s, when the collapse of world trade led to a collapse of trade with the West, the Soviet Union traded with the developed countries and with the United States in particular.[1] During this period, Soviet imports of Western raw materials and technology made an important contribution to Soviet growth, and a form of U.S.-Soviet economic interaction revived during the war years through U.S. lend-lease assistance.[2]

Some doubted the Soviet Union's interest in or ability to join the liberal multilateral system envisioned by the postwar planners.[3] United States officials, however, actively sought the Soviet Union's participation in the postwar economic order as a way to encourage political harmony, promote trade, and thereby encourage prosperity. Thus, the United States pressed for Soviet adherence to the Bretton Woods agreements and seriously considered giving a $10-million loan to the Soviet Union for postwar recovery.[4]

Western planners never questioned the participation of Eastern Europe in the postwar economic order. The countries of Eastern Europe had been closely integrated with the West, especially Western Europe, in the interwar period. In 1938, for example, Western Europe accounted for about 60 percent of Eastern Europe's exports and imports.[5] Czechoslovakia and Poland, which had been on the side of the Allies during the war, were invited to attend the international monetary and trade conferences. The United Nations Relief and Rehabilitation Administration was created in 1943 to help Eastern and Southern Europe recover after their liberation.[6] As late as 1947, Western European countries assumed "a substantial and ready resumption" of trade of principal goods with the East.[7]

Nevertheless, the economic relationship between the capitalist countries of the West and the Communist countries of the East became one of independence and confrontation. The Cold War led to an effort on both sides to separate the economies of East and West and to use that separation as a tool of political confrontation. The Soviet Union refused to join the Western economic order and, with the new Communist states of Eastern Europe, created a separate economic system. The Western states tried, for political and military reasons, to isolate the Communist economies and to integrate those of the developed market states.

The Creation of an Eastern Economic Bloc

The creation of a separate Eastern economic system was part of the Soviet Union's postwar policy of dominance in Eastern Europe and of its international political strategy.[8] Marxist ideology provided the justification for Soviet control. According to Marxist theory, the formation of a separate Eastern economic bloc would deepen the crisis of world capitalism and speed its inevitable demise. Stalin stated that denying the Eastern markets to the West would decrease Western exports, create idle industrial capacity, and lead to the inevitable internal economic and political collapse of capitalism.[9] The formation of a separate socialist bloc would insulate the East from the coming economic chaos in the West and enhance socialist economic development.[10] The primary motivation, however, was political. A separate Eastern economic bloc, in the Soviet Union's view, would provide a buffer zone of friendly, that is, Communist states on its borders and would prevent Germany or other "hostile" Western powers from posing a threat of military invasion. Furthermore, the Soviet Union would obtain access on favorable terms to the resources of Eastern Europe—raw materials and capital equipment—that could be used to rebuild the Soviet Union after the war and to advance its economic development.

Through wartime diplomacy, military occupation, and coups d'état, the Soviet Union established Communist satellite regimes in all the states of Eastern Europe.[11] The Soviet Union, in cooperation with national Communist leaders, restructured the economies of Eastern Europe, introducing state ownership of the means of production, central planning, and the Soviet model of economic growth based on self-sufficiency and all-around industrialization.[12] The Soviet Union also built a socialist international economic system centered on the Soviet Union, which had a low level of interaction with the West.

The Soviet Union refused to join the new international economic institutions created by the West and prevented eligible satellites from participating in Western institutions. Although the Soviet Union participated in the Bretton Woods conference, it refused to ratify the Bretton Woods agreements and become a member of the International Monetary Fund (IMF) or the International Bank for Reconstruction and Development (IBRD).[13] Czechoslovakia and Poland, which initially joined the fund and the bank, withdrew in 1950 and 1954, respectively, under strong Soviet pressure.[14]

Although invited, the Soviet Union refused to attend the preparatory meetings and international negotiations that led to the Havana Charter. Czechoslovakia and Poland participated in the Havana negotiations, although they did not ratify the charter. No Eastern states were contracting parties of the General Agreement on Tariffs and Trade (GATT).[15] The Soviet Union rejected the U.S. offer of aid under the Marshall Plan and refused to allow Poland and Czechoslovakia, the two Eastern states offered Marshall Plan aid, to accept U.S. aid and join the Organization for European Economic Cooperation (OEEC), the European organization established to coordinate European use of Marshall Plan funds.[16]

The institutional expression of the Eastern bloc was the Council for Mutual Economic Assistance (CMEA or Comecon). This economic organization, whose members included the Soviet Union and the states of Eastern Europe (except Yugoslavia), was established in 1949 as the Eastern response to the Marshall Plan. The communique issued at the time of its formation stated that the Eastern states formed Comecon in order to reinforce economic cooperation in the face of "the dictatorship of the Marshall Plan, which would have violated their sovereignty and the interests of their national economies."[17] Comecon pursued technical cooperation and joint planning, but its main function was to reorient trade eastward and to buttress the new political relationship between the Soviet Union and Eastern Europe.

Through Comecon and a series of bilateral trade agreements between the Soviet Union and the satellite countries, Eastern European trade was redirected from West to East. In 1938, 10 percent of Eastern exports went to Eastern countries including the Soviet Union, 68 percent to Western Europe, 4 percent to the United States and Canada, and 5 percent to Latin America. By 1953, 64 percent of Eastern exports went to Eastern countries, 14 percent to Western Europe, less than one percent to the United States, Canada, and Latin America.[18] In the first postwar decade, trade tended to benefit the Soviet Union, which was able to negotiate extremely favorable prices for its imports and exports.[19] One notorious example was the Polish-Soviet agreement under which Poland agreed to deliver large quantities of coal to the Soviet Union at a very favorable price.[20]

The Soviet Union's access to the planning process of the satellite countries also served to reorient economic flows. The Soviet Union's system of state ownership and central planning was imposed on Eastern Europe.[21] Eastern Europe's economic plans were prepared with the assistance of Soviet economic advisers by hand-picked economists trained in the Soviet

Union.[22] Because trade was controlled centrally, economic planners determined by administrative decisions to shift trade from West to East. Under their plans, Eastern European states produced and exported those products desired by the Soviet Union. Through long-term trade agreements, the Soviet Union obliged Czechoslovakia, for example, to emphasize production of heavy machinery, equipment, and arms instead of following the original Czech plan for more diversified production.[23]

Reparations imposed on the former Axis countries were an important element in the relationship between Eastern Europe and the Soviet Union. In East Germany, the Soviet Union unilaterally dismantled factories and claimed goods from current production for the Soviet army and the Soviet economy. The total value of these transfers has been estimated at $18 billion in 1950s dollars. In Hungary, Rumania, and Bulgaria, the Soviet Union also dismantled factories and claimed goods from current production, the total value of which has been estimated at close to $2 billion.[24]

Financial ties were also redirected from West to East. Eastern European currencies were made inconvertible (on inconvertibility, see below). The nationalization of foreign investment disrupted private capital flows. The Soviet Union and most of the satellites were not eligible for IMF or IBRD assistance, and they rejected Marshall Plan aid. The principal source of external financing for Eastern Europe was credit from the Soviet Union for the purchase of raw materials and equipment from the Soviet Union.[25]

Finally, after the war, the Soviet Union acquired as reparations numerous German industrial enterprises operating in Hungary, Rumania, and Bulgaria (former allies of Germany). These enterprises operated primarily as joint companies with the local national government. They enjoyed preferential taxes and access to foreign exchange and raw materials and often offered favorable prices to the Soviet Union. Because of their powerful and preferential position, these companies became a source of intrabloc conflict and were liquidated after 1954.[26]

Western economic warfare increased the East's self-imposed isolation. Following the establishment of Communist regimes in the Soviet-occupied states of Eastern Europe, Soviet pressure on Iran and Turkey, the outbreak of civil war in Greece, and political instability in Western Europe, U.S. policymakers concluded that their hopes for postwar cooperation with the Soviet Union were unrealistic. The East's rejection of Marshall Plan assistance, the coup in Czechoslovakia, and the Berlin blockade of 1948 confirmed the U.S. view that the Soviet Union was a political and military threat to the West.

In addition to building a united and prosperous Western economy and creating a powerful Western military alliance, the aim of United States and Western policy was to deny the Soviet Union and its allies economic resources that would enhance their military capability and political power. The Western strategic embargo began in full force with the passage of the

U.S. Export Control Act of 1949.[27] This act, which remained in force for twenty years, authorized the president to "prohibit or curtail" all commercial exports and to establish a licensing system to regulate exports to Communist countries. Any product that had military applicability or that would contribute to the military or economic potential of a Communist state was placed on the restricted list.[28]

The United States sought, with mixed success, to persuade other Western states to impose similar embargoes. In 1949 under U.S. pressure, the Coordinating Committee (Cocom) was set up to discuss and coordinate Western strategic embargo lists. Although it had no binding authority, Cocom succeeded in drawing up an international list of restricted items for its fifteen members.[29] However, the difference in views between the United States and its allies over the goals and content of the economic embargo became a source of tension throughout the postwar era. For the United States, the strategic embargo was intended to impair not only the East's military strength but also its political and economic power. The U.S. embargo therefore was directed at nonmilitary goods that would enhance economic performance and development as well as at military goods. The Europeans and Japanese, who had a greater economic stake in trade with the East than the United States did, felt that a broad embargo would encourage greater Eastern solidarity without hindering military and political capability. Thus, they advocated a more limited definition of strategic goods, namely, those with direct military implications.[30] As a result of allied resistance, the international list was less comprehensive than the U.S. control list.

The United States also used the Johnson Debt Default Act of 1934 to deny financial resources to the East. An effort to compel countries to repay World War I debts, the Johnson act prohibited private persons or institutions from extending credit to a foreign government in default on obligations to the United States. Following World War II, the act was amended to exempt members of the IMF and the World Bank, that is, virtually all states except those in the East. Yugoslavia, which was a member of the Fund and the Bank, and East Germany, Albania, and Bulgaria, which had no outstanding debts, were not affected.[31] The Johnson act's restrictions were reinforced by a disagreement between the United States and the Soviet Union on the settlement of the USSR's substantial World War II lend-lease debt.[32] Other NATO (North Atlantic Treaty Organization) countries did not restrict Eastern access to credit, and an effort by the United States to impose restrictions through international agreement failed.[33] Another form of economic warfare was to deny the East access to Western markets. In 1951 at the height of tensions in Korea, the U.S. Congress passed the Trade Agreements Extension Act, which withdrew all trade concessions negotiated with the Soviet Union and any Communist country (except Yugoslavia). As a result, products from Eastern countries remained subject to the onerous

Smoot-Hawley tariffs. Many European states also adopted restrictions on imports from Communist countries.[34]

Thus the East and West, mainly for political reasons, established separate international economic systems with separate institutions, rules, and patterns of interaction. At the height of economic separation during the Korean War, East-West trade was actually lower in absolute terms than it had been in 1937.[35] After the end of the Korean conflict and the death of Stalin in 1953, the political-security conflict eased somewhat. As a result, Eastern policies of regional economic isolation were modified; the West's control list was shortened; Western Europe, Canada, and Japan negotiated most-favored-nation agreements with Eastern Europe and the Soviet Union and reduced trade restrictions; and East-West trade increased.[36] From 1953 to 1958 Eastern exports to the West doubled, and from 1958 to 1963 they nearly doubled again.[37]

Nevertheless, as long as the Cold War continued, East-West trade remained unimportant as a percentage of both world trade and the total trade of East and West.[38] Although both Eastern and Western Europe favored greater commerce and took steps in that direction, the United States and the Soviet Union continued, for political reasons, to reject any major change in East-West economic relations. The large, self-sufficient economies of the superpowers enabled them to be less influenced by the potential economic advantages of interaction than their smaller and more trade-oriented partners were and more influenced by overriding political and security concerns.

Forces of Change in the East

The easing of political tensions as well as the growing problems of the Eastern economic system emerged as forces encouraging the East to end its isolation from the West. The end of the Cold War set the stage for change in both East and West. By the early 1970s, the Soviet Union had achieved effective equality with the United States in strategic weapons. Nuclear parity enabled Soviet leaders to view the West with more confidence, to modify the fear of military invasion, and to entertain the idea of limiting expenditures on strategic weapons. Because of the change in nuclear capability, the Soviet Union believed the West would be more willing to discuss arms limitations and to seek political accommodation. The combination of Soviet nuclear parity and greater Soviet flexibility in foreign policy led the United States and its Western allies to look more favorably on easing conflict with the Soviet Union.

While political changes were necessary, internal economic problems were the major motivation for opening economic relations with the West. Serious economic difficulties in agriculture and the industrial sector emerged in the 1960s and reached near-crisis proportions by the 1980s, particularly in the Soviet Union.

Agriculture was the first problem to affect the Soviet Union's international policy. Low agricultural productivity, a longstanding problem, had several causes: collectivization that destroyed the peasantry; excessive interference in local farm management by the large and unwieldy Soviet agricultural bureaucracy; inadequate infrastructure in many areas ranging from roads to storage facilities; and poor inputs from the industrial sector.[39] Periodic efforts to improve agricultural productivity have been undermined by the Soviet agricultural bureaucrats for whom any change in the prevailing system is a threat to their power. Despite significant capital investment in the years after 1960, productivity of the Soviet agricultural sector in the 1980s stood at 20 to 25 percent of U.S. productivity according to Soviet statistics and at 10 percent of U.S. productivity according to Western measures.[40]

In the 1960s, the Soviet Union, once a food exporter, became a net importer of food from the West (see Table 10-1). In part, this was because of a decision to improve the diet by increasing meat consumption which increased the need for grain for feedstock. Further, before 1960, the Soviet Union had adjusted to crop shortfalls by reducing domestic consumption. After 1960, Soviet leaders could no longer impose such hardships on their people without political risk. So, when shortfalls occurred, the Soviet Union turned to the international market to purchase grain.[41] Between 1960 and 1985 Soviet imports of food increased from $613 million to $16.4 billion—an increase of 2500 percent—while food exports increased 82 percent from $702 million to $1.3 billion.[42] The first major purchase—7 million tons—was made in 1964 following a disastrous crop in 1963. Subsequently, grain was regularly imported in large amounts—about 4 million tons per year—primarily from Canada (see Table 10-1). In 1972 another particularly bad harvest forced the Soviet Union to import over 19 million tons of grain from the United States and to make smaller purchases from other countries. The disruption caused by these large purchases led the United States to press the Soviet Union to sign a five-year agreement that stabilized Soviet purchases, committed the United States to make grain available up to fixed amounts, and provided for consultions on larger purchases. With the exception of the period of the grain embargo imposed after the invasion of Afghanistan (see below), the Soviet Union has made regular purchases of U.S. grain, and the grain agreement has been regularly renewed. By the 1980s, Soviet grain imports averaged approximately 37 million tons per year (see Table 10-1).

Industrial growth has also been a problem for the Eastern system. In the 1950s and 1960s, the Soviet Union and Eastern Europe achieved high rates of industrial growth by a significant expansion in the labor force—the employment of women, the transfer of labor from agriculture to industry,

Table 10-1   Soviet Grain Harvests, Exports, and Imports (millions of metric tons)

Year	Harvest	Export	Import
1950	81	2.9	0.2
1955	104	3.7	0.3
1956	125	3.2	0.5
1957	103	7.4	0.2
1958	135	5.1	0.8
1959	120	7.0	0.3
1960	126	6.8	0.2
1961	131	7.5	0.7
1962	140	7.8	—
1963	108	6.3	3.1
1964	152	3.5	7.3
1965	121	4.3	6.4
1966	171	3.6	7.7
1967	148	6.2	2.2
1968	170	5.4	1.6
1969	162	7.2	0.6
1970	187	5.7	2.2
1971	181	8.6	3.5
1972	168	4.6	15.5
1973	223	4.9	23.9
1974	196	7.0	7.1
1975	140	3.6	15.9
1976	224	1.5	20.6
1977	196	2.3[a]	18.9[a]
1978	237	2.8[a]	15.6[a]
1979	179	0.8[a]	31.0[a]
1980	189	0.5[a]	34.8[a]
1981	158	0.5[a]	46.0[a]
1982	187	0.5[a]	32.5[a]
1983	192	0.5[a]	32.9[a]
1984	173	1.0[a]	55.5[a]
1985	192	1.0[a]	29.0[a]
1986	210	1.0[a]	30.0[a]

[a]July to July of following year estimate of Department of Agriculture.
Source: Marshall Goldman, *Gorbachev's Challenge* (New York: W.W. Norton & Co., 1987), p. 33.

and long working hours—and by the rapid increase in capital formation at the expense of agriculture and of improvement in the standard of living.[43] By 1960, however, this type of expansion, known as extensive growth, began to reach its limits. Comecon's growth rates declined from an average of 6 percent per year in the 1950s to about 4 percent in the early 1970s.[44] By the early 1980s, growth had fallen to 1 to 2 percent (see Table 10–2).

Table 10-2 Real Gross National Product Growth (percent)

					Average Annual Rate of Growth[a]				
	1961–1965	1966–1970	1971–1975	1976–1980	1981–1985	1984	1985	1986	1987
Communist Countries									
USSR and Eastern Europe									
USSR[b]	4.9	5.1	3.1	2.2	1.8	1.4	.7	3.9	.5
Eastern Europe	3.9	3.8	4.9	1.9	1.2	3.6	.7	3.0	.6
Bulgaria	6.4	5.1	4.7	1.0	.7	3.2	– 3.5	5.0	.7
Czechoslovakia	2.4	3.4	3.4	2.2	1.2	2.4	.8	2.1	1.3
East Germany	3.0	3.1	3.5	2.0	1.9	3.5	2.8	1.5	2.2
Hungary	3.9	3.0	3.3	2.0	.6	2.6	– 2.6	2.1	1.2
Poland	4.5	4.0	6.5	.7	.6	3.6	1.0	2.8	– 2.5
Romania	5.4	4.9	6.7	3.9	1.9	6.0	1.3	5.8	3.1
Other									
China	NA	NA	5.5	6.1	9.2	12.0	12.0	7.8	9.4
North Korea	9.8	5.5	10.4	4.1	3.7	2.7	NA	NA	NA
Yugoslavia	NA	NA	4.6	5.5	1.2	2.1	.5	3.7	– .7

[a]GDP growth for the OECD countries.
[b]At factor cost.
SOURCE: Central Intelligence Agency, *Handbook of Economic Statistics 1988*, p. 33.

Growth slowed because it was no longer possible to increase quantity, as in the case of labor, and because the increase in quantity was no longer effective, as in the case of capital. The Eastern states needed to shift to intensive growth, which is achieved by improving productivity, that is, the efficiency of production. Intensive growth relies primarily on the application of technology: advanced machinery and production processes, modern computer and communications technology, sophisticated management techniques, and energy. Since the early 1960s, Eastern plans have emphasized the need to achieve growth through improved productivity and the development and application of technology, although there has been little practical application of this goal.

The Eastern system has encountered severe difficulties in improving productivity, largely because of the central planning system. In the West, markets by and large determine the allocation of resources. Supply and demand determine price which then determines production and consumption. In the East, planners allocate resources. They distribute resources for production and investment, determine production targets, and set prices.

Such a system discourages innovation, productivity, and quality. There is little incentive for plant managers to experiment with new technology. Rewards are based on fulfillment or overfulfillment of quantitative goals and not on improving the quality of the product or the production process. Indeed, there are disincentives to experiment with new methods because they threaten to interrupt production at least temporarily and thus to jeopardize fulfillment of the quantitative goals. Furthermore, the absence of competition and the existence of guaranteed markets eliminate incentives for managers to cut cost or improve quality. Above all, prices do not provide a guide to help managers determine what goods are needed by consumers and how to improve productivity by lowering costs.

Research and development have also been ineffective. Despite great emphasis on scientific research, there is little relationship between research and actual production. Unlike the West, where most research is carried out by private enterprise, research in the East is generally carried on in research institutes that have few links with production facilities. Scientists and engineers are thus not positioned to respond directly to the needs of industry or to make industry responsive to scientific development.[45] As a result of these system biases, the East has fallen far behind the West in the development of technology. For example, it has been estimated that the United States has a lead over the Soviet Union of eight to ten years in advanced microcircuits and nine to fifteen years in mainframe computers.[46]

In the 1960s and 1970s, the Eastern countries tried to solve the problem of technology and productivity through limited national economic reforms, intra-Comecon trade, and greater trade with the West. In the mid-1960s, managers were given greater freedom to decide what to produce and how, incentives were based on profit as well as quantitative goals, and prices were made more "rational." But the reforms did not go far enough. They were strongly opposed by party conservatives and government bureaucrats who saw their power threatened by the potential new power of the plant managers and who eventually reasserted centralized control.[47] The exception was Hungary, which for a time gave greater autonomy to individual enterprises and reformed its price system to reflect more closely supply and demand.[48] Other Eastern regimes were unwilling to risk real reform and introduced only mild changes. By 1970 many of these had been rescinded. Thus, the Eastern economies continued to stagnate.[49]

The East also attempted to solve the problem of technological development and intensive growth through Comecon. An effort began in the late 1950s to revitalize Comecon and change it from a tool of Soviet dominance to a tool of development. Attempts were made to increase trade within the bloc, as it was hoped that trade would lead to economies of scale, force competitiveness, and thus encourage modernization. Trade was encouraged by an agreement on methods for establishing trade prices, a clearing institution (the International Bank for Economic Co-operation), and programs for national specialization in production. Technological cooperation was also encouraged.[50] However, Comecon trade remained hampered for economic and political reasons by internal biases against trade other than bilateral trade: lack of complementarity with the Eastern economies, the poor quality of goods, unsatisfactory currency arrangements, and political unwillingness to delegate power to a supranational body—especially one in which the Soviet Union had a powerful voice. Trade within Comecon has been characterized by bilateral arrangements between the Soviet Union and Eastern European countries rather than multilateral integration among all Comecon nations.[51] Moreover, intrabloc technological cooperation was not up to the task of overcoming systemic biases against technological innovation. In the 1980s Comecon remained stagnant, although members agreed to establish diplomatic relations with the EC and expressed the desire to increase joint production efforts and improve the intra-Comecon trade pricing mechanisms.[52] But little was actually done to implement change.

Finally, the East sought to bridge the technology gap and achieve intensive growth by acquiring foreign technology. The Soviet Union's seven-year plan of 1959–1965 set the stage by calling for economic modernization through the development and application of technology and by allowing technological imports from the West to eliminate lags in technological development in the Soviet Union.[53] In 1959, Premier Nikita Khruschev announced that the Soviet Union intended to make major purchases of technology—patents, licenses, entire plants—from the West.[54] One example was a 1966 agreement with FIAT, the Italian automaker, to build an automobile plant in the Soviet Union. This $1.5 billion project involved the purchase of licenses and equipment, the training of Soviet technicians in Italy, and the use of Western personnel in the Soviet Union.[55] Industrial cooperation agreements between Western firms and Eastern European enterprises became increasingly important in the early 1970s. For the East, they were intended to provide Western technology, improve competitiveness in the West, and reduce foreign exchange needs. The West sought greater access to Eastern markets and the opportunity to reduce costs. West Germany, which was by far the most active in seeking such agreements, entered into more than 200 agreements with Comecon nations in the 1970s.[56] However, by the end of the decade both partners were disappointed with the results. The time lag for implementing projects was so long that by the time plants were built the technologies were no longer new. Some Western firms had only provided access to second-class technology, thus denying the East enhanced competitiveness in the West, and the scarcity of foreign exchange limited further agreements. The Western firms found that Third World industrializing countries with a more liberal investment climate offered the West better investment opportunities.

Western technology, however, had little impact on Soviet and Eastern European productivity and growth. As we shall see, there were financial constraints on the East's ability to purchase Western technology. Furthermore, despite the easing of Cocom controls, the West was not willing to sell sophisticated technologies that could contribute to the East's military strength. For example, Western computer and telecommunications technologies that are critical for modern production are also particularly sensitive for military reasons. Most important, foreign technology imports had little impact as long as there was no reform in the domestic economic system that would permit their effective use.

By the 1980s, the Eastern economic system was in need of drastic economic reform. Growth rates declined steadily, investment and productivity remained low. From 1981 to 1985, growth in the Soviet Union averaged only 1.8 percent and total factor productivity declined to 0.9 percent compared with 1.9 percent from 1975 to 1980.[57] Soviet agricultural problems were so great that some products were rationed and lines for goods became long in major Soviet cities. Between 1983 and 1985 the growth rate of agricultural production per capita actually fell 2 percent.[58] Shortages of all consumer products caused public dissatisfaction, creating a potential political challenge to the regime. At the same time, the Soviet Union faced a number of political reversals. The war in Afghanistan had become a costly economic drain that was unpopular at home and damaged Soviet relations abroad. In Poland, labor unrest arising in part from economic problems challenged the legitimacy of the Communist regime in that important Soviet ally.

In March 1985, Mikhail Gorbachev became General Secretary of the Communist Party and began a program to address these economic, political and foreign policy problems.[59] His first steps were tentative, especially in domestic economic matters. The earliest signs of change were in foreign policy. Gorbachev argued that the possibility of nuclear holocaust and the nature of contemporary world problems such as the environment made the world interdependent and called for a more cooperative foreign policy.[60] He adopted a defensive military strategy; signed an agreement with the United States on intermediate-range nuclear weapons and pursued negotiations on strategic and short-range nuclear weapons; announced a unilateral reduction of conventional forces in Europe; said he would accept greater autonomy in Eastern Europe; agreed to withdraw Soviet troops from Afghanistan; and took steps to improve relations with the People's Republic of China. These foreign policy initiatives not only eased political and military confrontations but also enabled the Soviet Union to focus more attention and resources on domestic economic reform. Under his domestic political policy known as *glasnost* or openness, Gorbachev improved his government's human rights policy including greater emigration, allowed more freedom in public discussion and the arts, and took steps toward greater democratization of the political process. In 1989, for example, he implemented a reform of the political system, creating a presidency and more open elections. Political reform was also designed to facilitate economic reform, in particular, by providing a popular check on the powerful, conservative bureaucracy.[61]

In the economic arena, Gorbachev announced a policy known as *perestroika*, or transformation of the Soviet economy.[62] Initially, perestroika was directed at "perfecting" the planning mechanisms and improving the planned economy through greater discipline. In 1987, it turned to systemic change. According to Gorbachev's plan for the industrial sector, decision making—with a number of exceptions—is to be decentralized from central planners to individual firms. Under the Law on State Enterprise adopted in June 1987, the central planning system is to be phased out by 1991 and replaced by annual plans drafted by individual firms. Central planners will develop voluntary guidelines for individual enterprises, establish long-term economic objectives, issue state orders for products of critical importance to the economy and national defense, and negotiate with firms to obtain those products. Instead of responding to obligatory targets set by central planners, firms will pursue revenue and profit. Individual enterprises will be responsible for production, sales, and investment. They will have more freedom to hire and fire workers and to set wages. Under the new law, they will also face the possibility of bankruptcy.

New markets responsive to these more autonomous enterprises are to be developed. Decisions on capital flows once made by state planners are to be made instead by newly liberalized financial markets. The existing system of centralized supply will be replaced by a wholesale distribution system that is to be responsive to the decisions of individual enterprises.

Reform of the agricultural system is also on the agenda. Gorbachev's "new agrarian policy" adopted in 1989 called for decentralization and a greater role for the private sector. The state bureaucracy is to be dismantled; decision making will be delegated to regional and local levels; agricultural enterprises, like industrial enterprises, are to pursue profits and to be self-financing; prices are to become more flexible; there is to be greater scope for private farming through lifetime leases of farms with the possibility of passing leases on to children.

The ability to implement these industrial and agricultural reforms remains to be seen. Many deadlines have been moved back even by Gorbachev. Perhaps the most difficult element of perestroika to implement will be a reform of the price system and associated subsidies. The announced intention is to move to a system in which prices reflect supply and demand. It is expected that there will be three types of prices: centrally fixed prices to cover only essential producer and consumer goods; prices allowed to fluctuate within established limits; and freely determined prices. The success of the industrial and agricultural reforms will depend heavily on the ability of the reformers to implement a more rational price system. But implementing that reform will call for difficult and disruptive changes. Without more accurate prices, individual industrial and agricultural managers will not be able to improve productivity and respond to economic needs as expressed through the price system.

Perestroika also has an international dimension. Part of Gorbachev's plan, albeit a minor part, is to improve trade and financial interaction with the West in order to speed the restructuring process. In general, many of the reforms designed to improve productivity and quality should help to promote exports and earn needed foreign exchange. In addition, in 1986, the Soviet Union announced a plan to decentralize the trade system and ended the monopoly of the Ministry of Foreign Trade over trade transactions. A number of ministries, authorities, and enterprises were authorized to conduct foreign trade directly through foreign trade organizations under their control. In 1986, the Soviet Union also requested observer status in the GATT, arguing that domestic economic reforms would remove impediments to its participation in a market-oriented organization. The Western countries, fearful that Soviet involvement would politicize the GATT, suspicious of Soviet motives, and wanting to see if reform really does move the Soviet Union toward a market-oriented economy, denied the request.[63]

The government has also aggressively pursued economic cooperation with Western firms in order to promote exports and to obtain Western technology. In a major departure from previous policy, the government issued new guidelines that will allow foreign equity and management participation in joint ventures. Some Western firms responded. For example, Combustion Engineering signed the first U.S.-Soviet joint venture in 1987 to manufacture instrumentation and control systems for petroleum refining. In 1989, the Soviet government and a consortium of five major U.S.

companies—RJR Nabisco, Eastman Kodak, Johnson & Johnson, Archer Daniels Midland, and Mercator—signed an agreement that enabled the companies to proceed with feasibility studies to explore joint ventures in a variety of sectors. Western Europeans have been quicker to initiate joint ventures than U.S. and Japanese firms. To finance these and other ventures, the Soviet Union increased its borrowing from Western financial institutions (see below on Eastern borrowing from the West). Finally, Soviet policymakers considered various schemes for making the ruble convertible, including the possibility of introducing a convertible or "hard" ruble for international transactions that could be backed by gold, foreign exchange, or exports (see below on ruble inconvertibility).[64]

In the wake of dramatic political changes in 1989 and growing economic problems, Eastern European countries can also be expected to move toward economic reform. Even before the political revolution of 1989, which ended the domination of the Communist Party, some Eastern European states had adopted economic reforms. Hungary had gone furthest by allowing more competitive pricing, reducing subsidies, introducing personal income and value-added taxes, liberalizing the financial sector and foreign trade sector, and introducing a bankruptcy law.[65] The impetus for Hungary's economic reform, which has come from some sectors within the Communist Party, was poor economic performance in the 1980s and the need to service the country's foreign debt. Political reform, aimed at allowing greater pluralism and the right of association, has gone hand in hand with economic reform and may even be outpacing it. Poland had gone furthest in political reform by legalizing Solidarity and other trade unions, introducing free elections, granting opposition parties seats in Parliament, and easing censorship of the press. Economic reform in Poland has moved more slowly, although there has been an attempt to make prices more responsive to international prices and to decentralize economic decision making.[66]

Forces of Change in the West

Whereas the Soviet Union's main interest in increased economic interaction with the West was economic, the West's main interest in ending isolation was political. For both political and economic reasons, Western Europe had long followed less restrictive policies than had the United States. Some Western European countries, notably France and Italy, have sizable Communist parties that favor closer economic (as well as political) relations with the Communist countries. West German government policy known as *Ostpolitik* has been based on the use of closer economic ties in order to promote better relations with the Communist countries. There is broad agreement among West Germans that economic interaction with East Germany will increase cultural and family interactions, improve political relations, and possibly lead to reunification.[67]

In addition, many Western European governments feel that they have a greater stake in good relations with the Soviet Union than does the United States because of their geographical proximity to the Soviet Union. Western European and Japanese proximity to the Soviet Union also makes Soviet markets and raw materials all that much more inviting. In the case of West Germany and several smaller European states, there is a history of economic ties with Eastern Europe that dates back far beyond Communist rule in the East.

Thus, the Soviet Union and Eastern Europe are much more important trading partners for these countries than they are for the United States; their exports to the East are almost exclusively manufactured goods and tend to be clustered in a few sectors in which Eastern orders sometimes have a very positive impact on employment and profits (see Table 10-3). On the import side, Soviet and other Eastern supplies of raw materials are a greater consideration for the Western Europeans than for the United States.[68]

For the United States economic forces for change were not significant. The most important economic factor was the belief that the United States was losing out on growing trade with the East because it maintained more restrictive export policies than its Western allies.[69] However, Eastern markets were important more to specific industries, such as those that hoped to sell technology or grain, than to the U.S. economy as a whole. It was the link between economic relations and political concerns that caused a change in policy.

One political factor was greater questioning of the effectiveness of the economic sanctions as a tool of foreign policy. The impact of the trade controls and of the financial restrictions on Eastern economic strength is difficult to determine and is a debated issue.[70] Premier Nikita Khrushchev said that it had been very costly, because it forced the Soviet Union to manufacture products that it could have obtained more cheaply through trade.[71] Some analysts argue that the West's economic warfare retarded Soviet growth in the long run by denying them access to Western technology.[72]

Other analysts believe that the economic impact was limited. The bloc's large size and the ability of its members to trade with one another shielded them from many negative economic consequences. Central planning made it easier for the bloc to make the rapid adjustments required by the embargo.[73] Some equipment was available from Western Europe and Japan. With the evolution of the Euromarket, it became more difficult to control financial flows to the East, because U.S. institutions could bypass the Johnson Debt Default Act restrictions by providing credit through foreign branches and subsidiaries. Furthermore, although the removal of most-favored-nation privileges hampered the export of Eastern European manufactured goods, it had little impact on Soviet exports, primarily raw materials not subject to tariffs.[74] In sum, the embargo policy seems to have held back Eastern growth over the long term, although it is difficult to measure. Furthermore, it was not without economic cost to the West—in the form of lost exports and the cost of administrative controls.[75] Due to the loss of exports and the reduction of investment and revenues for research and technology, some argue that export controls ultimately negatively affect the West's military capability.[76]

The sanctions also seem to have had little effect on the East's military capability. Because of its authoritarian system, the Soviet Union was able to direct massive expenditures into military development and to continue to emphasize heavy industry without political unrest. The embargo probably reinforced the power of those who viewed the West as hostile and who advocated high levels of military expenditures. The embargo did not prevent the Soviet Union from achieving effective strategic parity with the United States, although it probably delayed that achievement and made it more costly.

The political effects of economic isolation were also limited. Isolation provided an excuse for increased bloc autarchy and Soviet domination. It contributed, albeit not significantly, to intra-NATO tension arising from the conflict over Cocom lists and the assertion by the United States of extraterritorial jurisdiction over U.S. subsidiaries in cases of export control. Finally, it became increasingly ineffective as Western Europe and Japan eased their policies. In many cases, the East could obtain goods and technology from European and Japanese companies and even from subsidiaries of U.S. companies abroad.[77]

Gradually, many U.S. policymakers came to believe that the incentive of greater trade would be a more effective instrument of foreign policy than the denial of trade. In the mid-1960s, trade incentives were seen as a way to encourage greater independence of Eastern Europe from the Soviet Union and greater links with the West.[78] One example of this incentive was the admission of four East bloc countries—Czechoslovakia, Hungary, Poland, and Romania—to membership in the GATT. West Germany's *Ostpolitik*, or Eastern policy, was another prominent example of such a policy. Initiated in 1966, it used trade liberalization, participation in joint ventures with East European governments, credits, and technology transfers to renew political and diplomatic contacts between the Federal Republic and the East, especially East Germany.[79]

In the 1970s, under President Nixon and Secretary of State Kissinger, improvement in economic relations with the Soviet Union became an integral part of the policy of détente. Détente, meaning an easing of tensions, was an attempt to create a stable international system through greater cooperation between the United States and the Soviet Union. It was based

Table 10-3 Merchandise Trade of Selected Developed Countries with the Eastern Trading Area in 1963, 1973, and 1979–1987
(million dollars, exports f.o.b., imports c.i.f.)

Destination/Origin Reporting countries	Soviet Union			Eastern Europe			China			Total		
	EXPORTS	IMPORTS	BALANCE	EXPORTS	IMPORTS	BALANCE	EXPORTS	IMPORTS	BALANCE	EXPORTS	IMPORTS	BALANCE
United States 1963	23	23	0	143	64	79	0	0	0	166	87	79
1973	1192	233	959	605	324	281	690	70	620	2487	627	1860
1979	3604	353	3251	2067	1090	977	1716	654	1062	7387	2097	5290
1980	1510	415	1095	2340	1079	1261	3749	1161	2588	7599	2655	4944
1981	2357	355	2002	1904	1321	583	3599	2062	1537	7860	3738	4122
1982	2589	243	2346	1013	915	98	2905	2502	403	6507	3660	2847
1983	2002	373	1629	881	1100	−219	2163	2477	−314	5046	3950	1096
1984	3283	599	2684	894	1752	−858	2988	3381	−393	7165	5732	1433
1985	2438	441	1997	782	1670	−888	3796	4222	−426	7016	6333	683
1986	1247	450	797	718	1601	−883	3076	5243	−2167	5041	7294	−2253
1987	1477	470	1007	716	1648	−932	3460	6910	−3450	5653	9028	−3375
Japan 1963	158	162	−4	21	18	3	62	75	−13	241	255	−14
1973	485	1076	−591	326	154	172	1041	971	70	1852	2201	−349
1979	2461	1869	592	807	325	482	3699	2955	744	6967	5149	1818
1980	2778	1812	966	807	256	551	5078	4323	755	8663	6391	2272
1981	3259	1485	1774	758	230	528	5095	5292	−197	9112	7007	2105
1982	3899	1314	2585	584	200	384	3511	5352	−1841	7994	6866	1128
1983	2821	1348	1473	747	295	452	4912	5087	−175	8480	6730	1750
1984	2518	1330	1188	491	424	67	7216	5958	1258	10225	7712	2513
1985	2751	1275	1476	564	316	248	12479	6483	5996	15794	8074	7720
1986	3150	1585	1565	682	345	337	9856	5638	4218	13688	7568	6120
1987	2563	1922	641	717	476	241	8249	7386	863	11529	9784	1745
EC(12)ᵃ 1963	578	907	−329	1025	1161	−136	153	166	−13	1756	2234	−478
1973	2726	2457	269	5587	4800	787	743	689	54	9056	7946	1110
1979	9015	11942	−2927	12095	11345	750	3012	1980	1032	24122	25267	−1145
1980	10836	15996	−5160	13056	12537	519	2480	2752	−272	26372	31285	−4913

	(1)	(2)	(3)	(4)	(5)	(6)	(7)	(8)	(9)	(10)	(11)	(12)
1981	9173	15401	−6228	10951	10123	828	2172	2685	−513	22296	28209	−5913
1982	9042	17140	−8098	8377	9524	−1147	2097	2434	−337	19516	29098	−9582
1983	11052	16823	−5771	7607	9135	−1528	2540	2485	55	21199	28443	−7244
1984	9640	18334	−8494	7564	10058	−2494	2918	2642	276	20322	31034	−10712
1985	9510	15810	−6300	8415	10101	−1686	5458	2967	2491	23383	28878	−5495
1986	9693	13689	−3996	10174	11467	−1293	6399	4097	2302	26266	29253	−2987
1987	10606	14873	−4267	11551	13082	−1531	6349	5851	498	28506	33806	−5300
EFTA(6)												
1963	337	362	−25	356	377	−21	19	26	−7	712	765	−53
1973	776	989	−213	1499	1232	267	146	95	51	2421	2316	105
1979	2776	5064	−2288	3599	2770	829	387	211	176	6762	8045	−1283
1980	3852	6205	−2353	3689	3513	176	473	274	199	8014	9992	−1978
1981	4757	6310	−1553	3003	2970	33	298	280	18	8058	9560	−1502
1982	4763	6215	−1452	2645	3041	−396	337	252	85	7745	9508	−1763
1983	4557	5970	−1413	2534	3025	−491	368	251	117	7459	9246	−1787
1984	3871	5440	−1569	2547	3119	−572	500	273	227	6918	8832	−1914
1985	4265	5029	−764	2655	3132	−477	800	301	499	7720	8462	−742
1986	4721	4219	502	3180	3247	−67	948	407	581	8889	7873	1016
1987	4651	4695	−44	3869	3709	160	1055	764	291	9575	9168	407
Total of Above												
1963	1096	1454	−358	1545	1620	−75	234	267	−33	2875	3341	−466
1973	5179	4755	424	8017	6510	1507	2620	1825	795	15816	13090	2726
1979	17856	19228	−1372	18568	15530	3038	8814	5800	3014	45238	40558	4680
1980	18976	24428	−5452	19892	17385	2507	11780	8510	3270	50648	50323	325
1981	19546	24912	−4005	16616	14644	1972	11164	10319	845	47326	48514	−1188
1982	20293	24514	−4619	12619	13680	−1061	8850	10540	−1690	41762	49132	−7370
1983	20432	25703	−4082	11769	13555	−1786	9983	10300	−317	42184	48369	−6185
1984	19512	22555	−6191	11496	15353	−3857	13622	12254	1368	44630	53310	−8680
1985	18964	19943	−3591	12416	15219	−2803	22533	13973	8560	43913	51747	2166
1986	18811	21960	−1132	14754	16660	−1906	20319	15385	4934	53884	51988	1896
1987	19297		−2663	16853	18915	−2062	19113	20911	−1798	55263	61786	−6523

aExcluding trade between the Federal Republic of Germany and the German Democratic Republic.
SOURCE: GATT, *International Trade 1987–1988* (Geneva: GATT, 1988), Table AA5.

on the assessment that even though superpower competition would persist, that competition could be regulated by a mix of carrots and sticks. Détente was conceived as an ongoing and complex process of mutual relaxation of tensions in which numerous dimensions of U.S.-Soviet relations including political consultations, arms control negotiations, and economic relations would be linked to one another.[80]

United States policymakers believed that greater economic interaction between East and West would encourage a downward spiral in political tensions. The flow of trade and credits from the United States was expected to reinforce those internal forces in the Soviet Union that favored greater cooperation with the West, as opposed to those that opposed such cooperation. In addition, policymakers believed that U.S. economic concessions could be exchanged for Soviet political concessions. The East's desire for Western grain and technology could be linked, for example, with the West's interest in arms negotiations, Soviet pressure on North Vietnam to end the war in Vietnam, or human rights.[81]

Thus, in addition to political and security agreements between the United States and the Soviet Union, such as an agreement on the status of Berlin and the SALT I agreement, a number of economic agreements were part of the détente process. Agreements were reached to normalize U.S.-Soviet commercial relations; provide U.S. credit through the Commodity Credit Corporation for Soviet purchases of U.S. grain; settle the Soviet lend-lease debt; and sell major quantities of U.S. grain to the Soviet Union. As we shall discuss, political problems in Congress undermined some of these agreements, and the invasion of Afghanistan in 1979 ended the policy of détente. Nevertheless, by the end of the 1980s the emergence of Mikhail Gorbachev, with his moderate foreign policy and domestic reforms, renewed the interest in using economic links to promote political objectives. The dramatic political changes that swept Communist governments from power in 1989 led to a strategy of opening up economic relations with Eastern Europe (see below).

Barriers, East and West

Despite these important forces for ending East-West separation, equally important counterforces impeded change. For the East, the chronic shortage of foreign exchange was the primary barrier to change. To understand the foreign exchange constraint, it is necessary to examine the problems of inconvertibility and trade aversion under central planning.

Currencies of the Comecon countries are not convertible into Western currencies or into other Eastern currencies. In part, inconvertibility exists for the same reasons that Western countries sometimes impose limits on convertibility: balance-of-payments problems and lack of sufficient foreign exchange reserves. More important, convertibility would disrupt central planning and force price reforms the regimes are not yet prepared to accept. If foreigners could convert currencies into Russian rubles or Polish zlotys, for example, they could then seek to buy goods in these countries. If Easterners could convert rubles or zlotys into dollars or deutsche marks, they might buy goods abroad. Such free purchasing, however, cannot be permitted because it would disrupt the already precarious central plan under which production and distribution are carefully controlled. "Irrational" pricing in the East also makes inconvertibility necessary. As we have noted, prices in the East are planned; they are not related to market factors. Certain products are subsidized through artificially low prices, and others are given artificially high prices. Convertibility would enable foreigners to purchase goods that are deliberately kept inexpensive at home and would enable nationals to purchase abroad goods that are deliberately kept expensive. As a result of distortions in pricing at home, Eastern countries trade with the West and with one another in Comecon at world market prices.[82]

Because of inconvertibility, the only way for Eastern states to make purchases in the West or in other socialist states is by using hard, that is, convertible, Western currencies or by barter, known as countertrade. The principal way for the East to acquire these currencies is by selling its products in the West, that is, by exporting. The Eastern economies, however, have had problems in selling their products abroad. This is because central planning does not produce goods people want to buy.

Because of the characteristics of central planning as practiced in Eastern Europe and the Soviet Union, the East has found it difficult to produce manufactured goods that are competitive in Western markets.[83] While raw materials are relatively homogeneous and thus competitive and exportable, manufactured goods rarely meet Western standards. One reason is that central planners have only recently taken an interest in producing goods for export. More importantly, managers have little incentive to concentrate on quality because of the plan's reliance on quantitative, not qualitative, production goals.

This lack of interest in quality is bound up with the absence of competition in a planned system. Unlike the West, where free competition is part of the theory, if not always the reality, of the economic system, the plan directs production on a noncompetitive basis. Furthermore, sellers' markets have inhibited the production of high-quality manufactures. There is nowhere to turn if goods are shoddy and the quality is poor. Central planners have sought to use all factors of production to the maximum, committing resources fully and scheduling inputs and outputs tightly. This overfull employment planning often results in shortages and delays, producing a demand for virtually all goods produced, regardless of quality. The sellers' markets also inhibit the development of marketing skills, a barrier to dealing in foreign markets. Finally, centrally planned prices inhibit the production of competitive goods. For both ideological and policy reasons, prices do not reflect relative scarcities (that is, supply and demand), as they tend to do in market economies. Prices are based on the Marxist concept of the labor theory of value, which does not attribute value to capital inputs. Prices are also distorted by the use of the price system to subsidize certain items and to discourage the purchase of others through artificially set prices. Such irrational pricing prevents the efficient use of resources and inhibits low-cost, high-quality production.

The structure of the foreign trade system is also a barrier to trade. In most centrally planned economies, foreign trade is carried out not by producing enterprises but by a small number of large state organizations that have a monopoly of trade in certain types of products. These organizations make it difficult for enterprises that are not involved in trade to respond and adapt production to the various needs of potential foreign customers.

Over the years, the Soviet Union and Eastern Europe have had difficulty earning sufficient foreign exchange through exports to pay for their growing import appetite. Since 1960, foreign exchange shortages have severely limited the ability of the Eastern states to import Western goods. For example, in the early 1960s, Khrushchev's plan to import technology was curtailed when agricultural shortages necessitated wheat imports and strained the Soviet Union's limited foreign exchange reserves. Similarly, a shortage of foreign exchange plus slow growth led to a severe reduction of Comecon imports from the developed market economies in the early 1980s. From a peak of $42 billion in 1980, OECD exports to the East fell to $34 billion in 1985.[84]

One way out of the foreign exchange constraint has been to borrow in public and private Western markets. Some credits from Western European governments have been available. In particular, Western official agencies which finance exports—for example, the United Kingdom's Export Credits Guarantee Department and Japan's Export-Import Bank—guarantee or insure financing for exports to the Soviet Union and Eastern Europe. Financing by the U.S. Export-Import Bank has been blocked by the Jackson-Vanik provisions. More important was borrowing in private Western markets that began in a significant way in the 1970s. In 1971, publicly announced official and commercial credits to Eastern countries—primarily to Eastern Europe—amounted to $10 billion.[85] By 1975 they had climbed to $41 billion, and reached $137 billion by 1986 (see Table 10–4).

In the early 1980s, the Polish political and economic crisis—the emergence of the Solidarity movement in Poland, worker demonstrations, the decline in Polish industrial production, the drop in Poland's hard currency reserves, not to mention Soviet troop movements on Poland's eastern border—caused Western bankers to doubt all of Eastern Europe's political and economic stability.[86] At the same time, Eastern European governments took steps to moderate or reduce their debt, primarily by cutting imports. Consequently, by 1983 the net external debt for Eastern Europe and the Soviet Union had fallen by $8 billion (excluding Yugoslavia). These policies did reduce the debt, but at the cost of delayed modernization of plant and productivity loss.[87]

After 1984, the Soviet Union, which had not been a large borrower before, began to borrow from the West to finance a surge of imports. Between 1984 and 1986, the Soviet Union's net debt had increased 117 percent from $10 billion to $21.7 billion (see Table 10-4).

In the late 1980s some Soviet officials argued for even larger borrowing in order to import consumer goods to satisfy public demand during the disruptions to production caused by perestroika. Most of the increased lending has come from Western Europe and Japan—it is estimated that U.S. banks account for only 1.2 percent of the Soviet Union's outstanding bank loans to the West.[88] U.S. government officials have expressed concern that Western lending underwrites Soviet commitments to its client states and makes the West vulnerable to a Soviet debt repudiation. They argue the East has been able to take advantage of guaranteed export financing, which in effect lowers the cost of borrowing and subsidizes trade credits. In addition, they argue, the West should use credit as leverage to ensure greater respect for human rights.[89]

Industrial cooperation with Western companies is another way around the foreign exchange constraint.[90] Under such arrangements, Eastern firms have acquired Western technology and expertise through long-term agreements with Western firms. Industrial cooperation arrangements include licensing agreements and turnkey projects (supplying complete plants or production lines) for which Western firms are paid over time in goods produced. They also include more extensive coproduction agreements, joint ventures, and joint construction or other projects in third markets. In coproduction and joint ventures, Western partners typically provide the technology, managerial skills, markets, and sometimes capital, and the East provides the labor and raw materials. The Western firms are paid for their inputs by receiving a share of the final product, be it a raw material or a manufactured good. Coproduction and joint-venture schemes give the East ongoing access to Western technology and managerial skills, reduce the problem of foreign exchange shortage by payments in kind, and help overcome the East's lack of marketing expertise by giving the Western partner marketing responsibilities in Western markets.

The number of cooperative industrial ventures has been increasing in recent years, but there still are limits to such schemes. Until recently the East has been wary of Western equity participation. Joint ventures with Western participation are being promoted in each of the Eastern European countries except for East Germany. Whereas Western financial institutions

Table 10-4 External Debt of Soviet Union and Eastern European Countries: 1975 to 1986 (millions of dollars. Net debt represents gross debt minus assets held with Western commercial banks.)

Type and Source	1975	1979	1980	1981	1982	1983	1984	1985	1986
Gross debt, total	41,400	91,600	102,000	105,000	100,000	103,000	101,000	115,000	137,000
Soviet Union: Gross debt	11,600	19,700	18,800	20,000	19,500	20,900	21,500	28,200	36,700
Commercial debt	7,340	10,200	9,700	12,600	11,100	12,200	13,100	19,400	26,600
Official debt	4,300	9,480	9,140	7,420	8,370	8,740	8,440	8,790	10,100
Net debt	8,080	10,300	9,490	10,800	8,280	8,890	10,000	14,900	21,700
Bulgaria: Gross debt	2,640	4,030	3,550	3,050	2,750	2,390	2,260	3,610	4,880
Commercial debt	2,453	3,620	3,215	2,680	2,285	1,915	1,770	3,060	4,150
Official debt	187	410	335	370	465	475	490	550	730
Net debt	2,257	3,290	2,760	2,225	1,750	1,320	830	1,080	3,500
Czechoslovakia: Gross debt	1,132	4,100	4,920	4,500	4,050	3,950	3,600	3,830	4,480
Commercial debt	926	3,500	4,060	3,695	3,110	2,935	2,565	2,840	3,380
Official debt	206	600	860	805	940	1,015	1,035	990	1,100
Net debt	827	3,050	3,670	3,400	3,300	3,010	2,590	2,840	3,260
East Germany: Gross debt	5,388	12,300	14,100	14,900	13,000	12,840	12,150	13,900	16,750
Commercial debt	4,423	10,220	11,255	11,610	9,460	8,875	8,050	10,000	12,850
Official debt	965	2,080	2,845	3,290	3,540	3,965	4,100	3,900	3,900
Net debt	3,748	10,340	11,600	12,300	10,700	9,450	7,610	7,460	9,300
Hungary: Gross debt	3,135	8,140	9,090	8,700	7,700	8,260	8,840	11,760	15,090
Commercial debt	3,081	8,010	8,790	8,335	6,940	6,950	6,940	9,760	12,380
Official debt	54	130	300	365	525	740	760	830	1,090
BIS/IMF[1]	—	—	—	—	235	570	1,140	1,170	1,620
Net debt	2,195	6,910	7,000	7,050	6,600	6,690	6,740	8,860	12,010

Poland: Gross debt	8,014	22,669	25,000	25,500	24,800	26,400	26,800	29,300	33,500
Commercial debt	5,910	(NA)	14,900	14,215	13,640	10,900	9,400	10,600	12,100
Official debt	2,104	(NA)	10,100	11,285	11,160	15,500	17,400	18,700	21,400
Net debt	7,381	21,500	24,350	24,700	23,800	25,130	25,250	27,710	31,780
Romania: Gross debt	2,924	6,950	9,400	10,160	9,780	8,760	7,100	6,600	6,000
Commercial debt	2,024	5,100	6,545	6,167	5,415	4,770	3,430	2,900	2,700
Official debt	706	900	1,670	1,845	1,430	875	1,070	1,100	1,100
IMF/World Bank/CEMA bank[1]	194	950	1,185	2,148	2,935	3,115	2,600	2,600	2,200
Net debt	2,449	6,650	9,100	9,815	9,400	8,250	6,450	6,140	5,500
Yugoslavia: Gross debt	6,584	13,680	17,608	18,337	18,488	19,000	18,820	19,180	19,360
Commercial debt	4,280	10,150	12,911	12,200	11,928	10,315	8,955	7,780	7,390
Official debt	1,557	1,931	2,578	3,222	3,050	4,600	5,765	7,130	7,740
IMF/World Bank[1]	747	1,599	2,119	2,915	3,510	4,085	4,100	4,270	4,230
Net debt	5,804	12,477	16,237	16,830	17,718	18,080	17,660	17,700	17,900

—Represents zero. NA = Not available. [1]BIS = Bank of International Settlements. IMF = International Monetary Fund. CEMA = Council for Economic Mutual Assistance.

SOURCE: *U.S. Bureau of the Census, Statistical Abstract of the United States 1988* (Washington, D.C.: U.S. Government Printing Office, 1988), p. 823.

are willing to finance a number of small- and medium-sized projects, especially for manufacturing, in Eastern Europe they are often unwilling to undertake, without government backing, the massive projects for raw material production envisioned by the Soviet Union and some Eastern European states. Furthermore, Eastern projects compete for capital with other projects in countries that are more familiar, apparently more secure areas and where it is easier to operate. Thus, industrial cooperation, despite its increasing importance, is unlikely to have a major impact on the foreign exchange problem.

Whereas the Eastern barriers to trade are largely economic, the Western barriers are primarily political. The Western Europeans, for both economic and political reasons, have been more anxious to trade with the Soviet Union and its allies than has the United States. Japan has been constrained by ongoing political disputes over the Soviet occupation of several Japanese islands. United States policymakers have been caught between their desire to expand trade for economic and political reasons and their feeling that the East should not get something for nothing, that Western trade concessions should be linked to Eastern political concessions or to an easing in political and security relations. The experience of the past thirty years indicates that U.S. trade with Comecon countries is in large part a function of domestic political considerations in the United States and the state of diplomatic relations between the United States and the Soviet Union.

For example, in the mid-1960s, the Johnson administration tried to expand East-West trade in order to encourage greater pluralism in Eastern Europe and greater stability in relations between the United States and the Soviet Union. Beginning in 1966, the administration pushed for trade legislation to authorize the president to enter into commercial agreements with a Communist country and to grant most-favored-nation status to individual European countries not receiving such treatment (Yugoslavia and Poland were receiving it).[91] Despite strong administration support, Congress refused to pass such legislation and blocked the administration's policy because of concern about Soviet involvement in the war in Vietnam. After the Soviet invasion of Czechoslovakia in 1968, President Johnson abandoned the policy.

The early 1970s saw a renewal of U.S. interest in expanding East-West trade. In 1972, at the same time as the signing of the SALT I agreement, President Nixon and Chairman Brezhnev established a high-level, joint commercial commission that then negotiated a series of agreements designed to normalize U.S.-Soviet commercial relations and to open the way for increased trade and financial flows. Most important was an agreement on commerce and the settlement of the Soviet lend-lease debt. Because it was to open the way for Soviet access to private credits, this was of great economic importance to the Soviet Union. The United States agreement to grant most-favored-nation status to the Soviet Union had great political significance as a symbol of the end of the Soviet Union's exclusion from the West's international economic system. Other agreements made available U.S. Commodity Credit Corporation loans for Soviet purchase of U.S. grain exports and Export-Import Bank financing for exports to the Soviet Union.

Certain members of Congress, recognizing that these agreements gave the Soviet Union the financing it needed and a new level of political acceptance, sought to use the most-favored-nation status and Eximbank credits as a lever to force the Soviet Union to change its internal policies on emigration. Senator Henry Jackson and Representative Charles Vanik developed a proposal to link most-favored-nation treatment and Eximbank loans for the Soviet Union and Eastern Europe to freer policies of emigration in these countries. And they offered that proposal as an amendment to the U.S. trade bill which the administration needed to launch the Tokyo Round. After resisting the Jackson–Vanik amendment for two years, the Nixon administration capitulated on the assumption that the Soviet Union would change its policies in return for the inducements of credits and trade.[92] At the same time, Congress also enacted restrictions on Soviet access to Eximbank financing that would operate even if the Soviet Union satisfied emigration requirements.[93]

The Jackson-Vanik linkage plus the Eximbank restrictions proved to be more than the Soviet Union was willing to accept. The Eximbank provision meant that even a major capitulation such as permitting greater emigration would lead to only small credits. Furthermore, external commercial relations, no matter how important, were not worth the price of internal political change. The Soviet Union refused to give any assurances regarding emigration and charged the United States with interfering in its internal affairs. In January 1975 the United States and the Soviet Union agreed to nullify the 1972 commercial agreement.

The Carter administration policy followed a similar pattern. The administration early on indicated a desire for higher levels of U.S.-Soviet trade and urged the Congress to repeal restrictions on most-favored-nation status and Eximbank credits. Administration officials also indicated that "attempts to use economic pressure to achieve noneconomic concessions are likely to be ineffective."[94] This position was initially tested by the administration's concern over human rights in the Soviet Union. Following the jailing of political dissidents and slander conviction of U.S. journalists, President Carter proposed embargoing the export of computers and oil-drilling equipment to the Soviet Union. More important was the Soviet Union's invasion of Afghanistan in December 1979 which ended the Carter effort to expand economic relations.

The invasion of Afghanistan terminated the 1970s era of détente and led to a shift in U.S. policy from efforts to improve East-West economic relations to a return to economic sanctions. Before the invasion, Soviet expansionism in several Third World countries and the extensive Soviet military buildup of the 1970s created the feeling that U.S. policy toward the Soviet Union had created too many opportunities for Soviet foreign policy that had been left unanswered by the United States. After the invasion, further political conflicts—over Poland and the Soviet Union's shooting down of a Korean Airlines jet—plus a general hardening of Soviet-American relations led to a severe deterioration in U.S.-Soviet economic relations.

President Carter saw the invasion of Afghanistan as an indication of growing Soviet expansionism and particularly of Soviet designs on the nearby Persian Gulf oil fields. He withdrew the SALT II arms control treaty from consideration by the Senate and, in January 1980, announced new economic sanctions against the Soviet Union: an embargo on all sales of wheat and other grains to the Soviet Union above the amount authorized under the terms of the 1975 U.S.-Soviet grain agreement; an embargo on sales of high-technology goods to the Soviet Union; tightened restrictions on the sale of oil and gas exploration and production equipment to the Soviet Union; the suspension of service by the Soviet purchasing commission office in New York; and a more restrictive regime of access to U.S. ports for Soviet ships. [95] As a result, U.S. exports to the Soviet Union fell from $3.6 billion to $1.5 billion between 1979 and 1980.[96] Exports of U.S. grain to the Soviet Union fell from $2.8 billion in 1979 to $1.0 billion in 1980, accounting for most of the decline in U.S. exports.[97]

President Reagan adopted an even harder line with the Soviet Union, increasing military expenditures, initially downplaying arms control negotiations, and providing military support to anti-communist forces such as the Contras in Nicaragua.[98] The Reagan administration also sought to use trade as a stick to punish the East for policies such as the invasion of Afghanistan or the imposition of martial law in Poland and generally to deny to the East the Western technology and hard currency that would enhance the Soviet bloc's economic development and military strength.

Ironically, one of the first steps taken by the Reagan administration in early 1981 was to lift the grain embargo and to announce that the administration would not use grain as a foreign policy tool. The reason for this departure from President Reagan's hard-line policy was strictly political. The highly controversial grain embargo had become an issue in the 1980 campaign, with President Carter defending the embargo and candidate Reagan insisting that it was both ineffective and inequitable and that, if elected, he would end it. Despite the removal of the embargo, the Soviet Union, citing U.S. unreliability, refused to increase its purchases of U.S. grain and limited its imports to the amount it was committed to purchase under the terms of the grain agreement.

With this exception, the Reagan administration pursued a policy of economically isolating the Soviet Union. The administration maintained embargoes on the export of oil and gas exploration equipment and high-technology goods to the Soviet Union, tightened the enforcement of export controls generally, and favored more stringent export control legislation. The administration adopted a broad definition of the strategic goods that were to be denied to the Soviet Union, including not only defense or defense-related equipment but also many items that had either a limited or indirect impact on the East's military capability.

The Reagan administration also tried to use Cocom and NATO to impose this view of strategic exports on the West European allies. One such effort involved a U.S. attempt to stop its Western European allies from helping to build a pipeline from Siberian gas fields to customers in Western Europe. The United States viewed the plan to trade Western pipeline technology and credits for Soviet natural gas supplies as a dangerous extension of West European energy dependence on the Soviet Union and as a way of giving advanced technology to the Soviets, not only with reduced hard currency cost, but also with subsidized credits from Western governments. The Western European governments were unsympathetic to the U.S. position. From their viewpoint, energy dependence would be limited and manageable; indeed Soviet natural gas would reduce Europe's dependence on Middle Eastern oil. Furthermore, earnings and employment from the pipeline were important to the European economies, which were in the midst of a deep recession. From the European perspective, the United States was hypocritical in its efforts to block the pipeline deal when it was selling sorely needed grain to the Soviet Union.

After unsuccessfully trying to persuade the Cocom allies that they should not participate in the pipeline project, the Reagan administration imposed sanctions preventing U.S. or foreign companies using U.S.-licensed designs and technology from participating in the pipeline. Since many U.S. companies and U.S. technologies were already under contract to be used in the pipeline, this embargo brought immediate protests from Western European governments who ordered their national companies to fulfill their contracts with the Soviet Union. The United States retaliated with sanctions against those companies, forbidding them to deal with U.S. firms. After a year of heated controversy, the pipeline issue was settled: the Europeans agreed to a review of embargo policy and the U.S. agreed to lift the pipeline embargo.

By the late 1980s, the Reagan administration began to review its policy and to consider shifting from economic sanctions to economic inducements. The setting for this change was, as before, a thaw in East-West political-security relations. Gorbachev's foreign policy initiatives eliminated important sources of conflict such as the Soviet presence in Afghanistan and changes in some of the most aggressive aspects of Soviet military strategy. United States–Soviet Union summits were revived. Arms control talks led to the successful conclusion of the INF agreement that limited medium-range nuclear weapons in Europe and to progress on limiting conventional forces in Europe. Some administration officials came to believe that trade and finance could be used to support Gorbachev and his allies who supported the new thinking in foreign policy, glasnost and perestroika.[99] United States allies in Western Europe, less fearful of Gorbachev's Soviet Union and as usual interested in greater trade, urged a more moderate policy on the United States and specifically pressed for an easing of Cocom controls. Finally, the need to reduce the huge U.S. budget deficit led to pressure for reducing military expenditures, which could be justified in a more friendly East-West environment.

The Reagan administration's steps on the economic front were cautious: reestablishment of the U.S.-U.S.S.R. Joint Commercial Commission at ministerial level to discuss improving economic relations and encouragement of "commercially viable joint ventures complying with the laws and regulations of both countries."[100] Following the Soviet withdrawal from Afghanistan, the Bush administration eased export controls somewhat. With the political revolution in Eastern Europe in the fall of 1989, U.S. policy shifted toward using trade and investment to promote change in the East. At the Malta Summit in December 1989, President Bush called for opening markets to the Soviet Union and endorsed observer status for the USSR in the GATT after the completion of the Uruguay Round.

At the same time, Western European countries moved further and faster than the United States to increase economic flows with the East. For all the economic and political reasons we have discussed, many countries of Western Europe were more interested than the United States in economic and political rapprochment with the East. Furthermore, Gorbachev deliberately courted Western Europe, publicly advocating the concept of a "common European home."[101] Finally, at the 1989 summit meeting the European Community was given the lead Western role in opening relations with Eastern Europe.

One indication of this special focus on Europe was the official request by Comecon in 1988 for the establishment of diplomatic relations with the European Community. In addition, individual Comecon countries have sought preferential trade agreements with the EC. Such a relationship proved attractive to Western Europe in general and, in particular, to West Germany. As the leading trade partner of the Soviet Union and Eastern Europe and in continuing pursuit of its *Ostpolitik*, West Germany has taken a strong interest in increasing economic relations with the East, especially East Germany. West Germany responded positively to the interest of the East in increased political ties with the European Community; and German firms, with the support of their government, have aggressively pursued trade and joint-venture opportunities and signed numerous trade and joint-venture agreements with the Soviet Union.

China

For most of the postwar period, China, like the Soviet Union and Eastern Europe, was isolated from the Western trading and financial system. China pursued a policy of independent economic development that was based not only on Marxist-Leninist theory but also on China's historical experience with foreign occupation and exploitation beginning with the Opium Wars and unequal treaties of the nineteenth century and ending with the Japanese occupation in the twentieth century. Following the victory of the Communists in 1949, Mao Tse-tung declared that China would "lean to one side," that is, emphasize its relationship with the Soviet Union. A treaty of friendship, alliance, and mutual assistance against aggression by Japan or "any other state" (a veiled reference to the United States) was signed in February 1950. During the 1950s, China relied exclusively on the Soviet Union for technology transfers, capital equipment, and financial support. Originally, joint-stock companies in mining and other natural resources, like those in Eastern Europe after the war, were the preferred form of aid; these were liquidated after Stalin's death. In addition, the Soviet Union lent China $60 million a year from 1950 to 1955 and another $26 million a year from 1954 to 1959.[102] Thousands of Chinese went to Moscow for technical training, while thousands of Soviet technicians worked in China on over 330 industrial projects.[103] Domestically, Mao followed the Soviet model of urban-led industrialization based on the Marxist-Leninist tenets of collectivization, state ownership of the means of production, and central planning. China's strategy of independence was reinforced by its isolation by the West. The United States refused to recognize the Communist government and maintained diplomatic relations with the Nationalist government in Taiwan.

China's relations with the West were particularly strained as the Korean War developed. Following China's attack on U.S. troops in Korea in 1950, the United States imposed a complete embargo on China. The United Nations, which continued to recognize the Nationalist government in Taiwan until 1971, also imposed an embargo on the export of strategic materials to China in 1951 in response to their "aggression" in Korea.[104] As a result, trade with the West was minimal. China's total trade with all noncommunist countries amounted to only $550 million in 1952.[105]

As the fifties progressed, the Sino-Soviet alliance deteriorated. A history of border disputes and mistrust between the Soviet Union and China undergirded their differences, which were exacerbated in the 1950s by ideological disputes. When Khruschev began his de-Stalinization campaign and his policy of peaceful coexistence with the West, Mao accused him of revisionism. A struggle ensued over doctrinal purity and whether the Chinese or the Soviet Communist Party would be the rightful leader of the international Communist movement. Eventually the Soviet Union retracted its offer to help China develop nuclear weapons, and in 1960 all of the Soviet Union's technical and economic advisors were ordered to return to Moscow.

Beginning in the late 1950s, China had adopted a policy of self-sufficiency. China turned inward, and in 1958 it embarked on the Great Leap Forward, a plan to modernize its industry and increase output by way of structural changes and greater ideological purity. Agriculture had already been collectivized, but grain production had stagnated during the 1950s. Further concentration of collectives was encouraged to produce a mass mobilization of the energies of the rural laborers. The collectives were encouraged to place a priority on small-scale local industry to provide for the needs of the farmers. Economic management was decentralized and more responsibility was given to the local Communist parties. Although Mao believed that ideological incentives could unlock the potential of the workers, productivity declined as collectivization continued. This decline in productivity, combined with the withdrawal of Soviet advisors, the decentralization of the economy, and bad weather conditions, led to disaster for the Chinese economy. China's GNP decreased by one-third in 1960. The poor harvest resulted in large-scale starvation and malnutrition. The decentralization of the economy led to the breakdown of industry, transportation, and eventually to wide-scale demoralization. In 1959, the crisis reached such proportions that Mao was forced to step down from the Chairmanship of China (although he remained Chairman of the Communist Party). The communes were broken down, some private plots were restored, and control was returned to nonparty managers.

Although China's domestic economy began to recover in the mid-1960s, it suffered another major economic setback during the Cultural Revolution, from 1966 to 1969. In his search for ideological purity, Mao incited the public to rebel against the Party, which Mao felt had lost its revolutionary fervor. Major party leaders, educators, and factory managers were purged and parts of the country fell into anarchy. The economy was crippled as basic institutions fell apart. Eventually the army was forced to intervene to restore order. Throughout the 1960s China decreased its trade in real terms and repaid all of its outstanding loans in order to achieve complete self-sufficiency.[106] It had no diplomatic and few economic ties to the United States and continued to be subject to export controls and other restrictions on trade by the United States.

As the 1960s drew to a close, pressures for change began to force China away from its isolationism. The Great Leap Forward and the Cultural Revolution left China technologically backward and politically isolated. Population growth continued to strain China's ability to feed its people. The most important impetus for change at the time, however, was political. Relations with the Soviet Union had continued to deteriorate, and in 1969 the two countries came close to war on the Sino-Soviet border. In 1969,

China, motivated by its desire to form a tactical alliance against the Soviet Union, began sending diplomatic signals indicating its willingness to open relations with the West.

Improving relations with Beijing was an important component of Nixon and Kissinger's policy of détente. According to their view, China offered a counterbalance in the U.S. relations with the Soviet Union. Accordingly, the Nixon administration responded to China's signals and indicated its interest in improving relations. Some of the U.S. unilateral trade barriers were removed, and the United States voted to support the entry of China into the United Nations, although it voted against expelling Nationalist China. During President Nixon's dramatic visit to China in 1972, a joint statement, known as the Shanghai Communique, was issued to emphasize the areas of common interest between the two nations, while acknowledging continuing differences. At the same time, the United States and China signed a bilateral trade agreement, and trade resumed after a twenty-six-year interruption. Since that time, every U.S. administration has tried, with varying degrees of success, to play the "China card" in the balance-of-power game with the Soviet Union. Through the seventies, bilateral trade, although growing steadily, remained a small fraction of the overall trade balances of both nations. In 1978, the United States resumed its export of food to China, and the United States officially recognized the People's Republic of China. Bilateral trade grew rapidly, reaching $2.4 billion in 1979 (see Table 10–3).

During the 1970s Japanese-Chinese relations also improved. China's trade with Japan grew rapidly once diplomatic relations were reestablished in 1972. Total bilateral trade between Japan and China was $1 billion in 1972.[107] By 1979, bilateral trade had increased almost sevenfold, to $6.7 billion (see Table 10–3). This growth continued into the 1980s, growing fifteen times in value in fifteen years. China's main export to Japan was crude oil; Japan won contracts to build various chemical and steel plants in China.[108]

One of the most important events in recent Chinese history occurred in 1978, when Deng Xiaoping became vice-premier of the country and initiated a profound reform of the Chinese economy. China's need to embark on economic reform can be traced to many of the same inherent weaknesses of the Communist system that the Soviet Union has experienced. Under the socialist economic model, China's economy was forced to bear the burden of inefficient allocation of resources and lack of incentives for workers, resulting in poor agricultural and industrial performance. Flexibility and technological change were discouraged, resulting in an increasing technological gap between China and the West, which adversely affected its economic and military capabilities.

Deng's reforms affected both the domestic economy and China's external relations, and they focused on four areas: agriculture, industry, science and technology, and defense.[109] Beginning in the agricultural area, China implemented a "household responsibility system," which contracted work out to individuals and families and gave them more power to manage their own production decisions and more latitude to engage in economic activities outside the central state economy. Peasants were allowed to lease their own farm plots from their collectives and, after producing a certain quota for the state, to sell the rest of their production on an open market. China's 1982 constitution declared that the existence of an individual economy would complement, not threaten, the socialist economy. Another way in which agricultural production has been encouraged is through price reform. The government has allowed prices for agricultural products to increase across the board and has also stimulated production of certain products, such as vegetables and meat, by increasing their prices even further. In 1984 farmers were allowed to contract land from the communes for fifteen-year periods and transfer the rights to their farmland to other people, although the state still owned the means of production. In 1988, farmers were actually allowed to buy and sell "land use rights," the closest a socialist economy can come to allowing private ownership of land. The household responsibility system was extended into other sectors of the rural economy, such as light industry, fishing, and restaurants. Since 1985, purchase quotas for agricultural production have been replaced by open market transactions.

Reforms in the industrial sector focused on the development of light industry, to correct for previous overemphasis on heavy industry. In 1981, for the first time, production in light industries equaled that of heavy industries. The largest growth has been in small village enterprises. Firms have begun to be responsible for locating their own raw materials and customers. Their profits, although taxed by the state, are theirs to keep. Since 1985, 55 percent of all industrial products have been sold on the open market. The initial results of reform were strong. Agriculture improved from 4.2 percent average annual growth between 1953 and 1977 to 12.3 percent growth from 1978 to 1983. Industrial growth slowed from 10.8 percent to 6.8 percent in the respective periods, but overall national income increased from 6.1 percent average annual growth before the reforms to 8 percent growth from 1978 to 1983.[110]

As these reforms progressed and the government relinquished some of its central planning functions, it became evident that further price reform would also be necessary to allow the market to work. As private markets have developed in many products, the state has relinquished control over many prices but maintained control over others. This has created shortages and oversupply. Another important area of domestic reform is in the financial sector. Since 1986, innovations have occurred in the development of interbank markets in some cities and the opening of money markets in Beijing, Shenyang, and Shanghai.[111] New forms of financial intermediaries, such as insurance companies and leasing operations, have begun to function.

In its external affairs, China adopted a new open door policy that placed new emphasis on diplomatic relations with the West and the role of international trade, finance, and foreign investment in China's economic development. China's trade has increased rapidly in the seventies and eighties, after stagnating in the sixties. Its strategy has been to earn enough hard currency through its exports of textiles, petroleum, and other goods to support necessary capital and technology imports. China has also depended on receipts from tourism, foreign investments, and transfers from overseas Chinese to bolster its foreign exchange reserves. The most important imports have been heavy capital goods, iron and steel, oil- and gas-exploring and processing equipment, and, to a lesser extent, grain. Since 1984 regulations on imports of consumer goods have been relaxed, which has led to occasional trade deficits.

China's main trading partner is Japan (see above). Hong Kong is China's second largest trading partner, because of substantial indirect trade relations between China and other East Asian countries such as Taiwan and South Korea. Since no trade officially exists between these countries, the goods pass through Hong Kong. The EC as a whole is China's third largest trading partner, though the United States has more trade than any one EC country. Trade with the Communist bloc has decreased from 70 percent of China's total trade in the 1950s to approximately 8 percent today, though this may increase as Sino-Soviet relations improve.[112] China's total trade (exports and imports) quadrupled between 1976 and 1986.

United States-Chinese trade relations were cemented on July 7, 1979, when the two countries signed a trade agreement that granted China most-favored-nation trading status. The agreement both reduced U.S. tariffs on Chinese imports and made China eligible for Export-Import Bank financing. The pact also provided for the establishment of commercial trade offices in the two countries. President Reagan also played the China card by encouraging trade with that country. Export controls have also been relaxed, allowing for approximately one-third of U.S. exports to China in recent years to consist of high-technology equipment.[113] Under the Reagan administration, trade with China grew, and so by 1987, bilateral trade amounted to over $10.5 billion, compared with $2.4 billion in 1979 (see Table 10-3).[114]

In order to pursue a more active trade policy, China has had to restructure its internal trading system. Beginning in 1988, the system was decentralized so that state-owned trade corporations and manufacturers could make their own export and import plans. In addition, factories are now allowed to retain up to 80 percent of the export earnings that exceed their export targets. On the other hand, factories are increasingly responsible for their own losses. For foreign traders, the system is more difficult. Instead of negotiating with one central trade authority, as before, they must now court three organizations: the central trade authority, the provincial trading firms, and the manufacturers themselves. China's desire to increase its trade has also led it to apply to the GATT, an organization from which it withdrew in 1950.

In the financial realm, China signaled the end of its isolationism by joining the International Monetary Fund and World Bank in 1980. Financially, it has increased its borrowing from Western financial markets and international organizations, although it is wary of incurring an excessive debt burden. By the end of 1986, China's total public debt was approximately $22 billion.[115] China has also become a large aid recipient, both through multilateral organizations and through bilateral loans from the developed countries (especially Japan) that are intended to boost trade. Between 1982 and 1986 total official gross receipts of financial resources increased from $558 million to $1.9 billion.[116]

Another major change for China is its new interest in encouraging foreign direct investment and joint ventures with the West. As in many developing countries, China hopes to benefit from technology transfers embodied in these investments and also to take advantage of revenues generated from the exports created by these companies. China has taken many steps to encourage foreign investment but has found it difficult to provide an environment that is attractive to foreign investors. It has opened five special economic zones (SEZs), which encourage foreign investment and production for export by offering favorable tax treatment, special profit repatriation agreements, and other inducements to foreign investors. Fourteen other coastal cities offer similar incentives. A joint-venture law was passed in April 1988, to provide a legal framework for foreigners doing business in China. Modifications have been made in labor regulations to allow foreign companies to hire and fire employees freely; in general, Chinese companies must have permission to hire and fire workers. Although there were 2,185 joint and cooperative ventures agreed to in 1987, many barriers remain.[117] Primary among these is the inconvertibility of the remnimbi. China has very strict foreign exchange regulations that make foreign investment and profit repatriation very difficult. In addition, infrastructural problems, excessive bureaucracy, worker attitudes, and differences in management attitudes have been cited as barriers to more joint ventures. Negotiations are still taking place regarding fair dispute arbitration procedures.

Despite China's successes thus far, there are many barriers to continued change. Within the country, there is strong conservative opposition to the speed and extent of Deng's reforms, although the basic premise of reform is well accepted. High inflation rates in 1987 and 1988 resulted in fears of an overheated economy, which strengthened the position of the conservatives and allowed them to occasionally stop and even roll back the process of reform. Pressures for greater political reform have also increased. Thus far, China's reform process has been notable by the absence of political reform along the lines of Gorbachev's glasnost, but student demonstrations for more democratic politics became common in the 1980s before erupting into widespread demonstrations and demands for political liberalization in 1989. The confrontation between the students and the army in Tienanmen Square in June 1989 demonstrated the strength of the people's desire for political freedom—but it just as clearly demonstrated the government's determination not to allow it.

In addition to political opposition, there are other structural and ideological problems with the reform process. The riskiest part of the reform process, price reform, has been only partially implemented. It is unlikely that complete price reform will occur anytime in the near future. In the meantime, however, the half-adjusted system is placing strains on the economy. Transition problems in moving from centrally determined to market prices have resulted in severe shortages in some areas. The uneven development of different regions has also been unsettling to the country, resulting in regional discontent and internal migration problems. There have been a few highly publicized cases of corruption, and, in general, the ability of some workers and regions to profit handsomely while others do not seems to many to betray the socialist ideal. Fear of inflation and increased unemployment has also soured some Chinese on the new reforms. Finally, reform efforts may be slowed by bottlenecks in the energy and transportation sectors and general infrastructure, which has been neglected in recent years.

In mid-1989, China took a major step backward from its market-based reforms when Prime Minister Li Peng announced a return to central planning in many sectors of its economy. It was presented as a temporary austerity measure to regain control of the economy, but it is a stark reminder that China's road to reform will continue to be unpredictable. The main concerns of the government were the decentralization of power to the separate provinces, especially the wealthy special economic zones, and the social unrest that was symptomatic of the inequalities caused by the half-reformed economy. This step backward was accompanied by the apparent victory of the more conservative element of the Chinese government.

In terms of Chinese-U.S. relations, there are other barriers to improved relations. From the Chinese perspective, the continued friendly, but unofficial, relations of the United States with Taiwan and its arms sales to Taiwan are major issues. China has also accused the United States of excessive protectionism, and trade disputes regarding textiles and agricultural goods have marred the relationship. From the perspective of the United States, barriers to improved relations include political repression such as occurred in 1989, human rights issues (particularly in Tibet), China's abortion policy, and Chinese arms sales to the Middle East, including Iran and Syria. Nonetheless, significant parallel interests in the Far East ensure continued political relations between the two countries. Economic ties between China and the United States have become a more important part of the overall relationship, which may be a stabilizing force. China's economic opening to the West has been welcomed by Western businessmen who see the enormous potential of the Chinese market. China in turn has gained much technology and trade from relations with the West. Insofar as these relationships become regularized, they can become a force for continued openness.

Despite changes so far, China remains a highly centralized, socialist system. It has also been careful to maintain its independent course. China has studiously avoided allying itself too closely to the United States, and in the late 1980s it actually began a new rapprochement with the Soviet Union that led to a summit meeting between Gorbachev and Deng Xiaoping and may lead to new trade and financial ties between the two nations. Yet China remains a major independent power, perhaps a third superpower, and has been increasingly interested in becoming an international player. This alone has made it necessary for China to liberalize its trade and financial relations to pursue the modernization of its economy. In some ways China's reform has been easier than the Soviet Union's because it has a stronger tradition of entrepreneurship and because its Communist bureaucracy had not become as firmly entrenched as in the Soviet Union.[118] Nonetheless, the course of China's reform is impossible to predict.

East–West Economic Relations in the 1990s

The conflicting forces for and against greater East-West economic interaction will continue to shape the system in the 1990s. A key determinant of future relations will be the success or failure of economic reforms in the Eastern bloc and China. Success would encourage greater East-West interaction by creating a better political climate in East-West relations and reducing trade aversion. But success is far from assured. The economic challenges are massive and the disruption caused by economic reform can actually lead to a temporary decline in economic performance. Indeed, during the late 1980s, economic growth and per capita consumption in the Soviet Union stagnated and consumer dissatisfaction increased and became more vocal.[119] Political opposition could well undermine economic restructuring as it has thwarted less ambitious reform plans in the past. A major stumbling block will be opposition of the state and party bureaucracies, which stand to lose power through decentralization and greater reliance on market forces. Despite political reform, resistance to economic change may persist in Eastern Europe. In China, conservative resistance to political change could undermine the process of economic reform. Even if the forces of reform prevail, farmers and workers may have difficulty accepting and effectively operating in a more market-oriented system after nearly seventy years of a state-led economy in the Soviet Union and forty years in Eastern Europe and China.

Even a successful transformation will not assure East-West economic flows. Greater interaction will depend on political decisions about Eastern participation in the Western economic system. The amount of trade, investment, and financial flows will be shaped by Eastern policies regarding trade and investment and by Western policies regarding export controls and private and official financing. Greater Eastern integration into the market system will also be shaped by the role of the Eastern countries in the IMF, the World Bank, and the GATT. Several Eastern European countries have already joined these Western institutions and the system has been able to cope with their participation because they are small and because their role in the organizations has been marginal. The integration of China into the IMF/World Bank system has worked smoothly, but its integration into the GATT may prove a greater challenge to that market-oriented organization. The integration of the Soviet Union would pose far greater and perhaps insuperable challenges given the size of its economy and its political significance. The potential disruption of the functioning of these organizations that are at the heart of the Western economic system may be more than the developed market economies will allow. Finally, political-security conflicts could possibly lead to a renewal of economic warfare as has happened in the past. Despite Gorbachev's more conciliatory foreign policy, political conflict could erupt again. In East-West relations, political and not economic factors will continue to dominate.

A subsidiary issue in East-West relations will be how the two superpowers relate to their political allies on these issues. We have noted that part of Gorbachev's foreign policy reform has been to allow greater autonomy in Eastern Europe. This policy should provide room for greater interaction by Eastern Europe with the West as those countries pursue economic reforms. Such interaction could reinforce autonomy from the Soviet Union. However, some experts believe that greater autonomy in Eastern Europe may lead to greater political instability in that region as the threat of Soviet intervention becomes less of a deterrent to domestic political dissenters.[120] Whether and at what point the Soviet Union might seek to block a shift in the international economic relations of its Warsaw Pact allies or intervene in the case of political instability or change is uncertain.

The relationship among developed market economies will also be an important element in East-West economic relations. As we have seen, over the years, the United States and its Cocom allies have held different views about and policies toward trade with the East. Similar conflicts could well emerge in the future. As the 1990s evolve, the West will face important policy decisions regarding East-West economic interaction: the nature of national and multilateral export controls on critical technology; the desirability of greater trade with the East; Eastern access to public and private financing in the West; investment in joint ventures and special economic zones; and Eastern participation in Western economic institutions. All of these decisions could lead to conflict between the more conservative position of the United States and the more accommodative position of Western Europe. Furthermore, since many NICs, which increasingly produce sophisticated equipment, are not members of Cocom, their relationship with the East could become an issue in North-South relations.

Because political change has been significant and abrupt, it is difficult to predict the future of the East-West economic system. Although economic interaction is likely to increase significantly, it will not be central to the economies of the East or the West for the foreseeable future. For most OECD nations, trade with the East accounted for less than 4 percent of their exports and imports.[121] Although some members of the Eastern bloc may join Western institutions, there will be no imminent reintegration of the world economy and its management systems. Before that can happen, the East will have to undergo significant economic restructuring. Interaction will most likely grow in importance, but the separation caused by historical, economic, and political factors will remain a central characteristic of East-West economic relations.

NOTES

1. Marshall I. Goldman, *Détente and Dollars: Doing Business with the Soviets* (New York: Basic Books, 1975), pp. 4–20.

2. Anthony C. Sutton, *Western Technology and Soviet Economic Development, 1917 to 1930* (Stanford, Calif.: Hoover Institution on War, Revolution and Peace, 1968); Anthony C. Sutton, *Western Technology and Soviet Economic Development, 1930 to 1945* (Stanford, Calif.: Hoover Institution on War, Revolution and Peace, 1971).

3. See, for example, Jacob Viner, "International Relations Between State-Controlled National Economics," *American Economic Review*, 54 (1944), 315–329.

4. John Lewis Gaddis, *The United States and the Origins of the Cold War, 1941–1947* (New York: Columbia University Press, 1972), pp. 18–23, 174–197.

5. William Diebold, Jr., "East-West Trade and the Marshall Plan," *Foreign Affairs*, 26 (July 1948), 710.

6. On the United Nations Relief and Rehabilitation Administration, see E. F. Penrose, *Economic Planning for the Peace* (Princeton, N.J.: Princeton University Press, 1953), pp. 145–167.

7. Diebold, "East-West Trade and the Marshall Plan," p. 715.

8. For a discussion of motives and policies, see Zbigniew K. Brzezinski, *The Soviet Bloc: Unity and Conflict*, rev. ed. (Cambridge, Mass.: Harvard University Press, 1967), pp. 3–151.

9. Stalin, *Economic Problems of Socialism in the USSR*, pp. 26–30. Stalin was not alone in his predictions of postwar economic problems in the West. Many Western economists and policymakers were also concerned. See Gaddis, *The United States and the Origins of the Cold War, 1941–1947*.

10. On Marxist justification, see Zygmunt Nagorski, Jr., *The Psychology of East-West Trade* (New York: Mason & Lipscomb, 1974), pp. 58–59.

11. See, for example, Gaddis, *The United States and the Origins of the Cold War, 1941–1947*; Adam B. Ulam, *Expansion and Coexistence: The History of Soviet Foreign Policy, 1917–1967* (New York: Praeger, 1968), pp. 314–455.

12. See Nicholas Spulber, *The Economics of Communist Eastern Europe* (New York: Technology Press of MIT, John Wiley, 1957).

13. See Charles Prince, "The USSR's Role in International Finance," *Harvard Business Review*, 25 (Autumn 1946), 111–128.

14. See J. Keith Horsfield, ed., *The International Monetary Fund, 1945–1965, Volume 1: Chronicle* (Washington, D.C.: International Monetary Fund, 1969), pp. 263, 359–364.

15. Clair Wilcox, *A Charter for World Trade* (New York: Macmillan, 1949), pp. 164–167.

16. See Ulam, *Expansion and Coexistence*, pp. 432–440. It is debated whether or not the U.S. offer of aid to the Soviet Union was serious. In any case the Soviet rejection was clear. For a critical analysis of U.S. policy, see Joyce Kolko and Gabriel Kolko, *The Limits of Power: The World and the United States Foreign Policy*, 1945–1954 (New York: Harper & Row, 1972), pp. 359–383.

17. Michael Kaser, *Comecon: Integration Problems of the Planned Economies* (London: Oxford University Press, 1965), pp. 1–12.

18. Nicholas Spulber, "East-West Trade and the Paradoxes of the Strategic Embargo," in Alan A. Brown and Egon Neuberger, eds., *International Trade and Central Planning: An Analysis of Economic Interactions* (Berkeley and Los Angeles: University of California Press, 1968), p. 114.

19. Paul Marer, "The Political Economy of Soviet Relations with Eastern Europe," in Steven J. Rosen and James R. Kurth, eds., *Testing Theories of Economic Imperialism* (Lexington, Mass.: Lexington Books, 1974), pp. 244–245.

20. Ibid., p. 234. After the disturbances in Poland in 1956, the Soviet Union agreed to a reimbursement for the inequitable price of coal.

21. Under market systems like those in the West, the allocation of resources—decisions about what to produce, how to produce it, and to whom to distribute it—is determined mostly by private supply and demand. Under a centrally planned system, such decisions are made by a central state planning organization.

22. See Brzezinski, *The Soviet Bloc: Unity and Conflict*, p. 101.

23. Marer, "The Political Economy of Soviet Relations with Eastern Europe," pp. 247–249.

24. Ibid., pp. 233–235.

25. Spulber, *The Economics of Communist Eastern Europe*.

26. Ibid., pp. 166–223.

27. For a discussion of earlier actions, see Gunnar Adler-Karlsson, *Western Economic Warfare, 1947–1967: A Case Study in Foreign Economic Policy* (Stockholm: Almquist & Wiksell, 1968), p. 5 and, for the text of the Export Control Act, see pp. 217–219.

28. John P. Hardt and George Holliday, *U.S.–Soviet Commercial Relations: The Interplay of Economics, Technology Transfer, and Diplomacy*, for the Subcommittee on National Security Policy and Scientific Developments of the Committee on Foreign Affairs (Washington, D.C.: U.S. Government Printing Office, June 19, 1973), pp. 48–49.

29. Members were the United States, Canada, Japan, Belgium, Denmark, France, Greece, Italy, Luxembourg, the Netherlands, Norway, Portugal, Turkey, the United Kingdom, and West Germany (that is, all the NATO members except Iceland, plus Japan).

30. Adler-Karlsson, *Western Economic Warfare, 1947–1967*, pp. 1–6, 31–45. For a summary of Western European and Japanese views on Cocom, see Angela Stent, *East-West Technology Transfer: European Perspectives*, The Washington Papers, vol. 8, no. 75 (Beverly Hills, Calif.: Sage Publications, 1980); and Stephen Sternheimer, *East-West Technology Transfer: Japan and the Communist Bloc*, The Washington Papers, vol. 8, no. 76 (Beverly Hills, Calif.: Sage Publications, 1980), pp. 12–23.

31. Romania, Hungary, and Poland became eligible when they joined the International Monetary Fund and the World Bank in 1972, 1981, and 1986, respectively.

32. Hardt and Holliday, *U.S.–Soviet Commercial Relations*, pp. 55–58; Samuel Pisar, *Coexistence and Commerce Guidelines for Transactions Between East and West* (New York: McGraw-Hill, 1970), pp. 107–109.

33. See Goldman, *Détente and Dollars*, p. 52; Samuel Pisar, *Coexistence and Commerce*, pp. 111–114. The Berne Union, a group of governmental and private credit insurance organizations in the developed market economies, agreed to limit commercial credits to the East to five years and to require an initial cash payment of at least 20 percent of the purchase price. The agreement was nonbinding, however, and proved ineffective.

34. Pisar, *Coexistence and Commerce*, pp. 102–107. For other U.S. restrictions on imports, see Goldman, *Détente and Dollars*, pp. 98–102.

35. Spulber, "East-West Trade and the Paradoxes of the Strategic Embargo," p. 114.

36. Adler-Karlsson, *Western Economic Warfare, 1947–1967*, pp. 83–99; Franklyn D.

Holzman, *International Trade Under Communism—Politics and Economics* (New York: Basic Books, 1976), pp. 138–143.

37. Joseph Wilczynski, *The Economics and Politics of East-West Trade* (New York: Praeger, 1969), p. 56.

38. U.S. Department of State, *The Battle Act Report 1973*, Mutual Defense Assistance Control Act of 1951, Twenty-Sixth Report to Congress (Washington, D.C.: U.S. Government Printing Office, 1974), p. 22; Spulber, "East-West Trade and the Paradoxes of the Strategic Embargo," p. 114.

39. See Ann Goodman, Margaret Hughes, and Gertrude Schroeder, "Raising the Efficiency of Soviet Farm Labor: Problems and Prospects," in JEC, pp. 100–125.

40. Goodman, et al., p. 102.

41. See Goldman, *Détente and Dollars*, pp. 27–31.

42. Central Intelligence Agency, *Handbook of Economic Statistics 1987* (Washington D.C.: CIA), p. 100.

43. Joseph Wilczynski, *Socialist Economic Development and Reforms: From Extensive to Intensive Growth Under Central Planning in the USSR, Eastern Europe, and Yugoslavia* (New York: Praeger, 1972), pp. 26–33.

44. Franklyn D. Holzman and Robert Legvold, "The Economics and Politics of East-West Relations," *International Organization*, 29 (Winter 1975), 277–278.

45. See Wilczynski, *Socialist Economic Development and Reforms*, pp. 234–237; Goldman, *Détente and Dollars*, pp. 32–33; Holzman and Legvold, "The Economics and Politics of East-West Relations," p. 278. The problems of technology did not apply to the space and military sectors; rather, advances in these fields were made possible by the close relationship of research with end users, competition among research units and with the West, and preferences on supplies.

46. U.S. Congress, Joint Economic Committee, "The Soviet Economy in 1988: Gorbachev Changes Course," Report by the Central Intelligence Agency and Defense Intelligence Agency to the Subcommittee on National Security Economics, April 14, 1989; John P. Hardt and Richard F. Kaufman, "Gorbachev's Economic Plans: Prospects and Risks," in *Gorbachev's Economic Plans*, Volume 1, Study Papers submitted to the Joint Economic Committee, Congress of the United States, 110th Cong., 1st sess, November 23, 1987, p. IX.

47. Wilczynski, *Socialist Economic Development and Reforms*; Nagorski, *The Psychology of East-West Trade*, pp. 104–156.

48. Marshall Goldman, "Two Roads to Economic Reform: Hungary and the German Democratic Republic" in *Gorbachev's Challenge, Economic Reform in the Age of High Technology* (New York: W.W. Norton & Company, 1987), pp. 148–174; Ellen Comisso and Paul Marer, "The Economics and Politics of Reform in Hungary," *International Organization*, 40 (Spring 1986), pp. 421–454.

49. Holzman and Legvold, "The Economics and Politics of East-West Relations," p. 288.

50. See Wilczynski, *Socialist Economic Development and Reforms*, pp. 218–220, 252.

51. Josef Van Brabant, "CMEA Institutions and Policies versus Structural Adjustment: Comments on Chapter 5," in Josef C. Brada, Ed A. Hewett, and Thomas A. Wolf, eds., *Economic Adjustment and Reform in Eastern Europe and the Soviet Union* (London: Duke University Press, 1988), pp. 170–184.

52. For divergent views on Comecon policies in the 1980s see chapters by van Brabant and Marie Lavigne in *Economic Adjustment and Reform in Eastern Europe and the Soviet Union*, pp. 140–184.

53. Pisar, *Co-existence and Commerce*, p. 35.

54. John P. Hardt, George D. Holliday, and Young C. Kim, *Western Investment in Communist Economies: A Selected Survey on Economic Interdependence*, U.S. Senate, 93rd Cong., 2nd sess., Subcommittee on Multinational Corporations of the Committee on Foreign Relations, 1974, pp. 1–2.

55. See U.S. House, Committee on Banking and Currency, Subcommittee on International Trade, *The FIAT-Soviet Automobile Plant and Communist Economic Reforms*, 98th Cong., 2nd sess., 1967.

56. Klaus Bolz, "Industrial Cooperation," in Reinhard Rode and Hanns D. Jacobsen, eds., *Economic Warfare or Détente: An Assessment of East-West Economic Relations in the 1980s* (Boulder, Colo.: Westview Press, 1985), pp. 63–73.

57. Joint Economic Committee Report, p. ix.

58. UNCTAD, *Handbook of International Trade and Development Statistics 1988*, p. 452.

59. See Mikhail Gorbachev, *Perestroika: New Thinking for Our Country and the World* (New York: Harper & Row, 1987); Zbigniew Brzezinski, *The Grand Failure: The Birth and Death of Communism in the Twentieth Century* (New York: Charles Scribner's Sons, 1989).

60. See David Holloway, "Gorbachev's New Thinking," *Foreign Affairs*, 68 (Winter 1989), 66–81; Robert Legvold, "Soviet Foreign Policy," *Foreign Affairs*, op. cit., 82–98.

61. See Seweryn Bialer, "Gorbachev's Move," *Foreign Policy* (Fall 1987), 59–87.

62. Padma Desai, *Perestroika in Perspective: The Design and Dilemmas of Soviet Reform* (Princeton, N.J., Princeton University Press, 1989); see Ed A. Hewett, *Reforming the Soviet Economy: Equality versus Efficiency* (Washington, D.C.: Brookings Institution, 1988); Jerry F. Hough, *Opening Up the Soviet Economy* (Washington, D.C.: Brookings Institution, 1988).

63. Joan F. McIntyre, "Soviet Efforts to Revamp the Foreign Trade Sector," in *JEC*, pp. 501–503.

64. *Financial Times*, April 4, 1989, p.2.

65. On reforms in Hungary and East Germany see Marshall Goldman, *Gorbachev's Challenge*, pp. 148–173.

66. On reforms in Poland see Urszula Plowiec, "Economic Reform and Foreign Trade in Poland," in Josef Brada, Ed Hewitt, and Thomas Wolf, eds., *Economic Adjustment and Reform in Eastern Europe and the Soviet Union*, pp. 340–369.

67. For a good summary of these issues, see Angela Stent, *East-West Technology Transfer: European Perspectives*.

68. For an analysis of the implications of this difference in trade structure see Bruce Jentleson, "The Western Alliance and East-West Energy Trade," in Gary K. Bertsch, ed., *Controlling Technology Transfer* (Durham: Duke University Press, 1988).

69. U.S. Senate, *Export Expansion and Regulation*, hearings before the Subcommittee on International Finance of the Committee on Banking and Currency, 91st Cong., 1st sess., 1969, p. 92. U.S. Senate, *Authority for the Regulation of Exports—1972*, hearings before the Subcommittee on International Finance of the Committee on Banking, Housing, and Urban Affairs, 92nd Cong., 2nd sess., 1972.

70. For various viewpoints on the effect of export controls see Charles M. Perry and Robert L. Pfaltzgraff, Jr., eds. *Selling the Rope to Hang Capitalism? The Debate on East-West Trade and Technology Transfer* (Washington, D.C.: Pergamon-Brassey's International Defense Publishers, 1987).

71. Wilczynski, *The Economics and Politics of East-West Trade*, p. 284.

72. Goldman, *Détente and Dollars*, p. 46. See U.S. Department of Defense, "The Technology Security Program" (Washington D.C., 1986); Sutton, *Western Technology and Soviet Economic Development, 1917 to 1930* and *Western Technology and Soviet Economic Development, 1945 to 1965* (Stanford, Calif.: Hoover Institution on War, Revolution and Peace, 1973).

73. Wilczynski, *The Economics and Politics of East-West Trade*, pp. 283–288; Adler-Karlsson, *Western Economic Warfare, 1947–1967*, pp. 7–9.

74. Anton F. Malish, Jr., *United States-East European Trade: Considerations Involved in Granting Most Favored Nation Treatment to the Countries of Eastern Europe*, staff research studies, vol. 4 (Washington, D.C.: U.S. Tariff Commission, 1972).

75. Wilczynski, *The Economics and Politics of East-West Trade*, p. 289; Spulber, "East-West Trade and the Paradoxes of the Strategic Embargo."

76. See National Academy of Sciences Panel on the Impact of National Security Controls on International Technology Transfer, *Balancing the National Interest, U.S. National Security* (Washington, D.C.: National Academy Press, 1987).

77. In the Fruehof case, France forced the export of trucks to Czechoslovakia despite U.S. government opposition.

78. See, for example, President Johnson's Annual Message to the Congress on the State of the Union, "Lyndon B. Johnson," 1965, Book 1 (January 1, 1965–May 31, 1965), in *Public Papers of the Presidents of the United States* (Washington, D.C.: Office of the Federal Register, 1966), p. 3.

79. See Catherine M. Kelleher and Donald J. Puchala, "Germany, European Security,

348   The East-West System

and Arms Control," in William T. R. Fox and Warner R. Schilling, eds., *European Security and the Atlantic System* (New York: Columbia University Press, 1973), pp. 160–170.

80. U.S. Department of State, *The Bulletin*, 71 (October 14, 1974), 508. This statement by Secretary of State Kissinger is a good statement of the theory of détente.

81. Peterson, *U.S.-Soviet Commercial Relations in a New Era*, p. 3; U.S. Department of State, *The Bulletin*, 71 (October 14, 1974), 508.

82. Holzman, *International Trade Under Communism*, pp. 26–36, 42–43; Oscar Altman, "Russian Gold and the Ruble," International Monetary Fund, *Staff Papers*, 8 (April 1960), 415–438. For a discussion of convertibility and convertible-currency proposals see Franklyn Holzman, *The Economics of Soviet Bloc Trade and Finance* (London: Westview Press, 1987), p. 91.

83. Allen J. Lenz and Hedija H. Kravalis, "An Analysis of Recent and Potential Soviet and East European Exports to Fifteen Industrialized Western Countries," in U.S. Congress, Joint Economic Committee, *East European Economies Post-Helsinki* (Washington, D.C.: U.S. Government Printing Office, 1977), pp. 1055–1131; Hedija H. Kravalis, "Soviet-East European Export Potential to Western Countries," in U.S. Congress, Joint Economic Committee, *Issues in East-West Commercial Relations* (Washington, D.C.: U.S. Government Printing Office, 1979), pp. 91–112, 168–172; Edward Hewitt "Foreign Trade Outcomes in Eastern and Western Economies," in Paul Marer and John Michael Montias, eds., *East European Integration and East-West Trade*, pp. 41–68.

84. Amex Bank Review, *East European Reforms Impact on Trade, Growth and Finance*, April 27, 1988 (Vol. 15, No. 4), p. 2.

85. Central Intelligence Agency, *Handbook on Economic Statistics*, 1988, pp. 43 and 76.

86. Richard Portes, "East Europe's Debt to the West: Interdependence Is a Two-Way Street," *Foreign Affairs*, 55 (July 1977), 751–782; Joan Parpart Zoeter, "Eastern Europe: The Growing Hard Currency Debt," U.S. Congress, Joint Economic Committee, *East European Economies Post-Helsinki*, pp. 1350–1369.

87. Vienna Institute for Comparative Economic Studies, *Quarterly Report* (Vienna, Qtr. 3, Vienna Institute for Comparative Economic Studies, 1984), 29.

88. Statement by C.R. Neu, Senior Economist, The Rand Corporation before the Subcommittee on International Finance, Trade and Monetary Policy, Committee on Banking, Finance and Urban Affairs, U.S. House of Representatives on September 22, 1988.

89. See prepared statements by Senator Bill Bradley, Rep. Charles Schumer, Rep. Nancy Pelosi, and Rep. Jack Kemp before the Subcommittee on International Finance, Trade, and Monetary Policy of the Committee on Banking, Finance, and Urban Affairs, House of Representatives, *Bank Lending to Warsaw Pact Nations*, September 22, 1988. Report No. 100-92, pp. 57–66, 104–107, 114–115, and 382–385.

90. For an overview of the state of East-West industrial cooperation see the articles in "U.S.-Soviet Trade and Perestroika," *Columbia Journal of World Business*, Vol. 23 No. 2 (Summer 1988).

91. U.S. Senate, 89th Cong., 2nd sess., Bill 5–3363.

92. P.L. 93–618, the Trade Act of 1974.

93. The Export-Import Bank Act Amendments of 1974, P.L. 93–646.

94. "Appendix," in U.S. Congress, Joint Economic Committee, *Issues in East-West Commercial Relations*, p. 292. See also similar statements by Secretary of Commerce Juanita Kreps and a State Department spokesperson, pp. 290, 296–297.

95. See Zbigniew Brzezinski, *Power and Principle: Memoirs of the National Security Advisor, 1977–1981* (New York: Farrar, Straus, Giroux, 1983), especially Chapter 12, and Fred Halliday, *The Making of the Cold War* (London: Verso, 1983), for accounts of the development of President Carter's foreign policy. See also Raymond Garthoff, *Détente and Confrontation: American-Soviet Relations from Nixon to Reagan* (Washington, D.C.: Brookings Institution, 1985).

96. International Monetary Fund, *Direction of Trade Statistics, Yearbook 1983* (Washington, D.C.: International Monetary Fund, 1983), p. 399.

97. U.S. Department of Commerce, *Office of East European and Soviet Affairs* (Washington, D.C.: U.S. Government Printing Office, 1984).

98. Strobe Talbott and Michael Mandelbaum, *Reagan and Gorbachev* (New York: Vintage Books, 1987). For a more specific discussion of changes in U.S. East-West trade with

the Soviet Union, in Bruce Parrott, ed., *Trade, Technology and Soviet American Relations* (Bloomington: Indiana University Press, 1985).

99. See Marshall D. Shulman, "The Superpowers: Dance of the Dinosaurs," *Foreign Affairs*, 66 (Spring 1988), 494–550.

100. Department of State, "Joint Summit Statement," Bulletin, Dec. 10, 1987, p. 16.

101. Mikhail Gorbachev, *Perestroika: New Thinking for Our Country and the World*, op. cit., pp. 190–209.

102. John King Fairbank, *The United States and China*, 3rd ed. (Cambridge, Mass.: Harvard University Press, 1971), pp. 351–354.

103. Ibid.

104. Donald P. Whitaker and Rinn-Sup Shinn, *Area Handbook for the People's Republic of China* (Washington: U.S. Government Printing Office, 1972), p. 309.

105. U.S. Commerce Department statistics, cited in Congressional Quarterly, *China and U.S. Foreign Policy*, 2nd ed. (Washington, D.C.: Congressional Quarterly, 1973), p. 60.

106. Nicholas R. Lardy, *China's Entry Into the World Economy: Implications for Northeast Asia and the United States* (New York: University Press of America for the Asia Society 1987), p. 3.

107. Selzo Maysamuora, "Japan-China Trade in Retrospect—The 15th Anniversary of Normalizing Relations," in JETRO, *China Newsletter*, No. 72, January–February 1988, p. 19.

108. Ibid.

109. For a summary of China's reforms, see A. Doak Barnett and Ralph N. Clough, eds., *Modernizing China: Post Mao Reform and Development* (Boulder, Colo.: Westview Press, 1986), Harry Harding, *China's Second Revolution: Reform after Mao* (Washington, D.C.: Brookings Institution, 1987), and U.S. Congress, Joint Economic Committee, *China Under the Four Modernizations* (Washington, D.C.: U.S. Government Printing Office, 1982). See also U.S. Congress, Joint Economic Committee, *China's Economy Looks Toward the Year 2000* (Washington, D.C.: U.S. Government Printing Office, 1986).

110. Joint Economic Committee, *China's Economy Looks Toward the Year 2000*, pp. 44–47.

111. See Phillip Grub and Bryan L. Sudweeks, "Securities Markets and the People's Republic of China," in JETRO, *China Newsletter*, No. 74, May–June 1988, pp. 11–16.

112. Economists Intelligence Unit, *Country Profile: China, North Korea 1988-89*, p. 47.

113. Central Intelligence Agency, *China: Economic Performance in 1987 and Outlook for 1988* (Washington, D.C.: CIA, May 1988), p. 8.

114. On U.S.-China trade in general, see Eugene K. Lawson, ed., *U.S.-China Trade: Problems and Prospects* (New York: Praeger Press, 1988).

115. World Bank, *World Tables 1987* (Washington, D.C.: World Bank, 1988), p. 99.

116. OECD, *Geographical Distribution of Financial Flows to Developing Countries 1987* (Paris: OECD, 1987).

117. "China Data," *The China Business Review*, published by the National Council for U.S.-China Trade, May–June 1988, p. 57.

118. For a comparison of Soviet and Chinese reforms, see Marshall I. Goldman and Merle Goldman, "Soviet and Chinese Economic Reform," *Foreign Affairs*, 66 (America in the World 1987/88), 551–573.

119. U.S. Congress, Joint Economic Committee, *The Soviet Economy in 1988: Gorbachev Changes Course*.

120. Charles Gati, "Eastern Europe," *Foreign Affairs*, 68, (Fall 1989), 99–119.

121. U.S. Bureau of the Census, *Statistical Abstract of the U.S. 1988* (Washington, D.C.: Bureau of the Census, 1988), p. 820.

Conclusion: Toward a New International Economic Order?

This book has focused on two themes: the influence of politics on international economic relations and the political management of international economic relations in the years since World War II.

The examination of international economic relations since World War II has revealed the many ways in which political factors have shaped economic outcomes. We have seen that the postwar security system significantly affected the postwar economic system. The creation of a bipolar diplomatic-security system led to the separation of the Eastern and Western economic systems and provided a base for the dominant role of the United States in the Western system and of the Soviet Union in the Eastern system. The easing of political and security tensions, in turn, has encouraged greater East-West economic interaction. We have also seen the influence of domestic policymaking on international economic relations. Trade management, for example, has been hampered by the mobilization of interest groups in national policymaking. In the domestic policy process, overriding political concerns have often determined economic outcomes. The Marshall Plan and other aid programs, for example, were security policies as well as economic programs. Finally, and most importantly for us, international economic relations has itself been a political process of interaction in which state and nonstate actors try to manage conflict or to cooperate to seek common goals. The management of interdependence, the search for the end of dependence, and the creation of East-West independence, for example, were part of a process of political interaction in which actors sought markets, resources, power, and a multitude of other goals.

Our review of the political management of international economic relations in the years since World War II traced the system of political control established after World War II, the forces for change in the postwar order, and the factors affecting future international economic management.

It is to this last subject, the future of the international economic order, that this conclusion is devoted. Each chapter of this book has offered some conclusion about the future of management in particular areas—money, trade, investment—and in particular subsystems—West, North-South, East-West. It seems appropriate, therefore, to look at the future of the system as a whole and to suggest some answers to the question of whether it will be possible to develop new forms of political management that will be able to deal with the problems of our time.[1]

Political Conditions of Management

Any new international economic order will be based on political conditions different from the political bases of the Bretton Woods system: the concentration of power in a small number of states, the existence of a cluster of interests shared by those states, and the presence of a dominant power willing and able to assume a leadership role.

The future order will continue to rely on political management by a core of powerful, developed market states. The developed market economies and especially the "big five"—the United States, Japan, West Germany, France, and the United Kingdom—will remain the key actors in the system. The size and vitality of their economies will ensure their continuing leadership. Nevertheless, power relationships among the big five will change, affecting system management. Japan, as the second-largest developed market economy after the United States, will certainly seek to play a more important role. As we have seen, Japan has already staked out a greater role in international monetary relations and in foreign aid. At the same time, the big three countries of Western Europe—France, West Germany, and the United Kingdom—are seeking to enhance their economic power through the creation of an internal market among the twelve member states of the European Community. The ability of the EC to achieve its goal of a common economic system with a free flow of goods, services, money, and people will shape the role of its member states in the new order.

The management group, furthermore, will have to be broadened in some cases and some areas. Future management, if it is to be effective, will have to take account of new power centers. One case is the petroleum-exporting states. Some members of OPEC, for example, have a major say in energy issues. In the area of trade and foreign investment, the advanced developing countries whose economies are now closer to the developed core than to the rest of the Third World will have to play a greater role in international management. States such as Brazil, Mexico, South Korea, and Taiwan, whose trade is of great importance to the developed countries, which have huge amounts of foreign investment, and which often have significant financial relations with the North, will be in a position to demand and receive access to management. Their voices will be heard to a greater extent in trade negotiations as well as on the issue of LDC debt. The new rich may develop cooperative relations with or even join the Organization for Economic Cooperation and Development.

Whereas a few Third World countries will be involved to a greater extent in international economic decision making, the role of the other states of the Third World in international economic management is unlikely to change. These less-developed countries constitute a Fourth World whose only hope is not access to decision making but a greater ability to force the powerful to listen to their demands and to perceive that it is in their self-interest to respond to them. The South's weakness and increasing fragmentation are major obstacles to the Fourth World's ability to place its demands for equity on the international agenda.

Finally, Eastern countries may also pose important management challenges to the system. If the Soviet Union and China achieve their economic and political restructuring, and if the states of Eastern Europe follow suit with their own economic reforms, the Western states will be faced with the political decision and the economic challenge of breaking down the barriers to economic interaction that have separated East and West. Determining an appropriate management role—for example, membership in the IMF and GATT—as well as acceptable levels of economic flows will be a potential challenge for a new economic order.

Among the powerful core there will remain a recognized cluster of common interests. Despite conflicts raised by economic change and in particular by economic interdependence, the developed market economies will continue to support a liberal, capitalist international economy. The postwar experience has reinforced their belief in the need to cooperate to achieve that stable and prosperous economic system. The persistence of the shared goal of cooperation was demonstrated by the behavior of the developed states during the crises of the 1970s and 1980s. The restraint evidenced during the money, oil, and trade crises and the ability to achieve reform testify to the enduring consensus.

There are suggestions that the second tier of states—members of OPEC and the NICs among others—share the norm of cooperation. For example, the more pragmatic policies regarding trade and foreign investment may be signs of consensus. Nevertheless, it seems certain that the new rich will be more receptive to schemes for economic management at the international level. Despite the growing differentiation between the more-advanced and the least-developed Southern countries, the wealthier Southern states continue to support greater emphasis on international equity.

Although the goal of equity is not rejected by the industrial core, it is not seen as a primary goal of international economic management or as a responsibility of the developed market economies. Even though the South has succeeded in putting equity on the agenda of international economic management and the developed market economies are willing to carry out some redistributive or development programs, the North is unwilling to alter noticeably the established system's operation. Furthermore, some Northern critics have questioned whether equity, as demanded by the less-developed countries, is a legitimate goal. Some charge that redistribution as now conceived will benefit only a few or only a small stratum of the population of the less-developed countries and not the poorest in the poor countries. Without extensive internal political, social, and economic reform in the less-developed countries, international efforts at redistribution and development will be useless, according to many in both the North and the South. Conflict over equity and redistribution therefore is likely to continue to be a political dynamic in the new international economic order.

Finally, the new international economic order will be a system of multilateral management. In the past, the management of conflict and cooperation was carried out to a great extent by a single leader. In the nineteenth century, Great Britain was this leader, and in the postwar era, the United States took the part. The more even distribution of power among the core states in the future, however, will require the active participation of many states.

Multilateral management is difficult. Throughout history, agreement among sovereign powers in the absence of government has proved to be a difficult and often an impossible task. Several factors, however, enhance the possible success of multilateral economic management. The basic consensus among the powerful will be an important factor; so, too, will be the experience in cooperation since World War II. Multilateral management will be facilitated by a variety of formal and informal methods of multi-lateral decision making developed over the last four decades. A relatively sophisticated and complex structure of cooperative mechanisms has un-folded in the postwar era, and experience in using these mechanisms has grown.

Even within a multilateral system, however, leadership will be impor-tant. Existing institutions are simply insufficiently developed to manage the system alone. Most often, that leadership will have to come from the United States. Unless and until the European Community forms a political unit or Japan assumes a more assertive posture, the United States, by the very size of its economy, will be the most important international economic actor. Although the United States will be unable to manage the system by itself, management and reform will be impossible without it, and U.S. initiatives and support for the multilateral order will be crucial to its success.

The new management system will face a multitude of problems, many of which have been touched on in this book: monetary and trade reform, appropriate control of foreign investment, economic development, and renewed East-West economic interaction. Several, more general, points must be emphasized here. First, there are simply more issues on the agenda for international management than ever before. Interdependence, the demand for the end of dependence, and possibly less East-West independence place heavy strains on the political system of control. Second, because of greater international interdependence and dependence, the resolution of many issues on the management agenda will require states to relinquish some national control to international management, which is difficult for sovereign states to do. The conflict between national and international control will thus be a continuing dilemma.

The speed of change will aggravate all these problems. And the rapidity of change as well as its unpredictability will require flexible management mechanisms and understanding. The multiplicity of problems, their complexity, and the rapidity and unpredictability of change give observers and decision makers little time to analyze and understand, let alone prescribe, appropriate solutions and reach political agreement on those solutions. The problems of inflation and recession, the nature of economic development, and the impact of national policies on economic activity in other states all are insufficiently understood, but all must be confronted now if the future is to be in any way controlled.

Building a New International Economic Order

Because of the political setting and the nature of the task, the process of international economic reform will be piecemeal and evolutionary. Reform will result, in part, from international negotiations such as multilateral trade negotiations. It will arise from the evolution by negotiation of international institutions such as the IMF, IBRD, and GATT. Reform will also grow out of common law, the establishment of rules and procedures through trial and error and through *ad hoc* responses to problems. International monetary management through consultations among central bankers and finance ministers of the group of seven will most likely evolve through such a process. Reform will come not only from such international agreement and managed change but also from sporadic crises. It was the currency crises of the 1960s and 1970s, not international agreement, that led to the floating exchange rate system. And the near crises in Venezuela and Mexico led to a new approach to the debt problem. In the absence of agreed-upon rules, structures, and processes, such disturbances may multiply.

The outcome of these reform processes will not be a comprehensive international economic order. The political bases are too weak and the problems too complex to lead to anything approaching world economic management. In some areas, management will be effective and relatively comprehensive. Issues of interdependence will most likely be managed because they are of greatest concern to the developed market economies. As we have seen, work has progressed on guidelines for exchange rate management, rules on nontariff barriers, and codes for the behavior of multinationals. Because interaction will continue to be limited, progress on regulating East-West interaction is possible. The reduction of U.S. tariff barriers and guidelines for state trading behavior in international markets, for example, are likely.

But progress on international equity is much less likely. In most cases, the efforts of the less-developed countries to challenge the power and authority of the developed countries has failed. Evidence suggests that political weakness will continue to plague the South in the future. Some changes—aid for the least developed and greater market access in the North—will be offered by the developed market states. The Third World may also benefit indirectly from the management systems devised by the North for money, trade, and multinationals. No major redistribution, however, will occur. As a result, the confrontation between the haves and the have-nots will persist as an element of international economic relations.

Finally, it is not inevitable that a new international economic system will be established. Although the powerful core has shown a high level of cooperation, there is no assurance that this cooperation will continue or that it will be successful. The evolutionary process of reform is in many ways precarious, for it relies on mutual restraint and cooperation by the major powers until reform is achieved. Without agreed-upon rules, institutions, and procedures, a major economic shock could undermine cooperation and lead to economic warfare, as occurred in the 1930s. Indeed, it may be that the world will gradually evolve into a series of economic blocs: a Western hemisphere block centered on the United States and Canada; a European-African block based on the EC; and a Pacific block built around Japan. As we have seen, the U.S.-Canada Free Trade Agreement, the EC plan for an internal market, and the growing Japanese trade, investment, and financial role in Asia could create the basis for greater emphasis on regional management should multilateral management break down. Nevertheless, the postwar experience suggests that the will and ability to find mutual solutions exist and that cooperation among the powerful will continue.

NOTE

1. See, for example, David Calleo, *Beyond American Hegemony: The Future of the Western Alliance* (New York: Basic Books, 1987); Paul Kennedy, *The Rise and Fall of the Great Powers: Economic Change and Military Conflict from 1500 to 2000* (New York: Random House, 1987); Richard Rosecrance, *The Rise of the Trading State: Commerce and Conquest in the Modern World* (New York: Basic Books, 1986); Bruce Russett, "The Mysterious Case of Vanishing Hegemony: or, Is Mark Twain Really Dead?" *International Organization*, 39 (Spring 1985), 208–231; Susan Strange, "The Persistent Myth of Lost Hegemony," *International Oranization*, 41 (Autumn 1987), 551–574; Raymond Vernon and Debora Spar, *Beyond Globalism: Remaking American Foreign Economic Policy* (New York: Free Press, 1989).

Glossary

adjustment: The process by which countries correct deficits in their current accounts. Usually involves changes in expenditures, savings, and production that will produce capital inflows and stabilize the balance of payments situation.

balance of payments: An accounting of all economic transactions between one nation and the rest of the world, usually over a year. The balance of payments on current account includes the trade balance, which measures the movement of goods and some services; and the short-term capital account, which measures the flow of short-term investments and payments.

Bretton Woods: The agreement forged in Bretton Woods, New Hampshire, that shaped the postwar international monetary system until the United States suspended convertibility of dollars into gold in 1973. Bretton Woods participants set up the International Monetary Fund (IMF) and the International Bank for Reconstruction and Development (IBRD), or World Bank, to manage exchange rates and ensure international liquidity and deter balance-of-payments crisis.

capital formation: Capital formation occurs when a nation's capital stock increases. Unlike gross capital formation, net capital formation makes allowances for depreciation and repairs of the existing capital stock.

capital goods: Capital goods are manufactured products that are used to produce other goods.

capital markets: A nation's capital market includes such financial institutions as banks, insurance companies, and stock exchanges that channel long-term investment funds to commercial and industrial borrowers. Unlike the money market, on which lending is ordinarily short term, the capital market typically finances fixed investments like those in buildings and machinery.

cartel: An organization of producers seeking to limit or eliminate competition among its members, most often by agreeing to restrict output to keep prices higher than would occur under competitive conditions. Cartels are inherently unstable because of the potential for producers to defect from the agreement and capture larger markets by selling at lower prices.

central bank: Issues national currency, acts as a banker to both government and private banks, and oversees the financial system. Central banks administer national monetary policy, using their influence over the money supply and interest rates to implement macroeconomic policies.

comparative advantage: The theory that provides the basis for the argument for free-trade policies. Shows that a country can benefit from trade with another country even if it has only relative and not absolute advantage in efficiency of production of a certain good or service. Under a pure free-trade system, each country would use its resources optimally by specializing only in those goods or services that can be produced most efficiently and importing the rest.

competitiveness: The ability of an entity to operate efficiently and productively in relation to other similar entities. Competitiveness has been used most recently to describe the overall economic performance of a nation, particularly its level of productivity, its ability to export its goods and services and its maintenance of a high standard of living for its citizens.

customs union: A customs union is formed when two or more countries agree to remove all barriers to free trade with each other, while establishing a common external tariff against other nations. A free-trade area exists when nations remove trade barriers with each other while retaining individual tariffs against nonmembers.

debt rescheduling (debt restructuring): Debt rescheduling (debt restructuring) occurs when a borrower and a lender renegotiate the original terms of a loan, altering the payment schedule or debt-service charges. This usually occurs when debtor nations cannot meet the payments due on loans from creditors.

debt service: Debt service is the total amount of principal and interest due on a loan in a given period.

deficit: A national budget deficit occurs when a country's public spending exceeds government revenues. A current account deficit exists when exports and financial inflows from private and official transfers are worth less than the value of imports and transfer outflows.

depression: A depression is a prolonged and severe decline in national business activity, ordinarily occurring over several fiscal years. Depressions are characterized by sharply falling rates of production and capital investment; by the rapid contraction of credit; and by mass unemployment and high rates of business failure.

dumping: The practice of selling products below cost outside domestic markets, either to increase market share or to get rid of excess stocks. Government subsidies often are used to help absorb the losses, leading to friction among trading partners.

economic efficiency: Economically efficient production is organized to minimize the ratio of inputs to outputs. Production is economically efficient when goods are produced at minimum cost in money and resources. This typically occurs where input prices are used to find the least-expensive production process.

elasticity of demand: The elasticity of demand is the rate at which demand for a good changes in response to variables like price or supply. The price elasticity of demand, for instance, is the rate at which demand for a good varies with a price change. When demand for a good is price elastic, a relatively small change in price produces a relatively large change in demand. When demand is price inelastic, however, price changes will have little effect on demand.

Eurocurrencies: Currencies held outside their country of issue, such as dollars deposited in banks outside the United States (Eurodollars). Eurocurrency markets are generally free from most national controls, so they are a flexible outlet for deposits and a source of loans for major international corporations and for national governments. This is also true of Eurobonds, or securities issued on loosely controlled international markets.

exchange rate: The price of a currency expressed in terms of other currencies or gold. Fixed exchange rates prevail when governments agree to maintain the value of their currencies at pre-established levels. This is also known as maintaining parity. Floating exchange rates allow the market to determine the relative value of currencies.

external indebtedness: A nation's external indebtedness is the total amount of money owed by the government to lenders outside the country.

factor endowments: A nation's factor endowment is its original share of the inputs needed to produce other commodities. These inputs or factors of production are broadly classified into land, including the stock of natural resources; labor, or the supply of workers; and capital, or the supply of wealth available for productive investment. The availability of these factors of production helps set the price and determine the supply of commodities produced for domestic use and for international trade.

foreign direct investment: Foreign direct investment occurs when a corporation headquartered in one nation invests in a corporation located in another nation, either by purchasing an existing enterprise or by providing capital to start a new one. In portfolio investment, on the other hand, foreign investors purchase the stock of national corporations, but do not own the corporations themselves.

free trade: Free trade exists when the international exchange of goods is neither restricted nor encouraged by government-imposed trade barriers, and market forces determine the distribution and level of international trade.

gold standard: An international monetary system in which the value of a currency is fixed in terms of gold. A government whose currency is "on the gold standard" agrees to convert it to gold at a pre-established price. This creates a self-regulating mechanism for adjusting the balance of payments, since disequilibriums can be remedied by inflows and outflows of gold.

gross national product: The monetary value of a nation's total output of goods and services, usually over a year. Gross national product (GNP) at factor cost is based on the total earnings of all national factors of production (wages, rents, interest, profits). GNP at market cost is computed by adding total national expenditures on consumption, foreign and domestic investment, and government spending on goods and services. Unlike net national product (NNP), GNP makes no deductions for depreciation of the machinery used for production.

hard currencies: Freely convertible currencies that can be used to finance international trade, such as those held in national foreign exchange reserves, are called hard currencies. Soft currencies, on the other hand, are not freely convertible and are not held as reserve currencies.

inflation: A persistent rise in the price of goods and services that ordinarily reduces the purchasing power of the currency. Inflation resulting from government action to stimulate the economy is known as reflation. Disinflation is a downward movement of wages and prices that erases the effects of a previous round of price increases.

infrastructure: A nation's infrastructure consists of the communications networks, transportation systems, and public services needed to conduct business. These are called "public goods" because they are at least partly financed with public funds and are subject to government regulation. In some cases, "social infrastructure" refers to such human services as education and health care that affect the quality of the work force.

interest rate: The cost of money, rising and falling with changes in the demand for and supply of money. Also varies over length of loan or deposit and type of financial instrument.

intermediate inputs: Intermediate inputs are goods, like steel, that are used to produce finished products or "final goods," like automobiles. The value of intermediate inputs is not counted directly in calculating gross national product. Demand for these inputs (derived demand) is related to demand for the final goods they help to produce.

international commodity agreement: An agreement between producers and consumers to stabilize prices at a certain level, using buffer stocks and production or export quotas to smooth out sharply fluctuating commodity prices.

intervention: Actions taken on the part of one or more central banks in order to influence exchange rates. Since the move to a system of floating rates, the Group of Five (G-5), the United States, Japan, France, Germany, and Britain, has attempted to coordinate intervention in currency markets, usually by buying and selling currency, to achieve target rates.

macroeconomics: Macroeconomics is the branch of economics that analyzes patterns of change in aggregate economic indicators such as national product, the money supply, and the balance of payments. Governments attempt to influence these indicators by using macroeconomic policies. Fiscal policies are macroeconomic policies that determine the level and pattern of national expenditures and raise revenues through taxation and deficit financing. Monetary policies attempt to influence variables like the balance of payments, inflation, and employment, by increasing or decreasing interest rates and controlling the money supply.

market forces: The dynamic occurring when competition among firms determines the outcome in a given situation, and a supply-and-demand equilibrium is reached without government influence.

mercantilism: Originated in the seventeenth century, when certain trading states made it their goal to accumulate national economic wealth and thus national power by expanding exports and limiting imports. Some have charged that countries pursuing protectionist trade policies in the twentieth century are following a similar, neo-mercantilism strategy.

microeconomics: Microeconomics is the branch of economics that analyzes the market behavior of individual consumers and firms. The interaction of these individual decisionmakers creates patterns of supply and demand that fix the prices of goods and factors of production and determine how resources will be allocated among competing uses.

multinational corporation (MNC): A firm headquartered in one country but having operations in one or more other countries. Also known as a transnational corporation.

newly industrialized country (NIC) or newly industrialized economy (NIE): Countries that have a high level of economic growth and export expansion, outpacing the less-developed countries but not as industrialized as the developed countries. Middle-income countries like Mexico, Brazil, and Portugal are considered NICs, as are the "Four Tigers": South Korea, Singapore, Hong Kong, and Taiwan.

nonconcessional loans: Nonconcessional loans, or "hard loans," are offered on terms set by the market, so that interest rates and payment schedules are determined by the relative supply of investment funds. Concessional loans, or "soft loans," are offered on terms more generous than those prevailing in the market.

nontariff barriers (NTBs): Nontariff barriers attempt to protect domestic industries by restricting imports without levying taxes directly on merchandise. These barriers include quotas, by which the government determines the amount of a commodity that can be imported; and voluntary restraint agreements (VRAs), in which exporting nations agree to limit their exports of particular commodities and importing nations agree not to impose other types of protection. Other nontariff barriers include laws and regulations such as government procurement policies, customs procedures, and health and sanitary regulations. Regional policies, agricultural policies, and consumer and environmental protection standards are other examples of nontariff measures that may have trade-distorting effects. Nontariff barriers have contributed significantly to the growth of "the new protectionism" over the last decade and have proved challenging to negotiate under the General Agreement on Tariffs and Trade, in part because of the difficulty of assessing their protectionist impact.

oligopoly: An oligopoly exists when a few firms account for most of the output of a particular commodity. This concentration often leads to collusion among manufacturers, so that prices are set by agreement rather than by supply and demand. Competition among products occurs through marketing and advertising rather than through price.

price supports: Price supports are a form of government intervention in the market for commodities. The market price of certain goods is fixed at a level higher than that determined by the free interaction of supply and demand, and the government purchases surpluses that remain unsold at this artificially high price.

primary products: Unprocessed or partially processed goods, often used to produce other goods. They include commodities like grain and vegetables, and raw materials like iron ore and crude petroleum.

productivity: Productivity is the amount of product created by one unit of a given factor of production over a stated period of time. Productivity expresses the marginal relationship of inputs to outputs and measures the economic efficiency of production. Productivity indicators ordinarily relate output to a single factor of production, creating measures like "labor productivity," "capital productivity," and "land productivity."

recession: A short-term decline in national business activity, usually lasting for at least three consecutive quarters of a fiscal year. Recessions are characterized by rising unemployment rates and falling rates of production, capital investment, and economic growth, but these declines are not as severe nor as persistent as those that occur in depressions.

reserve currency: Reserve currencies are held by governments and institutions outside the country of issue and are used to finance international economic transactions, including trade and the payment of debts. Stable, easily convertible currencies issued by major trading nations like the United States, Germany, and Japan are generally included in national reserves.

revaluation: Revaluation is a change in the official rate at which one currency is exchanged for another or for gold. Devaluation reduces the relative value of the currency and creates a mechanism for adjusting balance of payments deficits, since it lowers the price of exports abroad and raises the price of imports at home. This mechanism will not function during periods of competitive devaluation when the devaluation of one currency causes other nations to follow suit.

services: Economic activities that are intangible, such as banking, tourism, insurance, and accounting, in contrast to goods that are tangible, such as automobiles and wheat. Services account for an ever-increasing part of the trade of the industrialized countries.

spot market: Commodities exchanged on the spot market sell at prices fixed by supply and demand at the time of sale. The forward market, on the other hand, exchanges promises to buy or sell commodities in the future at a pre-established "forward" price.

terms of trade: A nation's terms of trade is the relationship between the prices of its imports and those of its exports. Nations face declining terms of trade when import prices rise faster than export prices, while rising terms of trade occur when relative export prices grow faster.

trade barriers: Trade barriers are government restrictions on the free import or export of merchandise. Tariff barriers are taxes imposed on commodity imports based either on the value of the good or on a fixed price per unit, while nontariff barriers do not involve a direct tax. Protective tariffs attempt to shelter selected domestic industries by restricting the quantity and raising the price of competing imports, while revenue-producing tariffs are enacted mainly to increase government income.

Acronyms

AID	Agency for International Development
ASEAN	Association of Southeast Asian Nations
BIS	Bank for International Settlements
CAP	Common Agriculture Policy of the European Community
CMEA	Council for Mutual Economic Assistance (Comecon)
EC	European Community
ECOSOC	Economic and Social Council (United Nations)
ECU	European Currency Unit
EEC	European Economic Community
EMS	European Monetary System
EMU	European Monetary Union
FDI	Foreign Direct Investment
FTA	Free Trade Association
GATT	General Agreement on Tariffs and Trade
GDP	Gross Domestic Product
GNP	Gross National Product
GSP	Generalized System of Preferences
IBRD	International Bank for Reconstruction and Development (The World Bank)
ICA	International Commodity Agreement
IDA	International Development Association (United Nations)
IMF	International Monetary Fund
ITO	International Trade Organization
LDC	Less-Developed Country
MITI	Japan's Ministry of International Trade and Industry
MFA	Multi-Fibre Agreement

MFN	Most Favored Nation
MNC	Multinational Corporation
MTN	Multilateral Trade Negotiations
NATO	North Atlantic Treaty Organization
NIC	Newly Industrialized Country
NIEO	New International Economic Order
NTB	Nontariff Barrier to trade
OAS	Organization of American States
OAU	Organization of African Unity
OECD	Organization for Economic Cooperation and Development
OMA	Orderly Marketing Agreement
OPEC	Organization of Petroleum Exporting Countries
SDR	Special Drawing Right
UN	United Nations
UNCTAD	United Nations Conference on Trade and Development
VER	Voluntary Export Restraint
VRA	Voluntary Restraint Agreement
WTO	Warsaw Treaty Organization

Selected Bibliography

The bibliography reflects the organization of the book. The first section on general and theoretical works lists general studies and collections that encompass the broad subject of international political economy. The three bibliographical headings that follow denote the three-part division of the study: the Western system, the North-South system, and the East-West system. Each of these has a general subsection that cites works encompassing subtopics for the particular subsystem. Other subtopics correspond to the chapter subdivisions: money, trade, investment, and so on. With a few exceptions, individual articles from general works already cited under general subdivisions are not cited specifically under the various topical headings.

Publications by governmental and intergovernmental organizations are treated in three ways. Important official studies are included in the appropriate category in the first four sections. Important official serial publications are included in a separate category entitled official publications. Finally, because of space limitations some items are not listed. For example, because the U.S. Congressional hearings' bearing on the politics of international economic relations are voluminous they are not repeated here, but are, however, cited in the notes. Those who wish to pursue research in this field should note the significance of hearings such as the Bretton Woods agreements, the Marshall Plan, the North Atlantic Treaty Organization, various trade and foreign aid hearings, and hearings on the problems of the international monetary system, the influence of multinational corporations, and East-West relations. Similar material from international organizations has also been excluded from the bibliography. Researchers should note the importance of proceedings of the various United Nations bodies such as the General Assembly and UNCTAD and the voluminous material generated by international organizations such as the IMF and IBRD, the GATT, the OECD, and regional organizations.

Major newspapers and journals useful for the study of international political economy are cited in a final section.

General and Theory

Ashworth, William. *A Short History of the International Economy Since 1850.* London: Longman, 1975.

Axelrod, Robert. *The Evolution of Cooperation.* New York: Basic Books, 1984.

Baldwin, David A. *Economic Statecraft.* Princeton N.J.: Princeton University Press, 1985.

Baran, Paul A. *The Political Economy of Growth.* New York: Monthly Review, 1968.

————, and Paul M. Sweezy, *Monopoly Capital: An Essay on the American Economic and Social Order.* New York: Monthly Review, 1966.

Bergsten, C. Fred, and Lawrence B. Krause, eds. *World Politics and International Economics.* Washington, D.C.: The Brookings Institution, 1975.

Bhagwati, Jagdish N., ed. *Economics and World Order: From the 1970s to the 1990s.* New York: Macmillan, 1972.

Blake, David H., and Robert S. Walters. *The Politics of Global Economic Relations.* Englewood Cliffs, N.J.: Prentice-Hall, 1976.

Camps, Miriam, and Catherine Gwin. *Collective Management: The Reform of International Economic Organizations.* New York: McGraw-Hill, 1981.

Carr, Edward Hallet. *The Twenty Years' Crisis, 1919–1939: An Introduction to the Study of International Relations*, 2nd ed. New York: St Martin's, 1962.

Cooper, Richard N. "Economic Interdependence and Foreign Policy in the Seventies." *World Politics*, 24 (January 1972), 159–181.

————. *The Economics of Interdependence: Economic Policy in the Atlantic Community.* New York: McGraw-Hill, 1968.

Cox, Robert W. *Production, Power and World Order: Social Forces in the Making of History.* New York: Columbia University Press, 1987.

Gill, Stephen, and David Law. *The Global Political Economy: Perspectives, Problems and Policies.* Baltimore: Johns Hopkins University Press, 1988.

Gilpin, Robert. *The Political Economy of International Relations.* Princeton, N.J.: Princeton University Press, 1987.

————. *War and Change in World Politics.* Cambridge, Eng.: Cambridge University Press, 1983.

Gourevitch, Peter. *Politics in Hard Times: Comparative Responses to International Economic Crises.* Ithaca, N.Y.: Cornell University Press, 1986.

Hamilton, Alexander. "Report on the Subject of Manufactures," in Arthur Harrison Cole, ed. *Industrial and Commercial Correspondence of Alexander Hamilton Anticipating his Report on Manufacturing.* New York: Kelley, 1968.

Hawtrey, Ralph G. *Economic Aspects of Sovereignty*, 2nd ed. London: Longman, 1952.

Hecksher, Eli F. *Mercantilism.* 2 vols. Mendel Shapiro, transl. London: Allen & Unwin, 1935.

Hirsch, Fred, and John H. Goldthorpe, eds. *The Political Economy of Inflation.* Cambridge, Mass.: Harvard University Press, 1978.

Hirschman, Albert O. *National Power and the Structure of Foreign Trade.* Berkeley, Calif.: University of California Press, 1945.

Hoffmann, Stanley. "Obstinate or Obsolete? The Fate of the Nation-State and the Case of Western Europe." *Daedalus*, 45 (Summer 1966), 862–915.

Jacobson, Harold K. *Networks of Interdependence: International Organizations and the Global Political System*. New York: Knopf, 1979.

Kennedy, Paul. *The Rise and Fall of the Great Powers: Economic Change and Military Conflict from 1500 to 2000*. New York: Random House, 1987.

Keohane, Robert O. *Neo-Realism and its Critics*. New York: Columbia University Press, 1986.

——. *After Hegemony: Co-operation and Discord in the World Political Economy*. Princeton, N.J.: Princeton University Press, 1984.

——. "Transgovernmental Relations and International Organizations." *World Politics*, 27 (October 1974), 39–62.

——, and Joseph S. Nye, Jr. "Power and Interdependence Revisited." *International Organization*, 41 (Autumn, 1987), 725–753.

——, and Joseph S. Nye, Jr. *Power and Interdependence: World Politics in Transition*. Boston: Little, Brown, 1977.

Kindleberger, Charles P. *The International Economic Order: Essays on Financial Crisis and International Public Goods*. Cambridge: MIT Press, 1989.

——. *The World in Depression, 1929–1939*. Berkeley, Calif.: University of California Press, 1973.

——. *Power and Money: The Economics of International Politics and the Politics of International Economics*. New York: Basic Books, 1970.

Knorr, Klaus. *The Power of Nations: The Political Economy of International Relations*. New York: Basic Books, 1975.

——. *Power and Wealth: The Political Economy of International Power*. New York: Basic Books, 1973.

Krasner, Stephen, ed. *International Regimes*. Ithaca, N.Y.: Cornell University Press, 1983.

Lenin, V. I. *Imperialism: The Highest Stage of Capitalism*. New York: International Publishers, 1939 [1917].

Lewis, W. Arthur. *The Evolution of the International Economic Order*. Princeton, N.J.: Princeton University Press, 1978.

Lindblom, Charles E. *Politics and Markets: The World's Political-Economic System*. New York: Basic Books, 1977.

List, Friedrich. *The National System of Political Economy*. New York: Kelley, 1966.

Magdoff, Harry. *The Age of Imperialism: The Economics of U.S. Foreign Policy*. New York: Monthly Review, 1969.

Marx, Karl. *The Marx-Engels Reader*. Robert C. Tucker, ed. New York: W.W. Norton, 1972 [1848].

Morse, Edward L. *Modernization and the Transformation of International Relations*. New York: Free Press, 1976.

——. *Foreign Policy and Interdependence in Gaullist France*. Princeton, N.J.: Princeton University Press, 1973.

Olson, Mancur, Jr. *The Logic of Collective Action: Public Goods and the Theory of Groups*. Cambridge, Mass.: Harvard University Press, 1965, 1971.

——. *The Rise and Decline of Nations: Economic Growth, Stagflation, and Social Rigidities*. New Haven, Conn.: Yale University Press, 1982.

Oye, Kenneth, ed. *Cooperation Under Anarchy*. Princeton N.J.: Princeton University Press, 1986.

Perroux, François. *L'Economie du XXe Siècle*, 3rd ed. Paris: Presses Universitaires de France, 1961, 1969.

Robbins, Lionel. *The Economic Causes of War*. New York: Howard Fetig, 1968.

Rosecrance, Richard. *The Rise of the Trading State: Commerce and Conquest in the Modern World*. New York: Basic Books, 1986.

Russett, Bruce. "The Mysterious Case of Vanishing Hegemony; or is Mark Twain Really Dead?" *International Organization*, 39 (1985), 207–231.

Ruggie, John G., ed. *The Antinomies of Interdependence*. New York: Columbia University Press, 1983.

Schmitt, Hans O. "Mercantilism: A Modern Argument." *The Manchester School of Economic and Social Studies*, 47 (June 1979), 93–111.

Schumpeter, Joseph A. *Capitalism, Socialism and Democracy*. New York: Harper and Row, 1950.

Shonfield, Andrew. *Modern Capitalism: The Changing Balance of Public and Private Power*. London: Oxford University Press, 1969.

Smith, Adam. *An Inquiry into the Nature and Causes of the Wealth of Nations*. New York: Modern Library, 1937.

Snidal, Duncan. "The Limits of Hegemonic Stability Theory." *International Organization*, 39 (1985), 579–614.

Staley, Eugene. *War and the Private Investor*. Garden City, N.Y.: Doubleday, 1935.

Strange, Susan. "What Is Economic Power and Who Has It?" *International Journal* (Canada), 30 (Spring 1975), 207–224.

———."International Economics and International Relations: A Case of Mutual Neglect." *International Affairs*, 46 (April 1970), 304–315.

Tucker, Robert. *The Inequality of Nations*. New York: Basic Books, 1976.

Viner, Jacob. "Power vs. Plenty as Objectives of Foreign Policy in the Seventeenth and Eighteenth Centuries." *World Politics*, 1 (October 1948), 1–29.

Wallerstein, Immanuel. *The Modern World System: Capitalist Agriculture and the Origins of the European World-Economy in the Sixteenth Century*. New York: Academy Press, 1974.

Waltz, Kenneth N. *Theory of International Politics*. Reading, Mass.: Addison-Wesley, 1979.

Whitman, Marina V. N. *Reflections of Interdependence: Issues for Economic Theory and U.S. Policy*. Pittsburgh, Pa.: University of Pittsburgh Press, 1979.

Wu, Yuan-Li. *Economic Warfare*. Englewood Cliffs, N.J.: Prentice-Hall, 1952.

Young, Oran. "Interdependencies in World Politics." *International Journal*, 24 (Autumn 1969), 726–750.

The Western System

General

Bergsten, C. Fred, and William R. Cline. *The United States-Japan Economic Problem*. Policy Analysis in International Economics, n. 13. Washington, D.C.: Institute for International Economics, 1985.

Bressand, Albert. "Mastering the World Economy." *Foreign Affairs*, 16 (1983), 747–772.

Calingaert, Michael. *The 1992 Challenge from Europe: Development of the European Community's Internal Market*. Washington, D.C.: National Planning Association, 1988.

Calleo, David P. *Beyond American Hegemony: The Future of the Western Alliance*. New York: Basic Books, 1987.

Camps, Miriam. *"First World" Relationships: The Role of the OECD*. Paris: Atlantic Institute, 1975.

Cohen, Stephen D. *The Making of United States International Economic Policy*. New York: Praeger, 1977.

DeMenil, George, and Anthony M. Solomon. *Economic Summitry*. New York: Council on Foreign Relations, 1983.

Destler, I. M. *Making Foreign Economic Policy*. Washington, D.C.: The Brookings Institution, 1980.

Douglas, Gordon K., ed. *The New Interdependence: The European Community and the United States*. Lexington, Mass.: Lexington Books, 1979.

Gardner, Richard N. *Sterling-Dollar Diplomacy in Current Perspective: The Origins and Prospects of Our International Economic Order*. New York: Columbia University Press, 1980.

Gourevitch, Peter A., ed. *France in the Troubled World Economy*. London: Butterworth, 1983.

Inoguchi, Takashi, and Daniel I. Okimoto, eds. *The Political Economy of Japan. Volume II: The Changing International Context*. Stanford: Stanford University Press, 1988.

Katzenstein, Peter, ed. *Between Power and Plenty: Foreign Economic Policies of Advanced Industrial States*. Madison, Wisc.: University of Wisconsin Press, 1978.

Lincoln, Edward J. *Japan: Facing Economic Maturity*. Washington, D.C.: Brookings Institute, 1988.

McCracken, Paul W., et al. *Towards Full Employment and Price Stability: A Report to the OECD by a Group of Independent Experts*. Paris: OECD, 1972.

North, Douglass C. *Structure and Change in Economic History*. New York: W.W. Norton, 1981.

Promoting World Recovery: A Statement on Global Economic Strategy. Washington, D.C.: Institute for International Economics, 1982.

Putnam, Robert, and Nicholas Bayne. *Hanging Together: Cooperation and Conflict in the Seven-Power Summits*. Cambridge, Mass.: Harvard University Press, 1987.

Yamamura, Kozo, and Yasukichi Yasuba, eds. *The Political Economy of Japan. Volume I: The Domestic Transformation*. Stanford: Stanford University Press, 1987.

International Monetary System

Aliber, Robert Z. *The Political Economy of Monetary Reform*. London: Macmillan, 1977.

Aronson, Jonathan D. *Money and Power: Banks and the World Monetary System*. Beverly Hills, Cal.: Sage Library of Social Research, 1977.

Bergsten, C. Fred, and John Williamson. *The Multiple Reserve Currency System*. Cambridge, Mass.: MIT Press, 1983.

Bernstein, Edward M., et al. *Reflections on Jamaica*. Princeton, N.J.: International Finance Section, Department of Economics, Princeton University, 1976.

Block, Fred L. *The Origins of International Economic Disorder: A Study of United States International Monetary Policy From World War II to the Present*. Berkeley: University of California Press, 1977.

Bryant, Ralph C. *International Financial Mediation*. Washington, D.C.: Brookings, 1987.

Clark, Stephen V. O. *Central Bank Co-operation, 1924–1931*. New York: Federal Reserve Bank of New York, 1967.

Cline, William R. *International Debt: Systemic Risk and Policy Response*. Cambridge, Mass.: MIT Press, 1983.

Cohen, Benjamin J. *In Whose Interest?: International Banking and American Foreign Policy*. New Haven: Yale University Press, 1986.

Cohen, Stephen D. *International Monetary Reform, 1964–69*. New York: Praeger, 1970.

Cooper, Richard, et al. *The International Monetary System Under Flexible Exchange Rates: Global, Regional, National*. Cambridge, Mass.: Ballinger, 1982.

Dale, Richard with Richard P. Maltione. *Managing Global Debt*. Washington, D.C.: The Brookings Institution, 1983.

De Vries, Margaret G. *The International Monetary Fund, 1966–1971: The System Under Stress*. Washington, D.C.: International Monetary Fund, 1976.

Diebold, William, Jr. *Trade and Payments in Western Europe: A Study in Economic Cooperation, 1947–1951*. New York: Harper, 1952.

European Community, Committee for the Study of Economic and Monetary Union. *Report on Economic and Monetary Union in the European Community* (The Delors Report). Brussels: European Community, 1989.

Funabashi, Yoichi. *Managing the Dollar: From the Plaza to the Louvre*. Washington, D.C.: Institute for International Economics, 1988.

Gowa, Joanne. *Closing the Gold Window: Domestic Politics and the End of Bretton Woods*. Ithaca: Cornell University Press, 1983.

Group of Thirty. *The Problem of Exchange Rates: A Policy Statement*. New York: Group of Thirty, 1982.

Hewlett, Sylvia Ann, Henry Kaufman, and Peter B. Kenen. *The Global Repercussions of U.S. Monetary and Fiscal Policy*. New York: Ballinger, 1984.

Horsefield, J. Keith, ed. *The International Monetary Fund, 1945–65: Twenty Years of International Monetary Cooperation*. 3 vols. Washington, D.C.: International Monetary Fund, 1969.

King, Kenneth. *U.S. Monetary Policy and European Responses in the 1980's*, Chatham House Paper 16. London: Routledge, 1982.

Kojm, Christopher, ed. *The Problem of International Debt*. New York: H. W. Wilson, 1984.

Machlup, Fritz. *Remaking the International Monetary System: The Rio Agreement and Beyond*. Baltimore, Md.: Johns Hopkins Press, 1968.

Marris, Stephen. *Deficits and the Dollar: The World Economy at Risk*. Washington, D.C.: Institute for International Economics, 1987.

McKinnon, Ronald I. *The Eurocurrency Market*. Princeton, N.J.: International Finance Section, Department of Economics, Princeton University, 1977.

Mundell, Robert A., and Jacques J. Polak. *The New International Monetary System*. New York: Columbia University Press, 1977.

Odell, John. *U.S. International Monetary Policy: Markets, Power and Ideas As Sources of Change*. Princeton, N.J.: Princeton University Press, 1982.

Princeton University International Finance Section. "International Monetary Co-operation: Essays in Honor of Henry Wallich."*Essays in International Finance*, n. 169. Princeton: Princeton University International Finance Section, 1987.

Rowland, Benjamin M., ed. *Balance of Power or Hegemony: The Interwar Monetary System*. New York: New York University Press, 1976.

Shonfield, Andrew, ed. *International Economic Relations of the Western World, 1959-1971*. Vol. 2: *International Monetary Relations*. London: Oxford University Press, 1976.

———. *Sterling and British Policy: A Political Study of an International Currency in Decline*. New York: Oxford University Press, 1971.

Solomon, Robert. *The International Monetary System: 1945-1976: An Insider's View*. New York: Harper & Row, 1976.

Spero, Joan E. *The Failure of the Franklin National Bank: Challenge to the International Banking System*. New York: Columbia University Press, 1980.

Spindler, J. Andrew. *The Politics of International Credit*. Washington, D.C.: The Brookings Institution, 1984.

Stabler, Elizabeth. "The Dollar Devaluation of 1971 and 1973." *U.S. Commission of the Organization of the Government for the Conduct of Foreign Policy, Appendix*. Vol. 3. Washington, D.C.: Government Printing Office, 1976.

Strange, Susan. *Casino Capitalism*. Oxford and New York: Basil Blackwell, 1986.

Strange, Susan. "The Dollar Crisis 1971." *International Affairs*, 48 (April 1972), 191-215.

Triffin, Robert. "The International Role and Fate of the Dollar." *Foreign Affairs*, 57 (Winter 1978-79), 269-286.

———. *Evolution of the International Monetary System: Historical Reappraisal and Future Perspectives*. Princeton, N.J.: International Finance Section, Department of Economics, Princeton University, 1964.

———. *Gold and the Dollar Crisis: The Future of Convertibility*. New Haven, Conn.: Yale University Press, 1960.

———. *Europe and the Money Muddle: From Bilateralism to Near Convertibility, 1947-1956*. New Haven, Conn.: Yale University Press, 1957.

Tsoukalis, Loukas, ed. *The Political Economy of International Money*. London: Royal Institute of International Affairs/Sage Publications, 1985.

Ungerer, Horst. *The European Monetary System: Recent Developments*. Washington, D.C.: International Monetary Fund Occasional Papers No. 48, 1986.

Wachtel, Howard M. *The Money Mandarins: The Making of a Supranational Economic Order*. New York: Pantheon Books, 1986.

Wallich, Henry C., et al. *World Money and National Policies*. New York: Group of Thirty, 1983.

————. *The Failure of International Monetary Reform, 1971–74*. London: Nelson, 1977.

Williamson, John, and Marcus Miller. *Targets and Indicators: A Blueprint for International Coordination of Economic Policy*. Washington, D.C.: Institute for International Economics, 1987.

Trade among Developed Market Economies

Aggarwal, Vinod K. *Liberal Protectionism: The International Politics of Organized Textile Trade*. Berkeley: University of California Press, 1985.

Aho, C. Michael, and Jonathan David Aronson. *Trade Talks: America Better Listen!* New York: Council on Foreign Relations, 1985.

Baldwin, Robert E. *Non-Tariff Distortions of International Trade*. Washington, D.C.: The Brookings Institution, 1970.

Baldwin, Robert. *The Political Economy of U.S. Import Policy*. Cambridge, Mass.: MIT Press, 1986.

Bauer, Raymond A., Ithiel de Sola Pool, and Lewis Anthony Dexter. *American Business and Public Policy: The Politics of Foreign Trade*. Chicago: Aldine-Atherton, 1972.

Blackhurst, Richard, Nicolas Marian, and Jan Tumlir. *Adjustment, Trade and Growth in Developed and Developing Countries*. GATT Studies in International Trade, no. 6. Geneva: General Agreement on Tariffs and Trade, 1978.

Boltho, Andrea, ed. *The European Economy: Growth and Crisis*. Oxford: Oxford University Press, 1982.

Brown, William Adams, Jr. *The United States and the Restoration of World Trade: An Analysis and Appraisal of the ITO Charter and the General Agreement on Tariffs and Trade*. Washington, D.C.: The Brookings Institution, 1950.

Camps, Miriam, and William Diebold, Jr. *The New Multilateralism: Can the World Trading System Be Saved?* New York: Council on Foreign Relations, 1983.

Cline, William R. *Trade Policy in the 1980s*. Washington, D.C.: Institute for International Economics, 1983.

Conybeare, John A.C. *Trade Wars: The Theory and Practice of International Commercial Rivalry*. New York: Columbia University Press, 1987.

Curran, T. J. "Politics of Trade Liberalization in Japan." *Journal of International Affairs*, 37 (Summer 1983), 105–122.

Curzon, Gerard. *Multilateral Commercial Diplomacy: The General Agreements on Tariffs and Trade and its Impact on National Commercial Policies and Techniques*. London: Michael Joseph, 1965.

Dam, Kenneth W. *The GATT: Law and International Economic Organization*. Chicago: University of Chicago Press, 1970.

Destler, I.M. *American Trade Politics: System Under Stress*. Washington, D.C.: Institute for International Economics/New York: Twentieth Century Fund, 1986.

Diebold, William, Jr. "Adapting Economies to Structural Change: The International Aspect." *International Affairs* (London), 54 (October 1978), 573–588.

Diebold, William Jr. *Bilateralism, Multilateralism and Canada in U.S. Trade Policy*. Cambridge, Mass.: Ballinger, 1988.

————. *The End of the I.T.O.* Princeton, N.J.: International Finance Section, Department of Economics and Social Institutions, Princeton University, 1952.

Feketekuty, Geza. *International Trade in Services: An Overview and Blueprint for Negotiations.* Cambridge, Mass.: Ballinger/Washington: American Enterprise Institute, 1988.

Gadbaw, R. Michael, and Timothy J. Richards, eds. *Intellectual Property Rights: Global Consensus, Global Conflict?* Boulder, Colo.: Westview Press, 1988.

General Agreement on Tariffs and Trade. *The Tokyo Round: A Report by the Director-General of GATT.* Geneva: General Agreement on Tariffs and Trade, 1979.

Hathaway, Dale E. *Agriculture and the GATT: Rewriting the Rules.* Washington, D.C.: Institute for International Economics, 1987.

Hill, Brian. *The Common Agricultural Policy: Past, Present and Future.* New York: Methuen, 1989.

Hindley, Brian, and Eri Nicolaides. *Taking the New Protectionism Seriously,* Thames Essay No. 34. London: Trade Policy Research Centre, 1983.

Hine, R. C. *The Political Economy of European Trade: An Introduction to the Trade Policies of the EEC.* New York: St. Martin's Press, 1985.

Hopkins, Raymond F., and Donald J. Puchala. *Global Food Interdependence: Challenge to American Foreign Policy.* New York: Columbia University Press, 1980.

————, eds. "The Global Political Economy of Food." *International Organization,* 32 (Summer 1978), entire issue.

Hufbauer, Gary C., Diane T. Berliner, and Kimberly A. Elliot. *Trade Protection in the United States: Thirty-one Case Studies.* Washington, D.C.: Institute for International Economics, 1986.

Institute for Contemporary Studies. *Tariffs, Quotas and Trade: The Politics of Protectionism.* San Francisco: Institute for Contemporary Studies, 1979.

Johnson, Chalmers. *MITI and the Japanese Miracle: The Growth of Industrial Policy, 1925–1975.* Stanford, Calif.: Stanford University Press, 1982.

Koch, Karin. *International Trade Policy in the GATT, 1947–67.* Stockholm: Almquist and Wiksell, 1969.

Krasner, Stephen D. "The Tokyo Round: Particularistic Interests and Prospects for Stability in the Global Trading System." *International Studies Quarterly,* 23 (December 1979), 491–531.

————. "State Power and the Structure of International Trade." *World Politics,* 28 (April 1976), 317–343.

Krugman, Paul R., ed. *Strategic Trade Policy and the New International Economics.* Cambridge, Mass.: MIT Press, 1986.

Johnson, D. Gale, Kenzo Hemmi, and Pierre Lardinois. *Agricultural Policy and Trade: Adjusting Domestic Programs in an International Framework.* New York: New York University Press, 1986.

Lenway, Stefanie Ann. *The Politics of U.S. International Trade: Protection, Expansion and Escape.* Marshfield, Mass.: Pitman Publishing, 1985.

Metzger, Stanley D. *Lowering Nontariff Barriers: U.S. Law, Practice and Negotiating Objectives.* Washington, D.C.: The Brookings Institution, 1974.

Milner, Helen V. *Resisting the Protectionist Temptation: Global Industries and the Politics of International Trade.* Princeton: Princeton University Press, 1988.

Organization for Economic Cooperation and Development. *National Policies and Agricultural Trade*. Paris: OECD, 1987.

Ozaki, Robert S. *The Control of Imports and Foreign Capital in Japan*. New York: Praeger, 1972.

Paarlberg, Robert L. *Fixing Farm Trade: Policy Options for the United States*. Cambridge, Mass.: Ballinger, 1988.

Patterson, Gardener. *Discrimination in International Trade: The Policy Issues. 1945–65*. Princeton, N.J.: Princeton University Press, 1966.

Penrose, E.F. *Economic Planning for the Peace*. Princeton, N.J.: Princeton University Press, 1953.

Preeg, Ernest H. *Traders and Diplomats: An Analysis of the Kennedy Round Negotiations under the General Agreement on Tariffs and Trade*. Washington, D.C.: The Brookings Institution, 1970.

Reich, Robert B. "Beyond Free Trade." *Foreign Affairs*, 16 (1983), 747–772.

Schattschneider, E. E. *Politics, Pressures and the Tariff*. Englewood Cliffs, N.J.: Prentice-Hall, 1935.

Schonfield, Andrew, ed. *International Economic Relations of the Western World, 1959–1971*. Vol. 1: *Politics and Trade*. London: Oxford University Press, 1976.

Schott, Jeffrey J., and Murray G. Smith. *The Canada-United States Free Trade Agreement: The Global Impact*. Washington, D.C.: Institute for International Economics, 1988.

Strange, Susan. "The Management of Surplus Capacity: Or How Does Theory Stand Up to Protectionism 1970s Style?" *International Organization*, 33 (Summer 1979), 303–334.

Taylor, Paul. *The Limits of European Integration*. London: Croom Helm, 1983.

United States Congress. *The Mercantilist Challenge to the Liberal International Trade Order*. A study prepared for the use of the joint Economic Committee. Congress of the United States, December 29, 1982. Washington, D.C.: U.S. Government Printing Office, 1982.

Vogel, Ezra. *Japan as Number One*. Cambridge, Mass.: Harvard University Press, 1979.

Walter, Ingo. *Global Competition in Financial Services: Market Structure, Protection and Liberalization*. Cambridge, Mass.: Ballinger, 1988.

Wilcox, Clair. *A Charter for World Trade*. New York: Macmillan, 1949.

Winham, Gilbert R. *International Trade and the Tokyo Round Negotiations?* Princeton: Princeton University Press, 1987.

Zysman, John, and Laura Tyson. *American Industry in International Competition: Government Policies and Corporate Strategies*. Ithaca, N.Y.: Cornell University Press, 1983.

The Multinational Corporation in Developed Market Economies

Agmon, Tamir, and Charles P. Kindleberger. *Multinationals From Small Countries*. Cambridge, Mass.: M.I.T. Press, 1977.

Apter, David, and Louis W. Goodman, eds. *The Multinational Corporation and Social Change*. New York: Praeger, 1976.

Ball, George, ed. *Global Companies*. Englewood Cliffs, N.J.: Prentice-Hall, 1979.

Ball, George W. "Cosmocorp: The Importance of Being Stateless." *Columbia Journal of World Business*, 2 (November–December 1967), 25–30.

Baranson, Jack. *Technology and the Multinationals: Corporate Strategies and a Changing World Environment*. Lexington, Mass.: Lexington Books, 1978.

Barnet, Richard J., and Ronald E. Müller. *The Global Reach: The Power of the Multinational Corporations*. New York: Simon and Schuster, 1974.

Bassing, Reza. *Power v. Profit: Multinational Corporation-Nation State Interaction*. New York: Arno, 1980.

Behrman, Jack N. *U.S. International Business and Governments*. New York: McGraw-Hill, 1971.

Buckley, Peter J., and Mark Casson. *The Economic Theory of the Multinational Enterprise*. New York: St.Martin's Press, 1985.

Canada. Task Force on the Structure of Canadian Industry. *Foreign Ownership and the Structure of Canadian Industry*. Ottawa: Queen's Printer, 1968.

Cohen, Stephen S., and John Zysman. *Manufacturing Matters: The Myth of the Post-Industrial Economy*. New York: Basic Books, for the Council on Foreign Relations, 1987.

Cox, Robert W. "Labor and the Multinationals." *Foreign Affairs*, 54 (January 1976), 344–365.

Curzon, Gerard, and Victoria Curzon, eds. *The Multinational Enterprise in a Hostile World*. London: Macmillan, 1977.

Dunning, John H., ed. *The Multinational Enterprise*. London: Allen & Unwin, 1971.

Fayerweather, John. *Foreign Investment in Canada: Prospects for National Policy*. White Plains, N.Y.: International Arts and Sciences Press, 1973.

––––––. "Elite Attitudes Toward Multinational Firms: A Study of Britain, Canada, and France." *International Studies Quarterly*, 16 (December 1972), 472–490.

––––––. "International Transmission of Resources," in John Fayerweather, ed. *International Business Management: A Conceptual Framework*. New York: McGraw-Hill, 1969.

Gervais, Jacques. *La France face aux investissements étrangers: Analysé par secteurs*. Paris: Éditions de l'Enterprise Moderne, 1963.

Gilpin, Robert. *U.S. Power and the Multinational Corporation: The Political Economy of Foreign Direct Investment*. New York: Basic Books, 1975.

Goldberg, Paul M., and Charles P. Kindleberger. "Toward a GATT for Investment: A Proposal for Supervision of the International Corporation." *Law and Policy in International Business*, 2 (Summer 1970), 295–323.

Hedlund, Gunnar, and Lars Otterbeck. *The Multinational Corporation, the Nation State and the Trade Unions: A European Perspective*. Kent, Ohio: Comparative Administration Research Institute, 1977.

Hood, Neil, and Stephen Young. *The Economics of Multinational Enterprise*. London: Longman, 1979.

Huntington, Samuel P. "Transnational Organizations in World Politics." *World Politics*, 25 (April 1973), 333–368.

Hymer, Stephen. *The Multinational Corporation: A Radical Approach*. Ed. by Robert Cohen, et al. London: Cambridge University Press, 1979.

––––––. *The International Operations of National Firms: A Study of Direct Foreign Investment*. Cambridge, Mass.: M.I.T. Press, 1976.

———. "The Efficiency (Contradictions) of Multinational Corporations." *American Economic Review*, 60 (May 1970), 441–448.

Johnstone, Allan W. *U.S. Direct Investment in France: An Investigation of French Charges*. Cambridge, Mass.: M.I.T. Press, 1965.

Kojima, Kiyoshi. *Direct Foreign Investment: A Japanese Model of Multinational Business Operations*. London: Croom Helm, 1978.

Levitt, Kari. *Silent Surrender: The Multinational Corporation in Canada*. New York: St. Martin's, 1970.

Litvak, Isaiah A., and Christopher J. Maule, eds. *Foreign Investment: The Experience of Host Countries*. New York: Praeger, 1970.

Mandel, Ernest. *Europe vs. America: Contradictions of Imperialism*. New York: Monthly Review, 1970.

Patrick, Hugh, and Larry Meissner, eds. *Japan's High Technology Industries: Lessons and Limitations of Industrial Policy*. Seattle: University of Washington Press, 1987.

Robinson, John. *Multinationals and Political Control*. New York: St. Martin's, 1983.

Rubin, Seymour J. "Developments in the Law and Institutions of International Economic Relations: The Multinational Enterprise at Bay." *The American Journal of International Law*, 68 (July 1974), 475–488.

Safarian, A.E. *Governments and Multinationals: Policies in the Developed Countries*. Washington, D.C.: British North American Commission, 1983.

Servan-Schreiber, Jean-Jacques. *The American Challenge*, Ronald Steel, transl. New York: Atheneum, 1968.

Tolchin, Susan and Martin. *Buying into America: How Foreign Money Is Changing the Face of Our Nation*. New York: Times Books, 1988.

United Nations. *Report of the Group of Eminent Persons to Study the Impact of Multinational Corporations on Development and on International Relations*. New York: United Nations, 1974.

U.S. Senate Committee on Foreign Relations. *Multinational Corporations and United States Foreign Policy*. Hearings before the Subcommittee on Multinational Corporations of the Committee on Foreign Relations, 93rd and 94th Congresses, 1973–1976.

Vernon, Raymond. "Multinationals: No Strings Attached." *Foreign Policy*, 35 (1978), 121–134.

———. *Storm Over the Multinationals: The Real Issues*. Cambridge: Harvard University Press, 1977.

———. *Sovereignty at Bay: The Multinational Spread of U.S. Enterprises*. New York: Basic, 1971.

Vogel, Ezra. *Comeback Case by Case: Building the Resurgence of American Business*. New York: Simon and Schuster, 1985.

Wallace, Cynthia Day. *Legal Control of the Multinational Enterprise: National Regulatory Techniques and the Prospects for International Controls*. The Hague, Netherlands: Martinus Nijhoff, 1982.

Weinberg, Paul J. *European Labor and Multinationals*. New York: Praeger, 1978.

Wilkins, Mira. *The Maturing of the Multinational Enterprise: American Business Abroad from 1914 to 1970*. Cambridge, Mass.: Harvard University Press, 1975.

——. *The Emergence of Multinational Enterprise: American Business Abroad from the Colonial Era to 1914.* Cambridge, Mass.: Harvard University Press, 1970.

The North-South System

General and Theory

Amin, Samir. *Unequal Development: An Essay on the Social Formations of Peripheral Capitalism.* New York: Monthly Review, 1976.
——. *Accumulation on a World Scale.* New York: Monthly Review, 1974.
Apter, David. *Rethinking Development: Modernization, Dependency, and Postmodern Politics.* Beverly Hills: Sage Publications, 1987.
Baran, Paul A. *The Political Economy of Growth.* New York: Monthly Review, 1957.
Barratt-Brown, Michael. *The Economics of Imperialism.* Harmondsworth, Eng.: Penguin, 1974.
——. *After Imperialism*, rev. ed. New York: Humanities Press, 1970.
Bauer, Peter D. *Dissent on Development: Studies and Debates on Development Economics.* Cambridge, Mass.: Harvard University Press, 1972.
Bhagwati, Jagdish, ed. *The New International Economic Order: The North-South Debate.* Cambridge, Mass.: M.I.T. Press, 1977.
Bhagwati, Jagdish N., and John G. Ruggie, eds. *Power, Passions and Purpose: Prospects for North-South Negotiations.* Cambridge, Mass.: MIT Press, 1984.
Boulding, Kenneth, and Tapan Mukerjee, eds. *Economic Imperialism: A Book of Readings.* Ann Arbor, Mich.: University of Michigan Press, 1972.
Caporaso, James, ed. *A Changing International Division of Labor.* Boulder, Colo.: Lynne Rienner, 1987.
Caporaso, James, ed. "Dependence and Dependency in the Global System." *International Organization*, 32 (Winter 1978), entire issue.
Cockcroft, James D., André Gunder Frank, and Dale L. Johnson. *Dependence and Underdevelopment: Latin America's Political Economy.* Garden City, N.Y.: Anchor, 1972.
Cohen, Benjamin J. *The Question of Imperialism: The Political Economy of Dominance and Dependence.* New York: Basic Books, 1973.
Commins, Stephen, ed. *Africa's Development Challenge and the World Bank.* Boulder, Colo.: Lynne Rienner, 1988.
Cox, Robert W. "Ideologies and the New International Economic Order: Reflections on Some Recent Literature." *International Organization*, 33 (Spring 1979), 257–302.
Dos Santos, Theotonio. "The Structure of Dependence," in K. T. Fann and D. C. Hodges, eds., *Readings in U.S. Imperialism.* Boston: Sargent, 1971.
Emmanuel, Arghiri. *Unequal Exchange: A Study of the Imperialism of Trade.* New York: Monthly Review, 1972.
Erb, Guy F., and Valeriana Kallab, eds. *Beyond Dependence: The Developing World Speaks Out.* New York: Praeger, 1975.

Feinberg, Richard E., and Valeriana Kallab, eds. *Adjustment Crisis in the Third World*. Washington, D.C.: Overseas Development Council, 1984.

Fishlow, Albert, Carlos F. Diaz-Alejandro, Richard R. Fagen, and Roger D. Hansen. *Rich and Poor Nations in the World Economy*. New York: McGraw-Hill, 1978.

Frank, André Gunder. *Capitalism and Underdevelopment in Latin America: Historical Studies of Chile and Brazil*, rev. ed. New York: Monthly Review, 1969.

———. *Latin America: Underdevelopment or Revolution*. New York: Monthly Review, 1969.

Furtado, Celso. *Economic Development of Latin America*. London: Cambridge University Press, 1970.

———. *The Obstacles to Development in Latin America*. Charles Ekker, transl. Garden City, N.Y.: Anchor, 1970.

Galtung, J. "A Structural Theory of Imperialism." *Journal of Peace Research*, 2 (1971), 81–117.

Gosovic, Branislav, and John G. Ruggie. "On the Creation of a New International Economic Order." *International Organization*, 30 (Spring 1976), 309–345.

Hansen, Roger D. "North-South Policy—What is the Problem?" *Foreign Affairs*, 58 (Summer 1980), 1104–1128.

———. *Beyond the North-South Stalemate*. New York: McGraw-Hill, 1979.

Haq, Khadija, and Carlos Massad, eds. *Adjustment with Growth: A Search for an Equitable Solution*. Islamabad, Pakistan: North South Roundtable, 1984.

Haq, Mahbub ul. *The Poverty Curtain: Choices for the Third World*. New York: Columbia University Press, 1976.

Hart, Jeffrey. *The New International Economic Order: Conflict and Co-operation in North-South Economic Relations 1974–77*. New York: St. Martin's, 1983.

Helleiner, Gerald, and Carlos F. Díaz-Alejandro. *Handmaiden in Distress: World Trade in the 1980s*. Washington, D.C.: Overseas Development Council, 1982.

Hirschman, Albert O. *The Strategy of Economic Development*. New Haven, Conn.: Yale University Press, 1958.

Independent Commission on International Development Issues. *North-South: A Programme for Survival*. [Brandt Commission Report.] Cambridge: MIT. Press, 1980.

Independent Commission on International Development Issues. *Common Crisis North-South: Cooperation for World Recovery*. [Second Brandt Commission Report] Cambridge: MIT Press, 1983.

Jalée, Pierre. *Imperialism in the Seventies*, Raymond and Margaret Sokolov, transl. New York: Third World, 1972.

———. *The Third World in the World Economy*, Mary Klopper, transl. New York: Monthly Review, 1969.

———. *The Pillage of the Third World*, Mary Klopper, transl. New York: Monthly Review, 1968.

Johnson, Harry G. *Economic Policies Toward Less-Developed Countries*. New York: Praeger, 1967.

Kahler, Miles, ed. *The Politics of International Debt*. Ithaca, N.Y.: Cornell University Press, 1986.

Lewis, W. Arthur. "The Dual Economy Revisited." *The Manchester School of Economic and Social Studies*, 47 (September 1979), 211–229.

MacEwan, Arthur. "Capitalist Expansion, Ideology and Intervention." *Review of Radical Political Economics*, 4 (Spring 1972), 36–58.

Magdoff, Harry. *Imperialism: From the Colonial Age to the Present.* New York: Monthly Review, 1978.

Miller, S. M., Roy Bennett, and Cyril Alapatt. "Does the U.S. Economy Require Imperialism?" *Social Policy*, 1 (September-October, 1970), 12–19.

Myrdal, Gunnar. *Rich Lands and Poor: The Road to World Prosperity.* New York: Harper & Row, 1957.

———. *An International Economy: Problems and Prospects.* New York: Harper & Row, 1956.

Nabudere, Dan. *The Political Economy of Imperialism.* London: Zed Press, 1977.

Nurkse, Ragnar. *Equilibrium and Growth in the World Economy: Economic Essays.* Cambridge, Mass.: Harvard University Press, 1961.

———. *Problems of Capital Formation for Underdeveloped Countries.* New York: Oxford University Press, 1953.

Pearson, Lester B. *Partners in Development: Report of the Commission on International Development.* New York: Praeger, 1969.

Prebisch, Raúl. *The Economic Development of Latin America and its Principal Problems.* New York: United Nations, 1950.

Review of Radical Political Economy. "Facing the 1980s: New Directions in the Theory of Imperialism," 11 (Winter 1979), entire volume.

Review of Radical Political Economy. "Dependence and Foreign Domination," 4 (Winter 1972), entire volume.

Rosen, Steven J., and James R. Kurth, eds. *Testing Theories of Economic Imperialism.* Lexington, Mass.: Lexington Books, 1974.

Rothstein, Robert L. *Global Bargaining: UNCTAD and the Quest for a New International Economic Order.* Princeton, N.J.: Princeton University Press, 1979.

———. *The Weak in the World of the Strong: The Developing Countries in the International System.* New York: Columbia University Press, 1977.

Singer, H. W. *International Development: Growth and Change.* New York: McGraw-Hill, 1964.

Sunkel, Osvaldo. "Big Business and Dependence: A Latin American View." *Foreign Affairs*, 50 (April 1972) 517–532.

———. "National Development Policy and External Dependence in Latin America." Journal of Development Studies, 6 (October 1969), 23–48.

Sweezy, Paul M. *Modern Capitalism and Other Essays.* New York: Monthly Review, 1972.

Szymanski, Al. "Capital Accumulation on a World Scale and the Necessity of Imperialism." *The Insurgent Sociologist*, 7 (Spring 1977), 35–53.

Uri, Pierre. *Development Without Dependence.* New York: Praeger, 1976.

Vernon, Raymond, ed. *The Promise of Privatization: A Challenge for American Foreign Policy.* New York: Council on Foreign Relations, 1988.

Wallerstein, Immanuel. "Dependence in an Interdependent World." *African Studies Review*, 17 (April 1974), 1–26.

Weisskopf, Thomas E. "Theories of American Imperialism: A Critical Evaluation." *Review of Radical Political Economics*, 6 (Fall 1974), 41–60.

North-South Aid/International Financial Flows

Arnau, J. Sanchez, ed. *Debt and Development in Latin America*. New York: Praeger, 1982.

Bacha, Edmar Lisboa, and Carlos F. Diaz-Alejandro. *International Financial Intermediation: A Long and Tropical View*, Essays in International Finance, n. 47. Princeton, N.J.: Princeton University, International Finance Section; May, 1982.

Baldwin, David A. *Economic Development in American Foreign Policy, 1943-1962*. Chicago: University of Chicago Press, 1966.

Bauer, P.T. *Equality, the Third World, and Economic Delusion*. Cambridge, Mass.: Harvard University Press, 1981.

Bhagwati, Jagdish, and Richard S. Eckans, eds. *Foreign Aid*. Harmondsworth, Eng.: Penguin, 1970.

Bird, Graham. *The International Monetary System and the Less Developed Countries*. London: Macmillan, 1978.

Bitterman, Henry J. "Negotiation of the Bank for Reconstruction and Development." *The International Lawyer*, 5 (January 1971), 59–88.

Cassen, Robert and Associates. *Does Aid Work? Report to an Intergovernmental Task Force*. Oxford: Clarendon Press, 1986.

Cline, William. "Mexico's Crisis, the World's Peril." *Foreign Policy*, 49 (Winter 1982–83), 107–120.

Feinberg, Richard E., and Valeriana Kallab, eds. *Between Two Worlds: The World Bank's Next Decade*. New Brunswick, N.J.: Transaction Books, 1986.

Hayter, Teresa. *Aid as Imperialism*. Middlesex, Eng.: Penguin, 1971.

Hurni, Bettina S. *The Lending Policy of the World Bank in the 1970s*. Boulder, Colo.: Westview, 1980.

Kelleo, Peter M. with Nessanke E. Weerasinghe. *Multilateral Official Debt Rescheduling: Recent Experiences*. Washington, D.C.: International Monetary Fund, 1988.

Killick, Tony. *The IMF and Stabilization: Developing Country Experiences*. New York: St. Martin's, 1984.

Kuczynski, Pedro-Pablo. *Latin American Debt*. Baltimore: Johns Hopkins Press, 1988.

Lancaster, Carol, and John Williamson, eds. *African Debt and Financing*. Washington, D.C.: Institute for International Economics, 1986.

Levinson, Jerome, and Juan de Onis. *The Alliance that Lost its Way: A Critical Report on the Alliance for Progress*. New York: Quadrangle, 1970.

Little, I. D., and J. M. Clifford. *International Aid: A Discussion of the Flow of Public Resources from Rich to Poor Countries, with Particular Reference to British Policy*. London: Allen & Unwin, 1965.

Mason, Edward S., and Robert E. Asher. *The World Bank Since Bretton Woods*. Washington, D.C.: The Brookings Institution, 1973.

McNeill, Desmond. *The Contradictions of Foreign Aid*. London: Croom Helm, 1981.

Miller, Norman C. *International Reserves, Exchange Rates, and Developing Country Finance*. Lexington, Mass.: Lexington Books, 1982.

Millikan, Max F., and W. W. Rostow. *A Proposal: Key to an Effective Foreign Policy.* New York: Harper & Row, 1957.

Nelson, Joan M. *Aid, Influence and Foreign Policy.* New York: Macmillan, 1968.

Organization for Economic Cooperation and Development. *Twenty-five Years of Development Cooperation.* Paris: OECD, 1985.

Paarlberg, Robert L., "U.S. Agriculture and the Developing World." *Growth, Exports and Jobs in a Changing World Economy: Agenda 1988.* New Brunswick, N.J.: Transaction Books, 1988.

Packenham, R. A. *Liberal America and the Third World: Political Development Ideas in Foreign Aid and Social Science*, Princeton, N.J.: Princeton University Press, 1973.

Payer, Cheryl. *The Debt Trap: The International Monetary Fund and the Third World.* New York: Monthly Review, 1974.

Sachs, Jeffrey, and Harry Huizinga. "U.S. Commercial Banks and the Developing Country Debt Crisis," *Brookings Papers on Economic Activity*, Vol. 2. Washington, D.C.: Brookings, 1987.

Singer, Hans, John Wood, and Tony Jennings. *Food Aid: The Challenge and the Opportunity.* New York: Oxford University Press, 1987.

U.S. Senate. *Foreign Aid Program*, 1957. 85th Congress, 1st Sess. Washington, D.C.: Government Printing Office, 1957.

Wall, David. *The Charity of Nations: The Political Economy of Foreign Aid.* New York: Basic Books, 1973.

Walters, Robert S. *American and Soviet Aid: A Comparative Analysis.* Pittsburgh, Pa.: University of Pittsburgh Press, 1970.

Trade

Alting von Gesau, A. M., ed. *The Lomé Convention and a New International Economic Order.* Leiden, Netherlands: A. W. Sijthoff, 1977.

Behrman, Jere R. *International Commodity Agreements.* Washington, D.C.: Overseas Development Council, 1977.

Belassa, Bela. "The Developing Countries and the Tokyo Round." *Journal of World Trade Law*, 14 (March–April 1980), 93–118.

———. "Trade Policies in Developing Countries." *American Economic Review*, 61 (May 1971), 178–210.

Campos, Roberto de Oliveiro, et al. *Trends in International Trade: A Report by a Panel of Experts.* [Haberler Report] Geneva: The Contracting Parties to the General Agreement on Tariffs and Trade, October 1958.

Cordovez, Diego. "The Making of UNCTAD: Institutional Background and Legislative History." *Journal of World Trade Law*, 1 (May–June 1967), 243–328.

———. *UNCTAD and Development Diplomacy: From Confrontation to Strategy.* Twickenham, Eng.: Journal of World Trade Law, 1970.

Frank, Isaiah. "The 'Graduation' Issue for the Less Developed Countries." *Journal of World Trade Law*, 13 (July–August 1979), 289–302.

Friedeberg, A. S. *The United Nations Conference on Trade and Development of 1964: The Theory of the Peripheral Economy.* Rotterdam, Netherlands: Rotterdam University Press, 1969.

Goodwin, Geoffrey, and James Mayall, eds. *A New International Commodity Regime*. New York: St. Martin's, 1980.

Gosovic, Branislav. *UNCTAD, Conflict and Compromise: The Third World's Quest for an Equitable World Economic Order Through the United Nations*. Leiden, Netherlands: A. W. Sijthoff-Leiden, 1972.

Gruhn, Isebill V. "The Lomé Convention: Inching Towards Interdependence." *International Organization*, 30 (Spring 1976), 240–262.

Haberler, Gottfried. *International Trade and Economic Development*. Cairo: National Bank of Egypt, 1959.

Hudec, Robert. *Developing Countries in the GATT Legal System*. London: Trade Policy Research Center, 1987.

Law, Alton D. *International Commodity Agreements*. Lexington, Mass.: Lexington Books, 1975.

Levin, Jonathan V. *The Export Economies: Their Pattern of Development in Historical Perspective*. Cambridge, Mass.: Harvard University Press, 1964.

Linden, Steffan B. "The Significance of GATT for Underdeveloped Countries." *Proceedings of the United Nations Conference on Trade and Development*, 5 (1964), 502–532.

Maizels, Alfred. *Exports and Economic Growth of Developing Countries: A Theoretical and Empirical Study of the Relationship Between Exports and Economic Growth*. London: Cambridge University Press, 1968.

McMullen, Neil, and Louis Turner with Colin L. Bradford. *The Newly Industrializing Countries: Trade and Adjustment*. London: Allen & Unwin, 1982.

McNicol, David L. *Commodity Agreements and Price Stabilization*. Lexington, Mass.: Lexington Books, 1978.

Meadows, Donella H., et al. *The Limits to Growth: A Report for the Club of Rome's Project on the Predicament of Mankind*. New York: Universe, 1972.

Murray, Tracy. *Trade Preferences for Developing Countries*. New York: Wiley, 1977.

Nappi, Carmine. *Commodity Market Controls*. Lexington, Mass.: Lexington Books, 1979.

Nurkse, Ragnar. *Patterns of Trade and Development*. New York: Oxford University Press, 1961.

Organization for Economic Cooperation and Development. *The Newly Industrializing Countries: Challenge and Opportunity for OECD Countries*. Paris: OECD, 1988.

Payer, Cheryl. *Commodity Trade of the Third World*. London: Macmillan, 1975.

Prebisch, Raúl. "The Role of Commercial Policies in Underdeveloped Countries." *American Economic Review, Papers and Proceedings*, 49 (May 1959), 251–273.

Preeg, Ernest H., ed. *Hard Bargaining Ahead; U.S. Trade Policy and Developing Countries*. New Brunswick, N.J.: Transaction Books, 1985.

Reynolds, Paul D. *International Commodity Agreements and the Common Fund*. Lexington, Mass.: Lexington Books, 1978.

Sengupta, Arjun, ed. *Commodities, Finance and Trade: Issues in North-South Negotiations*. Westport, Conn.: Greenwood, 1980.

Sewell, John, Stuart K. Tucker, and contributors. *Growth, Exports and Jobs in a Changing World Economy: Agenda 1988*. New Brunswick, N.J.: Transaction Books, 1988.

Streeten, Paul, ed. *Trade Strategies for Development: Papers of the Ninth Cambridge Conference on Development Problems*, September 1972. New York: John Wiley, 1973.

———. *Toward a New Trade Policy for Development*. New York: United Nations, 1964.

Vastine, J. Robert. "United States International Commodity Policy." *Law and Policy in International Business*, 9 (1977), 401–477.

Yoffie, David. *Power and Protectionism: Strategies of the Newly Industrializing Countries*. New York: Columbia University Press, 1983.

Foreign Investment in Less-Developed Countries

Becker, David. *The New Bourgeoisie and the Limits of Dependency: Mining, Class, and Power in Revolutionary Peru*. Princeton, N.J.: Princeton University Press, 1983.

Biersteker, Thomas. *Multinationals, the State and Control of the Nigerian Economy*. Princeton: Princeton University Press, 1987.

———. *Distortion or Development? Contending Perspectives on the Multinational Corporation*. Cambridge, Mass.: MIT Press, 1978.

Evans, Peter. *Dependent Development: The Alliance of Multinational, State, and Local Capital in Brazil*. Princeton, N.J.: Princeton University Press, 1979.

Faundey, Julio, and Sol Picciotto, eds. *The Nationalization of Multinationals in Peripheral Economies*. London: Macmillan, 1978.

Frank, Isaiah. *Foreign Enterprise in Developing Countries*. Baltimore, Md.: Johns Hopkins Press, 1980.

Frieden, Jeffrey. "Third World Indebted Industrialization: International Finance and State Capitalism in Mexico, Brazil, Algeria, and South Korea." *International Organization*, Vol. 35 No. 3 (Summer 1981), 407–431.

Furnish, Dale B. "The Andean Common Market's Common Regime for Foreign Investments." *Vanderbilt Journal of Transnational Law*, 5 (Spring 1972), 313–339.

Gereffi, Gary. *The Pharmaceutical Industry and Dependency in the Third World*. Princeton, N.J.: Princeton University Press, 1983.

Goodsell, Charles T. *American Corporations and Peruvian Politics*. Cambridge, Mass.: Harvard University Press, 1974.

Hirschman, A. O. "How to Divest in Latin America and Why." Essays in International Finance, 74. Princeton, N.J.: International Finance Section, Department of Economics, Princeton University, 1969.

Hymer, Stephen. "The Multinational Corporation and the Law of Uneven Development," in Jagdish N. Bhagwati, ed., *Economics and World Order: From the 1970s to the 1990s*. New York: Macmillan, 1972.

International Labor Organization. *Multinational Enterprises and Social Policy*. Geneva: International Labor Organization, 1973.

Jröbel, Folker, Jürgen Heinrichs, and Otto Kreye. *The New International Division of Labor: Structural Employment in Industrialized Countries and Industrialization in Developing Countries*. Cambridge, Eng.: Cambridge University Press, 1980.

Kobrin, Stephen J. "Foreign Enterprise and Forced Divestment in LDCs." *International Organization*, 34 (Winter 1980), 65–88.

LaPalombara, Joseph, and Stephen Blank. *Multinational Corporations and Developing Countries*. New York: The Conference Board, 1979.

Marton, Katherin. *Multinationals, Technology and Industrialization: Implications and Impact in the Third World Countries*. Lexington, Mass.: Lexington Books, 1986.

Mikesell, Raymond F., William H. Bartsch, et al. *Multinational Corporations and the Politics of Dependence: Copper in Chile*. Princeton, N.J.: Princeton University Press, 1974.

————. *Foreign Investment in the Petroleum and Mineral Industries: Case Studies of Investor-Host Country Relations*. Baltimore, Md.: Johns Hopkins Press, 1971.

Moran, Theodore H. *Multinational Corporations: The Political Economy of Foreign Direct Investment*. Lexington, Mass.: Lexington Books, 1985.

Newfarmer, Richard S., ed. *Profits, Progress and Poverty: Case Studies of International Industries in Latin America*. Notre Dame, Ind.: University of Notre Dame Press, 1985.

Novak, Michael, and Michael P. Jackson. *Latin America: Dependency or Independence*? Washington, D.C.: American Enterprise Institute, 1985.

Oman, Charles. *New Forms of International Investment in Developing Countries*. Paris: OECD, 1982.

Penrose, Edith. "The State and the Multinational Enterprise in Less-Developed Countries," in John H. Dunning, ed., *The Multinational Enterprise*, London: Allen & Unwin, 1971.

Piñelo, Adalberto J. *The Multinational Corporation as a Force in Latin American Politics: A Case Study of the International Petroleum Company in Peru*. New York: Praeger, 1973.

Sampson, Anthony. *The Sovereign State of ITT*. New York: Stein & Day, 1973.

Sauvant, Karl, and Farid Lauipour, eds. *Controlling Multinational Enterprises: Problems, Strategies, Counter-Strategies*. Boulder, Colo.: Westview, 1976.

Singer, Hans W. "U.S. Foreign Investment in Underdeveloped Areas: The Distribution of Gains between Investing and Borrowing Countries." *American Economic Review*, 40 (May 1950), 473–485.

Sklar, Richard L. *Corporate Power in an African State: The Political Impact of Multinational Mining Companies in Zambia*. Berkeley, Calif.: University of California Press, 1975.

Turner, Louis. *Multinational Companies and the Third World*. New York: Hill and Wang, 1973.

United Nations. *Transnational Corporations in World Development: A Reexamination*. New York: United Nations, 1978.

United Nations, Center on Transnational Corporations. *Transnational Corporations in World Development: Trends and Prospects*. New York: United Nations, 1988.

United Nations. *Transnational Corporations in World Development, Third Survey*. New York: United Nations Center on Transnational Corporations, 1983.

U.S. Senate. Committee on Foreign Relations, Subcommittee on Multinational Corporations. *Multinational Corporations in Brazil and Mexico: Structural*

Sources of Economic and Noneconomic Power. Washington, D.C.: Government Printing Office, 1975.

Vernon, Raymond. "Conflict and Resolution Between Foreign Direct Investors and Less Developed Countries." *Public Policy*, 17 (1968), 333–351.

Widstrand, Carl, ed. *Multinational Firms in Africa*. Uppsala, Sweden: Scandinavian Institute of African Studies, 1975.

Oil and Commodity Cartels

Ahrari, Mohammed E. *OPEC: The Failing Giant*. Lexington: University Press of Kentucky, 1986.

Allen, Loring. *OPEC Oil*. Cambridge: Oelgeschlager, Gunn and Hain, 1979.

Alnasrawi, Abbas. "Collective Bargaining Power in OPEC." *Journal of World Trade Law*, 7 (March–April 1973), 188–207.

Bergsten, C. Fred. "The Threat from the Third World." *Foreign Policy*, II (Summer 1973), 102–124.

Blair, John M. *The Control of Oil*. New York: Pantheon, 1976.

Brown, Christopher. *The Political and Social Economy of Commodity Control*. London: Macmillan, 1980.

Chenery, Hollis B. "Restructuring the World Economy: Round II." *Foreign Affairs*, 59 (1981), 1102–1121.

Danielsen, Albert L. *The Evolution of OPEC*. New York: Harcourt Brace Jonanovich, 1982.

Deagle, Edwin A., Jr. *The Future of the International Oil Market*. New York: Group of Thirty, 1983.

Eckes, Alfred E., Jr. *The United States and the Global Struggle for Minerals*. Austin, Texas: University of Texas Press, 1979.

Engler, Robert. *The Brotherhood of Oil*. Chicago: University of Chicago Press, 1977.

———. *The Politics of Oil: Private Power and Democratic Directions*. Chicago: University of Chicago Press, 1961.

Finlayson, Jack A., and Mark W. Zacher. *Managing International Markets: Developing Countries and the Commodity Trade Regime*. New York: Columbia University Press, 1988.

Ghadar, Fariborz. *The Evolution of OPEC Strategy*. Lexington, Mass.: Lexington Books, 1977.

Goodwin, Geoffrey, and James Mayall, eds. *A New International Commodity Regime*. London: Croom Helm, 1982.

Griffin, James M., and David J. Teece. *OPEC Behavior and World Oil Prices*. London: George Allen & Unwin, 1982.

Hartshorn, J. E. *Oil Companies and Governments*, 2nd rev. ed. London: Faber, 1967.

Holloway, Steven Kendall. *The Aluminum Multinationals and the Bauxite Cartel*. New York: St. Martin's Press, 1988.

Hveem, Helge. *The Political Economy of Third World Producer Associations*. New York: Columbia University Press, 1978.

Krasner, Stephen D. *Defending the National Interest: Raw Materials Investments and U.S. Foreign Policy*. Princeton, N.J.: Princeton University Press, 1978.

————. "Oil Is the Exception." *Foreign Policy*, 14 (Spring 1974), 68–90.

Mikdashi, Zuhayr. *The Community of Oil Exporting Countries: A Study in Governmental Cooperation*. Ithaca, N.Y.: Cornell University Press, 1972.

————. *A Financial Analysis of Middle Eastern Oil Concessions: 1901–1965*. New York: Praeger, 1966.

Mikesell, Raymond F. *The World Copper Industry*. Baltimore, Md.: Johns Hopkins Press, 1979.

Nappi, Carmine. *Commodity Market Controls*. Lexington, Mass.: Lexington Books, 1979.

Noreng, Oystein. *Oil Politics in the 1980s: Patterns of International Cooperation*. New York: McGraw-Hill, 1978.

————. *The Pressures of Oil: A Strategy for Economic Revival*. New York: Harper and Row, 1978.

Nwoke, Chibuzo. *Third World Minerals and Global Pricing: A New Theory*. London: Zed Books, 1987.

Pearce, Joan, ed. *The Third Oil Shock: The Effects of Lower Oil Prices*. London: Royal Institute of International Affairs, 1983.

Penrose, Edith T. *The Large International Firm in Developing Countries: The International Petroleum Industry*. Cambridge, Mass.: MIT. Press, 1969.

Rangarajan, L. N. *Commodity Conflict: The Political Economy of International Commodity Agreements*. London: Croom Helm, 1978.

Rustow, Dankwart A., and John F. Mungo. *OPEC, Success and Prospects*. New York: New York University Press, 1976.

Sampson, Anthony. *The Seven Sisters: The Great Oil Companies and the World They Made*. New York: Viking, 1975.

Shwadran, Benjamin. *The Middle East, Oil and the Great Powers*. New York: Praeger, 1955.

Stobaugh, Robert, and Daniel Yergin. *Energy Future: Report of the Harvard Business School Energy Project*. New York: Random House, 1979.

Szyliowicz, Joseph S., and Bard E. O'Neill, eds. *The Energy Crisis and U.S. Foreign Policy*. New York: Praeger, 1975.

Takerichi, Kenji, John E. Strongman, Shunichi Maeda, and C. Suan Tan. *The World Copper Industry: Its Changing Structure and Future Prospects*. World Bank Staff Working Papers, no. 15. Washington, D.C.: World Bank, 1987.

Tanzer, Michael. *The Political Economy of International Oil and the Underdeveloped Countries*. Boston: Beacon, 1969.

Tilton, John E. "Cartels in Metal Industries." *Earth and Mineral Sciences*, 44 (March 1975), 41–44.

Tugwell, Franklin. *The Politics of Oil in Venezuela*. Stanford, Calif.: Stanford University Press, 1975.

Turner, Louis. *Oil Companies and the International System*. London: Allen & Unwin, 1978.

U.S. Federal Trade Commission. *International Petroleum Cartel*. Staff Report to the Federal Trade Commission, 82nd Congress, 2nd Sess. Washington, D.C.: Government Printing Office, 1952.

Vernon, Raymond. *Two Hungry Giants: The US and Japan in the Quest for Oil and Ores*. Cambridge, Mass.: Harvard University Press, 1983.

Woods, Douglas W., and James C. Burrows. *The World Aluminum-Bauxite Market: Policy Implications for the United States*. New York: Praeger, 1980.

Yager, Joseph A., and Eleanor B. Steinbert, et al. *Energy and U.S. Foreign Policy: A Report to the Energy Policy Project of the Ford Foundation*. Cambridge, Mass.: Ballinger, 1974.

Yergin, Daniel. *Energy Future*. New York: Ballantine, 1981.

East-West Economic Relations

Adler-Karlsson, Gunnar. *Western Economic Warfare*. 1946–1967. Stockholm. Sweden: Almquist and Wiksell, 1968.

Altman, Oscar. "Russians Gold and the Ruble." International Monetary Fund *Staff Papers*, 8 (April 1960), 415–438.

Bertsch, Gary, ed. *Controlling East-West Trade and Technology Transfer: Power, Politics and Policies* (Durham: Duke University Press, 1988.)

Blinken, Anthony. *Ally Versus Ally: America, Europe and the Siberian Pipeline Crisis*. New York: Praeger, 1987.

Brown, Alan A., and Egon Neuberger. *International Trade and Central Planning: An Analysis of Economic Interactions*. Berkeley, Calif.: University of Calif. Press 1968.

Clabaugh, Samuel F., and Richard V. Allen. *Trading with the Communists*. Washington, D.C.: Georgetown University Center for Strategic Studies, 1968.

———. *East-West Trade: Its Strategic Implications*. Washington, D.C.: Georgetown University, Center for Strategic Studies, 1964.

Fallenbuch, Z. M. "Comecon Integration." *Problems of Communism*. 22 (March–April 1973), 25–39.

Garland, John S. *Financing Foreign Trade in Eastern Europe: Problems of Bilateralism and Currency Inconvertibility*. New York: Praeger, 1977.

Giffen, James H. *The Legal and Practical Aspects of Trade with the Soviet Union*. New York: Praeger, 1969.

Goldman, Marshall I. *Détente and Dollars: Doing Business with the Soviets*. New York: Basic Books, 1975.

Grub, Phillip D., and Karel Holbik, eds. *American-East European Trade: Controversy, Progress, Prospects*. Washington, D.C.: National Press, 1969.

Harding, Harry. *China's Second Revolution: Reform After Mao*. Washington, D.C.: Brookings Institution, 1987.

Hewett, Ed. A. *Reforming the Soviet Economy: Equality versus Efficiency*. Washington, D.C.: Brookings Institution, 1988.

Hewett, Ed. A., and Thomas A. Wolf, eds. *Economic Adjustment and Reform in Eastern Europe and the Soviet Union*. London: Duke University Press, 1988.

Holzman, Franklyn D. *International Trade Under Communism—Politics and Economics*. New York: Basic Books, 1976.

Hoyt, Ronald E. *Winners and Losers in East-West Trade: A Behavioral Analysis of U.S.-Soviet Détente (1970–1980)*. New York: Praeger, 1983.

Hufbauer, Gary Clyde, and Jeffrey J. Schott. *Economic Sanctions Reconsidered: History and Current Policy*. Washington, D.C.: Institute for International Economics, 1985.

Kaldor, Mary. *The Disintegrating West*. New York: Hill and Wang, 1978.

Kaser, Michael. *Comecon: Integration Problems of the Planned Economies*. London: Oxford University Press, 1965.

Kostecki, M.M. *East-West Trade and the GATT System*. New York: St. Martin's, 1978.

Lardy, Nicholas R. *China's Entry into the World Economy: Implications for Northeast Asia and the United States*. New York: University Press of America for the Asia Society, 1987.

Lavigne, Marie, ed. *East-South Relations in the World Economy*. Boulder: Westview Press, 1988.

Lawson, Eugene K., ed. *U.S.-China Trade: Problems and Prospects*. New York: Praeger Press, 1988.

Malish, Anton F., Jr. "United States-East European Trade." *Staff Research Studies*, no. 4. Washington, D.C.: United States Tariff Commission, 1972.

Marer, Paul. "The Political Economy of Soviet Relations with Eastern Europe," in Steven J. Rosen and James R. Kurth, eds., *Testing Theories of Economic Imperialism*. Lexington, Mass.: Lexington Books, 1974.

Mikesell, Raymond F., and Jack N. Behrman. *Financing Free World Trade with the Sino-Soviet Bloc*. Princeton, N.J.: International Finance Section, Department of Economics, Princeton University, 1958.

National Academy of Science. *Balancing the National Interest: U.S. National Security Export Controls and Global Economic Competition*. Washington, D.C.: National Academy Press, 1987.

Nove, Alec. *East-West Trade: Problems, Prospects, Issues*. The Washington Papers, 6 no. 53. Beverly Hills, Cal.: Sage Publications, 1978.

Paarlberg, Robert. "Lessons of the Grain Embargo." *Foreign Affairs*, 59 (Fall 1980), 144–162.

Perry, Charles, and Robert Pfaltzcraft Jr., eds. *Selling the Rope to Hang Capitalism? The Debate on East-West Trade and Technology Transfer*. Washington, D.C.: Pergamon-Brassey, 1987.

Peterson, Peter G. *U.S.-Soviet Commercial Relationships in a New Era*. Washington, D.C.: Department of Commerce, August 1972.

Pisar, Samuel. *Coexistence and Commerce: Guidelines for Transactions Between East and West*. New York: McGraw-Hill, 1970.

Prince, Charles. "The U.S.S.R.'s Role in International Finance." *Harvard Business Review*, 25 (Autumn 1946), 111–128.

Rode, Reinhard, and Hanns-D. Jacobsen, eds. *Economic Warfare or Detente; An Assessment of East-West Relations in the 1980s*. Boulder, Colo.: Westview Press, 1985.

Roosa, Robert V., et al. *East/West Trade at the Crossroads: Economic Relations With the Soviet Union and Eastern Europe*, a task force report to the Trilateral Commission. New York: NYU Press, 1982.

Saunders, Christopher T., ed. *East-West-South: Economic Interactions Between Three Worlds*. London: Macmillan, 1981.

Schmitthoff, C.M., ed. *The Sources of the Law of International Trade, with Special Reference to East-West Trade*. New York: Praeger, 1964.

Schnitzer, Martin. *U.S. Business Involvement in Eastern Europe: Case Studies of Hungary, Poland, and Rumania*. New York: Praeger, 1980.

Shelton, Judy. *The Coming Soviet Crash: Gorbachev's Desperate Pursuit of Credit in Western Financial Markets*. New York: Free Press, 1989.

Sternheimer, Stephen. *East-West Technology Transfer: Japan and the Communist Bloc*. The Washington Papers, 8 no. 76. Beverly Hills, Calif.: Sage Publications, 1980.

Sutton, Anthony C. *Western Technology and Soviet Economic Development, 1945–1965*. Stanford, Calif.: Hoover Institution on War, Revolution and Peace, 1973.

——. *Western Technology and Soviet Economic Development, 1930 to 1945*. Stanford, Calif.: Hoover Institution on War, Revolution and Peace, 1971.

——. *Western Technology and Soviet Economic Development, 1917 to 1930*. Stanford, Calif.: Hoover Institution on War, Revolution and Peace, 1968.

U.S. Congress, Joint Economic Committee. *Issues in East-West Commercial Relations*. Washington, D.C.: Government Printing Office, 1979.

——. *East European Economics Post-Helsinki*. Washington, D.C.: Government Printing Office, 1977.

U.S. House Committee on Banking and Currency. *The FIAT-Soviet Automobile Plant and Communist Economic Reforms*. 88th Congress, 2nd Sess. Washington, D.C.: Government Printing Office, 1967.

Vernon, Raymond. "The Fragile Foundations of East-West Trade." *Foreign Affairs*, 57 (1979), 1035–1051.

Viner, Jacob. "International Relations Between State-Controlled National Economies." *American Economic Review*, 54 (1944), 315–329.

Wadekin, Karl-Eugen. "Soviet Agriculture's Dependence on the West." *Foreign Affairs*, 60 (1982), 882–903.

Watts, Nita G. M., ed. *Economic Relations Between East and West*. London: Macmillan, 1978.

Wilczynski, Joseph. *The Multinationals and East-West Relations*. Boulder, Colo.: Westview, 1976.

——. *Socialist Economic Development and Reforms: From Extensive to Intensive Growth Under Central Planning in the U.S.S.R., Eastern Europe and Yugoslavia*. New York: Praeger, 1972.

Wiles, P.J.D. *Communist International Economics*. New York: Praeger, 1968.

Yergin, Angela Stent. *East-West Technology Transfer: European Perspectives*. The Washington Papers, 8 no. 75. Beverly Hills, Calif.: Sage Publications, 1980.

Newspapers and Journals

American Economic Review.
American Journal of International Law.
American Political Science Review.
Amex Bank Review.
The Banker (London).

Columbia Journal of World Business.
The Economist.
Euromoney.
The Financial Times (London).
Foreign Affairs.
Foreign Policy.
Fortune.
Harvard Business Review.
International Affairs (London).
International Organization.
International Studies Quarterly.
Journal of Commerce.
Journal of Common Market Studies.
Journal of Development Studies.
Journal of International Affairs.
Journal of World Trade Law.
Law and Policy in International Business.
Monthly Review.
The New York Times.
Princeton Essays in International Finance.
Princeton Studies in International Finance.
Review of Radical Political Economics.
The Wall Street Journal.
World Business Weekly.
World Development.
The World Economy.
World Financial Markets (Morgan Guaranty Trust Co.).
World Politics.

Publications by Official Sources

Bank for International Settlements. *Annual Reports.*
International Bank for Reconstruction and Development. *World Bank Atlas.*
——. *World Debt Tables.*
——. *World Development Report.*
——. *World Social and Economic Indicators.*
International Bank for Reconstruction and Development and International Development Agency. *Annual Reports.*
International Monetary Fund. *Annual Reports.*
——. *Direction of Trade.*
——. *Finance and Development.*
——. *IMF Survey.*

————. *International Financial Statistics.*

————. *Selected Decisions of the Executive Directors and Selected Documents.*

————. *Staff Papers.*

————. *World Economic Report.*

Organization for Economic Cooperation and Development. *Flow of Financial Resources to Less-Developed Countries.*

————. *OECD Economic Outlook.*

————. *OECD Observer.*

————. Development Assistance Committee, *Development Cooperation. Review of Efforts and Policies of the Members of the Development Assistance Committee.*

————. *Statistics of Foreign Trade.*

————. *Stock of Private Direct Investments by DAC Countries in Developing Countries.*

————. *Trade by Commodities.*

United Nations Conference on Trade and Development. *Handbook of International Trade and Development Statistics.*

————. *Review of Trade and Development.*

United Nations Economic Commission for Europe. *Economic Survey of Europe.*

United Nations Economic Commission for Latin America. *Economic Survey of Latin America.*

U.S. Central Intelligence Agency. *Handbook of Economic Statistics.*

U.S. Department of Agriculture. *Foreign Agricultural Trade of the United States.*

U.S. Department of Commerce, Bureau of the Census. *Statistical Abstract of the United States.*

U.S. Department of Commerce. *Survey of Current Business.*

U.S. Department of State. *Bulletin.*

U.S. President's Council of Economic Advisors. *Economic Report of the President.*

U.S. Trade Representative. *Annual Report of the President of the United States on the Trade Agreements Program.*

Index